43 $\frac{50}{70C}$

C

DEVELOPMENT OF PERCEPTION

VOLUME 1
AUDITION, SOMATIC PERCEPTION,
AND THE CHEMICAL SENSES

BEHAVIORAL BIOLOGY

AN INTERNATIONAL SERIES

Series editors

James L. McGaugh

Department of Psychobiology
University of California
Irvine, California

John C. Fentress

Department of Psychology
Dalhousie University
Halifax, Canada

Joseph P. Hegmann

Department of Zoology
The University of Iowa
Iowa City, Iowa

DEVELOPMENT OF PERCEPTION

Psychobiological Perspectives
VOLUME 1
Audition, Somatic Perception,
and the Chemical Senses

Edited by
RICHARD N. ASLIN
JEFFREY R. ALBERTS
MICHAEL R. PETERSEN
Department of Psychology
Indiana University
Bloomington, Indiana

ACADEMIC PRESS
A Subsidiary of Harcourt Brace Jovanovich, Publishers
New York   London   Toronto   Sydney   San Francisco   1981

ACADEMIC PRESS, INC.
111 Fifth Avenue, New York, New York 10003

United Kingdom Edition published by
ACADEMIC PRESS, INC. (LONDON) LTD.
24/28 Oval Road, London NW1   7DX

Library of Congress Cataloging in Publication Data
Main entry under title:

The Development of perception.

    (Behavioral biology)
    Includes bibliographies and indexes.
    Contents: v. 1. Audition, somatic perception, and the
chemical senses -- v. 2. The visual system.
    1. Visual perception. 2. Neuropsychology. 3. Devel-
opmental psychobiology. I. Aslin, Richard N.
II. Alberts, Jeffrey E.   III. Petersen, Michael R.
IV. Series: Behavioral biology (New York, N.Y. : 1978)
[DNLM: 1. Visual perception. W1 705 D489]
QP491.D47   152.1'4   81-7946
ISBN 0-12-065301-X (v.1)   AACR2

Contents

PART A ANIMAL STUDIES OF AUDITORY DEVELOPMENT, 1

1 Roles of Early Experience in Species-Specific Perceptual Development

GILBERT GOTTLIEB

2 Development of Parent–Offspring Recognition in Birds

MICHAEL D. BEECHER

3 Perception of Acoustic Communication Signals by Animals: Developmental Perspectives and Implications

MICHAEL R. PETERSEN

15   Neurophysiological and Anatomical Aspects of Taste Development

CHARLOTTE M. MISTRETTA

Contributors

Numbers in parentheses indicate the pages on which the authors' contributions begin.

JEFFREY R. ALBERTS (321), Department of Psychology, Indiana University, Bloomington, Indiana 47405

RICHARD N. ASLIN (219), Department of Psychology, Indiana University, Bloomington, Indiana 47405

MICHAEL D. BEECHER (45), Department of Psychology, University of Washington, Seattle, Washington 98195

ELLIOTT M. BLASS (359), Department of Psychology, Johns Hopkins University, Baltimore, Maryland 21218

RACHEL CLIFTON (141), Department of Psychology, University of Massachusetts, Amherst, Massachusetts 01003

BEN M. CLOPTON (111), Department of Otolaryngology, School of Medicine, University of Washington, Seattle, Washington 98195

JOHN M. DOWD (141), Department of Psychology, University of Massachusetts, Amherst, Massachusetts 01003

DIANNE DURHAM (259), Department of Anatomy and Neurobiology, Washington University School of Medicine, St. Louis, Missouri 63110

JOHN C. FENTRESS (293), Departments of Psychology and Biology, Dalhousie University, Halifax, Nova Scotia B3H 4JI, Canada

BENNETT G. GALEF, JR. (411), Department of Psychology, McMaster University, Hamilton, Ontario L8S 4K1, Canada

GILBERT GOTTLIEB (5), North Carolina Division of Mental Health, Raleigh, North Carolina 27611

ROGER M. HARRIS* (259), Department of Anatomy, Washington University School of Medicine, St. Louis, Missouri 63110

* Present address: Department of Anatomy, University of California, San Francisco, School of Medicine, San Francisco, California 94143.

PETER W. JUSCZYK (191), Department of Psychology, University of Oregon, Eugene, Oregon 97403

RAYMOND D. KENT (161), Human Communication Laboratories, Boys Town Institutes, Omaha, Nebraska 68131

JOHN W. KULIG* (141), Department of Psychology, University of Massachusetts, Amherst, Massachusetts 01003

CHRISTIANA M. LEONARD (383), Department of Neuroscience, University of Florida, Gainesville, Florida 32610

CHARLOTTE M. MISTRETTA (433), Center for Human Growth and Development, Research Area, School of Nursing; and Department of Oral Biology, School of Dentristry, University of Michigan, Ann Arbor, Michigan 48109

BARBARA A. MORRONGIELLO (141), Department of Psychology, University of Massachusetts, Amherst, Massachusetts 01003

PATRICIA E. PEDERSEN (359), Department of Psychology, Johns Hopkins University, Baltimore, Maryland 21218

MICHAEL R. PETERSEN (67), Department of Psychology, Indiana University, Bloomington, Indiana 47405

DAVID B. PISONI (219), Department of Psychology, Indiana University, Bloomington, Indiana 47405

DANIEL J. SIMONS (259), Department of Anatomy and Neurobiology, Washington University School of Medicine, St. Louis, Missouri 63110

KAREN L. VALENTINO (259), Department of Anatomy and Neurobiology, Washington University School of Medicine, St. Louis, Missouri 63110

AMANDA C. WALLEY (219), Department of Psychology, Indiana University, Bloomington, Indiana 47405

THOMAS A. WOOLSEY (259), Department of Anatomy and Neurobiology, Washington University School of Medicine, St. Louis, Missouri 63110

* Present address: Department of Psychology, Northern Illinois University, DeKalb, Illinois 60115.

General Preface

The study of perceptual development has been approached from many different levels (from neurons to behavior), in different sensory modalities, and in a wide variety of species, and contemporary research has tended to travel down increasingly esoteric and reductionistic paths. Thus, articles, books, and research strategies are organized around rarified techniques, particular sensory modalities, or singular levels of analysis. We believe there is much to be gained by looking at perceptual development as a more broadly defined "field." Stepping back from the idiosyncracies of our own research and seeking out the commonalities that have been found across species and sensory modalities, we hope that overriding organizational principles will emerge to guide future research. The chapters in these volumes, disparate in origin and discipline, reflect a new surge of interest and activity in what can indeed be considered a field of scientific inquiry: the development of perception.

This two-volume set is a unique assemblage of chapters covering vision, audition, olfaction, taste, tactile sensitivity, and sensory-motor activity during ontogenesis. The chapters provide a comprehensive collection of overviews and an assortment of case histories that summarize the progress made in recent years. Within each sensory modality or content area there are different levels of analysis, varied research goals, and distinctive blends of theoretical integration. Our bias, as reflected in the title of this work, is to emphasize approaches to perceptual development that incorporate a psychobiological perspective, a term that we define to include analyses of phenomena at the mechanistic, physiological, behavioral, and evolutionary levels. Accordingly, the discussion of sensory and perceptual development must involve consideration of the multileveled network of causal factors that generate a unique, yet species-typical, organism. Studies of nonhuman species are essential, not only for ethical and methodological reasons, but also because the comparative approach allows us to take advantage of "natural experiments"—instances in which the timing, degree, and function of different developmental events can be varied by the appropriate choice of species. We hope that this broadened perspective will open new vistas for inquiry and encourage new methodologies with which we can address the persistent questions of perceptual development.

Acknowledgments

Many of the chapters in these volumes are outgrowths of a four-day meeting, the Brown County Conference, held in Nashville, Indiana, during October 7–12, 1979. More than sixty researchers from the United States, Canada, England, and Australia were assembled to share their data and thoughts on the complex interactions between genetic and experiential factors in determining the course of perceptual development. We want to thank the many people who made both the conference and the book possible. Support for the conference was provided by grants from the National Science Foundation (BNS 79-06204) and the Sloan Foundation (B1979-12). To those agencies we express our sincere appreciation. The mechanics of the conference were organized and coordinated in large part by Nancy Layman, who also provided invaluable assistance in the preparation of manuscripts during the succeeding months. We are most grateful for her efforts. Special thanks are also due to David Pisoni, one of the primary instigators of the conference, who helped to obtain funding and to oversee many of the organizational duties. Finally, we thank the graduate students at Indiana University who devoted their time and effort as hosts and shuttle bus drivers.

Preface

This volume contains both overviews and specific discussions of audition, somatic perception, and the chemical senses aimed at the anatomical, neurophysiological, and behavioral levels. It is organized into four parts; audition is given the greatest coverage as a result of a broader data base.

Parts A and B are devoted to aspects of auditory perceptual development in animals and humans, respectively. Gottlieb uses the development of species-specificity in duckling auditory perception as the vehicle for elucidating experiential processes in perceptual development. Beecher illustrates the functional role of auditory perception in parent–offspring recognition in birds. Petersen discusses basic ontogenetic issues that arise in nonhuman primates' perceptual biases for species-specific vocalizations. Clopton then reviews basic neurophysiological and anatomical development of the auditory system.

Three of the chapters on audition in human infants focus on specific topics. Clifton, Morrongiello, Kulig, and Dowd describe the development of auditory localization. The chapters by Kent and Jusczyk are concerned with the production and the processing of speech sounds, respectively. Walley, Pisoni, and Aslin address some of the more general issues in their analysis of experiential components in the development of speech perception.

Part C is an introduction to issues of somatosensory and sensorimotor development—important but relatively neglected areas. Woolsey, Durham, Harris, Simons, and Valentino describe pioneering studies of development and plasticity in the neural structures of specialized somatosensory areas. Fentress offers a review of questions, analyses, and integrative problems concerning sensorimotor development.

Part D contains chapters on the development of olfaction and taste. Alberts provides a broad overview of olfactory perceptual development. Pedersen and Blass focus on the perinatal factors involved in olfactory control of suckling in rats, an example of the recent, intense research interest in early behavior and olfaction. Leonard reviews olfactory neuroanatomical development and proposes a neurobiological model for the development of olfactory recognition. The chapters on gustatory development cover behavioral, anatomical, and neurophysiological levels of analysis. Galef discusses the social and nonsocial factors that determine diet preferences. Mistretta reviews anatomical and neurophysiological aspects of gustatory development.

Together, these chapters provide both an introduction to and a sampling of the progress, methods, problems, and concepts that characterize a broad spectrum of integrative studies of perceptual development.

Contents of Volume 2
The Visual System

PART C   VISUAL DEVELOPMENT IN HUMAN INFANTS

DEVELOPMENT OF PERCEPTION

VOLUME 1
AUDITION, SOMATIC PERCEPTION,
AND THE CHEMICAL SENSES

Animal Studies
of Auditory Development

Many animals live in highly social environments and, like man, co-ordinate their interactions by communicating with acoustic signals. In fact, the vocal behavior of many species, particularly that of birds and primates, is one of the most conspicuous attributes of their social behavior (as anyone who has walked through a deciduous forest while songbirds are in the midst of their spring mating rituals can readily attest). It should come as no surprise then that the bulk of the developmental studies with animals concerning sensory and perceptual processes in the auditory realm relate to the ontogeny of various aspects of acoustic communication, (e.g., Konishi & Nottebohm, 1969; Marler & Peters, 1977). Some of this work, particularly that of Marler and his associates on birdsong, has aroused considerable interest among those pursuing studies of human language development (e.g., Eimas & Tartter, 1979; Walley, Pisoni, & Aslin, Chapter 8, this volume) because certain aspects of animal vocal development parallel stages that children pass through while mastering a language. These similarities in rudimentary features of vocal development thus suggest that animal vocal behavior might serve as an experimental and conceptual model for some aspects of human language development. These gross similarities are, in turn, of interest to comparative psychologists and ethologists who seek to identify the adaptive significance of such traits in order to trace their evolution (e.g., Kroodsma, 1978). Three of the chapters in this section outline some of the more recent findings from research on the development of vocal-sound production and perception in birds and primates.

A question of some antiquity among those interested in the origins of behavior concerns the extent to which behavior is genetically versus experientially determined (e.g., see reviews by Kuo, 1921, 1967; Lehrman, 1953, 1970; Lorenz 1965, 1970; and Schneirla, 1956, 1966). The naive view is that behavior is an expression of *either* innate *or* learned capacities. Work has shown that such a view is generally incorrect. Behavior is an outcome of a complex set of interactions between innate predispositions and environmental variables; all behaviors are *both* genetically *and* environmentally determined—they differ primarily in the relative import of each factor in molding specific behaviors. One of the already classic illustrations of this principle comes from Gottlieb's work on the development of species-typical perceptual responses to maternal calls in wood and Peking ducklings. In summarizing nearly 20 years of research on this topic, Gottlieb points to the critical role of early embryological experiences in shaping the character of the newly hatched duckling's vocal perception. He then places his work in a more general context while presenting an updated and further differentiated explication of his conceptual model of behavioral development (cf. Gottlieb, 1976).

Whereas Gottlieb has concentrated on the development of what might be viewed as species recognition, Beecher's research is aimed at describing the processes involved in the development of offspring recognition by parents. In Chapter 2 work on this issue with different species of swallows is summarized. In Beecher's view, recognition of an individual entails two distinct processes—the production of individually distinctive cues by a sender and the perception of these cues by a receiver who then executes the recognition response. Most previous research on recognition phenomena has concentrated on one or the other of these two processes without explicitly treating their interrelation (e.g., Evans, 1970). In contrast, Beecher has made a deliberate attempt to elucidate the interplay between development of individually distinctive calls by a young bird and the recognition response of the parents. His work has clarified that there is an intimate linkage between the two for some species, but not in others. To account for the differences among species, he proposes a qualitative evolutionary model that explains the adaptive significance of parent–offspring recognition and therefore predicts whether a species will make use of the process depending on the ecological pressures they face.

Chapters 1 and 2 testify to the fact that our comprehension of the ontogeny of avian vocal behavior is very high indeed. In contrast, Petersen's contribution (Chapter 3) indicates how little we actually know about the development of primate vocal behavior. His critical review of developmental studies of avian vocal behavior and the small literature on primate vocal development points to specific topics that need additional research. In particular, lack of satisfactory methodology has hindered attempts to characterize the perception of vocalizations by communicatively competent primates; consequently, little is known about how the putative perceptual capacities develop. Petersen presents a case study of his efforts to uncover the mechanisms involved in the perception of vocalizations by subadult and adult Japanese monkeys. His studies show that they employ species-specific perceptual strategies that enable them to attend selectively to the communicatively significant dimensions of their vocalizations. This information sets the stage for attempts to trace the development of these traits and makes feasible the assessment of the relative roles of genetic and experiential factors.

The ultimate ideal of nearly any ontogenetic enterprise is to account for behavioral development in terms of neural change. Although little is known about the neural underpinnings of the perception of complex acoustic signals, such as animal vocalizations, some recent advances have been made in characterizing the development of those aspects of auditory neuroanatomy and physiology that seem to underlie the analysis of simple acoustic stimuli (e.g., see Rubel, 1978) such as pure tones and noise bands. Clopton (Chapter 4) presents a timely review of progress in this area and, in so doing, lays the groundwork for future investigations of neural development as it pertains to the perception of complex, multidimensional stimuli.

REFERENCES

Eimas, P. D., & Tartter, V. C. On the development of speech perception: Mechanisms and analogies. In H. W. Reese & L. P. Lipsitt (Eds.), *Advances in child development and behavior* (Vol. 13). New York: Academic Press, 1979.

Evans, R. M. Imprinting and mobility in young ring-billed gulls, *Larus delawarensis*. *Animal Behaviour Monographs,* 1970, **3**, 193–248.

Gottlieb, G. The roles of experience in the development of behavior and the nervous system. In G. Gottlieb (Ed.), *Neural and behavioral specificity*. New York: Academic Press, 1976. Pp. 25–54.

Konishi, M., & Nottebohm, F. Experimental studies in the ontogeny of avian vocalizations. In R. A. Hinde (Ed.), *Bird vocalizations*. London: Cambridge University Press, 1969. Pp. 29–48.

Kroodsma, D. Aspects of learning in the ontogeny of bird song: Where, from whom, when, how many, which and how accurately? In G. Burghardt & M. Bekoff (Eds.), *The development of behavior: comparative and evolutionary aspects*. New York: Garland, 1978. Pp. 215–230.

Kuo, Z. Y. Giving up instincts in psychology. *Journal of Philosophy,* 1921, **18**, 645–664.

Kuo, Z. Y. *The dynamics of behavior development*. New York: Random House, 1967.

Lehrman, D. S. A critique of Konrad Lorenz's theory of instinctive behavior. *Quarterly Review of Biology,* 1953, **28**, 337–363.

Lehrman, D. S. Semantic and conceptual issues in the nature–nurture problem. In L. R. Aronson, E. Tobach, D. S. Lehrman, & J. S. Rosenblatt (Eds.), *Development and evolution of behavior*. San Francisco: Freeman, 1970. Pp. 17–52.

Lorenz, K. *Evolution and modification of behavior*. Chicago: University of Chicago Press, 1965.

Lorenz, K. A consideration of methods of identification of species-specific instinctive behavior patterns in birds. In K. Lorenz (R.D. Martin, Trans.), *Studies in animal and human behavior* (Vol. 1). Cambridge, Mass.: Harvard University Press, 1970, (Originally published, 1932). Pp. 57–100.

Marler, P., & Peters, S. Selective vocal learning in a sparrow. *Science,* 1977, **198,** 519–521.

Rubel, E. W. Ontogeny of structure and function in the vertebrate auditory system. In M. Jacobson(Ed.), *Handbook of sensory physiology.* Berlin: Springer-Verlag, 1978. Pp. 135–237.

Schneirla, T. C. Interrelationships of the "innate" and the "acquired" in instinctive behavior. In P. P. Grassé (Ed.), *L'instinct dans le comportement des animaux et l'homme.* Paris: Masson, 1956. Pp. 387–452.

Schneirla, T. C. Behavioral development and comparative psychology. *Quarterly Review of Biology,* 1966, **41,** 283–302.

1

Roles of Early Experience in Species-Specific Perceptual Development

GILBERT GOTTLIEB
North Carolina Division of Mental Health

I. INTRODUCTION

When a young organism behaves in an adaptive species-typical fashion early in postnatal development, it is always tempting to label the behavior "innate" or "instinctive" and forego further analysis of the

5

possible experiential precursors to the behavior. This temptation arises most persuasively when (*a*) there is no immediately obvious experiential precursor; or (*b*) when the possible participation of conditioning or associative learning is nil. In the present chapter I shall strive to deal with both of these stumbling blocks to a full-fledged developmental approach to the problem of species-specific behavior. In the first case, I shall describe some nonobvious experiential precursors to species-specific behavior that would otherwise appear to be innate (i.e., independent of such experiences). On the second question, I shall present a theoretical framework of the various ways in which experience can foster the development of species-specific behavior outside of conventional associative mechanisms of learning. It is clear that traditional conceptions of learning have not been very useful in describing the contributions of experience to the species-typical development of behavior, so it is necessary to begin to formulate these contributions in a different way.

II. EARLY DEVELOPMENT OF SPECIES IDENTIFICATION IN PRECOCIAL AVIAN SPECIES

In nature, around the time of hatching, the duck embryo begins a sort of vocal dialogue with its parent, wherein the hen sporadically utters the maternal assembly call typical of her species. The hen later uses the same call to lure her brood from the nest (Gottlieb, 1963, 1965; Miller & Gottlieb, 1978). It is important to note that this assembly call is highly attractive to ducklings and chicks that have been hatched in incubators in the laboratory and thus have never before been exposed to it. In fact, as shown in Table 1.1, maternally naive ducklings and chicks are so selectively tuned to the maternal call of their species that in simultaneous choice tests they unerringly choose their own species maternal call over that of other species. A duckling in such a choice test is shown in Fig. 1.1.

The overriding significance of the call is further demonstrated in choice tests in which incubator-hatched birds of various precocial species are given the opportunity to follow a moving but nonvisible sound source emitting the maternal call of their species or a silent moving visual replica of the hen of their species: Without exception the young birds quickly choose to follow the call without any behavioral signs of conflict (Gottlieb, 1968, 1971).

It seems safe to conclude from these findings that the early sensory–perceptual basis of species identification is auditory in all avian

Table 1.1
The Outcome of Simultaneous Auditory Choice Tests in Which Maternally Naive (Incubator-Hatched) Birds Are Presented with the Maternal Assembly Call of Their Own and Other Species[a]

Species of hatchling	Calls in test and preference of hatchling (number choosing each call)	
	Mallard call versus pintail call	
Mallard duckling	18	1
Peking duckling		
(domesticated mallard)	19	0
	Mallard call versus wood duck call	
Mallard duckling	18	1
Peking duckling	24	3
	Mallard call versus chicken call	
Peking duckling	24	0
Domestic chick	1	19
	Wood duck call versus mandarin call	
Wood duckling	22	3
	Chicken call versus wood duck call	
Domestic chick	21	2
Jungle-fowl	11	0

[a] These figures were taken from Gottlieb, 1971, with the following exceptions that were added from unpublished test results. In the mallard versus chicken call test: 13 chicks. In the wood duck versus mandarin call test: 12 wood ducklings. In the chicken call versus wood duck call test: 12 domestic chicks and 11 jungle-fowl chicks. (Jungle-fowl is believed to be the wild progenitor of domestic strains of chicken.)

species studied to date. Thus, it becomes a matter of interest to trace the ontogenetic developmental basis of the avian neonate's special attraction to the maternal call of its species in advance of exposure to it. First, I shall discuss the field observations and experimental findings with the hole-nesting wood duckling (*Aix sponsa*) and then, for comparative purposes, I shall turn the discussion to the ground-nesting mallard (Peking) duckling (*Anas platyrhynchos*).

A. Wood Ducklings' Perception of Maternal Call of Their Species

In contrast to altricial species, in which the young are born in a very immature stage and must stay in the nest for a prolonged period, in precocial species such as the wood duck and mallard, the young are

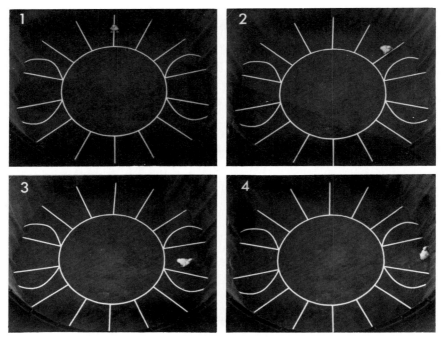

Fig. 1.1 Simultaneous auditory choice test. (1) Duckling placed equidistant between two speakers (not visible), in front of which are painted elliptical approach areas; (2) duckling on its way toward approach area on its left; (3) Duckling in approach area; (4) Duckling snuggling to curtain and orienting to nonvisible speaker broadcasting maternal call of its species. (From Gottlieb, 1975a, Figure 4. Copyright © 1975 by the American Psychological Association. Reprinted by permission.)

capable of leaving the nest with the maternal parent within a day or so after hatching. Whereas, in both duck species, the hen lures the young from the nest by uttering her species-specific maternal assembly call, the hole-nesting wood ducklings are unable to see the hen during the exodus, whereas the ground-nesting mallard ducklings are able both to hear and to see their hen as they leave the nest.

As one thinks about the prior experiential basis of the species-specific attraction of the hen's call even before the young are exposed to it, it becomes obvious that there must be particular acoustic features that invariably occur in the call and to which the young bird is always attracted. The investigation of nonobvious experiential precursors thus hinges on (*a*) a determination of the key acoustic features of the maternal call; and (*b*) an attempt to link those features to the young bird's early auditory experience (i.e., exposure to its own and sib vocalizations).

Are the critical acoustic features of the hen's maternal call somehow represented in the embryonic and neonatal vocalizations?

1. Determination of Key Acoustic Feature of Wood Duck Maternal Call

The rationale for determining the key acoustic features of the wood duck maternal call was as follows. The first step was to record the maternal calls of 11 wood duck hens as they called their young from nests in the field and subject these calls to an intensive acoustic analysis (Miller & Gottlieb, 1976). The acoustic features that showed little variation across hens would be the prime candidates for the critical perceptual features of the call used by maternally naive wood ducklings. That is, if the ducklings somehow are uniquely sensitive to the acoustic features of the generalized maternal call of their species in advance of exposure to a hen, these features would have to be rather stably represented in the calls of individual hens; otherwise, the ducklings' manifest ability to identify a maternal call of their species in advance of exposure to it would not be in evidence, as we know it is. (Evidence summarized in Table 1.1; further evidence in Gottlieb, 1971. Heaton, 1972, demonstrated differential behavioral responsiveness to wood duck and mallard maternal calls in the maternally naive wood duck embryo.)

a. Repetition Rate

The field study of the maternal calls of 11 wood duck hens indicated that the frequency modulation of the notes and the repetition rates of the calls were the most stable features across hens (Miller & Gottlieb, 1976). To examine the importance of repetition rate, an actual wood duck maternal call (Fig. 1.2) was altered by splicing blank pieces of tape between the notes to decrease the repetition rate of the call from 6.9 notes/sec to 4.0 notes/sec. Because the only feature altered was repetition rate, a preference shown by maternally naive birds for the 6.9 over the 4.0 rate in a simultaneous auditory choice test would indicate that repetition rate is one of the key perceptual features of the wood duck maternal call. However, if the birds did not show a preference in the test, the implication would be that repetition rate is not a particularly significant feature of the wood duck maternal call.

As can be seen in Fig. 1.3 (left), in a simultaneous choice test, the 14 maternally naive wood ducklings that made a choice did not show a preference for the normal (6.9) over the slowed (4.0) maternal call. Because the particular maternal call selected for this test was a bit slower than the modal repetition rate (8.8 notes/sec) of other hens recorded in the field (Miller & Gottlieb, 1976), an additional group of wood

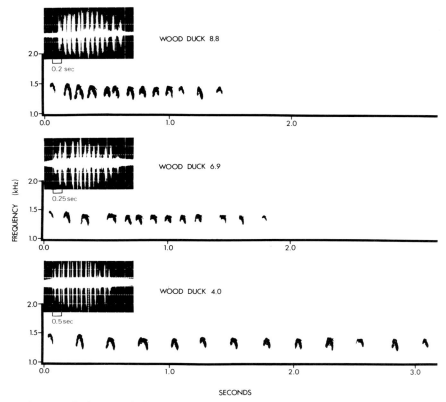

Fig. 1.2 Scale-magnified Sonagrams of wood duck maternal call at three different repetition rates. To speed or slow the normal call (6.9 notes/sec), it was necessary merely to delete space between the notes (8.8 notes/sec), or to add blank pieces of recording tape between the notes (4.0 notes/sec).

ducklings was tested with the same call at 6.9 notes/sec and a faster version of that call at 8.8 notes/sec.[1] (The faster version was made by deleting blank space between the notes, as shown in Figure 1.2.) The previously unpublished results of that test are shown in Figure 1.3 (right). Again, the 16 birds that made a choice did not prefer either repetition rate, that of the normal call (6.9), or the modal rate for the species (8.8). So, while repetition rate may not be completely unim-

[1]The figures for repetition rates given in this sentence are slightly different from those that appeared in Miller and Gottlieb (1976) and Gottlieb (1974), because of a difference in method of calculation. The present figures have been calculated by a more appropriate method (Scoville & Gottlieb, 1978).

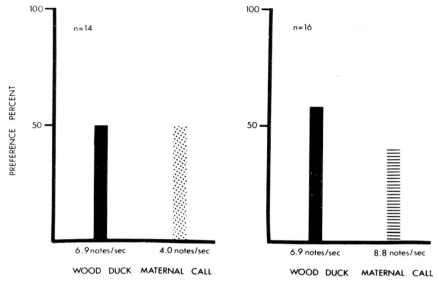

Fig. 1.3 Preferences of wood ducklings in simultaneous auditory choice tests with wood duck maternal call at three different repetition rates: 8.8 notes/sec (species mode), 6.9 notes/sec, and 4.0 notes/sec. (Results for 6.9 versus 4.0 replotted from Gottlieb, 1974, Table 5. Results for 8.8 versus 6.9, previously unpublished.)

portant, it is clearly not a key perceptual feature of the wood duck maternal call for maternally naive wood ducklings.

b.   Frequency Modulation

Because the frequency modulation (FM) of the notes of the wood duck maternal call was rather stable across the 11 wood duck hens that Miller and I (1976) recorded in the field, that was the next acoustic feature to be examined in the laboratory experiments. As can be seen in Fig. 1.4, we classified 661 notes from the 11 hens as primarily descending, primarily ascending, or symmetrically ascending–descending

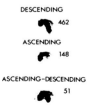

FREQUENCY MODULATION

DESCENDING

462

ASCENDING

148

ASCENDING–DESCENDING

51

Fig. 1.4 Tally of frequency modulation of 661 notes in maternal calls from 11 wood duck hens recorded during exodus from nest in the field. Of all the notes, 70% had a pronounced descending modulation (462). (Data abstracted from Miller & Gottlieb, 1976, Figure 4.)

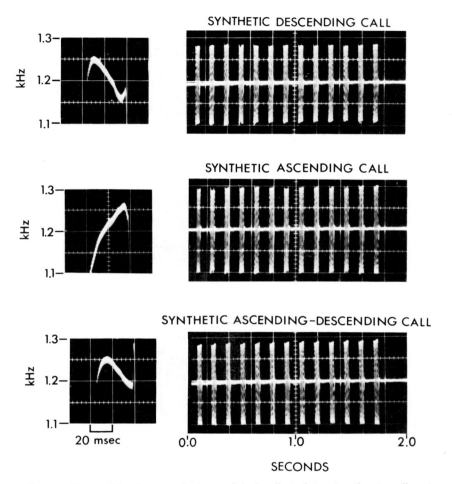

Fig. 1.5 Notes of the three synthetic wood duck calls to determine if maternally naive wood ducklings have a preference for the modal frequency modulation (descending). Each of the three calls contained 13 notes with a repetition rate of 6.9/sec to be equivalent in those respects to the natural wood duck call shown in Fig. 1.7. (Whereas the duration of notes in the natural wood duck call vary from 50–75 msec, all notes in the synthetic calls are a standard length.)

in FM, and 70% of the notes were mostly descending in modulation. All of the hens uttered descending notes, and all but one uttered many more descending notes than ascending or symmetrically ascending–descending notes (Fig. 4 in Miller & Gottlieb, 1976). The one exception uttered an almost equal number of descending and ascending notes.

If the descending FM of the notes is a critical perceptual feature, it should be possible to synthesize (fabricate) a call that is as attractive to wood ducklings as a natural call. To determine if the descending feature of the FM is indeed the critical aspect, maternally naive wood ducklings were tested for their preference among three synthetic calls: descending, ascending, and ascending–descending. It is important to realize that the call notes differed only in their FM; otherwise the calls were similar in frequency range, note length, burst length, and repetition rate (Fig. 1.5). As is evident in Fig. 1.5, each of the synthetic calls has an ascending and a descending component, with the ascending-descending call being closest to symmetrical in that respect, the descending call having a more pronounced descending component, and the ascending call having a greater ascending component.

As shown in Fig. 1.6, in simultaneous auditory choice tests, maternally naive wood ducklings preferred the synthetic descending call to the other synthetic calls. (Further analyses of these results and the ones immediately following appear in Gottlieb, 1974.) The next step in determining whether the descending synthetic call contained the critical components of the natural wood duck maternal call was to place the descending call in opposition to the natural wood duck maternal call in a simultaneous auditory choice test. The natural call was the one used earlier in the repetition-rate experiments. The detailed FM of the notes of the natural call is shown in Fig. 1.7, which can be contrasted to the descending synthetic call in Fig. 1.5. Both calls contained 13 notes and had a repetition rate of 6.9 notes/sec. If the synthetic call contained the critical perceptual components that underlie the attractiveness of the natural call, the ducklings should find the synthetic call as attractive as the natural call in the choice test. Otherwise, the birds would prefer the natural call.

As shown in Fig. 1.8 (left) maternally naive wood ducklings did not show a preference between the descending synthetic call and the natural wood duck call. To determine the specificity of the perceptual selectivity of the ducklings, another group of wood ducklings was tested with the ascending–descending synthetic call versus the natural call. In that case, the ducklings preferred the natural call to the synthetic one (Fig.

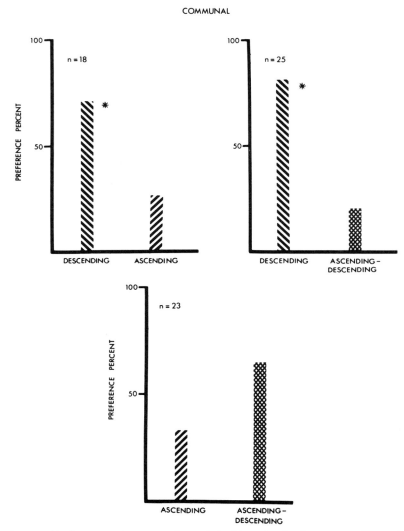

Fig. 1.6 Preferences of communal wood ducklings in simultaneous auditory choice tests with synthetic calls. *$p \leq .05$. (Data recast from Gottlieb, 1974, Table 1.)

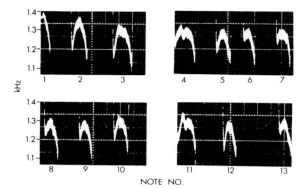

Fig. 1.7 Davis frequency chronogram of natural wood duck maternal call used in simultaneous choice tests with synthetic calls. Note that virtually all the notes of the natural call have a more pronounced descending component. Horizontal time scale = 50 msec/division. (Compare with synthetic calls in Fig. 1.5.)

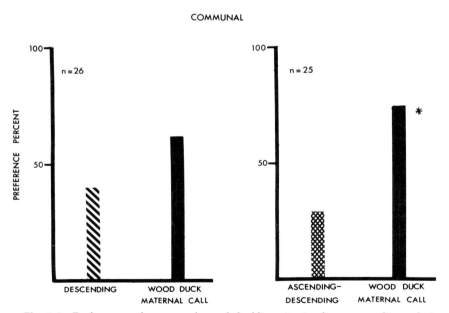

Fig. 1.8 Preferences of communal wood ducklings in simultaneous auditory choice tests with synthetic calls versus natural wood duck maternal call. *$p \leq .05$. (Data recast from Gottlieb, 1974, Table 3.)

1.8 (right). Therefore, the descending FM is a critical perceptual feature
of the wood duck maternal call.[2]

B. Effect of Auditory Deprivation on Species-Specific Perceptual Preference: Frequency Modulation

We are now in a position to ask what role, if any, prior auditory
experience plays in the development of the ducklings' selective response
to the descending frequency modulation of the wood duck maternal
call. According to the just presented results, maternally naive wood
ducklings identify the call of a hen of their species primarily on the
basis of its FM, the descending aspect being the pertinent cue. Given
the small differences in steepness and depth of descent between the
synthetic descending call and the synthetic ascending–descending call
used in the present experiments (Fig. 1.5), the manifest preference of
the wood ducklings for the former in a simultaneous choice test attests
not only to the importance of the descending modulation but to the
fineness of the ducklings' discriminative ability. The only vocal–auditory
experience the birds had before being tested was hearing their own
and sib vocalizations. Could this experience play a role in the development of their very keen perception of a key feature of the maternal
call?

As in many other species, the embryonic and neonatal wood duckling
is capable of uttering at least two acoustically distinct vocalizations:
contact–contentment and alarm–distress calls. (When the embryos
move into the air space at the large end of the egg a few days before
hatching, they begin breathing and thus can vocalize before hatching;
Gottlieb & Vandenbergh, 1968.) As shown in Fig. 1.9, the notes of both
the alarm–distress and contact–contentment vocalizations exhibit significant descending frequency modulations. In the case of the alarm
call, the descending component traverses almost 3000 Hz (from about
6000 to almost 3000 Hz). The descending FM of the contact–contentment
call goes from about 4500 to 2500 Hz. Both of these modulations are

[2]Ducklings respond to more than one acoustic feature of the maternal call. Some
features are more important than others, so there is a perceptual hierarchy of auditory
cues underlying species identification. Peking ducklings, for example, utilize repetition
rate and high-frequency components of their species' maternal call (Gottlieb, 1979), with
the former predominating over the latter (Gottlieb, 1978). Thus, both of these features
are "critical," and repetition rate seems to be more important than the high-frequency
components. The wood duckling does not utilize repetition rate within rather broad
limits; it does utilize frequency modulation, among other features not yet identified
(Gottlieb, 1974).

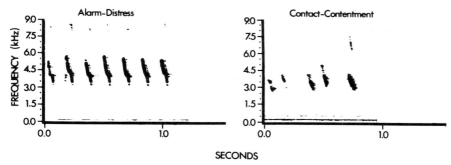

SECONDS

Fig. 1.9   Sonagrams of alarm–distress and contact–contentment calls of wood duck-lings. Note pronounced descending frequency modulation of each call extending over several thousand hertz. Notes of these calls are not in the same frequency range of the wood duck maternal call (compare Sonagram in Fig. 1.2).

considerably outside the range of the fundamental frequency of the maternal call, which is around 1300 Hz (Fig. 1.7). Could the birds be "abstracting" the descending FM from exposure to their own and sib vocalizations? The first step in answering that question would be to deprive the birds of hearing their own and sib vocalizations via em-bryonic devocalization, housing them in soundproof incubator com-partments, and then testing them, for example, with the descending versus ascending synthetic calls. If hearing the embryonic and neonatal vocalizations plays no role in the development of their preference for the descending FM, then such aurally deprived birds would prefer the descending call over the ascending one. If, however, exposure to the embryonic and neonatal vocalizations does play a significant role in the development of their perceptual preference, then aurally deprived wood ducklings might not show the normal preference for the descending call. That is the investigative strategy that I followed (Gottlieb, 1980b), with the exception of not muting the birds as embryos. Wood ducklings do not tolerate the muting operation as well as Peking ducklings (Gott-lieb, 1971), so I merely placed the birds in individual auditory isolation as embryos and tested them after hatching. Admittedly, this is not as precise a deprivation procedure as is devocalization, but it does work.

As can be seen in Fig. 1.10, the aurally isolated wood ducklings did not show the normal preference for the descending synthetic call. (These results and the ones to follow are abstracted from Gottlieb, 1980b, where the methods and results are presented in complete detail.)

The preceding results indicate that a certain amount of exposure to their own and/or conspecific vocalizations plays some role in the de-

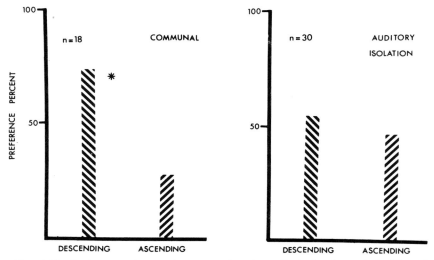

Fig. 1.10 Preference of normal communal and aurally isolated wood ducklings in simultaneous auditory choice test with descending and ascending synthetic calls. *$p \leq$ .05. (Data recast from Gottlieb, 1980b, Table 1.)

velopment of the wood duckling's species-specific perceptual preference for the descending FM characteristic of the wood duck maternal call. One of the roles normal experience could play is temporal regulation; that is, it may facilitate the appearance of the usual degree of perceptual specificity by a customary age. In that case, the absence of such experience would merely lead to a delay in the appearance of the ability. This has been observed, for example, in the Peking ducklings' response to the high-frequency components of the maternal call of its species: Isolates do not show the usual responsiveness to the high-frequency components at 24 hr after hatching, but they do show such responsiveness at 48 hr after hatching (Gottlieb, 1975c).

To determine if auditory deprivation merely slows the rate of normal perceptual development in wood ducklings, aurally isolated wood ducklings were tested in the next experiment with the descending versus ascending calls at 48 hr after hatching instead of at 24 hr as in the previous experiment.

As shown in Fig. 1.11, the aurally isolated wood ducklings did not show the preference for the descending FM when tested at 48 hr after hatching. Although it is possible that delaying testing beyond 48 hr might show the eventual appearance of the preference for the descending FM, in the previous instance where this was investigated (Gottlieb,

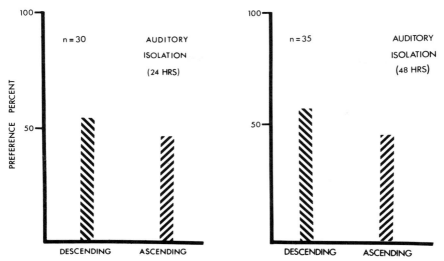

Fig. 1.11 Aurally isolated wood ducklings' preference in simultaneous auditory choice test with descending and ascending synthetic calls at 24 hr and 48 hr after hatching. (Data recast from Gottlieb, 1980b, Tables 1, 2.)

1975c), one in which there was improvement at 48 hr, there was a subsequent deterioration when the isolates were tested for the first time at 65 hr after hatching. In an unpublished experiment with wood ducklings related to this study, I examined the behavior of aural isolates 65 hr after hatching; their responsiveness in the test declined from 73% at 48 hr to 42% at 65 hr (and there was no evidence of improvement). Consequently, I did not pursue the investigation beyond 48 hr with the wood ducklings in the present study.

C. Specificity of Experiential Requirement to Maintain or Induce Species-Specific Frequency Modulation Preference

Whereas the wood ducklings show a preference for the descending call when they are incubated and brooded communally (communal group in Fig. 1.6), the question is whether it is exposure to their own and conspecific vocalizations that is specifically responsible for the preference. To examine this question, wood duck embryos were placed in individual auditory isolation, as in the previous experiments, and exposed to a repeated recording of a single burst of a wood duckling distress call (Fig. 1.12) for 5 min every hour until they were tested at 24 hr with the descending versus ascending calls. I chose to expose

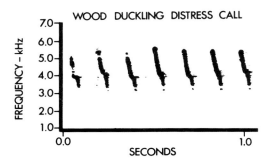

Fig. 1.12 Seven-note burst of wood duckling distress call. Aurally isolated wood ducklings were played this call either in the forward direction (descending modulation) or backward direction (ascending modulation) prior to testing to determine if such exposure would influence their choice of the descending versus ascending synthetic calls.

them to the alarm–distress call rather than to the contact–contentment call because I did not think a positive emotional connotation or association was necessarily required if such experience were to be effective, as has been theorized by Guyomarc'h (1972) in his extension of Schneirla's theory (1965). Because both the alarm–distress and contact–contentment calls are markedly descending in the FM of their notes, I thought it possible that one call might be just as effective as the other, if either proved to be effective.

It is significant to note that the embryos and hatchlings spend a great deal of time in sleep during the period of stimulation, and that the stimulation is of course not contingent on their state or activity. In another species (mallard), in which the eggs are plentiful and easy to obtain, it was possible to show that 5 min per hour of relevant stimulation could be confined to the embryonic period and remained effective up to 65 hr after hatching, the latest the birds were tested (Gottlieb, 1975b). Because wood duck eggs are neither plentiful nor easy to acquire, parametric study is not practical and I elected to continue the stimulation up to the time of testing rather than to terminate it around the time of hatching. As can be seen in Fig. 1.13 (left side), the isolates stimulated with the alarm–distress call showed the normal preference for the descending synthetic call.

To determine if the normal preference for the descending synthetic maternal call is specifically a consequence of the birds' experiencing the descending FM of the duckling alarm–distress call, in the next experiment isolated ducklings were exposed to the same alarm–distress call played backwards (i.e., ascending FM) on the same schedule as before

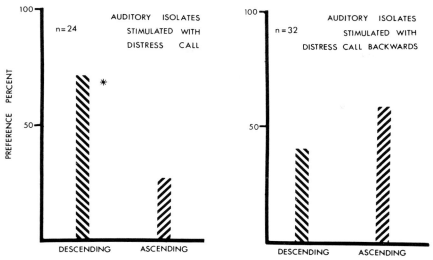

Fig. 1.13 Aurally isolated wood ducklings' preferences in simultaneous auditory choice tests with descending versus ascending synthetic calls after being exposed to a recording of the wood duckling distress call in the forward and backward direction. $*p < .05$. (Data recast from Gottlieb, 1980b, Table 3.)

and tested as before with the ascending versus descending synthetic calls at 24 hr after hatching.

There are several possible outcomes in the present experiment. If the experiential requirement is not specific, the alarm call played backwards would be sufficient for the manifestation of the normal preference for the descending synthetic maternal call. If the experiential requirement is specific, the birds in the present experiment would not show the normal preference. Furthermore, if the developing perceptual preference is relatively unconstrained in the direction of its development, stimulation with the alarm call in the backward direction could lead to a preference for the ascending synthetic call over the descending one. As shown in Fig. 1.13 (right side), the isolates stimulated with the alarm–distress call in the backward direction did not show the normal preference for the descending synthetic call, nor did they show a reliable preference for the ascending call.

There are several especially significant features in the present results. First and foremost, the development of the normal preference for a critical acoustic feature of the maternal call of the species is a highly specific consequence of the embryo and hatchling hearing their own and/or sib alarm–distress calls. Because the alarm–distress call is in a completely different frequency range than the maternal call, and its FM extends over a far greater range than the maternal call, the birds would appear to be "abstracting" the descending frequency modulation component when they subsequently respond to it in the maternal call.

The isolated ducklings did not develop a preference for the ascending frequency modulation when exposed to the duckling alarm–distress call played backward, thus suggesting a developmental constraint in the malleability of the FM preference. Because the isolated ducklings were not mute, at present we cannot rule out the interesting possibility that this constraint may be due to their hearing their own contentment and distress vocalizations (both having a descending FM), which could have buffered them against the effect of exposure to the ascending FM (distress call played backward). The other possibility is that the constraint stems entirely from endogenous auditory neuroanatomical and neurophysiological limiting factors that simply preclude the development of a preference for ascending FM.

D. Role of Experience

What role is experience playing in the present case? Because the isolated ducklings do not manifest the normal preference for a descending frequency modulation even if tested at a later age (Fig. 1.11), experience is not playing a *facilitative* role. That is, the isolates are not merely showing a lag in perceptual development as a consequence of experiential deprivation. Therefore, experience is serving either an *inductive* or a *maintenance* function (see Fig. 1.14). That issue can be decided by examining the response of embryos to the descending and ascending FMs in advance of normal auditory experience. If the embryos are responsive to both the descending and ascending FM calls, then auditory experience is inducing the normal postnatal preference for the descending call. If the embryos are responsive to the descending FM call and not to the ascending call, then auditory experience is serving a maintenance function. (The required experimental analysis is in progress.)

As will be described in more detail later, in another species (mallard) selective responsiveness to the species-typical repetition rate of the maternal call (4 notes/sec) develops in the embryo in advance of auditory experience, but the embryo requires specific exposure to its own vocalizations at 4 notes/sec to maintain the selective perceptual response into the postnatal period (Gottlieb, 1979, Gottlieb, 1980a). It is significant that a maintaining experience can have such a highly specific input requirement.

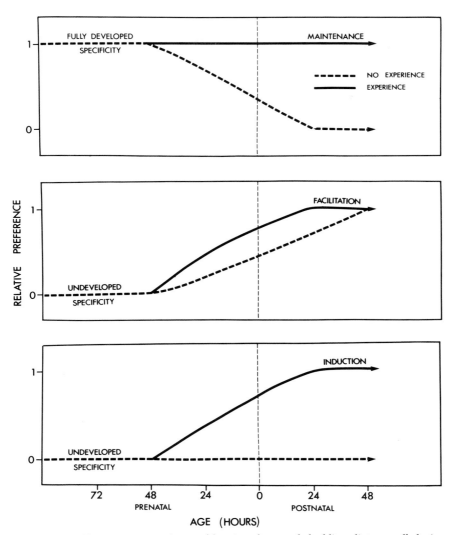

Fig. 1.14 Three ways experience of hearing the wood duckling distress call during the usual course of events could contribute to the normal development of the preference for the descending synthetic call. (See text for discussion.)

The latter result is the second such demonstration of a highly specific experiential requirement to maintain a selective or "finely tuned" feature of auditory perception. Earlier, I had found that the maintenance of normal high-frequency sensitivity (1500–2500 Hz) in ducklings at 65 hr after hatching required specific exposure of the embryo to its contact–contentment call, which contains just those frequencies. Exposure to calls above or below that range failed to preserve normal sensitivity in the 1500–2500 Hz range (Gottlieb, 1975b).

In the past, some theorists have assumed that the maintenance of "innate" behavior requires only rather general stimulation (see Bateson, 1976, for a review of this topic). The present evidence indicates that the experiential input requirement can be as specific for the *maintenance* of selective responsiveness as it is for the induction of selective responsiveness.

E. Nonobvious Experiential Precursors

As one examines the acoustic features of the wood duck maternal call and the wood duckling distress call (Figs. 1.7 and 1.12), it is far from obvious that the distress call could provide indispensable patterned "information" for the embryo and hatchling concerning a critical acoustic feature of the species' maternal call. If one were to make such an hypothesis prior to the present experiments, it would seem not only nonobvious but farfetched—superficially, the calls do not seem to share *any* common features. The invitation to search for nonobvious experiental precursors in the development of seemingly innate behavior, implicit and explicit in the writings of Kuo (1976), Schneirla (1956), and Lehrman (1953), has been largely ignored.

The finding of nonobvious precursors does not necessarily do away with the concept of innateness. Rather, what it does is force us to think in a new way about the role of experience in the development of species-specific or species-typical behavior. As discussed in the preceding sections and documented elsewhere (Gottlieb, 1976a,b), there is not only one role of experience during species-typical development, there are at least three: maintenance, facilitation, and induction. The interesting thing about these three modes is that (*a*) they do not fit the definition of traditional (i.e., associationistic) learning, and (*b*) they can entail specific *patterns* of stimulation to achieve the *species-typical* behavioral phenotype (e.g., Gottlieb, 1976b). Who would have thought, for example, that an already developed species-specific auditory perception would require a highly specific patterned experience to keep it functional (Gottlieb, 1980a)?

The search for nonobvious experiential precursors to unlearned behavior is in line with evolutionary considerations. Natural selection works on behavioral phenotypes; it is completely indifferent to the particular pathway taken by the phenotype during the course of development (Lehrman, 1970). Because all forms (pathways) of development involve genetic activity, natural selection need not favor one developmental pathway over another for the ontogenesis of unlearned behavior. Natural selection involves a selection for the entire developmental manifold, including both the organic and normally occurring stimulative features of ontogeny. Thus, nonobvious experiential precursors of a patterned kind may be much more widespread than heretofore realized. Only developmental investigations of unlearned behavior can answer that question.

F. Peking Ducklings' Perception of Maternal Call of Their Species

Because the specificity of the experiential background in the development of the wood ducklings' perception of a critical feature of its species maternal call might be regarded as unusual, I shall now turn to a discussion of a similar sort of specificity in another species and on another perceptual dimension. The maternally naive Peking duckling, a domestic form of mallard, relies primarily on the species-typical repetition rate of the mallard maternal call to identify it (evidence presented in the following). When the Peking duckling is muted embryonically and reared in auditory isolation, its usual narrow "tuning" to the species-typical repetition rate of the mallard maternal call (4 notes/sec) becomes so broad that, when tested after hatching, the mute Peking duckling actually "confuses" the mallard call with the chicken maternal call, the latter having a repetition rate of 2.3 notes/sec (Gottlieb, 1971). I was able to demonstrate experimentally that it is indeed a broadening of responsiveness on the dimension of repetition rate that is responsible for the mute Peking ducklings' inability to select the mallard over the chicken call (Gottlieb, 1978). Furthermore, the ducklings' normally highly selective repetition-rate bias is strictly dependent on the embryo's hearing its conspecific contact–contentment call at around 4 notes/sec (Gottlieb, 1980a). I shall now summarize those results.

G. Effect of Auditory Deprivation on Species-Specific Perceptual Preference: Repetition Rate

As can be seen in Fig. 1.15, whereas vocal–communal Peking ducklings show an exclusive preference for the mallard maternal call over

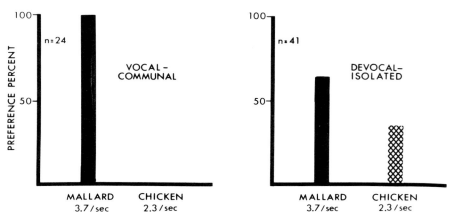

Fig. 1.15 Preference of vocal-communal and devocal-isolated Peking ducklings in simultaneous auditory choice test with mallard maternal call versus chicken maternal call. The normal repetition rate of these calls is 3.7 notes/sec and 2.3 notes/sec, respectively. (Data recast from Gottlieb, 1971, Table 35, and Gottlieb, 1978, Table 2.)

the chicken maternal call, the mute isolated ducklings find the calls equally attractive. A glance at sound spectrograms of the two calls (Fig. 1.16) shows that the calls differ on a number of acoustic dimensions (repetition rate, FM, high- and low-frequency components). Because the muted ducklings are positively responsive to the chicken maternal call in a behavioral test situation (Fig. 1.1) in which they have the option of not responding to it (the choice test apparatus is an open arena), they must be attracted to certain acoustic features of the chicken maternal call in the absence of normal exposure to their own and conspecific vocalizations. The question is, what acoustic attributes of the chicken call are the devocal–isolated ducklings responding to? Identification of the attribute(s) would pinpoint the change in species-specific perceptual development that occurs in the absence of normal auditory experience.

The mallard and chicken maternal calls share a dominant frequency band around 800 Hz, with the mallard call having higher-frequency components (around 1100, 1600, and 2300 Hz) and the chicken call having none (see Fig. 1.16). It was my first hypothesis that the de-vocal–isolated ducklings were responding to the 800-Hz band of energy in the chicken maternal call because devocalization had made them insensitive to the absence of the higher frequencies in the chicken call and the presence of them in the mallard call. Because the mallard call and the chicken call differ on other acoustic attributes besides frequency

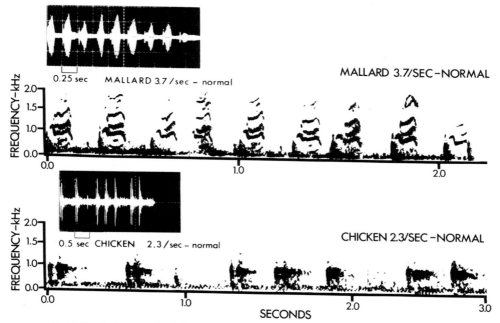

Fig. 1.16 Scale-magnified Sonagrams showing that the mallard and chicken maternal calls differ on various acoustic attributes (the presence of higher frequency bands and/ or harmonics, frequency modulation of the notes, etc.). The oscilloscopic insets depict the precise repetition rate of a burst of each call as used in the experiment described in the text. (From Gottlieb, 1978, Figure 1. Copyright © 1978 by the American Psychological Association. Reprinted by permission.)

components, a clear test of the high-frequency–insensitivity hypothesis required the use of high-frequency filtered versus nonfiltered mallard calls. Using such calls, earlier experiments have shown the high-frequency–insensitivity hypothesis to be correct at 24 hr but not at 48 hr after hatching (Gottlieb, 1975a,b,c). That is, the devocal birds were insensitive to the presence of the higher (> 800 Hz) frequency components of the mallard call at 24 hr after hatching, but they were preferentially responsive to those higher frequencies 48 hr after hatching. Because the latter is the age at which the mute birds "confuse" the chicken and mallard calls, and the chicken call does not contain frequencies over 800 Hz, it must be some other acoustic feature in the chicken call that the devocal–isolated ducklings find attractive 48 hr after hatching. Presumably, it is a feature that varies only slightly from the mallard call on some acoustic dimension critical to species identification. The next candidate I chose was repetition rate and that is the hypothesis to be evaluated in the following experiments.

1. Repetition-Rate Hypothesis

The species-typical repetition rate of the mallard maternal nest-exodus call is around 4 notes/sec (Miller & Gottlieb, 1978) and the typical rate for the domestic chicken (Collias & Joos, 1953) and wild jungle-fowl hen is around 3 notes/sec (Miller & Gottlieb, unpublished analysis of the maternal "cluck" calls of seven jungle-fowl hens recorded in the field during the exodus from the nest). The repetition rates of the particular calls used with the muted domestic mallard (Peking) ducklings were 3.7 notes/sec for the mallard and 2.3 notes/sec for the chicken. As these rates are fairly close to each other, it does not seem unreasonable to suppose that in the absence of the "fine tuning" ordinarily provided by exposure to their own and sibling vocalizations the devocal–isolated Peking ducklings might find them equally attractive (in the sense that they do not distinguish between them).[3] Heaton (1971) has identified repetition rate as a critical acoustic dimension of the mallard maternal call in vocal–communal Peking ducklings, so the repetition-rate hypothesis seemed especially worthy of investigation. It will be recalled that the devocal birds are sensitive to the high-frequency components (> 800 Hz) in the mallard call at 48 hr after hatching (i.e., they choose a mallard call with its high-frequency components intact over the same call with the high frequencies attenuated) (Gottlieb, 1975c), so the devocal birds must be disregarding the high-frequency difference in the mallard and chicken calls when they do not show a preference in the mallard–chicken call test 48 hr after hatching. The fact that the devocal ducklings are sensitive to the high-frequency difference but ignore it, indicates that their response in the mallard versus chicken call test is mediated by some other perceptual dimension (e.g., repetition rate) and that dimension takes precedence over frequency in controlling the devocal ducklings' response.

[3]There is a necessary ambiguity in the statement of the repetition-rate hypothesis. If the devocal ducklings find 3.7 notes/sec and 2.3 notes/sec equally attractive in the sense that they do not distinguish between them, that could be because (*a*) they are unable to discriminate between the two rates; or (*b*) their range of rate preferences has enlarged to embrace both rates. Alternative (*b*) does not imply a lack of discrimination, but a broadened range of positive responsiveness. Both alternatives lead to the same predictions in the present experiments, so the ambiguity cannot be resolved here. Other behavioral test procedures (e.g., stimulus generalization) are required to determine whether the devocal ducklings are able to discriminate between the rates.

The mallard and chicken maternal calls differ in several acoustic features other than repetition rate (e.g., frequency components, FM), thus, to make a precise test of the rate hypothesis, it was necessary to use temporal alterations of the mallard call itself as the basis of the choice test (i.e., to have only one acoustic feature, repetition rate, vary between the test calls).

If the rate hypothesis is correct, vocal–communal ducklings would show a preference for the normal mallard call at 3.7 notes/sec over a slowed version of that same call at 2.3 notes/sec, whereas the devocal–isolated birds would not show any preference (i.e., they would perform as they did in the mallard–chicken call test). Sonagrams and oscilloscopic verification of the repetition rates of the two calls are shown in Fig. 1.17. (The rate of the normal mallard call was slowed by inserting appropriately sized blank pieces of recording tape between the notes.)

As shown in Fig. 1.18, the vocal–communal ducklings showed a preference for the normal-rate mallard call, whereas the devocal–isolated ducklings did not, thus supporting the hypothesis that a broadening of repetition-rate preference occurs when the birds are deprived of hearing their own vocalizations.

H. Specificity of Experiential Requirement to Maintain Species-Specific Repetition-Rate Preference

After determining the broadening of the species-specific repetition-rate preference in the devocal–isolated ducklings, I undertook a study of the behavioral responsiveness of embryos to the mallard maternal call in advance of auditory experience (i.e., before they began vocalizing or were exposed to the vocalizations of conspecifics). The aurally inexperienced embryo was found to be responsive to the mallard call only at the rate of 2.7 notes/sec and not at other rates (Gottlieb, 1979). Thus, the broadening of a precise repetition-rate preference in the devocal–isolated ducklings reflects the failure of the maintenance of perceptual specificity in the absence of normally occurring auditory experience (exposure of the embryo to the vocalizations of self and siblings).

Because the embryo develops its highly specific responsiveness to the typical repetition rate of the species maternal call in advance of auditory experience, the original responsiveness can be viewed as "innate" and, thus, as the outcome of primarily endogenous processes of neural maturation. As Bateson (1976) has pointed out, some theorists

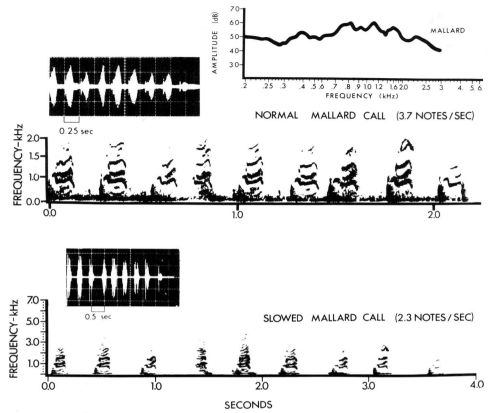

Fig. 1.17 Narrow-band Sonagrams and oscilloscopic depiction (insets) of the mallard maternal call at the normal (3.7 notes/sec) and slowed (2.3 notes/sec) repetition rates used in the experiments described in the text. (The necessity of greater photographic reduction makes the notes in mallard 2.3/sec appear shorter than in the other call.)

who concern themselves with innate behavior assume that the development of such behavior is not critically linked to any specific prior experience but that it will exhibit and maintain itself if rather general (nonspecific) life-sustaining conditions prevail during ontogeny. Thus, it is interesting to question whether the necessary auditory experiential contribution to keep the system "fine tuned" in the present instance could be of a rather general nature, as assumed by some theories of innate behavior development (e.g., Lorenz, 1965; Sperry, 1971), or whether the experiential requirement might be specific (i.e., the embryos having to hear their own vocalizations, which happen to be

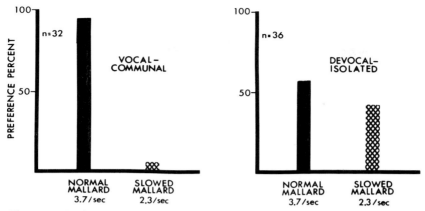

Fig. 1.18 Preference of vocal–communal and devocal–isolated Peking ducklings in simultaneous auditory choice test with mallard maternal call at normal and slowed repetition rates. (Data recast from Gottlieb, 1978, Table 3.)

around 4 notes/sec), as is assumed by other views of the development of species-specific behavior (Gottlieb, 1971, p. 156; Gottlieb, 1975b).

To examine the question of the requisite specificity of the embryonic auditory experience, in a recent study (Gottlieb, 1980a) devocalized–isolated embryos were given prior exposure to recordings of their species-typical embryonic contact–contentment call at three different repetition rates: the normal rate (4 notes/sec), slowed rate (2 notes/sec), or fast rate (6 notes/sec). These birds were subsequently tested after hatching for their preference in a simultaneous auditory choice test with the mallard maternal call at its normal rate (3.7 notes/ sec) versus the same call at an artificially slowed rate (2.3 notes/sec). As documented in the preceding, unstimulated devocalized ducklings do not show a preference in that test, whereas vocal ducklings prefer the 3.7/sec call over the slowed 2.3/sec call. If the embryonic auditory experiential requirement for the maintenance of the 4/sec preference is specific, the devocalized group receiving exposure to the contact–contentment call at 4 notes/sec would be the only one to show the normal preference for the species-typical rate of the maternal call. However, if the experiential requirement is not specific, all the stimulated groups should show the normal preference for the species-typical maternal rate. A third possibility is that the embryonic auditory exposure could modify the ducklings' normal repetition-rate preference. In the present case, that would signify a shift in preference from the normal maternal call to the one pulsed at 2.3 notes/sec in the group given previous exposure to the contact–contentment call at 2 notes/sec.

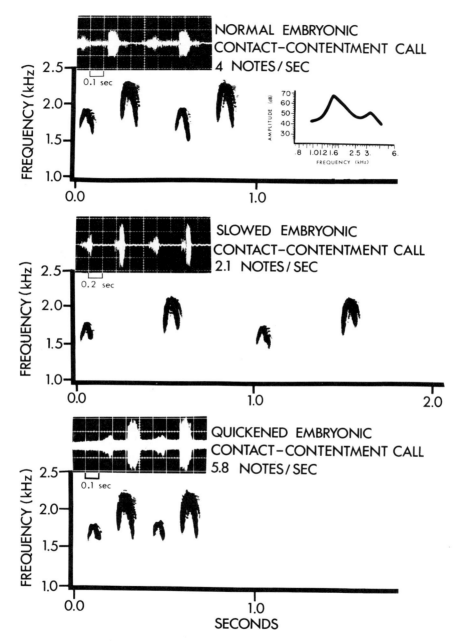

Fig. 1.19 Sonagram, oscilloscopic depiction, and peak frequency bands of embryonic contact–contentment call at 4 notes/sec (normal), 2.1 notes/sec, and 5.8 notes/sec. These

To determine if strictly embryonic experience was effective, the devocalized ducklings were exposed to the contact–contentment call for 5 min each hour for the last 2 days of the embryonic period (total stimulation: 4 hr) and tested at 48 hr after hatching. Naturally, they remained in quiet individual auditory isolation until the time of testing. (Further details are provided in Gottlieb, 1980a.)

As shown in Fig. 1.20, it was only the devocalized embryos stimulated with the contact–contentment call at 4 notes/sec that showed the species-typical preference for the normal maternal call over the slowed maternal call. The devocalized embryos stimulated with the contact–contentment call at either 2.1 notes/sec or 5.8 notes/sec did not show a preference in the choice tests, mirroring the performance of the unstimulated control embryos. Thus, prior exposure to the contact call at 2.1 notes/sec neither maintained the preference for the normal maternal call nor did it induce a preference for the 2.3 notes/sec maternal call, either of which seemed possible at the outset.

Consequently, if the ducklings are to show their normal preference for the maternal call at the species-typical repetition rate (4 notes/sec), they must be exposed to their own embryonic contact call at that rate. Exposure to the contact call at other rates fails to maintain this normal preference or to modify it (in the case of exposure to the embryonic call at 2 notes/sec). These results are all the more remarkable because the selective behavioral responsiveness to the maternal call at 4 notes/ sec arises in the embryo in advance of hearing its own or maternal vocalizations (Gottlieb, 1979). Thus, in the present instance, the maintenance of seemingly innate postnatal behavioral development is dependent upon a highly specific, normally occurring prior experience; it will not be maintained if only rather general (nonspecific) life-sustaining conditions prevail during ontogeny, as has been assumed in the past (Lorenz, 1965; Sperry, 1971).

The present results support the view that in the evolution of species-specific perception, natural selection has involved a selection for the entire developmental manifold, including both the organic and normally occurring stimulative features of ontogeny (Gottlieb, 1971, p. 156; Gottlieb, 1975b). That view is consonant with the conventionally accepted evolutionary assumption that natural selection operates on behavioral phenotypes, and behavioral phenotypes are the developmental out-

---

were the four-note bursts used to stimulate the devocal–isolated Peking duck embryos before they were tested with the normal and slowed mallard maternal call at 48 hr after hatching. (From Gottlieb, 1980a, Figure 1. Copyright © 1980 by the American Psychological Association. Reprinted by permission.)

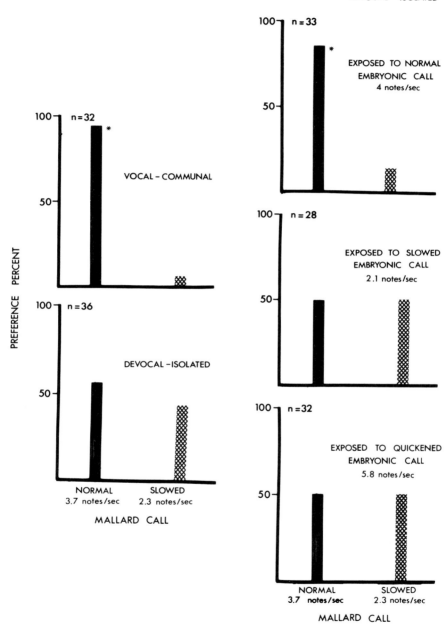

comes of individual organism–environment interactions. Just how highly specific such organism–environment interactions might necessarily be in the development and evolution of species-specific perception has not been appreciated. The embryonic developmental pathway of early species-typical adaptive behavior has not been the subject of much analytic experimental investigation, partly because it is technically difficult, but mostly because it has been regarded as a theoretically unrewarding enterprise. That is, we have assumed that we already know the unidirectional developmental pathway of "innate" behavior:

$$\begin{matrix} \text{genetic} \\ \text{activity} \end{matrix} \longrightarrow \begin{matrix} \text{neural} \\ \text{maturation} \end{matrix} \longrightarrow \text{species-typical behavior}$$

As I have argued elsewhere in some detail (Gottlieb, 1976a), the newly emerging view of species-typical behavioral development calls for the interpolation of experience as well as the bidirectionality of influences:

$$\begin{matrix} \text{genetic} \\ \text{activity} \end{matrix} \Longleftrightarrow \begin{matrix} \text{neural} \\ \text{maturation} \end{matrix} \Longleftrightarrow \text{experience} \Longleftrightarrow \text{species-typical behavior}$$

The present results assume greater generality when placed in the context of the other roles that experience plays in the development of species-typical behavior, namely facilitation and induction (Fig. 1.14). In a previous study (Gottlieb, 1975b), it was shown that, for the duckling to exhibit normal perceptual sensitivity to the higher-frequency components of the maternal call at the usual age after hatching, it had to be previously exposed to precisely those frequencies embryonically, and it happens that just those frequencies are present in their own embryonic contact–contentment call (1500–2500 Hz). In that case, the specific embryonic auditory experience *facilitates* the appearance of normal high-frequency perceptual sensitivity 24 hr after hatching, as well as maintains it 65 hr after hatching. The specificity of the experiential requirement for the *induction* of a perceptual preference for some feature of the maternal call as has been shown, for example, with early "habitat preferences" in developing amphibia (Wiens, 1970) must yet be determined. An opportunity to examine that question will present itself in

---

Fig. 1.20 Preference of vocal–communal and devocal–isolated Peking ducklings in simultaneous auditory choice test with normal and slowed mallard maternal call after prenatal exposure to embryonic contentment call at normal, slowed, and quickened repetition rates. $*p < .0001$. (Data recast from Gottlieb, 1980a, Table 1.)

the embryonic study of the development of ascending and descending FM preferences in wood ducklings in advance of auditory experience.

Although we have become accustomed to the high degree of experiential specificity required for the development of visual–motor coordinations (e.g., Hein & Diamond, 1972), in the present instance such specificity is shown to be necessary for the development of species-typical perception that involves no skilled or highly refined motor component.

Taken together with previous results, the present findings indicate that the development of species-specific auditory perception is a probabilistic phenomenon, in the sense that the threshold, timing, and ultimate normality of such perception are jointly regulated by sensory stimulative as well as organismic factors. In the usual course of development, the manifest changes and improvements in species-specific perception do not represent solely the unfolding of a fixed or predetermined organic substrate independent of normally occurring sensory stimulation.

It remains to note that, in lieu of the usual conceptions of learning, the present conception of the various roles of experience in the development of species-typical behavior (Fig. 1.14) has been found to be useful not only in the study of auditory perception in young birds (e.g., Evans, 1980; Kerr, Ostapoff, & Rubel, 1979) but in the development of speech perception in human infants (Aslin & Pisoni, 1980), olfactory experience and huddling preferences in rat pups (Brunjes & Alberts, 1979), and the maintenance of emotionality in gerbils (Clark & Galef, 1979), to specify several disparate examples. Traditional learning theory has not been useful in describing the contributions of experience to the species-typical development of behavior, so we must now begin to formulate these contributions in a different way.

III. ROLE OF EXPERIENCE

Three roles of experience in early neural and behavioral development have been described in some detail previously (Gottlieb, 1976a, 1976b). In light of recent evidence and for the sake of logical consistency, a change in the framework is required, as shown in Fig. 1.21.[4] Heretofore, (a), (b), and (c) in Fig. 1.21 were each regarded as a form of facilitation

---

[4]I have had especially useful discussions with colleagues on the roles of experience in behavioral development. I would like in particular to acknowledge David Miller, Timothy Johnston, Richard Aslin, Jeffrey Alberts.

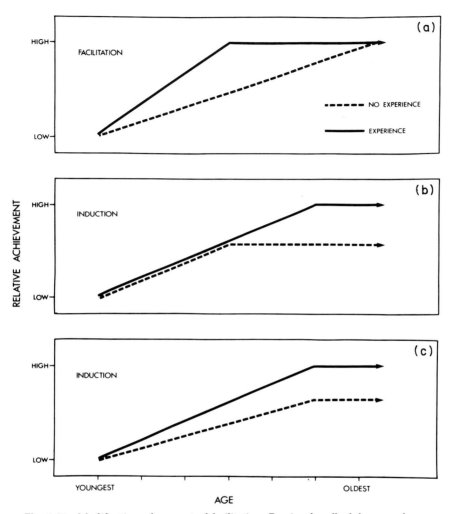

Fig. 1.21 Modification of concept of facilitation. Previously, all of these modes were considered facilitation (Gottlieb, 1976b). Facilitation is most appropriately applied to instances represented by (a), where experience causes accelerated development when compared to the absence of such experience. The key defining feature is that the same endpoint will eventually be realized even in the absence of the experience. In (b) and (c), the experience results in an elevated terminal level of achievement that is not reached in the absence of the experience, so these are most appropriately considered instances of induction instead of facilitation. In (b), the effect of the experience becomes manifest later than it does in (c).

(as indicated in Fig. 2 in Gottlieb, 1976b). For logical and definitional consistency, it is more appropriate to consider modes (b) and (c) as instances of induction rather than of facilitation. Induction refers to the role of experience when it completely determines whether a particular endpoint, level of achievement, degree of specificity, fine tuning, and so on will or will not be reached. These endpoints are not reached in the absence of experience as they are in the case where experience merely accelerates the appearance of an endpoint (Fig. 1.21a). Thus, facilitation now refers only to the temporal accelerating aspect of experience in all cases in which the same endpoint would eventually be reached in the absence of such experience. Instances in which the final level of achievement requires a necessary boost by experience (i.e., does not get there without experience) is logically and definitionally an inductive effect of experience (Fig. 1.21b,c).

The curves in Fig. 1.21 are purposely drawn to show some achievement in advance of, and without, experience. These are instances in which experience significantly *enhances* a degree of development that is already present in the system, as is well exemplified in a recent study of auditory perceptual development by Kerr, Ostapoff, and Rubel (1978). As shown in Fig. 1.22, young chicks deprived of normal auditory experience do not make as fine auditory discriminations as do chicks with normal auditory experience. Specifically, in the absence of normal

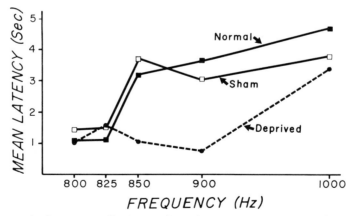

Fig. 1.22 Auditory generalization gradients in response to pure tones in normal and aurally deprived chicks. The chicks were habituated to 800-Hz tone and then tested with the other tones. Latency to resumption of cheeping was the measure of generalization. The aurally deprived chicks had ear plugs inserted bilaterally before hatching. The "sham" group had the same operation except the plugs were not inserted. (From Kerr, Ostapoff, & Rubel, 1979, Figure 7. Reproduced with permission of authors and publisher. Copyright © 1979 by the American Psychological Association.)

auditory experience, chicks can detect a difference between an 800-Hz tone and a 1000-Hz tone. With normal experience, that ability is significantly enhanced so that they can detect differences as small as 50 or 100 Hz from 800 Hz. In the literature on speech perception, this example could represent some degree of tuning in advance of experience, which is then perfected (enhanced, finely tuned) by exposure to speech sounds (Aslin & Pisoni, 1980). Of course, to discriminate between instances of facilitation and induction, it is still necessary to determine whether the finest degree of tuning would eventually occur even in the absence of experience. In the Kerr *et al.* study, the investigators recognized that they would have to test the aurally deprived chicks at later ages to determine whether or not their perception of tonal differences becomes as keen as that of aurally experienced chicks. Only in that way would they be able to conclude whether normal auditory experience plays an inductive or a facilitative role in the development of tonal discrimination in chicks.

To conclude, then, as shown in Fig. 1.23, the modified framework for interpreting the effects of early experience on development shows facilitation as solely a temporal regulative effect and induction as enhancing partially developed systems as well as relatively undeveloped ones. It is possible that, when considering the underlying neural mechanism, it may be best to discriminate instances of enhancement of partial development from those of rather incomplete development, but as yet we have no evidence of completely unbiased or indifferent motor or perceptual systems. That is, even systems that appear to be neutral or indifferent on initial study prove later to be more susceptible to being pushed in some directions rather than in other directions (e.g., Wiens, 1970). In any event, I leave this matter to eventual empirical and conceptual resolution. (This issue and other ones are further explicated in Aslin's Chapter 2, Volume 2.)

Another, and more pressing, fuzzy issue concerns maintenance and induction. An example of this problem is well illustrated by the experimental paradigm of the imprinting literature. Young, precocial, socially isolated birds are given a simultaneous choice test between two visually dissimilar objects at 48 hr after hatching. They approach and follow one or the other object indiscriminately and thus show no preference for either object as a group. Another group of birds is given an opportunity to follow one or the other object before the test at 48 hr. In this group, the birds prefer to follow the familiar object in the choice test. Because the control group showed no preference, and were as likely to follow one object as the other, it might be thought that the imprinting process merely *maintains* an already present response. In

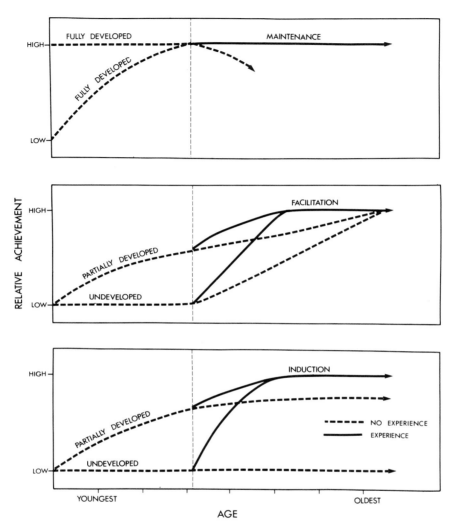

Fig. 1.23 Modified framework for interpreting the effects of early experience on species-typical behavioral development. Vertical dashed line indicates when experience starts. Terms fully developed, partially developed, and undeveloped refer to state of system prior to experience. See text for discussion. (Modified from Gottlieb, 1976b.)

this view the imprinted preference is the outcome of a selective maintenance process. I think this is an incorrect way to conceptualize the role of experience here, because it overlooks what must be going on during the exposure period. Namely, the bird is actively learning the characteristics of the object during the period of training or exposure, and that is what renders it familiar and allows the object to be discriminated and preferred in the later choice test. Thus, this is an example of induction, because it leads to the development of a preference (or perceptual specificity) that would not develop without the experience. Maintenance, on the other hand, concerns the preservation of already developed preferences or specificities. For example, from the research described earlier in this chapter we know that chicks are selectively responsive to the maternal call of their species in choice tests at 24 or 48 hr after hatching without the opportunity of previous exposure to the maternal call. The operation of maintenance in this connection has been shown by Graves (1973), who found that responsiveness to the maternal call wanes by 12 days of age unless the chicks are exposed to the call during Days 1–5. I would argue that the term maintenance is properly applied only when the specificity, preference, or selective responsiveness exists prior to the experience, so that the experience itself does not create or enhance the selective basis of the behavior but only preserves that which is already present. Thus, I think the use of the concept of maintenance to cover instances in which initially indiscriminate responding becomes selective [e.g., learning of individual parent calls by gull chicks (Evans, 1980; Impekoven, 1976)] overlooks the active learning (induction) that is going on during the familiarization process that leads to the selectivity of the response. The latter is necessarily based on a finer perception of the relevant cues than would be the case, for example, in the selective responsiveness to the generalized maternal call of the species. The experiential process involved in individual recognition is necessarily inductive, in the sense that the final selective response must be based on more cues, different cues, or a narrower specification of the original cues that mediated the initial selective response. Again, it would seem valuable to distinguish the two subtypes of induction: (*a*) enhancement of previously existing dimensions; and (*b*) the possible creation of new perceptual dimensions mediating the behavior.

Although I have discussed only a single example to try to explicate a subtle but crucial difference between maintenance and induction, I trust the reasoning is applicable to other behavioral phenomena. The concept of maintenance is properly applied only to instances where no further differentiation of perception or motor response occurs as a consequence of experience.

IV. SUMMARY AND CONCLUSIONS

The experimental results reviewed in this chapter confirm a hoary suspicion that normal embryonic or prenatal experience plays an essential role in the development of species-specific behavior after birth or hatching (behavior otherwise thought of as innate). In this century, Kuo (1921) was the first to raise the possibility that some features of the instinctive behavior of neonates may be a consequence of experience that occurred in the embryo and, building on Kuo's thoughts and the hypotheses stemming from his embryonic research, Lehrman (1953, 1970) and Schneirla (1956, 1965) kept the idea alive, although it was admittedly empirically unfounded.

Beyond confirming what seems to be almost an ancient issue in discussions of problems of early behavioral development, modifications are introduced into a recent framework for interpreting the various ways in which experience can influence the development of species-typical behavior. Because conventional associationistic conceptions of learning have not proven to be very useful in gaining an understanding of the function of experience in the development of species-typical behavior, it is necessary to begin to formulate the various contributions of experience in a different way. The present framework is a step in that direction.

ACKNOWLEDGMENTS

The research described in this chapter was supported by the North Carolina Division of Mental Health and Grant HD-00878 from the National Institute of Child Health and Human Development.

Jo Ann Bell, Mary Catharine Jackson, and Kathy Bobseine provided unstinting assistance with the laboratory experiments. I am also very grateful to David B. Miller for completing the collection of wood duck and mallard maternal calls in the field that I initiated in the early 1960s (Miller & Gottlieb, 1976, 1979). It was essential to know the modal features of these calls to assure that the experimental identification of their critical acoustic attributes in the laboratory was relevant to an understanding of species-typical behavior.

As the field and laboratory work recounted here summarizes the highlights of 20 years of especially gratifying labor, I thank my wife Nora for making life in a blind so much more endurable by her company in the spring of 1961.

REFERENCES

Aslin, R. N., & Pisoni, D. B. Some developmental processes in speech perception. In G. H. Yeni-Komshian, J. F. Kavanagh, & C. A. Ferguson (Eds.), *Child phonology.* New York: Academic Press, 1980.

Bateson, P. P. G. Specificity and the origins of behavior. In J. S. Rosenblatt, R. A. Hinde, E. Shaw, & C. Beer (Eds.), *Advances in the study of behavior* (Vol. 6). New York: Academic Press, 1976.

Brunjes, P. C., & Alberts, J. R. Olfactory stimulation induces filial preferences for huddling in rat pups. *Journal of Comparative and Physiological Psychology,* 1979, **93,** 548–555.

Clark, M. M., & Galef, B. G., Jr. A sensitive period for the maintenance of emotionality in Mongolian gerbils. *Journal of Comparative and Physiological Psychology,* 1979, **93,** 200–210.

Collias, N., & Joos, M. The spectrographic analysis of sound signals of the domestic fowl. *Behaviour,* 1953, **5,** 175–187.

Evans, R. M. Development of individual call recognition in young ring-billed gulls (*Larus delawarensis*): An effect of feeding. *Animal Behaviour,* 1980, **28,** 60—67.

Gottlieb, G. A naturalistic study of imprinting in wood ducklings (*Aix sponsa*). *Journal of Comparative and Physiological Psychology,* 1963, **56,** 86–91.

Gottlieb, G. Components of recognition in ducklings. *Natural History,* 1965, **74,** 12–19.

Gottlieb, G. Species recognition in ground-nesting and hole-nesting ducklings. *Ecology,* 1968, **49,** 87–95.

Gottlieb, G. *Development of species identification in birds.* Chicago: University of Chicago Press, 1971.

Gottlieb, G. On the acoustic basis of species identification in wood ducklings. *Journal of Comparative and Physiological Psychology,* 1974, **87,** 1038–1048.

Gottlieb, G. Development of species identification in ducklings: I. Nature of perceptual deficit caused by embryonic auditory deprivation. *Journal of Comparative and Physiological Psychology,* 1975, **89,** 387–399. (a)

Gottlieb, G. Development of species identification in ducklings: II. Experiential prevention of perceptual deficit caused by embryonic auditory deprivation. *Journal of Comparative and Physiological Psychology,* 1975, **89,** 675–684. (b)

Gottlieb, G. Development of species identification in ducklings: III. Maturational rectification of perceptual deficit caused by auditory deprivation. *Journal of Comparative and Physiological Psychology,* 1975, **89,** 899–912. (c)

Gottlieb, G. Conceptions of prenatal development: Behavioral embryology. *Psychological Review,* 1976, **83,** 215–234. (a)

Gottlieb, G. The roles of experience in the development of behavior and the nervous system. In G. Gottlieb (Ed.), *Neural and behavioral specificity.* New York: Academic Press, 1976. (b)

Gottlieb, G. Development of species identification in ducklings: IV. Change in species-specific perception caused by auditory deprivation. *Journal of Comparative and Physiological Psychology,* 1978, **92,** 375–387.

Gottlieb, G. Development of species identification in ducklings: V. Perceptual differentiation in the embryo. *Journal of Comparative and Physiological Psychology,* 1979, **93,** 831–854.

Gottlieb, G. Development of species identification in ducklings: VI. Specific embryonic experience required to maintain species-typical perception in Peking ducklings. *Journal of Comparative and Physiological Psychology,* 1980, **94,** 579–587. (a)

Gottlieb, G. Development of species identification in ducklings: VII. Highly specific early experience fosters species-specific perception in wood ducklings. *Journal of Comparative and Physiological Psychology*, 1980, **94**, 1019–1027. (b)

Gottlieb, G., & Vandenbergh, J. Ontogeny of vocalization in duck and chick embryos. *Journal of Experimental Zoology*, 1968, **168**, 307–325.

Graves, H. B. Early social responses in Gallus: A functional analysis. *Science*, 1973, **182**, 937–939.

Guyomarc'h, J.-C. Les bases ontogénétiques de l'attractivité du gloussement maternel chez la poule domestique. *Revue du Comportement Animal*, 1972, **6**, 79–94.

Heaton, M. B. *Stimulus coding in the species-specific perception of Peking ducklings*. Unpublished doctoral dissertation, North Carolina State University, 1971.

Heaton, M. B. Prenatal auditory discrimination in the wood duck. *Animal Behaviour*, 1972, **20**, 421–424.

Hein, A., & Diamond, R. M. Locomotory space as a prerequisite for acquiring visually guided reaching in kittens. *Journal of Comparative and Physiological Psychology*, 1972, **81**, 394–398.

Impekoven, M. Responses of laughing gull chicks (*Larus atricilla*) to parental attraction- and alarm-calls, and effects of prenatal auditory experience on the responsiveness to such calls. *Behaviour*, 1976, **56**, 250–278.

Kerr, L. M., Ostapoff, E. M., & Rubel, E. W. Influence of acoustic experience on the ontogeny of frequency generalization gradients in the chicken. *Journal of Experimental Psychology: Animal Behavior Processes*, 1979, **5**, 97–115.

Kuo, Z.-Y. Giving up instincts in psychology. *Journal of Philosophy*, 1921, **18**, 645–664.

Kuo, Z.-Y. *The dynamics of behavior development* (enlarged ed.). New York: Plenum, 1976.

Lehrman, D. S. A critique of Konrad Lorenz's theory of instinctive behavior. *Quarterly Review of Biology*, 1953, **28**, 337–363.

Lehrman, D. S. Semantic and conceptual issues in the nature–nurture problem. In L. R. Aronson, E. Tobach, D. S. Lehrman, & J. S. Rosenblatt (Eds.), *Development and evolution of behavior*. San Francisco: Freeman, 1970.

Lorenz, K. *Evolution and modification of behavior*. Chicago: University of Chicago Press, 1965.

Miller, D. B., & Gottlieb, G. Acoustic features of wood duck (*Aix sponsa*) maternal calls. *Behaviour*, 1976, **57**, 260–280.

Miller, D. B., & Gottlieb, G. Maternal vocalizations of mallard ducks (*Anas platyrhynchos*). *Animal Behaviour*, 1978, **26**, 1178–1194.

Schneirla, T. C. Interrelationships of the "innate" and the "acquired" in instinctive behavior. In P.-P. Grassé (Ed.), *L'Instinct dans le comportement des animaux et de l'homme*. Paris: Masson, 1956.

Schneirla, T. C. Aspects of stimulation and organization in approach/withdrawal processes underlying vertebrate behavioral development. In D. S. Lehrman, R. A. Hinde, & E. Shaw (Eds.), *Advances in the study of behavior* (Vol. 1). New York: Academic Press, 1965.

Scoville, R., & Gottlieb, G. The calculation of repetition rate in avian vocalizations. *Animal Behaviour*, 1978, **26**, 962–963.

Sperry, R. W. How a developing brain gets itself properly wired for adaptive function. In E. Tobach, L. R. Aronson, & E. Shaw (Eds.), *The biopsychology of development*. New York: Academic Press, 1971.

Wiens, J. A. Effects of early experience on substrate pattern selection in *Rana aurora* tadpoles. *Copeia*, 1970, No. 3, 543–548.

2

Development of Parent–Offspring Recognition in Birds

MICHAEL D. BEECHER
University of Washington

I. INTRODUCTION

Individual recognition may be defined as the discrimination of a particular individual from others, based on individually distinctive characteristics rather than on circumstantial evidence. Consider parent–offspring recognition. Generally, a parent returning to the nest (den, etc.) can be virtually certain that the young there are its own,

45

and individual recognition is not required. To find offspring away from the nest in a group of similar-aged young, however, the parent must utilize individually distinctive characteristics to locate them (or alternatively, the offspring must recognize the parent by individual characteristics). I emphasize in this chapter that recognition actually consists of two distinct processes: identification (the sender providing cues to its identity) and actual recognition (the receiver perceiving these cues).

Most studies of the development of recognition have focused on the learning of species-typical characteristics. Two representative examples are the learning of species-specific song by white-crowned sparrows (Marler, 1970) and the learning of the maternal call by wood ducklings (Gottlieb, 1974, and Chapter 1, this volume). In most such cases, the distinctive characteristics are learned through specific experiences occurring during a sensitive period. As in the two cases mentioned, innate constraints on what is learned are usually found. Some of these studies have indicated that individual or class-distinctive characteristics are learned in addition to species-distinctive characteristics, although in general the adaptive significance of this specificity is still uncertain. For example, white-crowned sparrows learn local dialects (Marler, 1970) and female zebra finches learn the individual characteristics of their father's song, which they still recognize on reaching sexual maturity (Miller, 1979). Thus the studies on the development of species recognition can be seen to blend into the studies on the development of individual recognition.

In this chapter I describe our continuing research on the development of parent–offspring recognition in bank swallows (*Riparia riparia*) (Beecher, Beecher, & Hahn, 1981; Beecher, Beecher, & Lumpkin, 1981; Beecher & Beecher, in preparation). This research has been carried out primarily in the field; we are just beginning to study aspects of the individual recognition process in the laboratory and these efforts are described briefly. Previous studies on parent–offspring recognition have made three points. First, parent–offspring recognition is not an inevitable consequence of an extended parent–offspring relationship: There appear to be at least some cases in which recognition does not develop (e.g., Emlen, 1941; Vehrencamp, 1977). The problems of negative evidence notwithstanding, it is generally presumed that these failures of recognition are understandable in terms of the species' particular natural history and ecology, that is, in such species the appropriate selection pressures are absent. Second, when the developmental timetable for recognition has been determined by exchanging young of various ages between like-aged broods, it has been found that parent-offspring recognition develops very shortly before it is needed. Thus recognition develops on about Day 5 in herring gulls (Tinbergen, 1953) and not until after about 5 weeks in kittiwake gulls (Cullen, 1957); in both cases, these ages correspond approximately to the onset of the intermingling of young of different broods. Third, the development of recognition appears to be an imprinting-like process, with the parent (or offspring) learning the characteristics of the offspring (or parent) during some brief sensitive period.

II. PARENT–OFFSPRING RECOGNITION IN BANK SWALLOWS

A. Natural Contexts

Parent–offspring recognition is a critical component of the social behavior of bank swallows. A summary of the natural contexts in which it occurs follows (Beecher, Beecher, & Lumpkin, 1981). Bank swallows live in colonies that typically contain at least 20 but more generally at least 100 pairs. The birds dig burrows in sand banks, constructing the nest at the back of the burrow. These burrows are tightly packed, being separated by an average distance of 0.5 m. This highly social existence produces at least four important contexts in which parent–offspring recognition is needed:

1. In bank swallows, there is a period of 4–7 days during which the young can fly but are not completely emancipated from their parents or their natal burrow. During this period, they leave and return to the bank frequently, often returning to the wrong burrow. Because these burrows themselves typically contain similar-aged young, the parent at that nest will return from foraging to find an alien chick among its own. Bank swallow parents give clear evidence of recognition in this situation by "evicting" the alien chick from its nest.

2. Parents give further evidence of recognition by searching for and retrieving their chicks during this stage.

3. Fledgling birds are often left by their parents in large groups of young similar to the crèches seen in many colonial species. These aggregations are usually on power lines near the colony and may contain hundreds of birds. The parent returns to this aggregation, finds its own chicks, and feeds them there; we have never seen a parent feed a chick other than its own in this situation.

4. Parents and offspring continue to associate for some time after vacating the burrow, although we cannot describe this stage in any detail nor state how long it lasts.

B. Development of Parental Recognition

Our field observations on bank swallows indicate that (*a*) parents do not need to recognize their offspring before 14 days, because alien chicks rarely fly into pre-14 day nests, but are conspicuous merely by their age when they do; (*b*) recognition is required at 18 days, when the chicks begin to fly; and (*c*) a call given by the chick appears to be involved in recognition by the parent. Consequently, one would predict recognition of a chick by its parent to develop some time between 14 and 18 days, and to be correlated with the development of some cue, perhaps the chick call.

We carried out experiments in which we exchanged chicks between broods that were approximately the same age (Beecher, Beecher, & Hahn, 1981). All chicks from a brood were removed from the burrow, banded, and color-marked. Two chicks from one brood were then exchanged with two chicks from a likeaged brood. The remaining chicks in each brood (usually 3) were then returned to their original nest. Because the returned chicks were treated similarly to the exchanged chicks in all other respects, they are "sham exchanges" or controls. We marked 41 experimental (exchanged) chicks and 52 control (returned) chicks. All 52 sham exchanges were reaccepted by their parents, illustrating that there is no effect of removing, handling, and marking the young. The fate of the 41 experimental birds depended on their ages. All birds 15 days old or younger ($N = 23$) were adopted by the host. That the adoption was complete and symmetrical was revealed by three cases in which adopted chicks subsequently happened to fly back into their natal burrow (at 21, 21, and 22 days, respectively): In all three cases, the birds were evicted by their natural parents. A mixed response was seen with the 16–17-day-old transfers ($N = 10$): Four were adopted, four were immediately evicted, and circumstantial evidence strongly indicates that the remaining two were also evicted later. Seven of the eight 18-day-old transfers flew from the foster burrow within 30 min of the transfer; all seven were observed back at the home burrow by the next day. The only bird that remained in the nest long enough (90 min) was evicted by the resident adult. Birds typically begin to fly at 18–19 days, so experimental exchanges at this point are not really feasible. However, as mentioned in the previous section, there are many natural occurrences of birds 18 days or older flying into alien nests, and the parents typically evict these intruders. Thus the results indicate that parental recognition is completely absent before 16 days, but is essentially complete by 18 days.

On the basis of this experiment and our field observations, we hypothesized that the distinguishing cue, which we will call the chick's "signature," develops at about Day 15–17. The parent learns this signature in what we suppose is an irreversible, imprinting-like process. The parental learning process must lag the chick's development of the signature, by perhaps a day or so. Since the exchange experiments provided us with a measure of the development of parental recognition (although not unconfounded by chick recognition), we attempted to subsequent experiments to ascertain if the chick call mentioned earlier might (a) have signature qualities, that is, be individually distinctive; (b) be a sufficient cue for recognition by the parents; and (c) develop according to the timetable suggested by our hypothesis, that is, a day or so in advance of the development of parental recognition.

C. The Chick's Signature Call

The mobility of swallows makes recording of their calls away from the burrow a hit-or-miss proposition. However, we are able to get quite good recordings from the birds in the burrow, using small dynamic microphones secured near the entrance. The birds quickly habituate to these foreign objects and the quality of the recordings obtained compares favorably with our best recordings obtained outside the burrow with the usual condensor microphone. We first noted that calls recorded when the birds were quite young (immature calls) differed markedly from calls recorded in the days shortly before fledging (mature calls); examples of these two types of calls are given in Fig. 2.1. A variety of tests in which we had naive human observers attempt to identify birds from sonagrams of their calls revealed this to be an easy task when mature calls were judged, but essentially impossible for immature calls. We have begun an objective acoustic analysis of the mature calls (signature calls) and so far have found five acoustic parameters for which interindividual variation is significantly greater than intraindividual variation (Beecher, Beecher, & Hahn, 1981). We believe that there are more such parameters, but the task of extracting dimensions from complex patterns is not a simple one, and we are still at work on this problem. Having shown that the information for individual recognition was present in the mature call, we had next to show that the parents could indeed extract this information.

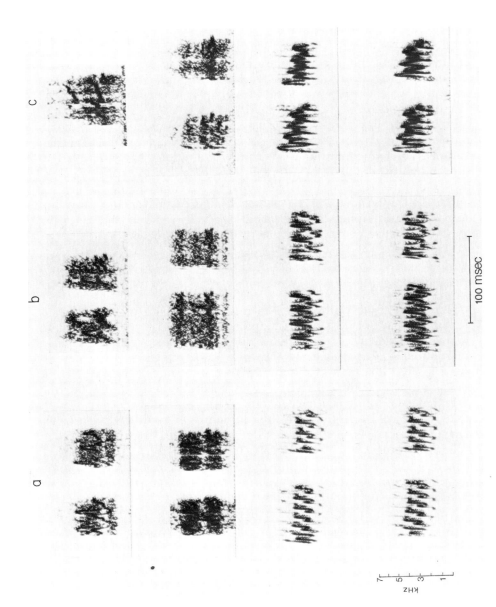

a   b   c

100 msec

7
5
3
1
KHz

D. Playback Experiments

To obtain direct evidence that the signature call is used by parents to recognize their young, we conducted a playback experiment (Beecher, Beecher, & Hahn, 1981). This procedure (a) isolates the call from other possible cues given by the chick; and (b) eliminates the effects of recognition by the chick of parent, siblings, nest, etc. The experiments were carried out at a time when the young in a nest were 18–21 days of age, a time when they are apt to fly into an alien burrow, and when parents are often observed searching for lost young. On the day before a test, we recorded from the particular burrow to be tested. We then analyzed these recordings on the Sonagraph, selected three different calls, and made a tape loop. In the playback test, small speakers were placed in each of two burrows on either side of the experimental burrow, approximately 3–4 m apart. For the duration of the test, all young from the experimental nest were removed, to stimulate searching by the parents. On a trial, calls were broadcast simultaneously from the two speakers: from one, the experimental tape, and from the other, a control tape (i.e., from another burrow). Each tape loop was used once as an experimental tape and once as a control tape. A test consisted of four trials, with each tape played from each side twice. Positive responses to a speaker were scored when an adult hovered in front of a speaker for at least two 15-sec periods. Responses were often much more vigorous, as when the parent tried to push past the speaker into the burrow. Although, in theory, a parent could respond to both speakers on a given trial, this, in fact, never happened. We performed this test at eight nests where the young were 18–21 days old; all female parents and five of the male parents were marked. Of these 13 parents, 12 preferred the experimental tape to the control tape (41 trials to 0), that is, preferred the calls of their own chicks to those of alien chicks; the thirteenth parent failed to respond at all. These results clearly indicate that the signature call contains sufficient information for recognition of the chick by the parent.

Fig. 2.1 Vocalizations recorded at three nests. Each column (a, b, and c) represents a single individual. The top two rows are calls recorded at ages 12–14 days. The bottom two rows are calls recorded on Days 17–21. The former are categorized as "immature" calls because of their basically wide-band, noisy nature. The latter are characterized as signature calls because of (a) their more clearly defined acoustic structure, identifiable in the distinct frequency sweeps (figures); and (b) their consistency, or minimal intraindividual variability. Occasionally, only the first note of the two-note signature call is given. Similarly, the immature begging call may be given as either a single-note or a two-note call. (From Beecher, Beecher, & Hahn, 1981.)

E. Development of the Signature Call

The hypothesis given in the preceding section suggests that the development of the signature call should precede the development of parental recognition, as revealed by the chick exchange experiments. To measure the ontogeny of the call, we recorded from each of 12 nests in one colony every second or third day and calculated the proportion of signature (mature) calls relative to immature begging calls. Three human observers independently classified each call as mature or immature (examples of each are shown in Fig. 2.1). There was complete agreement on 1242 of the 1258 calls; the remaining 16 calls were classified according to the majority judgment.

The development of the signature call is shown in Fig. 2.2. Ages are mean brood ages (individual ages within the asynchronously hatching brood were within ± 1 day of the mean age). The ages are plotted in 2-day blocks to provide an N of 8–12 nests per point, and also because of an uncertainty of approximately ± 1 day in the assigned mean brood age.

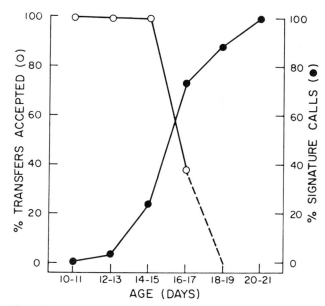

Fig. 2.2 The right axis is the percentage of signature calls (relative to immature calls). The left axis is the percentage of exchanged chicks accepted. The curve for the latter is extrapolated to zero in the 18–19 day age range on the basis of natural observations in addition to the experimental results. (From Beecher, Beecher, & Hahn, 1981.)

It can be seen in Fig. 2.2 that the signature calls begin to appear on Day 14–15 and, by Day 18–19, virtually all calls are signature calls. It appears that the major development takes place in the 16–17 day mean brood age range. The curve would undoubtedly be more quantal in form if our data had been obtained from individuals of precisely known developmental age. It is likely that the few signature calls in the 14–15 mean brood age range were given by older chicks in the brood (possibly 16 days old) and the immature calls in the 16–17 mean brood age range by younger chicks in the brood (possibly 15 days old). Some broods have a runt, and it may be this sibling that gives the few immature calls seen on Day 18–19.

Also plotted in Fig. 2.2 are the results of the chick exchange experiments already described (it should be emphasized that these were independent studies). The horizontal axis refers to the age of the exchanged chicks. It can be seen that the curves describing the development of the signature call and the development of parent–offspring recognition both break at 16–17 days. Thus, these data are consistent with the hypothesis that the call is a signature by which the parent recognizes its young, and that the development of parental recognition depends on the development of the chick call.

F. Comparative Study of Rough-winged Swallows

Swallows (Hirundinidae) are an interesting group for the study of adaptations to coloniality, as they range from highly colonial to more or less solitary species. Bank swallows belong at one end of this continuum, as they are typically found in dense colonies of hundreds of individuals. The rough-winged swallow (*Stelgidopteryx ruficollis*) falls at the opposite end of this continuum. They appropriate natural cavities, often burrows dug by other hole-nesting birds, and are found nesting solitarily or in small, happenstance groups. Bank and rough-winged swallows are ideal for comparative study because they are so similar in many fundamental aspects: their breeding cycles are virtually identical, they both forage on the wing for the same groups of insects, they both build their nests at the backs of burrows dug into sand banks (at least in some areas, including our study sites in Michigan and Massachusetts), and they are very similar in size and appearance (inexperienced bird-watchers confuse the two).

Our intention in the comparative study of bank and rough-winged swallows was to explicitly address the extent to which parent–offspring recognition can be considered a true adaptation to the specific selection pressures correlated with colonial life, as opposed to simply a facultative developmental response to different proximate environmental conditions. This distinction between the proximate and ultimate effects of the species-typical environment is often ignored. For example, consider the classic herring gull versus kittiwake contrast. Cullen (1957) found that kittiwakes show no signs of parent–offspring recognition in contexts comparable to those in which herring gulls do (Tinbergen, 1953) and attributed this difference to the fact that the herring gull breeding grounds allow intermingling of young, whereas this is not possible in the cliff ledge-nesting kittiwakes. It has generally been presumed that this nesting habitat difference has exerted its influence on recognition in the species's evolutionary past (ultimate cause) by selecting for or against discrimination–recognition mechanisms. Thus, we would expect the two species to differ in terms of the specific mechanisms by which they do (or do not) accomplish parent–offspring recognition. But it could well be that the nesting habitat difference has its influence on a developmental time scale (proximate cause): The two closely related species could, in fact, share the same open developmental program so that, depending on the particular environmental conditions, the appropriate adaptive responses develop. Some support for the latter interpretation comes from a report that herring gulls nesting on cliff ledges do not recognize their chicks at an age (1–2 weeks) when their ground-nesting conspecifics do (Von Rautenfeld, 1978). Thus, all gull species may have the capacity for recognition at an earlier age (4–5 days), such recognition occurring as a facultative response to the appropriate environmental conditions (e.g., kittiwakes nesting on flat ground might likewise develop the ability and/or tendency to recognize their young at 4–5 days). Except for those fortunate cases in which the two species can be found in both sets of environmental circumstances (e.g., both species found nesting on ledges and in the open), the only way to differentiate between these two hypotheses is to examine directly the specific behavioral mechanisms and their development.

We have taken this latter approach in our comparative study of bank swallows and rough-winged swallows (Beecher & Beecher, in preparation). At our Michigan study sites, we were able to find both bank and rough-winged swallows nesting in close proximity; a single rough-winged pair was often found on the periphery of a bank swallow colony. Thus some of the proximate aspects of the environment are matched in this comparison. The critical features, however, are not. The various problems facing bank swallow parents are simply not present for rough-wing parents: (*a*) rough-winged young fledge as a group and are not apt to fly into other burrows; (*b*) other young rough-wings do not fly into their nests; (c) parents do not have to find their young in large aggregations of other young rough-wings, and so on. However, rough-wings nesting near bank swallows are faced with a special problem: young bank swallows may fly into their nests. In this situation, rough-wings show an amazing lack of discrimination. For example, in one such "experiment of nature" we watched two rough-winged parents feed at least five different bank swallows that flew into their nest over a 50-hr period, for a total of 48 visible feedings; they gave no hint of rejection during this entire period. To examine this phenomenon under controlled conditions, we performed 12 single-bird interspecific transfers. All transfers were 10–15 days old. In this experiment, we removed one nestling from a rough-winged nest and exchanged it with a bank swallow from a bank swallow nest. As before, to control for the effects of handling, banding, and color marking, we removed all or most of the remainder of the brood, performed the same manipulations, and returned them to their home nests. Again, none of these sham-exchanged birds were rejected by their parents. An exchanged chick was considered to have been accepted by its foster parent if it was fed and remained there until at least 19 days of age (fledging normally occurs at 21–22 days in both species). Five of the six rough-wings transferred into bank swallow burrows were rejected, whereas all six bank swallows transferred into rough-winged burrows were accepted ($p = .0076$, Fisher exact probability). Three of the rough-wing transfers were not fed by their bank swallow hosts, two were fed until 16 days of age and were then rejected, and the single rough-wing that was unequivocally accepted at the bank swallow burrow remained there from 13 days until fledging at 20 days.

Our interpretation of these results is that rough-winged swallows are not sensitive to those characteristics and behaviors of chicks that reveal their genetic relatedness or lack of it; we of course cannot tell from these data whether they do not perceive these differences, or perceive but simply do not respond to them. Bank swallows, however, are sensitive to these characteristics, although the mixed results in these interspecific transfers suggest that selectivity increases with the age of the brood and is somewhat labile (one rough-wing was accepted and two others were accepted for a time). Interspecific exchanges, however, are rather radical experiments, and it is possible that they can be explained by some other rough-winged–bank swallow asymmetry. However, the results of *intra*specific exchange experiments, which are free from this criticism, are consistent with our interpretation. We have already described our intraspecific bank swallow exchange experiments: these indicated that parental recognition developed at around 16–17 days. Hoogland and Sherman (1976) carried out intraspecific transfer experiments with rough-wings. The 17 rough-winged young that they transferred were "able or almost able to fly," that is, presumably in the 15–19-day age bracket. They found no indication that rough-winged parents could discriminate between these transfers and their own young.

Considering just the results of the intraspecific transfer experiments, our data are comparable to the classic herring gull–kittiwake contrast discussed earlier. Considering, however, the similarity of the rough-winged swallow and bank swallow nesting conditions at our study site, and the different reactions of parents of the two species to interspecific exchanges, it seems clear that bank swallow parents show an increasing selectivity with brood age that rough-wing parents do not. Because our bank swallow studies indicated that the development of parental recognition was keyed to the development of the chick signature call, we decided to examine rough-wing chick vocalizations. Rough-wings do have a homologous begging call that they give under similar conditions. It, too, develops with age, although it appears earlier. Our data are not complete enough to precisely date the first appearance of the mature form of the call, but it probably occurs at about 11–14 days. The most dramatic difference between rough-winged and bank swallow calls is the simpler structure and apparent lack of individuality of the rough-wing calls. Figure 2.3 shows calls from four bank swallows and from four rough-wings. All rough-wing calls are simply a series of upward frequency sweeps. We are working on an objective acoustic analysis of the rough-wing calls, but although we were easily able to extract five parameters from the bank swallow calls to test for individual distinctiveness (see Section II-C), we simply have been unable to extract more than two for the rough-wing calls and individual rough-wings do not differ greatly on these dimensions.

We would summarize our findings on rough-winged and bank swallows as follows. First, as has been shown before, parent–offspring recognition develops only if it is demanded by the ecological circumstances of the species, and then only shortly before it is, in fact, needed. Second, the species difference in this case appears not to be simply a fortuitous consequence of a particular, open developmental program. Rather, it is dependent on several specializations found in bank swallows. These probably include: (a) the distinctive call by which the chick identifies itself; (b) the apparent tendency of the parent to learn this call within a brief period after the chick begins to give it; and (c) a correlated set of behaviors, such as the "eviction" response, by which recognition is translated into restriction of parental care to offspring.

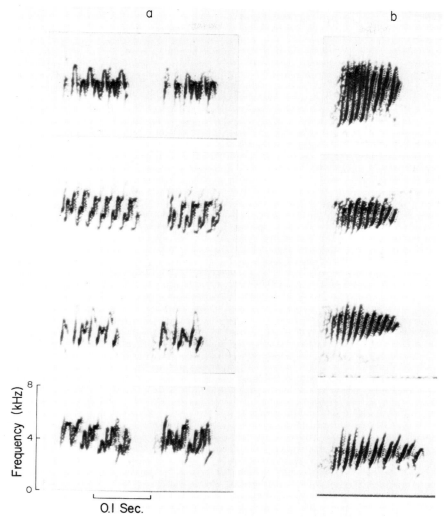

Fig. 2.3 (a) Signature calls from four different bank swallows and (b) homologous calls from four different rough-winged swallows.

G. Studies in Progress

We are now beginning an examination of the two developmental processes that are critical to the development of parent–offspring recognition in bank swallows—the development of the chick signature call and the development of parental recognition. (We also plan to examine other possible components of parent–offspring recognition, including recognition of parent by chick.) Some characteristics of the development of parental recognition of calls are already clear. First, there is a critical learning period at about Days 16–17. Second, the rough-wing transfer experiments suggest a limitation on what sort of call the bank swallow parent will learn, although altogether other characteristics of the rough-wing chicks may cause the bank swallow to reject the chick. The critical period and the possible constraints on what bank swallow parents will learn represent an interesting parallel with previous studies on imprinting phenomena (e.g., the Marler & Gottlieb studies referred to earlier). However, the development of parental recognition is a phenomenon that cannot be brought into the laboratory; we will have to study it using indirect methods in the field.

The development of the chick signature, which may have a learning component, can be studied in the laboratory. As will be discussed further in the following sections, it may be adaptive for chicks to imitate some external model, the two possibilities being the parent and their siblings. The latter is a possibility in bank swallows, as the brood hatches asynchronously, thus older chicks begin to call before their younger siblings. The calls of siblings generally resemble one another, although this could be due entirely to their genetic relatedness. In 1979, we hand-raised 15 chicks taken from the nest at 9–10 days (about the earliest they can be removed from the 1 m deep burrows). They were raised in isolation or with a foster sibling. We tested the hypothesis that they imitate the calls of older sibs by tutoring them on a model chick call for 10–12 hr per day, 1 call per 6 sec. Three different model calls were utilized. Once every day we recorded the calls of the chicks (hand-raised birds, unlike wild ones, call quite readily in this situation). Inspection of sonagrams does not support the imitation hypothesis. However, we consider this negative conclusion tentative because (a) we are not yet sure that we provided the optimal conditions for learning; and (b) we have not yet completed the objective acoustic analysis of these calls, which may reveal subtle features of imitation that are not obvious from visual inspection of sonagrams. We plan to repeat these experiments with some modifications and to test the adult call as a model as well.

It is also possible to study in the laboratory the development of recognition of siblings and parents by the chicks. Six of the isolated tutored chicks just described were tested for their preference for their tutor call versus the two calls used as models for other birds. Under these isolation conditions, the tutor call is equivalent to the call of a sibling, being the only other call the isolate hears besides its own. Each bird was placed in the center of an alley with a speaker at each end. The bird's tutor call was played from one speaker and one of the other tutor calls was played from the other speaker; positions were changed randomly from trial to trial. Each of the six chicks showed a significant preference for the tutor call it had been raised on. These data suggest that chicks normally come to recognize the calls of their siblings. We have additional observations on this point: When removed temporarily from the nest, chicks gave a stronger antiphonal vocal response to calls of their siblings than they did to the calls of unrelated chicks (Beecher & Beecher, in preparation).

H.   Conclusions

We have isolated two developmental aspects of the complex of behavioral interactions involved in parent–offspring recognition in bank swallows: the development of the chick signature call and of parental learning of that call. When fully analyzed, we suspect that the pattern of these developmental processes will resemble those of other recent ethological–developmental studies (e.g., Emlen, 1975; Gottlieb, 1974; Marler, 1970): a complex interweaving of genetic and experiential factors that defies the old innate–learned dichotomy.

III.   THEORETICAL ASPECTS OF PARENT–OFFSPRING RECOGNITION

I will now consider parent–offspring recognition from a different, theoretical perspective, in which I raise questions concerning the selective factors that have shaped the evolution of the underlying genetic–developmental programs. I do this in the conviction that concern with the "whys" (ultimate causation) of development complements the more traditional concern with the "hows" (proximate mechanisms). Although we do not have sufficient comparative data to evaluate the hypotheses I will develop here, this theoretical approach can be valuable for directing subsequent research.

A.   Advantages and Disadvantages of Recognition

The fundamental expectation concerning parent–offspring recognition is that because, as Williams puts it, individuals are "designed to reproduce themselves, not their species" (1966, p. 189), natural selection will favor parents that are discriminating in their parental care (i.e, that restrict it to their own young). The argument goes: (a) offspring of discriminating parents will tend to carry genes for discrimination; (b) they will be fed more than offspring of nondiscriminating parents, as both their parents and nondiscriminating parents will feed them; hence (c) genes for discrimination will spread in the population. According to this argument, there is an interesting asymmetry in the relationship: selection will act directly on parents to recognize their young, but only indirectly on offspring to recognize their parents. A parent increases its inclusive fitness by restricting parental care to its own offspring, and withholding it from unrelated offspring. Offspring, however, benefit equally whether the donor of parental care is their parent or an un-related adult. Thus an offspring should discriminate its own parent from other potential donors of parental care *only* if the latter are likely to recognize the chick and rebuff it. By the same line of reasoning, one could argue that recognition by the chick need not be as sophisticated as that by the parent; it may suffice, in fact, for a lost chick simply to announce its location by a call that the searching parent can hear, rather than to search out and be able to recognize its parent.

The preceding argument suggests that parent–offspring recognition should generally be asymmetrical in this sense, and one might suppose that cases of parent–offspring recognition will generally be primarily recognition of offspring by parent. Interestingly, however, considering those species in which the direction has been demonstrated, there appear to be about as many cases of recognition of parent by offspring as the reverse. In fact, the data on colonial gulls suggest that recognition of parent by chick may be much more acute than the reverse process. For example, Beer (1979) has found that laughing gull parents do *not* discriminate the calls of their own chicks from those of alien chicks, when tested in a situation parallel to that in which chicks show a clear preference for the calls of their own parents (Beer, 1970). Beer duly notes the clash between his findings and the conventional selection argument just given. Although generalizing from negative results in problematic, I believe this finding may hold in general for other gulls. In ring-billed gulls, Evans (1970) has shown that chicks recognize the calls of their parents. However, Miller and Emlen (1975) found that muting ring-billed chicks does not disturb parent–offspring recognition, and gross alteration of chicks' visual markings produces only a tem-porary rejection response by the parents, which wanes when the chicks continue to approach their parents. Most of the Miller and Emlen experiments indicate that it is basically the chick that recognizes its nest and parent; parental rejection, when it occurs, may be based primarily on changes in the comportment of the chick, chiefly the fear and avoidance responses made by the chick.

The selection argument given previously is misleading in several respects. First, it implicitly assumes that the recognition process is under selective control but the identification process is not. Second, it considers the benefit of parental discrimination while ignoring its potential costs. Third, it considers the benefit of offspring nondiscrimination while ignoring its potential costs. The benefits and costs of discrimination will vary with the ecological circumstances. These three points are elaborated on here.

In any particular instance in which a parent must make the decision of whether or not to feed a chick, the parent should do so only if the benefit (assuming the chick is its own), multiplied by the probability that the chick *is* in fact its own, exceeds the cost of feeding. This is the key point, for it means that any act or trait of the chick that reduces its parent's uncertainty as to kinship—whether this be staying in the nest, remaining close to the parent all the time, or having a distinctive appearance—will be favored by natural selection. We are interested in particular in any signature traits the chick may provide (a distinctive physical appearance, call, or odor). The parent's ability to evaluate the probability of kinship will depend not only on its own ability to detect cues as to the chick's identity, but *also* on the chick's ability to provide such signature cues. Thus we arrive at the conclusion that selection should act equally on the parent to recognize its own chick and on the chick to identify itself. Note that in this situation the chick is, in effect, as selective as the parent: by broadcasting its identity, it is increasing the probability that its parent will feed it but simultaneously reducing the probability that any other adult will do so. The offspring cannot have it both ways. Moreover, if it "cheats" and identifies itself only to its own parent, but somehow "lies" to other unrelated adults, this reduces the critical probability just discussed, and parents will be selected to take the signature "with a grain of salt." Note again that selection for individual identification by the chick will not occur without prior selection for individual recognition of chick by parent, and that recognition of the parent by the chick is not required.

Why, then, does individual recognition of the parent by the chick occur in some species, very possibly in the absence of individual recognition of the chick by the parent? The following is essentially a post hoc argument, but makes clear predictions concerning the direction of parent–offspring recognition for future studies. The argument so far has considered only the benefits of recognition by the parent. However, there is always the potential cost of making a mistake of the second kind, that is, rejecting one's own offspring. I believe this cost may be the reason why parent–offspring recognition typically does not develop until shortly before the offspring leave the nest, as noted earlier. Before chick mobility, homing to the nest by the parent is sufficient to guarantee that the young are its own; true interlopers can be recognized by their advanced ages.

Consideration of the *cost* of parental recognition suggests that, in certain ecological circumstances, it may be more advantageous for the chick to recognize its parent than vice-versa. This seems to be the case in (at least some) gulls. The critical difference between gulls and other colonial birds that have been studied is that gull chicks either remain in the home territory, or, when older, remain in close association with the parents; in most of the other colonial birds studied, the young are either left in a creche or have extensive opportunity to intermingle with other young. Thus in a gullery, a gull chick that attempts to "free-load" must either leave its territory to enter another territory, or leave its family group to attach to another family group. In the average case, this will only result in a decrease in the rate at which the chick is fed—even assuming *no* discrimination by the host—because the group it will have joined will thereby be larger on average than the chick's natal group. (The smaller the average brood size, the greater the effect will be.) Thus a chick is under *direct* selection to recognize its own parent. In turn, a parent may be favored *not* to detect any cues other than general cues indicating alien chicks (e.g., age discrepancies). Thus, in the gullery situation, recognition of parent by chick will be under selection as direct as the reverse process. And once selection has begun to act in one direction, selection pressure in the other direction is reduced. The crèche situation is of course quite different, and more closely resembles the general situation imagined in the conventional selection argument. In the crèche, a chick can solicit a feeding from an unrelated adult without the cost of foregoing a feeding from its own parent; the chick has nothing to lose by begging from any adult that arrives with food (other than the effort entailed). Thus, in this situation, the original argument pertains and we should expect that selection should favor parents that recognize offspring and offspring that identify themselves. This prediction is consistent with the differences found to date in gulls and in crèche-forming colonial birds, but it must be tested in future studies.

B. The Development of Recognition: Why Do Parents Learn the Signature?

In all examples of parent–offspring recognition that have been studied sufficiently, the parent learns the offspring's signature (or the offspring learns the parent's). Why is the signature always learned? Wu, Holmes, Medina, and Sackett (1980), for example, found evidence for "innate" recognition by half-sibling pigtailed macaques. These half-sibs had been reared in total isolation from one another yet showed a significant preference for the half-sib over a similarly reared but unrelated individual. Another evident example of innate kin recognition has recently been reported in sweat bees (Greenberg, 1979). Whatever may be the proximate mechanisms of kin recognition in these two cases, both studies demonstrate innate recognition in the sense that recognition of individuals occurs without prior experience with those particular individuals (I shall use the term in this sense in the remainder of the discussion). Is such innate recognition likely in the parent–offspring context?

Let us call the mechanism by which the parent decides the signature is that of its own offspring a "template." The parent matches an observed signature to the template, makes a statistical decision as to the goodness of fit, and takes an appropriate action (does or does not provide parental care). Now, although a parent will in fact share more genes with its offspring than with an unrelated chick, making an innate mechanism feasible, it is also the case that a parent will have had *some* experience with its offspring (although, in precocial species, perhaps not much) before it finds itself in a situation requiring discrimination of its own from alien young. Thus, in general, a parent will do better to learn its chick's signature de novo, rather than using an innate mechanism: a "learned" template will be better than an innate template simply because it can more closely resemble the real thing. Any innate mechanism has the basic limitation that the parent passes on *only* one half of its genes to its offspring.

Innate recognition, however, can still occur as an incidental (or selected) consequence of a genetically specified signature and it may have certain advantages in special circumstances, for example, where the father provides parental care but may be uncertain of paternity (e.g., bank swallows, Beecher & Beecher, 1979), or in sibling recognition between individuals from different years' broods (e.g., Belding's ground squirrels, Sherman, 1980). If the signature is a polygenic trait, relatives will share more signature genes than will nonrelatives (I discuss genetic models of signature systems elsewhere, Beecher, 1981). Thus, an individual that has never encountered a particular relative (e.g., an older half-sib, from a previous year's brood), may recognize it on the basis of the similarity of their signatures. Although such recognition cannot be as precise as it would be had the individual had the opportunity to learn the signature (e.g., as would have been possible had they been raised together), such innate recognition will be favored in any ecological circumstance that requires kin recognition but in which there is no opportunity for prior experience with that particular class of kin. However, it should be noted that innate recognition need imply neither a genetic signature nor a genetic recognition mechanism. For example, suppose that an animal imitates the signature of its mother. Then it might later recognize a half-sib from a different year's litter (mother's side) who similarly acquired its signature. We need only assume, then, a preference for or a tendency to behave altruistically toward individuals perceived as similar with respect to the signature trait; the signature and the means of recognizing need not be innate at all in the usual sense of the word.

C.   Imitation of Signatures?

Regardless of whether or not there is a genetic component to the signature, it may be advantageous for offspring (in a multioffspring brood) to imitate one another's signatures or some other common model such as the parent. Such imitation would cause the signatures of brood members to be more alike than could be expected merely from the fact that they are genetically related. The parents' discrimination task is made easier, as they can match a signature to a single template; presumably fewer nonrelated chick signatures will match this template than would match five different templates (brood size of five). We are presently beginning to evaluate this imitation hypothesis in bank swallows with isolation experiments of the sort described earlier and with cross-fostering experiments in the field.

REFERENCES

Beecher, M. D. Signature systems and kin recognition. *American Zoologist*, 1981, in press.
Beecher, M. D., & Beecher, I. M. Sociobiology of bank swallows: Reproductive strategy of the male. *Science*, 1979, **205**, 1282–1285.
Beecher, M. D., Beecher, I. M., & Lumpkin, S. Parent–offspring recognition in bank swallows: I. Natural history. *Animal Behaviour*, 1981, **29**, 86–94.

Beecher, M. D., Beecher, I. M., & Hahn, S. Parent–offspring recognition in bank swallows. II. Development and acoustic basis. *Animal Behaviour,* 1981, **29,** 95–101.

Beer, C. G. Individual recognition of voice in the social behavior of birds. In D. S. Lehrman, R. A. Hinde, & E. Shaw (Eds.), *Advances in the study of behavior,* Academic Press: 1979, **3,** 27–74.

Beer, C. G. Vocal communication between laughing gull parents and chicks. *Behaviour,* 1979, **70,** 118–146.

Cullen, E. Adaptations in the kittiwake to cliff-nesting. *Ibis,* 1957, **99,** 275–302.

Emlen, J. T., Jr. An experimental analysis of the breeding cycle of the tricolored redwing. *Condor,* 1941, **43,** 209–219.

Emlen, S. T. The stellar-orientation system of a migratory bird. *Scientific American,* 1975, **223,** 102–111.

Evans, R. M. Imprinting and mobility in young ring-billed gulls, *Larus delawarensis. Animal Behaviour Monographs,* 1970, **3,** 193–248.

Gottlieb, G. On the acoustic basis of species identification in wood ducklings (*Aix sponsa*). *Journal of Comparative and Physiological Psychology,* 1974, **87,** 1038–1048.

Greenberg, L. Genetic component of bee odor in kin recognition. *Science,* 1979, **206,** 1095–1097.

Hoogland, J. L., & Sherman, P. W. Advantages and disadvantages of bank swallow (*Riparia riparia*) coloniality. *Ecological Monographs,* 1976, **46,** 33–58.

Marler, P. A comparative approach to vocal learning: Song development in white-crowned sparrows. *Journal of Comparative and Physiological Psychology,* 1970, **71,** 1–25.

Miller, D. E., & Emlen, J. T., Jr. Individual chick recognition and family integrity in the ring-billed gull. *Behaviour,* 1975, **52,** 124–144.

Miller, D. B. Long-term recognition of father's song by female zebra finches. *Nature,* 1979, **280,** 389–391.

von Rautenfeld, D. B. Bemerkungen zur Austauschbarkeit von kueken der silbermoewe (*Larus argentatus*) nach der ersten lebelswoche. *Zeitschrift für Tierpsychologie,* 1978, **47,** 180–181.

Sherman, P. W. The limits of ground squirrel nepotism. In G. W. Barlow & J. Silverberg (Eds.), *Sociobiology: Beyond nature–nurture.* Washington, D.C.: AAAS, 1980.

Tinbergen, N. *The herring gull's world.* London: Collins, 1953.

Vehrencamp, S. L. Relative fecundity and parental effort in communally nesting anis (*Crotophaga sulcirostris*). *Science,* 1977, **197,** 403–405.

Williams, G. C. *Adaptation and natural selection.* Princeton, N.J.: Princeton University Press, 1966.

Wu, M. M. H., Holmes, W. G., Medina, S. R., & Sackett, G. P. Kin preference in infant *Macaca nemestrina. Nature,* 1980, **285,** 225–227.

Perception of Acoustic Communication Signals by Animals: Developmental Perspectives and Implications

MICHAEL R. PETERSEN
Indiana University

I. INTRODUCTION

In its most fundamental form, acoustic communication is a simple, two-component process comprising production of a signal by a sender and perception of the signal by a receiver. Animal behaviorists have traditionally directed their efforts toward various aspects of signal production and, until very recently, enjoyed little success in elucidating the processes enlisted by the receiver to perceive these events. This is particularly true of research conducted with birds and primates—the two most highly vocal and extensively studied animal taxa. Thus, although richly detailed compilations of the vocal repertoires of a variety of birds (e.g., Kroodsma, 1977; Orians & Christman, 1968) and primate species (e.g., Gautier & Gautier, 1977; Green, 1975a) are available, we have little sense of the character of the perceptual network or mechanisms employed to interpret, comprehend, categorize, and discriminate the individual vocalizations within a species' lexicon. This predilection to study vocal output doubtless derives in large part from the fact that sound production is an *overt* behavior that can be easily observed, recorded, and quantified, often in highly sophisticated ways. Perception, however, is a subtle, *covert* process that does not always produce changes in behavior. Following the path of least resistance then, investigators have opted to study the more readily observable, generative features of animal communication systems.

Given the bias toward the study of vocal production it is not surprising that attempts to trace the development of communicative competence and the mechanisms underlying this process have centered on the acquisition of signals from a species' repertoire rather than on the ontogeny of the corresponding perceptual capacities (e.g., Marler, 1970; Nottebohm, 1970). The central problem is that we simply do not know enough about how mature adult birds and primates perceive their vocalizations. Once we do it will be possible to design critical experiments to: (a) chart the normal pattern of development of the perceptual phenomena discovered; and (b) assess the relative roles of genetic predispositions and environmental experiences in determining the pattern of perceptual development and the character of perception in the mature organism. Hence, the charge to those interested in the ontogeny of vocal-sound perception is clear: Collect normative perceptual data from adult birds and primates and use it to guide studies of the development of the receptive aspects of acoustic communication.

I shall first briefly summarize what has already been learned about the development of acoustic communication in birds and primates as a way of providing some hints of what we might expect to find when more is known about the production and, particularly, the perception of vocalizations by adults. In the process I shall point to some problems with certain traditional approaches to the study of vocal-sound perception and its development. Then, in an effort to illustrate a different approach to the difficult task of characterizing such perceptual processes, I shall outline a series of studies I conducted in collaboration with several colleagues (Beecher, Petersen, Zoloth, Moody, & Stebbins, 1979; Petersen, Beecher, Zoloth, Moody, & Stebbins, 1978; Petersen, 1981; Petersen, Beecher, Zoloth, Green, Marler, Moody, & Stebbins, 1981a,b; Zoloth, Petersen, Beecher, Green, Marler, Moody, & Stebbins, 1979) on the perception of species-specific vocalizations by subadult and adult monkeys. The studies are of interest in a developmental context because they were successful in identifying some specific characteristics of vocal-sound perception in adult primates, thus setting the stage for studies of their ontogeny. The studies are of further relevance because they uncovered clear species differences in the perceptual strategies adopted by animals processing their own species' vocalizations versus those of alien species. These findings raise the question of the extent to which the disparity among species in perception represents a difference in genetic (phylogenetic) endowment as opposed to experience in the use of such signals in social interactions. The potential implications of this discovery for future ontogenetic research in highly vocal primates will be discussed.

II.   THE DEVELOPMENT OF AVIAN ACOUSTIC COMMUNICATION

A.   Production

Avian vocal behavior has served as the principal animal model for studies of the ontogenesis of the expressive aspects of acoustic communication. Most developmental psychologists and biologists are well aware of the classic work of Konishi, Marler, Nottebohm, and their associates along this line (e.g., Konishi & Nottebohm, 1969; Marler, 1970; Marler, Mundinger, Lutjen, & Waser, 1972; Marler & Peters, 1977; Marler & Waser, 1977; Nottebohm, 1970; Nottebohm, 1977; Nottebohm & Nottebohm, 1978; Waser & Marler, 1977). I shall not attempt to provide a comprehensive review of that literature because several excellent accounts are already available (e.g., Kroodsma, 1978; Marler, Dooling, & Zoloth, 1980; Marler & Mundinger, 1971; Marler & Peters, 1981). Developmental studies of avian vocal behavior have provided numerous examples of the insufficiency of either experiential or nativistic accounts alone in explaining how vocal competence is attained. Most young birds seem to come to the world with a set of genetic predispositions that place boundaries on the range of acoustic features that an animal will learn to produce. Within these constraints, however, the animal learns vocalizations that are both individually and/or group distinctive and in conformance with the species' basic sound patterns. Furthermore, for many species, the acquisition of certain vocalizations depends critically on exposure early in life to signals that conform to the prototypic species pattern. Without such experiences the animal eventually produces acoustically impoverished signals containing only rudiments of the species-specific vocal signal.

B. Perception

Progress in directly tracing the development of the receptive aspects of vocal communication in birds has only recently been made. Historically, researchers have opted to infer the characteristics of the perceptual apparatus by assessing the effects of various sensory interventions on the development of vocal *output*. The underlying assumption is that an animal's ability to learn to produce subtle acoustic nuances is constrained by its ability to perceive these features in the model's vocalizations. Thus, investigators have found that deafening the young of certain bird species before the end of the critical period for song learning severely disrupted the acoustic character of the mature species-typical song (e.g., Konishi & Nottebohm, 1969; Marler, 1970; Marler & Waser, 1977). In other experiments, birds exposed to the vocalizations of conspecifics and alien species learned the former but not the latter (e.g., Marler, 1970). In refined versions of this experiment, birds were exposed to syllables from a species-typical song delivered either in the natural species-specific temporal pattern or in a perturbed form that falls outside the range of patterns ordinarily observed for the species (Marler & Peters, 1977; 1981). The birds were extraordinarily selective in such situations, rejecting the aberrant song and learning the more natural one. On the basis of these and other studies using vocal output as an index of perceptual processes, Marler (1970, 1975, 1976) has argued that a sensory template is responsible for the analysis of species-specific song. The template acts as a sort of filter that provides information to the perceptual apparatus about those features of the vocal signal that are within the bounds of a prototypical species-specific song and ought, therefore, to be modeled by the young bird.

However, the problem with using vocal output as an index of the perceptual process (one which is appreciated by workers in this area) is that it may reflect only those properties of the receptive apparatus that interact with (e.g., guide) the motor acts involved in producing the vocalization. That is, one is only able to characterize that portion of the perceptual process that is expressed in motor output; it is entirely possible that the perceptual network is able to appreciate much more about the signals that it analyzes than is reflected in an animal's vocal behavior. The importance of this point is illustrated by considering results of recent research in comparative linguistics. Although native English speakers make use of only a subset of the total possible number of phonetic contrasts available to them, they nonetheless retain the capacity to classify and discriminate among speech sounds that employ such cues (Pisoni, Aslin, Perey, & Hennessy, in press; Walley, Pisoni, & Aslin, Chapter 8, this volume). If linguists had relied on vocal output alone, they would have grossly underestimated the sensory and perceptual capabilities of such speakers. In the same way we must remain guarded about viewing the songbird's productions as faithful representations of its perceptual capabilities.

It is certainly conceivable in this context, that the sensory–perceptual mechanisms guiding vocal development in birds are not responsible for all aspects of vocal-sound perception. Research on human speech perception indicates that the speech signal undergoes several stages of analysis during the course of perceptual processing (e.g., Pisoni, 1978; Wood, 1974, 1975). Some of these stages are responsible for simple acoustic analyses of an utterance whereas others are specialized for extracting phonetic, syntactic, and semantic features. Moreover, these different processing stages have distinct operating characteristics that can be revealed through various psychoacoustic testing techniques. For instance, convergent evidence suggests that, in the phonetic stage, acoustic stimuli are processed in a categorical manner, whereas, in the acoustic stage, processing occurs in a continuous fashion (e.g., Pisoni, 1973; 1975). Each of these types of processing contributes to the overall perception of the speech signal: The acoustic stage, for instance, is more heavily involved in processing vowels and the paralinguistic dimensions (e.g., pitch) of speech whereas the phonetic stage is critical for the perception of consonants. Might not such a multistage model of perception apply to certain aspects of birdsong as well? More specifically, one might imagine that the acquisition of song is governed by output from the rudimentary, lower levels of the perceptual process, whereas actual interpretation of songs in a communicative context requires more higher-level processing. Indeed, researchers have found that songbirds raised in acoustic isolation learn a highly impoverished song that manifests only the most fundamental structural features of the species-typical song without the rich detail and subtle acoustic nuances of a normal song (Marler, 1970; Marler & Waser, 1977). Of course, further work will be required to definitively test notions of this sort, but so little is known about the perception of birdsong that one can hardly rule out any reasonable possibility. The important point is that, if multistage processing schemes are characteristic of birdsong perception, it is possible that only some of the stages are involved in directing the motor program for song acquisition. If this proves true, vocal output would provide an inadequate portrait of the perceptual process as a whole.

Recent research by West and her colleagues (see West, King, & Eastzer, 1981, for a review) on the factors influencing song acquisition by cowbirds suggests an additional reason for having reservations about assessing perceptual capacities by measuring vocal output. They report that the vocal behavior exhibited by an adult cowbird depended not only on its early acoustic experiences but was linked to its social environment as well. Birds raised in social isolation developed more potent songs (as measured by the song's effectiveness in eliciting copulatory displays from female cowbirds) than animals raised with conspecifics. It appears that being raised with others suppresses the expression of certain acoustic components that contribute to a song's potency because they often elicit attacks from male companions. In any event, the very fact that the acoustic nature of the vocalization is so critically dependent on such a nonperceptual factor would seem to compromise its utility as a measure of perceptual processes. In this regard, it is worth mentioning that the technique developed by West and her associates (King & West, 1977; West, King, Eastzer, & Staddon, 1979) for testing the perception of normal and isolate birdsong holds great promise for future work in this area. Marler and his colleagues (Searcy & Marler, 1981) have recently devised a similar test for use with more frenetic songbird species so we can soon expect to see some of the inferences about perception drawn from vocal output put to direct experimental tests.

The lesson, then, is that using vocal output as an indication of perceptual abilities might lead to incorrect inferences about the bird's perceptual capacities. Although studies using such an approach have provided valuable information about the role of sensory–perceptual processes in guiding vocal development, they do not offer a detailed enough picture of the limitations and specific characteristics of the perceptual network independent of the constraints that operate on production.

Many advances have been made in developing procedures to more directly measure perceptual processes in young animals. Gottlieb (1975a,b,c; 1978, 1979, 1980a,b; Chapter 1, this volume) has conducted a most elegant series of perceptual studies on the ontogeny of species recognition in Peking and wood ducks. He takes advantage of the ducklings' natural proclivity to approach the source of a maternal call to test its ability, following exposure to various acoustic rearing conditions, to discriminate playbacks of signals that approximate (to varying degrees) the acoustic character of this call. Using this approach, he discovered that the duckling exhibited normal responsiveness to the species-specific maternal call only when it received exposure as an embryo to specific acoustic features of that call which, interestingly, are ordinarily also present in the embryo's own vocalizations. For example, if the embryo was both muted and held in acoustic isolation, development of the usual response to the maternal call after hatching was greatly retarded. Taken together, Gottlieb's series of experiments along this line represent the most comprehensive analysis of the development of vocal-sound perception in animals conducted to date. His work has already had an impact on the conceptualization, design, and interpretation of ontogenetic studies of vocal-sound perception in other species, most notably the perception of speech by human infants (Aslin & Pisoni, 1980), and it is likely to continue influencing the field for some time to come. The principal reservation that comes to mind is methodological and pertains only to the generalizability of the playback technique (see the following section) to perceptual studies of other less "evocative" vocal signals. Whereas it is clear that the conceptual framework suggested for ontogenetic studies by Gottlieb's work transcends methodology, the formidable problem of measuring perceptual development for signals that do not reliably elicit reflexive responses remains to be dealt with. Some variant of the operant procedures used in the study of human infant auditory and visual perception, and that have recently been applied to the measurement of infant monkey visual capacities (see Booth, Chapter 7, Volume 2), might provide a way to circumvent this problem.

Taking quite a different tack, Dooling and Searcy (1980) have assessed vocal-sound perception in young swamp and song sparrows by using changes in the cardiac orienting profile in response to different acoustic signals. With this technique, they found that young swamp sparrows could discriminate the songs of song sparrows from swamp sparrows whereas young song sparrows could not. If this technique proves to be robust enough for use with other species it will be an important tool for testing the validity of inferences about the existence of innate sensory templates that were originally made on the basis of the quality of vocal output. For instance, prior to the Dooling and Searcy studies, Marler and Peters (1977) showed that swamp sparrows are highly discriminating when learning a song—they learn to produce only syllables with properties characteristic of those found in the species-specific song pattern. Song sparrows, however, are not nearly so selective and will learn songs that contain either swamp or song sparrow syllables. The inference drawn by Marler and Peters, and verified to some extent by Dooling and Searcy, was that the swamp sparrow possesses a highly selective innate template for its species' song, whereas the song sparrow does not. It is important to recognize, nonetheless, that inferences about perception made on the basis of vocal behavior always require this sort of independent corroboration before they can be accepted as valid. In any event, it is clear that significant progress has been made in developing effective paradigms for assessing perceptual sensitivities in young birds, and we can expect that, over the next several years, we shall learn much about this facet of avian acoustic communication.

III. THE DEVELOPMENT OF PRIMATE VOCAL COMMUNICATION

A. Discrete versus Graded Repertoires

Astonishingly little is known about the ontogeny of primate vocal behavior. Only one review of research in the field has been published (Newman & Symmes, in press) and, although it was accurate and comprehensive, its most potent message was that not much has been learned about the development of either vocal production or perception in primates.

The sheer complexity of primate vocal behavior has to some extent impeded research on vocal development. In comparison, most avian vocalizations are delivered as part of a highly stereotyped motor pattern resulting in utterances that, from one iteration to the next, vary little in their acoustic properties. This high degree of stereotypy in production results in a vocalization composed of several discrete, easily identifiable acoustic units that can be readily quantified. Thus the investigator's task of characterizing the total repertoire is relatively straightforward in the sense that separate categories can be erected for these acoustically distinct patterns and renditions from different individuals or by the same individual at different times can be sorted into them. Because there is generally very little overlap between what appear to be functionally distinct sound morphs, vocalizations can usually be assigned to one category or another with little ambiguity.

The generally small range of variability in the acoustic properties of bird vocalizations also greatly simplifies attempts to chart the development of vocal competence in young animals. Typically, investigators note whether particular acoustic units are present or absent, they measure changes in the amount of acoustic variability as signals are mastered, and they determine how closely individual notes approximate the targeted mature forms in terms of features such as frequency content, harmonic structure, amplitude and frequency modulation, duration, sequence of notes, etc.

In contrast, primate field researchers are finding that one of the most conspicuous and consistent features of primate acoustic communication systems is the large amount of acoustic variability both within and between classes of vocalizations which appear to serve distinct functions (e.g., Gautier, 1974; Green, 1975b; Richman, 1976). This pervasive variability greatly complicates the job of identifying distinct categories of call types. Although it is possible to suggest potential distinctive features when defining categories, there is often much variability within a category around the modal value of the specific feature or complex of features, as well as some degree of overlap between apparently separate categories lying at different points along acoustic continua. In addition, this variability in the acoustic features that appears to differentiate individual vocal categories is overlaid by variability in the other dimensions that constitute the call. Thus, variations in certain acoustic features occur because they depend on individual differences in vocal tract properties. For example, the fundamental frequency of an animal's voice depends on its age and sex, and the amplitude of a call varies with the quality and intensity of an individuals affective or motivational state. When attempting to catalog graded sounds of this sort, the field biologist must perceptually normalize the variability so that the calls can be placed into appropriate categories. It probably goes without saying that this is an extraordinarily taxing procedure. One must decide, on the basis of the social and ecological context within which particular sounds are produced, whether the call belongs to one of several closely related categories. Obviously, one of the central problems with this approach is that the human sorts the calls on the basis of the percepts he has imposed on the communication signals of another species. Thus, the cataloging process is valid only to the extent that the human's categorization scheme is consistent with that used by the species that ordinarily produces and perceives these signals. This is, of course, true of any attempt to classify another species' vocalization by human ears and eyes, but problems are greatly exacerbated when one is dealing with signals that acoustically intergrade with one another. It is often difficult to discern where one category ends and another begins. Indeed, one does not even know whether a species parcels its continuously varying acoustic signals into discrete perceptual or cognitive categories. This is certainly one possibility, but perhaps the variability in the signal encodes information of relevance to both the sender and the receiver. That is, the vocalizer may transmit information about a continuously changing state by continuously varying acoustic features that signify the condition. The listener may in turn be sensitive to these subtle variations and intergradations, using them actively to interpret and comprehend the sender's message. A choice among these possibilities can be made only if we begin to obtain information from the animals themselves about their perception of categories and to what extent acoustic variability in the signal is of communicative significance.

Of special interest in the present context is that the acoustic variability seen in the vocalizations of adult primates is even more pronounced in the vocal signals of developing animals (Gautier, 1974; Green, 1981). Thus, in addition to facing the variability of signals produced by communicatively competent adults, the field biologist must somehow deal with the additional variability in the signals of animals acquiring the ability to communicate effectively. Largely as a result of this very difficult problem, little progress, with the exception of a few very recent studies, has been made in tracing the ontogeny of graded vocalizations in primates. Because perceptual studies generally follow on the heels of successful cataloging efforts, essentially no attempt has been made to trace the ontogeny of the complementary perceptual processes used to analyze such signals.

B. Recent Advances: Longitudinal versus Age-Sampling Approaches

The primate's lengthy period of maturation has discouraged most investigators from following the lead of birdsong researchers by longitudinally tracking the vocal development of individual animals. In one of the few studies of this kind, Gautier and Gautier (1977) diligently followed the pitch changes in the voices of individual male *Cercopithecus pogonias* monkeys over a 7-year period. They observed an abrupt lowering of pitch during puberty—a phenomenon that directly parallels the voice-deepening phenomenon seen in human males.

In perhaps the most exhaustive study of this type to date, Lieblich, Symmes, Newman, and Shapiro (1980) traced the development of the isolation peep in several squirrel monkeys over the first 2 years of life. They found that the essential structural features of the adult isolation call were present even in 1-day-old infants, but that there was a consistent trend across animals to show progressive changes in specific features during development. The communicative (i.e., functional and perceptual) significance of these changes has yet to be assessed.

The more typical approach of late has been to sample the vocal behavior of individuals of various ages ranging from infancy to adulthood. Green (1981), for example, examined the development of sex-specific vocalizations in Japanese and lion-tailed monkeys using such an approach and found that it allowed him to distinguish among a number of different conditions that might account for the ontogeny of sex differences in vocalization behavior. Differences between males and females in the usage of certain vocalizations might appear because of: (a) sex-specific anatomical or morphological constraints on productions of certain sounds; (b) sex differences in the likelihood of exposure to circumstances that are ordinarily linked with particular vocalizations; (c) differences in hormonal conditions; and (d) active social suppression of certain vocalizations for one sex and not the other in different situations. However, to identify specifically those conditions actually responsible for these differences, it will be necessary to experimentally test the alternative explanations. It will also be important to determine if there are sex differences in perception paralleling those in production.

Using this age-sampling strategy, Seyfarth, Cheney, and Marler (1980a,b) studied the usage of different classes of predator alarm calls in various age groups of the vervet monkey (Cercopithecus aethiops). They first confirmed Struhsaker's (1967) preliminary observation that the vervets use four acoustically distinct alarm vocalizations to announce sightings of their four primary predators: martial eagles, pythons, leopards, and baboons. Then, playback experiments with the first three alarms showed that each call leads to a unique set of responses that is adaptive for thwarting the hunting strategy of a particular predator. When vervets were on the ground, snake alarms caused them to stand up, look and/or approach the snake to mob it, eagle alarms prompted them to look up or run into bushes, and leopard alarms caused them to run into trees. When monkeys were in trees, the leopard alarm elicited no consistent response; the eagle alarm caused them to look up or run out of the tree; and the snake alarm prompted them to look down and/or approach the predator. On the basis of these findings, Seyfarth, Cheney, and Marler (1980a,b) suggested that these alarm calls represent semantic signals in the sense that they arbitrarily and symbolically signify specific objects in a noniconic way.

Inasmuch as this is the first report that a nonhuman species uses a natural semantic signaling system, it has attracted the interest of many who wonder how far the parallels with human speech extend. In an ontogenetic context, questions have been raised about how the use of alarm calls develops and to what extent it is a learned or inherited phenomenon. In follow-up studies, Seyfarth and Cheney (1980) and Seyfarth, Cheney, and Marler (1980b) found that, as compared to adults, infant and juvenile vervets give these alarm calls to a significantly wider variety of species. Interestingly though, the young monkeys did not respond arbitrarily to the alarm-eliciting stimuli they encountered. Infants gave eagle alarms to birds and certain other airborne objects, snake alarms to reptiles, and leopard alarms to certain terrestrial mammals. With increasing age and experience, there was a narrowing of the categories of species eliciting the different alarms until, eventually, only those spcecies that constitute a real predatory threat elicited the appropriate signal. Preliminary observations by Seyfarth, Cheney, & Marler (1980b) and Seyfarth & Cheney (1980) suggest, in addition, that infants learned proper usage of the alarms by attending to other individuals in the troop (particularly their mothers) during alarm-calling episodes. Thus, the evidence points to a role for both genetic and experiential factors in shaping the production of alarms: The nonarbitrary nature of even the infant's calling behavior suggests that it is born prepared to make associations between the individual calls and specific, albeit broad, classes of stimuli. These tendencies then serve as the basis for a selective sharpening of responses to particular predator species through learning.

Playbacks of the different alarm signals to infants also produced a wider variety of perceptual responses than was seen in adults. Infants often responded maladaptively to the alarms in the sense that they did not always adopt an escape strategy that would have effectively coped with the predator who elicited the call. For example, when on the ground, an infant vervet might have responded to a leopard alarm by running into some bushes, whereas the adults would take to the trees. The infant's response was maladaptive because leopards often hide in bushes when hunting. As with the development of alarm call production, this variability of perceptual response to alarms diminished with increasing age and experience. Analyses of films taken during alarm playbacks suggested that the infants learn the appropriate behavior by receiving cues from the behavior of other individuals. Alarm playbacks increased the amounts of time infants spent looking at their mothers, thus increasing the chances that they could obtain information about the appropriate response. Furthermore, infants who were near their mothers when they heard the alarm were less likely to respond maladaptively than those who were far away—presumably because information exchange between them was better when in close proximity.

C. Development of Acoustic Structure versus Situational Usage

The work with vervets raises an important issue relevant to the characterization of the development of vocal behavior. Ordinarily, researchers concentrate on changes in the structural features of different vocalizations and tacitly assume that organisms become communicatively competent when the signal reaches adult form. This is particularly true of the work with birdsong and much of the small body of work with primate vocalizations. However, it is important to keep the issue of the development of the acoustic form and structure of a call separate from the acquisition of the ability to use the call in appropriate circumstances. As the studies of Seyfarth and Cheney (1980) and Seyfarth, Cheney, and Marler (1980b) illustrate, an animal may actually be able to produce a structurally mature signal before it can competently discriminate the conditions under which such a call is appropriate. This raises the questions of an important difference between primate and avian vocal behavior. Compared to birds, primates generally have much larger vocal repertoires and have the potential for a richer variety of social interactions. Consequently, there is a greater likelihood of errors wherein specific vocalizations appear at the wrong time or place. Especially when studying the development of vocal behavior in primates, then, one must remain cognizant of the fact that development can occur in at least two domains: (a) acoustic structure; and, (b) situational usage. This is not to deny that similar distinctions apply for birds, only that they are even more critical for primates. If researchers of avian vocal behavior began to attend to the propriety of usage of bird vocalizations, they too might discover important ontogenetic effects. It would be interesting to know, for example, whether birds allowed to model their species-specific song in social isolation (and who thus have acquired a structurally intact signal) would be able to use their song in situationally appropriate ways. The studies by West and her colleagues reviewed earlier suggest that such rearing conditions do not interfere with the cowbird's usage of vocalizations under fairly restricted laboratory conditions. Whether their results generalize to other more typical songbirds (the cowbird is a nest parasite; therefore, the process of song acquisition occurs under quite different conditions than it does for the more common nonparasitic species) is an open issue. Smith's (e.g., 1965) discovery that the meaning of bird sounds varies with context suggests at least the possibility that animals learn to produce signals in particular situations and to adjust their interpretations as a function of ambient circumstances. In any event, additional research is clearly needed if we are to tease apart the development of acoustic form and situational usage in birds.

The preliminary ontogenetic studies with vervets (Seyfarth & Cheney, 1980; Seyfarth, Cheney, & Marler, 1980b) constitute the only published attempts to differentiate usage from structure with primates. The need to properly evaluate these two aspects of vocal development is demonstrated by considering findings from studies aimed at assessing the importance of inheritance versus experience in shaping primate vocal repertoires. For example, Winter, Handley, Ploog, & Schott (1973) found that squirrel monkeys produced nearly all the sounds seen in the adult repertoire within the first week of life and that the structural aspects of the vocal output of infants raised in isolation with devocalized mothers were essentially normal. However, the question of whether these signals were, or even could be, used in appropriate contexts was not addressed. It is conceivable, for instance, that although the acoustic properties of the call developed normally, the animals' usage was somehow aberrant.

Newman and Symmes' (1973) finding that socially deprived rhesus monkeys develop structurally abnormal vocalizations suggests at least some role for social experience in shaping the acoustic properties of vocal signals. Unfortunately, this study is difficult to interpret because the animals' early rearing conditions have been shown to result in a variety of behavioral, motivational, and emotional pathologies (Harlow, Harlow, & Suomi, 1971) that might have indirectly influenced vocal behavior. Perhaps a better approach would be to ensure nearly normal infant–mother relations by following the paradigm of Winter et al. (1973), but then to assess the ontogeny of both structure and usage.

At least some support for the notion that vocal usage is influenced by social factors comes from Green's (1975b) report of dialect differences in the food calls used by geographically isolated troops of Japanese macaques. Each of three artificially food-provisioned troops uttered a locale-specific vocalization during feeding. The vocalization at each site derived from the tonal coo-like sounds produced by all Japanese macaques, however, each troop introduced a different modification on one of these vocalizations resulting in a group-specific sound. The calls were heard only during provisioning and, interestingly, older animals who were not provisioned as infants or juveniles did not produce the vocalizations. Furthermore, animals younger than 6 months did not produce it. This suggests, but by no means proves, that the signals were acquired by the different troops to communicate about the provisioning situation and that, within a troop, the signal is both culturally transmitted and acquired. If nothing else, this finding points to the need for additional attention to the role of social influence on the ontogeny of vocal behavior.

Given the special importance of social interaction to primates and the fact that vocalizations are a principal mode of modulating these interactions, it is clear that primates must be able to identify the circumstances in which vocalizations with specific acoustic properties are appropriate. It is important, first, that we learn how both facets of this capability develop and, second, how important genetic predispositions and social experience are to the process.

D. Future Directions

In summary, whereas few systematic attempts have been made to follow the development of vocal production and perception in primates, the observations made thus far offer a tantalizing preview of the prospects and potential directions of future research. Simply stated, we need more data of the following kinds: (a) comprehensive descriptions of adult signal production and, especially perception, to provide a frame of reference for developmental studies; (b) information on the structural development of vocalizations within the repertoire; (c) efforts to assess the development of signal usage; and, (d) attempts to assess the development of perception in the context of (b) and (c).

In an effort to illustrate a potentially viable approach to meeting part of objective (a), the remainder of this chapter is a case-study description of research conducted by my colleagues and I (Beecher et al., 1979; Petersen, 1981; Petersen et al., 1978, 1981a,b; Zoloth et al., 1979) that sought to characterize the perceptual processes used by adult monkeys when discriminating and categorizing their vocalizations. Given the paucity of data on monkey vocal-sound perception, this work represented a logical first step in a long-term effort to trace the development of this process. As we shall see, some of our initial findings were particularly intriguing because they suggested the possibility that the study species, the Japanese macaque (Macaca fuscata), enlists species-specific perceptual strategies and mechanisms. We shall outline a series of experiments designed to delineate the processes and mechanisms underlying this species-specificity and then point to the need for developmental studies: (a) to ascertain the relative roles of genetic and environmental factors in shaping the species-specific nature of the processes; and (b) to trace the normal course of development of vocal sound perception.

IV. VOCAL PERCEPTION IN JAPANESE MONKEYS: A CASE STUDY

A. Introduction

During the past 10 years, significant advances have been made in the study of primate vocal behavior. In addition to developing taxonomies of the vocalizations used by different species, primatologists have succeeded in providing detailed descriptions of the different social contexts within which specific acoustically distinct signals are likely to occur (Gautier & Gautier, 1977; Green, 1975a; Robinson, 1979). They have also examined the organization of different species' vocal communication systems and are able to account for variations in repertoire complexity with reference to particular characteristics of the species' socioecology (e.g., Marler, 1975; Zoloth & Green, 1979). Some are even involved in analyses of the syntactic properties of sequences composed of several different utterances and have discovered that certain primates make use of a subset of the rules that govern sequences of human speech sounds (e.g., Robinson, 1979). Finally, as already discussed, they have provided evidence that some primate vocal signals serve semantic functions in the sense that they label or signify external objects and events (Seyfarth, Cheney, & Marler, 1980a,b), rather than functioning exclusively (as many had believed) as correlative indices of internal arousal levels (e.g., Myers, 1976).

Progress in characterizing the perceptual strategies and mechanisms used by primates to interpret their vocal signals has, however, been stymied because of methodological inadequacies. One technique that has proved somewhat effective in testing the perception of certain signals is the sound playback method. In a typical playback experiment, recorded exemplars of particular vocalizations are broadcast from a speaker and the overt responses of the listeners are noted and treated as indices of the animals' perception of the signal. The paradigm has been used quite successfully to answer myriad questions including how vocal communication is used in mate attraction and selection (Marler & Mundinger, 1971; West, King, & Easter, in press), individual recognition (e.g., Cheney & Seyfarth, 1980; Emlen, 1971; Falls, 1969; Waser, 1976), species recognition (e.g., Emlen, 1972; Thompson, 1969) and subspecies (dialect) discrimination (e.g., Lemon, 1967). However, the method is limited to the study of vocalizations that reliably elicit easily observable changes in behavior. It simply cannot be used to characterize the perception of the many signals used by animals that do not occasion highly stereotyped responses from a recipient. This shortcoming is particularly noticeable in the study of primate vocal perception. A major portion of a typical primate's repertoire is produced in the course of fairly calm, quiet interactions among individuals within a social unit; the sounds often do not evoke overt responses from listeners. Much like the speech sounds exchanged between participants in a conversation do not necessarily evoke immediate or obvious changes in behavior, nonhuman primates detect and presumably process vocal sounds uttered during complex social interactions to which they do not instantaneously or even inevitably react. Consequently, a different paradigm is needed to assay the perception of such signals. An encouraging development in this regard is a recent report by Sinnott (1980) of successful use of an operant paradigm to study selective attention to biologically significant portions of species-specific sounds by red-winged blackbirds and brown-headed cowbirds. This approach appears to be particularly promising because it allows one to assess the perception of essentially any signal by arranging nearly arbitrary relations among various stimuli, responses, and rewards. That is, one may condition an animal to emit overt discriminative responses to stimuli that ordinarily elicit no reliably observable behavior, thereby providing a window through which to view a typically covert process. Independently of Sinnott (1980), my colleagues and I (Beecher et al., 1979; Petersen, 1981; Petersen et al., 1978, 1981a,b; Zoloth et al., 1979) developed an operant procedure to assess primate vocal perception by modifying a same–different task originally devised by Stebbins (1973; 1975) to measure auditory difference thresholds.

B. Discrimination Procedure

Animals are seated in a restraint chair inside a soundproof booth during testing. Earphones are attached to the chair and aligned carefully over the animal's external ear canal. A feeder chute is mounted directly in front of the animal's mouth providing easy access to food pellets that are dispensed as rewards. The monkeys are trained to reach out and grasp a contact-sensitive metal tube located just in front of the chair when a cue light imbedded in the lumen of the tube begins to flash. Contact with the tube initiates a series of background stimuli from one vocal category; after a randomly determined number of background stimuli have been presented, a comparison stimulus from another category is inserted into the series. The monkey's task is to maintain contact with the tube during the background stimulus and to release it within 2 sec of a comparison stimulus. Correct reports of the comparison stimulus are rewarded. If the subject fails to report the comparison signal, the background series resumes. False alarms (releases of the tube at any time other than within 2 sec of a comparison stimulus) produce an 8-sec time-out period during which the sound booth lights are extinguished and the animal is not allowed to earn any food. The well-trained subject quickly grasps the tube when the cue light flashes, holds it through several background signal presentations, and releases it only on hearing a signal from the comparison category.

C.   Discrimination of Coo Vocalizations

All the experiments completed to date have focused on characterizing the perception of a pair of vocalizations, the smooth early high (SE) and smooth late high (SL) coos, from the Japanese macaques' (*Macaca fuscata*) repertoire. Selection of *fuscata* as the study species was dictated by several considerations. First, we were able to undertake the perceptual studies because Green (1975a) had just completed a field study of the *fuscata's* vocal communication system and had compiled a descriptive catalog of their signals that was far more thorough than those available for any other primate species. Second, the audio recordings made by Green in the field were of relatively high quality and were available for use in these studies. Finally, a good deal was known about the basic psychoacoustic capacities of other Old World monkey species; all studies suggested that their absolute and differential sensitivities, at least for frequency and intensity, were very similar (e.g., Stebbins, 1973). This was critical, since it meant that we could compare essentially any Old World species with the *fuscata* in experiments with *fuscata* sounds, and thereby determine the species-specificity of any perceptual strategies we might find, without undue concern that species differences were due to mismatches in sensory capabilities.

Sonagrams of the SE and SL coos used as the core stimulus set for the studies are shown in Fig. 3.1. The calls were distinguished by Green (1975a) on the basis of function *and* acoustic structure. Coo vocalizations are, in general, produced in affinitive, contact-seeking situations. The SE and SL coos are but two of the seven different coo types, each of which is produced within a rather distinctive context.

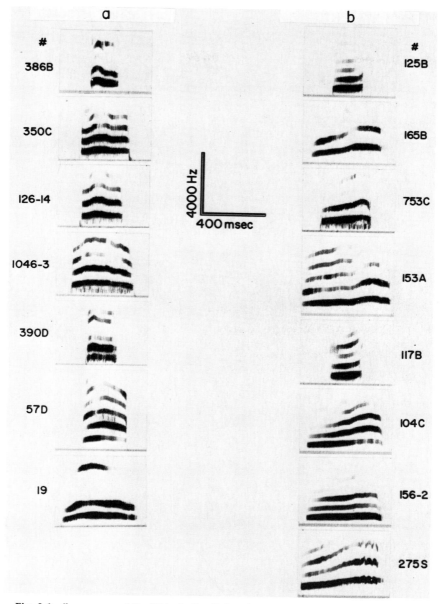

Fig. 3.1 Sonagrams of the 15 test stimuli showing (a) smooth early highs; (b) smooth late highs. The dark bands indicate energy present at different frequencies over time.

The SL is produced primarily by estrus females as a sexual solicitation to adult males. It is also occasionally produced by subordinate males and females in deference to dominant troop members. The SE is typically produced by solitary animals who have become detached from their principal social units. For example, it is uttered by infants separated from their mothers. Acoustically, both calls are characterized by an ascending–descending frequency modulation (FM), termed the *peak* of the call. The fundamental distinction between the calls is the relative temporal location of the peak: for SEs, it occurs before two thirds of the call has transpired, for the SL's it occurs after this point.

Because these calls appear to be both acoustically and functionally distinct, Green's classification scheme suggested that *fuscata* ought to treat them as though they belonged to different categories. The question then was could *fuscata* discriminate these two signals on an acoustic basis devoid of all the redundant and supplementary contextual information ordinarily available in the wild? Furthermore, could they do so with greater ease than other monkey species who do not appear to use such distinctions in their own repertoires? A failure to find a difference between species would suggest that the conditions of the experiment promoted classification of the stimuli, perhaps independently of their communicative significance. A species difference in discriminability, however, might be due to the special communicative importance of these signals to *fuscata*. To test these notions, three *fuscata* and three comparison monkeys (a pigtail macaque (*M. nemestrina*), a bonnet macaque (*M. radiata*) and a vervet) were tested in a discrimination task involving the signals shown in Fig. 3.1. Initially, the animals were trained to discriminate the uppermost SL and SE from one another; the SL served as a background stimulus, the SE as a comparison stimulus. When the animals fulfilled a set of performance criteria (see Zoloth, Petersen, Beecher, Green, Marler, Moody, and Stebbins, 1979, for details) additional stimuli were added progressively to the discrimination set until, eventually, the monkeys were discriminating eight SLs from seven SEs.

The rate of acquisition of the peak discrimination is summarized in the form of learning curves shown in Fig. 3.2 for each subject. The cumulative number of sessions necessary to meet the performance criteria is plotted for successive stages of the discrimination. The left and right numbers in each of the dyads along the abscissa designate the total number of SL and SE stimuli, respectively, among which the subjects were required to discriminate during different stages of the experiment. During the 1 versus 1 stage (1 SL versus 1 SE), subjects could have solved the discrimination by attending to any one of the

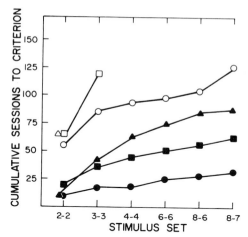

Fig. 3.2 Cumulative learning curves for six animals on the peak discrimination: M35 *M. nemestrina* (○); M58 *C. aethiops* (□); M88 *M. radiata* (△); M98 *M. fuscata* (●); M99 *M. fuscata* (■); M100 *M. fuscata* (▲). Each point represents the cumulative number of sessions required to meet the performance criteria and advance to the next stage. The left and right number in each dyad along the abscissa indicates the total number of SL and SE stimuli, respectively, the subject was required to discriminate among at that stage of the problem.

several acoustic dimensions along which the two calls, 386B and 125B, differed. However, in all subsequent stages, the only consistent distinctive feature was peak position. Thus, the cumulative learning curves for the discrimination of peak position begin with the 2 versus 2 phase, the first point at which the only reliable cue was peak position.

The most prominent aspect of the data was the clear difference that emerged between the discrimination learning rates for *fuscata* and the comparison animals. All three *fuscata* learned the discrimination more rapidly than did the most proficient comparison animal (M35). Indeed, whereas all *fuscata* eventually learned to discriminate among the maximum of 8 SLs and 7 SEs, only one of the three comparison animals (M35) ever reached this stage. The other two comparison animals, M88 and M58, showed little indication of improvement during the 2 versus 2 and 3 versus 3 stages, respectively, and were finally removed from the experiment. It is also noteworthy that the comparison animal and *fuscata* learning functions first diverge dramatically at the 2 versus 2 stage, with the comparison animals all requiring nearly three times as many sessions to meet the criterion at this point. This suggests that the comparison animals had more difficulty attending to the peak cue per se, resulting in poor transfer from the 1 versus 1 stage, where attention to any acoustic difference was sufficient to learn the discrimination, to the 2 versus 2 stage, where attention to the peak cue was the best solution to the problem.

Another important species difference emerged upon analysis of each animal's performance on the individual stimuli from the test set. When transferred from one stimulus set to the next, more complex set, the *fuscata* typically responded correctly almost immediately to presentations of novel SL and SE signals, whereas M35 (the other comparison animals did not complete enough stages to establish a trend) simply failed to respond at all. However, after several presentations of the new stimuli, ranging anywhere from 10 to several hundred, M35 would finally begin to respond correctly to a progressively larger proportion of the stimuli until he finally reached criterion levels of accuracy. This suggests that, whereas the *fuscata* were attending specifically to peak position and classifying signals on that basis, the comparison animals were mastering the task by attending to some other aspect of the signals (which, therefore, impeded their learning) or by memorizing the signals in a rote fashion.

An additional, rather disturbing, observation made during the analysis of performance on individual stimuli was that one of the SE signals (350C) proved to be a most difficult stimulus for all animals to discriminate. Unfortunately, this signal was introduced at the 2 versus 2 stage—exactly where the first difference between species was predicted to appear. Whether species differences in discriminating 350C alone were entirely responsible for the overall difference in learning rate or whether, because it was inherently more difficult to discriminate, 350C simply potentiated differences which would have appeared anyway, were two possibilities which could not be distinguished in this initial study.

To address this problem we simply rearranged the stimulus set so that 350C would not be used until the late stages of the task. We then tested two experimentally naive *fuscata* and two comparison animals (the two from the first study who had failed to advance beyond the 3 versus 3 stage) on the new stimulus set. As Fig. 3.3 shows, the pattern of results paralleled that of the first study. The *fuscata* acquired the discrimination more quickly than the comparison animals and the learning curves first separated at the 2 versus 2 stage with the comparison animals requiring twice as many sessions to reach criterion as the *fuscata*. A comparison of the learning curves in Fig. 3.2 and 3.3 suggests that introduction of 350C early in the task simply potentiated (by a factor of four) the difficulty of the discrimination without affecting the relative performance of the *fuscata* and comparison animals.

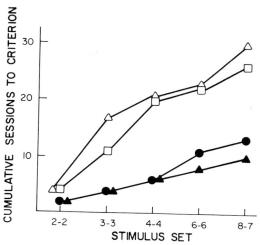

Fig. 3.3 Cumulative learning curves for the four animals tested on the second peak discrimination: M58 *C. aethiops* (△); M88 *M. radiata* (□); M120 *M. fuscata* (●); M121 *M. fuscata* (▲). See Fig. 3.2 for additional details.

In summary, the two studies together clearly show that the *fuscata* are readily capable of performing a discrimination between classes of complex communication sounds distinguished by a subtle, but socio-behaviorally relevant acoustic cue. This finding, at the very least, suggests that they have the capacity to classify and presumably to recognize or identify stimuli on the basis of acoustic parameters postulated by Green (1975a) to be of communicative significance to the species. In a sense, then, the results of the study might be viewed as psycho-acoustical support for the plausibility of Green's classification of these particular coo subtypes, and, by inference, for the classification system as a whole. This inference, however, clearly requires empirical verification with systematic replications of this experiment using other classes of vocalizations from the *fuscata* vocal repertoire.

The strongest interpretation of the substantial difference in learning rate between the *fuscata* and comparison animals, most apparent in the early (2 versus 2, 3 versus 3) stages of the task, is a suggestion that *fuscata* are differentially prepared to attend to acoustic features that signal distinctions between conspecific vocalizations. To clarify, consider the subject's task as a problem in concept formation. During the 1 versus 1 stage, as noted earlier, the subject could solve the discrimination by attending to any of the several acoustic differences between the natural exemplars, 386B and 125B. However, upon introduction of two additional stimuli in the 2 versus 2 stage (and for each subsequent stage), the only reliable acoustic distinction between the stimulus classes was the relative temporal position of the peak frequency. On the assumption that *fuscata* are perceptually predisposed to attend to this very subtle (at least to the human ear) cue, we should expect that they would be superior to the comparison animals, who do not share this predisposition, in forming a concept based on this cue. Our finding that the differences appear at the 2 versus 2 stage, the first point at which the animals were forced to attend to the peak cue, seems to confirm this prediction. Presumably because of its communicative significance to the *fuscata*, the peak dimension is higher in their attentional hierarchy than it is in that of the comparison animals. Thus, when the animals were transferred from a stage in which they could attend to any acoustic cue to a stage in which they were required to attend to the peak cue, the *fuscata* had less difficulty because they were predisposed to attend to this dimension. Whether this potential predisposition derives from innate sensory–perceptual proclivities or is experientially based, or, more probably, represents the interaction of the two, is an intriguing but as yet unanswered question.

All of this discussion rests, of course, on the assumption that *fuscata* is not selectively endowed with either superior auditory capabilities or special capacities to form complex auditory concepts. Although the first assumption has not been directly tested for *fuscata*, Stebbins (1973) reports that all Old World monkey species tested thus far have approximately the same absolute and differential auditory sensitivities. Nonetheless, in view of the novelty of the present finding, it is important that standard measures of auditory sensitivity eventually be made on *fuscata* to ensure that the learning advantage is not attributable to some simple difference in basic psychoacoustic capacities. Studies of this sort are currently underway in my laboratory. The second assumption, that the *fuscata* are not inherently better at forming auditory concepts, was addressed by testing the animals on a different auditory concept formation task.

D. Selective Attention to Communicatively Potent Dimensions

The stimulus set for this new task was formed by grouping the signals from Fig. 3.1 according to the values of their onset frequencies. These measures (and some others to be discussed in following sections) are shown in Table 3.1. We shall treat onset frequency as an estimate of the pitch of each call, a dimension that carries some information about the age, sex, and/or affective demeanor of the vocalizer (Green, 1981). It does not, however, seem as communicatively potent as other di-

Table 3.1
Summary of Acoustic Measurements Made on Test Stimuli

Stimulus	Relative peak position[a]	Onset frequency (Hz)	Peak frequency (Hz)	Duration (msec)
SE				
386B	0.14	675	760	156
350C	0.31	650	870	276
126-14	0.38	750	920	228
1046-3	0.32	700	850	348
390D	0.20	550	600	168
57D	0.49	675	850	252
19	0.18	525	800	432
SL				
125B	1.00	500	915	168
165B	0.61	675	935	384
753C	0.81	725	925	276
153A	0.77	750	1120	504
117B	1.00	535	725	180
104C	0.80	500	780	432
156-2	0.70	500	600	432
275S	0.76	700	1350	468

[a] Relative peak position $= \dfrac{\text{Temporal position of peak frequency (msec)}}{\text{Call duration (msec)}}$.

mensions, such as peak position, which differentiate functionally distinct call types. Stimuli with onset frequencies ≥ 600 Hz defined a high-pitched group, those with onset frequencies < 600 Hz formed a low-pitched group. Because 9 of the 15 stimuli fell into the high-pitched group, 3 of them were eliminated. This resulted in a high-pitched set with 3 SEs and 3 SLs and a low-pitched group with 4 SLs and 2 SEs. The low-pitched stimuli were arbitrarily designated as background signals, the high-pitched signals as comparison stimuli. Four animals (two *fuscata* and two comparison animals) were tested on this task and on the peak task. The order of exposure to the tasks was counterbalanced across animals.

Learning curves for each discrimination are shown for individual animals in Fig. 3.4. Order of exposure to the tasks did not affect the basic pattern of results. The animals' performance on the peak task replicated the earlier findings of *fuscata* superiority. However, there was a complete reversal of superiority on the pitch task: The two comparison animals learned more readily than did the *fuscata*. This finding thus refutes the claim that the *fuscata* superiority in the earlier peak tasks was due to a special ability for forming concepts about complex

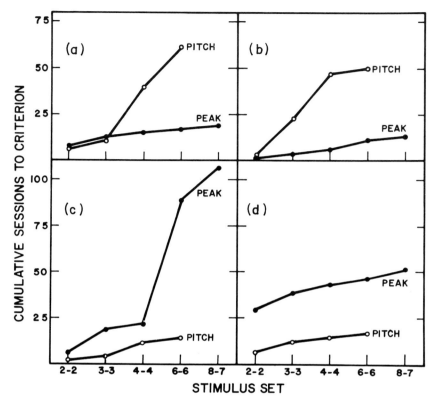

Fig. 3.4 Cumulative learning curves from the peak and pitch discrimination tasks for four subjects. Each point represents the cumulative number of sessions necessary to meet the performance criteria and to advance beyond that stage of the problem. The left and right numbers in each dyad along the abscissa indicate the total number of S− and S+ stimuli, respectively, that the subjects were required to discriminate at that stage. (a) M122 *M. fuscata* and (c) M93 *M. nemestrina* were tested on the pitch task first. (b) M120 *M. fuscata* and (d) M133 *M. radiata* experienced the peak task first.

auditory stimuli. A comparison of the peak learning curves for *fuscata* with the pitch learning curves of the comparison animals shows that all animals were capable of acquiring such concepts. The principal difference between the two groups of animals apparently lies in their "preparedness" (e.g., Hinde & Stevenson, 1973; Seligman & Hager, 1972) to discriminate particular acoustic cues.

The results are consistent with the hypothesis that the *fuscata* attended preferentially to the peak dimension of these calls. To illustrate we can again consider the animal's task in these two discriminations as problems in concept formation. Every call used in the discriminations was taken from field recordings and, therefore, manifested all the natural variability in acoustic dimensions other than those critical to the distinction between SE and SL. That is, although each call was classified as an SE or SL on the basis of the temporal position of the peak frequency, the calls varied asystematically in duration, pitch, harmonic structure, etc. (see Fig. 3.1 and Table 3.1). In the peak discrimination, then, the subjects were required to form a concept for SE and for SL and to classify background and target stimuli accordingly while ignoring "irrelevant" variations in other acoustic dimensions, including pitch value. Similarly, in the pitch task, the animals were required to form a high-pitched and low-pitched concept and sort the calls on that basis while ignoring irrelevant variations in other parameters, including peak position. On this view, the supposed attentional preference of *fuscata* for the peak cue facilitated performance of the peak task but, because peak was varied orthogonally across the pitch classes, it interfered with acquisition of the pitch task. The comparison species, however, lacked the attentional preference for peak and presumably attended to a more acoustically salient feature of the call. On the assumption that pitch is a more salient feature than peak, such a strategy would favor acquisition of the pitch task and interfere with performance on the peak discrimination.

The finding of selective attention to the acoustic dimension cueing the difference between vocal call types is strikingly similar to a phenomenon reported in the speech literature. When tested for their ability to classify speech sounds on the basis of some phonetic cue in the face of irrelevant variation of some paralinguistic acoustic dimension (pitch), infant listeners had no difficulty. However, when asked to classify stimuli on the paralinguistic dimension in the face of irrelevant, orthogonal variation of a phonetic cue, they had considerable difficulty (Fodor, Garrett, & Brill, 1975; Kuhl, 1976). It is argued that the phonetic aspect of the speech stimulus is an inherently more prominent dimension of the signal that arrests the subject's attention whether the discrimination is based on phonetic or acoustic aspects of the sound (see Carrell, Smith, & Pisoni, 1981, for an alternative view). On this account, preferential attention to the phonetic cue facilitates performance on a task requiring classification on a phonetic basis but interferes with the classification of the same sounds on the basis of some nonphonetic acoustic dimension. This of course raises the interesting question of whether infant *fuscata* might also show attentional preferences for the class-distinctive features of their species' signals. We hope to begin pursuing this question in the very near future.

E.   Perceptual Lateralization: A Neural Basis for Selective Attention?

The suggestion that the *fuscata* are using species-specific perceptual strategies seems secure in view of the findings just summarized. However, the notion would be strengthened even further if it were possible to show that the strategies reflect the operation of a specialized neural network. Research over the last 100 years on the neural bases of language has pointed to a preeminent role for the temporal regions of the left cerebral hemisphere in the perception and production of speech. Cognizant of the possibility that a similar condition might be responsible for the species-specificity in *fuscata* vocal perception, we took steps from the outset of our studies to measure perceptual lateralization effects. One of the standard techniques used in speech perception research for this purpose is to compare the accuracy of the right ear versus the left ear in discriminating or categorizing speech sounds. The typical finding for most humans is that words, consonants, and, under certain conditions, vowels, are identified more accurately when presented to the right ear than to the left ear (e.g., Kimura, 1967; Springer, 1973). Since physiological evidence suggests that each ear functionally projects primarily to the contralateral hemisphere (Cowley & Dewson, 1972; Pribram, Rosner, & Rosenblith, 1954), the finding of a right ear advantage for speech is interpreted as evidence that the left cerebral hemisphere is dominant for this function.

In the first three studies discussed earlier, stimuli were delivered monaurally to either the left or right ear, thereby producing separate accuracy scores for each ear with which to determine whether the subjects were employing neurally lateralized processing mechanisms. In the first two studies, the animal's task of discriminating stimuli on the basis of an acoustic distinction of communicative relevance to the *fuscata* was essentially analogous to the conventional listening tasks given human subjects to study the lateralization of speech sounds. The third experiment, which compared discrimination of two different acoustic features of the same set of vocalizations, permitted a test of whether any lateralized processing observed was specific to the analysis of a communicatively relevant acoustic distinction. This approach parallels the work of Wood, Goff, and Day (1971) who studied the role of lateralized processors in analyzing the phonetic and nonphonetic acoustic features of the same speech signal in human adults.

Following each session, a percentage correct score, rounded to the nearest whole number, was computed for left-ear and right-ear presentations of each stimulus. Then, for each stimulus, the right and left-ear scores were compared and classified as revealing a left ear performance advantage (LEA), a right ear advantage (REA), or no ear advantage (NEA). The total number of cases that fell into each of these categories is shown in the appropriate column of Table 3.2. The peak discrimination data of the first three studies are shown in the upper portion of Table 3.2; the lower part presents data from the pitch discrimination of the third study.

A metric expressing the overall performance differences between the ears was calculated by determining the proportion, designated P, of the total number of cases that were REA cases. Columns 8 and 9 present the results of two different ways of calculating the P proportion. Proportions P_1 were calculated by assigning one-half of the NEA cases to the REA category and the other half to the LEA. This approach was based on the assumption that there should always be performance differences between the ears but that our measurement techniques were occasionally insensitive to them. The second method of calculating the proportion was based on the same assumption, but instead of dividing the NEA cases equally between REA and LEA categories, they were simply discarded. This approach ensured that any statistical difference obtained would not be the result of artificially inflating the total sample size. For both of these methods of calculating the P measure, a P of 0.5 suggested no performance advantage for either ear, a $P > 0.5$ represented an overall right-ear advantage, and a $P < 0.5$ indicated an overall left-ear advantage. All obtained proportions were then statistically compared, using the normal approximation to the binomial distribution (Siegel, 1956), to determine whether apparent ear advantages were significantly different from what would be expected through chance variation. Asterisks designate those proportions that proved statistically different from 0.5. The pattern of results was identical for each P measure. On the peak discrimination task, all five *fuscata* but only one of the five comparison animals showed a significant REA. Of the other four comparison animals, three (M35, M88 and M93) showed a small but insignificant REA, and one (M133) showed a nonsignificant LEA. On the pitch discrimination, one of the *fuscata* showed a significant LEA, whereas the other *fuscata* and both comparison animals showed no significant ear advantage. A test of the difference in P values obtained on the peak and pitch tasks, shown in the last two columns revealed no significant change for the comparison animals, whereas relative to the peak task, the *fuscata* showed a significant reduction in P on the pitch tasks.

Thus, when the discrimination task required analysis of peak position, a communicatively relevant acoustic dimension for the *fuscata*, all five of them and only one of the five comparison animals showed

Table 3.2

Frequency of Left-Ear Performance Advantage (LEA), Right-Ear Advantage (REA), and No Ear Advantage (NEA) Classifications for Each Subject[a]

(1) Subject	(2) Sex	(3) Age	(4) Species	(5) LEA	(6) REA	(7) NEA	(8) P_1[b]	(9) P_2[c]	(10) Peak$_{P_1}$-Pitch$_{P_1}$	(11) Peak$_{P_2}$-Pitch$_{P_2}$
Peak discrimination										
M35	M	Adult	*Macaca nemestrina*	177	197	65	0.52	0.53		
M58	M	Adult	*Cercopithecus aethiops*	36	61	15	0.61*	0.63*		
M88	M	Subadult	*M. radiata*	44	51	31	0.53	0.54		
M93	M	Subadult	*M. nemestrina*	160	168	265	0.51	0.51		
M133	M	Subadult	*M. radiata*	90	76	24	0.46	0.46		
M98	M	Subadult	*M. fuscata*	33	56	36	0.59*	0.63*		
M99	M	Subadult	*M. fuscata*	44	150	34	0.73*	0.77*		
M100	M	Subadult	*M. fuscata*	123	198	36	0.61*	0.62*		
M120	F	Subadult	*M. fuscata*	8	24	32	0.63*	0.75*		
M122	F	Subadult	*M. fuscata*	36	66	28	0.61*	0.65*		
Pitch discrimination										
M93	M	Subadult	*M. nemestrina*	16	19	21	0.53	0.54	−0.02	−0.03
M133	M	Subadult	*M. radiata*	23	24	8	0.51	0.51	−0.05	−0.05
M120	F	Subadult	*M. fuscata*	76	38	68	0.40*	0.37*	+0.23*	+0.38*
M122	F	Subadult	*M. fuscata*	100	104	77	0.51	0.51	+0.10*	+0.14*

[a] The proportion (P_1 or P_2) of the total cases classified as REA is also shown.

[b] $P_1 = \dfrac{REA + 1/2\ NEA}{(REA + 1/2\ NEA) + (LEA + 1/2\ NEA)} = \dfrac{REA + 1/2\ NEA}{REA + LEA + NEA}$.

[c] $P_2 = \dfrac{REA}{LEA + REA}$.

* $p < .05$.

statistically significant REAs. Furthermore, when asked to attend to a different, presumably less communicatively relevant cue of the same stimuli neither the *fuscata* nor the comparison animals showed evidence of right-ear superiority. These findings directly parallel those reported by Wood *et al.* (1971). In that study, humans were required in different tasks to attend to the phonetic or nonphonetic aspects of the same speech sounds. Average evoked responses recorded from the temporal regions of both hemispheres suggested that the left hemisphere (which receives its primary projection from the right ear) was predominantly involved in the phonetic discrimination, while both hemispheres participated equally in processing of the nonphonetic dimension. Similarly, the *fuscata* showed a REA, at least implicating left hemisphere dominance, in the processing of a communicatively relevant dimension and either a NEA or a LEA implicating either both hemispheres or predominantly the right, in the processing of the less critical (in a communicative sense) dimension. Neither of these dimensions were of communicative relevance to the comparison animals and, with but one exception, they showed no ear performance advantage and, by implication, no hemispheric dominance for the processing of these cues.

Although the discussion thus far has concentrated on the relative communicative significance of the peak and pitch cues, it should be noted that the lateralized processing could just as well reflect a fundamental difference in the acoustic character of the two cues. The peak feature is a very subtle cue that requires attention to both the spectral and temporal structure of the signals whereas, by comparison, the pitch cue requires only a simple frequency analysis. This perspective is consistent with the more contemporary account of auditory neural lateralization, holding that the left hemisphere is specialized to deal with the complex temporal and acoustic cues contained in speech sounds rather than some ill-defined "communicative" character of the sounds (e.g., Blechner, 1976; Halperin, Nachson, & Carmon, 1973; Natale, 1977; Papcun, Krashen, Terbeek, Remington, & Harshman, 1974; Schwartz & Tallal, 1980; see Bradshaw & Nettleton, 1981, for a review).

This point of view raises a critical question concerning the species-specific nature of the selective attention and perceptual lateralization findings. Specifically, the failure of the comparison animals to show neural lateralization might have reflected either a failure to attend to the peak dimension at all *or* the use of a different set of nonlateralized processes when attending to this cue. If the comparison animals were attending to some aspect of the signal other than peak, perhaps that cue did not require lateralized processing. However, it is possible that the comparison animals were attending to the peak cue by the time they reached the later stages of the peak task but did not enlist later-alized processors when doing so. On reflection, it is difficult to believe that the comparison animals who succeeded in solving the advanced phases of the peak task, albeit slowly, could have done it without eventually attending to peak position. Although they may have had no natural predilection to attend to this cue, it seems likely that at some time during the last stages of the discrimination, they would have adopted such a strategy. The central issue, then, is whether or not the comparison animals were attending to peak position by the time they reached the final stages of the discrimination. We reasoned that if they were, they ought to have little difficulty classifying additional, novel SE and SL vocalizations. To assess this notion, four animals (two *fuscata* and two comparison) who had reached the 8 versus 7 stage of the peak task and were reliably classifying all 15 stimuli, were tested for gen-eralization to a total of 27 novel coo signals with relative peak positions ranging continuously from early to late.

During the generalization test, the animals continued to perform on the basic discrimination task with the usual reward contingencies for the 15 core stimuli in force. During each testing session a small subset of the generalization stimuli was used and occasionally one of them was inserted into a trial sequence in place of a comparison stimulus. Releases in response to any of the generalization stimuli were rewarded to eliminate bias in the animal's response in either direction. The hope was that, as highly practiced as these animals were, they would be resistant to releasing to SL-like stimuli and thus would be less likely to sample the reward contingencies for such stimuli in comparison to the SE-like stimuli. To reduce contamination of the generalization re-sults with long-term learning effects that would probably appear with prolonged testing, we examined responses only to the first 10 pres-entations of each signal. The results are shown in Fig. 3.5. All four animals showed the same pattern of generalization to the novel signals: Coos with early peaks evoked more responding than did those with late peaks. The responding of all animals appeared to be under precise control of the peak cue suggesting that, by the time the comparison animals reached the 8 versus 7 stage on the peak task, they were indeed attending to the peak cue. (Precisely when the comparison animals began attending to peak is a question that merits further study.) Un-fortunately, the laterality index used in the concept-formation studies is not reliable with as few trials as we could administer with the gen-eralization stimuli. So, we have no direct measure of laterality in the generalization tests. However, laterality measures made during pro-longed testing of these four subjects on the 8 versus 7 stimulus set just

NATURAL   COO   GENERALIZATION

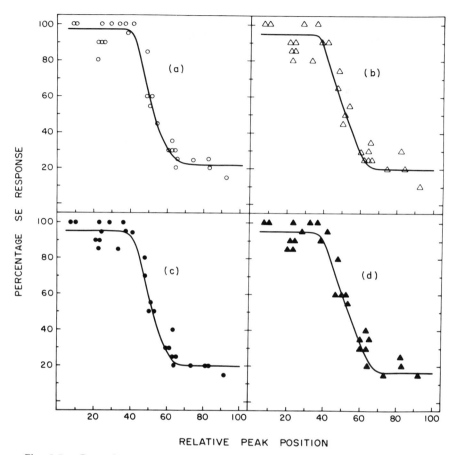

Fig. 3.5   Generalization data for the 27 novel, natural signals with relative peak positions ranging from 0.05 to 1.00. (a) M35 *M. nemestrina;* (b) M88 *M. radiata;* (c) M98 *M. fuscata;* (d) M100 *M. fuscata.*

prior to the generalization test were consistent with the pattern shown in Table 3.2: Both *fuscata* showed a REA ($P = 0.59$ for M98 and 0.58 for M100) whereas neither comparison animal showed an ear advantage ($P = 0.50$ for M35 and 0.51 for M88). This fact, together with the generalization data, suggests that, although both sets of animals were attending to the peak cue during at least the 8 versus 7 stage, they were using different neural processing strategies to perform the task.

To further substantiate the claim that the animals were attending specifically to the peak cue we conducted another generalization test. In all the experiments described to this point we had used signals originally recorded in the wild. Thus, they had all the characteristics of natural vocalizations—background noise, apparently asystematic variability along multiple acoustic dimensions (see Table 3.1) and so on. It was conceivable, therefore, that in solving the peak task the animals may have been attending to some dimension that only inci-

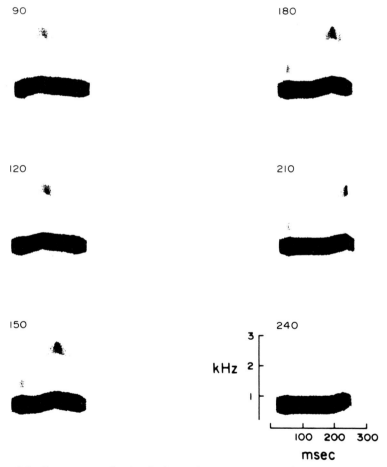

Fig. 3.6 Sonagrams of stimuli from the computer synthesized smooth–early–smooth–late continuum. The number above each sonagram designates, in msec, the position of the peak frequency.

dentally correlated or covaried with the peak position rather than listening to the peak cue per se. To control for this possibility, we generated a set of synthetic vocalizations with a computer and held all
acoustic properties except peak position constant. Sonograms of these
synthetic signals are shown in Fig. 3.6. A continuum of peak position
values was produced by moving the peak through the call in 15 msec
steps. The signals were then presented in a generalization test format
to the animals who had participated in the first test. Two of the animals
were tested as before—any response to a generalization stimulus was
rewarded. The other two animals were tested differently—responses
to any generalization stimulus were never rewarded. The results shown
in Fig. 3.7 confirm that all the animals were under the control of the
peak cue. Synthetic stimuli with peak positions in the SE range were
classified as SEs; those in the SL range were treated as SLs. Therefore,
it appears that, because both sets of animals were attending specifically
to peak position, but only the *fuscata* showed evidence of neural lateralization, each set was using a different neural process to perceive
the same cue.

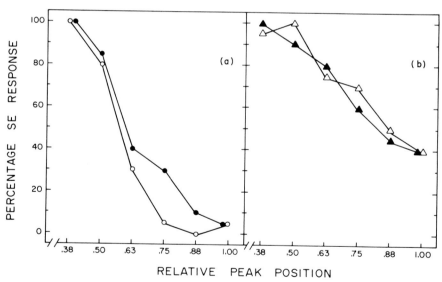

Fig. 3.7 Generalization data for the 6 synthetic coo sounds. Animals in (b), M88 *M.
radiata* (△) and M100 *M. fuscata* (▲), were tested with a reinforcement procedure wherein
a response to any of the signals was rewarded. Animals in (a), M35 *M. nemestrina* (○)
and M99 *M. fuscata* (●), were tested with an extinction procedure wherein a response
to the signals was never followed by a reward.

F. Conclusion

Considered together, these studies indicate that the *fuscata* are per-ceptually predisposed to attend to the communicatively potent dimen-sions of their vocalizations. With sufficient training, comparison species can be induced to attend to these same cues and thus to classify novel signals appropriately. However, even when the comparison animals and the *fuscata* appear to be attending to the same cue (which is of biological significance to *fuscata* alone) they seem to employ different neural processing strategies. The implication is that the *fuscata's* genetic endowment, its experience with social usage of the cue, or some com-bination of these influences is responsible for the species-specificity of the neural processes. Obviously, there is now an acute need for de-velopmental studies of these phenomena to determine how and when the species-specific perceptual and neural processes arise.

Some studies of the ontogenetic emergence of lateralization in hu-mans provide evidence that neuroanatomical asymmetries that seem to underly perceptual lateralization in adults are present in newborns (Witelson & Pallie, 1973; see Witelson, 1977 for a review). In addition, Molfese, Freeman, & Palermo (1975) have reported asymmetries in the auditory evoked potentials of newborns listening to speech that are similar to those recorded from adults (Wood *et al.*, 1971). Thus, it appears that the human nervous system is already significantly later-alized early in life. How this fact relates to the trends seen in the development of speech perception capacities from infancy to adulthood is not at all clear. Cross-language research shows that different world languages employ various subsets of the total range of phonetic con-trasts available to the human speaker/listener (Lisker & Abramson, 1964). Furthermore, developmental and cross-cultural research seems to suggest that, although the human infant is perceptually equipped to attend to any of these contrasts, more attention is eventually directed to those acoustic cues used in the phonetic contrasts of the child's native language (Aslin, Hennessy, Pisoni, & Perey, in press; Strange & Jenkins, 1978; Streeter, 1976; Williams, 1974). Human adults do, however, retain the ability to sense and perceive contrasts not used in their native language (Pisoni, Aslin, Perey, & Hennessy, in press). Is it possible that the neurally lateralized processors present at birth pro-vide the physiological bases for attending to the wide range of phonetic contrasts with which the child might be confronted? If so, does this network become finely tuned (in an attentional sense) to the phonetic contrasts relevant to one's native language as competence in the use of that language is acquired? Does this fine tuning then appear in the form of selective attention to these language relevant cues? These are important questions that need to be answered if we are to have a clearer understanding of the relation between neural lateralization and language development. Similar questions, of course, apply to the ontogeny of species-specific vocal perception in *fuscata*. We expect that the answers to such queries will be as intriguing as the findings that have prompted them.

V. SUMMARY

A consistent theme emerging from this selective review is the need for additional research on the development of the perceptual processes invoked to analyze species-specific vocalizations. Although our understanding of the ontogeny of vocal production in birds is ever increasing, and new techniques are revealing much about the development of the complementary perceptual capacities in this group, we still know virtually nothing about the acquisition of communicative competence in nonhuman primates. Historically, the complexity of primate vocal behavior has impeded attempts to characterize the repertoires of most species and the lack of such information has, in turn, blocked progress in identifying the nature of the corresponding perceptual processes. Consequently, we know little about the sequence or character of developmental events for this important aspect of social behavior. Recent progress in the cataloging of primate vocalizations is cause for optimism, however. As we begin to understand more about the organization of different species' acoustic communication systems and the necessary perceptual studies are performed, the proper course to follow in studying ontogenetic processes will become clearer. It is in this context that the research with *fuscata* that we have described is particularly relevant. Studies of this sort identify the phenomena characteristic of perception in the adult that the young animal must eventually acquire. Once the adult perceptual capacities are known and at least partially characterized, investigators will have a more concrete notion of which aspects of the young animal's behavior are of particular interest, at least with respect to the development of adult characteristics, and can conduct the suggested experiments.

For example, the *fuscata* research has uncovered two perceptual phenomena in the adult—selective attention and neural lateralization—both of which appear to be species-specific. The natural questions raised by this research revolve around when and how these phenomena arise in the young animal and how communicative experience and genetic predispositions interact to produce the species-specific patterns of perception. Future studies of the normative development of these characteristics, as well as experiments with social isolates and animals raised by foster parents of a different species will be necessary to answer such questions. In addition, further perceptual experiments with adults are likely to uncover other important processes worthy of developmental study. Finally, application of the paradigms used with *fuscata* to other primate species may provide some insight into the perceptual strategies adopted by different animals in response to specific social and ecological challenges, as well as setting the stage for comparative studies of the ontogenesis of such characteristics.

ACKNOWLEDGMENTS

During preparation of this chapter the author was supported by NSF grant BNS 79-24477 and Biomedical Research Support Grant PHS SO7 RR7031. The research reported here was funded by those grants as well as NSF grants BNS 77-19254 to M. Beecher, W. Stebbins, and D. Moody; and BNS 75-19431 to P. Marler. The author gratefully acknowledges the advice and support of the individuals listed as well as S. Zoloth and S. Green. N. Layman provided expert secretarial assistance. The manuscript profitted from comments by R. Aslin, J. Alberts, M. Owren, and J. Sinnott.

REFERENCES

Aslin, R., Hennessy, B., Pisoni, D., & Perey, A. Individual infants' discrimination of VOT: Evidence for three modes of voicing. *Child Development*, in press.

Aslin, R., & Pisoni, D. Some developmental processes in speech perception. In G. Yeni-Komshian, J. Kavanagh, & C. Ferguson (Eds.), *Child Phonology: Perception and Production*. New York: Academic Press. 1980, pp. 67–96.

Beecher, M., Petersen, M., Zoloth, S., Moody, D., & Stebbins, W. Perception of conspecific vocalizations by Japanese macaques: Evidence for selective attention and neural lateralization. *Brain, Behavior and Evolution*, 1979, **16**, 443–460.

Blechner, M. J. Right-ear advantage for musical stimuli differing in rise time. *Haskin Laboratories Status Reports*, 1976, **47**, 63–70.

Bradshaw, J. and Nettleton, N. The nature of hemispheric specialization in man. *The Behavioral and Brain Sciences*, 1981, **4**, 51–91.

Carrell, T., Smith, L., & Pisoni, D. Some perceptual dependencies in speeded classification of vowel color and pitch. *Perception & Psychophysics*, 1981, **29**, 1–10.

Cheney, D., & Seyfarth, R. Vocal recognition in free-ranging vervet monkeys. *Animal Behaviour*, 1980, **28**, 362–367.

Cowey, A., & Dewson, J. Effects of unilateral ablation of superior temporal cortex on auditory sequence discrimination in *Macaca mulatta*. *Neuropsychologia*, 1972, **10**, 279–289.

Dooling, R., & Searcy, M. A. Early perceptual selectivity in the swamp sparrow. *Developmental Psychobiology*, 1980, **13**, 499–506.

Emlen, S. T. The role of song in individual recognition in the Indigo bunting. *Zeitschrift fur Tierpsychologie,* 1971, **28,** 24–246.

Emlen, S. T. An experimental analysis of the parameters of bird song eliciting species-recognition. *Behaviour,* 1972, **41,** 130–171.

Falls, B. Functions of territorial song in the white-throated sparrow. In R. Hinde (Ed.), *Bird vocalizations.* Cambridge: Cambridge University Press, 1969, pp. 207–232.

Fodor, J., Garrett, M., & Brill, S. The perception of speech sounds by pre-linguistic infants. *Perception & Psychophysics,* 1975, **18,** 74–78.

Gautier, J.-P. Field and laboratory studies of talapoin monkeys (*Miopithecus talapoin*). *Behaviour,* 1974, **51,** 209–273.

Gautier, J., & Gautier, A. Communication in Old World monkeys. In T. Sebeok (Ed.), *How animals communicate.* Bloomington: Indiana University Press, 1977, pp. 890–964.

Gottlieb, G. Development of species identification in ducklings: I. Nature of perceptual deficit caused by embryonic auditory deprivation. *Journal of Comparative and Physiological Psychology,* 1975, **89,** 387–399. (a)

Gottlieb, G. Development of species identification in ducklings. II. Experiential prevention of perceptual deficit caused by embryonic auditory deprivation. *Journal of Comparative and Physiological Psychology,* 1975, **89,** 675–684. (b)

Gottlieb, G. Development of species identification in ducklings: III. Maturational rectification of perceptual deficit caused by auditory deprivation. *Journal of Comparative and Physiological Psychology,* 1975, **89,** 899–912. (c)

Gottlieb, G. Development of species identification in ducklings: IV. Change in species-specific perception caused by auditory deprivation. *Journal of Comparative and Physiological Psychology,* 1978, **92,** 375–387.

Gottlieb, G. Development of species identification in ducklings: V. Perceptual differentiation in the embryo. *Journal of Comparative and Physiological Psychology,* 1979, **93,** 831–854.

Gottlieb, G. Development of species identification in ducklings: VI. Specific embryonic experience required to maintain species-typical perception in Peking ducklings. *Journal of Comparative and Physiological psychology,* 1980, **94,** 579–587. (a).

Gottlieb, G. Development of species identification in ducklings: VII. Highly specific early experience fosters species-specific perception in wood ducklings. *Journal of Comparative and Physiological Psychology,* 1980, **94,** 1019–1022. (b)

Green, S. The variation of vocal pattern with social situation in the Japanese monkey (*Macaca fuscata*): A field study. In L. Rosenblum (Ed.), *Primate behavior* (Vol. 4). New York: Academic Press, 1975, pp. 1–102. (a)

Green, S. Dialects in Japanese monkeys: Vocal learning and cultural transmission of locale-specific behavior? *Zeitschrift fur Tierpsychologie,* 1975, **38,** 304–314. (b)

Green, S. Sex differences and age gradations in vocalizations of Japanese and lion-tailed monkeys. *American Zoologist,* 1981, **21.**

Halperin, Y., Nachson, I., & Carmon, A. Shift of ear superiority in dichotic listening to temporally patterned nonverbal stimuli. *Journal of the Acoustical Society of America,* 1973, **53,** 46–50.

Harlow, H., Harlow, M., & Suomi, S. From thought to therapy: Lessons from a primate laboratory. *American Scientist,* 1971, **59,** 538–549.

Hinde, R., & Stevenson-Hinde, S. *Constraints on learning.* New York: Academic Press, 1973.

Kimura, D. Functional asymmetry of the brain in dichotic listening. *Cortex,* 1967, **3,** 163–178.

King, A. & West, M. Species identification in the North American cowbird: Appropriate responses to abnormal song. *Science,* 1977, **195,** 1002–1004.

Konishi, M., & Nottebohm, R. Experimental studies in the ontogeny of avian vocalizations. In R. A. Hinde, (Ed.), *Bird vocalizations*. London: Cambridge University Press, 1969, pp. 29–48.

Kroodsma, D. Correlates of song organization among North American wrens. *American Naturalist*, 1977, **111**, 995–1008.

Kroodsma, D. Aspects of learning in the ontogeny of bird song: Where, from whom, when, how many, which and how accurately? In G. Burghardt & M. Bekoff (Eds.), *The development of behavior: Comparative and evolutionary aspects*. New York: Garland, 1978, pp. 215–230.

Kuhl, P. Speech perception in early infancy: The acquisition of speech categories. In S. Hirsch, D. Eldredge, I. Hirsch, & S. Silverman (Eds.), *Hearing and Davis: Essays honoring Hallowell Davis*. St. Louis: Washington University Press, 1976, pp. 265–280.

Lemon, R. The response of cardinals to songs of different dialects. *Animal Behaviour*, 1967, **15**, 538–545.

Lieblich, A., Symmes, D., Newman, J., & Shapiro, M. Development of the isolation peep in laboratory-bred squirrel monkeys. *Animal Behaviour*, 1980, **28**, 1–9.

Lisker, L., & Abramson, A. A cross-language study of voicing in initial stops: Acoustical measurements. *Word*, 1964, **20**, 384–422.

Marler, P. A comparative approach to vocal development: Song learning in the white-crowned sparrow. *Journal of Comparative and Physiological Psychology*, 1970, **71**(2), 1–25.

Marler, P. On the origins of speech from animal sounds. In J. Kavanagh (Ed.), *The role of speech in language*. Cambridge, Mass.: MIT. Press, 1975, pp. 11–40.

Marler, P. An ethological theory of the origin of vocal learning. *Annals of the New York Academy of Sciences*, 1976, **280**, pp. 386–395.

Marler, P., Dooling, R., & Zoloth, S. Comparative perspectives on ethology and behavioral development. In M. Bornstein (Ed.), *Comparative methods in psychology*. Hillsdale, N.J.: Erlbaum, 1980, pp. 189–230.

Marler, P. & Mundinger, P. Vocal learning in birds. In H. Moltz (Ed.), *The ontogeny of vertebrate behavior*. New York: Academic Press, 1971, 389–449.

Marler, P., & Peters, S. Selective vocal learning in a sparrow. *Science*, 1977, **198**, 519–521.

Marler, P., Mundinger, P., Lutjen, A., & Waser, M. Effects of acoustical stimulation and deprivation on song development in red-winged blackbirds. *Animal Behaviour*, 1972, **20**, 586–606.

Marler, P. & Peters, S. Birdsong and speech: Evidence for special processing. In P. Eimas and J. Miller (Eds.) *Perspectives on the study of speech*. Hillsdale, New Jersey: Erlbaum, 1981, pp. 75–112.

Marler, P., & Waser, M. Role of feedback in canary song development. *Journal of Comparative and Physiological Psychology*, 1977, **91**, 8–16.

Molfese, D., Freeman, R., & Palermo, D. The ontogeny of brain lateralization for speech and nonspeech stimuli. *Brain and Language*, 1975, **2**, 356–368.

Myers, R. E. Comparative neurology of vocalization and speech: Proof of a dichotomy. *Annals of the New York Academy of Sciences*, 1976, **280**, 745–757.

Natale, M. Perception of nonlinguistic auditory rhythms by the speech hemisphere. *Brain and Language*, 1977, **4**, 32–44.

Newman, J., & Symmes, D. Vocal pathology in socially deprived monkeys. *Developmental Psychobiology*, 1973, **7**, 351–358.

Newman, J., & Symmes, D. Inheritance and experience in the acquisition of primate acoustic behavior. In C. Snowdon, C. Brown, & M. Petersen (Eds.), *Primate communication*. New York: Cambridge University Press, in press.

Nottebohm, F. The ontogeny of bird song. *Science*, 1970, **1967**, 950–956.

Nottebohm, F. Asymmetries in neural control of vocalization in the canary. In S. Harnad, R. Doty, L. Goldstein, J. Jaynes, & G. Krauthamer (Eds.). *Lateralization in the nervous system.* New York: Academic Press, 1977, pp. 23–44.

Nottebohm, F. & Nottebohm, M. Relationship between song repertoire and age in the canary. *Serinus canarius. Zeitschrift fur Tierpsychologie,* 1978, **46**, 298–305.

Orians, G. M., & Christman, G. M. A comparative study of the behavior of red-winged, tricolored and yellow-headed blackbirds. *University of California Publications in Zoology,* 1968, **84**, 1–85.

Papcun, G., Krashen, S., Terbeek, D., Remington, R., & Harshman, R. Is the left hemisphere specialized for speech, language and/or something else? *Journal of the Acoustical Society of America,* 1974, **55**, 319–327.

Petersen, M. The perception of species-specific vocalizations by primates: A conceptual framework. In C. Snowdon, C. Brown, & M. Petersen (Eds.) *Primate communication.* New York: Cambridge University Press, 1981, in press.

Petersen, M. Beecher, M., Zoloth, S., Moody, D., & Stebbins, W. Neural lateralization of species-specific vocalizations by Japanese macaques (*Macaca fuscata*). *Science,* 1978, **202**, 324–327.

Petersen, M. Beecher, M. Zoloth, S., Green, S., Marler, P., Moody, D., & Stebbins, W. Monkeys employ different neural mechanisms when processing their own versus another species' vocalizations. Under editorial review, 1981a.

Petersen, M., Beecher, M., Zoloth, S., Green, S., Marler, P., Moody, D. & Stebbins, W. Comparative studies of the perception of vocalizations by primates: Neural lateralization, perceptual constancy, and categorization. Under editorial review, 1981b.

Pisoni, D. B. Auditory and phonetic codes in the discrimination of consonants and vowels. *Perception & Psychophysics,* 1973, **13**, 253–260.

Pisoni, D. B. Auditory short-term memory and vowel perception. *Memory and Cognition,* 1975, **3**, 7–18.

Pisoni, D. B. Speech perception. In W. K. Estes (Ed.), *Handbook of learning and cognitive processes* (Vol. 6). Hillsdale, N.J.: Erlbaum, 1978, pp. 167–233.

Pisoni, D. Aslin, R., Perey, A., & Hennessy, B. Identification and discrimination of a new linguistic contrast: Some effects of laboratory training on speech perception. *Journal of Experimental Psychology: Human Perception and Performance,* in press.

Pribram, K., Rosner, B., & Rosenblith, W. Electrical responses to acoustic clicks in monkey: Extent of neocortex activated. *Journal of Neurophysiology,* 1954, **17**, 336–344.

Richman, B. Some vocal distinctive features used by gelada baboons, *Journal of the Acoustical Society of America,* 1976, **60**, 718–724.

Robinson, J. G. An analysis of the organization of vocal communication in the Titi monkey, *Callicebus moloch. Zeitschrift fur Tierpsychologie,* 1979, **49**, 381–405.

Schwartz, J. & Tallal, P. Rate of acoustic change may underlie hemispheric specialization for speech perception. *Science,* 1980, **207**, 1380–1381.

Searcy, W. & Marler, P. A test of responsiveness to song structure and programming in female sparrows. *Science,* 1981, **213**, 926–928.

Seligman, M., & Hager, J. *Biological boundaries of learning.* New York: Appleton-Century-Crofts, 1972.

Seyfarth, R. M., & Cheney, D. L. The ontogeny of vervet monkey alarm calling behavior: A preliminary report. *Zeitschrift fur Tierpsychologie,* 1980, **54**, 37–56.

Seyfarth, R., Cheney, D., & Marler, P. Vervet monkey alarm calls: Semantic communication in a free-ranging primate. *Animal Behaviour,* 1980, **28**, 1070–1094. (a)

Seyfarth, R., Cheney, D., & Marler, P. Monkey responses to three different alarm calls: Evidence of predator classification and semantic communication. *Science,* 1980, **210**, 801–803. (b)

Siegel, S. *Nonparametric statistics for the behavioral sciences.* New York: McGraw-Hill, 1956.

Sinnott, J. Species-specific coding in bird song. *Journal of the Acoustical Society of America,* 1980, **60,** 494–497.

Smith, W. J. Message, meaning and context in ethology. *American Naturalist,* 1965, **99,** 405–409.

Springer, S. Hemispheric specialization for speech opposed by contralateral noise. *Perception & Psychophysics,* 1973, **13,** 391–393.

Stebbins, W. Hearing of Old World monkeys (Cercopithecidae). *American Journal of Physical Anthropology,* 1973, **38,** 357–364.

Stebbins, W. C. Hearing of the anthropoid primates: A behavioral analysis. In D. B. Tower (Ed.), *The nervous system* (Vol. 3): *Human communication and its disorders.* Raven, 1975, pp. 113–124.

Strange, W., & Jenkins, J. The role of linguistic experience in the perception of speech. In H. L. Pick & R. D. Walk (Eds.), *Perception and Experience,* New York: Plenum, 1978.

Streeter, L. Language perception of 2-month-old infants shows effect of both innate mechanisms and experience. *Nature,* 1976, **259,** 39–41.

Struhsaker, T. Auditory communication among vervet monkeys (*Cercopithecus aethiops*). In S. Altmann (Ed.), *Social communication among primates,* Chicago: University of Chicago Press, 1967.

Symmes, D., Newman, J., Talmage-Riggs, G., & Lieblich, A. Individuality and stability of isolation peeps in squirrel monkeys. *Animal Behavior,* 1979, **27,** 1142–1152.

Thompson, W. Song recognition by territorial male buntings (*Passerina*). *Animal Behavior,* 1969, **17,** 658–663.

Waser, M. & Marler, P. Song learning in canaries. *Journal of Comparative and Physiological Psychology,* 1977, **91,** 1–7.

Waser, P. Individual recognition, intragroup cohesion, and intergroup spacing: Evidence from sound playback to forest monkeys. *Behaviour,* 1976, **60,** 28–74.

West, M. J., King, A. P., & Eastzer, D. H. The cowbird: Reflections on development from an unlikely source. *American Scientist,* 1981, **69,** 56–66.

West, M. J., King, A. P., & Eastzer, D. H. Validating the female bioassay of cowbird song: Relating differences in song potency to mating success. *Animal Behaviour,* in press.

West, M., King, A., Eastzer, D., & Staddon, J. A bioassay of isolate cowbird song. *Journal of Comparative and Physiological Psychology,* 1979, **93,** 124–133.

Williams, C. L. Speech perception and production as a function of exposure to a second language. Doctoral Dissertation, Harvard University, 1974.

Winter, P., Handley, P., Ploog, D., & Schott, D. Ontogeny of squirrel monkey calls under normal conditions and under acoustic isolation. *Behaviour,* 1973, **47,** 320–329.

Witelson, S. Early hemispheric specialization and interhemisphere plasticity: An empirical and theoretical review. In *Language Development and Neurological Theory.* New York: Academic Press, 1977, pp. 213–287.

Witelson, S., & Pallie, W. Left hemisphere specialization for language in the newborn: Neuroanatomical evidence of asymmetry. *Brain,* 1973, **96,** 641–647.

Wood, C. Parallel processing of auditory and phonetic information in speech perception. *Perception & Psychophysics,* 1974, **15,** 501–508.

Wood, C. Auditory and phonetic levels of processing in speech perception: Neurophysiological and information-processing analyses. *Journal of Experimental Psychology: Human Perception and Performance,* 1975, **104,** 3–20.

Wood, C., Goff, W., & Day, R. Auditory evoked potentials during speech perception. *Science,* 1971, **173,** 1248–1251.

Zoloth, S., & Green, S. Monkey vocalizations and human speech: Parallels in perception? *Brain, Behavior and Evolution,* 1979, **16,** 430–442.

Zoloth, S., Petersen, M., Beecher, M., Green, S., Marler, P., Moody, D., & Stebbins, W. Species-specific perceptual processing of vocal sounds by Old World monkeys. *Science,* 1979, **204,** 870–873.

4

Neurophysiological and Anatomical Aspects of Auditory Development

BEN M. CLOPTON
University of Washington

111

I. INTRODUCTION

The sequence of auditory development as reflected in the structure and neural activity of various stations along the auditory pathway from the cochlea to the auditory cortex is considered in this chapter. This development has importance for understanding the hearing process because the limits of our detection, discrimination, and recognition of sounds are determined by limits on peripheral and central processing. These limits, in turn, are dependent on the early environmental conditions that provide the organism with initial auditory stimulation.

Because of the broad scope and interpretive controversies that characterize this topic, the aim is to introduce the reader to the problems of auditory development in mammalian species as they appear today. A nascent literature represents research at peripheral and central sites, so the author feels justified in selectively summarizing current knowledge and pointing out interesting directions for future research. References included at the end provide a more diverse and detailed introduction to the field (e.g., Clopton, 1979, 1980; Rubel, 1978).

A. Strategies in Auditory Research

The auditory system presents challenges for relating neural and perceptual phenomena because the analysis and encoding of complex sounds are not well understood despite extensive and often prolonged, productive investigations. Physiological studies of the auditory system have primarily employed transient, presumptively elementary stimuli such as brief tones and clicks. The rationale for using simple auditory stimuli is that knowledge of the responses of a linear system to such stimuli allows prediction of its responses to more complex stimuli. Although many events in auditory processing are surprisingly linear over a large dynamic range at the periphery (von Békésy, 1960), very important nonlinearities exist at middle-ear and cochlear sites (e.g., Sachs & Abbas, 1974; Sachs & Kiang, 1968), and central processing abounds with nonlinearities. The manner in which speech, music, and species-specific sounds are analyzed by the auditory system is largely determined by properties that are inherently difficult to describe (Sachs & Young, 1980). Much auditory research at present is concerned with descriptions of interactions between elementary stimuli, for example, two-tone interaction, and other manifestations of complex signal processing in the auditory pathways. The number of organizing concepts for explaining auditory phenomena is increasing, but observations on adult and immature hearing mechanisms must be tempered with the knowledge that we cannot rigorously define and manipulate much of the sound information that the ear and central auditory pathways normally extract. The search for mechanisms that extract features from complex sounds has met with little success (Abeles & Goldstein, 1972; Newman & Wollberg, 1973; Winter & Funkenstein, 1973). The following discussion will stress the anatomical and neurophysiological changes occurring at brainstem and cochlear sites that are introduced by early sound environments. Very basic processing characteristics of the auditory pathways change with development and are subject to modification as a result of early sound experience.

B. Developmental Plasticity in Auditory Pathways

There is ample evidence that the auditory system of adult mammals is both structurally and functionally influenced by auditory experience during early postnatal development. Because of the large numbers of people who are deaf at birth or soon afterward, an especially important area of investigation concerns the effect of early auditory deprivation on central development (Clopton, 1980). Efforts to establish or reestablish hearing using electrical activation of the auditory nerve through a cochlear prosthetic may be frustrated in the case of those patients who were deaf at an early age because viable central auditory processing has atrophied or failed to develop due to a lack of early stimulation (Bilger, Black, Hopkinson, Myers, Vega, & Wolf, 1977). At the other extreme, the possibility that early sound experience can optimize or selectively direct auditory development has received little attention (Clopton & Winfield, 1976).

Deprivation of sound during development can severely affect subsequent adult hearing capacities. Early studies suggested changes in absolute threshold and behavioral discrimination abilities (Batkin, Groth, Watson, & Ansberry, 1970; Tees, 1967a,b). Clinical evidence from humans has raised many concerns about early conductive losses having retardant effects on language development (Downs, 1975, 1977). Anatomical and neurophysiological studies have confirmed structural (Coleman & O'Conner, 1979; Webster & Webster, 1977) and functional (Clopton, 1980; Clopton & Silverman, 1977; Clopton & Silverman, 1978; Silverman & Clopton, 1977) brainstem correlates of auditory deprivation. This research points clearly to critical periods during development when sound input is necessary for the achievement of normal function and structure. There is little evidence concerning the effect of exposure to specific sound environments on brainstem auditory development (Clopton & Winfield, 1976; Moore & Aitkin, 1975). Because there is uncertainty about the potency of various dimensions and features of auditory experience in different species, enhancing that experience is not a straightforward task.

C.   Research Techniques in Auditory Development

In children, the clinical entity that accounts for most of conductive hearing loss is recurring otitis media. This loss of hearing due to middle ear effusions may result in a maximum attenuation of approximately 30 dB for airborne sounds. It is greater at high frequencies and often fluctuates over short periods of time due to the nature of the pathology. It has been argued that a loss of 10–15 dB in a young child is inconsequential (Eagles, 1964; Kessner, Snow, & Singer, 1973), but growing clinical and experimental observations have prompted concern about even these minimal, discontinuous losses.

Experimental techniques have been developed to produce both reversible and irreversible conductive losses that approximate the degree of attenuation caused by otitis media. Neurophysiological experiments that require normal activation of the system after a period of deprivation have employed reversible blocks, whereas anatomical observations following early sound blocks do not necessarily require a reversibility. With the growing concern for producing delimited periods of deprivation to delineate critical periods, reversible blocks are indicated for both anatomical and physiological studies.

An irreversible conductive block can be produced by removing the blastema of the external auditory meatus and the middle-ear ossicles soon after birth (Coleman & O'Conner, 1979; Webster & Webster, 1977). Reversible blocks have been produced by inserting removable ear plugs (Batkin *et al.*, 1970; Tees, 1967a,b) and by ligation of the external auditory meatus. Both methods have problems. Ear plugs often meet with tissue reactions and other complications due to an accumulation of ear wax and epithelial debris in the meatus. For this reason, they must be removed periodically for inspection and clearing of the meatus. Ligation of the meatus in a young animal is a minor surgical procedure, but blockage of the meatus in this way also causes an accumulation of wax and debris between the ligation and the eardrum. As a result, there is an increasing chance of damage to the tympanic membrane or middle ear resulting in an irreversible loss of middle-ear conductive efficiency. No method of conductive loss will completely exclude sounds due to bone conduction, the maximum attenuation being 30–35 dB. Also, low-frequency, self-generated sounds are relatively unaffected by this type of deprivation. A combination of conductive blockage and housing in a low-noise environment is undoubtedly the best method for achieving high levels of reversible deprivation. The optimal method of deprivation will depend on the hearing capacities of the experimental species chosen, especially the extent to which they are sensitive to low frequencies, as these are the most difficult to exclude.

D. Choice of Species

Terrestrial vertebrates vary significantly not only in their hearing capacities but also in the details of auditory development (Foss & Flottorp, 1974). Among the mammals, the time of the onset of hearing ranges from months before birth for the precocial human (Johansson, Wedenberg, & Westin, 1964; Murphy & Smyth, 1962; Sakabe, Arayama, & Suzuki, 1969) to altricial species that begin to hear weeks after birth or in excess of a month after birth in the case of marsupials (McCrady, Wever, & Bray, 1937). The rate of maturation for the hearing process also is variable across species. The laboratory rat has been the most popular experimental species for work on auditory development (e.g., Bosher & Warren, 1971; Coleman & O'Conner, 1979; Silverman & Clopton, 1977) perhaps due to its availability, 21-day gestation time, prolificacy, and hardiness, but the rapid and relatively predictable events associated with the onset of hearing function, as illustrated in Fig. 4.1, also contribute to its being a convenient animal model. Similar developmental sequences are characteristic of most myomorph rodents; the hamster (Bock & Saunders, 1977; Bock & Seifter, 1978) and mouse (Webster & Webster, 1977; Willott & Shnerson, 1978) are others of this group that have been studied. All have a period of 2 to 3 weeks after birth before they lose the benefit of parental protection, so the utility of their having mature sensory systems after this period is evident.

The cat has been the primary animal model for neurophysiological investigation, and it has provided the vast majority of data gathered during the recent, rapid delineation of the neural plasticity associated with visual development. Its schedule of cochlear development is more prolonged than the rat's (Fernandez & Hinojosa, 1974). Fewer studies on auditory development have used the cat than might be expected from its history (Aitkin & Moore, 1975; Aitkin & Reynolds, 1975; Brugge, 1975; Brugge, Javel, & Kitzes, 1978; Moore & Aitkin, 1975). Other species such as the chick (Rubel, 1978) offer unique advantages such as known and precise developmental stages and ease of prenatal experimental manipulation. The growing data base for avian auditory neurophysiology promises to encourage further the use of birds as a nonmammalian alternative.

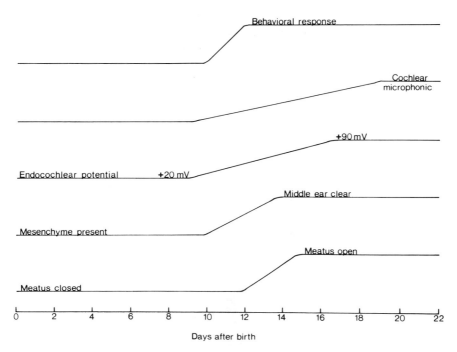

Fig. 4.1 A summary of the major events characterizing the onset of hearing in the laboratory rat and similar myomorph rodents. The behavioral reponse is a startle response evoked by very intense transient sounds such as a handclap near the ear. The cochlear microphonic and endocochlear potentials are referenced to adult values. Individuals within a litter may vary 1 or 2 days on all measures, and a difference of a day is common between ears within an individual for many of these events. The gradients shown are designed to illustrate those observed in the author's laboratory and to summarize published observations.

II. PERIPHERAL DEVELOPMENT

The analysis of sounds at the auditory periphery is based on mechanical responses to vibration, and these are determined by the dimensions, masses, elasticities, and other structural characteristics of the cochlea and middle ear. The dimensions and ossification of the cochlea do not change after birth in the human, in fact, the otic capsule is fully ossified by the fifth month of fetal development, and the bony spiral lamina to which the basilar membrane is attached becomes ossified soon afterwards (Bast & Anson, 1949). Thus, the supporting structures of the cochlea are established early in human development. There is still some uncertainty about the micromechanical events in the developing cochlea, as will be discussed. In addition, much needs to be learned about the maturational processes of hair-cell transduction and the neural transmission process.

The conduction of auditory energy to the inner ear may represent a severe limitation on hearing by developing mammals. The conducting apparatus of the middle ear is an impedance-matching arrangement that efficiently transfers sound energy from the air to the much denser fluids of the inner ear. This function is not needed in the intrauterine environment; the relatively intense sounds of the womb provide a potentially potent stimulus to the inner ear through direct bone and tissue conduction (Armitage, Baldwin, & Vince, 1980; Bench, 1968; Johansson et al., 1964; Murphy & Smyth, 1962). There is uncertainty about how well these sounds activate the inner ear because the middle ear is filled with gelatinous mesenchyme during much of this period. This material may restrict movement of both the round and oval windows, the two openings between the middle and inner ears. Structures on the basilar membrane necessary for neural activation depend on a pressure-induced exchange of fluid volumes between the round and oval windows, so fixation of the ossicles and round window probably restricts the effectiveness of prenatal sound stimulation.

A. Onset of Peripheral Function

Hearing onset appears to be limited by the beginning of auditory function at the periphery. Behavioral indices of hearing, such as the Preyer reflex (Foss & Flottorp, 1974), are in agreement with physiological indices such as the cochlear microphonic and evoked potentials (Crowley & Hepp-Reymond, 1966; Jewett & Romano, 1972) in pinpointing the onset of hearing in rodents. Therefore, it is convenient to specify the onset of hearing in terms of the initial afferent transmission of information from the cochlea.

The transduction of sound to neural activity occurs through the mechanical, electrophysiological, and neural events of the cochlea (see Miller & Towe, 1979; Miller, Towe, Pfingst, Clopton, & Snyder, 1979 for more details and references on cochlear transduction). Figure 4.2 illustrates a cross section through one turn of the cochlea revealing the three fluid-filled compartments of the inner ear. The scala tympani and scala vestibuli are filled with perilymph, a fluid that is similar to the extracellular medium in that it is high in sodium and low in potassium. The fluid filling the scala media is called endolymph and is characterized by a high potassium content and a low sodium content. The endolymph supports an endocochlear potential of approximately 90 mV relative to the average extracellular voltage. In contrast, the intracellular potential

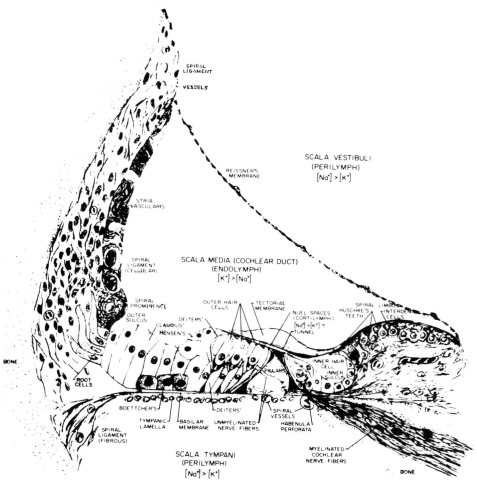

Fig. 4.2 Cross-sectional view of the cochlea illustrating the anatomical structures and their roles in excitation of the hair cells. Part of a midmodiolar section of the cochlea shows the three fluid compartments and their relative sodium–potassium concentrations. Neurons of the spiral ganglion have cell bodies situated within bone to the right and send dendrites to innervate, primarily the one row of inner hair cells and to a lesser extent the three rows of outer hair cells at their bases that are anchored on the basilar membrane. At the tops of the hair cells are stereocilia projecting toward or into the tectorial membrane.

of the hair cells resting on the organ of Corti at one side of the scala media is -60 mV. A potential difference thus exists in the neighborhood of the tectorial membrane and tops of the hair cells that approaches 150 mV. This is probably the largest biological potential in the human body and has been proposed to serve as the driving force for electrical currents intimately involved in the transduction process. Davis's theory of auditory transduction (Davis, 1965) proposes a modulation of currents across the potential interface by a variable resistance in the hair cells. This variable resistance reflects the shearing activity between the tectorial membrane and the tops of the hair cells, the bottoms of which rest on the basilar membrane. This shearing activity depends on the independent hinging of the tectorial and basilar membranes at points above and below the inner spiral sulcus as shown in Fig. 4.3.

Micromechanical, electrochemical, and neural events at the organ of Corti appear to limit the onset of transduction from sound pressure in cochlear fluids to afferent, eighth-nerve activity. Observations concerning these events have come primarily from mammals that begin to hear after birth. An example is the rise of the endocochlear potential in the inner ear (Bosher & Warren, 1971; Fernandez & Hinojosa, 1974). In kittens and rat pups, the endocochlear potential has been observed to rise over the course of hearing onset. In the rat this rise is dramatic, going from about 10 mV to 70 or 90 mV during the second week of life when the cochlea undergoes rapid maturational change (Bosher & Warren, 1971). This event depends on the maturation of the stria vascularis (Fernandez & Hinojosa, 1974; Pujol & Hilding, 1973) which performs as an ionic pump at the outer boundary of the scala media, and on the electrical properties of other boundary tissues.

In the nineteenth century, a mass of cells lying within the inner spiral sulcus were observed in the immature cochlea by Kölliker (1861). This

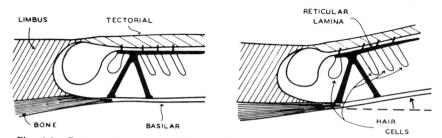

Fig. 4.3 Cross-sectional view of the cochlea. Movement of the tectorial membrane over the stereocilia and the reticular lamina that rigidly anchors the tops of the hair cells is believed to be crucial for the transduction of mechanical disturbances into neural activity.

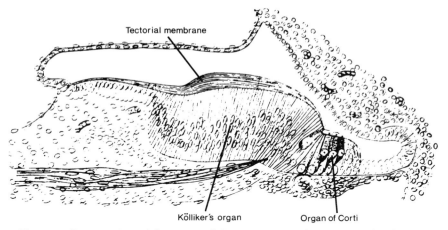

Fig. 4.4 Cross section of the organ of Corti in a prenatal inner ear. The absence of the inner spiral sulcus in the developing ear is due to the existence of Kölliker's organ, an extensive mass of columnar cells to the inside (left) of the organ of Corti. The scala media has not expanded in the young ear and appears largely to be filled with the tectorial membrane, Kölliker's organ, and the organ of Corti. The tectorial membrane is in extensive contact with Kölliker's organ, and the arrangement for independent movement relative to the basilar membrane, so obvious in the adult, appears to be severely compromised. The separation of the tectorial membrane and the hair cells in the adult is due to fixation artifact. (From Retzius, 1884.)

anatomical structure, termed Kölliker's organ and illustrated in Fig. 4.4, regresses through autophagocytosis during the first month of life in the kitten (Hinojosa, 1977). The shrinkage of Kölliker's organ through a reduction in cellular cytoplasm progresses from base to apex and is likely to permit an increasing mobility of the basilar membrane (Fig. 4.5). The filling of the inner spiral sulcus by this structure in the immature cochlea probably restricts or prevents the independent hinging and thereby the movement of the tectorial and basilar membranes (Hinojosa, 1977). This would, in turn, prevent the independent shearing action at the interface of the hair cells and tectorial membrane that is considered to be central to transduction within the cochlea (Davis, 1965; von Békésy, 1960). As Kölliker's organ regresses, a fine network of filaments connecting it and the overlying tectorial membrane is lost (Hinojosa, 1977). It is very probable that an increased sensitivity, and perhaps changes in frequency selectivity and temporal encoding, result from these events in the developing cochlea.

The inner and outer hair cells of the organ of Corti transduce shearing forces at one end to synaptic transmission and consequent eighth-nerve activity at the other. The relative contribution of the inner and outer

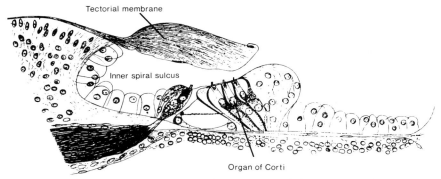

Tectorial membrane

Inner spiral sulcus

Organ of Corti

Fig. 4.5   Cross section of the organ of Corti in an adult inner ear. (From Retzius, 1884.)

hair cells is uncertain, but 90% or more of afferent innervation arises from inner hair cells (Spoendlin, 1971). Dallos and Harris (1978) among others, suggest that the outer hair cells transduce low-intensity stimulation, whereas the inner hair cells transduce high-intensity inputs in the adult. The sharp-frequency tuning of afferent, eighth-nerve fibers at low intensities are thus considered to reflect outer hair-cell function. There is indirect evidence based on the development of masked tuning curves derived from evoked potentials that the outer hair cells become functional later than do the inner hair cells (Carlier & Pujol, 1978). Hair cells are approached by afferent dendrites of the spiral ganglion cells relatively soon after their differentiation, but synaptic formation is prolonged (Kikuchi & Hilding, 1965). Cochlear microphonics and action potentials from the eighth nerve appear at about the time of synaptic maturation (Alford & Ruben, 1963; Crowley & Hepp-Reymond, 1966), the last major event being the arrival of efferent fibers (Kikuchi & Hilding, 1965).

Maturational processes in the cochlea usually follow a base-to-apex sequence. This would seem to suggest that high-frequency sensitivity should precede the development of low-frequency sensitivity, but this is not the case. Responses to high-intensity tones of low frequencies appear first (Crowley & Hepp-Reymond, 1966; Fink, Schneck, & Hartman, 1972; Pujol & Marty, 1970). This may be partially due to damping of ossicular motion in the middle ear by mesenchyme, but mechanical and electrophysiological developments within the cochlea are also likely to contribute to this pattern of functional onset. Numerous changes occur at the time of increasing sensitivity including alterations in vascular supply to the cochlea, rising magnitudes of cochlear microphonics associated with the growing endocochlear and intracellular hair cell potentials (Bosher & Warren, 1971; Fernandez & Hinojosa, 1974), arrival of efferent innervation (Kikuchi & Hilding, 1965), regression of mesenchyme from the middle ear (Crowley & Hepp-Reymond, 1966; Fink, Schneck, & Hartman, 1972; Pujol & Marty, 1970), opening of the external auditory meatus in many mammalian species, opening of the internal spiral sulcus and mobilization of the tectorial membrane (Hinojosa, 1977), and cytologic events within cochlear structures (Nakai, 1970). Experimental differentiation of the contribution of each of these changes to the beginning of functional hearing has not been attempted, but it is reasonable to anticipate multiple, coordinated effects converging to initiate peripheral auditory function.

B. Early Acoustic Trauma and Fatigue

Exposure to intense sounds early in life may have exceptionally fatiguing or damaging effects on the cochlea. Evidence from animals indicates that the cochlea goes through a critical period of development during which exposure to intense noise causes a greater permanent loss in hearing or temporary shift in sensitivity than would be expected for adults exposed to the same sounds (Bock & Saunders, 1977; Bock & Seifter, 1978; Falk, Cook, Haseman, & Sanders, 1974). This critical period extends for about the first month after the onset of hearing in hamsters, that is, to 70 days after birth. Because cochlear function is affected, as reflected in changes of threshold in the cochlear microphonic, the impact of sound exposure appears to be peripheral. Observations with light microscopy (Stephens, 1972) show that cochlear maturation is complete well before this critical period. The implication is that maturational processes unobserved in anatomical events continue at the cochlea, and these processes are vulnerable to excessive stimulation (Bock & Saunders, 1977).

C. Afferent Neural Activity

The appearance of whole-nerve action potentials a day or two after the rise of cochlear microphonic amplitude indicates that afferent transmission of sound information begins at this time (Jewett & Romano, 1972; Pujol & Hilding, 1973). The processes of spiral ganglion neurons begin to undergo myelinization at about this time also (Raymond, Sans, Romand, & Marty, 1976; Wada, 1923). This envelopment of the axons of the eighth nerve by Schwann cells must contribute to increased conduction velocities and correlated decrements in the latencies of neural responses (Hecox & Galambos, 1974; Jewett & Romano, 1972). Figure 4.6 compares the changes in latencies for brainstem evoked responses in rat, cat, and human. Little direct information is available about the activity of fibers of the eighth nerve at this stage of development, but unit recording at the cochlear nuclei (Brugge *et al.*, 1978; Clopton, 1980) and inferior colliculus (Willott & Schnerson, 1978) indicates that frequency tuning is present although minimum thresholds may be 100 dB SPL or more and frequency selectivity does not approach that of the adult. Figure 4.7 illustrates the sequence of development for unit tuning curves in the rat based on published reports using single-unit recording (Clopton, 1980; Willott & Schnerson, 1978) and

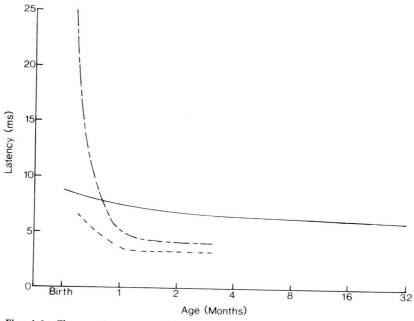

Fig. 4.6 Changes in response latencies for click-evoked potentials are shown for human (—), cat (– – –), and rat (- - -) as a function of log age. The latency measured was associated with the potential originating from the inferior colliculus as observed in the brainstem evoked response for each species. The final, asymptotic value differs due to the size of the brain and corresponding distances of neural transmission in the adult. Vastly different time courses of development are suggested by these changes in response latency. Much of the decline in the human curve occurs before birth in agreement with the early maturation of the human auditory system, whereas postnatal maturation characterizes the cat and rat.

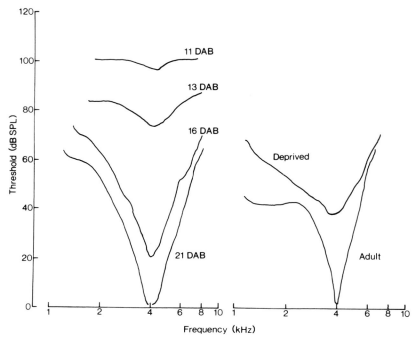

Fig. 4.7 Sequence of development for some major features of single-unit tuning curves in the brainstem of myomorph rodents. Each curve represents the frequency–intensity coordinates for tone bursts just eliciting spiking above a spontaneous rate, if any. A dramatic decline in minimal threshold occurs in the period from 10 days after birth (DAB) to the time of weaning at about 21 DAB. An increase in frequency selectivity for single-unit tuning also occurs in conjunction with this increased absolute sensitivity. Young rats deprived of sound for 2 weeks during the initial onset of hearing have tuning curves for many units at the cochlear nuclei with significantly increased thresholds and decreased frequency selectivity as shown. All curves have been centered at 4 kHz for purposes of illustration.

tone-on-tone masked tuning curves from evoked potentials (Carlier, Lenoir, & Pujol, 1979). The observations on rodents and cats show not only that frequency tuning and maximum sensitivity increase, as mentioned, but temporal locking to sinusoids also becomes more secure with development (Brugge, 1975; Brugge *et al.*, 1978). The relative contribution of maturational processes to these changes at the cochlea as opposed to the developmental progression of synaptic connectivity and function at brainstem sites intervening between the cochlea and the site of recording is not known.

D. Summary

The peripheral development of the auditory system, briefly and selectively traced here, limits the onset of hearing. Although the physical
dimensions of the inner ear reach adult values rapidly in mammals,
a number of anatomical and physiological indicators are correlated with
prolonged onset and consolidation of the analysis and transduction
processes of the cochlea. The maintenance of normal cochlear function
very possibly depends on early stimulation and is particularly subject
to disruption by excessive stimulation. Future research may reveal either
(a) subcellular correlates of extended maturational processes that correspond to these physiological observations; or (b) efferent influences
from central sites changed by an excess or lack of stimulation; or (c)
both. The adult cochlea is not easily manipulated or observed, and the
neonatal cochlea presents many additional problems. However, new
experimental techniques offer promise for revealing cochlear function
even in the developing system. Important areas for clarification subject
to recently developed techniques or approaches include the mechanics
of the basilar membrane in the developing cochlea (e.g., Rhode, 1971),
differential function and maturation of the inner and outer hair cells
(Carlier & Pujol, 1978), metabolic labeling with amino acids and 2-
deoxyglucose (Kelly, Hudspeth, & Kennedy, 1978), and, as previously
discussed, changes in cochlear function specific to early deprivation or
overstimulation.

III. CENTRAL DEVELOPMENT

A. Prenatal Structural Events

The histogenesis, migration, death, and synaptic formation of neurons in auditory brain centers have been studied only sparsely. An
outline can be given of the events characterizing the developing central
auditory system. Histogenesis for the large cells occurs first (Pierce,
1967). These are the cells that become the principal neurons of auditory
nuclei and project their axons beyond the limits of the nucleus. Golgi
II neurons appear later in histogenesis. At the cochlear nuclei, these
cells migrate into position in great numbers so that the initial total
exceeds that of the adult. The loss of excess neurons through cell death
occurs at different times for the ventral and dorsal cochlear nuclei
(Mlonyeni, 1967). It is not known if the formation of functional connections plays a role in cellular survival. It is an intriguing possibility

that early afferent stimulation may play a role in functional validation that selectively determines which neurons survive in the auditory nervous system.

B.   Postnatal Structural Changes

Anatomical changes other than cell migration and death continue to occur after birth in the central auditory pathways. Information about these changes come primarily from work by Morest (1968, 1969a, 1969b). Large axons entering the medial trapezoid body have been observed to continue their processes of establishing very large synaptic endings called calyces of Held weeks after birth in some species. Some observations suggest a continued capacity for modification in these synapses. The dendrites of Golgi II neurons at the medial geniculate body continue to grow throughout adulthood. These initial observations indicate a significant capacity for growth and restructuring in auditory pathways after birth.

It should be noted that principal neurons, those that project axons to other nuclei, are the first to migrate to a nuclear area and demonstrate signs of stability. Golgi II neurons that have smaller cell bodies and mediate intranuclear processing have a later histogenesis, arrive later at the nuclear site, and apparently retain dendritic and axonal flexibility longer than do the larger cells (Morest, 1969a; Pierce, 1967).

C.   Gross Potential Correlates of Development

Electrical field potentials evoked by transient auditory stimuli provide an indication of auditory activation (Jewett & Romano, 1972). Their interpretation must be tempered by the knowledge that they can arise from divergent cell types in differing locations and from presynaptic or postsynaptic events. They may add or subtract at the point of recording so that designating a correspondence between parts of the wave form and unit activity is tenuous at best. However, with modern computer averaging techniques, careful attention to latencies, and experimental verification, they can provide some information about sites of origin, limits of sensitivity, and certain response growth and latency functions relevant to development of the auditory system (Buchwald & Huang, 1975; Hecox & Galambos, 1974).

From studies using gross potentials, maturation in the cochlea appears to be the limiting event in the activation of central auditory nuclei. Electrical stimulation of the auditory pathways indicates that they can transmit information from the thalamus to the cortex before cochlear maturation (Hassmannová & Mysliveček, 1967). Onset of function at the cochlea is soon followed by neural responses to transient stimuli that can be observed throughout the auditory pathways. These early responses have very large latencies and wave form features suggesting immaturity (Jewett & Romano, 1972). The latencies decline rapidly at a rate characteristic of the species' maturational schedule as shown in Fig. 4.6. The basis for this decline, once again, is undoubtedly a combination of factors including peripheral changes, myelination of axons, and increasing security of synaptic transmission.

Evoked responses in the central nervous system are observed at about the same time that the first behavioral responses to intense sounds appear (Jewett & Romano, 1972). There is no indication that thalamo-cortical levels of auditory processing lag in their absolute responsiveness by any appreciable amount. Responses to tone bursts at these sites parallel the development of frequency sensitivity measured at the cochlea. They are first evoked by high-intensity stimuli in the low-to-middle frequency range of hearing for an animal, and then develop increasing sensitivity to all frequencies along with an increase in the frequency range of hearing (Crowley & Hepp-Reymond, 1966; Foss & Flottorp, 1974).

D. Single-Unit Activity

Single-unit activity at the brainstem level of developing animals yields many indicators that change with maturation. Some of these changes are probably caused by cochlear events discussed previously. For example, Brugge et al. (1978) recorded from units of the anteroventral cochlear nucleus in the cat. These units have "primary" responses and are considered to mirror the response characteristics of eighth-nerve fibers. Their tuning during the first week after birth resembles that for rodents shown in Fig. 4.7, that is, they tended to be broadly tuned with high thresholds. The sharpness of the high-frequency cut-off, so representative of adult tuning curves, was missing. The spontaneous rate of units of the anteroventral cochlear nucleus was very low for the first few weeks after birth, and response patterns suggestive of strong inhibitory processes have been observed (Pujol, 1972). This inhibition of responding was often in excess of 100 msec in contrast to an average suppression of responding of about 30 msec in adults. In addition, tones of long duration evoked bursting activity that probably arose due to cyclic inhibitory activity. The bursting effect moderated and largely disappeared with age.

Although tuning rapidly approximates that in the adult for units of the anteroventral cochlear nucleus, the maximum spike rate evoked by high-intensity tones, maximum sensitivity, and latency of the first spike to a tone burst continue to approach adult values for 20–30 days after birth in the cat (Brugge *et al.*, 1978). Temporal locking to the phase of low-frequency tones is very weak during the first week, the upper frequency of locking being 700–1000 Hz. Phase locking continues to improve at least through the first month in the cat and possibly beyond.

Neurons in the cochlear nuclei are currently classified into a number of categories based on their shape, connectivity, location in the nuclei, association with distinctive electrical potentials, and response patterns to selected elementary stimuli (Kiang, Morest, Godfrey, Guinan, & Kane, 1973). It is reasonable to anticipate differences in the developmental processes for these cell types. As more is learned about their contribution to adult auditory processing, their study in the developing system will be useful for both an understanding of development as well as the bases for adult processing.

Observations of single units at the inferior colliculus in rats and cats indicate that even complex processing such as comparison of sounds at the two ears is present to some degree in very young animals (Aitkin & Reynolds, 1975; Clopton & Silverman, 1977). Binaural interaction in the rat consists of unit responses evoked by sounds to the ear opposite the colliculus recorded from and suppression of this responding by clicks presented to the ear on the same side (Silverman & Clopton, 1977). This response suppression by ipsilateral input is present in rat pups at 14 days after birth, just a few days after the onset of hearing. In fact, the degree of ipsilateral suppression appears to be greater than in the adult. It seems likely that experience with binaural sounds plays a role in fine tuning the binaural system under conditions of normal sound experience, as will be discussed.

E.   Summary

These observations clearly point to an organized projection of frequency-analyzed sound information into the auditory system soon after the onset of hearing. This analysis is apparently limited at first by maturational processes at the cochlea and middle ear, but the central connectivity forming the basis of tonotopic organization does not depend on sharply tuned afferent neural activity for its organization. Inhibitory processes at the cochlear nuclei may be especially active then, and coupled with immaturity of excitatory synaptic functions, this could account for the very low spontaneous activity of neurons. Temporal patterns of sounds are very poorly represented in central activity at this early stage, and this measure of stimulus encoding is one of the more sensitive ones to disparities between the immature and adult auditory systems. At least some aspects of more complex auditory processing, such as binaural interaction, are also present near the onset of hearing.

IV. EXPERIENTIAL EFFECTS

A. Anatomy

In mice experimentally deprived of early sound stimulation, significant decrements in cell size and cell number have been observed for certain neuronal subpopulations of the cochlear nuclei (Webster & Webster, 1977). Globular cells of the ventral cochlear nucleus are significantly smaller in deprived animals, and the neuronal density of the dorsal cochlear nucleus is reduced. In addition, neurons of the medial nucleus of the trapezoid body are smaller in deprived animals. A comparison of these same areas in a human deafened at an early age due to maternal rubella has also revealed reductions in neuronal size at the cochlear nuclei and superior olivary complex.

Observations on the size of spherical neurons in the anteroventral cochlear nucleus of rats monoaurally or binaurally deprived clearly indicate that even monaurally activated neurons are subject to binaural deprivation effects (Coleman & O'Conner, 1979). Monaural deprivation from 10 days after birth, the onset of hearing in the rat, results in a 17% size reduction on the deprived side and a 4% increase in size on the nondeprived side. Binaural deprivation has little or no result. Deprivation monaurally from 16 days after birth has less of an effect, pointing to the initial importance of balanced binaural hearing during the first few days after peripheral function begins. The spherical neurons are believed to receive only monaural input, but they project to the medial superior olive, a site of binaural interaction. Fusiform cells in the same area as the spherical cells did not undergo size changes. A probable basis for the anatomical changes caused by deprivation is a competitive interaction of the axonal projections of the spherical cells at the medial superior olive. These and other observations (Silverman & Clopton, 1977) support the concept of binaural competition during the initial stages of auditory function.

B. Monaural Processing

Restriction of input to one ear in rat pups 10 days after birth significantly increases the latency and changes the form of unit responding in the colliculus opposite to that ear (Clopton & Silverman, 1978). This increase in latency, two to three times that for nondeprived ears, was not observed in the gross potentials associated with eighth-nerve activation, so the most likely mechanism is a slowing of synaptic transmission in brainstem nuclei. Latency changes were not seen if adults were deprived. The effects of deprivation on latency of unit responding were almost exclusively restricted to neurons with characteristic frequencies above 10 kHz. These high-frequency neurons are candidates for the mediation of fine timing information from low frequencies (Deatherage, Eldredge, & Davis, 1959; Deatherage & Hirsh, 1959), so slowing of afferent transmission from one side can be expected to have serious consequences for binaural processing which is capable of resolving interaural time differences of less than 100 μsec. In addition, the encoding of high-frequency envelope information, important for both binaural and complex wave-form processing, is undoubtedly compromised by temporal distortions within the high-frequency pathways.

In addition to changes in latency, a change in the form of responding resulted from early sound deprivation (Clopton & Silverman, 1978). Again, the change was seen predominantly in high-frequency units, and it consisted of a briefer neural response to clicks. Units activated through a deprived ear responded with bursts of spikes over only about 2 msec, whereas units responding to clicks presented to a nondeprived ear gave bursts of spikes averaging 3 msec. Although this change is difficult to interpret in relation to auditory processing due to our ignorance of the meaning of duration and patterns in unit responding, it suggests that more detailed measures of response patterns are likely to reflect early deprivation.

Threshold tuning curves for units at the cochlear nuclei are also affected by sound deprivation during development (Clopton, 1980). Tuning, which is present in the rat soon after the onset of hearing, is degraded by deprivation with a consequent lessening of frequency selectivity and increase in threshold at the characteristic frequency of the unit. This is illustrated in Fig. 4.7. Whereas thresholds to pure tones at the cochlear nuclei may increase by 20 to 40 dB due to deprivation, thresholds for the activation of collicular units by click stimulation show changes of only 5–10 dB (Silverman & Clopton, 1977). This discrepancy may arise from an inadequacy of pure-tone thresholds for representing auditory processing of broadband spectra characteristic of clicks.

C. Binaural Processing

The interaction of afferent activity from the two ears can greatly enhance temporal and intensity differences in sounds at the two ears.

This results in neural cues to the locus of sound sources. Asymmetry in the encoding of sound wave form intensity for the afferent pathways will obviously affect binaural interaction, so distortions of brainstem binaural processing is predictable from the previous discussion of monaural sequelae of early deprivation. Investigations with rats confirm this prediction. Moreover, the results parallel the anatomical observations mentioned in previous sections.

Binaural interaction was measured in adult rats with experimentally varied deprivation experiences during development (Clopton & Silverman, 1977; Silverman & Clopton, 1977). The results are summarized in Fig. 4.8 for the relevant conditions. Monaural deprivation from 10 days after birth resulted in a loss of ipsilateral suppression by the deprived ear of unit responding at the inferior colliculus. The deprived ear continued to evoke responses in the contralateral colliculus with a minimal loss of effectiveness, but the nondeprived ear provided much more ipsilateral suppression of that evoked activity. The loss of ipsilateral suppression from the ear that was deprived of sound from the onset of hearing is clearly a dramatic effect. This result was dependent on the time that deprivation is started; the actual duration of deprivation being the same in all cases. Deprivation from 30 days after birth produced less of a reduction in ipsilateral suppression, and waiting until 60 days after birth produced an increase in ipsilateral suppression. Bilateral deprivation had about the same effect.

These findings parallel the anatomical changes established at the anteroventral cochlear nucleus with early deprivation (Coleman & O'Conner, 1979) although an association of neuronal types and functions at the cochlear nuclei and binaural interaction is tenuous at the present.

D. Summary

A critical period clearly exists within the first few weeks of hearing in the rat during which sound stimulation profoundly affects structural and functional outcomes of auditory development in the brainstem. The binaural observations strongly suggest competitive processes between the projections of the cochlear nuclei. This competition appears to determine the relative balance between the ipsilateral suppression provided by stimulation of the ears. In the context of synaptic elimination during development (Purves, 1980), these observations implicate sites within the brainstem, very probably at the superior olivary complex, where dynamic rearrangements of synaptic fields occur with early sound-induced activity playing a significant role. Changes in neuronal

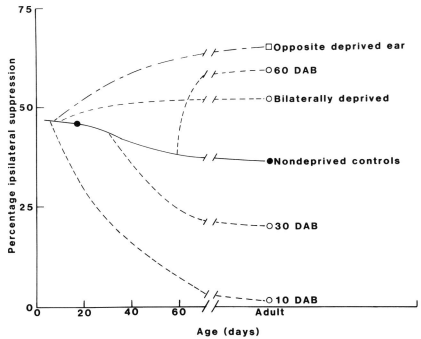

Fig. 4.8 Ipsilateral suppression of unit responding at the inferior colliculus versus age as a function of conditions of sound deprivation. In the rat, clicks to one ear (contralateral) produce unit responding in the opposite colliculus. Clicks to the other (ipsilateral) ear tend to suppress this responding, a process termed ipsilateral suppression. Ipsilateral suppression is very susceptible to sound deprivation during development. Deprivation was accomplished by ligation of the external auditory meatus at 10, 30, or 60 DAB. Both unilateral and bilateral deprivation was used in different animals. The filled circles and solid line illustrate the observed values and inferred time function of ipsilateral suppression during normal development. Early, unilateral deprivation greatly reduced or eliminated ipsilateral suppression, whereas other experimental conditions led to an enhancement. These results point to plasticities in binaural processing, especially a dependence on early stimulation for the maintenance of ipsilateral suppression.

somas at the cochlear nuclei may reflect these synaptic events at their axonal projection fields.

V.   SUMMARY AND CONCLUSIONS: FUTURE DIRECTIONS

Research on the influence of the early sound environment on the structure and function of the auditory system has raised many interesting questions. Cochlear processing, long held to be stable and predetermined, is increasingly being embued with vulnerabilities (e.g., Evans, 1974) and nonlinearities in the mature state. Measures of auditory information encoding at the most peripheral sites in the central auditory pathways indicate progressive changes with maturation. There is a distinct possibility that cochlear processing may be influenced by early sound stimulation, either directly or as a result of experiential modifications in efferent activity. Structural correlates of early auditory deprivation are well documented at the cochlear nuclei. These effects are differentially distributed within neuronal subpopulations, neuronal size being influenced in some groups of neurons and neuronal density in others. Associating deprivational effects observed anatomically with specific functional measures is difficult, and remains as a goal for future research.

The mechanisms of functional plasticity at the present time appear to extend beyond the mere lessening of synaptic efficacy caused by inactivity. Neurons of specific structural and presumably functional types appear to react to the relative activity of other neurons. This may occur because of a sharing of spaces of axonal projection by two neuronal groups with a subsequent dynamic reorganization due to competitive processes. In the case of binaural interaction, the neuronal groups appear as subpopulations of the two cochlear nuclei, and the site of competitive interaction is probably within the superior olivary complex.

The most fruitful attempts at defining normal sequences of development and plasticity in the auditory system have been at the auditory periphery and within the auditory brainstem pathways. It is likely that this trend will continue because the changes observed in auditory processing are extensive at the brainstem stations and inherently difficult to independently identify in observations at higher levels. A better understanding of the manner in which complex auditory stimuli are encoded and processed in the adult will greatly facilitate investigations on the developing auditory system. Questions with significant meaning in relation to complex stimuli are only beginning to be asked of the mature auditory system, so much work remains for the immature system.

REFERENCES

Abeles, M., & Goldstein, M. H., Jr. Responses of single units in the primary auditory cortex of the cat to tones and tone pairs. *Brain Research,* 1972, **42,** 337–352.
Aitkin, L. M., & Moore, D. R. Inferior colliculus II: Development of tuning characteristics

and tonotopic organization in central nucleus of the neonatal cat. *Journal of Neurophysiology*, 1975, **38**, 1208–1216.

Aitkin, L. M., & Reynolds, A. Development of binaural responses in the kitten inferior colliculus. *Neuroscience Letters*, 1975, **1**, 315–319.

Alford, B. R., & Ruben, R. J. Physiological, behavioral and anatomical correlates of the development of hearing in the mouse. *Annals of Otolaryngology*, 1963, **72**, 237–274.

Armitage, S., Baldwin, B. A., & Vince, M. A. The fetal sound environment of sheep. *Science*, 1980, **208**, 1173–1174.

Bast, T. H., & Anson, B. J. *The temporal bone and the ear.* Springfield, Ill.: Charles C Thomas, 1949.

Batkin, S., Groth, H., Watson, J. R., & Ansberry, M. Effects of auditory deprivation on the development of auditory sensitivity in albino rats. *Electroencephalography and Clinical Neurophysiology*, 1970, **28**, 351–359.

Bench, J. Sound transmission to the human foetus through the maternal abdominal wall. *Journal of Genetic Psychology*, 1968, **113**, 85–87.

Bilger, R. C., Black, F. O., Hopkinson, N. T., Myers, E. N., Vega, A., & Wolf, R. V. Evaluation of subjects presently fitted with implanted auditory prosthesis. *Annals of Otology Rhinology & Laryngology*, 1977, **36**, Supplement 38.

Bock, G. R., & Saunders, J. C. A critical period for acoustic trauma in the hamster and its relation to cochlear development. *Science*, 1977, **197**, 396–398.

Bock, G. R., & Seifter, E. J. Developmental changes of susceptibility to auditory fatigue in young hamsters. *Audiology*, 1978, **17**, 193–203.

Bosher, S. K., & Warren, R. L. A study of the electrochemistry and osmotic relationships of the cochlear fluids in the neonatal rat at the time of the development of the endocochlear potential. *Journal of Physiology (London)*, 1971, **212**, 739–761.

Brugge, J. F. Mechanisms of coding information in the auditory system. *Acta Symbolica*, 1975, **6**, (Part I), 35–64.

Brugge, J. F., Javel, E., & Kitzes, L. M. Signs of functional maturation of peripheral auditory system in discharge patterns of neurons in anteroventral cochlear nucleus of kitten. *Journal of Neurophysiology*, 1978, **41**, 1557–1579.

Buchwald, J. S., & Huang, C. M. Far-field acoustic response: Origins in the cat. *Science*, 1975, **189**, 382–384.

Carlier, E., Lenoir, M., & Pujol, R. Development of cochlear frequency selectivity tested by compound action potential tuning curves. *Hearing Research*, 1979, **1**, 197–201.

Carlier, E., & Pujol, R. Role of inner and outer hair cells in coding sound intensity: an ontogenetic approach. *Brain Research*, 1978, **147**, 174–176.

Clopton, B. M. The development of hearing. In T. Ruch & H. D. Patton (Eds.), *Physiology and biophysics*, Philadelphia: Saunders, 1979, pp. 411–417.

Clopton, B. M. Neurophysiology of auditory deprivation. In Gulf Shores State Park Resort, Alabama, October, 1980, The National Foundation, *Morphogenesis and malformation series workshop on the ear.*

Clopton, B. M., & Silverman, M. S. Changes in latency and duration of neural responding following developmental auditory deprivation. *Experimental Brain Research*, 1978, **32**, 39–47.

Clopton, B. M., & Silverman, M. S. Plasticity of binaural interaction II: Critical period and changes in midline response. *Journal of Neurophysiology*, 1977, **40**, 1275–1280.

Clopton, B. M., & Winfield, J. A. Effect of early exposure to patterned sound on unit activity in rat inferior colliculus. *Journal of Neurophysiology*, 1976, **39**, 1081–1089.

Coleman, J. R., & O'Conner, I. P. Effects of monaural and binaural sound deprivation on cell development in the anteroventral cochlear nucleus of rats. *Experimental Neurology,* 1979, **64,** 553–566.

Crowley, D. E., & Hepp-Reymond, M. C. Development of cochlear function in the ear of the infant rat. *Journal of Comparative and Physiological Psychology,* 1966, **62,** 427–432.

Dallos, P., & Harris, D. Properties of auditory nerve responses in absence of outer hair cells. *Journal of Neurophysiology,* 1978, **41,** 365–383.

Davis, H. A model for transducer action of the cochlea. *Cold Spring Harbor Symposium on Quantitative Biology,* 1965, **30,** 181–190.

Deatherage, B. H., Eldredge, D. H., & Davis, H. Latency of action potentials in the cochlea of the guinea pig. *Journal of the Acoustical Society of America,* 1959, **31,** 379–386.

Deatherage, B. H., & Hirsh, I. J. Auditory localization of clicks. *Journal of the Acoustical Society of America,* 1959, **31,** 486–492.

Downs, M. P. Hearing loss: definition, epidemiology and prevention. *Public Health Reviews,* 1975, **4,** 225–280.

Downs, M. P. The expanding imperatives of early identification. In F. H. Bess (Ed.), *Childhood deafness.* New York: Grune & Stratton, 1977, pp. 95–106.

Eagles, E. The survey. In Proceedings of the Conference on the Collection of Statistics of Severe Hearing Impairment and Deafness in the United States. Washington, D.C.: Public Health Service Publication No. 1227, **43, 44,** 1964.

Evans, E. F. The effects of hypoxia on the tuning of single cochlear nerve fibres. *Journal of Physiology,* 1974, **238,** 65–67.

Falk, S. A., Cook, R. O., Haseman, J. K., & Sanders, G. M. Noise-induced inner ear damage in newborn and adult guinea pigs. *Laryngoscope,* 1974, **84,** 444–453.

Fernández, C., & Hinojosa, R. Postnatal development of endocochlear potential and stria vascularis in the cat. *Acta Oto-Laryngologica,* 1974, **78,** 173–186.

Fink, A., Schneck, C. D., & Hartman, A. F. Development of cochlear function in the neonate mongolian gerbil (*Meriones uniquicalatus*). *Journal of Comparative and Physiological Psychology,* 1972, **78,** 375–380.

Foss, I., & Flottorp, G. A comparative study of the development of hearing and vision in various species commonly used in experiments. *Acta Oto-Laryngologica,* 1974, **77,** 202–214.

Hassmannová, J., & Mysliveček, J. Maturation of the primary cortical response to stimulation of medial geniculate body. *Electroencephalography and Clinical Neurophysiology,* 1967, **22,** 547–555.

Hecox, K., & Galambos, R. Brainstem auditory evoked responses in human infants and adults. *Archives of Otolaryngology,* 1974, **99,** 30–33.

Hinojosa, R. A note on development of Corti's organ. *Acta Otolaryngology,* 1977, **84,** 238–251.

Jewett, D. L., & Romano, M. N. Neonatal development of auditory system potentials averaged from the scalp of rat and cat. *Brain Research,* 1972, **36,** 101–115.

Johansson, B., Wedenberg, E., & Westin, B. Measurement of tone response by the human foetus. *Acta Oto-Laryngologica,* 1964, **57,** 188–192.

Kelly, J. P., Hudspeth, A. J., & Kennedy, S. Transneuronal transport in the auditory system of the cat. *Brain Research,* 1978, **158,** 207–212.

Kessner, D. M., Snow, C. K., & Singer, J. *Assessment of medical care in children: Contrasts in health status* (Vol. 3). Washington D.C.: National Academy of Sciences, 1973.

Kiang, N. Y. S., Morest, D. K., Godfrey, D. A., Guinan, J. J., Jr., & Kane, E. C. Stimulus coding at caudal levels of the cat's auditory nervous system: I. Response characteristics of single units. In A. R. Moller (Ed.), *Basic mechanisms in hearing.* New York: Academic Press, 1972, pp. 455–478.

Kikuchi, K., & Hilding, D. The development of the organ of Corti in the mouse. *Acta Oto-Laryngologica*, 1965, **60**, 207–222.

Killackey, H., & Ryugo, D. K. Effects of neonatal peripheral auditory system damage on the structure of the inferior colliculus. *Anatomical Record*, 1977, **87**, 624.

Kölliker, A. *Entwicklungsgeschichte des Menschen und der Hoheren Thiere.* Leipzig: Engelmann, 1861.

Kuijpers, W. Na-k-ATPase activity in the cochlea of the rat during development. *Acta Oto-Laryngolica*, 1974, **78**, 341–344.

McCrady, E., Jr., Wever, E. G., & Bray, C. W. The development of hearing in the opossum. *Journal of Experimental Zoology*, 1937, **75**, 503–517.

Miller, J., & Towe, A. L. Audition: structural and acoustical properties. In T. Ruch & H. D. Patton (Eds.), *Physiology and biophysics.* Philadelphia: Saunders, 1979, pp. 339–375.

Miller, J. M., Towe, A. L., Pfingst, B. E., Clopton, B. M., & Snyder, J. M. The auditory system: transduction and central processes. In T. Ruch & H. D. Patton (Eds.), *Physiology and biophysics.* Philadelphia: Saunders, 1979, pp. 376–434.

Mlonyeni, M. The late stages of the development of the primary cochlear nuclei in mice. *Brain Research*, 1967, **4**, 334–344.

Moore, D. R., & Aitkin, L. M. Rearing in an acoustically unusual environment—effects on neural auditory responses. *Neuroscience Letters*, 1975, **1**, 29–34.

Morest, D. K. The growth of synaptic endings in the mammalian brain: A study of the calyces of the trapezoid body. *Zeitschrift fuer Anatomie und Entwicklungsgeschichte.* 1968, **127**, 201–220.

Morest, D. K. The differentiation of cerebral dendrites: A study of the post-migratory neuroblast in the medial nucleus of the trapezoid body. *Zeitschrift fuer Anatomie und Entwicklungsgeschichte*, 1969, **128**, 271–289. (a)

Morest, D. K. The growth of dendrites in the mammalian brain. *Zeitschrift fuer Anatomie und Entwicklungsgeschichte*, 1969, **128**, 290–316. (b)

Murphy, K. P., & Smyth, C. N. Response of foetus to auditory stimulation. *Lancet*, 1962, **5**, 972–973.

Nakai, Y. An electron microscopic study of the human fetus cochlea. *Practica Oto-Rhino-Laryngologica* 1970, **32**, 257–267.

Nakai, Y., & Hilding, D. Cochlear development. Some electron microscopic observations of maturation of hair cells, spiral ganglion and Reissner's membrane. *Acta Oto-Laryngologica*, 1968, **66**, 369–385.

Newman, J. D., & Wollberg, Z. Multiple coding of species-specific vocalizations in the auditory cortex of squirrel monkeys. *Brain Research*, 1973, **54**, 287–304.

Pierce, E. T. Histogenesis of the dorsal and ventral cochlear nuclei in the mouse: An autoradiographic study. *Journal of Comparative Neurology*, 1967, **131**, 27–54.

Pujol, R. Development of tone–burst responses along the auditory pathway in the cat. *Acta Otolaryngolica*, 1972, **74**, 383–391.

Pujol, R., & Hilding, D. Anatomy and physiology of the onset of auditory function. *Acta Oto-Laryngologica*, 1973, **76**, 1–10.

Pujol, R., & Marty, R. Postnatal maturation in the cochlea of the cat. *Journal of Comparative Neurology*, 1970, **139**, 115–126.

Purves, D., & Lichtman, J. W. Elimination of synapses in the developing nervous system. *Science*, 1980, **210**, 153–157.

Raymond, R., Sans, A., Romand, M. R., & Marty, R. The structural maturation of the stato-acoustic nerve in the cat. *Journal of Comparative Neurology*, 1976, **170**, 1–16.

Retzius, G. Das Gehororgan der Wirbeltiere II. *Das Gehororgen der Reptilien, der Vogel und der Saugetiere.* Stockholm: Samson and Wallin, 1884.

Rhode, W. S. Observations of the vibration of the basilar membrane in squirrel monkeys using the Mossbauer technique. *Journal of the Acoustical Society of America,* 1971, **49,** 1218–1231.

Rubel, E. W. Ontogeny of structure and function in the vertebrate auditory system. In M. Jacobson (Ed.), *Handbook of sensory physiology,* Berlin: Springer-Verlag, 1978, pp. 135–237.

Sachs, M. B., & Abbas, P. J. Rate versus level functions for auditory nerve fibers in cats: Tone–burst stimuli. *Journal of the Acoustical Society of America,* 1974, **56,** 1835–1847.

Sachs, M. B., & Kiang, N. Y. S. Two-tone inhibition in auditory-nerve fibers. *Journal of the Acoustical Society of America,* 1968, **43,** 1120–1128.

Sachs, M. D., & Young, E. D. Effects of nonlinearities on speech encoding in the auditory nerve. *Journal of the Acoustical Society of America,* 1980, **68,** 858–875.

Sakabe, N., Arayama, T., & Suzuki, T. Human fetal evoked response to acoustic stimulation. *Acta Oto-Laryngolica,* 1969, Supplement **252,** 29–36.

Silverman, M. S., & Clopton, B. M. Plasticity of binaural interactions I. Effect of early auditory deprivation. *Journal of Neurophysiology,* 1977, **40,** 1266–1274.

Spoendlin, H. Degeneration behavior of cochlear nerve. *Archiv fuer Ohren-, Nasen- und Kehlkopfheilkunde,* 1971, **200,** 275–291.

Stephens, C. B. Development of the middle and inner ear in the golden hamster (*Mesocricetus auratus*). *Acta Oto-Laryngologica* 1972, Supplement **296.**

Tees, R. C. The effects of early auditory restriction in the rat on adult duration discrimination. *Journal of Auditory Research,* 1967, **7,** 195–207. (a)

Tees, R. C. Effects of early auditory restriction in the rat on adult pattern discrimination. *Journal of Comparative and Physiological Psychology,* 1967, **63,** 389–393. (b)

von Békésy, G. *Experiments in hearing,* New York: McGraw-Hill, 1960.

Wada, T. Anatomical and physiological studies on the growth of the inner ear of the albino rat. *American Anatomical Memoirs,* 1923, **10.**

Webster, D. B., & Webster, M. Neonatal sound deprivation affects brainstem auditory nuclei. *Archives Oto-Laryngology,* 1977, **103,** 392–396.

Willott, J. F., & Shnerson, A. Rapid development of tuning characteristics of inferior colliculus neurons of mouse pups. *Brain Research,* 1978, **148,** 230–233.

Winter, P., & Funkenstein, H. H. The effect of species-specific vocalizations on the discharge of auditory cortical cells in the awake squirrel monkey. *Experimental Brain Research,* 1973, **18,** 498–504.

Worden, F. G., & Galambos, R. (Eds.). Auditory processing of biologically significant sounds. *Neuroscience Research Progress Bulletin,* 1972, **10.**

Audition and Speech
Perception
in Human Infants

The basic auditory abilities of human infants have long been a topic of considerable interest to researchers in a wide variety of disciplines. The systematic study of such abilities, however, has not proceeded as rapidly as has that of the infant's visual system. For example, the study of speech perception in human infants began just 10 years ago (Eimas, Siqueland, Jusczyk, & Vigorito, 1971; Moffitt, 1971), whereas detailed studies of infant visual perception began over 2 decades ago (Fantz, 1958). The greater difficulty in studying auditory development stems in part from the absence of behavioral responses, such as the presence of eye movements and fixations in the visual modality, that are uniquely linked to the pickup of auditory inputs. However, researchers have measured orienting responses by newborns presented with laterally located sounds (Chapter 5 by Clifton, Morrongiello, Kulig, & Dowd in this volume; Muir & Field, 1979). Clifton, *et al.* summarize these data, which provide a systematic documentation of an auditory localization ability that many others have not observed until the fourth or fifth postnatal month.

In addition to orienting responses, the human infant begins to use a complicated neuromuscular system to produce the sounds that will be utilized in verbal communication. Chapter 6 by Kent describes the process of development of underlying mechanisms involved in artic- ulatory gestures, particularly with reference to the anatomical and neurophysiological changes that occur during the first 2 postnatal years. The relationship between sensory and perceptual processes and the motor programs involved in articulation provides an example of the complex set of sensorimotor interactions involved in the simultaneous development of afferent and efferent systems.

Chapter 7 by Jusczyk briefly reviews the history of the area of infant speech perception and proposes a nonlinguistically based model to account for the performance of infants in past studies of speech perception. This model suggests that there are constraints on the processing of all complex acoustic signals. The model is elaborated on in Chapter 8 by Walley, Pisoni, and Aslin. They describe the possible mechanisms by which early linguistic input may influence the acquisition of sensitivities to speech signals and the formation of speech-sound categories. Reviews of the area of infant speech perception (see Eilers, 1980; Eimas & Tartter, 1979; Morse, 1978; Trehub, 1979) have tended to follow the traditional theory that speech signals are processed in a specialized manner compared to nonspeech. Chapters 7 and 8 propose an alternative position, similar to Kuhl's (1978), that a specialized speech-processing mechanism in infants should not be posited until appropriate nonspeech and foreign speech controls are performed, as well as studies of speech perception in nonhuman species.

REFERENCES

Eilers, R. Infant speech perception: History and mystery. In G. H. Yeni-Komshian, J. Kavanagh, & C. A. Ferguson (Eds.), *Child phonology: perception and production* (Vol. 1). New York: Academic Press, 1980.
Eimas, P. D., Siqueland, E. R., Jusczyk, P., & Vigorito, J. Speech perception in infants. *Science*, 1971, **171**, 303–306.
Eimas, P. D., & Tartter, V. C. On the development of speech perception: Mechanisms and analogies. In H. W. Reese & L. P. Lipsitt (Eds.), *Advances in child development and behavior* (Vol. 13). New York: Academic Press, 1979.
Fantz, R. L. Pattern vision in young infants. *Psychological Record*, 1958, **8**, 43–47.
Kuhl, P. K. Predispositions for the perception of speech-sound categories: A species-specific phenomenon? In F. D. Minifie & L. L. Lloyd (Eds.), *Communicative and cognitive abilities: Early behavioral assessment.* Baltimore, Md.: University Park Press, 1978.
Moffitt, A. R. Consonant cue perception by twenty- to twenty-four-week-old infants. *Child Development*, 1971, **42**, 717–731.
Morse, P. A. Infant speech perception: Origins, processes and *Alpha Centauri.* In F. D. Minifie & L. L. Lloyd (Eds.), *Communicative and cognitive abilities: Early behavioral assessment.* Baltimore, Md.: University Park Press, 1978.
Muir, D., & Field, J. Newborn infants orient to sounds. *Child Development*, 1979, **50**, 431–436.
Trehub, S. E. Reflections on the development of speech perception. *Canadian Journal of Psychology*, 1979, **33**, 368–381.

5

Developmental Changes
in Auditory Localization
in Infancy

RACHEL CLIFTON
BARBARA A. MORRONGIELLO
JOHN W. KULIG
JOHN M. DOWD
University of Massachusetts

I. INTRODUCTION

An organism's ability to locate the source of a sound in the environment is extremely basic and adaptive for its survival. Erulkar (1972) pointed out that animals "from insects to primates" that have developed a hearing mechanism sensitive to sound waves are also capable of localizing sounds. The evolutionary significance of detecting sound directionality lies in its enabling an animal to find prey, escape enemies, and locate mates. Despite its obvious importance, the development of perceptual abilities involved in auditory localization are little understood in the human infant. This chapter reports a series of studies exploring

141

DEVELOPMENT OF PERCEPTION
Volume 1

temporal and frequency parameters of auditory localization between birth and 6 months of age.

Before introducing this research, we remind the reader of the two major binaural cues that help to specify a sound's locus in space: (a) differences in phase due to different times of arrival at the two ears; and (b) differential intensity at the ears produced by the head acting as a sound shield (Green, 1976; Moore, 1977). The method by which pure tones are localized binaurally in space differs with frequency of the tone. Low-frequency tones (below 1500 Hz) arrive at the two ears differing in phase, whereas higher-frequency tones (greater than 1500 Hz) can produce interaural intensity differences as large as 20 dB. Both of these cues are present for various frequencies in different degrees, with frequencies in the range between 1500 and 5000 Hz being most difficult to localize (see Mills, 1972; Moore, 1977, for reviews of this problem).

Sound localization is an interesting auditory skill to follow developmentally because both binaural input and higher central nervous system (CNS) manipulations of that input seem to be required to find the locus of a sound (Masterton & Diamond, 1973; Mountcastle, 1974). In discussing the effect of cortical lesions on various auditory discriminations, Elliott and Trahiotis (1972) described sound localization as a more complex and difficult task than discrimination of frequency or intensity, as these latter discriminative abilities remain after large bilateral ablations of the auditory cortex, whereas sound localization is disturbed. For many years the auditory cortex was considered to be necessary for successful localization of sound, but within the past decade a number of refinements have been added to this picture. Early work by Neff and Diamond (1958), and Neff, Fisher, Diamond, and Yela (1956) showed that cats with bilateral ablations of the auditory cortex were unable to run toward a sound source that signaled food. However, unilateral ablations left this ability unimpaired, and no behavioral deficit was observed as long as either the right or left auditory cortex remained.

A. Precedence Effect

More recently, a unilateral ablation effect was obtained utilizing a phenomenon known as the precedence effect. To produce the phenomenon, the same signal is fed through two loudspeakers located on opposite sides of the listener's head, but the onset of one signal is delayed by several milliseconds. The listener experiences a single sound located at the leading loudspeaker; the lagging sound is not heard at all, although it has the same intensity as the other. Whitfield, Cranford, Ravizza, and Diamond (1972) first established that intact cats would treat sounds that came from one loudspeaker located to the right (R) and sounds that came from both loudspeakers with the right leading the other by 5 msec (RL) as perceptually equivalent. [The corresponding equivalence between the left-only loudspeaker (L) and delayed sounds with the left leading (LR) was also trained.] The delayed sound stimuli were designed to produce the precedence effect, and the cats did respond equally to both types of sound, treating them as equivalents when indicating which sound box held the food. After removal of one auditory cortex, however, the cats failed to locate the sound source on precedence effect trials when the leading loudspeaker was contralateral to the lesioned side. For example, a right-lesioned cat failed to respond appropriately to LR sounds but could run toward an RL sound. As in previous research with unilaterally lesioned cats, responses to single-source signals from either right or left were unimpaired. The authors concluded that the precedence effect probably involves a neuronal mechanism of cortical origin that responds to temporal order of sound produced from the left or the right of the body. In support of this hypothesis, Whitfield (1974) found single units in the cat's auditory cortex that were responsive to delayed clicks when the contralateral click led by 5 to 10 msec.

The precedence effect has also been investigated with human adults (see Gardner, 1968). Mills (1972) described it in terms of echo suppression, saying that "listening in ordinary rooms . . . would be acoustic bedlam [p. 341]" if it were not for the precedence effect. In normal acoustic environments, echoes reverberate from many surfaces and would if we heard them confuse the location of the original sound. In fact, we perceive only the original sound unless the reflected sound arrives at the ear after a critical time limit, in which case we do experience an echo. The precise threshold for hearing two distinct sounds depends on the direction of sounds in relation to the head, the kind of signal (brief clicks versus more complex, time-varying sounds such as speech or music), and intensity differences between the primary sound and reflected sound. In man, estimates of the intersound time ranges for perceiving the precedence effect vary between 1 and 35 msec (Wallach, Newman, & Rosenzweig, 1949), 1 and 50 msec (Gardner, 1968), and 600 μsec to 50 msec (Blauert, 1971). At time intervals shorter than 1 or 2 msec, a single sound is heard but is located at some intermediate position between the two sources, whereas simultaneous onsets result in the sound localized in the center between the loudspeakers.

Whatever the exact neural locus of processing temporal events involved in the precedence effect, the animal literature indicates that more complex neural processing is required than when stimuli come from a single source in the environment. By comparing precedence effect sounds with single-source sounds, we can introduce two levels of difficulty in perceptual discrimination while holding constant other task requirements. The simultaneous development of perceptual, cognitive, and motor systems in the months following birth makes interpretation of developmental differences ambiguous unless task requirements are kept constant. In our research, which is presented later in this chapter, we have looked for developmental changes in the ways infants respond to two types of stimuli. We hypothesized that infants would show head turning and other discriminative responses to single source sounds earlier than to precedence-effect sounds, because of the more complex neural processing required by the latter.

B. Special Considerations

A major problem faced in this research was the selection of a response. Research on sound localization with animals frequently requires them to move about the room, physically locating an acoustic stimulus to receive a reward. Research with human adults relies primarily on verbal responses or button presses, with the strong assumption that the subjects could physically locate the stimulus if asked to do so. In such tasks, the assumption appears to be that auditory localization implies some knowledge of the sound source's spatial location. The degree of accuracy could vary from the grossest division of space into hemifields, to the minimum audible angle (i.e., the smallest detectable change in azimuth). Sound localization should be distinguished from the discrimination of perceptual cues underlying the localization process, such as differences in interaural arrival time and intensity. These cues can be manipulated via earphones, producing a sensation of the sound shifting in location within or around the head rather than "out there" in surrounding space. The time parameters for detecting interaural differences with earphones are of a different order of magnitude from sound localization in a free field, and the task is sometimes called lateralizing to distinguish it from localizing (Masterton & Diamond, 1973; Mills, 1972). There is no doubt that lateralizing and localizing a sound make different demands on the organism. The initial comparison of binaural phase and intensity disparities is accomplished by the superior olivary complex (Boudreau & Tsuchitani, 1970; Masterton, Thompson, Bechtold, & Robards, 1975), so it is not surprising to find that monkeys deprived of both auditory cortices are still capable of correctly pressing keys to discriminate sounds presented from right or left (Heffner & Masterton, 1975). However, these monkeys could not physically locate the sound in the room, leading the authors to conclude that ablation of the auditory cortex resulted in an auditory–motor deficit. More specifically, the auditory cortex is not necessary for sensory discrimination of the acoustic cues underlying sound localization, but rather is responsible for integrating information regarding sound locus with some motor response.

The preceding considerations are critical when interpreting infant behavior. Because infants cannot verbally identify the locus of a sound some behavioral response indicating the directionality of the stimulus is necessary. Responses such as eye widening, heart-rate change, respiratory change, and auditory evoked potentials can provide evidence of the detection of a change or shift in location, but cannot be considered as instances of sound localization. Until infants begin reaching for objects emitting sound (but unseen), or locomoting on their own, we are left with an extremely limited response repertoire. For infants under 6 to 8 months, eye movements and head turning toward sound appear to be the only directional responses available. Both of these responses have been reported in newborns, 1 to 3 days of age. Researchers recording newborn eye movements have usually stabilized or restricted head movement, their major purpose being to investigate auditory–visual coordination of space (Butterworth & Castillo, 1976; McGurk, Turnure, & Creighton, 1977; Mendelson & Haith, 1976; Turkewitz, Birch, Moreau, Levy, & Cornwell, 1966; Wertheimer, 1961). Head turning toward a rattle sound (Muir & Field, 1979) and human speech (Alegria & Noirot, 1978; Turner & Macfarlane, 1978) have been reported, despite earlier claims that this response was not reliably present until around 6 months of age (Chun, Pawsat, & Forster, 1960; Ewing & Ewing, 1944).

We adopted many aspects of Muir and Field's (1979) procedure because it resulted in head turning on 74% of the stimulus presentations, a far higher percentage than other investigators have observed. Several factors appear to be responsible for their success, including the stimulus itself, careful attention to the infant's state of arousal, and a relatively long time period in which the baby was allowed to respond. To give credit where it is due, Muir and Field were actually inspired by an item on the Brazelton Neonatal Assessment Scale (Brazelton, 1973) in which the examiner holds the baby in one hand while shaking a rattle off to one side for several seconds. Newborns must respond with an ipsilateral head turn to pass this item. Muir and Field (1979) modified this procedure, instituting several important controls. The rattle sound was

tape-recorded and presented over loudspeakers; the experimenter holding the baby wore masking earphones, which prevented him or her
from knowing the spatial origin of the sound; and the infant's behavior
was videotaped and scored later by two "blind" observers who were
not informed about the location of the sound from trial to trial. The
baby was held by an experimenter throughout this procedure, with the
head cradled in one hand and the lower body supported by the other
hand. Between trials, the baby was lifted to the experimenter's shoulder
and talked to, and trials were initiated only when the baby appeared
to be alert. The rattle sound was presented for 20 sec, giving the baby
a much longer time to respond than previous studies had allowed. We
have used these same features in our newborn study of sound localization. We compared head turning to a rattle sound from a single
loudspeaker to the same sound presented through two loudspeakers
with one onset delayed by 7 msec to produce the precedence effect.

II. DEVELOPMENTAL STUDIES OF AUDITORY
LOCALIZATION IN INFANTS

A. Study I: Newborns

Muir and Field (1979) indicated that newborns would reliably turn
their heads toward the source of a rattle sound. We hypothesized that
newborns would fail to turn toward the leading sound on precedence
effect trials, because this perceptual effect appears to require cortical
processing. The ability to localize precedence effect stimuli would presumably be beyond the limited capabilities of the newborn's immature
auditory system, but would be expected to develop in the months
following birth as the brain undergoes rapid growth (Conel, 1963; Dekaban, 1970). In Study I (Clifton, Morrongiello, Kulig, & Dowd, 1981)
we presented 18 newborns with the rattle sound under three different
trial conditions:

1. Single source trials, as used by Muir and Field (1979), in which
a single loudspeaker produced a sound whose source was easily localized by adults.
2. Precedence effect trials in which the same signal was fed through
two loudspeakers, with one signal leading the other by 7 msec; adults
perceive this sound as exclusively localized on the side of the leading
sound.
3. Control trials in which the same signal was fed simultaneously
through both loudspeakers. Adults experience this as one sound lo-

calized in the middle plane midway between the loudspeakers (the so-called "phantom speaker" effect because a sound is localized where there is no loudspeaker). These trials controlled for possible activating effects of sound that might generally increase head turning.

Head turning on precedence effect and control trials was not expected to differ, as behavior on these trials should reflect spontaneous activity that is not directed toward a sound source.

The rattle sound was produced by rhythmically shaking a plastic bottle partially filled with popcorn kernels. Muir and Field (1979) used a similar rattle, adopting it from the Brazelton Neonatal Assessment Scale. A spectrographic analysis revealed the rattle to be a broadband stimulus comprising frequencies ranging from 50 to 7000 Hz (peak frequency = 2700 Hz). This sound was recorded on a tape loop, then passed through two channels of a device that could delay the output of one channel by 7 msec to produce the precedence effect. The delay of 7 msec was chosen on the basis of work with animals and human adults (Wallach et al., 1949; Whitfield et al., 1972). On control and single source trials the signal was passed through one channel of the delay device to control for any possible alterations in signal quality.

Eighteen healthy, full-term newborns were tested in an alert, calm state. Each infant received 12 trials divided into four blocks, with each block composed of 1 trial of each type: single source, precedence, and control. Order of trial types was balanced so that each type appeared equally often in various ordinal positions. Each stimulus presentation lasted for 20 sec or was terminated if the baby made a 90 deg head turn. During stimulus presentations infants were held with their heads equidistant between two KLH loudspeakers, located 60 cm from each ear at a 90 deg angle from the infant's midline. During intertrial intervals, the experimenter typically raised the baby to her shoulder, rocked, and spoke to the baby to maintain an alert state. Trials were initiated only when a minimum of 15 sec from the previous stimulus had elapsed (mean = 25 sec) and the experimenter holding the baby indicated that a trial should begin.

Videotape records were scored by two observers without knowledge of direction or type of sound. Head turns were defined as lateral movements greater than 10 deg from midline; latency of head turn was defined as the number of seconds from sound onset until initiation of head turn, and response duration as the time from initiation of a turn until it was completed. For precedence-effect trials, a head turn was considered "correct" if the baby turned toward the leading loudspeaker; for control trials a "correct" side was assigned by using the same left–right sequence as presented for the single-source trials.

Table 5.1
Frequency of Correct and Incorrect Head Turns by Newborns

Trial[a]	Correct	Incorrect
Precedence-effect trials	3	5
Single-source trials	40	2
Control trials	8	4

[a]Each type of trial was presented 4 times to each infant, yielding a group total of 72 trials. Total number of subjects = 18.

For all comparisons reported here, an alpha level of $p < .05$ or better was used. Table 5.1 categorizes all head turns into trial types and appropriateness of direction. The data are striking in the high incidence of head turning on single-source trials compared to either precedence or control trials. Newborns turned their heads on 58% of single-source trials, and 95% of these turns were in the appropriate direction. On precedence trials, head turning occurred on 11% of the trials, and only 38% were in the direction of the leading loudspeaker. Behavior on control trials was similar to that in precedence trials in that incidence of head turning was 17% with 67% of these turns in the "correct" direction.

Both frequency and directionality of head turning clearly depended on the type of auditory stimulus being offered, but other characteristics of head turning also differed. Head turns on precedence trials had a longer latency (mean = 11.0 sec) and a longer duration (mean = 9.33 sec) than turns on single source trials (mean = 7.58 sec and 3.5 sec for latency and duration, respectively). Behaviors other than head turning, such as alerting and looking up during stimulus presentations, did not occur differentially among trial types.

B.   Study II: 5-Month to 6-Month-Old Infants

By using the same motor response and auditory stimulus across three conditions, we were able to show that newborns make directionally appropriate responses toward spatial locations of sound under simple conditions, but do not when complex temporal processing is required. Infants 5 to 6 months of age seemed likely to show head turning toward precedence effect as well as toward single-source sounds. Brain maturation, including cortical development, proceeds rapidly between birth and 6 months, with brain weight virtually doubling and myelination progressing markedly (Dekaban, 1970). If 6-month-old infants responded equivalently to single-source and precedence-effect sounds, this could be taken as indirect evidence of a functional correlate of brain development during this period.

Sixteen infants between 5 and 6 months of age were given 16 trials, 8 precedence-effect and 8 single-source. Order of presentation was balanced across infants, with half getting precedence-effect trials first and half single-source trials first. The stimuli were dc clicks, of 3 msec duration, presented at a rate of 5 clicks/sec. Click trains rather than the rattle sound were used because signal onset and other acoustic characteristics could be more specifically defined. Additionally, pilot work indicated that clicks were very attention-getting for infants of this age group. Each trial consisted of a series of clicks presented for 8 sec, followed by an 8-sec intertrial interval.

The results were quite clear. Babies turned their heads just as readily to precedence-effect stimuli (43 of 128 trials) as to single-source stimuli (48 of 128 trials). Infants showed rapid habituation of attention to this repetitive, nonsignal stimulus, with most head turning occurring in the first half of the session regardless of trial type. We concluded that, by 5 months of age, infants seem to process the differential time cues of precedence-effect stimuli in a manner similar to adults, as they turned vigorously toward the leading loudspeaker, showing no hesitation or contralateral turning. In neither this study nor the newborn study did a side bias for left or right emerge.

C.   Study III: 6–9-Week-Olds

If newborns turned their heads correctly toward single-source sounds but not to precedence-effect sounds, and 5-month-olds turned their heads toward both types of sounds, there should be a point in between when infants first begin to respond to the precedence effect. We ran two studies with 6–9-week–olds, one with speech stimuli and one using clicks, each type of stimulus presented as both single-source and precedence-effect trials. For a number of reasons, results are equivocal from both of these studies. Because the stimuli are most comparable to those used with 5-month-olds, only responses to the click stimuli will be presented here.

Infants at this age are difficult to test because they often cry and fuss when placed in infant seats for durations longer than 4 or 5 min. For this reason, every effort was made to keep the experimental session short. Rather than using discrete trials with several seconds of silence between each trial, we adopted a procedure developed by Leavitt, Brown, Morse, & Graham (1976). The stimulus was presented continuously from one side (right or left) for 30 sec, then shifted to the other side. Presentation from one side constituted a trial, each infant receiving a block of four single-source and a block of four precedence-effect trials. Between the first and second block of trials, 30 sec of silence intervened.

Head turning was expected to be less frequent than in previous studies, as Field, Muir, Pilon, Sinclair, & Dodwell (1980) reported decreased head turning for infants at this age relative to either newborns or 3-month-olds. They repeatedly presented the Brazelton rattle to the same babies from birth to 3 months, and found suppressed responding at 2 months. Thus, an additional response measure, heart rate change, seemed imperative, as the shift in sound location might elicit a reliable heart rate response even though head turning was not observed. Heart rate deceleration has been observed to onset of auditory stimuli and changes in stimulation by a number of investigators (Berg & Berg, 1978; Clifton, 1978; Leavitt et al., 1976). In this study, we expected heart rate deceleration to stimulus onset of the first trial and to the shift in location from one side to the other.

As in Study II, square wave click trains served as stimuli. The rate of click presentation was 2 clicks/sec, somewhat slower than in Study II to allow time for shifting the sound from one side to the other between clicks with no interruption of rhythm. Ten infants received the block of four precedence-effect trials first (Group P-SS) and ten received the block of four single-source trials first (Group SS-P).

As expected, overall frequency of head turning was lower than in the two previous studies (25% and 16% of single-source and precedence-effect trials, respectively). In addition, these infants made more contralateral turns compared to newborns or 5-month-olds, so that correct head turning was not significantly different from chance.

The cardiac data revealed differential responding to the trial types. Reliable heart rate deceleration occurred to the onset of the *first* precedence-effect trial, regardless of order, but the first single source trial failed to elicit a response. Change in location did not produce reliable cardiac responses to either stimulus type. These results tentatively suggest that precedence-effect stimuli were more effective in eliciting cardiac orienting from 6–9-week-old infants than the same sound, played at the same intensity, from a single loudspeaker.

These results leave many questions unresolved about 6–9-week-olds' discrimination of sound location. First, in regard to their reaction to single-source sounds, head turning toward the sound was much less frequent, supporting Field et al.'s longitudinal data (1980). To indulge in an interesting speculation, perhaps newborn head turning is a reflexive response, controlled at the brainstem level, and has no implication that the newborn "knows" where the sound is originating in the environment. This initial head turning may represent an innately organized response that seeks to maximize changes in binaural stimulation by moving the head through the sound field, somewhat analogous to newborn visual scanning of edges and angles. Newborn head turning characteristically has a long latency slow movement, accompanied sometimes but not always by open eyes, and no habituation for at least 12 trials (Study I). In contrast, by 5 months of age the infant appears to be conducting a visual search for an unseen sounding object, a response that quickly habituates if it is not rewarded in some way. Interestingly, congenitally blind infants are reported to turn toward sound at about 5 months but soon adopt a centered head position with little mobility, perhaps caused by lack of visual reinforcement (Fraiberg, 1977, pp. 212–219). If there is a shift from innately organized head turning to more voluntary turning at 5 months, 6 to 9 weeks of age may be an in-between state when reflexive behavior is suppressed by the developing cortex but voluntary search behavior has not yet been achieved. We are proposing a progression that many other behaviors show during infancy. For example, the stepping reflex is present in the newborn, is suppressed around 3 or 4 months, and is replaced by voluntary walking in later infancy (Taft & Cohen, 1967). In the visual modality, Bronson (1974) proposed that the infant's earliest visual behavior is mediated by phylogenetically older components, whereas more sophisticated behavior during the second and third months of life reflects the growing influence of neocortical components. Head turning to sound has not previously been recognized as a neonatal reflex, but the problem of how and when controlled head turns toward sound develop is an important problem in its own right. Extensive analysis of videotaped behavior from birth to 6 months is needed to resolve these questions.

Second, the reaction of infants to precedence effect stimuli in Study III presented a quandary. Why should these stimuli be more effective in eliciting heart rate deceleration than the same sound presented over one loudspeaker? This finding did *not* indicate that the babies were localizing precedence-effect stimuli because no directional head movements accompanied the cardiac response. Rather, it seemed to indicate that precedence stimuli were somehow more salient, or at least discriminable from single source stimuli. The basis of this differential responding is unknown, and frankly very surprising. In subsequent pilot work we found that adults have difficulty in identifying which type of signal is presented on a particular trial, although they improve with training and feedback.

D.   Study IV: The Role of Frequency in Localization

The effectiveness of the Brazelton rattle in eliciting newborn head turning is somewhat a mystery. Muir and Field's (1979) study was the first experimental demonstration that newborn head turning toward sound was a reliable event with a high probability of occurrence on each trial. Many different types of auditory stimuli have been administered to newborns over the past 20 years (see Clifton & Nelson, 1976; Eisenberg, 1976, for tabled summaries of these studies), and head turning toward sound has not been a reliable response. Part of this failure is undoubtedly due to (a) testing infants in their cribs with loudspeakers not placed on the interaural axis of the infant's ears; (b) paying little attention to body posture, especially head positions involving possible ear occlusion; and (c) failing to test infants when they are spontaneously alert. However, beyond these important methodological differences, the rattle stimulus itself appears to have special eliciting properties that other stimuli lack. Having used square waves and dc clicks for many years and preferring the experimental control that is possible over the production and specification of these stimuli, we attempted to elicit head turning in newborns using all aspects of Muir & Field's procedure except the rattle stimulus. Our failure to observe head turning to the same clicks that readily produce the response in 5-month-olds, led to an analysis of the acoustic properties that might underlie the rattle's power to elicit neonatal head turning. Possibilities abound, including the rattle's continuous sound versus the discontinuous brief duration clicks, the pulsating rhythm produced by manual shaking, and frequency characteristics. Recall that the rattle is a broadband stimulus containing frequencies between 50 and 7000 Hz, peaking somewhat symmetrically around 2700 Hz. Morrongiello (1980) proposed and conducted a study that compared newborns' and older infants' differential responding to the rattle filtered to alter its frequency composition.

Three types of stimuli were generated by passing the rattle sound through a Brüel and Kjaer spectrum shaper: a low-frequency bandpass rattle limited to frequencies less than 1600 Hz, a mid-frequency bandpass rattle (1000–3000 Hz), and a high-frequency bandpass rattle (over 1800 Hz). The original unfiltered rattle was retained as a control stimulus. All stimuli were single-source, that is, presented through one loudspeaker, throughout this experiment.

Newborns and 5-month-olds, 24 children at each age, were tested in a spontaneously alert, quiet state. All infants received 12 trials, three presentations each of the four stimulus types, counterbalanced over subjects for order and left–right position. Sound pressure level (SPL)

was randomly varied across trials to prevent possible confounding of
loudness changes with frequency changes. We do not know if equal
loudness curves are the same for infants as they are for adults, and
varying SPL on every trial seemed to be the best means of eliminating
responses consistent with loudness rather than frequency variations.
Because the hearing threshold at birth is elevated by at least 5–10 dB
over that of 5-month-olds (Berg & Berg, 1978), somewhat greater SPLs
were used with the younger infants. For newborns, SPL values ranged
from 76 to 82 dB, whereas 5-month-olds received variations between
68 and 74 dB (re 0.0002 dynes/cm^2, calibrated using the A scale of a
General Radio sound level meter). Heart rate was recorded and overt
behavior was videotaped for later scoring, as in earlier studies. Morrongiello's study was the only one in this series to directly compare
the behavior of newborns with that of older infants, using the same
stimuli and procedures.

Overall, head turning toward sound was more frequent in 5-month-
olds (55% of the trials) than in newborns (43%). Although older infants
turned more than newborns toward stimuli of all frequencies, this difference was most pronounced for the low-frequency bandpass stimulus
(see Figure 5.1). Age differences at other frequencies were not statistically reliable. Both age groups turned more to higher frequencies,
with the high-frequency and broadband stimuli eliciting more head
turning from all infants. Matched t-tests for pairwise comparisons produced the following reliable rank orderings for newborns: The low-
frequency stimulus elicited less responding than any other stimulus;
the medium-frequency stimulus elicited less response than high- and

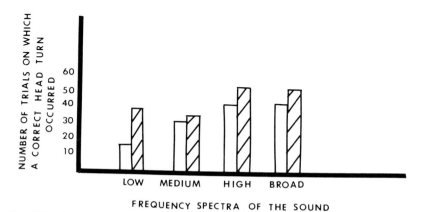

Fig. 5.1 The number of trials on which a correct head turn occurred as a function
of age and frequency spectra of sound. Newborn, □; 5-month-old, □.

broadband frequencies, which did not differ from one another. For 5-month-olds, head turning toward low and medium frequencies was significantly less than toward high and broad frequencies, with no further comparisons reliably different. It is important to emphasize that differential head turning in this situation does not indicate either discrimination or lack of discrimination among these frequency bandwidths, as that was not directly tested. Rather, the results indicate differential eliciting properties of these frequencies for a response that is assumed to reflect sound localization (i.e., head turning).

Heart rate response to these stimuli was deceleration in both age groups, and did not differ with frequency. Cardiac orienting was shown to all stimuli, suggesting that all frequencies were attended to. Heart rate response did differ when head movement was involved, a finding that replicated previous work (Clifton, 1978; Pomerleau-Malcuit & Clifton, 1973). In this analysis, single trials with and without head turning were selected from each frequency block for each subject. Because so few newborns made head turns to low-frequency stimuli, only 14 infants from each age group contributed to the following analysis. For both groups, heart rate deceleration was evident on trials when no head turn occurred, but movement blocked the deceleration response for newborns (see Figure 5.2). Heart rate deceleration was maintained by 5-month-olds when making head turns, but magnitude was less than on trials without movement. Cardiac–somatic coupling may be stronger in newborns because they have fewer resources to meet energy

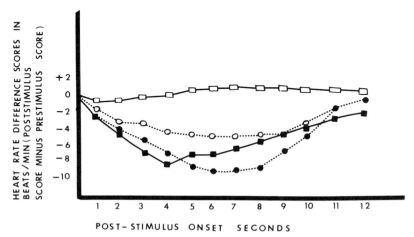

Fig. 5.2   Heart rate responses to sound of newborns and 5-month-old infants on trials accompanied and not accompanied by head turns. Newborns: No head turn, ■; head turn, □. Five-month-olds: no head turn, ●; head turn, ○.

demands made by body movements. Cardiac rate at every age can be influenced by somatic activity as a wealth of adult literature attests (Lacey & Lacey, 1974; Obrist, 1976), but movements of the immature organism may tax the system relatively more, a state that may be reflected in greater cardiac change than that observed at older ages. Exquisite time locking of heart rate acceleration with each burst of nonnutritive sucking has been found in newborns (Nelson, Clifton, Dowd, & Field, 1979), suggesting that even small motor movements can produce concomitant cardiac activity in this age infant.

That low-frequency stimuli were less likely to elicit head turning, particularly in newborns, supports the growing evidence that sensitivity to frequency varies with age. Trehub, Schneider, & Endman (1980) tested threshold sensitivity for octave band noises with center frequencies varying between 200 and 10,000 Hz. Infants at 6 months of age displayed thresholds about 5–8 dB higher than 12–18-month-olds for frequencies between 200 and 2000 Hz. Compared to adults, 6-month-olds' thresholds were 20–30 dB higher throughout this frequency range. All infants' thresholds approached that of adults at 10,000 Hz. Schneider, Trehub, & Bull (1980) extended the range to 19,000 Hz, and found comparable thresholds for infants and adults at this very high frequency. Morrongiello's data (1980) indicate that, even when sounds are presented well above threshold, infants remain less behaviorally responsive to frequencies in the lower range (under 1600 Hz).

Both Trehub et al. and Morrongiello used a localization response, head turning toward sound, to assess sensitivity across frequencies. Less sensitivity to lower frequencies may be specific to localization responses, and may not reflect hearing sensitivity in general. Cardiac deceleration has been standardly used as an index of stimulus detection and attention in infants for many years (for research reviews see Clifton, 1974; Graham & Jackson, 1970). In Morrongiello's study, cardiac deceleration occurred to all frequencies in both age groups, but did *not* differ among frequencies. Why might sound localization be frequency dependent although other measures of hearing sensitivity are not? Recall that the major cue for localization of frequencies under 1500 Hz is a binaural difference in time of arrival, whereas higher frequencies produce binaural intensity differences and spectrum changes as the sound moves over the head and pinna (Green, 1976, pp. 204–205; Mills, 1972). Infants may simply be able to utilize the binaural intensity cue (arising from high frequencies) for localizing sound earlier than interaural arrival time differences (arising from low frequencies). Interaural arrival time will change with head growth by a significant factor, so this cue is changing throughout early childhood. Because of its relation to sound localization, greater sensitivity to high frequencies may only be apparent when the infant is required to perform a task involving localizing responses. An assessment of the validity of this conclusion awaits further research.

At least one study does not support the view that infants develop sensitivity to interaural intensity differences before interaural arrival time differences. Bundy (1980) tested infants in a lateralization task, measuring their discrimination of each binaural cue separately by delivering sound over earphones manipulated to produce apparent changes in location. Although 16-week-olds appeared to discriminate changes in both binaural cues, 8-week-olds responded only to changes in interaural arrival time. These data are inconclusive, however, because of a methodological problem involving the habituation–dishabituation paradigm used by Bundy (1980). The younger babies in the interaural intensity group showed very little response decrement over successive habituation trials, making increased responding to the dishabituation stimulus or change trial less possible. If all infants had been required to meet an habituation criterion before the stimulus was changed, discrimination of both cues might have been demonstrated (see Clifton & Nelson, 1976, for fuller discussion of this issue).

To summarize, current data indicate that infants are more responsive to high than to low frequencies, but we do not know whether this finding is tied to sound localization cues and responses or is a general aspect of the infant's hearing sensitivity.

III. CONCLUSIONS

In the studies reported here we explored sound localization in infants from birth to 5 months of age. Newborn head turning is elicited only under highly specific stimulus conditions, and is behaviorally different from head turning in older infants. Newborns can discriminate and respond directionally to sounds coming from a single source in the environment, but appear unable to discriminate the direction of the leading sound in the more complex stimulus created by delayed onset signals. By 5 months, infants turned their heads equally toward single-source and delayed-onset sounds, appearing to localize both types of signals in an adult-like manner. The precedence effect involves sensory inhibition of the delayed signal, and is thought to require processing at the cortical level. We propose that the developmental change in responding to the precedence effect is a functional correlate of early brain development. A converging research strategy is needed to confirm this hypothesis. Again drawing on neurophysiological studies of animals and clinical studies of brain-injured human adults, we find that other auditory phenomena have been related to cortical functioning. For example, discrimination and localization of very brief stimuli are prone to disruption following loss of the auditory cortex (Cranford, 1979; Gersuni, 1971, p. 87; Scharlock, Neff, & Strominger, 1965). Diamond (1974) suggested that there are two levels at which the auditory cortex functions, depending on signal duration.

1. The most "primitive" level allows the organism to "track" a sound, perhaps through changes in intensity as head and body movements are made in the process of locating the sound. This process would require a fairly long signal duration.

2. A "more refined" level allows the organism to localize brief sounds with durations of 25 msec or less. Diamond saw this second level as a later evolutionary development and dependent upon an expanded auditory neocortex.

An interesting analogy might be drawn with head turning toward sound during infancy. If newborn head turning is like a tracking response that relies on continuously available sound to guide it, the sound must remain on while the infant is turning. The act of head turning induces changes in sensory input for both binaural intensity and time cues, guiding the head through the sound field. Ipsilateral turning rather than contralateral turning is more adaptive because turning toward the sound brings the head into the position with the greatest acuity or resolution for sound localization (i.e., the sound is straight ahead; Mills, 1972, p. 309). As noted earlier, newborn head turning may be analogous to neonatal visual behavior in which eye movements scan the field for contrasting edges and patterns. The older baby's head turn is based on a more sophisticated sound localization process, and may represent more voluntary behavior under intentional control.

These ideas are readily testable. If newborn head turning is based on sensory change in the ongoing sound, one would expect a turn to be disrupted if the sound were turned off at initiation of the turn. In addition, one might predict no directionally appropriate head turn to be initiated to very brief duration stimuli if indeed the auditory cortex is necessary for this localization. Systematic variation of stimulus parameters, task demands, and age of subjects should lead us to a better understanding of auditory development in infancy. Ultimately, we hope to relate developmental changes in auditory functioning to the broader concern of early maturation in the CNS.

ACKNOWLEDGMENTS

This research was supported by grant HD-06753 to Rachel Clifton. We are grateful to the staff of Baystate Medical Center, Springfield, Massachusetts, and to the parents of infants who participated in this research for their cooperation. We thank Gilbert Tolhurst for his advice and help in preparing the auditory stimuli used in these studies.

REFERENCES

Alegria, J., & Noirot, E. Neonate orientation behavior towards human voice. *International Journal of Behavior Development*, 1978, **1**, 291–312.

Berg, W. K., & Berg, K. M. Psychophysiological development in infancy: State, sensory function and attention. In J. Osofsky (Ed.), *Handbook of infant development*, New York: Wiley, 1978.

Blauert, J. Localization and the law of the first wavefront in the median plane. *Journal of the Acoustical Society of America*, 1971, **50**, 466–470.

Boudreau, J., & Tsuchitani, C. Cat superior olive S-segment cell discharge to tonal stimulation. In W. Neff (Ed.), *Contributions to sensory physiology* (Vol. 4). New York: Academic Press, 1970, pp. 143–213.

Brazelton, T. *Brazelton neonatal assessment scale*. London: Spastics International Medical Publications, 1973.

Bronson, G. The postnatal growth of visual capacity. *Child Development*, 1974, **45**, 873–890.

Bundy, R. S. Discrimination of sound localization cues in young infants. *Child Development*, 1980, **51**, 292–294.

Butterworth, G., & Castillo, M. Coordination of auditory visual space in newborn human infants. *Perception*, 1976, **5**, 155–160.

Chun, R., Pawsat, R., & Forster, F. Sound localization in infancy. *Journal of Nervous & Mental Disease*, 1960, **130**, 472–477.

Clifton, R. Cardiac conditioning and orienting in infants. In P. Obrist, A. Black, J. Brener, & L. DiCara. *Cardiovascular psychophysiology: Current issues in response mechanisms, biofeedback, and methodology*. Chicago: Aldine, 1974, pp. 479–504.

Clifton, R. The relation of infant cardiac responding to behavioral state and motor activity. In W. A. Collins (Ed.), *Minnesota Symposia on child psychology* (Vol. 11). New York: Harper & Row, 1978.

Clifton, R., & Nelson, M. Developmental study of habituation in infants: The importance of paradigm, response system and state. In T. Tighe & R. Leaton (Eds.), *Habituation: Perspectives from child development, animal behavior and neurophysiology*. Hillsdale, N.J.: Erlbaum, 1976.

Clifton, R., Morrongiello, B., Kulig, J., & Dowd, J. Newborns' orientation toward sound: Possible implications for cortical development. *Child Development*, 1981, **52**, 833–838.

Conel, J. L. The postnatal development of the human cerebral cortex (Vol. 1). *The cortex of the newborn*. Cambridge, Mass.: Harvard University Press, 1963.

Cranford, J. L. Detection versus discrimination of brief tones by cats with auditory cortex lesions. *Journal of the Acoustical Society of America*, 1979, **65**, (6), 1573–1575.

Dekaban, A. *Neurology of early childhood*. Baltimore: Williams & Wilkins, 1970.

Diamond, I. T. Structure and function of auditory thalamus and cortex. *Archives of Otolaryngology*, 1974, **98**, 408–411.

Eisenberg, R. B. *Auditory competence in early life.* Baltimore, Md.: University Park Press, 1976.

Elliott, D., & Trahiotis, C. Cortical lesions and auditory discrimination. *Psychological Bulletin,* 1972, **77**, 198–222.

Erulkar, S. D. Comparative aspects of spatial localization of sound. *Physiological Review,* 1972, **52**, 237–360.

Ewing, I. R., & Ewing, A. W. G. The ascertainment of deafness in infancy and early childhood. *Journal of Laryngology and Otology,* 1944, **59**, 309–333.

Field, J., Muir, D., Pilon, R., Sinclair, M., & Dodwell, P. Infants' orientation to lateral sounds from birth to three months. *Child Development,* 1980, **51**, 295–298.

Fraiberg, S. *Insights from the blind.* New York: Basic Books, 1977.

Gardner, M. B. Historical background of the Haas and/or precedence effect. *Journal of the Acoustical Society of America,* 1968, **43**, 1243–1248.

Gersuni, G. Temporal organization of the auditory function. In G. V. Gersuni (Ed.), *Sensory processes at the neuronal and behavioral levels.* New York: Academic Press, 1971, pp. 85–114.

Graham, F. K., & Jackson, J. C. Arousal systems and infant heart rate responses. In H. Reese & L. P. Lipsitt (Eds.), *Advances in child development and behavior* (Vol. 5). New York: Academic Press, 1970.

Green, D. *An introduction to hearing.* Hillsdale, N.J.: Erlbaum, 1976.

Heffner, H., & Masterton, B. Contribution of auditory cortex to sound localization in the monkey (*Macaca mulatta*). *Journal of Neurophysiology,* 1975, **38**, 1340–1358.

Lacey, J., & Lacey, B. Studies of heart rate and other bodily processes in sensorimotor behavior. In P. Obrist, A. Black, J. Brener, & L. DiCara (Eds.), *Cardiovascular psychophysiology: Current issues in response mechanisms, biofeedback, and methodology.* Chicago: Aldine, 1974.

Leavitt, L., Brown, J., Morse, P., & Graham, F. Cardiac orienting and auditory discrimination in 6-week infants. *Developmental Psychology,* 1976, **12**, 514–523.

Masterton, B., & Diamond, I. Hearing: Central neural mechanisms. In *Handbook of perception III.* New York: Academic Press, 1973, pp. 407–448.

Masterton, B., Thompson, G., Bechtold, J., & Robards, J. Neuroanatomical basis of binaural phase-difference analysis for sound localization: A comparative study. *Journal of Comparative and Physiological Psychology,* 1975, **89**, 379–385.

McGurk, H., Turnure, C., & Creighton, S. J. Auditory–visual coordination in neonates. *Child Development,* 1977, **48**, 138–143.

Mendelson, J. J., & Haith, M. M. The relation between audition and vision in the human newborn. *Monographs of the Society for Research in Child Development,* 1976, **41**, (4, Serial No. 167).

Mills, A. W. Auditory localization. In J. V. Tobias (Ed.), *Foundations of modern auditory theory* (Vol. 2). New York: Academic Press, 1972, pp. 301–345.

Moore, B. C. *Introduction to the psychology of hearing.* Baltimore, Md.: University Park Press, 1977.

Morrongiello, B. *Developmental changes in cardiac–somatic relations and infants' orientation to complex sounds as a function of frequency.* Unpublished Master's thesis, University of Massachusetts, Amherst, Mass., 1980.

Mountcastle, V. B. Central neural mechanisms in hearing. In V. Mountcastle (Ed.), *Medical physiology,* St. Louis: C. V. Mosby, 1974, pp. 412–439.

Muir, D., & Field, J. Newborn infants orient to sounds. *Child Development,* 1979, **50**, 431–436.

Neff, W. D., & Diamond, I. T. The neural basis of auditory discrimination. In H. R. Harlow & C. N. Woolsey (Eds.), *Biological and biochemical bases for behavior.* Madison, Wis.: University of Wisconsin Press, 1958, pp. 101–126.

Neff, W. D., Fisher, J. F., Diamond, I. T., & Yela, M. Role of auditory cortex in discrimination requiring localization of sound in space. *Journal of Neurophysiology,* 1956, **19,** 500–512.

Nelson, M., Clifton, R., Dowd, J., & Field, T. Cardiac responding to auditory stimuli in newborn infants: Why pacifiers should not be used when heart rate is the major dependent variable. *Infant Behavior and Development,* 1978, **1,** 277–290.

Obrist, P. The cardiovascular–behavioral interaction as it appears today. *Psychophysiology,* 1976, **13,** 95–107.

Pomerleau-Malcuit, A., & Clifton, R. K. Neonatal heart rate response to tactile, auditory, and vestibular stimulation in different states. *Child Development,* 1973, **44,** 485–496.

Scharlock, D., Neff, W., & Strominger, N. Distinction of tone duration after bilateral ablation of cortical auditory areas. *Journal of Neurophysiology,* 1965, **28,** 673–681.

Schneider, B., Trehub, S., & Bull, D. High-frequency sensitivity in infants. *Science,* 1980, **207,** 1003–1004.

Taft, L. T., & Cohen, H. J. Neonatal and infant reflexology. In J. Hellmuth (Ed.), *The exceptional infant* (Vol. 1). New York: Brunner/Mazel, 1967.

Trehub, S., Schneider, B., & Endman, M. Developmental changes in infants' sensitivity to octave-band noises. *Journal of Experimental Child Psychology,* 1980, **29,** 282–293.

Turner, S., & Macfarlane, A. Localization of human speech by the newborn baby and the effects of pethidine ("meperidine"). *Developmental Medicine and Child Neurology,* 1978, **20,** 727–734.

Turkewitz, G., Birch, H., Moreau, T., Levy, L., & Cornwell, A. Effect of intensity of auditory stimulation on directional eye movements in the human neonate. *Animal Behavior,* 1966, **14,** 93–101.

Wallach, H., Newman, E., & Rosenzweig, J. The precedence effect in sound localization. *American Journal of Psychology,* 1949, **62,** 315–336.

Wertheimer, M. Psychomotor coordination of auditory and visual space at birth. *Science,* 1961, **134,** 1692.

Whitfield, I., Cranford, J., Ravizza, R., & Diamond, I. Effects of unilateral ablation of auditory cortex in cat on complex sound localization. *Journal of Neurophysiology,* 1972, **35,** 718–731.

Whitfield, I. C. A possible neurophysiological basis for the precedence effect. *Federation Proceedings,* 1974, **33,** (8), 1915–1916.

6

Sensorimotor Aspects of Speech Development

RAYMOND D. KENT
Human Communication Laboratories

The thesis of this chapter is that the interplay of genetic and experiential factors is necessary for the acquisition of the motor patterns of speech. The thesis endorses neither the nativist argument that the child begins to speak automatically and inevitably as the genetic plan unfolds, nor the experientialist claim that genetic influences are minor compared to factors in the child's environment. Rather, the argument is that essential backdrops for speech development are: (*a*) a biological predisposition; and (*b*) a musculoskeletal and neuromotor maturation that is strongly conditioned by experience or use. When these two factors are combined with the child's emerging auditory–motor awareness of vocalization, the stage is set for voluntary and intentional oral communication. Given this backdrop, it is argued that the acquisition of speech as a motor skill may be explained in part by a schema theory of motor learning (Schmidt, 1975).

161

DEVELOPMENT OF PERCEPTION
Volume 1

I. OBSTACLES TO SPEECH DEVELOPMENT IN THE NEONATE

To appreciate fully the obstacles that naturally lie in the path of speech development, one has to begin at least at the neonatal stage. Actually, our study could begin even earlier, with the prenatal organism, but for present purposes it suffices, and is complicated enough, to start with the neonate, or the child within the first 3 months of postnatal life.

The human organism of this age differs markedly from the adult who easily coordinates about 100 muscles to produce speech at rates of 10–15 phonemes per sec. A description of the neonate might be as follows:

1. *Split-brained,* for it lacks the commissure development needed for communication between hemispheres (Gazzaniga, 1970);

2. *Primarily subcortical,* for it lacks cortical cell myelination and dendritic branching (Conel, 1939, 1941,a,b, 1947);

3. *Essentially reflexive* in overall behavior (Capute, Accardo, Vining, Rubinstein, & Harriman, 1978; Dekaban, 1970; Fiorentino, 1972; Taft & Cohen, 1967; Wyke, 1975);

4. *Basically nonhuman mammalian in head anatomy* (Bosma, 1975; DuBrul, 1977); and

5. *Undergoing massive remodeling of its musculoskeletal anatomy and rapid development of the central nervous system (CNS)* (Bosma, 1975; Netsell, 1979; Woodruff, 1978).

Not only is the neonate anatomically ill-equipped to produce speech, but it would seem a major blunder of nature for the organism to learn skilled motor control of a mechanism that is being so drastically remodeled. In a sense, the neonate's immature CNS and predominantly reflexive behavior could save it the trouble of learning elaborate motor control strategies that would be quickly made obsolete by the severe remodeling of the musculoskeletal system. However, it is not implied that performance continuity is entirely impossible in the face of a changing anatomy. Bosma (1975) writes as follows on the relationship between oral function and a plastic anatomy.

> The gestures of prelinguistic sounds and of early speech are accomplished by structures at their current moment of development in histology, in form and dimension, and in spatial arrangement within this region. A month later, speech is accomplished by a different anatomy. And yet expressive speech and the basic functions of this region are performance in continuity.
>
> The developmental changes in these performances reflect maturation in their central representations. Thus, each item of performance is the net product of current central maturation, within the category of that performance, and

the current maturation of the motor effectors. These two components of motor performance are linked. As in the limbs, motor functions generate their performance anatomy by stimulating the growth and structural adaptation of the fascia, tendons, bones, and articulations upon which the muscles act. Growth and adaptation of the motor effector apparatus continues throughout development [p. 469].

If we take a moment to study how anatomic remodeling affects the speech apparatus, we find that the neonate's vocal tract differs from that of the adult in several important respects. As depicted in Fig. 6.1, the infant has a flat oral cavity that is nearly filled by the tongue, a relatively anterior tongue mass, a gradually sloping connection of the rather poorly differentiated oral and pharyngeal cavities, a short pharynx, and a larynx positioned high in the neck (Bosma, 1975; Fletcher, 1973; Goldstein, 1979). One of the most significant anatomic constraints on a neonate's vocal efforts is the engagement of larynx and nasopharynx (Sasaki, Levine, Laitman, & Crelin, 1977), which probably persists until the neonate acquires the distinctively human craniovertebral angle (DuBrul, 1977). Functionally, the larynx–nasopharynx

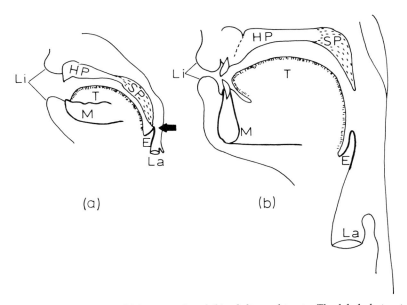

(a)   (b)

Fig. 6.1 Comparison of (a) neonatal and (b) adult vocal tracts. The labeled structures are Li, lips; HP, hard palate; SP, soft palate (or velum); T, tongue; M, mandible (or jaw); E, epiglottis; and La, larynx. Note in particular the neonate's epiglottic–velic contact (indicated by arrow) in contrast to the marked separation of these structures in the adult. The nasopharynx is the portion of the pharynx in the vicinity of the soft palate.

engagement forces the neonate to be an obligate nasal breather (Sasaki
et al., 1977), and, therefore, a nasal vocalizer (Oller, 1978). Only after
the larynx has descended into the neck, and the epiglottic–velic contact
has been broken, does the infant have the capability for two essential
properties of speech: (a) exclusively oral radiation of sound energy, as
required for almost all sounds except nasal consonants and vowels in
nasal contexts; and (b) the reliable impounding of intraoral air pressure
required for plosives and fricatives. Interestingly, the disengagement
of larynx and nasopharynx apparently occurs at about 4–6 months
postterm (Sasaki et al., 1977), at about the same time as the following
significant developments in the infant's life: the disappearance of many
reflexes (Capute et al., 1978), Dekaban, 1970; Fiorentino, 1972; Taft &
Cohen, 1967), marked changes in visual behavior (Bronson, 1974); functional connection of the hemispheres (Gazzaniga, 1970); fairly extensive
myelination and dendritic branching of cortical cells (Conel, 1939, 1941,
1947); appearance of a predominantly occipital rhythm of about 3–4 Hz
in the electroencephalogram (EEG) (Woodruff, 1978); and the onset of
nonnasalized or "true" babbling with alternating closures and openings
of the vocal tract (Oller, 1978). The list could be extended, but the point
is simply that when the infant has the vocal tract anatomy appropriate
for speech, he or she also has made other developmental strides that
make for timely support of the venture into the complex voluntary
motor behavior of speech. (For some cognitive prerequisites of intentional vocalization, see Harding & Golinkoff, 1979.)

Table 6.1 shows how phonetic development may be linked to anatomic and physiological changes in the child's speech mechanism. Major
stages of phonetic development listed in the middle column (from Oller,
1978) appear to be associated with the anatomic and physiological features listed in the right-hand column. Thus, many aspects of phonetic
development are timed by the appearance of the requisite anatomy and
physiology. Brief definitions of the terms used by Oller are as follows:

1. *Quasi-resonant nucleus:* vocalizations with normal phonation but
possessing no consonants and lacking the full vocalic resonance of
mature vowels; generally nasalized.

2. *Fully resonant nucleus:* vocalizations with normal phonation and
oral resonance; an example is a vowel-like sound that might be phonetically transcribed as [a].

3. *Raspberry:* vibrants or trills.

4. *Squeal* and *growl:* vocalizations with extreme pitch variations; the
maximal f_0 of squealed utterances is often higher than 500 Hz and the
f_0 of growled utterances often is lower than 150 Hz.

5. *Yelling:* vocalizations with systematic manipulations of amplitude.

Table 6.1
Parallels between Stages of Phonetic Development and Significant Anatomic–Physiological Changes of Speech Apparatus.[a]

Age of infant	Phonetic development	Anatomic–physiological correlate
0–1 month (phonation stage)	Quasi-resonant nucleus	Nasal breathing and nasalized vocalization because of engagement of larynx and nasopharynx. Tongue has mostly back-and-forth motions and nearly fills the oral cavity.
2–3 months (GOOing stage)	Quasi-resonant nucleus plus velar or uvular constrictions	Some change in shape of oral cavity and an increase in mobility of tongue; but tongue motion is still constrained by larynx–nasopharynx engagement.
4–6 months (expansion stage)	Fully resonant nuclei	Disengagement of larynx and nasopharynx allows increased separation of oral and nasal cavities, so that nonnasal vowels are readily produced.
	Raspberry (Labial)	The intraoral air pressure necessary for fricative-like productions can be developed with some regularity because of larynx–nasopharynx disengagement. Raspberry results from forcing air through lips, which close after each air burst because of natural restoring forces.
	Squeal and growl	Contrasts in vocal pitch are heightened perhaps because descent of larynx into neck makes the vocal folds more vulnerable to forces of supra-laryngeal muscles.
	Yelling	Better coordination of respiratory system and larynx, together with prolonged oral radiation of sound, permit loud voice.
	Marginal babble	Alternation of full opening and closure of vocal tract is enhanced by larynx–nasopharynx disengagement.

[a] From Kent, 1979; Oller, 1978.

6. *Marginal babble:* sequences of fully resonant vowels alternating with closures of the vocal tract; timing characteristics differ from mature speech in that transitions are slow and variable.

II. SENSORIMOTOR FACTORS

A. Genetic and Experiential Considerations

Even if it is correct that the development of speech as a motor skill is largely forestalled during the first 3 months of life, a similar statement probably cannot be made about the auditory perception of speech. Whether through the separate or combined actions of innate and learned processes, it is clear that the neonate has considerable capacity to make discriminations of speech or speechlike sounds (see Chapters 7 and 8). Because normal speech is an integrated sensorimotor performance, we need to keep in mind both the perceptual and productive capabilities of the child. Hemispheric differences in cortical responses to speech appear to exist within a few hours after birth (Molfese & Molfese, 1979), and it is clear that infants of less than 3 months can make several auditory discriminations pertinent to speech perception by adults (Kuhl, 1979). Perhaps the general mammalian auditory system is capable of basically the same discriminations as those reported for the infant (e.g., Kuhl & Miller, 1975), which may indicate the extent of hard wiring in the human auditory nervous system. Whatever the relative contributions of genetic and experiential factors might be in these early auditory discriminations, it is clear that the child can make reliable auditory discriminations of speech cues before she or he can reliably produce the same cues with the speech mechanism.

Some idea about the relative influence of genetic and experiential factors in speech development can be obtained through comparisons of the early behavior of normal infants and infants born blind, deaf, or both. It has been reported that children born deaf do enter a babbling period (Lenneberg, 1967; Mavilya, 1972) although they do not pass from this kind of vocal activity into imitation or child–parent exchanges.

Furthermore, there is evidence that some rudiments of expression do not depend on sensory experience. Eibl-Eibesfeldt (1974) reported that children born both blind and deaf laugh, smile, cry, frown, and stomp their feet in anger much as other children do. Moreover, children born blind cover their faces with their hands when embarrassed and blind infants stare in the direction of familiar voices. Although these behaviors are not necessarily communicative in intent or function, their appearance in the face of sensory deprivation may indicate a strong genetic component in some aspects of communicative behavior. Arguments for genetic preprogramming of vocal patterns for laughing and crying have been posed by Jürgens and Ploog (1981).

There is some evidence that a kind of sensory hegemony for communication may evolve in the normal infant in that auditory information outweighs visual information in a communicative setting. Volkmar, Hoder, and Siegel (1977) reported that when 12–14-month-old infants were presented with contradictory messages in the auditory and visual channels, the auditory channel was given dominance. Mayo and La France (1978) also noted that joking messages such as combinations of visual-positive and vocal-negative are not understood by young children because they do not integrate sensory channels. These authors concluded that "in keeping with Piaget's description of perceptual centration in the concrete operational stage of cognitive development, young children cannot focus on several dimensions of a situation [p. 217]." Thus, with the normally developing child, auditory information in a communicative setting may come to have a preferential shaping role. This role perhaps is reflected in such behaviors as conversational turn taking. A kind of turn-taking pattern, one of alternating voice style, has been observed between mothers and young infants (Bateson, 1975; Stern, Faffe, Beebe, & Bennett, 1975). In addition, slow motion film analyses (Condon & Sander, 1974) showed that infants made fine coordinated changes in movement with changes in a speaker's speech pattern. Mayo and La France pointed to an implication of this sensitivity to speech patterns: "It may be through such constant exposure to a particular speech stream that an infant becomes habituated to the speech rhythms in his or her native language [p. 223]." The auditory awareness of the infant is further illustrated by the report of a 6-week-old infant who was exposed more to bird calls than to human speech and subsequently "began to make high-pitched shrieks similar to the bird calls [Sweeney, 1973, p. 490]."

B. The Acoustic and Articulatory Variance of Speech

To learn speech, the child must relate the auditory representation of his or her vocalization to the underlying motor patterns. The child also has to establish equivalence classes between his or her acoustic patterns and those of the adult models. Equivalence classes have to be formed because the child's short vocal tract cannot produce exact acoustic replicas of adult speech sounds. This problem is illustrated for vowels in Fig. 6.2, which shows the first and second vocal-tract resonances (formants) for vowels produced by men, women, 6-year-old children, and 4-year-old children. The second-formant frequency (F_2) can be over 1000 Hz higher for a young child than for an adult male. Thus, unlike the mynah bird, which apparently produces speech that is spectrally similar to the modeled speech (Klatt & Stefanski, 1974), the child learns speech in the face of a considerable acoustic disparity between his or her speech and that of the adult models. The speech of a young child differs from that of an adult in both spectral and temporal structure (Eguchi & Hirsh, 1969; Pentz, Gilbert, & Zawadzki, 1979).

A spectrographic comparison of speech produced by adult and child (aged 3:9) is given in Fig. 6.3. The utterance, transcribed phonetically,

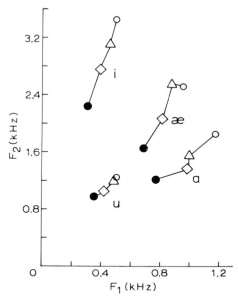

Fig. 6.2 Frequencies of the first formant (F_1) and second formant (F_2) for the vowels /i/ (h*ea*t), /æ/ (h*a*t), /a/ (h*o*t), and /u/ (h*oo*t) produced by men (●), by women (◇), and by children aged 4 years (○), and by children aged 6 years (△). The data points represent means for 5 men, 5 women, and 10 children in each of the two younger age groups. The graph shows that the same vowel is produced with a different formant structure by speakers of different sex and ages.

at the bottom of the figure, is "took a spoon." The numbers identify the major acoustic–phonetic segments bounded by the vertical lines. Although young children typically have longer utterance durations than do adults (Kent & Forner, 1980), the lengthening does not apply uniformly to all acoustic segments. For example, the spectrograms in Fig. 6.3 show that the child actually has a shorter voice onset time (VOT) (the sum of segments 1 and 2) than the adult, although many other segments are longer in the child's utterance (for instance, segments 3, 4, 6, and 8). The spectrograms also reveal the higher frequencies of the child's vocal-tract resonances. For example, whereas the adult's first- and second-formant (F_1 and F_2) frequencies for Segment 6 (the *schwa* vowel) are about 500 and 1500 Hz, respectively, the corresponding values for the child are about 750 and 2200 Hz. Similarly, the child's /s/ frication (Segment 7) has higher-frequency energy than the adult's /s/. The comparison makes it clear that a child's speech is not a spectral or temporal replica of adults' speech. Certain relational patterns may

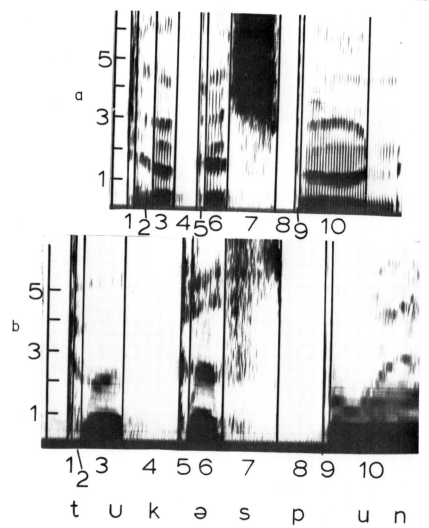

Fig. 6.3 (a) Spectrogram of an adult's and (b) a child's production of the phrase *took a spoon*, transcribed phonetically at the bottom of the figure. Frequency in kHz is scaled on the ordinate. The numbered segments are: (1) release burst for /t/, (2) aspiration noise for /t/, (3) vocalic nucleus of the word *took*, (4) stop gap for /k/, (5) release burst and aspiration for /k/, (6) *schwa* vowel, (7) frication for /s/, (8) stop gap for /p/, (9) voice onset time (including release burst) for /p/, and (10) vocalic nucleus for /u/ in *spoon*. The acoustic pattern for the child is longer in duration than that of the adult, and individual spectral features have higher frequencies in the child's production.

be the same, but little definitive work has been done to reveal what these patterns are, or the age at which they are established.

Acoustic segmentation of the word *box*, recited four times in sentence context by 10 adults and 10 4-year-old children is shown in Fig. 6.4. The segments shown are voice onset time for /b/, duration of the vocalic nucleus (including transitions into and out of the vowel), duration of closure (stop gap) for /k/, and the duration of the combined noise energy for /k/ release and /s/ frication. The patterns for the children show a general lengthening relative to the patterns for the adults. In addition, the children are more variable, both within and across subjects. Some insight into the articulatory patterns associated with segment lengthening can be gained by a closer look at the spectrograms. For example, Fig. 6.5 shows that, whereas adults exhibit anticipatory coarticulation in the form of a continuously rising F_2 during the vowel segment in *box*, this coarticulation often was not evident in the children's productions. Apparently, the adults tended to produce the vowel, not as a genuine steady state, but as a gradually changing articulation that was directed toward (or coproduced with) the following velar stop /k/. However, the children produced a vowel segment with a well-defined

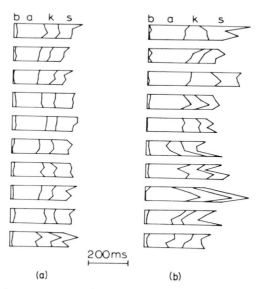

(a)   (b)

Fig. 6.4 Acoustic segmentation of the word *box*, produced four times each by (a) 10 adults and (b) 10 4-year-old children. The four segments within the word are (1) voice onset time for /b/; (2) vocalic nucleus for the vowel; (3) stop gap for /k/; and (4) release burst for /k/ plus frication for /s/. The acoustic segments for a given talker are graphically enclosed to highlight their appearance. Note the generally longer duration of the word for the children. The word was extracted from the sentence *The box is blue and red*.

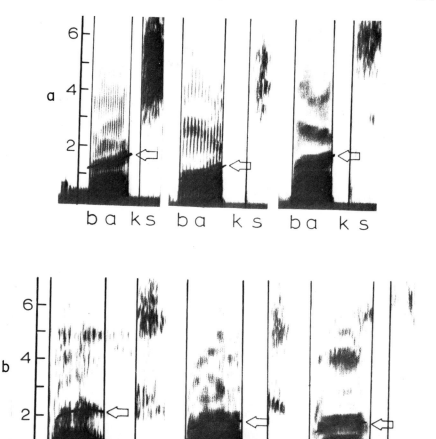

Fig. 6.5 Wide-band spectrograms of the word *box* for (a) three young adults and (b) three 4-year-old children. Frequency in kHz is scaled on the ordinate. Note the almost continuously rising second formant (arrow) in the adults' productions in contrast to the flat, or steady-state second formant in the children's productions.

steady-state characteristic. This comparison of adults' and children's productions shows that, even after children have acquired *phonemically* correct articulation, the motor patterns continue to change to permit a more rapid and more highly coarticulated sequence of gestures. Thus, the motor learning of speech, at least beyond the one-word stage, might be considered in two phases: (*a*) an early phase in which the major segments are phonemically correct but not tightly coarticulated; and

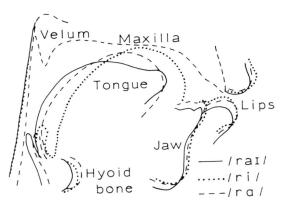

Fig. 6.6 Articulatory positions for consonant /r/ in three phonetic contexts. The composite of the vocal-tract shapes shows that a given phoneme can be associated with a variety of articulatory patterns and hence a number of underlying motor control specifications.

(b) a later phase in which rate is increased and contextual variation in articulatory pattern is maximized without sacrificing intelligibility. After a certain articulatory phonemic proficiency is mastered, the child learns the permissible ranges of articulation that are associated with rapid coarticulated speech.

Another aspect of the problem of acoustic–phonetic equivalence is that a given phonetic feature often can be accomplished with a variety of articulatory configurations (Kent, 1976a). A simple example is shown in Fig. 6.6, which illustrates the vocal tract shapes for three prevocalic r-sounds uttered by the same speaker. Notice the variety of positions of the tongue, lips, and jaw for segments all possessing the quality of r-coloring. Little wonder that the r-sound is one of the last to be mastered in speech development. To master this sound, the child has to recognize its distinguishing acoustic features, such as F_2–F_3 convergence, and to learn the associated vocal-tract shapes, often adjusted to phonetic context.

III. SCHEMA THEORY APPLIED TO SPEECH DEVELOPMENT

A. General Properties of Motor Skill Acquisition of Speech

The picture that emerges from these musculoskeletal, neural, and sensory–perceptual considerations is that the infant of about 6 months has (a) adequately remodeled the vocal-tract anatomy for speech production; (b) acquired many of the cortical and subcortical neural connections required for motor skill acquisition; and (c) developed an acute auditory awareness of his or her own vocalizations as well as the speech patterns of adult models. The task that lies ahead is to learn the appropriate categories of speech perception and speech production. To some degree, the learning of motor patterns for speech may be guided by inherent nonlinearities in the conversion of articulation (vocal-tract shaping) to the acoustic speech signal. (See, for example, the quantal theory described by Stevens, 1972, and the discussion in Kent, 1979.) But even if there is a predisposition for certain articulations, the child still has a complex motor skill to learn.

In discussing the motor development of speech, it is useful to observe several distinctions made by Connolly (1979) with regard to motor skill development. Applying his basic terminology to the problem of speech development, we have the following distinctions. The *motor skill* of speech is the organization of certain articulatory movements into a purposeful plan that is executed with economy. A skill is developed by constructing a program of action directed toward attainment of a goal. An *action* is a higher-level description from which a skill is developed and executed. *Thus, a skill is an organization of movements in space and time in the context of a program of action.*

Bruner (1973) viewed the development of a motor skill as the construction of serially ordered acts, the performance of which is modified to achieve diminishing variability, increased anticipation, and improved economy. These same goals may be applied to the development of speech, which is characterized by a diminishing variability of segment durations and spectra (DiSimoni, 1974a,b,c; Eguchi & Hirsh, 1969; Kent, 1976b; Kent & Forner, 1980; Tingley & Allen, 1975), a general reduction of segment durations (Kent & Forner, 1980; Smith, 1978; Subtelny, Worth, & Sakuda, 1977), and increased anticipatory coarticulation (Thompson & Hixon, 1979). Children, compared with adults, give more time to individual speech segments and they have a relatively large error in controlling segment duration in repeated performances. In addition, children appear to anticipate less than adults, so that anticipatory assimilation, such as nasalization and palatalization, may have smaller temporal ranges for children.

B. Motor Schema Theory

Because one major part of the acquisition of speech is the learning of the requisite motor skill, it may be helpful to consider speech in the light of theories of motor skill learning. One such theory that recently has been given a good deal of attention is Schmidt's (1975) *schema theory.* In proposing this theory, Schmidt attempted to describe how a motor skill is learned, and to resolve three major problems in motor control: (a) the problem of how a person can recognize errors and correct for them in subsequent responses; (b) the storage problem that results from the assumption that a vast number of motor programs are required to control complex motor behavior; and (c) the so-called novelty problem that arises from the recognition that no two apparently identical movements are really the same. These same problems have received considerable discussion in the literature on speech production, although the first rarely has been couched in terms of motor skill acquisition. The storage problem as it applies to speech has been widely discussed (e.g., Kent, 1976a; MacNeilage, 1970; MacNeilage & MacNeilage, 1973; Wickelgren, 1969). MacNeilage and MacNeilage (1973) estimated that the production of English speech with appropriate intonation and accent would require something on the order of 100,000 sound units. Perhaps the brain is capable of handling this number of control units in speech production, but a search persists for a more elegant solution to the control problem. The novelty problem has been a central issue in many discussions about speech, and many attempts to demonstrate invariances in the motor control of speech have failed (MacNeilage, 1970).

Schema theory recognizes four types of information to accomplish skilled movements:

1. Initial conditions for the movement, for example, for speech, the instantaneous positions of the articulators.

2. Response specifications for a motor program, for example, the basic motor plan for a phonetic sequence.

3. Sensory consequences, for example, the kinesthetic feedback produced by the motor response.

4. Response outcome, for example, the actual outcome (knowledge of results or KR) of the articulatory program.

Schema theory operates with two types of memory. Recall memory is essential to the generation of motor commands, and recognition memory serves for the evaluation of response-produced feedback to derive error information. Schmidt also assumes that the CNS constructs generalized motor programs that "contain stored muscle commands with all of the details necessary to carry out a movement [p. 46]." A recall schema is an experience-based relationship among past actual outcomes. Each time a person executes a movement pertinent to a particular motor skill, the relationship among these variables is refined until eventually the schema is well established. Once the schema is established, response specifications for a novel movement are generated with the desired outcome and the initial conditions as the only input.

A recognition schema is an experience-based relationship among initial conditions, sensory consequences, and actual outcomes. This schema allows a person to predict the sensory consequences of a movement, and then, by comparing the expected and actual sensory consequences, to detect errors even when KR is not available.

Although experimental tests of schema theory have not been wholly supportive, some of its predictions have been satisfied in experiments on arm and hand movements. The variability of practice hypothesis states that (a) variable practice will lead to better performance on transfer to a novel task; and that (b) variable practice will promote rapid improvement in performance of the novel task. Moxley (1979) concluded from experiments with 6–8-year-old children that the first part of the hypothesis was supported, but the second was not. Because schema theory takes the generation of response specifications during learning to be essential to the development of recall memory, another prediction of the theory is that active practice is necessary for motor skill learning. In a test of this prediction, Wallace and McGhee (1979) concluded that, although active practice generally is required to develop recall memory (in agreement with schema theory) there was evidence that *passive* experience with sensory feedback also helps to develop recall memory.

Gerson and Thomas (1977) combined schema theory and neo-Piagetian theory (Pascual-Leone, 1970) to account for the performance of 5- and 6-year-old children in a curvilinear repositioning task designed to test motor recall of a novel response. The neo-Piagetian theory combines Piaget's (1952) stages of child development with a quantitative parameter that explains how children move to progressively higher stages. The quantitative parameter is assigned to a central computing space (mental space or M-space) that integrates or transforms the information from a child's behavioral repertoire to meet environmental demands. Gerson and Thomas's data supported schema theory's prediction of symmetry of motor memory across varying spatial locations. Neo-Piagetian theory also was supported in its prediction that high M-processors would perform better than low M-processors. Gerson and Thomas pointed out several similarities between the constructs of schema theory and neo-Piagetian theory and concluded that neo-Piagetian theory "seems to need the addition of at least some aspects of schema theory to adequately explain psychomotor performance [p. 133]."

C. Motor Schema for Speech

Figure 6.7 is a representation of schema theory applied to speech production. The desired outcome, a phonetic target, is one input and the initial conditions, the current state of the vocal tract, is the other.

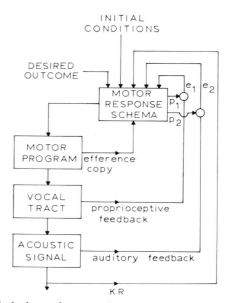

Fig. 6.7 A model of schema theory applied to speech production. The motor response schema generates a motor program (response specifications) given the desired outcome, initial conditions, and past experience with response specifications and actual outcomes. The desired outcome is any particular phonetic goal or state, and the initial conditions describe the instantaneous positions of the articulators. Efference copy, generated by the evolving movement, informs the motor response schema that the movement is underway. Proprioceptive feedback and auditory feedback from the motor response are compared with predicted proprioceptive feedback (p_1) and predicted auditory feedback (p_2) to obtain the error signals e_1 and e_2. The error signals are used to revise the motor schema as needed for future movements. Knowledge of results (KR) can be any external evaluation of articulatory performance, such as a parent's reaction.

These two inputs are essential to response recognition. The child learning speech determines from past outcomes and response specifications the set of specifications for any particular desired outcome and set of initial conditions. A motor program, possibly novel, is then executed. The child also generates the expected sensory consequences, for example, the predicted auditory feedback (p_2) and the expected proprioceptive feedback (p_1). The expected feedback is compared with actual feedback to derive error information, e_1 and e_2. The desired outcome can be an auditory pattern, as in imitating an adult model, or an internal phonetic goal, as in spontaneous vocalization.

Depending on the stage of acquisition and the articulatory requirements of a particular phonetic target, the emerging motor schema must deal with at least three major types of feedback (and hence three major types of feedback prediction in the recognition schema): tactile, kinesthetic, and auditory. In the early stages of speech acquisition, probably all three types of feedback are closely monitored. But as skill develops (i.e., the motor schemata are well established), the child may lessen dependence on the slow-loop auditory channel and rely to a greater degree on tactile and kinesthetic feedback. This changing emphasis on feedback modality may explain why the so-called "functional" articulation errors, like *w* for *r* and voiceless *th* for *s*, often are resistant to change when an attempt is made to draw the child's attention to the auditory distinction between the error production and the correct production. Locke and Kutz (1975) reported that children who substitute *w* for *r* can distinguish these sounds as said by an adult but hear their own tape-recorded *w–r* productions as *w*. Once the motor skill of speech is developed, continuous auditory processing probably is not necessary. However, long-term deprivation of auditory feedback, as in the case of acquired hearing impairment, frequently leads to a deterioration of articulation. Apparently, some degree of auditory monitoring is needed to maintain speech articulation (Zimmerman & Rettaliata, 1981).

In studying speech production in novel conditions, we have been impressed by the "one-trial" learning ability of adult speakers. For example, in experiments on the imitation of computer-generated non-English vowels (Kent, 1973, 1974), subjects frequently remarked that, after their first attempt at imitation, they felt that they knew immediately how to imitate the target more successfully. Similarly, when a subject is asked to produce a test utterance after the jaw has been restrained at various degrees of opening, the first attempt sometimes is characterized by tentative, searching movements of the articulators, but the second-trial production has a much more fluent execution (Netsell, Kent, & Abbs, 1978). In these tasks of producing a novel target (imitation) or producing a known target under novel conditions (jaw restraint), the subject apparently can correct for production errors given adequate feedback from one trial. In terms of schema theory, one trial is needed to obtain error information by comparison of the predicted and actual sensory consequences.

In a motor schema view of speech development, the child learns recall schemata to generate the response specifications for articulations and learns recognition schemata to derive error information from the comparison of predicted and actual sensory consequences of an articulation. The child acquires speech without a great deal of deliberate "speech instruction" from parents because he or she learns to recognize errors and to correct them in subsequent productions. Also within this view, early misarticulations vary with phonetic context (Curtis & Hardy, 1959; Gallagher & Shriner, 1975a,b) because the schemata for some pairings of initial conditions and desired outcomes are better developed than others. Indeed, a major aspect of speech development as a motor (articulation) skill is the ability to generate response specifications adapted to a particular set of initial conditions and a particular desired outcome. The stress given here to motor skill interpretations of speech development is not intended to exclude linguistic considerations (House, 1981) but to complement them. Naturally, a full account of the processes of speech development must address a variety of issues. The present emphasis on sensorimotor factors is an attempt to correct for an apparent neglect of these factors in many considerations of speech development.

Babbling, at least in its early appearances, does not strictly qualify as a motor skill for phonetic purposes because it does not itself produce the recall and recognition schemata needed for speech. In this view, it is not surprising that the ostensible "phonetic" development during babbling is somewhat discontinuous with the subsequent mastery of sounds in early words. Of course, some parallels may obtain because of differential sensorimotor maturation of the relevant musculature. For example, the lips have a relatively early neuromotor maturation. However, the repetitive movements in reduplicated babbling (/da da da/) are not the stuff of which context-sensitive allophones are made. The child has mastered a phoneme only when he or she can produce the desired acoustic–phonetic consequence in many different phonetic contexts and with a potentially large number of speech-muscle contraction patterns. To the extent that speech is controlled by abstract discrete units, such as phonemes, the process of speech articulation is one of continual change in initial conditions and desired outcomes (articulatory targets). But even though babbling, by this argument, is not a motor skill that is entirely predictive of later phonetic acquisition, it certainly has a sensorimotor relevance to, and some continuity with, later speech learning. Babbling gives the infant experience in moving the articulators and in hearing the consequences of these movements (Kent, 1979). In addition, early vocalization experience contributes to the respiratory and laryngeal support required for speech (Crystal, 1973; Wilder & Baken, 1978), and may share with developing speech some articulatory preferences (Oller, Wieman, Doyle, & Ross, 1976).

The idea that the motor control of speech articulation is based on schemata that are gradually acquired through articulatory practice in a variety of phonetic environments is compatible with recent research on phonological development in children at the one-word stage. Leon-ard, Newhoff, and Mesalem (1980) observed highly individual inter-actions between phonological patterns and lexical acquisition in children aged 1:4 to 1:10. They summarized their results as follows:

> Initially, children learn words, and *more incidentally, corresponding articulations.* Thus, the early oppositions in children's speech will be in terms of words, not sounds. Such words will not be strictly phonemically principled and vari-ability may be seen in a child's production of the same word. Certain per-ceptual or production constraints may operate on children's selection and use of these early words. In addition, *because of the primacy of lexical learning, associated articulations may be learned more incidentally and may be poorly remembered* [p. 28, emphasis added].

The Labovs' analysis of their daughter's first words *cat* and *mama* (Labov & Labov, 1978) also shows that early vocalizations do not con-stitute a phonemic motoric mastery that is obviously carried into later acquisition of phonology. Their account is not one of gradual and per-sistent phonetic growth but one of phonetic growth *and decay:* "We can observe a steady increment in the complexity of the system throughout this first half of the *cat* and *mama* period. But the rise was followed by an even more dramatic decline. At many points in this account of the phonetics of *cat* and *mama,* we have seen words appear and disappear, phonetic elements integrated into words and then abandoned, phon-ological contrasts constructed and then neglected [p. 843]." They con-cluded that "the grammar of *cat* and *mama* is not a list of words or phonemes . . . [but] a set of operating principles of linguistic analysis and linguistic structure [p. 850]."

A child's first words, then, may be motoric units; they may not have phonetic components that are easily transferred to other phonetic con-texts. Motor control that is adapted to the production of phonetic seg-ments in a variety of phonetic contexts in different words perhaps comes about as the child discards the principle of preparing word-sized motor sequences for each word in his or her lexicon. That is, the child is forced to a segmental (phonetic) motor organization through sheer force of economy and manageability.

The schema is a means by which an abstract linguistic unit such as the phoneme can make contact with the physical events of articulatory control. Just as the phoneme is a useful abstraction in phonology, so is the schema a useful abstraction in describing speech motor control. Articulatory definition of the phoneme is constantly frustrated by the variance of its articulatory correlates (MacNeilage, 1970). But it is pre-cisely this variance that a motor schema is suited to explain. The

schema, receiving as input the desired outcome specified by a performance phonology (i.e., a behaviorally constrained phonology), examines the initial or current conditions of the articulatory apparatus, and
determines from past experience the appropriate response specifications. Specifications associated with a given speech unit (either a phoneme or an allophone specified by the phonology) will vary from production to production because of (a) changes in the desired outcomes
dictated by the performance phonology; (b) differences in the initial
(current) conditions; and (c) errors or inaccuracies in the generation of
response specifications that may be novel to the child as new words
are attempted.

This proposal of speech motor learning (presented here only in outline form) makes certain predictions which should be amenable to empirical tests. First, the model predicts that coarticulation, or overlapping
patterns of articulation for a phonetic sequence, will increase both temporally and spatially (i.e., involving more articulators at one time) with
age and speech experience. A second prediction of the model is that
coarticulation is not limited to segments with relatively independent
muscle activations. In contrast, "coproduction" theories (Fowler, 1980;
Fowler, Rubin, Remez, & Turvey, 1980; Ohman, 1966, 1967; Perkell,
1969) propose that coarticulation occurs primarily between segments
that make noncompeting demands on the musculature of the speech
apparatus. The model envisaged here should account for coarticulation
between segments that are motorically noncompeting and also for coarticulation between segments that make similar or competing demands
on the speech motor system. The need to account for both types of
coarticulation is discussed by Kent and Minifie (1977) and Kent (1980).
A third prediction, akin to the variability-of-practice hypothesis discussed earlier, is that schemata for articulation are acquired through
speech motor practice in the production of sounds in different contexts.
Thus, it is expected that the motor skill for production of a given speech
sound is not well developed until that sound has been articulated in
a range of phonetic environments that essentially matches the contextual demands of the speaker's language. A fourth prediction is that
speech motor control will be susceptible to various short-term and long-
term disruptions in afference. That is, assuming that speech motor
control is acquired and maintained partly through "recognition schemata," disruptions in feedback (especially of long-term, but sometimes
of short-term as well) will have deleterious effects on motor learning
for speech *and* the preservation of acquired articulatory patterns. In
contrast, a proposal that speech articulation is based on the organization
of reflexive motor responses does not immediately predict strong re-

liance on different forms of feedback—position, movement, and audition. A corollary prediction of the model proposed here is that, as recognition schemata deteriorate, a speaker's ability for error correction will suffer.

IV. MOTOR PROGRAMS FOR SPEECH: THEIR NATURE AND CONTENT

As Semjen (1977) noted in his review of sensorimotor learning processes, evidence for motor programs derives primarily from three research areas: deafferentation studies showing that relatively complex motor sequences can be performed even after the interruption of presumably relevant feedback; movement initiation studies showing that reaction time in motor activation is influenced by factors apparently related to motor programming requirements; and movement time studies showing that the time for the execution of many movements is shorter than the loop delay of pertinent feedback. Semjen recognized that motor programs and rapidly acting regulatory loops (like alpha–gamma linkage) are not contradictory, in that motor programs may involve the *"preparatory presetting of the amplification and timing characteristics of the automatic regulatory loops* [p. 186, emphasis in the original]."

Two important characteristics of the sensorimotor bases of speech movements are that (*a*) these movements have a high degree of freedom in serial timing (Lashley, 1951; Semjen, 1977); and (*b*) articulatory movements are based on an internalized representation of a desired action or state (Kent, 1976a). Thus, speech production is the execution of highly flexible movement sequences reflecting internalized (phonetic) goals or states. A motor schema might be particularly advantageous to this kind of motor skill for the reasons discussed by Semjen (1977):

Another possibility, already evoked by Glencross (1975) and Schmidt (1975), is to consider that learned motor sequences are jointly controlled by a motor program and by an internal reference representing the sensory consequences of an action reaching a desired environmental goal. The former would ensure the initiation and the execution of the motor sequences and would operate in either an open-loop fashion or with the assistance of regulatory proprioceptive feedback loops. The latter would control whether the ongoing action meets its environmental goal, by evaluating the sensory consequences of the motor sequence. As long as the error signal generated in this system remained below a critical value, the motor sequence would continue as determined by the program. Beyond this critical value, the error signal would stop the ongoing action and/or call for a new program, which would be better able to fulfill the desired environmental goal [pp. 190–191].

In this conception, the suitability of motor programs for speech (or other motor behavior) is determined by *reference schemata,* which represent "the best possible estimate of the sensory consequences associated with the action likely to attain this goal [Semjen, 1977, p. 190]." For speech, reference schemata would be developed for both auditory feedback (long-loop delay) and proprioceptive feedback (various loops of short-to-moderate delay).

In very early speech development, when the child has a small number of single words, the child works with relatively simple motor programs that can be regarded as movement sequences identified with individual words, and not necessarily based on anything like phonemes or phonetic segments. That is, the program structure is (in phonetic terms) almost unitary at the word level. As the child's lexicon grows, movement sequences begin to be associated with segments (vowels and consonants) that can be inserted with considerable articulatory flexibility in different words. For example, Labov and Labov (1978) summarize the phonetic development of their child during the one-word stage in this way: "In the course of these five months, J seemed to have acquired a competence in phonological contrast, canonical forms, and consonantal articulation; and she had fully outlined the shape of the vowel space she would use later on. Furthermore, she had explored the iconic value of vowels and consonants, and gradually moved away from those values toward more arbitrary representations more typical of adult use [p. 850]." As the lexicon increases and the child acquires syntactic and semantic competence, the organization of speech motor behavior is accordingly more complicated, involving the "integration of syntactic form and semantic content with segmental and suprasegmental specifications at an underlying level of organization and planning [Branigan, 1979, p. 419]."

Eventually, the motor program must be structured to deal with at least the following (from Branigan, 1979): (*a*) a set of articulatory targets (or goals) corresponding to the intended phonemic sequence; (*b*) assignment of stress to the syllables contained within the sequence; (*c*) syllable-duration sensitivities to stress, segmental composition and position in utterance; (*d*) junctural features including transitions between elements and terminal juncture at the end of the planned unit; and (*e*) internal ordering of words as it reflects syntactic form to express semantic intentions. See Fig. 6.8 and its caption for an illustration of these effects. The sensitivity and complexity of motor programs for speech is indicated by the large number of factors that influence the duration of individual phonetic elements (Klatt, 1976). Obviously, motor programs are structured to contain a large amount of information, in-

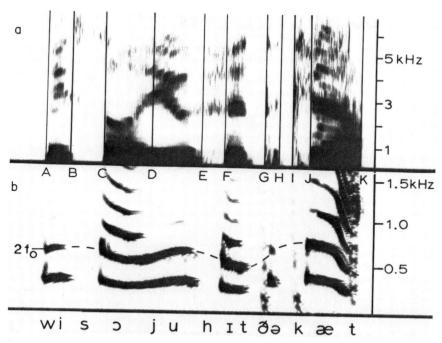

Fig. 6.8 (a) Wide-band and (b) narrow-band spectrograms of a 4-year-old's production of the sentence *We saw you hit the cat.* Major time points marked on the wide-band pattern are: (A) onset of phonation for *we;* (B) onset of /s/ frication; (C) end of /s/ frication and beginning of voicing for vowel in *saw;* (D) approximate onset of articulation of /j/ in *you;* (E) onset of /h/ frication for *hit;* (F) beginning of voicing for vowel in *hit;* (G) release of initial consonant in *the;* (H) end of vowel in *the;* (I) release burst of /k/ in *cat;* (J) onset of voicing for vowel in *cat;* and (K) end of voicing for vowel in *cat:* The wide-band pattern shows the rapid, essentially continuous, changes in articulation and also makes evident the large differences in segment duration. For example, compare the vowel durations in the words *hit the cat.* The narrow-band pattern shows the f_0 contour through resolution of the laryngeal harmonics. For example, the highlighted second harmonic ($2f_0$) shows how f_0 changes over time and how it falls markedly during *cat* to signal terminal juncture. The spectrogram gives some idea about the complexity of motor programs required for speech.

cluding some information that usually is considered to belong to high-level language processing.

A motor program that really has the capability of controlling long motor sequences without peripheral feedback must determine:

a) the identity of the effector units (muscles or groups of muscles to be activated, b) the specific function of the selected units (agonistic-antagonistic; phasic-tonic), c) the intensity and duration of their activation, and d) the

temporal order and the specific temporal structure which control the timing
of the selected units [Semjen, 1977, p. 184].

The temporal or serial-timing requirement is particularly interesting in
speech development. As Glencross (1975) has observed, this requirement has two aspects: sequencing (or the temporal order of the units)
and phasing (the details of temporal structure aside from seriation of
units). It is perhaps in phasing that the adult and child speakers represented in Fig. 6.5 differ. The children have accomplished sequencing
(ordering of the phonetic segments) but not phasing (the details of
temporal control, including many phenomena collectively known as
coarticulation). It seems logical that sequencing is an earlier objective
in motor skill learning than is phasing.

Possibly much of a child's progress in reaching adult rates of speech
production depends on mastery of phasing. It has been known for
some time that speech rate is strongly affected by age. McNeil (1974)
reported speech rates of slightly over 3 words per sec for adults, 2.5
words per sec for 4–5-year-old children, 1.6 words per sec for 2-year-
olds. These differences in rate are reflected in duration of individual
segments (Kent & Forner, 1980). Bonvillian, Raeburn, and Horan (1979)
determined that children more successfully imitated sentences spoken
at a rate nearer to their own than sentences produced at faster or slower
rates. Perhaps optimal productive and perceptual performances for
speech share the same event rate, in which case, motor programs would
have a distinct perceptual relevance. Once the child has attained reasonable mastery of segmental production, the motor programs are gradually refined until the rate of utterance approaches the adult rate (see
again the comparison of utterance for child and adult in Fig. 6.3, which
shows differences in temporal structure).

V. SUMMARY

The path to speech development begins in the neonatal period with
a substantial remodeling of the vocal tract and an apparent capability
to make speech-sound discriminations relevant to adult speech perception. The performance anatomy (i.e., anatomy shaped by experience
and use) of the vocal tract is an important consideration in determining
when the infant has sufficient musculoskeletal stability to learn skilled
motor control of the speech organs. Although the vocal-tract anatomy
continues to change even into puberty, the essential structure needed
to make oral (nonnasal) sounds is established by about 4–6 months,

at which age true babbling begins. Babbling provides the child with auditory and motor experience of the sound-producing mechanism but it does not yield the recall and recognition schemata needed for speech motor skill per se.

These schemata are gradually acquired as the child learns to achieve a particular desired outcome (phonetic goal) in the face of different initial conditions (different phonetic contexts). As the motor schema develops, the child learns to recognize his or her own errors and to alter motor programs accordingly. Motor schema theory may explain imitation (observational) learning and the child's ability to produce novel sounds and to use "directed trials and errors" in learning the motor skill of speech. Finally, as Semjen (1977) observed, motor schema theory allows us to consider motor-skill learning and sensorimotor co-ordination learning in a common theoretical framework.

ACKNOWLEDGMENT

Ronald Netsell and Charles Watson made many helpful comments on a draft of this chapter.

REFERENCES

Bateson, M. C. Mother–infant exchanges: the epigenesis of conversational interactions. *Annals of the New York Academy of Sciences,* 1975, **47,** 1079–1088.

Bonvillian, J. D., Raeburn, V. P., & Horan, E. A. Talking to children: the effects of rate, intonation, and length on children's sentence imitation. *Journal of Child Language,* 1979, **6,** 459–467.

Bosma, J. F. Anatomic and physiologic development of the speech apparatus. In D. B. Tower (Ed.), *The nervous system* (Vol. 3): *Human communication and its disorders.* New York: Raven, 1975.

Branigan, G. Some reasons why successive single word utterances are not. *Journal of Child Language,* 1979, **6,** 411–421.

Bronson, G. The postnatal growth of visual capacity. *Child Development,* 1974, **45,** 873–890.

Bruner, J. S. Organization of early skilled action. *Child Development,* 1973, **44,** 1–11.

Capute, A. J., Accardo, P. J., Vining, E. P. G., Rubenstein, J. E., & Harryman, S. *Primitive reflex profile. Monographs in developmental pediatrics* (Vol. 1). Baltimore, Md.: University Park Press, 1978.

Condon, W. S., & Sander, L. W. Synchrony demonstrated between movements of the neonate and adult speech. *Child Development,* 1974, **45,** 456–462.

Conel, J. L. *The postnatal development of the human cerebral cortex* (Vol. 1): *The cortex of the new born.* Cambridge, Mass.: Harvard University Press, 1939.

Conel, J. L. *The postnatal development of the human cerebral cortex* (Vol. 2): *The cortex of the one month infant.* Cambridge, Mass.: Harvard University Press, 1941.

Conel, J. L. *The postnatal development of the human cerebral cortex* (Vol. 3): *The Cortex of the three month infant.* Cambridge, Mass.: Harvard University Press, 1947.

Connolly, K. The nature of motor skill development. *Journal of Human Movement Studies,* 1977, **3,** 128–143.

Curtis, J. F., & Hardy, J. C. A phonetic study of /r/. *Journal of Speech and Hearing Research,* 1959, **2,** 244–257.

Crystal, D. Non-segmental phonology in language acquisition: a review of the issues. *Lingua,* 1973, **32,** 1–45.

Dekaban, A. *Neurology of early childhood.* Baltimore: Williams & Wilkins, 1970.

DiSimoni, F. G. Influence of vowel environment on the duration of consonants in the speech of three-, six-, and nine-year-old children. *Journal of the Acoustical Society of America,* 1974, **55,** 360–361. (a)

DiSimoni, F. G. Influence of consonant environment on duration of vowels in the speech of three-, six-, and nine-year-old children. *Journal of the Acoustical Society of America,* 1974, **55,** 362–363. (b)

DiSimoni, F. G. Influence of utterance length upon bilabial closure for /p/ in three-, six-, and nine-year-old children. *Journal of the Acoustical Society of America,* 1974, **55,** 1353–1354. (c)

DuBrul, E. L. Origin of the speech apparatus and its reconstruction in fossils. *Brain & Language,* 1977, **4,** 365–381.

Eguchi, S., & Hirsh, I. J. Development of speech sounds in children. *Acta Otolaryngologica,* 1969, Supplement **257.**

Eibl-Eibesfeldt, I. *Love and hate: The natural history of behavior patterns.* New York: Shocken, 1974.

Fiorentino, M. R. *Normal and abnormal development: The influence of primary reflexes on motor development.* Springfield, Ill.: Charles C Thomas, 1972.

Fletcher, S. G. Maturation of the speech mechanism. *Folia Phoniatrica,* 1973, **25,** 161–172.

Fowler, C. A. Coarticulation and theories of extrinsic timing. *Journal of Phonetics,* 1980, **8,** 113–133.

Fowler, C. A., Rubin, P., Remez, R., & Turvey, M. T. Implications for speech of a general theory of action. In B. Butterworth (Ed.), *Speech production.* New York: Academic Press, 1980.

Gallagher, T. M., & Shriner, T. H. Articulatory inconsistencies in the speech of normal children. *Journal of Speech and Hearing Research,* 1975, **18,** 168–175. (a)

Gallagher, T. M., & Shriner, T. H. Contextual variables related to inconsistent /s/ and /z/ production in the spontaneous speech of children. *Journal of Speech and Hearing Research,* 1975, **18,** 623–633. (b)

Gazzaniga, M. S. *The Bisected Brain.* New York: Appleton-Century-Crofts, 1970.

Gerson, R. F., & Thomas, J. R. Schema theory and practice variability within a neo-Piagetian framework. *Journal of Motor Behavior,* 1977, **9,** 127–134.

Gilbert, J. H. V., & Purves, B. A. Temporal constraints on consonant clusters in child speech production. *Journal of Child Language,* 1977, **4,** 417–432.

Glencross, D. J. The effect of changes in task conditions on temporal organization of a repetitive speed skill. *Ergonomics,* 1975, **18,** 17–28.

Goldstein, U. *Modeling children's vocal tracts.* Paper presented at the 97th Meeting of the Acoustical Society of America, Cambridge, Mass., 1979.

Harding, C. G., & Golinkoff, R. M. The origins of intentional vocalizations in prelinguistic infants. *Child Development,* 1979, **50,** 33–40.

Hawkins, S. Temporal coordination of consonants in the speech of children: preliminary data. *Journal of Phonetics,* 1973, **1,** 181–218.

House, A. S. Reflections on a double negative: misarticulation and inconsistency. *Journal of Speech and Hearing Research*, 1981, **24**, 98–103.

Jürgens, U., & Ploog, D. On the neural control of mammalian vocalization. *Trends in Neurosciences*, 1981, **4**, 77–80.

Kent, R. D. The imitation of synthetic vowels and some implications for speech memory. *Phonetica*, 1973, **28**, 1–25.

Kent, R. D. Auditory–motor formant tracking: a study of speech imitation. *Journal of Speech and Hearing Research*, 1974, **17**, 203–222.

Kent, R. D. Models of speech production. In N. J. Lass (Ed.), *Contemporary issues in experimental phonetics*. New York: Academic Press, 1976. (a)

Kent, R. D. Anatomical and neuromuscular maturation of the speech mechanism: evidence from acoustic studies. *Journal of Speech and Hearing Research*, 1976, **19**, 421–447. (b)

Kent, R. D. *Articulatory–acoustic perspectives on speech development*. Paper presented at the Johnson and Johnson Pediatric Roundtable Conference on Language Behavior in Infancy and Early Childhood, Santa Barbara, Calif., 1979.

Kent, R. D. *Segmental organization of speech*. Paper presented at Conference on Speech Production, University of Texas, Austin, Texas, April 28–30, 1980.

Kent, R. D., & Forner, L. L. Speech segment durations in sentence recitations by children and adults. *Journal of Phonetics*, 1980, **8**, 157–168.

Kent, R. D., & Minifie, F. D. Coarticulation in recent speech production models. *Journal of Phonetics*, 1977, **5**, 115–133.

Klatt, D. H. Linguistic uses of segmental duration in English: Acoustic and perceptual evidence. *Journal of the Acoustical Society of America*, 1976, **59**, 1208–1221.

Klatt, D. H., & Stephanski, R. A. How does a mynah bird imitate human speech? *Journal of the Acoustical Society of America*, 1974, **55**, 822–832.

Kuhl, P. K., & Miller, J. D. Speech perception by the chinchilla: Voiced–voiceless distinction in alveolar plosive consonants. *Science*, 1975, **190**, 69–72.

Kuhl, P. K. The perception of speech in early infancy. In N. J. Lass (Ed.), *Speech and language: Advances in basic research and practice* (Vol. 1). New York: Academic Press, 1979.

Labov, W., & Labov, T. The phonetics of *cat* and *mama*. *Language*, 1978, **4**, 816–852.

Lashley, K. S. The problem of serial order in behavior. In L. A. Jeffres (Ed.), *Cerebral mechanisms in behavior*. New York: Wiley, 1951.

Lenneberg, E. H. *Biological foundations of language*. New York: Wiley, 1967.

Leonard, L. B., Newhoff, M., & Mesalam, L. Individual differences in early child phonology. *Applied Psycholinguistics*, 1980, **1**, 7–30.

Locke, J. L., & Kutz, K. J. Memory for speech and speech for memory. *Journal of Speech and Hearing Research*, 1975, **18**, 176–191.

MacNeilage, P. F. Motor control of serial ordering of speech. *Psychological Review*, 1970, **77**, 182–196.

MacNeilage, P. F., & MacNeilage, L. A. Central processes controlling speech production during sleep and waking. In F. J. McGuigan & R. A. Schoonover (Eds.), *The psychophysiology of thinking*. New York: Academic Press, 1973.

Mavilya, M. Spontaneous vocalization and babbling in hearing impaired infants. In G. Fant (Ed.), *International symposium on speech communication ability and profound deafness*. Washington, D.C.: Alexander Graham Bell Association for the Deaf, 1972.

Mayo, C., & La France, M. On the acquisition of nonverbal communication: a review. *Merrill-Palmer Quarterly*, 1978, **4**, 213–228.

McNeill, D. The two-fold way for speech. In *Problemes Actuels en Psycholinguistique*. Paris: Editions du Centre National de la Recherche Scientifique, 1974.

Molfese, D. L., & Molfese, V. J. Hemisphere and stimulus differences as reflected in the cortical responses of newborn infants to speech stimuli. *Developmental Psychology*, 1979, **15**, 505–511.

Moxley, S. E. Schema: the variability of practice hypothesis. *Journal of Motor Behavior*, 1979, **11**, 65–70.

Naeser, M. A. *The American child's acquisition of differential vowel duration*. The Wisconsin Research and Development Center for Cognitive Learning, Report No. 144, Parts 1 and 2, Madison, Wis., 1970.

Netsell, R. *The acquisition of speech motor control: A perspective with directions for research*. Paper presented at the Johnson and Johnson Roundtable Conference on Language Behavior in Infancy and Early Childhood, Santa Barbara, Calif., 1979.

Netsell, R., Kent, R. D., & Abbs, J. H. *Adjustments of the tongue and lips to fixed jaw positions during speech: A preliminary report*. Paper presented to Conference on Speech Motor Control, University of Wisconsin, Madison, Wis., 1978.

Ohman, S. E. G., Coarticulation in VCV utterances: Spectrographic measurements. *Journal of the Acoustical Society of America*, 1966, **39**, 151–168.

Ohman, S. E. G. Numerical model of coarticulation. *Journal of the Acoustical Society of America*, 1967, **41**, 310–320.

Oller, D. K. Infant vocalizations and the development of speech. *Allied Health & Behavioral Sciences*, 1978, **1**, 523–549.

Oller, D. K., Wieman, L. A., Doyle, W. J., & Ross, C. Infant babbling and speech. *Journal of Child Language*, 1976, **3**, 1–11.

Pascual-Leone, J. A mathematical model for the transition rule in Piaget's development stages. *Acta Psychologica*, 1970, **32**, 301–345.

Perkell, J. S. *Physiology of speech production: Results and implications of a quantitative cineradiographic study*. Research Monograph No. 53. Cambridge, Mass.: MIT Press, 1969.

Pentz, A., Gilbert, H. R., & Zawadzki, P. Spectral properties of fricative consonants in children. *Journal of Acoustical Society of America*, 1979, **66**, 1891–1892.

Piaget, J. *The origins of intelligence in children*. New York: International Universities Press, 1952.

Sasaki, C. T., Levine, F. A., Laitman, J. T., & Crelin, E. S. Postnatal descent of the epiglottis in man. *Archives of Otolaryngology*, 1977, **103**, 169–171.

Schmidt, R. A. A schema theory of discrete motor skill learning. *Psychological Review*, 1975, **82**, 225–260.

Schmidt, R. A. The schema as a solution to some persistent problems in motor learning theory. In G. E. Stelmach (Ed.), *Motor control: Issues and trends*. New York: Academic Press, 1976.

Semjen, A. From motor learning to sensorimotor skill acquisition. *Journal of Human Movement Studies*, 1977, **3**, 182–191.

Smith, B. L. Temporal aspects of English speech production: a developmental perspective. *Journal of Phonetics*, 1978, **6**, 37–68.

Stern, D. N., Faffe, J., Beebe, B., & Bennett, S. L. Vocalizing in unison and in alternation: two modes of communication within the mother–infant dyad. *Annals of the New York Academy of Sciences*, 1975, **263**, 89–100.

Stevens, K. N. The quantal nature of speech: Evidence from articulatory–acoustic data. In P. B. Denes & E. E. Davis (Eds.), *Human Communication, A Unified View*. New York: McGraw-Hill, 1972.

Subtelny, J. D., Worth, J. H., & Sakuda, M. Intraoral pressure and rate of flow during speech. *Journal of Speech and Hearing Research*, 1966, **9**, 498–518.

Sweeney, S. The importance of imitation in the early stages of speech acquisition: a case report. *Journal of Speech and Hearing Disorders*, 1973, **38**, 490–494.

Taft, L. T., & Cohen, H. J. Neonatal and infant reflexology. In J. Hellmuth (Ed.), *Exceptional infant* (Vol. 1): *The normal infant.* Seattle, Wash.: Special Child Publications, 1967.

Thompson, A. E., & Hixon, T. J. Nasal air flow during normal speech production. *Cleft Palate Journal*, 1979, **16**, 412–420.

Tingley, B. M., & Allen, G. D. Development of speech timing control in children. *Child Development*, 1975, **46**, 186–194.

Volkmar, F. R., Hoder, E. L., & Siegel, A. E. *Discrepant social communications.* Paper presented at the Biennial Meeting of the Society for Research in Child Development, New Orleans, La., 1977.

Wallace, S. A., & McGhee, R. C. The independence of recall and recognition in motor learning. *Journal of Motor Behavior*, 1979, **11**, 141–151.

Wickelgren, W. A. Context sensitive coding, associative memory, and serial order in (speech) behavior. *Psychological Review*, 1969, **76**, 1–15.

Wilder, C. N., & Baken, R. J. Some developmental aspects of infant cry. *Journal of Genetic Psychology*, 1978, **132**, 225–230.

Woodruff, D. A. Brain electrical activity and behavior relationships over the life span. In P. B. Baltes (Ed.), *Life-span development and behavior* (Vol. 1). New York: Academic Press, 1978.

Wyke, B. The neurological basis of movement—a developmental review. In K. S. Holt (Ed.), *Movement and child development.* London: Heinemann, 1975.

Zimmerman, G., & Rettaliata, P. Articulatory patterns of an adventitiously deaf speaker: implications for the role of auditory information in speech production. *Journal of Speech and Hearing Research*, 1981, **24**, 169–178.

7

The Processing of Speech and Nonspeech Sounds by Infants: Some Implications

PETER W. JUSCZYK
University of Oregon

What are the implications of the remarkable capacities that infants have shown for discriminating speech sounds? Do 2-month-old infants have specialized mechanisms devoted exclusively to processing human speech? Or, can all of the findings from infant speech perception studies be accounted for by recourse to general features of the auditory processing system in humans? These questions have been a source of great concern in the field of infant speech perception ever since its inception. Moreover, it is likely that researchers in the field will continue to seek satisfactory answers to these questions for some years to come. In this

DEVELOPMENT OF PERCEPTION
Volume 1

chapter, I review some of the background that has led to the interest in understanding the nature of the mechanisms underlying the infant's speech perception capacities, and then focus on the efforts to elucidate these mechanisms. I close with a discussion of the implications that results from infant studies have for our understanding of the development of speech perception.

I.   EARLY EVIDENCE FAVORING A SPECIALIZED SPEECH MODE

The most parsimonious way of dealing with speech perception would be to explain it by reference to general principles of auditory perception. If this were possible, there would be no need to postulate a specialized mode for the perception of speech. Thus, the reason for investigators' speculations about a specialized speech mode was that there were certain facts about speech perception that could not be accommodated within the framework of existing theories of auditory perception. In presenting their case for a specialized mode of processing for speech, Liberman, Cooper, Shankweiler, and Studdert-Kennedy (1967) enumerated a number of ways in which speech sounds were apparently processed differently from other acoustic signals. For example, they pointed to the lack of simple acoustic invariants for speech sounds; the same speech sound (e.g., [d]) might be cued by different features in different phonetic environments (e.g., as in [du] and [di]), or worse, that the same acoustic cue (e.g., a burst of noise) might give rise to the perception of two different phones (i.e., [p] or [k]) depending on what vowel (e.g., [i] or [a]) followed it. Among other findings cited in support of their claim, the most relevant to the present discussion concerned differences in the identification and discrimination of speech and non-speech sounds.

It is a well-known psychophysical fact that for variations along a single acoustic continuum, listeners can discriminate many more stimuli than they can absolutely identify. For example, in a range where most listeners can discriminate about 1200 different pitches, they are able to identify absolutely only about 7 of them (Miller, 1956). The results from early studies suggested that this is not the case for many speech sounds. Instead, it was found (see Fig. 7.1) that when speech sounds were varied along a particular phonetic dimension (e.g., place or voicing) the ability of listeners to discriminate these sounds was only slightly better than their ability to identify the sounds absolutely (e.g., Liberman, Harris, Hoffman, & Griffith, 1957; Liberman, Harris, Kinney, & Lane,

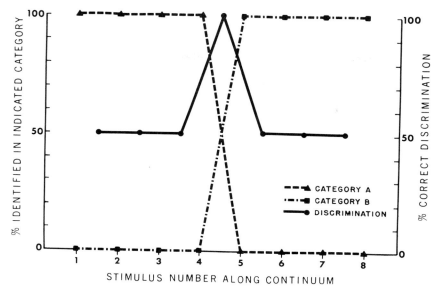

Fig. 7.1 Idealized form of categorical perception showing the identification function (left ordinate) and the discrimination function (right ordinate). (From Studdert-Kennedy, Liberman, Harris, & Cooper, 1970. Copyright © by the American Psychological Association.)

1961). It was as if listeners' ability to discriminate between speech sounds was no better than their ability to assign these sounds to different phonetic categories. Hence, the name "categorical perception" was applied to the way in which listeners responded to information varying along a single phonetic dimension. By contrast, the name given to the type of performance shown by subjects in response to variations along simple acoustic continua such as pitch, was "continuous perception."

Direct comparisons between subjects' responses to speech continua and simple acoustic continua are complicated because speech stimuli are more complex acoustically than the simple acoustic stimuli used in measuring responsiveness to pitch. Thus, categorical perception might simply indicate the way humans respond to all complex acoustic signals, rather than refer to a mode of perception peculiar to speech. For this reason, the researchers at Haskins Laboratories recognized the necessity of employing nonspeech stimuli of equivalent complexity to the speech stimuli they were using. Several interesting attempts were made along these lines. The first of these was that of Liberman *et al.* (1961) who compared subjects' performance with synthetic speech stimuli to that with nonspeech versions of the same stimuli. The speech stimuli were chosen to represent a voicing continuum between [do] and [to]. Voicing refers to the relationship between vocal cord vibration and release from articulatory closure. For voiced sounds like [do], vocal cord vibration begins nearly simultaneously with the release from articulatory closure, whereas for voiceless sounds like [to], the release precedes the initiation of vocal cord vibration. The nonspeech version of this continuum was created by inverting the speech stimuli and altering one of the formants slightly. Both sets of stimuli consisted of hand-painted spectrograms that were converted to sound via a pattern playback device. Although both identification and discrimination data were collected for the speech stimuli, only discrimination data were gathered for the nonspeech stimuli. Comparisons of discrimination performance indicated that the speech sounds were better discriminated than were the nonspeech sounds by a wide margin. Moreover, the discrimination functions for the speech sounds showed prominent peaks in the region of the phonetic boundary, whereas no such peaks were present in the functions for the nonspeech sounds. These results suggested that the same information present in both speech and nonspeech stimuli might be processed differently in the two cases. However, Liberman et al. tempered their conclusion somewhat because there were certain acoustic differences between the speech and nonspeech stimuli that may have affected performance. In particular, for the speech stimuli, the onset time of the first formant was varied relative to that of the second formant, whereas, for the nonspeech stimuli, the onset time of the third formant was varied with respect to the second formant. Thus, although supportive of a difference in processing for speech and nonspeech sounds, Liberman et al.'s study was by no means definitive.

In an effort to circumvent some of the difficulties that hampered the interpretation of the earlier study, Mattingly, Liberman, Syrdal, and Halwes (1971) addressed the speech–nonspeech question using different sorts of nonspeech control stimuli. They began by creating a place-of-articulation continuum that ranged from [bae] to [dae] to [gae]. The stimuli they employed were two-formant synthetic speech sounds that varied only with respect to the starting point of the second-formant transitions. These differences in second-formant transition were sufficient to cue the perception of [bae], [dae] and [gae]. To observe whether or not the information contained in the transitions was processed differently in nonspeech contexts, Mattingly et al. simply presented their subjects with isolated versions of the second-formant transitions. (see Fig. 7.2). They reasoned that these isolated second-formant transitions, called "chirps," would serve as appropriate nonspeech controls since

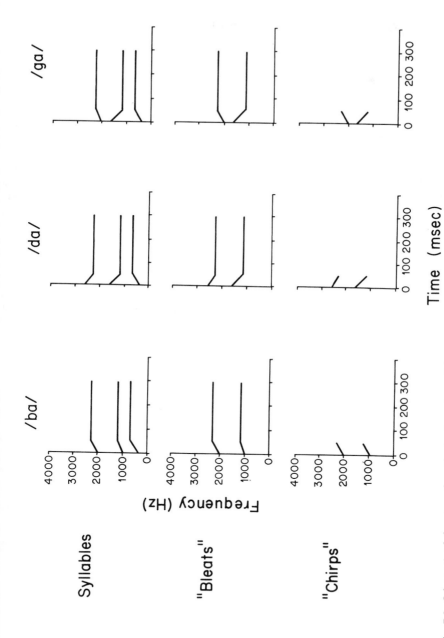

Fig. 7.2 Schematized drawing of synthesized versions of the syllables /ba/, /da/, and /ga/ and the derivative two-formant "bleat" and "chirp" patterns for these syllables.

they constituted the only source of variance between the speech sounds. Hence, it would be possible to observe subjects responding to the same information in both speech and nonspeech contexts.[1]

Once again discrimination performance diverged for the speech and nonspeech stimuli. The discrimination functions for the speech stimuli were marked by sharp peaks in the regions of the phonetic boundaries, whereas the same functions for the nonspeech stimuli exhibited no such peaks (although overall discrimination performance for this condition was better than chance).

Mattingly *et al.* attempted to extend their findings in a second experiment by employing a second type of nonspeech control stimulus ("bleats") in addition to the chirp stimuli. The bleats consisted of the complete second-formant patterns, as opposed to the chirps, which contained just the transitions (see Fig. 7.2). The bleats were employed to control for the possibility that the steady-state portion of the second formant might provide a useful reference point in discriminating the stimulus. If this were the case, any differences observed in discrimination performance for the speech and chirp stimuli might be attributed to the lack of such a reference point in the latter. Apparently, the presence of the steady-state portion of the second formant was of little consequence, because discrimination performance was essentially the same for both the chirps and the bleats. Again there was no evidence of peaks in the discrimination functions for either group. However, there were two curious findings in this experiment. First, although sharp peaks were present in the discrimination functions for consonant–vowel syllables, there were no peaks for vowel–consonant syllables. Second, discrimination performance was actually better for the comparable chirps and bleats than for the vowel–consonant syllables. Still, in light of the differences in discrimination performance for the speech and nonspeech stimuli, Mattingly *et al.* interpreted their results "to be evidence for the existence of a speech mode that differs in interesting ways from the auditory mode [p. 152]."

To summarize to this point, the early investigations tended to support the contention that speech sounds were processed differently from nonspeech sounds. The main grounds for this claim were the repeated demonstrations that speech sounds were perceived in a categorical manner with sharp peaks in discrimination functions in the vicinity of

---

[1] The assumption here is that what is critical for the listener is the absolute frequency level for the second-formant transition, and not some relation between the second and first formants. As will become apparent in later discussion, there is some reason to question this assumption.

the phonetic boundary. By contrast, investigations of various nonspeech continua yielded flat discrimination functions, suggesting continuous perception for these sounds.

II.   EVIDENCE FOR A SPEECH MODE IN INFANTS

The belief that the perception of speech may rely on specialized processes led quite naturally to an interest in the possible origins of these processes. One early suggestion (Liberman *et al.*, 1961) was that the heightened discriminability of speech sounds in the vicinity of phonemic boundaries might reflect "acquired distinctiveness" gained in learning the phonemic categories. Another plausible suggestion was that innate mechanisms might be responsible for categorical perception. Consequently, it is not surprising that, when suitable techniques were developed for tapping the perceptual capacities of young infants, one of the first issues to be addressed was whether or not they had categorical perception for speech sounds.

The first attempt to investigate categorical perception in infants was the study by Eimas, Siqueland, Jusczyk, and Vigorito (1971). By presenting infants with speech sounds differing along a voice-onset-time (VOT) continuum, these investigators sought to determine whether infants would exhibit better discrimination of speech sounds chosen from the phonetic boundary region between [ba] and [pa].[2]

In English, the VOT boundary between [ba] and [pa] has been estimated to be about 25 msec, such that syllables with VOTs of less than 25 msec are perceived as [ba] and ones with VOTs greater than 25 msec are perceived as [pa] (Lisker & Abramson, 1970). To determine whether infants were more sensitive to VOT differences in the vicinity of the phonetic boundary, Eimas *et al.* tested infants' abilities to discriminate two different types of contrasts. The "between categories" pair pitted syllables with VOTs from opposite sides of the phonetic boundary (e.g., a [ba] with a VOT of +20 msec versus a [pa] with a VOT of +40 msec). The "within categories" pairs opposed two syllables from the same side of the phonetic boundary (e.g., a [pa] with a VOT of +60 msec versus a [pa] with a VOT of +80 msec). The procedure used to assess dis-

---

[2] In articulatory terms, *voice onset time* has been defined as the interval between onset of phonation (i.e., when the vocal cords begin to vibrate) and release from articulatory closure (in the case of [ba] and [pa], when the lips are parted). With regard to the stimuli used by Eimas *et al.*, voice onset time was approximated by the interval between the onset of the first formant relative to that of the second formant.

crimination in the infant was a modified version of the high-amplitude sucking (HAS) technique devised by Siqueland and DeLucia (1969). The technique involves making the presentation of one of a pair of auditory stimuli contingent upon the infant's rate of sucking, such that a suck exceeding a predetermined criterion level will trigger the presentation of one speech sound. Generally, the infant's rate of sucking will show a slow but steady increase after the introduction of the auditory contingency. At some point, the sucking rate levels off and then begins to decline toward a baseline level. When the rate has declined by some prearranged amount, the auditory stimulus is changed to the second member of the pair. The infant's discrimination of the pair is inferred from an increase in sucking rate (relative to that of control subjects) upon the presentation of the second stimulus.

Eimas *et al.* found that infants produced significant increases in sucking after shifts from one member of the between categories pair to the other, but not after shifts involving members of the within categories pairs. Thus, like adults, the infants displayed a greater sensitivity to discriminating VOT differences in the region of the phonetic boundary.

On the basis of these results from discrimination tests, Eimas *et al.* concluded that infants had categorical perception for VOT differences.[3] Furthermore, because the infants they tested were as young as 1 month of age, Eimas *et al.* argued that categorical perception has an innate rather than a learned basis. Moreover, because categorical perception had as yet only been demonstrated for speech sounds, Eimas *et al.* suggested that the innate mechanisms underlying categorical perception were specialized for processing speech.

Although Eimas *et al.*'s study suggested that infants might respond to speech in a special way, it did not provide a direct comparison of responses to speech and nonspeech sounds. By using nonspeech chirps, as well as speech syllables, Morse (1972) attempted to determine how infants respond to the same acoustical differences in speech and nonspeech contexts. He examined a syllable pair ([ba] versus [ga]), which contrasts in place of articulation. In this instance, the place-of-articu-

---

[3] Strictly speaking, this claim was premature, because Eimas *et al.* (1971) were not able to collect data on the way in which infants labeled these stimuli (regretably, nor has anyone else managed to do so in the interim, although not for the lack of effort). Since the accepted definition of categorical perception (Studdert-Kennedy, Liberman, Harris, & Cooper, 1970) requires both identification and discrimination data, it is perhaps more appropriate to describe Eimas *et al.*'s results as demonstrating "categorical discrimination." Of course, Eimas *et al.* had based their claim on the parallel they observed between the discrimination performance of the infants they tested with that of adults (e.g., Lisker & Abramson, 1970).

lation contrast was cued by differences in the second- and third-formant transitions of each syllable. Nonspeech chirps were created by presenting only the transition portions from the second and third formants. Morse did not directly assess whether infants showed categorical discrimination for the speech and nonspeech stimuli. Rather, he looked for any differences in the infants' discrimination performance for the speech and nonspeech stimuli. The overall analysis of his results indicated that there was no difference in the infants' responsiveness to the speech and nonspeech stimuli. Still, discrimination performance for the nonspeech sounds was bimodally distributed with about half of the infants giving evidence of discrimination, and the remainder not. On this basis, Morse argued that infants were responding differently to speech and nonspeech sounds (for further discussion of this point, see Jusczyk, 1981).

A more successful demonstration of infants responding differentially to speech and nonspeech contexts was provided by Eimas (1974). Drawing on the early work with adults (Liberman et al., 1961; Mattingly et al., 1971), Eimas examined infants' abilities to display categorical discrimination of the same acoustic differences in both speech and nonspeech contexts. For this purpose, he selected syllables and chirps from the stimuli used by Mattingly et al. (1971). Specifically, he chose his speech stimuli to provide between category (e.g., [bae] versus [dae]) or within category (e.g., [bae$_1$] versus [bae$_2$]) comparisons. Because these were two-formant syllables, the comparable nonspeech test pairs were created by utilizing only the second-formant transitions of the syllables. Thus, for each pairing of speech syllables, there was a comparable nonspeech chirp pairing. The results indicated that the infants' discrimination of the speech contrasts was categorical: Pairings of syllables from opposite sides of the adult phonetic boundary were discriminated, whereas pairings of syllables from the same side of the boundary were not. Such was not the case for the nonspeech contrasts. Although infants were able to discriminate the chirps, there was no indication that the chirps corresponding to between category pairs were better discriminated than ones corresponding to within category pairs.

Because these results seemed to show that infants respond differentially to the same acoustic information in speech and nonspeech contexts, they lent credence to the earlier claims of Eimas et al. (1971) that infants possessed innate mechanisms specialized for processing speech. Moreover, this claim was also bolstered by the results of other studies subsequently conducted by Till (1976) and by Eimas (1975).

Like Eimas (1974), Till (1976) also investigated the infant's discrimination of acoustic cues for place of articulation (i.e., [ba] versus [da]) in both speech and nonspeech contexts. However, unlike Eimas, Till employed a nonspeech control that involved inverting the first formant pattern. Hence, as opposed to the chirps that Eimas had used, Till's patterns contained information in the general region of the first formant and were equivalent in duration to the speech stimuli. Although he used a different measure of discrimination,[4] and different nonspeech control stimuli, Till's findings were essentially the same as those of Eimas (1974). That is, categorical discrimination was present for the speech sounds, but not for the nonspeech sounds.

Eimas (1975) extended previous findings in this area, by showing that speech–nonspeech differences could be obtained for acoustic cues other than those used to signal place of articulation. This time Eimas (1975) focused on the acoustic differences that serve to distinguish [ra] from [la]. Previous work with adults by Miyawaki, Strange, Verbrugge, Liberman, Jenkins, and Fujimura (1975) had shown that changes in the initial steady-state frequency of the third formant were sufficient to cue a distinction between [ra] and [la]. Moreover, for American listeners, although not for Japanese listeners, the third-formant cue was perceived categorically in the speech context but continuously in a nonspeech context, as in an isolated bleat.[5]

The results of Eimas's (1975) study were in line with what Miyawaki *et al.* observed for American adults. The infants displayed categorical discrimination for the speech but not for the nonspeech sounds. Again these results suggested the notion that infants processed speech and nonspeech sounds differently. Furthermore, because categorical discrimination was present for American infants but not for Japanese adults, there was some suggestion that the ability to discriminate certain kinds of phonetic contrasts might be lost, or at least reduced, in the absence of specific experience with these contrasts.

To this juncture, the evidence from both the infant and adult studies pointed to differences in the way in which speech and nonspeech sounds are processed. It appeared that categorical perception, at least in the auditory realm, was limited to speech sounds, and that the same

---

[4] The heart rate dishabituation procedure as employed by Till (1976) involves presenting infants with a sequence of 40 stimuli: 20 of one type followed by 20 of another type. Heart rate activity is monitored during this presentation sequence and discrimination is inferred from a change in heart rate activity immediately after the change to the second stimulus in trial 21. (For further details of this procedure, consult Miller, Morse, & Dorman, 1977).

[5] Even though the [ra]–[la] contrast is not native to their linguistic environment, Japanese listeners also showed a difference in their discrimination performance for the speech and nonspeech contrast: The discriminability of the nonspeech pairs was higher.

acoustic information was perceived differently in speech and nonspeech contexts. However, more recent developments forced a reexamination of these claims. We now turn to these.

III. ANOTHER LOOK AT THE EVIDENCE FOR A SPEECH–NONSPEECH DISTINCTION

The speech–nonspeech issue is a difficult one to resolve. Just when the evidence seems to be decisive in favor of one position, some additional finding comes to light that is not readily explicable within that framework. In this section, some of that shifting evidence is examined; first, results undercutting the view that speech is special and then findings that seem to reaffirm claims for a special speech mode of perception. Some studies with adults are considered, followed by a review of some pertinent studies with infants.

A. Research with Adults

Perhaps the main challenge to the existence of a specialized mode of processing for speech was the demonstration of categorical perception for certain nonspeech continua (e.g., Cutting & Rosner, 1974; Miller, Wier, Pastore, Kelly, & Dooling, 1976; Pisoni, 1977). For instance, Cutting and Rosner (1974) varied the rise times of sawtooth wave stimuli. The resulting stimuli sounded as though they had been generated by musical stringed instruments. Sawtooth waves with rapid rise times (under 35 msec) were labeled by subjects as emanating from a "plucked" stringed instrument, whereas those with more gradual rise times (greater than 35 msec) were attributed to a "bowed" stringed instrument. The use of a nonspeech continuum whose endpoints were so readily labelable as "plucks" and "bows" enabled Cutting and Rosner to obtain both identification and discrimination data for their stimuli. Moreover, since the rise-time dimension also serves as a cue for distinguishing certain speech contrasts (such as [tʃa] and [ʃa]), Cutting and Rosner were able to observe how the same cue was perceived in both speech and nonspeech contexts. Their results showed that both the speech and nonspeech sounds were perceived categorically. Subsequently, further research by Cutting, Rosner, and Foard (1976) indicated that like speech sounds, the pluck and bow stimuli were susceptible to selective adaptation.[6]

[6] Selective adaptation occurs as a result of repeated exposure to a member of a phonetic category (the adapter). After such exposure, the locus of the phonetic boundary shifts

Thus, the work of Cutting and his colleagues suggested that categorical perception could no longer be assumed to be the sole province of speech perception. Instead, it appears that categorical perception is a consequence of the way in which the human auditory system processes complex acoustic information. In this view, the mechanisms used in speech perception are not necessarily unique to speech but are part of a general set used in basic auditory processing.

Any doubts that Cutting and Rosner's results were a quirk of either the particular stimuli or stimulus dimension they chose were put to rest by other demonstrations of categorical perception for nonspeech sounds. Both Miller *et al.* (1976) and Pisoni (1977) investigated the perception of nonspeech dimensions analogous to the VOT dimension for speech. We will focus on Pisoni's work as there is a direct parallel to it in the infant speech perception literature (i.e., Jusczyk, Pisoni, Walley, & Murray, 1980).

Pisoni (1977) drew on earlier research by Hirsh (1959) and Hirsh and Sherrick (1961) showing that the auditory system responds differently when the onsets of two events occur within 20–25 msec of one another than it does when their onsets are separated by more than 25 msec. Specifically, subjects are unable to identify the temporal order of two distinct acoustic events when their onsets occur within 25 msec of each other. However, when the onsets are spaced by more than 25 msec, the two events are perceived as occurring successively and ordered in time. Pisoni speculated that this basic property of the auditory system in responding to the temporal order of acoustic events might underlie the perception of VOT differences in speech. To test his hypothesis, he created a nonspeech continuum consisting of two-component tone stimuli. Each stimulus was composed of a 500 Hz tone and a 1500 Hz tone. The nonspeech continuum was derived by systematically varying the relative onset times of the two tones. For example, the 500 Hz tone could lead the 1500 Hz by 50 msec, lag behind the 1500 Hz tone by 50 msec, or the two tones could occur simultaneously (see Fig. 7.3). Pisoni found that listeners displayed categorical perception for these sounds. Furthermore, there was a remarkable similarity in the identification functions for the tone onset time (TOT) stimuli and those observed previously in studies of VOT. Pisoni's listeners displayed three

---

toward the adapting stimulus. For example, after selective adaptation with a bow stimulus, the pluck–bow boundary would shift toward the bow end of the continuum. A natural result of such a shift would be that stimuli from the boundary region prior to adaptation would be perceived to be plucks after adaptation to a bow adapter.

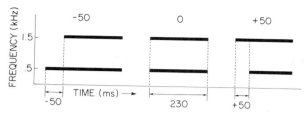

Fig. 7.3 Schematic representations of three stimulae differing in relative onset time: leading (−50 msec), simultaneous (0 msec), and lagging (+50 msec). (From Pisoni, 1977. Copyright © by the American Institute of Physics.)

categories for the TOT continuum corresponding to leading, simultaneous, and lagging onsets. The boundaries for these categories occurred at approximately −25 and +25 msec, which fit well with the boundary locations for the categories observed with VOT stimuli (Lisker & Abramson, 1970). Hence, Pisoni's results provide support for the view that categorical perception of VOT may be the consequence of mechanisms attuned to psychophysical properties in the acoustic signal.

Clearly there are parallels between the way in which adults perceive speech sounds and the way in which they perceive certain types of nonspeech sounds. A question to consider at this point is why previous studies of speech and nonspeech sounds suggested important differences in the way in which these sounds are perceived. One obvious possibility is that the nonspeech stimuli used as controls in the earlier experiments were inappropriate in some respect such that critical information may have been omitted from the nonspeech stimuli. Liberman et al. (1961) did raise this possibility with respect to the nonspeech stimuli they chose. Likewise, Mattingly et al. (1971) expressed similar qualms about their chirp stimuli, although they thought that they had circumvented these difficulties with their bleat stimuli. Nevertheless, both the chirps and the bleats lacked first-formant transition information. This information was omitted because it is typically redundant across the speech continuum under examination and because the chirps sound less speechlike without it. However, recent research by Jusczyk, Smith, and Murphy (1981) suggests that the presence of first-formant transitions has a critical effect on the way in which adults classify chirps. One implication of their work is that it may be the relationship between the formants rather than the absolute values of the formants that is crucial to the listener's perception of these sounds.

A central problem in this area is how to determine when a given set of nonspeech stimuli constitutes an adequate control for a particular speech dimension. Unfortunately, it is almost impossible to know a priori whether nonspeech controls are appropriate. Yet, if one must depend upon the results of one's investigation to determine the appropriateness of the control, then settling the argument as to whether an independent mode of perception exists for speech is problematic. For example, consider the case when the results for the speech and nonspeech sounds diverge. One can always claim that critical information was altered or omitted from the nonspeech sounds. However, if the pattern of results is the same for speech and nonspeech stimuli, one could argue that both sets of sounds were processed by the speech processor (i.e., it was tricked into processing the nonspeech sounds as if they were speech).

There would seem to be few ways out of this conundrum. One tack for proponents of the view that there is no special speech mode would be to demonstrate that other species respond to speech continua in approximately the same way as do humans. Indeed, precisely this sort of result has been observed for the perception of VOT by chinchillas (Kuhl & Miller, 1975; Kuhl & Miller, 1978). If similar evidence emerged for the perception of other speech dimensions such as place of articulation, one would be led to believe that the categories used in speech reflect basic capacities of the mammalian auditory system.

Proponents of a special mode for speech perception can try to uncover instances in which animals and humans diverge in their responsiveness to speech sounds. The difficulty here is that one would be placed in the position of proving that no animals respond to a particular speech dimension in the same way as do humans. A more fruitful course might be to show that labeling a given stimulus set as speech or nonspeech produces entirely different effects in the listener. Such a result would seem to implicate at least two distinct modes of perception (although it would still be necessary to determine if the mode used for speech might not also serve in analyzing other types of acoustic signals). Recently, there have been several reports that the same acoustic signals could be perceived in more than one way. The first of these involved the perception of sine wave analogues to speech stimuli (Bailey, Summerfield, & Dorman, 1977). Bailey *et al.* created a set of nonspeech stimuli by replacing the formant structure of synthetic speech syllables with frequency- and amplitude-modulated sine waves. Their objective was to ascertain whether the spectro–temporal characteristics of these nonspeech stimuli would be sufficient to account for categorization along the place-of-articulation continuum. If so, the psychophysical boundaries for the nonspeech stimuli should coincide with the phonetic boundaries for the comparable speech stimuli. In fact, there was some indication that the phonetic boundary did not coincide with the psychophysical boundary. Of more significance was the result obtained when Bailey *et al.* varied the instruction set for the nonspeech sounds. After being tested with the sine-wave stimuli under nonspeech instructions, all subjects were retested under instructions to hear the sounds as speech syllables. Remarkably, there were significant shifts in subjects' category boundaries under the two instruction sets.[7] However, in a second experiment, there was little evidence for a difference in the performance of subjects who heard the sine waves as nonspeech. Therefore, though suggestive that instructions to hear sounds as speech or nonspeech have important consequences for perception of the same stimuli, Bailey *et al.*'s results require additional replication and elaboration.

A different sort of demonstration comes from experiments involving "duplex perception" (Isenberg & Liberman, 1978; Liberman, 1979; Rand, 1974). In these experiments, listeners report hearing the same acoustic signal as speech and nonspeech *simultaneously*. The experimental manipulation is one which involves the dichotic presentation of two portions of a speech syllable. For example, the third-formant transition might be played to one ear and the remainder of a syllable to the other ear. The resulting perception is one of a completed speech syllable plus a nonspeech chirp. Hence, in this case, the third-formant transition is perceived both as a speech and nonspeech cue at the same time. Moreover, in their study, Isenberg and Liberman (1978) showed that varying the intensity of the third-formant transition affected only judgments about the perceived loudness of the chirp, and not of the overall syllable. Thus, judgments about the third formant's contribution to the fused-speech percept seem to be independent of those made about the nonspeech chirp percept. The implication here is that the third-formant transition has undergone two different modes of processing, and that one of these modes is used in the analysis of acoustic signals as speech.

Research on duplex perception has only begun. To the extent that future studies of this phenomenon yield similar results, the evidence would seem to support claims for at least two modes of processing for acoustic signals. At least one of these modes would be utilized for processing complex acoustic signals like speech. Yet, whether the domain of this mode of perception is limited to speech signals or whether

---

[7] One confound in this study is the fact that all subjects were tested on sine-wave series first under nonspeech instructions, then under speech instructions. This raises the possibility that subjects' performance might have changed simply as a result of greater familiarity with the stimuli during the second test rather than as a consequence of the change in the instruction set.

it includes all complex acoustic signals of possible ecological significance to the organism would still be uncertain.

In summary, the original grounds for postulating a speech–nonspeech distinction in the processing of acoustic information has been undercut by findings from recent research with nonspeech sounds. At the same time, new evidence has surfaced suggesting that speech sounds may undergo some form of special processing. Whether this specialized processing is exclusive to speech remains unresolved at present.

B. Research with Infants

What are the origins of categorical perception for certain classes of nonspeech sounds? One possibility is that categorical perception for nonspeech sounds is a consequence of the underlying sensory mechanisms for basic auditory processing in humans. An alternative view is that categorical perception for certain nonspeech dimensions arises because adults are able to label the stimuli by relating and comparing them to highly familiar speech categories. One way to explore this issue is to utilize a group of subjects who are unlikely to have well-developed category labels (e.g., infants). If young infants display categorical discrimination for nonspeech sounds, the implication is that the infants' performance reflects the operation of mechanisms attuned to the psychophysical properties of the acoustic signal.

The first indication that infants do display categorical discrimination for certain classes of nonspeech sounds came from the work of Jusczyk, Rosner, Cutting, Foard, and Smith (1977). These investigators employed the same sine-wave stimuli that adults had labeled as plucks and bows in the study by Cutting and Rosner (1974). Jusczyk et al. used the HAS technique and tested 2-month-old infants on pairs of sine-wave stimuli differing in rise times. The pairs were selected so that some comparisons involved stimuli chosen from within the same category (e.g., 0 msec versus 30 msec of rise time; both of which are perceived as plucks), whereas other comparisons involved members from opposite sides of the adult category boundary (e.g., 30 msec versus 60 msec of rise time; perceived as pluck and bow, respectively). Jusczyk et al. found that only the between categories pairing was discriminated by the infants. Therefore, like adults, the infant's discrimination of the rise-time dimension for nonspeech sounds is categorical. Consequently, categorical discrimination by infants is not uniquely limited to speech. Thus, the existence of categorical discrimination for speech sounds is not a sufficient basis for claiming that infants possess specialized speech-processing mechanisms.

The finding that infants exhibit categorical discrimination of certain nonspeech continua lead quite naturally to a consideration of how they would respond to other nonspeech continua, particularly those proposed as an underlying basis for a given speech dimension. The most likely candidate for such an investigation was the tone-onset-time (TOT) continuum. Recall that Pisoni (1977) had employed this continuum in his exploration of whether or not responses to temporal order information could account for the way in which VOT information is perceived. The remarkable correspondence he found between the location of category boundaries for the TOT and VOT continua suggested that a common perceptual basis for the two might exist in the way in which the human auditory system responds to temporally ordered events. To further investigate this issue, Jusczyk, Pisoni, Walley, and Murray (1980) presented 2-month-old infants with contrasts between stimuli from various points along the TOT continuum. Three of the stimulus pairings consisted of items chosen from within the same category for adults (i.e., $lead_1/lead_2$, $simultaneous_1/simultaneous_2$, lag_1/lag_2), while the remaining two involved contrasts between stimuli from different categories (i.e., lead/simultaneous, simultaneous/lag). The infants demonstrated that they were sensitive to temporal order information and that, like adults, they appear to divide the TOT continuum into three categories. However, for the infants the regions of highest discriminability along the continuum were shifted to slightly larger stimulus values than those observed for adults. In particular, the infants only gave evidence of discriminating the $-70/-40$ msec and $+40/+70$ msec contrasts; both of which were, for adults, within category contrasts (between lagging and leading stimuli, respectively). Jusczyk *et al.* had predicted that the infants would discriminate only those pairs that crossed the adult category boundaries at -20 msec and $+20$ msec. Thus, in contrast to the studies with adults, which showed a close correspondence in the locations of the TOT and VOT boundaries, the studies with infants indicated a slight discrepancy in the location of their boundaries for the speech and nonspeech stimuli.[8] Specifically the infants' boundary for the voiced–voiceless portion of the VOT continuum is somewhere in the region of 20 to 40 msec, whereas the comparable TOT boundary is apparently located between 40 and 70 msec. In fact, the HAS technique only permits a rather crude estimate of the infant's category boundaries, so some caution is necessary in inter-

---

[8] Note that the infant's category boundaries must be inferred from the discrimination data, as there are no direct observations available on the infant's identification of the stimuli.

preting the discrepancy between the TOT and VOT series. Nevertheless, it seems likely that temporal order information does *not* provide the sole basis for the infant's discrimination of VOT. Rather, temporal order information is probably but one of several acoustic cues that might be used in combination to produce the perception of VOT differences (Lisker, 1975; Lisker, 1978).

Thus, recent research on the perception of nonspeech sounds by infants indicates that categorical discrimination occurs for certain nonspeech continua. These findings undermine the view that categorical discrimination for speech sounds is evidence for the presence of specialized linguistic processing mechanisms for infants. However, attempts to determine the psychophysical properties underlying the discrimination of certain speech contrasts, although promising, have not been completely successful. For this reason, one still cannot entirely preclude the possibility that infants might possess some specialized processing mechanisms for the perception of speech.

IV. EVALUATING THE EVIDENCE: ONE POSSIBLE INTERPRETATION OF INFANT SPEECH PERCEPTION

We have reviewed only a small and selective portion of the research on infant speech perception. The main body of research in the field over the past decade has consistently demonstrated that the human infant possesses a remarkable range of abilities for analyzing the speech signal. So, for example, there is evidence that infants are capable of distinguishing speech sounds along a variety of different phonetic dimensions such as voicing (e.g., Eimas *et al.*, 1971), place of articulation (e.g., Morse, 1972), nasality (Trehub, 1976), laterality (e.g., Eimas, 1975), etc. Moreover, the infant's capacity for distinguishing phonetic segments is not limited to the occurrence of these segments in the initial positions of syllables. The infant is sensitive to phonetic contrasts present in the medial (e.g., Jusczyk & Thompson, 1978) and final (Jusczyk, 1977) positions of utterances as well. Furthermore, recent investigations of perceptual constancy suggest that infants are able to preserve information about phonetic contrasts in the face of irrelevant variations in pitch, speaker's voice, and vowel context (e.g., Katz & Jusczyk, 1980; Kuhl, 1979).

The studies we have focused on in this chapter are those that have been directed toward understanding the nature of the mechanisms underlying the infant's remarkable speech perception capacities. A logical first step in such an enterprise is to delineate boundaries for the infant's perceptual capacities. Are there commonalities that exist between the way in which the infant responds to complex acoustic signals and to speech sounds? If so, then general auditory processing mechanisms may be sufficient to account for the way in which the infant responds to speech contrasts.

An explanation of the infant's speech perception capacities in terms of general properties of the auditory system is attractive for several reasons. First, it would provide a unified account of why categorical discrimination is observed for both speech and nonspeech sounds. Second, it would help to explain why nonhuman species such as chinchillas exhibit categorical perception for VOT (Kuhl & Miller, 1978). Third, it offers a reasonable account of why infants from diverse linguistic environments display similar patterns of discrimination along speech continua despite cross-language differences in the location of phonetic boundaries by adults (e.g., Aslin, Hennessy, Pisoni, & Perey, 1979; Lasky, Syrdal-Lasky, & Klein, 1975; Streeter, 1976).

One version of a psychophysical explanation for infant speech perception might be framed as follows. Initially, the infant's sensitivity to contrasts between phonetic segments is governed by the way in which the auditory system responds to psychophysical properties inherent in the acoustic wave form. In this sense, the infant would not be responding to speech contrasts in any way differently than to contrasts that might occur between other sounds in its environment.[9] Nevertheless, the innate capacities that the infant has for analyzing complex acoustic signals would provide an initial partitioning of speech sounds into categories based on their acoustic characteristics. Because the basic capacities reflect the way in which the human auditory system is structured, it is quite natural to expect that any initial partitioning of speech sounds according to acoustic characteristics should lead to essentially the same categories even among infants from diverse language backgrounds. Yet, at the same time, we know from research conducted with adults (e.g., Lisker & Abramson, 1970; Williams, 1977), that cross-language differences do eventually develop in the perception of phonetic contrasts. How might these cross-language differences come about?

Given the model we have been considering, there are two ways in which cross-language differences in the perception of speech could be

---

[9] In fact, careful examination of data from my own studies over the past 5 years revealed no discernible differences in the way in which infants tested with the HAS technique responded to speech and nonspeech stimuli. The infants appear to satiate to both types of sounds at approximately the same rates and display similar increases in sucking rate following shifts to a second stimulus.

handled. One alternative is to assume that mere exposure to the sounds of a particular language serves to bias the responding of the underlying auditory mechanisms in a particular direction, resulting ultimately in a shift in the sensitivity of these mechanisms. This view, favored by Aslin and Pisoni (1980), draws heavily on parallels to visual system development wherein varying the amount of passive exposure to visual patterns has been shown to influence the responsiveness of neural mechanisms serving vision. However, as MacKain (1979) has noted, it is difficult to assess the plausibility of this approach in the absence of any data regarding the frequency of occurrence of phonetic tokens across different languages.

The alternative view, favored here, postulates that cross-language differences in the perception of speech sounds are unlikely until after these sounds begin to take on significance for the infant in a communicative context. Thus, only after the infant becomes actively engaged in trying to attach meaning to the utterances that he or she hears would cross-language differences be expected to emerge. By tying a set of phonetic tokens to a particular meaning, the child is in a position to observe which variations among the tokens he uses or hears have an important impact in conveying that meaning. Those acoustic attributes that are most prominent in the phonetic environments as defined by the phonological constraints of the specific language are the ones which the infant utilizes in his analysis of speech as language. It is hard to imagine that these phonological constraints could have much relevance for the infant outside of the important role that they serve in the communicative context. The view here, then, is that the impetus to attach meaning to utterances promotes the assignment of different weightings to various acoustic cues according to their salience in marking a distinctive contrast in the language the infant is acquiring. The actual assignment of these weightings might translate into no more than a bias to focus more closely on one region of the acoustic spectrum rather than another. Changes in the relative weightings of the acoustic cues underlying a particular phonetic contrast could shift the region of highest discriminability along some selected stimulus continuum. Because phonological constraints do differ from language to language, the weightings assigned to the acoustic cues would also differ, thus resulting in cross-language differences in the perception of various speech continua.

The view put forth here has interesting implications for questions about the existence of a speech mode of perception. Rather than involving a set of specialized mechanisms, the speech mode would exist as an interpretive schema that overlays the output of general auditory processing mechanisms. In other words, when the speech mode of perception is engaged, one employs the set of weightings derived for speech, otherwise the weightings chosen would be different ones.[10] An account along these lines provides a straightforward explanation of why Bailey *et al.*'s (1977) subjects produced different labeling functions depending upon whether they heard the sine-wave stimuli as speech or as nonspeech.[11] One need only to assume that subjects employ different criteria for weighting the information in the two cases.

Therefore, rather than ruling out a specialized speech mode, the psychophysical account of infant speech perception suggests that the speech mode develops when the child begins to view language as a vehicle for communication.

V. SOME POTENTIAL PITFALLS FOR A PSYCHOPHYSICAL ACCOUNT OF INFANT SPEECH PERCEPTION

It is tempting to conclude at this point that a psychophysical explanation can provide a complete account of infant speech perception abilities. However, there are several cases in which such an account may prove to be deficient. One potentially difficult problem for the psychophysical approach is how it could handle results demonstrating perceptual constancy for speech sounds. As noted earlier, there are indications that infants are able to preserve information concerning the identity of phonetic segments despite variations in pitch and speakers' voices (Holmberg *et al.* 1977; Kuhl, 1979) and, to some extent, despite variations in vowel context (Holmberg *et al.*, 1977; Katz & Jusczyk, 1980). Whereas, a psychophysical explanation for the infant's discrimination of speech contrasts is relatively direct, accounting for perceptual

---

[10] Although we have focused exclusively on aspects of the acoustic analysis of the speech signal and phonological constraints as determining weightings for speech perception, other factors, such as information about articulatory constraints, may also affect the assignment of weightings. A slightly different approach, but along the same lines, has been proposed by Oden and Massaro (1978).

[11] Even within the speech mode itself, there are indications that subjects will selectively weight the incoming acoustic information. Carden, Levitt, Jusczyk, and Walley (1981) found that changing a subject's set as to the manner of articulation resulted in a change in the way in which acoustic cues for place of articulation were perceived, even though the physical stimulus itself was not altered in any way. Because these shifts in the perceived place of articulation occurred in the absence of any alterations to the physical stimulus, Carden *et al.* argued that the processing of the place feature depends not directly upon the actual acoustic information for manner, but rather on the *interpretation* that the listener gives to this information.

constancy for speech segments is more complicated. The problem arises because of the absence of invariant physical cues in the acoustic wave forms common to all utterances of a given phonetic segment (see Liberman et al., 1967 for a review). Attempts to address this issue have focused on the relations between components of the overall spectral patterns in an effort to find some configurational properties that might serve to signal a particular phonetic segment in all its potential contexts (e.g., Searle, Jacobson, & Rayment, 1979; Stevens & Blumstein, 1978). Should these attempts prove to be successful, one implication would be that the human auditory system is sensitive to patterns with configurational properties of this sort. Findings demonstrating such sensitivity in infants would suggest an innate rather than learned basis for perceptual constancy.[12] Given the existence of this sensitivity to configurational patterns corresponding to phonetic categories, the question arises as to whether it would not be appropriate to claim that the infant possesses mechanisms specialized for the perception of speech. To show otherwise would require either a demonstration that the same mechanisms have applicability in establishing constancy for nonspeech sounds or that nonhuman species display similar abilities. In fact, there is some evidence that both the dog (Baru, 1975) and the chinchilla (Burdick & Miller, 1975) are able to ignore irrelevant variation in pitch contour and speakers' voice. Should a similar tendency also be observed for responding to the same phonetic segment across different vowel contexts, it would implicate a source for perceptual constancy for speech in general properties of the mammalian auditory system. Still, any attempted conclusions about the eventual resolution of this issue are premature at this point, especially since there is only relatively weak evidence that human infants exhibit perceptual constancy when vowel context is varied.[13]

A second set of findings that may prove to be difficult within the framework of a psychophysical model comes from recent research on the infant's perception of place-of-articulation distinctions between fricatives. Jusczyk, Murray, Murphy, Levitt, and Carden (in preparation) examined 2-month-old infants' sensitivity to acoustic cue signaling a contrast between [fa] and [θa]. For purposes of the present discussion,

---

[12] The innate rather than learned basis is favored here because there is no reason to believe that the infant is reinforced for such things as grouping all words that begin with "b," for example, into the same category. In fact, it is much more likely that the infant would be reinforced for grouping together words without common phonetic segments such as "cat," "dog," and "horse."

[13] Katz and Jusczyk (1980) found evidence for constancy when only two vowel contexts were used but not when four vowel contexts were used.

their most interesting finding concerned the way in which infants responded to information carried in the formant transitions. To determine whether differences in formant transitions would be sufficient to signal the distinction between [fa] and [θa], Jusczyk *et al.* removed the frication portion of natural speech tokens of these syllables. The remaining portions of the [fa] and [θa] syllables, consisting of formant transitions and steady-state patterns, were both perceived by adults as sounding like "ba." Infants showed no evidence of discriminating between these truncated syllables.[14] However, Jusczyk *et al.* also conducted an additional test in which they appended the same frication noise (from a [fa]) to the truncated version of each syllable. Despite the fact that the same acoustic information was added to each syllable, the infants were now able to discriminate the syllables. (Interestingly enough, the addition of this common frication noise to each truncated syllable enabled adults to hear them as "fa" and "θa.") Clearly, then, the frication noise provides a context in which the formant transition differences can be distinguished.

One possible reason as to why the context is effective in this case is because it serves as a cue to manner of articulation. Thus infants, like adults tested by Carden *et al.* (see Footnote 11), may interpret the formant transition cues differently according to their perception of manner of articulation. If so, we would have to attribute the infant with sophisticated mechanisms for processing speech.

Alternatively, one might hypothesize a psychophysical account for the context effect. For instance, perhaps the frication noise serves as a reference point that helps to simplify the comparison of the formant transitions. If this were so, the substitution of another noise with similar spectral characteristics might produce equivalent results. There is some indication from another experiment by Jusczyk *et al.* (in preparation) that the psychophysical account of the context effect may not work, but further testing is required to resolve the issue.

VI. CONCLUSIONS

I have reviewed those studies of the perception of speech and non-speech sounds that seem to be most pertinent to an understanding of

---

[14] A reasonable expectation at this point was that the [fa]–[θa] distinction must be signaled by a difference in the frication portion of the syllables. Jusczyk *et al.* tested this hypothesis and found that the infants could discriminate the frication portions of each syllable.

the underpinnings for the infant's speech perception abilities. The issue as to whether it is necessary to credit the infant with specialized processing mechanisms used exclusively for speech perception is one which remains with us today. However, at the present time, the weight of the evidence seems to favor an account of infant speech perception based on the operation of generalized auditory mechanisms. Accordingly, I have proposed a model that attributes no specialized speech processing mechanisms to the infant. Instead, the infant's initial discriminations of speech contrasts are dictated by the way in which the human auditory system responds to certain well-defined psychophysical properties. In time, speech sounds do receive special treatment by the developing infant, ultimately leading to the development of a special mode of perception for speech. But this speech mode does not make its appearance until the infant begins trying to attach meaning to speech.

Finally, some potential difficulties for a psychophysical account of infant speech perception were also considered. Ultimately, the validity of the proposed model may rest on its capacity to deal effectively with problems of this nature.

ACKNOWLEDGMENTS

Preparation of this manuscript was supported by an N.S.E.R.C. grant A-0282 to the author. I wish to thank Nancy Beattie for the excellent job she did in typing earlier versions of the present manuscript.

REFERENCES

Aslin, R. N., Hennessy, B., Pisoni, D. B., & Perey, A. J. *Individual infant's discrimination of voice onset time: Evidence for three modes of voicing.* Paper presented at the Biennial Meeting of the Society for Research in Child Development, San Francisco, Calif., 1979.

Aslin, R. N., & Pisoni, D. B. Some developmental processes in speech perception. In G. H. Yeni-Komshian, J. Kavanagh, and C. A. Ferguson (Eds.), *Child Phonology: Perception and Production* II. New York: Academic Press, 1980.

Bailey, P. J., Summerfield, Q., & Dorman, M. On the identification of sine-wave analogues of certain speech sounds. *Haskins Laboratories: Status Report on Speech Research*, SR-51/52, 1977.

Baru, A. V. Discrimination of synthesized vowels [a] and [i] with varying parameters in dog. In G. Fant and M. A. A. Tatham (Eds.). Auditory Analysis and the Perception of Speech. London: Academic Press, 1975.

Burdick, C. K., & Miller, J. D. Speech perception by the chinchilla: Discrimination of the sustained /a/ and /i/. *Journal of the Acoustical Society of America,* 1975, **58**, 415–427.

Carden, G., Levitt, A., Jusczyk, P. W., & Walley, A. Evidence for phonetic processing of cues to place of articulation: Perceived manner affects perceived place. *Perception & Psychophysics*, 1981, **29**, 26–36.

Cutting, J. E., & Rosner, B. S. Categories and boundaries in speech and music. *Perception & Psychophysics*, 1974, **16**, 564–571.

Cutting, J. E., Rosner, B. S., & Foard, C. F. Perceptual categories for musiclike sounds: Implications for theories of speech perception. *Quarterly Journal of Experimental Psychology*, 1976, **28**, 361–378.

Eimas, P. D. Auditory and linguistic processing of cues for place of articulation by infants. *Perception & Psychophysics*, 1974, **16**, 513–521.

Eimas, P. D. Auditory and phonetic coding of the cues for speech: Discrimination of the [r–1] distinction by young infants. *Perception & Psychophysics*, 1975, **18**, 341–347.

Eimas, P. D., Siqueland, E. R., Jusczyk, P., & Vigorito, J. Speech perception in infants. *Science*, 1971, **71**, 303–306.

Hirsh, I. J. Auditory perception of temporal order. *Journal of the Acoustical Society of America*, 1959, **31**, 759–767.

Hirsh, I. J., & Sherrick, C. E. Perceived order in different sense modalities. *Journal of Experimental Psychology*, 1961, **62**, 423–432.

Holmberg, T. L., Morgan, K. A., & Kuhl, P. K. *Speech perception in early infancy: Discrimination of fricative consonants.* Paper presented at the 94th Meeting of the Acoustical Society of America, Miami Beach, December 16, 1977.

Isenberg, D. & Liberman, A. M. Speech and nonspeech percepts from the same sound. *Journal of the Acoustical Society of America*, 1978, Supplement No. 1, J20.

Jusczyk, P. W. Perception of syllable-final stop consonants by two-month old infants. *Perception & Psychophysics*, 1977, **21**, 450–454.

Jusczyk, P. W. Infant speech perception: A critical appraisal. In P. D. Eimas & J. L. Miller (Eds.), *Perspectives on the studies of speech.* Hillsdale, N.J.: Erlbaum, 1981.

Jusczyk, P. W., Murray, J., Murphy, C., Levitt, A., & Carden, G. The perception of place of articulation in fricatives by two-month-old infants. (In preparation.)

Jusczyk, P. W., Pisoni, D. B., Walley, A., & Murray, J. Discrimination of relative onset time of two-component tones by infants. *Journal of the Acoustical Society of America*, 1980, **67**, 262–270.

Jusczyk, P. W., Rosner, B. S., Cutting, J. E., Foard, C. F., & Smith, L. B. Categorical perception of nonspeech sounds by two-month old infants. *Perception & Psychophysics*, 1977, **21**, 50–54.

Jusczyk, P. W., Smith, L. B., & Murphy, C. *The perceptual classification of speech. Perception & Psychophysics*, 1981, **30**, 10–23.

Jusczyk, P. W., & Thompson, E. Perception of a phonetic contrast in multisyllabic utterances by 2-month old infants. *Perception & Psychophysics*, 1978, **23**, 105–109.

Katz, J., & Jusczyk, P. W. *Do six-month olds have perceptual constancy for phonetic segments?* Paper presented at the International Conference on Infant Studies, New Haven, Conn., 1980.

Kuhl, P. K. Speech perception in early infancy: Perceptual constancy for spectrally dissimilar vowel categories. *Journal of the Acoustical Society of America*, 1979, **66**, 1668–1679.

Kuhl, P. K., & Miller, J. D. Speech perception by the chinchilla: Voiced–voiceless distinction in alveolar–plosive consonants. *Science*, 1975, **190**, 69–72.

Kuhl, P. K., & Miller, J. D. Speech perception by the chinchilla: Identification functions for synthetic VOT stimuli. *Journal of the Acoustical Society of America*, 1978, **63**, 905–917.

Lasky, R. E., Syrdal-Lasky, A., Klein, R. E. VOT discrimination by four and six and a half month old infants from Spanish environments. *Journal of Experimental Child Psychology*, 1975, **20**, 215–225.

Liberman, A. M. *Duplex perception and integration of cues: Evidence that speech is different from nonspeech and similar to language.* Paper presented at the Ninth International Congress of Phonetic Sciences, Copenhagen, 1979.

Liberman, A. M., Cooper, F. S., Shankweiler, D. D., & Studdert-Kennedy, M. Perception of the speech code. *Psychological Review*, 1967, **74**, 431–461.

Liberman, A. M., Harris, K. S., Hoffman, H. S., & Griffith, B. C. The discrimination of speech sounds within and across phoneme boundaries. *Journal of Experimental Psychology*, 1957, **54**, 358–368.

Liberman, A. M., Harris, K. S., Kinney, J. A., & Lane, H. The discrimination of relative onset time of the components of certain speech and nonspeech patterns. *Journal of Experimental Psychology*, 1961, **61**, 379–388.

Lisker, L. Is it a VOT or a first-formant transition detector? *Journal of the Acoustical Society of America*, 1975, **57**, 1547–1551.

Lisker, L. In qualified defense of VOT. *Language and Speech*, 1978, **21**, 375–383.

Lisker, L., & Abramson, A. S. The voicing dimension: Some experiments in comparative phonetics. In *Proceedings of the sixth international congress of phonetic sciences*, Prague, 1967, Prague: Academia, 1970.

MacKain, K. S. *On assessing the role of experience in infant speech discrimination.* Unpublished manuscript (Haskins Laboratories), 1979.

Mattingly, I. G., Liberman, A. M., Syrdal, A. K., & Halwes, T. Discrimination in speech and nonspeech modes. *Cognitive Psychology*, 1971, **2**, 131–157.

Miller, C., Morse, P., & Dorman, M. Cardiac indices of infant speech perception: Orienting and burst discrimination. *Quarterly Journal of Experimental Psychology*, 1977, **29**, 533–545.

Miller, G. A. The magical number seven, plus or minus two, or some limits on our capacity for processing information. *Psychological Review*, 1956, **63**, 81–96.

Miller, J. D., Wier, L., Pastore, R., Kelly, W., & Dooling, R. Discrimination and labeling of noise–buzz sequences with varying noise–lead times. *Journal of the Acoustical Society of America*, 1976, **60**, 410–417.

Miyawaki, K., Strange, W., Verbrugge, R., Liberman, A. M., Jenkins, J. J., & Fujimura, O. An effect of linguistic experience: The discrimination of [r] and [1] by native speakers of Japanese and English. *Perception & Psychophysics*, 1975, **18**, 331–340.

Morse, P. A. The discrimination of speech and nonspeech stimuli in early infancy. *Journal of Experimental Child Psychology*, 1972, **14**, 477–492.

Oden, G. C., & Massaro, D. W. Integration of featural information in speech perception. *Psychological Review*, 1978, **85**, 172–191.

Pisoni, D. B. Identification and discrimination of the relative onset time of two-component tones: Implications for voicing perception in stops. *Journal of the Acoustical Society of America*, 1977, **61**, 1352–1361.

Rand, T. C. Dichotic release from masking for speech. *Journal of the Acoustical Society of America*, 1974, **55**, 678–680.

Searle, C. L., Jacobson, J. E., & Rayment, S. G. Phoneme recognition based on human audition. *Journal of the Acoustical Society of America*, 1979, **65**, 799–809.

Siqueland, E. R., & DeLucia, C. A. Visual reinforcement of non-nutritive sucking in human infants. *Science*, 1969, **165**, 1144–1146.

Stevens, K. N., & Blumstein, S. E. Invariant cues for place of articulation in stop consonants. *Journal of the Acoustical Society of America*, 1978, **64**, 1358–1368.

Streeter, L. A. Language perception of 2-month old infants shows effects of both innate mechanisms and experience. *Nature*, 1976, **259**, 39–41.

Studdert-Kennedy, M., Liberman, A. M., Harris, K. S., & Cooper, F. S. Motor theory of speech perception: A reply to Lane's critical review. *Psychological Review*, 1970, **77**, 234–249.

Till, J. A. *Infants' discrimination of speech and nonspeech stimuli*. Paper presented at the annual meeting of the American Speech and Hearing Association, Houston, Texas, November, 1976.

Trehub, S. E. The discrimination of foreign speech contrasts by infants and adults. *Child Development*, 1976, **47**, 466–472.

Williams, L. The perception of stop consonant by Spanish–English bilinguals. *Perception & Psychophysics*, 1977, **21**, 289–297.

8

The Role
of Early Experience
in the Development
of Speech Perception

AMANDA C. WALLEY
DAVID B. PISONI
RICHARD N. ASLIN
Indiana University

I. INTRODUCTION

A substantial body of information has accumulated over the past 10 years concerning the speech-processing capacities of prelinguistic infants. Some of the major theoretical issues surrounding the precise nature of these capacities, particularly the extent of their innate specification and the role of early experience in their development, will be discussed in this chapter. In addition, several theories that attempt to

DEVELOPMENT OF PERCEPTION
Volume 1

explain these capacities will be summarized. A conceptual framework will be presented for evaluating these theories and, within this context, some of the processes and mechanisms underlying the perception of segmental contrasts will be examined. Particular emphasis is placed on the perception of voicing and place of articulation in stop consonants—two phonetic distinctions that have received considerable attention in both adult and infant speech perception research. However, the general approach to problems of perceptual development to be advocated here can be extended to other classes of speech sounds and other aspects of the phonology of natural language that eventually become part of the linguistic knowledge of all mature speaker–hearers.

II. BACKGROUND

The pioneering work of Eimas, Siqueland, Jusczyk, and Vigorito (1971) demonstrated that prelinguistic infants could discriminate speech sounds differing in voice onset time (VOT)—a major cue to voicing. VOT has been defined for word-initial stop consonants as the interval between the onset of the release burst and the onset of laryngeal pulsing (Lisker & Abramson, 1964). Stop consonants are those speech sounds that are produced by achieving complete closure of the relevant articulators and thus complete and brief obstruction of the airstream. The Eimas et al. study was motivated, in part, by two previous empirical findings concerning VOT. The first of these was that adults perceive variations in VOT categorically (e.g., Liberman, Harris, Kinney, & Lane, 1961); in contrast to the perception of other auditory stimuli, the discriminability of variations in these speech sounds appears to be limited by the listener's ability to identify them differentially. The second was that speakers' productions, sampled from 11 diverse languages, cluster around the same three modal values of VOT (Lisker & Abramson, 1964). These two findings suggested the existence of innate constraints on perception and production of the voicing contrast. Because infants represent a linguistically naive population, they seemed to provide an excellent opportunity for studying the roles of genetic and experiential factors in perceptual development. The finding that infants discriminated VOT differences categorically led Eimas et al. to conclude that infants were perceiving these sounds in a manner approximating categorical perception in adults. This in turn was interpreted as support for the inference that the perceptual categories of the young infant closely resemble those of the adult and that these perceptual categories are genetically specified, because infants have had little experience in the language-learning environment. Moreover, since the predominant view at the time was that categorical perception was unique to the perception of speech signals, Eimas *et al.* also argued that the infants perceived the sounds in a linguistic mode and that the mechanisms underlying speech perception were therefore part of the human's biological makeup (i.e., phonetic categories were thought to be innately specified). This view acknowledged, therefore, little, if any, influence of nongenetic, experiential factors in the development of speech perception. In a more recent discussion of infant speech perception, Eimas (1980) has essentially reasserted these claims and ignored theoretical arguments for integrating the role of early experience in accounts of the development of speech perception (Aslin & Pisoni, 1980b).

A.   Level of Analysis

The results from several lines of research in speech perception necessitate a substantial tempering and modification of the conclusions originally drawn from the Eimas *et al.* study. For example, it is now well established that categorical perception does not necessarily imply the operation of a linguistic mode of processing. First, categorical perception is not, as was once thought, unique to the perception of speech signals. Several studies (Cutting & Rosner, 1974; Miller, Wier, Pastore, Kelley, & Dooling, 1976; Pisoni, 1977) have demonstrated quite conclusively that there are classes of complex nonspeech signals that can be perceived categorically by adults. Moreover, it has been found that infants discriminate these same nonspeech signals categorically (Jusczyk, Pisoni, Walley, & Murray, 1980; Jusczyk, Rosner, Cutting, Foard, & Smith, 1977). In fact, this line of research has led to the proposal that psychophysical constraints on the resolution of temporal order underlie VOT perception (Hirsh, 1959; Pisoni, 1977). Jusczyk (1980; Chapter 7, this volume) has offered a psychophysical explanation of the stop/glide (e.g., /ba/ versus /wa/) distinction. Thus, the original claim that the infant's categorical discrimination indicates processing at a linguistic level is certainly not supported by evidence of uniqueness, because nonspeech signals are also discriminated categorically.

A second argument against the claim that categorical perception is mediated by linguistic analysis follows from the demonstration that categorical perception is not limited to human perception. Kuhl and Miller (1975, 1978) have shown that chinchillas exhibit discrimination of stop consonants that is similar to humans' even though such perception in chinchillas is obviously not mediated by the phonological system of any natural language. These two findings concerning categorical perception clearly render untenable the strong contention (Eimas *et al.*, 1971) that categorical-like perception implies perception in a linguistically relevant manner. The demonstration of categorical discrimination in infants is not, therefore, sufficient to warrant the claim that speech signals are processed by specialized perceptual mechanisms or that the infant's discrimination is directly constrained by the phonological structure of any particular natural language. Rather, it appears that there are general constraints on the mammalian auditory system and that infants (and chinchillas, for that matter) may simply be responding to the psychophysical or sensory properties of speech signals without any subsequent linguistic interpretation of these signals. It seems quite plausible, however, that certain languages have, in the manner that Stevens (1972) has suggested, exploited various properties of the auditory system in selecting the inventory of speech sounds to be used as phonological distinctions.

B.   Innate Specification of Perceptual Categories

These findings concerning categorical perception raise serious doubts about the inference that specific adult-like phonetic categories exist as such for the infant. The second of Eimas's claims—that the perceptual categories underlying phonetic segments, at least those for stop consonants, are innately specified is also subject to criticism. The original basis for this nativistic claim was twofold. First, although the precise locations of the boundaries between phonological categories for stops differed somewhat across languages, Lisker and Abramson (1964, 1967) found that production and perceptual categories tended to fall around at least one of three modal values along the VOT continuum corresponding to long-lead, short-lag, or long-lag distinctions in voicing. These investigators proposed, therefore, that VOT is a universal dimension for realizing voicing distinctions and is closely tied to the way in which laryngeal and supralaryngeal events are controlled in speech production. Second, because of the close correspondence between the infant's discrimination performance for the synthetic VOT stimuli and the Lisker and Abramson adult English perceptual data, Eimas (1975, 1978) argued that prelinguistic infants are predisposed to process VOT information and that this processing is achieved via the operation of an innately specified linguistic feature detector system that is independent of the infant's linguistic environment.

Despite the apparently sound reasoning behind this strong nativistic position, Eimas overlooked several important empirical findings. First, the precise location of the voicing boundaries described by Lisker and Abramson *do* differ somewhat from language to language, indicating that some fine tuning or realignment of perceptual categories must occur in development—an implication that Eimas (1975) later realized and discussed briefly. Indeed, this sort of perceptual modification might explain why Eimas failed to find any evidence for the discrimination of the prevoiced–voiced distinction in English infants (i.e., even the limited exposure that 2-month-olds have had to their native language might have exerted a change in sensitivity to this particular contrast). However, several studies have suggested that such a period of exposure is unlikely to produce any pronounced change in sensitivity along the VOT continuum and that infants are, in fact, sensitive to this contrast (but see Eilers, Gavin, & Wilson, 1979, for an exception to this position). Lasky, Syrdal-Lasky, and Klein (1975) found that infants raised in a Spanish-speaking environment do discriminate voicing contrasts that are not discriminated by Spanish-speaking adults, but that these infants fail to discriminate the contrast that straddles the Spanish adult voicing boundary. Additional evidence for the discrimination of voicing contrasts not found in the linguistic environment has been obtained by Streeter (1976) for Kikuyu infants and by Aslin, Pisoni, Hennessy, and Perey (1981) for English infants. Although Eimas's innate feature detector model can account for the ability of all infants to discriminate all three of the VOT contrasts, there certainly must be some influence exerted by experience during development. Moreover, the features used in discrimination are most likely auditory, and not phonetic.

A second problem with Eimas's argument is his use of the correspondence between the English adult and infant discrimination data to support the claim that voicing categories are perceived by infants in a linguistically relevant manner and are, therefore, genetically specified. If such a correspondence between the data from English infants and adults supports a linguistic level of analysis in these infants, at what level do Spanish infants, whose data do not correspond to that of Spanish adults, analyze these same stimuli? Apparently, Eimas did not see any conflict in the lack of correspondence between the Spanish adult and infant data. Yet, this lack of correspondence would seem to invalidate the claim that English infants process speech sounds (at least those differing in VOT) at a linguistic level.

Although the nativistic account of speech perception proposed by Eimas might be thought of as representing a significant advance over previous views of perceptual development that have assumed that speech production precedes or parallels perception (e.g., Fry, 1966), it seems clear that experience must, at some point in development, exert an influence on perception to produce the adult perceptual categories appropriate for speech. Indeed, the necessity of such environmental influence on language acquisition was obvious to Hockett (1958), who identified several essential "design features" that characterize all spoken languages and set them apart from communication systems of other organisms. Specifically, Hockett observed that inherent in all natural languages is a "duality of patterning." That is, there is a syntactic level of representation that consists of the arrangement of meaningful elements (morphemes or words), differences in which are realized by variations in the arrangement of meaningless elements (phonemes) at the phonological level of representation. The arbitrary relationship between sound and meaning in human language, and the resulting variability that exists across linguistic communities, necessitates the cultural transmission of any particular language. Cultural transmission of a language in turn requires a substantial amount of plasticity in learning and susceptibility to the influence of experiential factors in the language learner. However, what mechanisms underlie such responsiveness to environmental input, what precise effects linguistic experience exerts on perception, and when during development these experiential influences are most significant, have not yet been specified.

C. Mechanisms

Clearly, there is some selective modification during the course of phonological development. This is evidenced by the fact that different languages have different phonological systems and by the apparent difficulty adults have in recognizing phonetic contrasts that are phonologically irrelevant in their native language. The cross-language research of Lisker and Abramson (1967) supports the contention that only phonologically distinctive perceptual categories are perceived by adults and that linguistic experience plays a significant role in the categorization of speech sounds. As can be seen in Fig. 8.1, English, Thai, and Spanish adults are only able to differentially label those speech sounds that are used contrastively in their language. Cross-language research by Miyawaki, Strange, Verbrugge, Liberman, Jenkins, and Fujimura (1975) also provides support for the view that the phonologically distinctive /r/–/l/ contrast in English is perceived by English adults, but not by Japanese adults who do not use this contrast in their language.

Fig. 8.1 Adult labeling functions for synthetic labial, apical, and velar stop consonants differing in VOT obtained from native speakers of English, Thai, and Spanish. (Redrawn from Lisker & Abramson, 1967.)

VELARS

APICALS

LABIALS

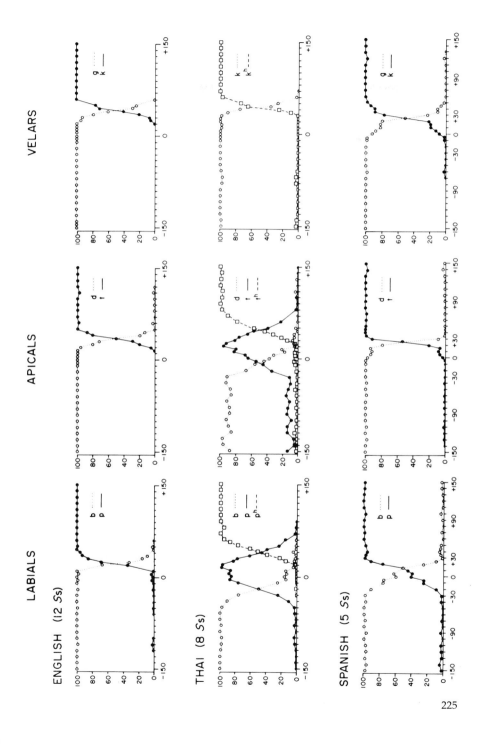

ENGLISH (12 Ss)

THAI (8 Ss)

SPANISH (5 Ss)

Training studies such as those summarized by Strange and Jenkins (1978) suggest further that, although the ability to perceive a phonologically irrelevant contrast may have been present at birth, adults who have lost or failed to develop the ability to discriminate that contrast are probably incapable of (re)acquiring it. Findings such as these have been interpreted as evidence that a neural substrate for the perception of phonologically irrelevant contrasts either failed to form during a critical or sensitive period or atrophied in the absence of experience with that contrast (Eimas, 1975). This neural theory of phonological development is passive, in the sense that it assumes that little, if any involvement, either attentional or productive, is required to maintain or create a particular perceptual ability. It cannot, therefore, explain how a child eventually realizes that different acoustic cues signal differences at the morphological level of language.

An alternative to this passive or strictly receptive account of the role of early experience in speech perception is the view that the failure to actively engage an attentional or productive system in the use of a particular phonetic contrast only depresses or attenuates subsequent discrimination performance on that contrast. The apparent difficulty adults have in discrimination may not be due to the degradation of any sensory or neural process per se, but may simply be a consequence of an attentional deficit similar to the process of acquired equivalence— a perceptual mode that involves learning to ignore distinctive differences among stimuli (Riley, 1968). This view assumes that perception of the relevant distinctive contrasts is so automatic as a result of processing strategies or mechanisms previously acquired by the listener that reacquisition of a phonologically irrelevant contrast is difficult, if not impossible, to obtain reliably in untrained adults who have had little experience in the laboratory (see Shiffrin & Schneider, 1977).

Pisoni, Aslin, Perey, and Hennessy (1982) have conducted several experiments showing that monolingual adult speakers of English are able to acquire a new voicing contrast. In one condition, the subjects had three response categories corresponding to prevoiced /ba/, /pa/, and /ba/. All subjects were consistent in labeling the synthetic VOT stimuli into three perceptual categories, despite the absence of highly prevoiced stops in syllable-initial position in English and despite the very limited exposure and training experience that preceded the labeling task. Prior to testing in this condition, subjects listened to several repetitions of the -70, 0, and $+70$ msec VOT stimuli (prevoiced /ba/, /ba/, and /pa/, respectively) to familiarize themselves with the stimulus contrasts and the appropriate responses. However, no overt response was required at this time and no feedback was provided, nor was any attempt made to train subjects in any explicit way. The identification results from this three-category labeling task are particularly striking when compared to the identification results from the more traditional two-alternative forced-choice task in which subjects simply categorized the stimuli into two groups corresponding to English /ba/ and /pa/ (see Fig. 8.2).

Note the classic two-category identification functions obtained in this task for /ba/ and /pa/ responses. The ABX discrimination functions for subjects in both conditions reveal two peaks in discrimination (see Fig. 8.2); i.e., even subjects in the two-category labeling condition discriminate stimuli in the voicing-lead region of the stimulus continuum despite the fact that these stimuli were all identified as belonging to the same phonological category (/ba/). This result was also obtained for subjects tested without prior labeling experience and without feedback. Apparently, phonologically irrelevant categories (such as prevoiced /ba/, for speakers of English) can be consistently categorized by adults even without very extensive training. Thus, the lack of exposure to specific phonetic contrasts during infancy and childhood does not appear to result in a complete neural loss or atrophy of the feature detectors that have been assumed to underlie phonetic categorization (Eimas, 1975).

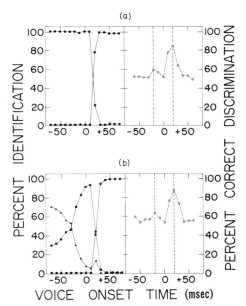

Fig. 8.2   Average identification and ABX discrimination functions for (a) two-category ($N = 10$) and (b) three-category ($N = 15$) labeling of synthetic VOT. (From Pisoni *et al.*, 1982.)

These new findings call into question the strong conclusions of Strange and Jenkins (1978) concerning the negligible effects of laboratory training on speech perception. Moreover, given that subjects could use three response categories consistently and without extensive training in the Pisoni *et al.* study, it is difficult to argue that there was any appreciable "selective" loss in perceptual sensitivity by these subjects in processing voicing information. The performance decrements observed in earlier studies on voicing discrimination may simply have been the result of criterion shifts and response constraints that were a part of the different subject strategies used in these tasks (see Carney, Widin, & Viemeister, 1977; Pisoni & Lazarus, 1974).

III. ROLE OF EARLY EXPERIENCE IN PERCEPTUAL DEVELOPMENT

There still exists a strong tendency toward theoretical simplification in describing the ontogeny of various infant speech-processing capacities (i.e., toward explaining them either in vague terms of learning or by recourse to strong nativistic accounts). In contrast, several researchers working in the area of visual system development have begun to appreciate the many diverse and interactive roles that genetic and experiential factors can play in the development of sensory and perceptual systems. For example, some of the neural mechanisms underlying visual functioning are not present at birth, nor do they emerge during development as a simple consequence of a genetically controlled plan or schedule. Instead, early visual experience does have some influence on the course of visual system development (see Chapters 1,2,3, and 4, Volume 2). This experience does not, however, totally control the outcome of visual system development as some genetically specified limits are clearly placed on how much and at what point such early experience can influence visual system functioning (for general reviews, see Blakemore, 1976; Grobstein & Chow, 1976).

It has become clear from the study of visual system function and its development that a simple dichotomy between nativistic and empiricist accounts of the process of development is simply inadequate to capture the multiple and seemingly complex genetic and environmental interactions that underlie normal perceptual development (see Chapter 2, Volume 2). Similarly, the following discussion is motivated primarily by the concern for providing a more explicit and coherent framework from which to view the course of perceptual development—particularly the development of speech perception. The need for such a framework in understanding the development of speech perception is particularly pressing in light of the many seemingly diverse and conflicting empirical findings that have appeared in the infant speech perception literature in recent years, some of which will be reviewed in following sections (see also Jusczyk, 1980; Chapter 7, this volume).

Gottlieb (1976a,b; Chapter 1, this volume) has provided an account of some of the possible roles that early experience can play in behavioral development. His conceptualization of these experiential processes seems to be particularly relevant and amenable to discussions of the development of speech perception (Aslin & Pisoni, 1980b). According to our application of Gottlieb's framework, there are four basic ways in which early experience could influence the development of speech-processing abilities. These possibilities are illustrated in Fig. 8.3.

First, a perceptual ability may be present at birth but require certain specific types of early experience to maintain the integrity of that ability. The absence or degradation of the requisite early experience can result in either a partial or a complete loss of the perceptual ability, a loss that may be irreversible despite subsequent experience. For example, the work of Hubel and Wiesel (1965, 1970) on the visual system of the kitten showed, among other things, that the full complement of neural cells responsible for binocular vision was present at birth, although

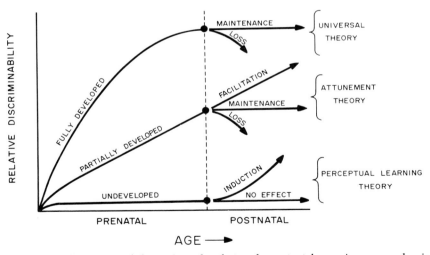

Fig. 8.3   Illustration of the major roles that early postnatal experience can play in modifying the relative discriminability of speech sounds. Three general classes of theories are shown here to account for the development of speech-sound discrimination: universal theory, attunement theory, and perceptual learning theory. (From Aslin & Pisoni, 1980b.)

they lost their function if the kittens were deprived of binocular vision during a sensitive period. Early experience in this case served then to maintain the functional integrity of the mechanisms underlying binocular vision (see also Blakemore, 1978).

Second, an ability may be only partially developed at birth, requiring specific types of early experience to facilitate or attune the further development of that perceptual ability. The lack of early experience with these stimuli that may serve a facilitating function could result either in the absence of any further development or a loss of that ability when compared to its level at birth. As an example of a facilitating effect of experience, Gottlieb himself has shown that ducklings modify their subsequent preference and recognition of species-specific calls by their own vocalizations prior to and shortly after hatching (Gottlieb, 1976a). If these self-produced vocalizations are prevented from occurring (through devocalization techniques) in the early stages of development, the developmental rate of preference for species-specific calls declines and the ability to discriminate and recognize particular calls is substantially reduced (Gottlieb, 1975).

Third, a perceptual ability may be absent at birth, and its development may depend on a process of induction based on specific early experiences of the organism. The presence of a particular ability, then, would depend to a large extent upon the presence of a particular type of early experience. For example, it is well known that specific early experience presented to young ducklings leads to imprinting to a particular stimulus object and can be taken as an instance of inducing a behavioral preference (Hess, 1972). Thus, in this case, the presence of a particular early experience is *necessary* for the subsequent development of a particular preference or tendency.

Finally, early experience may, of course, exert no role at all in the development of a particular perceptual ability. That is, the ability may be either present or absent at birth and it may remain, decline, or improve in the absence of any particular type of early experience. Absence of experiential effects is difficult to identify and often leads to unwarranted conclusions, especially those that assume an induction process might be operative. For example, it is quite common for investigators to argue that if an ability is absent at birth, but then observed to be present sometime after birth, the ability must have been learned (see Eilers *et al.*, 1979). In terms of the conceptual framework just outlined, this could be an instance of induction. Yet it is quite possible that the ability simply unfolded developmentally according to a genetically specified maturational schedule—a schedule that required no particular type of early experience in the environment. Fantz, Fagen, & Miranda (1975) provide an example of this by demonstrating a visual preference for patterned stimuli in both full-term and premature infants. This unfolding of an ability may be subsumed under the general class of maturational theories of development. As another example, although general motor activity is necessary to prevent the atrophy of various muscle systems, many of the classic studies by Gesell in the 1930s demonstrated that no specific training experience was necessary for infants to acquire the ability to walk (Gesell & Ames, 1940). Thus, the complexity of these numerous alternatives—maintenance, facilitation, induction, and maturation—and their possible interactions should serve to caution researchers against drawing premature conclusions about the developmental course of specific perceptual abilities.

To make clear the relevance of Gottlieb's scheme of the roles of early experience to the development of speech perception, four general classes of theories of perceptual development that parallel the effects of early experience as described by Gottlieb will be outlined. After the assumptions of these perceptual theories are described, several examples from the infant speech perception literature will be selected to illustrate the usefulness of this conceptualization. The classes of theories of perceptual development to be considered here are universal theory, attunement theory, perceptual learning theory, and maturational theory.

Universal theory assumes that, at birth, infants are capable of discriminating all the possible phonetic contrasts that may be used phonologically in any natural language. According to this view, early experience functions to maintain the ability to discriminate phonologically relevant distinctions—those actually presented to the infant in the environment. However, the absence of exposure to phonologically irrelevant contrasts results in a selective loss of the ability to discriminate those specific contrasts. The perceptual mechanisms responsible for this loss of sensitivity may be either neural or attentional or both. These two alternatives also make several specific predictions concerning the possible reacquisition of discriminative abilities in adults, an important topic in its own right, as mentioned previously.

Attunement theory assumes that, at birth, all infants are capable of discriminating at least some of the possible phonetic contrasts contained in the world's languages, but that the infant's discriminative capacities are incompletely developed and/or possibly quite broadly tuned. Early experience, therefore, functions to align and/or to sharpen these partially developed discriminative abilities. Phonologically relevant contrasts in the language-learning environment would then become more finely tuned with experience and phonologically irrelevant contrasts would either remain broadly tuned or become attenuated in the absence of specific environmental stimulation.

In contrast with the other two views, perceptual learning theory assumes that the ability to discriminate any particular phonetic contrast is dependent on specific early experience with that contrast in the language-learning environment. The rate of development could be very fast or very slow depending on the relative importance of the phonetic contrasts during early life, the relative psychophysical discriminability of the acoustic cues underlying the phonetic contrast compared with other phonetic contrasts, and the attentional state of the infant. According to this view, however, phonologically irrelevant contrasts would never be discriminated better than the phonologically relevant ones present in the language-learning environment.

Finally, maturational theory assumes that the ability to discriminate a particular phonetic contrast is independent of any specific early experience and simply unfolds according to a predetermined developmental schedule. All possible phonetic contrasts would be discriminated equally well irrespective of the language environment, although the age at which specific phonetic contrasts could be discriminated would depend on the developmental level of the underlying sensory mechanism. For example, if infants did not show sensitivity to high frequencies until later in development, one would not expect them to discriminate phonetic contrasts that are differentiated by high-frequency information.

These classes of theories of perceptual development make rather specific predictions concerning the developmental course of speech perception in infants and young children. It is important to note here that probably no single class of theory will uniquely account for the development of all speech contrasts. Rather, it may be the case that some hybrid of the theories provides the best description of the development of specific classes of speech-sound discrimination. In fact, this view of parallel developmental processes appears to be supported by current empirical findings.

A. Voicing in Stop Consonants

The Eimas *et al.* (1971) study generated a great deal of interest in the infant's speech-processing capacities (see Jusczyk, 1980; Chapter 7, this volume). Since then, infants' discrimination of over two dozen VOT contrasts has been studied and positive evidence of discrimination has been obtained for all contrasts that crossed the English voiced–voiceless boundary. However, for contrasts that crossed a prevoiced–voiced boundary, the only positive evidence of discrimination was obtained with infants whose native language environment contained this phonological contrast for stop consonants (see Eilers *et al.*, 1979; see also Aslin & Pisoni, 1980a, for an important critique of this study).

Whereas these results on the discrimination of voicing contrasts by infants might appear to provide strong support for perceptual learning theory, there are findings that clearly conflict with the theory's predictions. For example, several contrasts have been tested with infants whose native language environment was not English (e.g., Lasky *et al.*, 1975; Streeter, 1976). Positive discrimination on the majority of these contrasts was observed despite the fact that these specific contrasts were not phonologically distinctive and therefore were unlikely to occur in the infants' language-learning environment. However, other VOT studies have failed to provide evidence that infants discriminate contrasts that are present in their language-learning environment (e.g., Lasky *et al.*, 1975). Within the conceptual framework being proposed here, these seemingly contradictory results can be reconciled and a systematic account of them offered in terms of what is currently known about the psychophysical properties of these speech signals and the developmental processes responsible for realizing the discrimination.

There is now sufficient evidence to suggest that the basis for VOT discrimination by infants is probably not directly related to phonetic categorization or a linguistic mode of analysis (see Stevens & Klatt, 1974). Pisoni (1977) has demonstrated that when the relative onset times of two-component tones are varied, adults perceive such variations in these nonspeech stimuli categorically. The identification data indicate that the tone-onset-time (TOT) continuum is parsed into three discrete categories; stimuli with onset differences greater than 20 msec are perceived as having either leading or lagging onsets, and those with onset differences less than 20 msec as having simultaneous onsets. Pisoni (1977) has also shown that the peaks in the discrimination functions for these stimuli coincide quite closely with these values.

Similar discrimination performance with these TOT stimuli has been observed in infants, although the precise location of the infants' category boundaries (as inferred from the discrimination data) differs somewhat from the adults' (Jusczyk *et al.*, 1980). The adult category boundary values observed by Pisoni for the TOT continuum also correspond very closely to the loci along the VOT continuum of the three voicing categories found earlier by Lisker and Abramson (1964, 1967) across a wide variety of languages. This correspondence, together with the infant and chinchilla data, suggests that the categorical perception of VOT information may simply reflect an inherent limitation of the mammalian auditory system to resolve temporal differences between two acoustic events—specifically, in the case of voicing, between laryngeal and supralaryngeal ones. The resolution of the temporal relation between these two events is greater at certain regions (± 20 msec) along the VOT stimulus continuum that correspond roughly to the psychophysical threshold for resolving these differences (Hirsh, 1959).

This psychophysical account of VOT perception is attractive in that it can account for both the infant and chinchilla data without recourse to the assumption of innate linguistic (i.e., phonetic) knowledge. Moreover, it can account for the cross-language similarities that have been observed for infant perception. However, two questions are immediately apparent from this analysis. First, why is there so little evidence for the discrimination of VOT in the -20 msec region of voicing-lead in the infant literature? Second, what role does the environment play in tuning the perceptual mechanism responsible for processing temporal order information? In other words, what accounts for cross-language differences in the adult perceptual data?

The first question can be addressed by observing that, even with nonspeech signals differing in relative onset time, discrimination of onset differences is better in the positive region of the stimulus continuum than in the negative region. The same relation can be found in the original Lisker and Abramson (1967) discrimination data obtained with Thai subjects (see Fig. 8.4a). The smaller incidence of discrimination of VOT differences in the region of voicing-lead is probably due to the generally poorer ability of the auditory system to resolve temporal differences in which a lower-frequency component precedes a higher one (Danaher, Osberger, & Pickett, 1973).

Lower discriminability of stimuli in the minus region of the VOT continuum cannot completely account for the overall performance of infants, because all three positive instances of discrimination of prevoiced and voiced stop contrasts reported in the literature involved infants from linguistic environments where this contrast is used. Thus, it can be further argued that early linguistic experience must play some role in modifying the discriminability of speech stimuli depending on the relative predominance of certain VOT values in the productions of adults.

Differences in the relative discriminability of VOT contrasts are yet another indication that early environmental experience plays an important role in perceptual development. Although there are two regions of high discriminability even in the functions obtained from speakers of English, a language that does not have the prevoiced–voiced contrast,

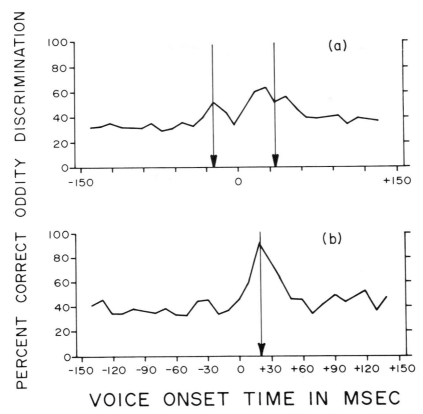

Fig. 8.4   Oddity discrimination data obtained from adult speakers of (a) Thai (N = 8) and (b) English (N = 5) for synthetic bilabial stop consonants differing in VOT. (Pooled 2-step labial discrimination data from Lisker & Abramson, 1967.)

the peak in the minus region is substantially lower than the Thai discrimination data (see Fig. 8.4a). A very similar finding is apparent in the discrimination data of Williams (1974) for Spanish and English subjects and in the data of Pisoni *et al.* (1982) with naive adult English subjects (see Fig. 8.2). The Spanish subjects in the Williams study displayed a much broader region of heightened discriminability extending well into the area encompassing the location of the English voicing boundary.

The available data on the development of voicing perception, therefore, provide good support for the attunement theory outlined earlier, as there appears to be a partially specified ability at birth to process temporal order information. Perceptual sensitivity to temporal order differences such as those present in synthetic stimuli is, however, susceptible to the influence of early experience, which apparently selectively modifies the distinctiveness and location of the regions of sensitivity along a stimulus continuum such as VOT.

Jusczyk (1980; Chapter 7, this volume) has suggested how such modification might be achieved. Experience in a particular linguistic environment could direct the infant or child to make use of other prominent acoustic cues to voicing that occur regularly in certain phonetic environments as a consequence of phonological constraints specific to that language. This experience would result in a differential perceptual weighting of the various cues to voicing and produce a change in the perceptual salience and location of regions of sensitivity along the VOT continuum. Although Jusczyk has proposed that the infant may only begin to attend to relevant acoustic cues for phonetic contrasts when speech begins to assume a communicative (i.e., meaning-related) purpose, it is also quite possible that a communicative context (i.e., dyadic interchange) acts as a vehicle for directing the child's attention to the subtle acoustic features of the speech signal. If the latter explanation is correct, one role of social interaction is to *focus* the child's perceptual capacities and attention, rather than to trigger a new level of analysis related to referential skills. Clearly, these issues require extensive study of infants during the early months of speech production (12–18 months of age) and, unfortunately, such studies are virtually absent from the speech perception literature.

B. Place of Articulation for Stop Consonants

Because the acoustic cues to place of articulation have in the past so successfully eluded any simple characterization, this phonetic contrast has been the subject of extensive research and the resulting information about place perception has been of major importance in the formulation of speech perception theories. Although several acoustic properties, such as formant transitions, burst spectra, and direction of rapid spectrum change following consonantal release, have been implicated in the perception of place of articulation (e.g., Cooper, Delattre, Liberman, Borst, & Gerstman, 1952; Liberman, Cooper, Shankweiler, & Studdert-Kennedy, 1967; Stevens, 1975; Stevens & Blumstein, 1975), attempts to state unequivocally which acoustic properties or correlates constitute the primary perceptual cue for this feature have been complicated by the fact that all of these acoustic features may vary for a given place of articulation in different phonetic contexts. The failure to find an absolute, invariant set of acoustic properties that correspond to place of articulation in all environments has led some theorists to argue more generally that invariant cues do not exist for phonetic features—that the relation between the acoustic signal and the phonetic percept is not a direct one (e.g., Liberman *et al.*, 1967). Rather, it is claimed that the invariance of the phonetic percept results from the interpretation of acoustic cues in a manner that is context dependent. To explain how such contextually determined interpretation could be achieved, one class of speech perception theories has viewed the speech perception process as an active one in which the identification of phonetic segments depends on some sort of computational or look-up procedure that involves higher-level linguistic knowledge that imposes structure on the incoming speech waveform (e.g., Chomsky & Miller, 1963; Chomsky & Halle, 1968; Liberman *et al.*, 1967; Stevens & Halle, 1967; Stevens & House, 1972).

In support of context dependent views of speech perception is the finding that vastly different acoustic cues may give rise to the same phonetic percept, and the converse finding that the same acoustic segment in different contexts may give rise to the perception of different phonetic segments (Liberman *et al.*, 1967; Liberman, Delattre, & Cooper, 1952; Schatz, 1954). Moreover, the finding that potential cues for place of articulation are context dependent has been an important justification for the claim that speech perception involves specialized processing mechanisms (e.g., Liberman & Studdert-Kennedy, 1978). Several studies have shown that infants discriminate place contrasts categorically in speech contexts, but not in nonspeech contexts (for a summary, see Jusczyk, 1980), providing additional support for this type of theory.

There are, however, two potential sources of evidence against such context dependent views of speech perception. First, if linguistic knowledge is actually a prerequisite for the perception of speech, this would seem to require that experience in speech perception and/or production is necessary for the perception of specific contextual dependencies. However, this implication is challenged to some extent by the results of infant speech perception studies showing that infants, with only very limited exposure to the numerous phonetic distinctions employed by various languages and with virtually no experience in the consistent articulation of these distinctions, are capable of discriminating certain acoustic variations across adult phonemic categories while ignoring within-category variations. Although active theories of speech perception might still account for these abilities by positing innate knowledge of phonological rules, Eimas (1975) has proposed instead that the infant data is better accommodated by simply assuming the existence of a linguistic feature detector system. He has argued that the human auditory system might be endowed with feature or property detectors that are sensitive to the restricted ranges of acoustic information that signal phonetic features (see also Stevens, 1975). Thus, infants may be predisposed to perceive certain speech stimuli in a linguistically relevant way. As discussed previously, it is more parsimonious to attribute categorical perception, at least of the VOT continuum, to basic psychophysical constraints on the auditory system, rather than to linguistically oriented feature detectors.

A second source of evidence against context dependent theories of speech perception derives from research that attempts to specify in detail the psychoacoustic constraints on the mammalian auditory system. The importance of these constraints is that they provide the basis for a mode of perception that accounts, in part, for the invariance of the phonetic (voicing) percept and thus the child's ability to acquire voicing as a phonemic contrast. Although it seems reasonable to assume that a psychophysical basis for the categorical perception of variations in the cues to place of articulation may also exist, such a basis is less obvious in view of the greater contextual variability of the hypothesized cues for this feature. Indeed, Bailey, Summerfield, and Dorman (1977) have provided evidence that the psychophysical boundaries obtained for a set of nonspeech frequency- and amplitude-modulated sine waves, which were modeled after the formant structure of stop consonant–vowel (CV) syllables, do not correspond to the phonetic boundaries obtained for the speech stimuli. Thus, they interpret this finding as support for the existence of some specialized speech-processing mechanism. However, Pisoni (1979), using comparable nonspeech stimuli, has shown that the location and extent of perceptual categories are not necessarily rigidly controlled by any simple physically defined invariant, such as the direction of frequency change but are influenced by contextual information as well. This finding may account for the boundary differences obtained by Bailey *et al.* In any event, a number of investigators (Kewley-Port, 1980; Searle, Jacobson, & Rayment, 1979; Stevens & Blumstein, 1978, 1980) who have employed new methods of speech analysis that attempt to incorporate known psychophysical and psychophysiological properties of the human peripheral auditory system into models of the initial stages of speech processing, have been more successful in finding invariant acoustic cues for place of articulation. This work would seem to argue strongly against active, context dependent theories of speech perception.

Whereas the results of studies of infant perception of place of articulation might be expected to address the viability of active, context dependent theories of speech perception, only a few studies have actually addressed the question of whether or not the perceptual equivalence of different and/or contextually varying acoustic features exists for infants (Eilers, 1977; Fodor, Garrett, & Brill, 1975; Kuhl, 1979). Investigations of infant speech perception have, for the most part, only examined discrimination of stimuli varying along a single acoustic dimension. Thus, although it has been shown that infants are capable of categorically discriminating place distinctions (for a review, see Jusczyk, 1980), it is not yet clear from these investigations that the perceptual equivalence of different and/or contextually varying acoustic segments exists for infants, nor that these infant data can be used to refute active, context dependent theories.

The recent work of Stevens and Blumstein (1978, 1980) represents the most substantial theoretical account of the infant's perception of place of articulation. Because several studies have shown that infants can discriminate place-of-articulation differences (e.g., Bush & Williams, 1978; Eimas, 1974; Leavitt, Brown, Morse, & Graham, 1976; Miller & Morse, 1976; Moffitt, 1971; Morse, 1972), Stevens and Blumstein object to the view, entailed in active speech perception theories, that only after learning to organize contextually diverse and variable acoustic features into their appropriate adult phonemic categories, does the child come to perceive place-of-articulation distinctions. Instead, they propose that some innate mechanism must mediate the invariance that they assume is entailed in the discrimination of such distinctions by infants. It should be emphasized, however, that studies to date have merely shown that infants are capable of discriminating place-of-articulation differences in stimuli varying along a particular acoustic dimension (i.e., formant starting frequency and direction). They have not demonstrated that infants perceive syllables such as /da/ and /di/ as being similar with respect to the initial phonetic segment and evidence for perceptual constancy cannot, therefore, be inferred from any of these simple discrimination studies. Until it is shown that infants are able to sort different and/or contextually variant acoustic features into their appropriate adult phonemic categories, theories that require experience in the perception and/or production of these features are not, as Eimas (1975) contends, and Stevens and Blumstein implicitly assume, invalidated on the basis of the current data from infant speech perception research (but see Pisoni, 1978, for other criticisms of these theories).

Whereas it has not yet been demonstrated that infants have any initial basis for recognizing that contextual variations in acoustic features belong to certain phonetic categories, Stevens and Blumstein are reluctant to abandon the notion that some invariant property exists in the acoustic correlates of each particular place-of-articulation category. They have argued that, even though various context dependent features, such as starting frequency and direction of formant transitions and release bursts, are separately observable in spectrograms, the auditory system does not necessarily process these features independently of one another. Instead, Stevens and Blumstein claim that the auditory system integrates these features in such a way that the gross spectral properties associated with each place-of-articulation category provide the acoustic invariance that underlies the constancy of the phonetic percept and that must, in their opinion, mediate infant perception. The search for invariant acoustic correlates of phonetic features, and thus for a means of automatic, passive recognition of phonetic distinctions, represents a notable digression from earlier proposals that speech perception proceeds primarily via the active operations entailed, for example, in analysis-by-synthesis (Stevens & Halle, 1967; Stevens & House, 1972) or by reference to motor–articulatory patterns (e.g., Liberman *et al.*, 1967).

Stevens and Blumstein's (1978, 1980) assertion that there are distinctive and context independent acoustic properties associated with different places of stop consonant articulation derives from both theoretically based expectations about the gross shape of the short-term spectrum sampled at consonantal release and spectral analyses they have carried out on natural speech. According to these criteria, labials (/b/, /p/) are characterized by a diffuse–falling spectrum, alveolars (/d/, /t/) by a diffuse–rising spectrum, and velars (/g/, /k/) by a prominent midfrequency spectral peak. Examples of these are shown in Fig. 8.5. These putatively invariant acoustic cues for place of articulation—location and diffuseness of spectral energy at stimulus onset—are, of course, very similar to the compact versus diffuse and grave versus acute features originally proposed by Jakobson, Fant, and Halle (1952). Stevens and Blumstein have also maintained that these spectral properties may be used to characterize nasals of different places of articulation and that the spectrum sampled at vowel offset of a VC syllable should exhibit the same properties as the onset spectrum for a given place of articulation. The characteristics of onset spectra are determined by the burst spectrum and the initial portions of the formant transitions at voicing onset. The same spectral shapes can be obtained for synthetic

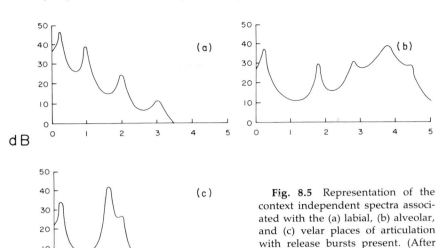

dB

FREQUENCY (kHz)

Fig. 8.5 Representation of the context independent spectra associated with the (a) labial, (b) alveolar, and (c) velar places of articulation with release bursts present. (After Stevens & Blumstein, 1978.)

stimuli containing only formant transitions and no burst, but these shapes are enhanced by the presence of the burst. Stimuli with only the release burst present do not yield these distinctive spectral shapes.

Because Stevens and Blumstein (1978) found that only those synthetic stimuli with distinctive spectral characteristics were identified consistently by adults according to place of articulation, they proposed that the auditory system also performs a short-term spectral analysis at stimulus onset for a stop consonant. According to their account, formant transitions are not the primary cue to place of articulation in CV syllables. Rather, identification of this phonetic feature is achieved through the operation of property detectors that, at the peripheral stage of auditory processing, are tuned to the invariant properties of the onset spectrum. They argue that it is the operation of these detectors that accounts for the infant's ability to discriminate stimuli with different places of articulation—particularly when these stimuli contain both formant transitions and release bursts. This assertion concerning the relative discriminability of stimuli with and without release bursts is based on the earlier work of Bush and Williams (1978) and may not be valid, as these investigators failed to actually examine discrimination of pairs of stimuli with and without bursts.

The claim that the context independent properties just described provide the basis for perception of a given place of articulation might be challenged by the finding that adults are able to identify differentially two-formant synthetic stimuli with respect to place of articulation (Cooper *et al.*, 1952; Delattre, Liberman, & Cooper, 1955; Liberman *et al.*, 1952). These stimuli do not, as Stevens and Blumstein claim (1978), yield spectra with the distinctive, contextually invariant shapes that purportedly underlie the perception of this phonetic feature. Stevens and Blumstein agree that, in two-formant stimuli, only the second-formant transition can signal differences in place of articulation. They attempt to explain the adult's ability to use this context dependent cue in terms of the co-occurrence of the primary, invariant, and secondary, context dependent features in the full-formant stimuli. Because adults have learned the co-occurrences between primary and secondary cues through repeated exposure to them in the linguistic environment, they can, in the absence or distortion of the primary attributes of the stimulus, use the secondary cue of starting frequency and direction of formant transitions to identify place of articulation. In terms of the theories previously outlined, Stevens and Blumstein's account incorporates certain aspects of both universal and perceptual learning theory. Perception of place of articulation is claimed to be mediated by innately specified mechanisms sensitive to the onset spectra of stimuli. By this account, experience presumably functions to maintain the integrity of these perceptual categories. However, perception of place of articulation is eventually also mediated by the detection of formant transition information, once sensitivity to this information is induced by linguistic experience—specifically, by virtue of the co-occurrence of these secondary cues with the primary stimulus attributes that determine the overall shape of the spectrum at stimulus onset.

By proposing that formant transitions constitute a secondary, learned cue to place of articulation, Stevens and Blumstein's theory makes several predictions about infants' perception of place of articulation (see Walley, 1979). Foremost of these is the prediction that infants should not be able to discriminate place of articulation differences in two-formant stimuli, as these stimuli do not, according to Stevens and Blumstein, yield the distinctive, contextually invariant spectra of their full-formant counterparts and only contain formant-transition information. According to Stevens and Blumstein's theory, formant transitions provide only a secondary, learned cue to place of articulation and infants should not, therefore, be able to use this cue to discriminate two-formant stimuli differing in place of articulation in the same way that adults do. If, however, formant transitions *do* constitute the major cue for this phonetic feature, infants should be able to discriminate differences in two-formant stimuli even without specific experience with them.

With regard to previous demonstrations that infants discriminate place of articulation differences (Leavitt et al., 1976; Miller & Morse, 1976; Moffitt, 1971; Morse, 1972), Stevens and Blumstein would, of course, assert that it is the distinctive shape of the onset spectra of the three-formant stimuli employed in these studies that underlies the infant's discrimination. However, Eimas (1974) found that infants presented with two-formant stimuli could discriminate labial versus alveolar stops that were differentiated solely by the second-formant transition. It cannot be asserted that discrimination here is mediated by a divergence in spectral shape if stimuli containing only the first two formants do not possess the distinctive and invariant spectra contained in three-formant stimuli. Rather, this suggests that it is the second-formant transition that provides the basis for the infant's discrimination, although, according to Stevens and Blumstein, infants should not be able to use this cue exclusively in discrimination of place of articulation.

Walley (1979) recently attempted to establish which of these two theories offers the best account of place perception by conducting a more extensive examination of infants' discrimination of place differences in synthetic two-formant stimuli. After the two-formant stimuli for this test were constructed and their onset spectra analyzed, it was observed, however, that the onset spectra of the labial and velar stimuli (see Fig. 8.6) were, contrary to Stevens and Blumstein's report, very similar in overall shape to those of their full-formant counterparts—a discrepancy that is perhaps due to the superior quality of the more recent digital synthesizer and the extensive spectrographic analyses used in the construction of Walley's stimuli. Of course, the two-formant alveolar stimulus differed from the full-formant one (an obvious consequence of removing the upper formants) and was actually very similar to the two-formant velar stimulus.

These initial findings concerning the onset spectra of the two-formant stimuli clearly render Stevens and Blumstein's proposal that formant transitions constitute secondary, learned cues to place of articulation of little predictive value. It may well be that spectral attributes mediate place perception, but because the putatively primary, invariant spectral cues typically are present even in so-called degraded (i.e., two-formant) stimuli, there would seem to be no necessity for an infant to learn to use contextually diverse formant-transition starting frequency and direction as an additional cue to place of articulation (at least in the case

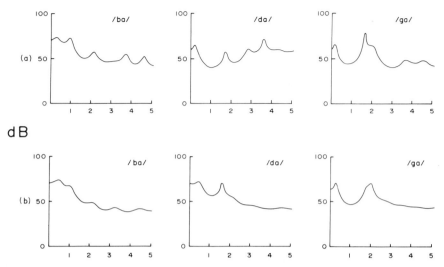

Fig. 8.6 Onset spectra for the (a) full cue and (b) partial cue labial, alveolar, and velar stimuli used by Walley (1979).

of the labial versus alveolar and labial versus velar two-formant contrasts). Thus, an account in terms of perceptual learning seems to be ruled out. Moreover, if, as Stevens and Blumstein maintain, it is differential sensitivity to spectral shape that mediates perception of place-of-articulation differences, infants should indeed be able to discriminate the labial versus alveolar and labial versus velar contrasts in the two-formant stimuli. Although Stevens and Blumstein's theory actually makes the same predictions about infants' discrimination of two-formant stimuli as does the notion that formant transitions provide the primary cue to this feature, Walley still hoped to differentiate the two accounts on the basis of their predictions concerning infants' discrimination of the alveolar versus velar two-formant contrast. Because the spectra for these two stimuli are very similar, infants should not, according to Stevens and Blumstein's theory, be able to make this discrimination. If formant-transition starting frequency and direction are used as cues to place of articulation, infants might be expected to discriminate this contrast as well.

Using a variation of the operant head-turning (OHT) procedure (Moore, Wilson, & Thompson, 1977), in which the infant learns to make a directional head turn in anticipation of the presentation of a visual stimulus that serves as a reinforcer whenever a change in a speech stimulus occurs (see Fig. 8.7 for an illustration of the experimental

Fig. 8.7   Testing set-up in the sound-attenuated booth employed for testing infants' discrimination in the operant head-turning paradigm. (From Walley, 1979.)

setup), Walley (1979) assessed infants' discrimination of place-of-articulation differences. She was able to verify previous reports that prelinguistic infants can discriminate full-cue exemplars of CV syllables differing in place of articulation (/ba/, /da/, and /ga/). In addition, infants were found to be capable of discriminating these contrasts when they are specified by only two-formant, partial-cue stimuli. Most important with respect to Stevens and Blumstein's theory, a number of infants were able to discriminate the partial-cue alveolar versus velar contrast. This result is not predicted by Stevens and Blumstein, since the onset spectra for these stimuli are very similar. Moreover, this result would seem to suggest that for the other two contrasts (labial versus alveolar and labial versus velar), where onset spectra and formant-transition cues are confounded, it may be the latter cue that mediates discrimination.

The infant data on discrimination of place-of-articulation differences in two-formant stimuli argue rather strongly against one of the main assertions of Stevens and Blumstein's theory—namely, that formant transitions constitute only secondary, learned cues to place of articulation perception in stop consonants and that onset spectra differences are the primary mediator of place discrimination. If formant-transition starting frequency and direction can cue place of articulation, obviously, these cues are not learned in any traditional sense, because infants can, indeed, discriminate two-formant stimuli at an early age. Because formant-transition information is contextually variable, presumably the child would have to learn how contextual variations in these cues can continue to signal the same place of articulation—a requirement that is probably most in accord with either universal or attunement theory. (However, note that it has not been determined that infants can discriminate contextual variations in formant transitions for a given place of articulation. For example, it is not known whether they can discriminate /da/ versus /di/ on the basis of information contained only in the formant transitions.) Even if onset spectra do mediate place perception and experience functions simply to maintain sensitivity to this cue, it appears that contextually invariant and distinctive spectral cues generally characterize even such degraded stimuli as two-formant ones and logically there would, therefore, be little reason for learning to use the secondary cues. It would, of course, be important to examine the spectra of other two-formant stimuli containing different vowels to ensure that this observation can be generalized to other contexts. Regardless of which cue infants use to discriminate place differences, Stevens and Blumstein's distinction between primary, innate versus secondary, learned cues does not seem to be a valid or useful one for understanding the perception of place of articulation or its development. (For further criticisms of Stevens and Blumstein's static theory, see Kewley-Port, 1980.)

A strong test of Stevens and Blumstein's theory would entail manipulating spectral and transitional cues independently of one another in labial, alveolar, and velar stimuli and ascertaining which cue controls perception. Although Walley's (1979) work revealed that this is not possible with two-formant stimuli, Walley and Carrell (1980) have gathered identification data from adults for synthetic stimuli containing conflicting spectral onset and transition cues to place of articulation. In general, their results indicate that listeners use dynamic transition information more often than they do the spectral information in identifying place of articulation. The notion that listeners use the dynamic information contained in the onsets of CV syllables (i.e., *changes* in spectral energy over time, as opposed to the static spectral sample at stimulus onset proposed by Stevens and Blumstein), has served as the basis for Kewley-Port's (1980) work. Fig. 8.8 shows examples of the running spectral displays used by Kewley-Port who has found that these representations contain time-varying features that provide an invariant description of place of articulation for voiced stop consonants.

IV. SUMMARY AND CONCLUSIONS

From this consideration of voicing and place perception, it should be apparent that none of the major roles of experience discussed pre-

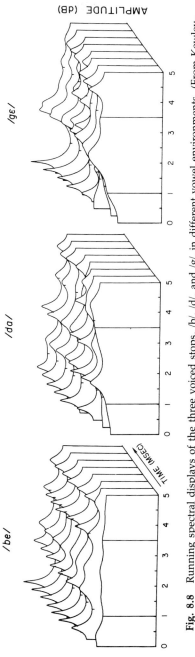

Fig. 8.8 Running spectral displays of the three voiced stops, /b/, /d/, and /g/, in different vowel environments. (From Kewley-Port, 1980.)

247

viously can be uniformly invoked to account for the development of the abilities needed to discriminate the various contrasts found in spoken language. Perception of voicing appears to be best described by attunement theory and is subject to retuning and alignment effects as a result of linguistic experience. Perception of place of articulation, however, may best be accounted for by universal theory, where the effect of experience is to maintain or collapse already specified perceptual categories. Unfortunately, there is, at the present time, no cross-linguistic adult or infant data on the perception of place of articulation to further clarify the role of experience in the development of this distinction. However, this view of the diverse effects of experience on the development of speech perception is buttressed by an examination of the course of perceptual development for other classes of speech sounds, such as fricatives, liquids, and vowels, within the framework being proposed (for a discussion, see Aslin & Pisoni, 1980b). For example, the auditory system of humans may well be specialized for processing certain very specific types of acoustic attributes at an early age. If some phonetic contrasts in language happen to have these distinctive acoustic properties in common, the infant should be able to discriminate these speech signals with practically no experience in the language-learning environment short of sensory deprivation. If, however, a certain amount of neural maturation or specific early experience is required for discrimination, a delay or developmental lag in discrimination of these contrasts might be anticipated.

This parallel interactive view of the role of early experience in the development of speech perception has a precedent in recent work on visual system development (see Aslin & Dumais, 1980). This work emphasizes the fact that parallel developmental mechanisms (analogous to three of the general classes of speech theories discussed) can operate upon different aspects of the same sensory input. However, only a very detailed description of the development of discriminative abilities will permit a distinction between the various types of complex interactions between genetic and experiential factors in determining speech-processing capacities. Such a description requires a better understanding of the infant's basic auditory capacities and more sophisticated experimental procedures for measuring discrimination and other aspects of perceptual analysis. For example, more detailed information about the infant's frequency-resolving capabilities is necessary before a really complete understanding of the infant's perception of more complex speech stimuli, such as those involving place contrasts, can be obtained. Fortunately, these problems are beginning to be addressed by some researchers (Sinnott, Pisoni, & Aslin, 1981; Trehub, Schneider, & Endman, 1980). In addition, if questions about the discriminative abilities of infants to resolve small differences between speech signals at a purely sensory level are to be answered, many more data points from individual subjects need to be obtained to produce more detailed and reliable discrimination functions (see Aslin *et al.*, 1981; Aslin & Pisoni, 1980b). Furthermore, to study questions surrounding the development of perceptual constancy and categorization of speech signals—abilities that are probably more relevant to the larger task of language acquisition, measures of generalization, and perceptual similarity analogous to adult identification tasks are required. These measures may prove to be particularly important to the understanding of language acquisition if they involve the active engagement of the infant's perceptual, attentional, and cognitive capacities. All of the current measures of infant speech discrimination capitalize on reflexive (orienting) response systems to indicate perceptual sensitivity. More volitional responses, such as manual responding, may provide a better indication of when the infant is attentive to the task of responding to various auditory stimuli in a two-choice paradigm. Such measures, however, will of necessity involve much older infants.

Finally, the issue of species-specificity in human speech perception demands careful analysis and a cautious approach to the interpretation of data gathered from infants. The analogy between song learning in various species of birds and speech perception by human infants (e.g., Marler, 1970) is quite seductive. Songbirds are apparently predisposed to encode, at a preproductive age, a prototypic "song" that is characteristic of their species. Human infants also appear capable of perceiving the "appropriate" categories of human speech long before they can actually produce these sounds. Yet, there is not a single piece of evidence that any subgroup of the human species, when raised in the natural language environment of another subgroup, fails to acquire the speech perception skills required for that "new" language. Moreover, in the case of VOT, it is quite clear that basic species-specific perceptual abilities are essentially invariant across a wide variety of linguistic environments. The cross-language data suggest only that these basic perceptual sensitivities are modified slightly and occasionally suppressed if they are not required by a particular language system. The simple fact that members of a particular language environment can, even at later ages, acquire new phonological systems and communicate effectively (albeit with some productive deficiencies) argues strongly against the "template" analogy used in the birdsong literature.

The issue of species-specificity in human speech perception is also related to the debate over what level of analysis is operative in early speech perception. If an aspect of a human adult's performance appears to be unique to speech, it is absolutely essential that appropriate controls are used before concluding that speech signals are processed in a special way and that this specialized processing is related to the phonological rule system of a natural language. For example, categorical perception was initially thought to be unique to speech. Later, however, three types of control studies rendered this claim equivocal. First, nonspeech signals, perceived by adults as meaningless auditory signals, yielded categorical identification and discrimination functions. Second, nonhumans, who do not use human speech signals in a communicative manner, produced similar categorical discrimination data. Third, studies of adults from different language environments, when presented with phonologically irrelevant speech signals, also yielded categorical data. To claim, therefore, that the categorical nature of the infant speech perception data supports a specialized, *phonetic* mode of processing that has a biological basis (i.e., is species-specific), is clearly unjustified at the present time. Similarly, more recent claims (Eimas, 1980; Eimas & Miller, 1980) concerning the "unique" context dependent nature of the perception of certain speech sounds must again be evaluated with considerable caution until the appropriate control studies have been conducted (e.g., see Carrell, Pisoni, & Gans, 1980). If context dependency is present in nonspeech signals, in nonhumans, and in adults from other language communities, then this "specialized" speech mechanism will also have to join the ranks of those general characteristics of the mammalian auditory system that are used by the phonological systems of natural languages to support the perception (and perhaps production) of speech. To claim that human infants perceive speech phonetically because their discrimination data indicate contextual dependency effects makes the same premature and logical error that characterized the first infant studies on voicing perception. A remarkable amount of empirical data on infant speech perception has been gathered since the first studies in the early 1970s, but research in this field must strive for the methodological and interpretive rigor that is found in other areas of experimental psychology.

ACKNOWLEDGMENTS

Preparation of this chapter was partially supported by grants from NICHHD (HD-11915-03) and NIMH (MN-24027-06) and by a doctoral fellowship awarded to Amanda C. Walley from the Social Sciences and Humanities Research Council of Canada.

REFERENCES

Aslin, R. N., & Dumais, S. T. Binocular vision in infants: A review and a theoretical framework. In H. Reese & L. Lipsitt (Eds.), *Advances in child development and behavior* (Vol. 15). New York: Academic Press, 1980.

Aslin, R. N., & Pisoni, D. B. Effects of early linguistic experience on speech discrimination by infants: A critique of Eilers, Gavin, and Wilson (1979). *Child Development*, 1980, **51**, 107–112. (a)

Aslin, R. N., & Pisoni, D. B. Some developmental processes in speech perception. In G. Yeni-Komshian, J. F. Kavanagh, & C. A. Ferguson (Eds.), *Child phonology, Volume 2: Perception.* New York: Academic Press, 1980. (b)

Aslin, R. N., Pisoni, D. B., Hennessy, B. L., & Perey, A. J. Discrimination of voice-onset-time by human infants: New findings and implications for the effects of early experience. *Child Development*, 1981, in press.

Bailey, P. J., Summerfield, Q., & Dorman, M. On the identification of sine-wave analogues of certain speech sounds. *Haskins laboratories: Status report on speech research*, SR-51/52, 1977.

Blakemore, C. The conditions required for the maintenance of binocularity in kittens' visual cortex. *Journal of Physiology (London)*, 1976, **261**, 432–444.

Bush, L., & Williams, M. Discrimination by young infants of voiced stop consonants with and without release bursts. *Journal of the Acoustical Society of America*, 1978, **63**(4), 1223–1226.

Carney, A. E., Widin, G. P., & Viemeister, N. F. Noncategorical perception of stop consonants differing in VOT. *Journal of the Acoustical Society of America*, 1977, **62**, 961–970.

Carrell, T. D., Pisoni, D. B., & Gans, S. J. Perception of the duration of rapid spectrum changes: Evidence for context effects with speech and nonspeech signals. *Journal of the Acoustical Society of America*, 1980, **68**, S1, S49.

Chomsky, N., & Halle, M. *The sound pattern of English.* New York: Harper & Row, 1968.

Chomsky, N., & Miller, G. A. Introduction to the formal analysis of natural languages. In R. D. Luce, R. Bush, & E. Galanter (Eds.), *Handbook of mathematical psychology* (Vol. 2). New York: Wiley, 1963, pp. 269–231.

Cooper, F. S., Delattre, P. C., Liberman, A. M., Borst, J. M., & Gerstman, L. J. Some experiments on the perception of synthetic speech sounds. *Journal of the Acoustical Society of America*, 1952, **24**(6), 597–606.

Cutting, J. E., & Rosner, B. S. Categories and boundaries in speech and music. *Perception & Psychophysics*, 1974, **16**, 564–570.

Danaher, E. M., Osberger, M. J., & Pickett, J. M. Discrimination of formant frequency transitions in synthetic vowels. *Journal of Speech and Hearing Research*, 1973, **16**, 439–451.

Delattre, P. C., Liberman, A. M., & Cooper, F. S. Acoustic loci and transitional cues for consonants. *Journal of the Acoustical Society of America*, 1955, **27**(4), 769–773.

Eilers, R. E. Context sensitive perception of naturally produced stop and fricative consonants by infants. *Journal of the Acoustical Society of America*, 1977, **61**(5), 1321–1336.

Eilers, R. E., Gavin, W., & Wilson, W. R. Linguistic experience and phonemic perception in infancy: a cross-linguistic study. *Child Development*, 1979, **50**, 14–18.

Eimas, P. D. Auditory and linguistic processing of cues for place of articulation by infants. *Perception & Psychophysics*, 1974, **16**(3), 513–521.

Eimas, P. D. Speech perception in early infancy. In L. B. Cohen & P. Salapatek (Eds.), *Infant perception: From sensation to cognition* (Vol. 2). New York: Academic Press, 1975.

Eimas, P. D. Developmental aspects of speech perception. In R. Held, H. W. Leibowitz, & H.-L. Teuber (Eds.), *Handbook of Sensory Physiology VIII: Perception.* Berlin: Springer-Verlag, 1978.

Eimas, P. D. *Infant speech perception: Issues and models.* Paper presented at the C. N. R. S. Conference in Paris, France, June 15–18, 1980.

Eimas, P. D., & Miller, J. Contextual effects in infants speech perception. *Science,* 1980, **209,** 1140–1141.

Eimas, P. D., Siqueland, E. R., Jusczyk, P. W., & Vigorito, J. Speech perception in infants. *Science,* 1971, **171,** 303–306.

Fantz, R. L., Fagan, J. F., III, & Miranda, S. B. Early visual sensitivity. In L. B. Cohen & P. Salapatek (Eds.), *Infant perception: From sensation to cognition* (Vol. 1). New York: Academic Press, 1975.

Fodor, J. A., Garrett, M. F., & Brill, S. L. Pi ka pu: The perception of speech sounds by prelinguistic infants. *Perception & Psychophysics,* 1975, **18,** 74–78.

Fry, D. B. The development of the phonological system in the normal and deaf child. In F. Smith & G. A. Miller (Eds.), *The genesis of language.* Cambridge, Mass.: MIT Press, 1966.

Gesell, A. L., & Ames, L. B. The ontogenetic organization of prone behavior in human infancy. *Journal of Genetic Psychology,* 1940, **56,** 247–263.

Gottlieb, G. Development of species identification in ducklings: I. Nature of perceptual deficit caused by embryonic auditory deprivation. *Journal of Comparative and Physiological Psychology,* 1975, **89,** 387–399.

Gottlieb, G. Conceptions of prenatal development: Behavioral embryology. *Psychological Review,* 1976, **83,** 215–234. (a)

Gottlieb, G. The roles of experience in the development of behavior and the nervous system. In G. Gottlieb (Ed.), *Neural and behavioral specificity.* New York: Academic Press, 1976. (b)

Grobstein, P., & Chow, K. Receptive field organization in the mammalian visual cortex: The role of individual experience in development. In G. Gottlieb (Ed.), *Neural and behavioral specificity.* New York: Academic Press, 1976.

Hess, E. H. "Imprinting" in a natural laboratory. *Scientific American,* 1972, **227,** 24–31.

Hirsh, I. J. Auditory perception of temporal order. *Journal of the Acoustical Society of America,* 1959, **31,** 759–767.

Hockett, C. F. *A course in modern linguistics.* New York: Macmillan, 1958.

Hubel, D. H., & Wiesel, T. N. Binocular interaction in striate cortex of kittens reared with visual squint. *Journal of Neurophysiology,* 1965, **28,** 1041–1059.

Hubel, D. H., & Wiesel, T. N. The period of susceptibility to the physiological effects of unilateral eye closure in kittens. *Journal of Physiology (London),* 1970, **206,** 419–436.

Jakobson, R., Fant, C. G. M., & Halle, M. *Preliminaries to speech analysis.* Technical Report No. 13 Acoustics Laboratory, Massachusetts Institute of Technology, May, 1952.

Jusczyk, P. W. Infant speech perception: A critical appraisal. In P. D. Eimas & J. L. Miller (Eds.)., *Perspectives on the study of speech.* Hillsdale, N.J.: Erlbaum, 1980.

Jusczyk, P. W., Pisoni, D. B., Walley, A., & Murray, J. Discrimination of relative onset time of two-component tones by infants. *Journal of the Acoustical Society of America,* 1980, **67,** 262–270.

Jusczyk, P. W., Rosner, B. S., Cutting, J. E., Foard, C. F., & Smith, L. B. Categorical perception of non-speech sounds by two-month-old infants. *Perception & Psychophysics,* 1977, **21,** 50–54.

Kewley-Port, D. Representations of spectral change as cues to place of articulation in stop consonants. *Research on speech perception.* Technical Report No. 3, Indiana University, 1980, p. 263.

Kuhl, P. K. Speech perception in early infancy: The acquisition of speech-sound categories. In S. K. Hirsh, D. H. Eldredge, I. J. Hirsh, & S. R. Silverman (Eds.), *Hearing and Davis; Essays honoring Hallowell Davis.* St. Louis, Mo.: Washington University Press, 1976.

Kuhl, P. K., & Miller, J. D. Speech perception in the chinchilla: Voiced–voiceless distinction in alveolar plosive consonants. *Science,* 1975, **190,** 69–72.

Kuhl, P. K., and Miller, J. D. Speech perception by the chinchilla: Identification functions for synthetic VOT stimuli. *Journal of the Acoustical Society of America,* 1978, **63,** 905–917.

Lasky, R. E., Syrdal-Lasky, A., & Klein, R. E. VOT discrimination by four- and six-and-a-half-month-old infants from Spanish environments. *Journal of Experimental Child Psychology,* 1975, **20,** 215–225.

Leavitt, L. A., Brown, J. A., Morse, P. A., & Graham, F. K. Cardiac orienting and auditory discrimination in 6-week infants. *Developmental Psychology,* 1976, **12,** 514–523.

Liberman, A. M., Cooper, F. S., Shankweiler, D. P., & Studdert-Kennedy, M. Perception of the speech code. *Psychological Review,* 1967, **74,** 431–461.

Liberman, A. M., Delattre, P. C., & Cooper, F. S. The role of selected stimulus variables in the perception of the unvoiced stop consonants. *American Journal of Psychology,* 1952, **65,** 497–516.

Liberman, A. M., Harris, K. S., Kinney, J. A., & Lane, H. The discrimination of relative onset time of the components of certain speech and nonspeech patterns. *Journal of Experimental Psychology,* 1961, **61,** 379–388.

Liberman, A. M. & Studdert-Kennedy, M. Phonetic perception. In R. Held, H. Leibowitz, & H. L. Teuber (Eds.), *Handbook of sensory physiology: Perception VIII.* Berlin: Springer–Verlag, 1978.

Lisker, L., & Abramson, A. S. A cross language study of voicing in initial stops: Acoustical measurements. *Word,* 1964, **20,** 384–422.

Lisker, L., & Abramson, A. S. The voicing dimension: Some experiments in comparative phonetics. In *Proceedings of the sixth international congress of phonetic sciences,* Prague, 1967. Prague: Academia, 1970.

Marler, P. A comparative approach to vocal learning: Song development in white-crowned sparrows. *Journal of Comparative and Physiological Psychology, Monograph,* 1970, **71(2),** Part 2, 1–25.

Miller, C. L., & Morse, P. A. The "heart" of categorical speech discrimination in young infants. *Journal of Speech and Hearing Research,* 1976, **19,** 578–589.

Miller, J. D., Wier, C. C., Pastore, R., Kelley, W. J., & Dooling, R. J. Discrimination and labeling of noise–buzz sequences with varying noise-lead times: An example of categorical perception. *Journal of the Acoustical Society of America,* 1976, **60(2),** 410–417.

Miyawaki, K., Strange, W., Verbrugge, R., Liberman, A. M., Jenkins, J. J., & Fujimura, O. An effect of linguistic experience: The discrimination of [r] and [l] by native speakers of Japanese and English. *Perception & Psychophysics,* 1975, **18,** 331–340.

Moffitt, A. R. Consonant cue perception by twenty- to twenty-four-week-old infants. *Child Development,* 1971, **42,** 717–731.

Moore, J. M., Wilson, W. R., & Thompson, G. Visual reinforcement of head-turn responses in infants under twelve months of age. *Journal of Speech and Hearing Research,* 1977, **42,** 328–334.

Morse, P. A. The discrimination of speech and nonspeech stimuli in early infancy. *Journal of Experimental Child Psychology,* 1972, **14,** 477–492.

Pisoni, D. B. Identification and discrimination of the relative onset of two-component tones: Implications for the perception of voicing in stops. *Journal of the Acoustical Society of America,* 1977, **61,** 1352–1361.

Pisoni, D. B. Speech perception. In W. K. Estes (Ed.), *Handbook of learning and cognitive processes* (Vol. 6). Hillsdale, N.J.: Erlbaum, 1978.

Pisoni, D. B. Some remarks on the perception of speech and nonspeech signals. *Proceedings of the Ninth International Congress of Phonetic Sciences,* Copenhagen, August, 1979. Copenhagen: Institute of Phonetics, University of Copenhagen, 1980, pp. 301–312.

Pisoni, D. B., Aslin, R. N., Perey, A. J., & Hennessy, B. L. Some effects of laboratory training on identification and discrimination of voicing contrasts in stop consonants. *Journal of Experimental Psychology: Human Perception and Performance,* 1982, in press.

Pisoni, D. B., & Lazarus, J. H. Categorical and noncategorical modes of speech perception along the voicing continuum. *Journal of the Acoustical Society of America,* 1974, **55,** 328–333.

Riley, D. A. *Discrimination learning.* Boston: Allyn & Bacon, 1968.

Schatz, C. The role of context in the perception of stops. *Language,* 1954, **30,** 47–56.

Searle, C. L., Jacobson, J. E., & Rayment, S. G. Phoneme recognition based on human audition. *Journal of the Acoustical Society of America,* 1979, **65,** 799–809.

Shiffrin, R. M., & Schneider, W. Controlled and automatic human information processing: II. Perceptual learning, automatic attending and a general theory. *Psychological Review,* 1977, **84,** 127–190.

Sinnott, J. M., Pisoni, D. B., & Aslin, R. N. A comparison of pure tone auditory thresholds in human infants and adults. *Infant Behavior & Development,* 1981, in press.

Stevens, K. N. The quantal nature of speech: Evidence from articulatory–acoustic data. In E. E. David, Jr. & P. B. Denes (Eds.), *Human communication: A unified view.* New York: McGraw-Hill, 1972.

Stevens, K. N. The potential role of property detectors in the perception of consonants. In G. Fant & M. A. A. Tatham (Eds.), *Auditory analysis and perception of speech.* New York: Academic Press, 1975.

Stevens, K. N., & Blumstein, S. E. Quantal aspects of consonant production and perception: A study of retroflex consonants. *Journal of Phonetics,* 1975, **3,** 215–234.

Stevens, K. N., & Blumstein, S. E. Invariant cues for place of articulation in stop consonants. *Journal of the Acoustical Society of America,* 1978, **64**(5), 1358–1368.

Stevens, K. N., & Blumstein, S. E. Perceptual invariance and onset spectra for stop consonants in different vowel environments. *Journal of the Acoustical Society of America,* 1980, **67**(2), 648–662.

Stevens, K. N., & Halle, M. Remarks on analysis-by-synthesis and distinctive features. In W. Wathen-Dunn (Ed.), *Models for the perception of speech visual form.* Cambridge, Mass.: MIT Press, 1967.

Stevens, K. N., & House, A. S. Speech perception. In J. Tobias (Ed.), *Foundations of modern auditory theory II.* New York: Academic Press, 1972.

Stevens, K. N., & Klatt, D. H. Role of formant transitions in the voiced–voiceless distinction for stops. *Journal of the Acoustical Society of America,* 1974, **55,** 653–659.

Strange, W., & Jenkins, J. J. The role of linguistic experience in the perception of speech. In R. D. Walk & H. L. Pick, Jr. (Eds.), *Perception and experience.* New York: Plenum, 1978.

Streeter, L. A. Language perception of two-month-old infants shows effects of both innate mechanisms and experience. *Nature,* 1976, **259,** 39–41.

Trehub, S. E., Schneider, B. A., & Endman, M. Developmental changes in infants' sensitivity to octave-band noises. *Journal of Experimental Child Psychology,* 1980, **29,** 282–293.

Walley, A. Infants' discrimination of full and partial cues to place of articulation in stop consonants. *Research on speech perception*. Progress Report No. 5, Indiana University, 1979, 85–1-45.

Walley, A. C., & Carrell, T. D. *Onset spectra versus formant transitions as cues to place of articulation. Journal of the Acoustical Society of America*, 1980, **68,** S1, S49–S50.

Williams, C. L. *Speech perception and production as a function of exposure to a second language.* Doctoral Dissertation, Harvard University, 1974.

Somatosensory
and Sensorimotor
Development

The two chapters that constitute Part C, on somatosensory and sensorimotor development, help to fill an unfortunate void in our general considerations of perceptual ontogenesis. Tactile sensitivity is believed to be the first sensory modality to begin to function during vertebrate maturation (cf., Gottlieb, 1971 for a particularly broad and thorough review). There are numerous indications that specific and general forms of early cutaneous stimulation are crucial inputs for normal development. Nevertheless, the skin as an organ, "the largest organ of the body" (Montagu, 1971) has received little attention in perceptual studies and especially in developmental analyses. Perhaps the very early onset of function of cutaneous sensitivity has been a deterrent; prehatching and prenatal studies present a distinct order of technical difficulties.

The relatively recent elucidation of the fine isomorphisms between peripheral tactile sensory fields and the arrangement of barrel cells in the central nervous system (CNS) of rodents provided a needed impetus for intensive experimental analyses of somatosensory function and organization. Woolsey and his associates, contemporary pioneers in this area, provide a broad and up-to-date summary of this exciting new work in Chapter 9.

Chapter 10 by Fentress, on sensorimotor development is broadly integrative. Again, this is an area of the most basic concerns, one which can represent the beginning of analysis of organized behavior in response to external and internal stimuli. Interestingly, early "developmental psychobiologists" such as G. E. Coghill, viewed the problems of sensorimotor development as central issues of their science (see Oppenheim, 1978, for an insightful and scholarly discussion of Coghill, his work and its intellectual framework). The classic studies by Coghill (e.g., 1929) and Windle (e.g., 1940) remain foundation stones for current considerations that have a vital air of eclecticism. Fentress's Chapter 10 is a fine introduction to many of the exciting and elusive issues in this relatively uncharted area.

REFERENCES

Coghill, G. E. *Anatomy and the problem of behavior.* New York: Hafner, 1964. (Originally published, 1929.)
Gottlieb, G. Ontogenesis of sensory function in birds and mammals. In: E. Tobach, L. R. Aronson, & E. Shaw (Eds.), *The biopsychology of development,* New York: Academic Press, 1971, pp. 67–128.
Montagu, A. Touching: *The human significance of the skin.* New York: Harper & Row, 1971.
Oppenheim, R. W. G. E. Coghill (1872–1941): Pioneer neuroembryologist and developmental psychobiologist. *Perspectives in biology and medicine,* 1978, **22,** 44–64.
Windle, W. F. *Physiology of the fetus: Origin and extent of function in prenatal life.* Philadelphia: Saunders, 1940.

9

Somatosensory Development

THOMAS A. WOOLSEY
DIANNE DURHAM
ROGER M. HARRIS
DANIEL J. SIMONS
KAREN L. VALENTINO
Washington University School of Medicine

I. INTRODUCTION

Our understanding of the anatomical, the physiological, and the behavioral development of the somatosensory system is generally less detailed than it is for other sensory systems. The reasons for this are numerous. The peripheral organization of the somatosensory system is established early in ontogeny. In contrast to the retina, the organ of Corti, the olfactory epithelium, or the taste buds of the oropharynx, the somatosensory periphery is not a simple two-dimensional sheet having a stereotyped structure confined to a specific organ or small group of organs that can be easily isolated. There are many somatosensory nerves and receptor specializations disturbed nonuniformly, both with respect to body parts and to their location within them (e.g., Andres & Von Düring, 1973). Within the central nervous system (CNS),

259

the somatosensory pathways are poorly isolated from those of other systems especially in the spinal cord and brain stem (e.g., Brodal, 1981). Thus, despite its obvious importance to the organism, the somatosensory system of adult animals in many ways is relatively difficult to study. Accordingly, experimental manipulations directed toward understanding the development of the somatosensory system would seem to be particularly problematical.

Nevertheless, the arrangement of somatic inputs from the face, especially in rodents, has allowed us and others to study details of the morphological and the functional development of the somatosensory system. For reasons that will become apparent, in this chapter we have chosen to focus on the development of the trigeminal system in mice and rats—specifically the large whiskers and their central representations. We shall consider the following aspects of the system: (*a*) its organization; (*b*) its morphogenesis; (*c*) its response to experimental manipulation; and (*d*) certain genetic and environmental influences on its development.

II. ORGANIZATION OF THE SOMATOSENSORY PATHWAY

Many animals have large tactile hairs on the face that are called whiskers, vibrissae, or sinus hairs. These are especially prominent in rodents (Woolsey, Welker, & Schwartz, 1975). In rats and mice, the largest vibrissae are organized in five distinct rows composed of at least four to seven individual hairs on the upper lip (see Fig. 9.4). In some species, including rats and mice, these mystacial (mystacial = moustache) vibrissae are actively whisked or vibrated back and forth in a stereotypical fashion as the animals explore their environments (Fig. 9.1; Vincent, 1912; Welker, 1964). Each hair arises from a hair follicle;

Fig. 9.1   Mice and rats actively explore their environment by moving their whiskers to and fro in a stereotyped fashion. This figure shows the results of an analysis of this behavior from high-speed motion pictures of a behaving mouse. (c) Two adjacent frames from a motion picture show the mouse from above. (a) Tracings of five such sequential frames of a motion picture occurring approximately at 20 msec intervals. The whiskers move forward in a movement called *protraction,* which is somewhat longer than their movement backwards called *retraction.* The change in position of different groups of whiskers is shown in (b) as a function of motion picture frame number. These data were obtained by measuring the angle of different rostrocaudal groups of whiskers to the midline as shown in (c). Note that all whiskers on both sides of the face seem to move at the same frequency, although the excursion of whiskers on different sides of the face differs. Whiskers on each side of the face move in synchrony. The maximum excursion whiskers measured in this analysis was approximately 50 deg; the maximum frequency was about 15 Hz. In regard to the latter, the frequency with which mice whisk is about twice that reported by Welker (1964) in the rat.

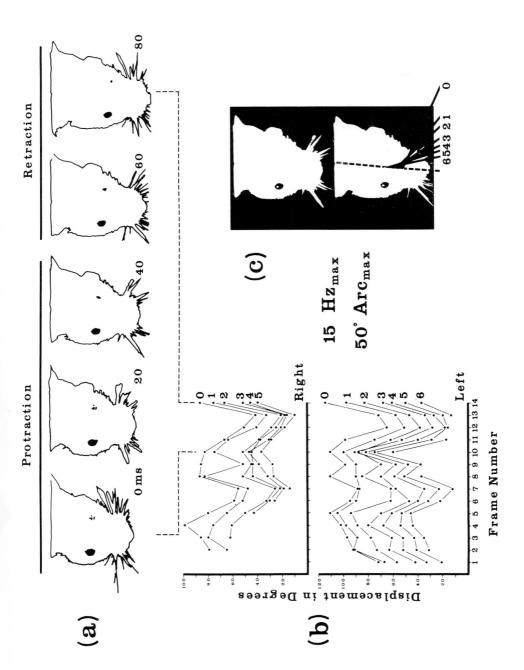

Protraction Retraction

(a)

0 ms   20   40   60   80

(b)

Displacement in Degrees

Right

0 1 2 3 4 5

Left

0 1 2 3 4 5 6

1 2 3 4 5 6 7 8 9 10 11 12 13 14

Frame Number

(c)

15 Hz$_{max}$

50° Arc$_{max}$

0 1 2 3 4 5 6

each follicle has a complex structural organization; and each follicle contains a number of morphologically distinct mechanoreceptor endings, including Merkel discs, lanceolate endings, Golgi-Mazzoni endings, and free nerve endings (Andres, 1966). The follicles receive a substantial and segregated innervation from the maxillary branch of the trigeminal nerve (Fig. 9.2; Woolsey, 1978). There may be as many as 200 myelinated nerve fibers supplying a single vibrissa (Lee & Woolsey, 1975; Vincent, 1913). The cell bodies of these primary afferents are located in a cranial equivalent of the dorsal root ganglia, the trigeminal ganglion. Physiological studies have shown that the fibers innervating the vibrissae have complicated response properties and, importantly, that a single afferent fiber innervates only one vibrissa (Dykes, 1975;

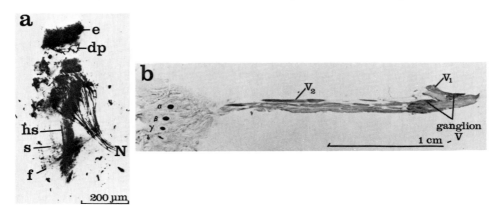

Fig. 9.2   The organization of innervation to a single whisker and the trigeminal nerve: (a) a single dissected whisker from a mouse that was stained by the Winkelmann method to reveal axons. The hair shaft (hs) rests in connective tissue (f) and is surrounded by a blood sinus (s). Presumably by inflating or deflating the blood sinus, the animal can adjust the relative threshold of mechanoreceptors. Each follicle has two striated muscle groups attached to its sheath, the contraction of which produces the whisking behavior shown in Fig. 9.1. The silver stain shows a single bundle of nerve fibers (N) entering the follicle from behind and densely innervating the midportion of the hair shaft; just below the epidermal surface (e) is a dermal plexus (dp) of nerves. Electron micrographs of single vibrissal nerves show that, in addition to the myelinated fibers, there are unmyelinated nerve fibers that typically number about one-third of the myelinated fibers. The myelinated fibers are assumed to arise from cells in the trigeminal ganglion; the origin of the unmyelinated fibers is unknown. Each whisker then has a heavy and isolated pattern of innervation. (b) A longitudinal section of the trigeminal nerve (maxillary = V_2; ophthalmic = V_1) of the rat stained with the Nissl stain. This nerve conveys axons traveling in individual nerve bundles from each whisker (e.g., α–δ) to the CNS. The cell bodies of these neurons are located in the trigeminal ganglion (ganglion V). Unlike the other portions of this pathway, the neurons in the trigeminal ganglion are not anatomically segregated.

Gottschaldt, Iggo, & Young, 1973; Zucker & Welker, 1969). Peripheral fibers innervating the small pelage hairs between the whiskers on the mystacial pad have been observed by anatomists (e.g., Andres, 1966) but have only very rarely been recorded from by physiologists (Zucker & Welker, 1969).

The discrete and punctate nature of the mystacial pad is reflected in the anatomical and physiological organization of the whole afferent pathway from the periphery to the cerebral cortex. The trigeminal ganglion cells (which are the only components in the system that are not obviously segregated anatomically; Gregg & Dixon, 1973) project to the principal sensory nucleus of V and two parts of the spinal nucleus of the fifth nerve in the brainstem (Fig. 9.3). There they terminate in discrete groupings that are demonstrable by the succinic dehydrogenase (SDH) histochemical technique (Belford & Killackey, 1979) that stains the mitochondria (Nachlas, Tsou, deSouza, Cheng, & Seligman, 1957) that are particularly numerous in axon terminals (Peters, Palay, & Webster, 1976). The spatial organization of these terminal patches is similar to the arrangement of whiskers on the face (Fig. 9.4) and in general agrees with physiologically determined "maps" of the vibrassae in the brain stem (Nord, 1967; Shipley, 1974). The second-order brainstem neurons project to the somatosensory ventroposteromedial thalamus or ventrobasal complex (VB) after crossing the midline near the decussation of the medial lemniscus (Erzurumlu & Killackey, 1980). In the thalamus there is a clearly defined physiological (Emmers, 1965; Waite, 1973) and anatomical arrangement of both afferent fibers (Belford & Killackey, 1979) and cells—called barreloids—(Van der Loos, 1976; Woolsey, Anderson, Wann, & Stanfield, 1979) which, as in the brainstem, closely parallels the spatial arrangement of the contralateral vibrissae (Fig. 9.3). Third-order fibers leave the thalamus via the rodent equivalent of the internal capsule to terminate principally in Layer IV of the sensorimotor (SmI) cortex (Cragg, 1975; Donaldson, Hand, & Morrison, 1975; Killackey, 1973; Labedsky & Lierse, 1968; Petrovickey & Druga, 1972; White, 1978; White & De Amicis, 1977; Woolsey, 1978). The region of the SmI cortex that receives these fibers is characterized by discrete cellular aggregates extending throughout the thickness of Layer IV (Woolsey, 1967). Because of their three-dimensiomal shape, these cellular groupings are called "barrels" (Welker & Woolsey, 1974; Woolsey & Van der Loos, 1970). As in lower centers, the anatomical arrangement of the barrels is "isomorphic" (Szentágothai, 1975) to the organization of the sensory periphery, and a one-to-one correspondence between a given mystacial vibrissa and its corresponding cortical barrel can be demonstrated by both physiological and anatomical methods

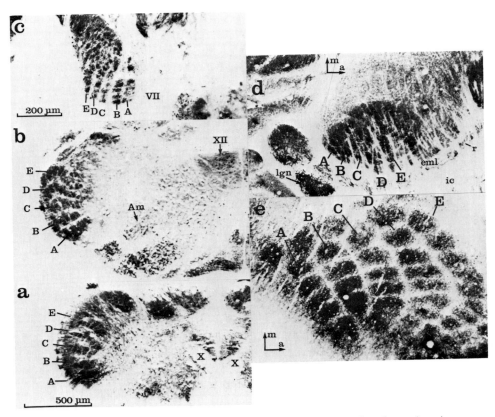

Fig. 9.3 The pattern of central projections of the trigeminal pathway in mice as revealed by the succinic dehydrogenase (SDH) histochemical method. The trigeminal pathway in rodents stains intensely with this method and shows segmentation at all levels that is isomorphic to the organization of the sensory periphery. (a) The trigeminal representation at the level of the nucleus caudalis of the spinal trigeminal complex. In this and other figures, the association with the rows of whiskers is indicated as summarized in Fig. 9.4. (b) The interpolaris subdivision of the spinal trigeminal complex in which a second isomorphic representation is present. (c) The organization of the principal nucleus of the fifth nerve. (d) The organization of the representation in the ventromedial nucleus of the thalamus, also known as the ventrobasal complex (VB). (e) The organization of the projection patterns in the cerebral cortex. Figures (a) through (c) are transverse sections of the brainstem; (d) is a modified horizontal section through the thalamus; and (e) is tangential to the pial surface overlying SmI. For comparison, parts (a), (b), (d), and (e) are all presented at the same scale. (c) is shown at a higher magnification. The brainstem representations come from the left side of the brain; the thalamus and cortex are from the right side. For orientation, the decussation of the corticospinal tract in (a) is shown by x; the nucleus ambiguus and hypoglossal nuclei are shown in (b) by Am and xii, respectively; in (c), the position of the facial nerve is shown by vii. In (d), the position of the reticular nucleus of the thalamus is given by r, lateral geniculate by lgn,

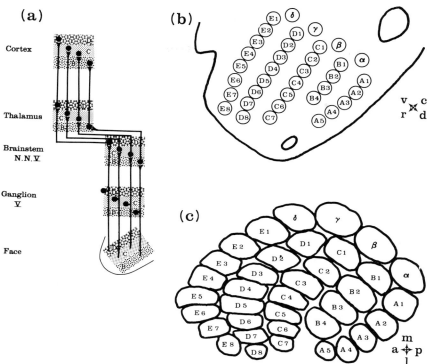

Fig. 9.4 Summary of the schematic organization of the pathway showing the nomenclature applied to both the sensory periphery and central pathways. (a) The general organization of the sensory pathway is shown schematically. With the exception of the trigeminal ganglion, all parts of the system are clearly organized anatomically as shown in Fig. 9.3. The pathway from the periphery to the cortex contains three synapses occurring in the brainstem, thalamus, and cortex. The thalamus and cortex are contralateral to the preceding substations. (b) The nomenclature employed for the whiskers and their central representations. In (b), the whiskers on the face are arranged in five rows labeled from dorsal to ventral A–E. Within each row, whiskers are numbered from 1 up caudal to rostral. Whiskers within each row having the same number constitute an arc according to the terminology of Rice and Van der Loos (1977). Caudally, four whiskers straddle each of these rows α–δ. In each central representation such as that shown in Fig. 9.3, a similar arrangement occurs. This is shown schematically in (c) for the PMBSF barrels in the contralateral cerebral cortex.

external medullary lamina by eml, and internal capsule is given by ic. The arrows indicate medial up and anterior to the right. In (e), the orientation is identical to that in (d). Note that, at each location on the pathway, the central projections are largely isomorphic to the sensory periphery and, given the appropriate plane of section, can be relatively easily demonstrated. Note also that, in the thalamus, shown in (d), the pattern of staining is complicated by bundles of fibers contributing to the internal capsule and distorting the pattern of the histochemical stain.

(Figs. 9.3, 9.7; Simons, 1978; Simons & Woolsey, 1979; Welker, 1976; Van der Loos & Woolsey, 1973). The isomorphism is not only qualitative but quantitative. For instance, in mice, it has been shown that there is a direct proportionality between the number of myelinated nerve fibers innervating a vibrissa and the number of neurons in the barrel to which it projects (Lee & Woolsey, 1975).

The overall organization of the rodent trigeminal system is summarized schematically in Fig. 9.4. The figure illustrates a basic feature of this afferent pathway that like other sensory pathways, has a recepterotopic or somatotopic organization whereby the two-dimensional relationships in the sensory periphery are preserved in the orderly arrangement of central fibers and cell bodies. A major advantage in studying the vibrissal system is that it is characterized by easily identified punctate receptor organs—the vibrissae of the mystacial pad—and by their isomorphic central projections in the brainstem, thalamus, and cortex that can be demonstrated by straightforward histological methods.

We assume that the massive peripheral innervation of the vibrissae and the relatively large volume of CNS devoted to processing vibrissal inputs is an index of the behavioral importance of this sensory system for the rodents, analogous to the visual system of "higher" primates. The vibrissal system is like the primate visual system in that the vibrissae are actually small tactile organs with segregated or "disjunctive" projections in the CNS (Johnson & Welker, 1965). The two eyes are separate sense organs each with segregated or disjunctive projections in the CNS but only for the binocular visual field (e.g., Guillery, 1972; Hubel & Wiesel, 1977). The vibrissal and the visual pathways are also similar in the sense that inputs from different sense organs are sharply segregated until they reach the cortex. This is of particular value for interpreting anatomical and functional studies. The pathways differ, however, in that the inputs from the different vibrissae are arranged to represent inputs from one side of the body only, whereas those from the two eyes are segregated so that the corresponding parts of the two retinae can be interdigitated appropriately.

III. NORMAL DEVELOPMENT OF THE VIBRISSAL SYSTEM

For rats and mice, detailed data are available describing the development of various components in the somatosensory system. The time course of two developmental "events" at various locations in the vibrissal pathway is shown in Table 9.1. The two events are: (a) the time

Table 9.1
Time Course of Developmental Events in Mouse Somatosensory System

Level	Birthdays[a]	Gradient(s)[a]	Form	Authors
Mystacial vibrissae	E 12[b]	C → R	E 12	Dun (1959)
Trigeminal ganglion[c]	E 11–13	?	By PND-1	Yamakado & Yohro (1979) Forbes & Welt (1981)
Brainstem nuclei	E 10–11	V → D "C → R"	By PND-1	Waite & Cragg (1979) Taber (1963)
Ventrobasal complex	E 10–14	V → D L → M C → R	By PND-2	Angevine (1970) Woolsey et al. (1979)
Cortical barrels	E 15–17	W → P L → M? R → C?	By PND-5	Rice (1974) Rice & Van der Loos (1977)

[a] As determined from ³H Thymidine labeling, E = embryonic day; gradients are mapped in various directions (i.e., R = rostral; C = caudal; L = lateral; M = medial; V = ventral; D = dorsal; W = white matter; P = pia).

[b] Vibrissae first seen in histological sections and the scanning electron microscope (SEM).

[c] This study is from the rat. Forbes and Welt postulate that a few large neurons could be "born" on E10 or E9.

of final mitosis as indicated by ^{3}H-thymidine autoradiography, which determines when the relevant neurons are generated; and (b) the time when a structure begins to resemble its form in the adult, which indicates when the relevant neurons are completing their postmitotic migration and differentiation. The time course of both events suggests an outside-to-inside sequence of development in this pathway.

The vibrissal follicles develop early in intrauterine life. This has been shown by light microscopy (e.g., Dun, 1959) amd more recently by scanning electron microscopy (Yamakoto & Yohro, 1979). The vibrissae are induced by the dermis (Dhouailly, 1977) and arise on both the nasal and maxillary processes of the developing face (Rows A and B on the former and Rows C through E on the latter; see Fig. 9.4 [Yamakoto & Yohro, 1979]). There is a dramatic and rapid transition in their development from embryonic Day E-11 when hair follicles are not recognizable, to embryonic Day E-12 when they are clearly present. By embryonic Day 13, the follicles can be seen to have small hairs emerging from them. The mechanoreceptor specializations described in the preceding section are not present until several days later (e.g., English, Burgess, & Kavka-Van Norman, 1980). In the rat, and presumably in the mouse also, the trigeminal ganglion neurons undergo a final mitosis at about the same time (E-12 and 14; but see Fig. 229 in Theiler, 1972). Therefore the peripheral processes of most of the trigeminal ganglion cells are not present in the periphery at the time that the vibrissae are formed (but see Van Exan & Hardy, 1980). The development of the mystacial pad is independent of (Dhouailly, 1977) and probably precedes its innervation.

Neurons in the brainstem (e.g., Taber, 1963), the thalamus (e.g., Angevine, 1970; Scheibel, Davies & Scheibel, 1976), and the cortex (Angevine & Sidman, 1961; Rice, 1974) are generated either concurrently, or after those in the trigeminal ganglion; but the farther one proceeds centrally, the later into embryogenesis the final mitotic events occur. Paralleling this outside-to-inside sequence of final mitosis is the pattern in which the various substations begin to resemble their final cytoarchitectonic form. For example, in mice and rats, the trigeminal ganglion and the brainstem nuclei are clearly recognizable in their adult form on the day of birth (Waite & Cragg, 1979). The thalamus becomes adult-like several days later (approximately postnatal Day-3 [PND-3]; Woolsey et al., 1979) and, in the cortex, the barrels in Layer IV are not recognizable until at least 5 days after birth (Rice & Van der Loos, 1977; Weller, 1972; Woolsey et al., 1979). An important correlate of cortical cytoarchitectonic differentiation is the ingrowth of the thalamocortical fibers. Although present in an unsegregated fashion in the subcortical white matter of rats as early as the second day of life, the thalamocortical fibers do not segregate and grow into Layer IV until approximately PND-5 (Wise & Jones, 1978). Similar patterns of "instruction" by ingrowing extrinsic fibers may be operant in subcortical locales, but these data are not yet available.

To summarize, it appears that the sensory periphery develops in several important ways prior to the arrival of the trigeminal nerve fibers (Table 9.1). The central neural structures associated with the vibrissal pathway follow a clear ouside-to-inside sequence of neuronogenesis and morphogenesis, with the cerebral cortex being the last to attain its characteristic form. Similar outside–inside sequences of neuronogenesis, including developmental gradients, have been described in other sensory systems and in other species (e.g., Hendrickson & Rakic, 1977; Rakic, 1977a,b). The *timing* of these events, particularly morphogenesis, occurs in such a way that one structure could dictate the details of organization in the next. For example, the whisker pad could "instruct" the partitioning of the central fibers of the trigeminal ganglion cells. In the case of the cortex, the available observations support this possibility (Woolsey, 1978).

As shown in Table 9.1, both neuronogenesis and morphogenesis occur in the mouse and the rat with incredible rapidity (e.g., Yamakoto & Yohru, 1979)—particularly when contrasted with similar events in the primate (Rakic, 1977a). Although this shortens the "turnaround" times of certain experiments, it severely limits their temporal resolution. Finally, from Table 9.1, the morphogenesis of the more central aspects of the vibrissal system is incomplete at birth. This suggests that it might be possible to perturb the system postpartum to learn more about its *development.*

IV. EXPERIMENTAL ALTERATIONS OF THE VIBRISSAL PATHWAY

Damage to the vibrissae by electrocautery in neonatal animals produces a significant and predictable alteration in the normal arrangement of the cortical barrels (see Fig. 9.6; Van der Loos & Woolsey, 1973). This experiment was the first proof of the direct relationship between vibrissae and barrels. Of greater interest for developmental studies is the observation that damage to receptor organs can be manifest so dramatically in cells three synapses up the pathway. This finding has since been replicated numerous times by different workers in various species (Killackey, Belford, Ryugo, & Ryugo, 1976; Verley & Axelrad,

1977; Weller, 1979; Weller & Johnson, 1975; Woolsey & Wann, 1976). It has been demonstrated that these alterations in the cortex are present from the time that the barrels can be first recognized, and are not the result of a reorganization of a previously normal pattern (Jeanmonod, Rice, & Van der Loos, 1977; Killackey & Belford, 1979).

To define more precisely the postnatal susceptibility of the differentiating cortex to manipulation of the sensory periphery, we examined the brains of mice whose whiskers had been cauterized on different postnatal ages (Woolsey & Wann, 1976). Figure 9.6 summarizes the progressive and graded responses to peripheral damage produced at successively later ages and shows that on the seventh day of life lesions to the vibrissae fail to alter the cytoarchitectonic pattern in the cortex. Experiments such as these define a "critical" or "sensitive" period ending between the fifth and sixth days of life during which cytoarchitectonic development can be affected. Furthermore, the cytoarchitectonic results observed parallel the temporal patterns of segregation of the specific thalamocortical afferents that are also altered by neonatal whisker damage (Killackey & Belford, 1979; Woolsey, 1978). Namely, the time of first arrival of the specific thalamocortical fibers to this region (at least in rats) correlates well with the time at which the barrels can first be recognized (Rice & Van der Loos, 1977; Wise & Jones, 1978).

Qualitatively similar alterations can be observed in the ventrobasal thalamus where the "barreloids" can be recognized (Figs. 9.5 and 9.6). The "critical period" during which this structure can be affected by peripheral damage terminates about 48 hours *before* it does in the cortex (Woolsey *et al.*, 1979; but see Belford & Killackey, 1980). Alterations in the organization of the afferent fibers to the brainstem, the thalamus, and the cortex can be seen with the SDH stain (Fig. 9.5). Interpretation of these experiments in the brainstem trigeminal complex is complicated by the fact that the centrally projecting fibers from the trigeminal ganglion are undergoing degeneration as a consequence of the peripheral damage (Aldskogius & Arvidsson, 1978; Waite & Cragg, 1979). In the brainstem nuclei in which these centrally projecting axons terminate, there is a paling of the appropriate zones of projection but there is no substantial alteration in the dimensions of the segregated patterns of their termination such as is seen in thalamus and cortex, even when vibrissal damage is made on the first day of life (Fig. 9.5). Thus, there is a remarkable parallel between the temporal sequence of effects that peripheral lesions have on the ascending pathway and the sequence of the system's morphogenesis. Those centers in the pathway that are located most centrally and attain their full development latest, are those

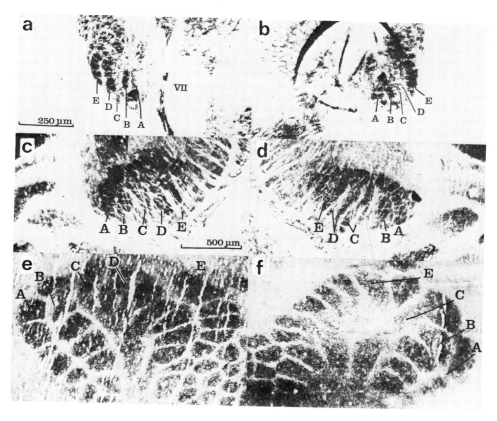

Fig. 9.5   The anatomical consequences of early damage to the sensory periphery in the mouse. This animal had the middle row, C, of whiskers damaged on the left face and Rows C and D damaged on the right face on the third day of life. (a and b) The left and right principal nucleus of V, respectively. In (a), there is paling in the zone normally occupied by Row C as a consequence of the whisker damage. In (b), paling exists in the Row C and D representations. Although the zone is paled, presumably because of the degeneration of the central projections from the trigeminal ganglion cells, there is no change in the dimensions of the projections from the intact vibrissae. (c and d) The ventrobasal thalami from this same animal. Although it is possible that the total area of the central projection of the damaged whiskers is attenuated, there is evidence for the segregation of these projections both into rows and into arcs, which is in contrast to the appearance of the cortex shown below. (e and f) The cortices of this animal. In (e), Row C is attenuated and lacks segmentation into individual barrels. In (f), the same features are present. Note that the C and D rows are unsegregated and, furthermore, that the representation associated with the E whiskers is somewhat enlarged. These data suggest a sequential susceptibility to peripheral damage in this system. For the time course of these changes, see Fig. 9.6. (Unpublished data from D. Durham.)

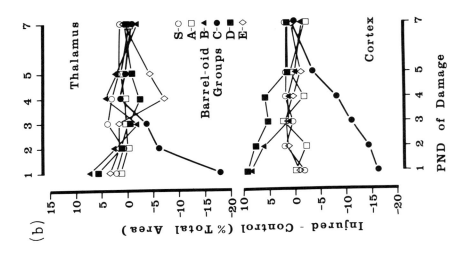

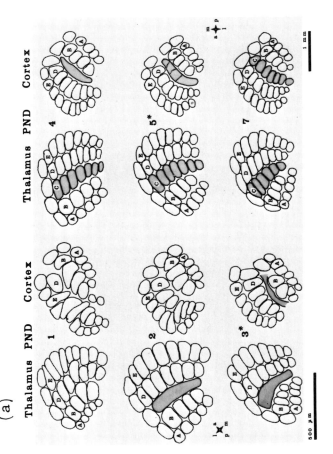

that remain susceptible to perturbations several synapses away for the longest period of time after birth.

We should discuss two other aspects of our results with respect to the barrels that are related to well-known developmental mechanisms in the CNS (e.g., Cowan, 1979). The first is programmed neuronal death. This phenomenon is well known and dramatic in a number of vertebrate nervous systems, especially in the spinal cord (e.g., Hollyday & Hamburger, 1977). It is possible that neuronal death could account for the anatomical changes we have seen in the cortex after whisker damage. The contributions of this mechanism, if any, are probably very small as the total area of the posteromedial barrel sub-field (PMBSF) (see Fig. 9.4) is unaltered after the experiment and, qualitatively, neuronal cell density does not appear to be diminished (Woolsey & Wann, 1976). However, careful (and tedious) counts of cortical cells are needed to decide the point.

The second class of observations is related to the role of developmental gradients in establishing order in central projections (e.g., Jacobson, 1978). The arrangement of vibrissae into a "grid" on the mystacial pad allows manipulations of patterns of damage to test for antero–posterior, mediolateral, etc, gradients of development in the central projections. When groups of whiskers are damaged, the barrels to which they should have sent projections are either missing or diminutive. In these experiments, the adjacent barrels became enlarged seemingly to "compensate" for the areal loss produced by the whisker damage. The pattern of this "compensation" varies as a function of the time and the pattern of the peripheral damage (see Fig. 9.7). For instance, if a *row* of barrels is altered after a *row* of whiskers is damaged, the adjacent anterior row of barrels retains the capacity to compensate later in life than the adjacent posterior row of barrels does. This seems to correspond to a caudal to rostral developmental gradient described for the thalamus. No such gradient has been described in the cortex. (Table 9.1). If the whiskers in an arc (i.e., across rows) are damaged,

---

Fig. 9.6 A comparison of the developmental consequences of whisker damage in the thalamus and cortex of mice: qualitative and quantitative. (a) The schematic reconstructions of the thalamus and cortex of animals in which whiskers were damaged on different days. These data are derived from cytoarchitectonic studies of these centers as reported by Woolsey *et al.* (1979). In particular, note the difference between the time course of events in the thalamus, as shown to the left, and the cortex, as shown to the right, which is consistent with the data as shown in the previous figure. These results are shown graphically in (b) of this figure. Note that, in the thalamus, the "critical" or "sensitive" period to the peripheral damage ends a day or two before that in the cortex. Furthermore, in both centers, there seems to be a "compensation" for the loss of areal representation in those parts of the brain associated with the damaged whiskers.

the more medially placed barrels become enlarged (Valentino, Woolsey & Wilson, 1978). This pattern of compensation seems to correspond to the lateral to medial developmental gradient described in Table 9.1 for the cortex. Finally, our experiments in which all whiskers are damaged suggest that there is a stepwise or sequential segregation of the thalamocortical inputs. The division of these fibers to represent the rows of whiskers on the face precedes the segregation of fibers within a row for the representation of individual whiskers (Fig. 9.7). This stepwise segregation of the thalamocortical afferents and the cells to which they project has certain correlates with the function of this cortex (Simons, 1978; Simons & Woolsey, 1979). Of greater interest here is that the sequences of fiber segregation in this system may permit a direct experimental investigation of the factors involved in partitioning CNS pathways.

V. SOME DETAILS IN THE CORTEX

The descriptions in the preceding sections have concerned patterns of cellular and axonal aggregation. Several other experiments provide information about how the system develops at the cellular level.

The appearance of normal cortical barrels in Golgi stains is quite striking (Lorente de Nó, 1922; Stefan, 1976; Woolsey & Dierker, 1978; Woolsey, Dierker, & Wann, 1975a). In mice, many cells have extremely eccentric dendritic fields and about 80% of all cells in Layer IV have their dendritic processes restricted to a single barrel. All impregnated cells can be classified into two major groups according to both qualitative (e.g., presence of dendritic spines) or quantitative (e.g., measures of dendritic and axonal arbors and somal areas) criteria (Woolsey et al., 1975a). Similar criteria have been used to classify barrel neurons in rats (Simons & Woolsey, 1978). Interestingly, in both species, two types of extracellularly recorded units can be distinguished physiologically in Layer IV and most respond to deflections of only a single whisker (Simons, 1978; Simons & Woolsey, 1979). Qualitative and quantitative analyses of Golgi-impregnated barrel neurons in mice whose Row-C whiskers were cauterized at different postnatal ages have recently been completed (see Fig. 9.8; Harris & Woolsey, 1981; Stefan & Van der Loos, 1980). The dendritic fields of cells in the expanded Row-D and -B barrels still respect barrel boundaries as seen in normal animals. By contrast, the dendritic fields of impregnated neurons in the Row-C zone extend into adjacent Rows-B and -D when peripheral damage is produced on PND-1. These become progressively more confined to the

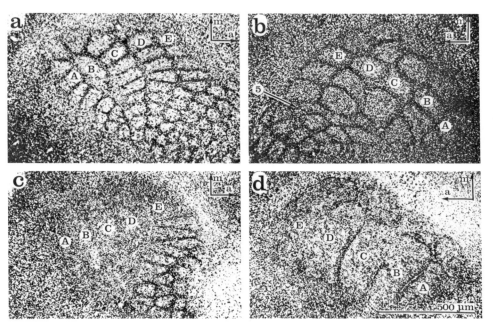

Fig. 9.7   The results of different patterns of whisker damage in the cortex of the mouse at selected time points using the Nissl stain for cell bodies. Other studies show that the pattern of cells seen here correlates well with the pattern of specific thalamo-cortical afferents to this part of the brain. (a) The whiskers of Row B were damaged on the second day of life. Note the absence of formation of individual barrels in the B zone of the cortex and some enlargement of the barrels in neighboring rows A and C to "compensate" for the loss of area of projection seen in Row B. (b) The whiskers of Arc 5 were damaged on the first day of life in this animal. The resultant cytoarchitectonic pattern shows severe attenuation of the Arc 5 barrels in the cortex with enlargement or "compensation" by the barrels that lie medial to those barrels affected by the damage. In (a) there is a caudal to rostral "compensation," whereas in (b) there is a lateral to medial compensation for the loss of cortical area as a consequence of the peripheral damage. In (c), all whiskers except some in Row E were damaged on the second day of life. Although there is a clear delineation of the somatosensory cortex as shown by the increased cell density, the organization of cells into distinct patterns is not sharp. However, cellular condensations indicate that rows are forming. (d) One day later all whiskers were damaged, and here the pattern of rows is clearly delineated from the organization of cortical cell bodies. These and other data suggest a pattern of "compensation" within the cortex that correlates with some developmental gradients described in Table 9.1. Furthermore, the data suggest stepwise, or sequential, segregation of cortical cells and the thalamocortical fibers projecting to them, such that the system is first segregated into rows and, second, segregated into individual barrels associated with single vibrissae. Data from Valentino *et al.* (1978).

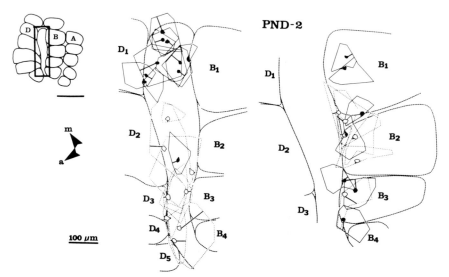

Fig. 9.8 A schematic diagram showing the orientation of barrel neuron dendritic trees after whisker damage. To the left is shown the related damaged zone. Although the processes of these cells are largely confined to this area, some "spill" over into adjacent barrels. On the right are shown the dendritic territories of cells that normally would have been in the C zone. The dendrites of these cells now orient toward the B barrels suggesting that the growth of dendrites of these cells is strongly influenced by the projections to them from the thalamus, which in turn might have functional meaning. (Data from Harris & Woolsey, 1981. Reproduced with permission.)

Row-C zone as damage is done at later postnatal ages, achieving a normal pattern following damage at PND-4 and -5. This correlates with the critical period for altering barrel cytoarchitecture. Quantitative data about somal area, dendritic branches, and lengths do not differ among normal and vibrissa-damaged animals, regardless of the age at which the damage is accomplished. These findings are consistent with the suggestion that these latter features of barrel neuronal morphology are intrinsically determined, whereas those of dendritic orientation are strongly influenced by extrinsic factors such as the ingrowing thalamocortical fibers. These efferents appear to instruct the dendritic outgrowth of barrel cells in a manner analogous to the relationship between the ingrowing olfactory filia and mitral cell apical dendrites in the olfactory bulb (Hinds, 1972).

A number of studies have reported the *functional* changes in the cortex of mice and rats following damage to the vibrissae on the first or second postnatal day. Although this would seem to be a straightforward experiment, the reported results vary widely. After lesioning individual vibrissal row(s), Killackey, Ivy, and Cunningham (1978) reported the following "changes" of the receptive fields in cortex in anesthetized rats: Cells were driven by more whiskers than normal and a representation of the down or pelage hairs between the whiskers appeared. Pidoux, Verley, Farkas, and Scherrer (1979) removed all of the vibrissae individually and reported that mouse whisker cortex was invaded by a central representation of the down hairs between the whiskers which, according to them, is normally represented somewhat anterolaterally in the SmI of normal mice. (It should be noted that the central representation of these hairs in *normal* animals has not been confirmed by any other laboratory, including our own.) Finally, Waite and Taylor (1978) produced very large lesions on the faces of newborn rats that presumably destroyed the innervation of the whiskers and whatever innervation exists for the pelage hairs. From their widely spaced cortical electrode penetrations, they concluded that the central representation of the bridge of the nose, the cheek, and upper lip occupied, with some overlap, the cortex that normally would contain the representation of the vibrissae. Although it is not surprising that different results are obtained in animals subjected to different patterns of peripheral damage (*vide supra*), some of the results, such as the detection of "novel" neurons responding to more than one whisker, are open to other interpretations. For instance, it is known that, in normal cortex, neurons in the supra- and infragranular layers are driven by more than one whisker (Simons, 1978). Appropriate histological controls could resolve this issue, as well as documenting the extent and severity of the peripheral damage. In addition, histology would help to locate the position of the electrode penetrations within the context of the altered cytoarchitectonic organization of the somatosensory cortex. Unfortunately, these data are not available for any of the previously mentioned studies.

In our own functional studies of animals that had had their whiskers damaged early in life, we have been careful to localize our findings with respect to the cytoarchitectonic organization of the barrels in both the horizontal and vertical dimensions and to determine the pattern and extent of the peripheral damage from histological sections. Our first functional studies of vibrissa damaged animals employed Sokoloff's (Sokoloff *et al.*, 1977) 2-DG method. In normal behaving animals, simply removing whiskers reduces glucose utilization in cortex associated with and including the appropriate barrels (Durham & Woolsey, 1978; Durham, Woolsey & Kruger, 1981). In similar experiments in rats and mice, in which the middle row (Row C) of whiskers was damaged in early life, the functional activity so demonstrated always obeys the altered cytoarchitectonic boundaries (Durham, Welt, & Woolsey, 1978). That is, if the whiskers in the adjacent Rows -B and -D are left intact, higher 2-DG concentrations are found in these barrels but not extending into the experimentally altered cortical zones (or in the converse experiment shown in Fig. 9.9). From our Golgi studies, this result was expected. The 2-DG method is not adequate, however, to distinguish whether or not there are abnormal projections of body surfaces into the altered

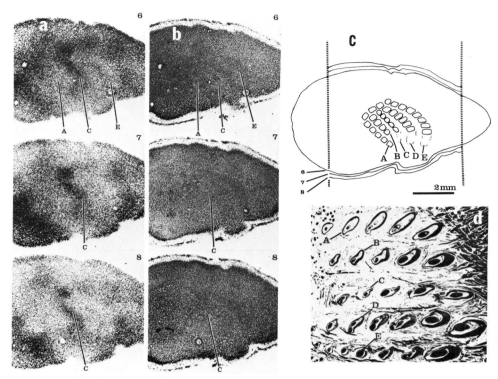

Fig. 9.9 The functional consequences of whisker damage in a rat after the whiskers in Row C were damaged on the first day of life. (a) X-ray autoradiograms of ^{14}C-2-deoxyglucose localization after the whiskers in all rows except the damaged Row C were removed; (b) the histological sections; (c) anatomical reconstruction from this brain; and (d) a histological picture of the pattern in the periphery as shown by H and E staining. Even though the Row C whiskers were damaged and are attenuated as shown by the histology, they are still present. The autoradiograms in (a) show that the C whiskers that were damaged are still capable of activating the relevant part of the cortex. When restricted to Layer IV, the regional activity is confined to the appropriate barrels. Experiments in which the converse was done, namely, the B and D whiskers were left intact, show a similar correspondence between the cytoarchitectonic pattern seen in Layer IV and the area of activation as demonstrated by the 2-DG technique. These data suggest that the architectonic subdivisions seen in the cortex are obeyed even though the sensory periphery has been manipulated, but they do not provide evidence about the nature of activation of the cells in this cortex. (Data from Durham *et al.*, 1978.)

cortex or to provide information as to whether neurons are receiving inputs from abnormal numbers of whiskers.

To examine these questions directly, we recorded single units from rats and mice in which the middle row of whiskers was damaged on different postnatal days. All units were localized anatomically with respect to their position in the horizontal direction using the barrels, as well as in the vertical direction using the cortical layers as cytoarchitectonic markers (Simons, Durham, & Woolsey, 1980). The data from some 1400 single units all lead to the same fundamental conclusions. Some of the data are shown in Fig. 9.10. First, appropriate whiskers activate cells in appropriate barrels even though the latter may be substantially enlarged. This result is in accord with the findings of Welt (1977), who studied the same problem in anesthetized animals with the necessary histological controls; and it is in accord with the 2-DG studies (Durham et al., 1978). Second, when cortical laminar boundaries are accounted for, there is no abnormality in the number of whiskers that will activate a cortical cell. In these animals as in normals, most of the multiwhisker cells are located in the nongranular layers and show convergence only from whiskers that are physically adjacent on the face. Third, we found no evidence for a representation of other body parts in the altered cortex. Fourth, although we did find an abnormality in that some of the cortical cells reponded to pelage hairs after whisker damage, a majority of these are also driven strongly by adjacent intact whiskers. That these abnormal units are more prevalent in the smaller mice than the larger rats suggests to us that peripheral sprouting of the primary afferents may be taking place rather than a rearrangement or significant modification in the development of the central pathways. Finally, when microelectrodes are in that part of Layer IV, which is associated with the damaged vibrissae, a very high percentage of the units exhibit sluggish responses, are undrivable at all by peripheral stimuli, or are silent unless "injured" by the microelectrode. As expected from the anatomy (Woolsey & Wann, 1976), the dimensions of this "undrivable" zone increase with later damage to the whiskers; and as expected from normal physiology (Simons, 1978; Simons & Woolsey, 1979), the dimensions of the "undrivable" zone are smaller in the nongranular layers where cells receive convergent inputs from neurons associated with the intact vibrissae.

If there is a general impression from these experiments, it is that the experimentally altered cortex is surprisingly *normal*. Specifically, adjacent points on the body surface have adjacent central representations despite the experimental manipulations. When laminar boundaries are taken into account, there are no qualitative distinctions between the behavior of units in normal and whisker damaged animals. These re-

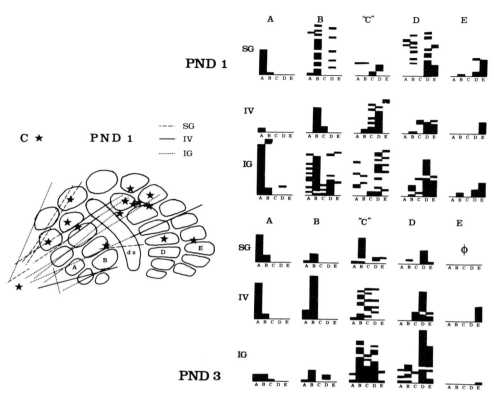

Fig. 9.10 Some response properties of cells in the cerebral cortex of mice in which the middle row (Row C) of whiskers were damaged at different postnatal days. To the left is a schematic diagram of the position of electrode tracks through the cortices of a number of animals whose middle Row C of whiskers was damaged on the first day of life. For schematic purposes, the zone associated with these damaged whiskers is somewhat enlarged, as indicated by dz. Electrode tracks were located in histological sections and were made either normal to or parallel to the surface of the pia. To the right the response properties of single units recorded in these cortices is summarized. On the abscissa are shown the anatomical locations of the units with respect to barrel Rows A through E; and on the ordinate are the numbers of units responding to whiskers in different rows on the face as well as the cortical layer in which those units were recorded. Units from Rows A and B are quite normal; the whiskers related to the relevant barrels are those most likely to drive cells in any layer. If the units are recorded in the zone associated with the damaged whiskers, the pattern is quite abnormal in that either the units are undrivable by peripheral stimuli or that they are, if driven, most likely excited by stimulation of the whiskers in adjacent rows. What the data do not show is that the majority of units recorded in the C zone were undrivable by any form of natural peripheral stimulation. In none of these experiments did we find abnormal parts of the sensory periphery being represented in the CNS. In a few cases, the C whiskers were present as in the previous figure and drove the units and the appropriate barrels accordingly. Note that in the supra-(SG-) and infragranular (IG) layers, there is a convergence of

sults are all consistent with the observed anatomy and with the notion that, during development, the CNS receives cues allowing it to accurately assess the status of the sensory periphery and to map this periphery in a spatially coherent fashion. In the rodent somatosensory cortex, this effect is mediated by the segregation of the specific thalamic cortical afferents, which in turn influence the growth of cortical neuronal processes (Harris & Woolsey, 1981). Furthermore, our results suggest that the factors that are important for the establishment of basic intracortical connectivity, as determined from an analysis of the laminar locations of single units, may be relatively insensitive to gross manipulation of the sensory periphery.

VI. GENETIC CONTROL

What evidence exists for genetic control of somatosensory development? Mice are the mammals of choice for genetic studies, and a number of results have been reported that are of importance for the genetic control of the development of the somatosensory periphery as well as of the CNS.

There are several reports that are relevant for the consideration of genetic controls in the sensory periphery. First, there are two papers documenting that mice with supernumerary vibrissae have an appropriate extra barrel in the contralateral cerebral cortex (Van der Loos & Dörfl, 1978; Yamakoto & Yohro, 1979). These observations are of interest because they, in a sense, represent the converse of the experimental manipulations just described. Yamakoto and Yohro (1979) observed "extra" whiskers in certain strains of mice and noted that these whiskers appeared along the nasolacrimal fold—the line of fusion between the nasal and maxillary processes. Appropriately the extra barrel in the cortex was located between rows -B and -C. This phenomenon is probably related to a genetic predisposition to a congenital anomaly, rather than a genetic specification of additional whiskers in the developing whisker pad.

A second line of evidence comes from studies of different species that must be genetically distinct (Woolsey et al., 1975b). In certain rodents such as the gerbil, there are more rows of whiskers on the face than in mice and rats, although different gerbils have the same number

inputs as occurs in the normal cortex. We conclude from these experiments that the cytoarchitectonic boundaries constitute functional boundaries and, furthermore, that the pattern of intracortical connectivity is preserved despite the peripheral insult. (Data from Simons et al., 1980.)

of whisker rows. As in mice and rats, the pattern of the periphery is faithfully repeated in the gerbil cortex, which has more rows of PMBSF barrels.

Third, Dun and Frazier (1958) showed that the number of vibrissae of the house mouse is under the control of at least two genes. Their conclusion was that there are factors present in the skin that controlled the genesis of the vibrissal follicles. The tabby mutation is particularly interesting, because this gene is X-linked. The Lyon hypothesis (Lyon, 1961) predicts an intermediate number of reduced vibrissae in females, due to the expression of the wild type and the tabby genes in adjacent areas of skin. Indeed, this is what was found; and, although the cortices of these animals have not been examined, it is quite likely from other evidence that the numbers of barrels in the cortex would match the pattern of whiskers in the periphery. Thus the CNS apparently reads the pattern of the periphery and can adapt to somatic changes or mutations without any genetic requirement to alter the details in forming CNS pathways. The value of such a mechanism, even in humans, can be appreciated for a variety of genetic conditions such as polydactally (e.g., McKusick, Egeland, Eldridge, & Krusen, 1964).

With respect to genetic factors in the development of the CNS, there are a number of mutations in mice that produce profound derangements in CNS structure including the cytoarchitecture of the cerebral cortex (Sidman, Green, & Appel, 1965). For instance, in reeler (an autosomal recessive mutant) the pattern of thalamocortical afferents to the barrels and some cytoarchitectonic structures resembling the barrels have been described (Caviness, Frost, & Hayes, 1976; Welt & Steindler, 1977). In these animals, the course that the thalamocortical afferents take to the cortex is very abnormal, proceeding to the pial surface before projecting deep into the cortical mantle (Caviness, 1976). Even though the cellular arrangements in the cortex and the course of fibers to them are abnormal, the projection patterns (and possibly the same afferent–target cell interactions) remain intact. The further study of reeler and other mutants may provide a useful handle in breaking down genetic control of the assembly of CNS somatosensory pathways. Evidence suggests that the function of cortical neurons in the visual cortex of the reeler is surprisingly normal even given the very distorted cytoarchitecture (Dräger, 1977; Lemmon & Pearlman, 1981).

VII. ENVIRONMENTAL CONSIDERATIONS

From the results described in Sections IV and V, it would seem logical to examine the results of a "pure sensory deprivation" produced by chronic whisker removal. We have shown, in behaving animals injected with 2-deoxyglucose, that following *acute* removal of only the whisker hairs there is a significant reduction in the utilization of glucose in the appropriate barrels and in the cortex above and below them (Durham & Woolsey, 1978; Durham *et al.*, 1981). This result indicates that if activity has a role in the development and maintenance of central cortical connections, then one might expect to find changes in the cortex. Experiments in which a chronic sensory deprivation is produced by whisker hair removal are complicated by the rate at which the hairs grow back. Nevertheless, a number of studies using this approach have failed to demonstrate any gross or obvious alterations in the cytoarchitecture of the barrels (e.g., Woolsey & Wann, 1976). Despite these observations, studies indicate that chronic whisker removal alone does reduce levels of enzymes associated with aerobic metabolism (Dietrich, Durham, Lowry, & Woolsey, 1980, 1981; Wong-Riley, 1980; (Wong-Riley & Welt, 1980; see Fig. 9.11), but whether there is a change in the functional properties of cortical neurons analogous to those following various forms of visual deprivation remains an open question. Certainly it is easy to conceive of a number of experiments for the vibrissal system that are analogous to the selective deprivation experiments described for the visual system (see other chapters in volume 2), but the execution of these studies is at best difficult.

There are other important factors in the "environment" that affect the CNS, including somatosensory development. Environmental effects on the barrels have been demonstrated in several studies. Welker (1973) examined rats exposed to a powerful teratogen during gestation to produce microencephalic animals. Her unit cluster analyses showed that the functional connections from the vibrissae to the somatosensory cortex were intact. Furthermore, barrels in these microencephalic animals, although very abnormal for rats, were present in the appropriate pattern. Recently, Vongdokmai (1980) showed that young mice whose mothers were exposed to low protein diets prior to, during and after gestation, have a 2-day *delay* of the appearance of barrels in the cortex. The brain weights of these animals are significantly below their control littermates; the total area of the barrel field is diminished; and the number of cortical neurons associated with each of the barrels is reduced. This study is interesting because of the possibilities it raises for developmental manipulation of the barrels, but also points to nutritional variables in studies of plasticity that have largely been ignored. The implications of Vongdokmai's findings for the human population of the world are self-evident.

The effects of intrauterine X-irradiation on parts of the vibrissal system have been examined. Rats irradiated on the seventeenth day of

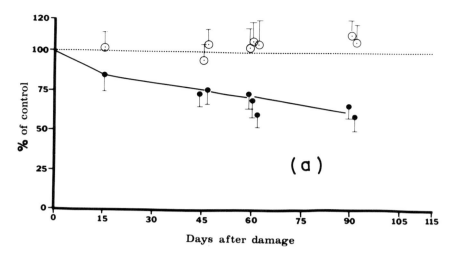

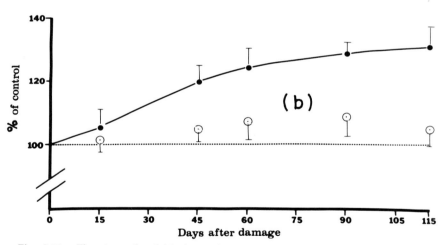

Fig. 9.11   The time-related biochemical responses of the somatosensory cortex to damage to the sensory periphery in the adult. In animals such as these, no anatomical changes have been reported. Yet, microanalysis of the appropriate barrels, indicated by ●, shows that there are significant changes in levels of two enzymes, (a) citrate synthase and (b) glycogen phosphorylase, associated with energy metabolism. These are dependent on the time after the damage was produced in the adult and suggest a kind of metabolic plasticity in response to loss of activity in the relevant neurons. Citrate synthase control = 5.28 ± 0.15 M/kg dry wt/hr. Glycogen phosphorylase control = 374' ± 31.4 mM/kg dry wt/hr. Controls are designated by ⊙. (Data from Dietrich *et al.*, 1980.)

gestation fail to develop cortical Layers IV through II (compare with Table 9.1). Electrophsiological studies of the somatosensory cortex of these animals indicate that, as in normal animals, there is an orderly projection of the sensory periphery to this abnormal cortex even though the usual principal targets of the thalamocortical projection are absent (Ito, Kawataba, & Shoji, 1979). At the periphery, X-irradiation of mice on the twelfth day of gestation will prevent the development of the whiskers (Jacobson, 1966). Similar treatment before or after this time is not effective, suggesting that this perturbation interfers with the normal interaction between the dermis and epidermis that is required to generate the vibrissae (Dhouailly, 1977). Thus, X-irradiation, like the dietary manipulation just described, is an experimental method that can be used to investigate the principals of development in the somatosensory system.

VIII. COMMENTARY

We have focused our discussion on the development of a particular somatosensory system and how it can be modified by a variety of experimental manipulations. Although these data are taken from one specialized system, there is no reason to doubt that they can be applied to the patterns of generation of somatosensory systems or other sensory systems in other animals (see Rakic, 1977a). Quite a bit less is known about the role of development in the establishment of behaviors and discriminative capacities of the organism (Gustafson & Felbain-Keramidis, 1977). Although crude electrophysiological studies indicate that the pathways that we have described can be activated at the time they are generated (Armstrong-James, 1973; Verley & Axelrad, 1975, 1977a,b), what is of greater interest is exactly when the animal is likely to begin to make behavioral use of these pathways. The well-described exploratory behavior in rats and mice first appears in a form that resembles the adult at about the twelfth or thirteenth day of life (Welker, 1964; Weller, 1972). In the rat, the onset of this behavior is correlated with the appearance of heavy myelination in the infraorbital nerve (Waite & Cragg, 1979). The importance of the vibrissae in certain free-field behaviors such as visual-cliff discrimination or maze running has been determined (Schiffman, Lore, Passifiume, & Neeb, 1970). However, it seems to us that the system is particularly amenable to psychophysical studies, in part because of its importance to the animal, but also because the whiskers are relatively easy to observe in a controlled setting. An index of the social importance of the whiskers is that, in rodent communities, dominant individuals bite off the whiskers of subordinate individuals (Bugbee & Eichelman, 1972; Gregoire & Smith, 1975; Long, 1972).

For the purposes of this overview, some of the details of the various experimental paradigms have not been emphasized. This is not a trivial issue. Results vary across different laboratories and different animals, namely the rat and the mouse. We have found that the timing of the whisker lesions is absolutely critical and is not easy to control with respect to the "age" of the animal. Studies of embryo staging that use morphological markers suggest that littermates in a particular rat or mouse pregnancy can differ by as much as 23 to 48 hours (Grünberg, 1943; Juurlink & Fedoroff, 1979; Long & Burlingame, 1937). For a rapidly developing system, such temporal differences can be significant. Second, in particular, the severity of the central effects that result from peripheral damage is difficult to control across different animals. In our experience, this constitutes a major problem in comparing experiments across different laboratories.

There are now a number of studies in the literature using cell to cell adhesivity and contact assays that indicate the appropriate topographic affinities between a projection source and its target (e.g., Gottlieb, Merrel, Rock, Littman, Santala, & Glaser, 1977). This is indirect experimental support for an early hypothesis of Ramón y Cajal (e.g., 1928) who suggested that the problems in neuronal recognition may be similar to that of an antibody to an antigen as expressed in the host response to bacterial infection. Furthermore, various compounds, such as the nerve growth factor, have been demonstrated to be important in the establishment of certain connections with the CNS (Hamburger, Brunso-Bechtold, & Yip, 1981). The somatosensory system does offer some possibilities in defining similar phenomena, particularly as biochemical technology becomes better at dealing with minute amounts of identified molecules. The genetic studies of Dun and Fraser (1958), for instancĕ, strongly suggest a biochemical markers that, if not directly responsible for establishing the patterns of organization of the sensory periphery, may be a part of the expression of those genes that control the morphogenesis of the whiskers. Although an oversimplification, it may be that whatever these markers are they could be used throughout the developing somatosensory pathway to provide organizational instructions to target neural tissues.

ACKNOWLEDGMENTS

This work was supported by NIH Grants NS 10244 and NS 15070 and by a grant from the Research and Technology Foundation of the Paralyzed Veterans of America. Durham,

Simons, and Valentino were supported by an NIH Training Grant NS 07057. We wish to thank Nhan Van Huang for histology, Bob Freund for photography, Monica Herk for figures and bibliography, and Mary Murphy for typing.

REFERENCES

Aldskogius, H., & Arvidsson, J. Nerve cell degeneration and death in trigeminal ganglion of adult rat following peripheral nerve transection. *Journal of Neurocytology*, 1978, **7**, 229–250.

Andres, K. H. Über die Feinstruktur der Rezeptoren an Sinus-Haaren. *Zeitschrift für Zellforschung*, 1966, **75**, 339–365.

Andres, K. H., & von Düring, M. Morphology of cutaneous receptors. In A. Iggo (Ed.), *Handbook of sensory physiology II. Somatosensory system.* New York: Springer-Verlag, 1973, pp. 3–28.

Angevine, J. B., Jr. Time of neuron origin in the diencephalon of the mouse. An autoradiographic study. *Journal of Comparative Neurology*, 1970, **139**, 129–188.

Angevine, J. B., Jr., & Sidman, R. L. Autoradiographic study of cell migration during histogenesis of cerebral cortex in the mouse. *Nature*, 1961, **192**, 766–768.

Armstrong-James, M. Functional integrity of neonatal rat cerebral cortex. *Foetal and neonatal physiology.* Cambridge: Cambridge University Press, The Sir Joseph Babcroft Centenary Symposium, 1973, pp. 28–32.

Belford, G. R., & Killackey, H. P. Vibrissae representation in subcortical trigeminal centers of the neonatal rat. *Journal of Comparative Neurology*, 1979, **183**, 305–322.

Belford, G. R., & Killackey, H. P. The sensitive period in the development of the trigeminal system of the rat. *Journal of Comparative Neurology*, 1980, **193**, 335–350.

Brodal, A. *Neurological anatomy in relation to clinical medicine* (3rd ed.). Oxford: Oxford University Press, 1981.

Bugbee, N. M., & Eichelman, B. S., Jr. Sensory alterations and aggressive behavior in the rat. *Physiology and Behavior*, 1972, **8**, 981–985.

Cajal, S. Ramón y. [*Degeneration and regeneration of the nervous system*]. (R. M. May, trans.). New York: Hafner, 1959. (Originally published, 1928.)

Caviness, V. S. Patterns of cell and fiber distribution in the neocortex of the reeler mutant mouse. *Journal of Comparative Neurology*, 1976, **170**, 435–448.

Caviness, V. S., Jr., Frost, D. O., & Hayes, N. L. Barrels in somatosensory cortex of normal and reeler mutant mice. *Neuroscience Letters*, 1976, **3**, 7–14.

Cowan, W. M. The development of the brain. *Scientific American*, 1979, **241**(3), 112–133.

Cragg, B. G. Absence of barrels and disorganization of thalamic afferent distribution in the sensory cortex of reeler mice. *Experimental Neurology*, 1975, **49**, 858–862.

Dhouailly, D. Regional specification of cutaneous appendages in mammals. *Wilhelm Roux's Archives of Developmental Biology*, 1977, **181**, 3–10.

Dietrich, W. D., Durham, D., Lowry, O. H., & Woolsey, T. A. Quantitative histochemical analysis of single identified barrels in the mouse SmI cortex. *Society for Neuroscience Abstracts*, 1980, **6**, 666.

Dietrich, W. D., Durham, D., Lowry, O. H., & Woolsey, T. A. Quantitative histochemical effects of whisker damage on single identified cortical barrels in the adult mouse. *Journal of Neuroscience*, 1981, **1**, 929–935.

Donaldson, L., Hand, P. J., & Morrison, A. R. Cortico–thalamic relationships in the rat. *Experimental Neurology*, 1975, **47**, 448–458.

Dräger, U. Reeler mutant mice: Physiology in primary visual cortex. In G. S. Stent (Ed.),

Function and formation of neural systems: Report of the Dahlem Workshop on function and formation of neural systems. Berlin: Dahlem, 1977, pp. 274–276.

Dun, R. B. The development and growth of vibrissae in the house mouse with particular reference to the time of action on the tabby (Ta) and ragged (Ra) genes. *Australian Journal of Biological Science,* 1959, **12**, 312–330.

Dun, R. B., & Fraser, A. S. Selection for an invariant character—"vibrissa number" in the house mouse. *Nature,* 1958, **181**, 1018–1019.

Durham, D., Welt, C., & Woolsey, T. A. 2-deoxyglucose studies of mouse and rat SmI barrel cortex following early lesions of the vibrissae. *Society for Neuroscience Abstracts,* 1978, **4**, 471.

Durham, D., & Woolsey, T. A. Acute whisker removal reduces neuronal activity in barrels of mouse SmI cortex. *Journal of Comparative Neurology,* 1978, **178**, 629–644.

Durham, D., Woolsey, T. A., & Kruger, L. Cellular localization of 2-[³H]deoxy-D-glucose from paraffin-embedded brains. *Journal of Neuroscience,* 1981, **1**, 519–526.

Dykes, R. W. Afferent fibers from mystacial vibrissae of cats and seals. *Journal of Neurophysiology,* 1975, **38**, 650–662.

Emmers, R. Organization of the first and the second somesthetic regions (SI and SII) in the rat thalamus. *Journal of Comparative Neurology,* 1965, **124**, 214–228.

English, K. B., Burgess, P. R., & Kavka-van Norman, D. Development of rat Merkel cells. *Journal of Comparative Neurology,* 1980, **194**, 475–496.

Erzurumlu, R. S., & Killackey, H. P. Diencephalic projections of the subnucleus interpolaris of the brainstem trigeminal complex in the rat. *Neuroscience,* 1980, **5**, 1891–1901.

Forbes, D. J., & Welt, C. Neurogenesis in the trigeminal ganglion of the albino rat: A quantitative autoradiographic study. *Journal of Comparative Neurology,* 1981, **199**, 133–147.

Gottlieb, D. I., Merrell, R., Rock, K., Littman, D., Santala, R., & Glaser, L. Studies on cell recognition in the developing brain. In Z. Hall, R. Kelly, & C. F. Fox (Eds.), *Cellular neurobiology.* New York: Liss, 1977, pp. 139–146.

Gottschaldt, K. M., Iggo, A., & Young, D. W. Functional characteristics of mechanoreceptors in sinus hair follicles of the cat. *Journal of Physiology,* 1973, **235**, 287–315.

Gregg, J. M., & Dixon, A. D. Somatotopic organization of the trigeminal ganglion in the rat. *Archives of Oral Biology,* 1973, **18**, 487–498.

Gregoire, S. E., & Smith, D. E. Mouse-killing behavior in the rat: effects of sensory deficits on attack behavior and stereotyped biting. *Animal Behavior,* 1975, **23**, 186–191.

Grüneberg, H. The development of some external features in mouse embryos. *Journal of Heredity,* 1943, **34**, 89–92.

Guillery, R. W. Binocular competition in the control of geniculate cell growth. *Journal of Comparative Neurology,* 1972, **144**, 117–130.

Gustafson, J. W., & Felbain-Keramidas, S. Behavioral and neural approaches to the function of the mystacial vibrissae. *Psychological Bulletin,* 1977, **84**, 477–488.

Hamburger, V., Brunso-Bechtold, J. K., & Yip, J. W. Neuronal death in the spinal ganglia of the chick embryo and its reduction by nerve growth factor. *Journal of Neuroscience,* 1981, **1**, 60–71.

Harris, R. M., & Woolsey, T. A. Dendritic plasticity in mouse barrel cortex following postnatal vibrissa follicle damage. *Journal of Comparative Neurology,* 1981, **196**, 357–376.

Hendrickson, A. E., & Rakic, P. Histogenesis and synaptogenesis in the dorsal lateral geniculate nucleus (LGd) of the fetal monkey brain. *Anatomical Record,* 1977, **187**, 602.

Hinds, J. W. Early differentiation in the mouse olfactory bulb: II. Electron microscopy. *Journal of Comparative Neurology*, 1972, **146**, 253–276.

Hollyday, M., & Hamburger, V. An autoradiographic study of the formation of the lateral motor column in the chick embryo. *Brain Research*, 1977, **132**, 197–208.

Hubel, D. H., & Wiesel, T. N. Functional architecture of macaque monkey visual cortex. *Proceedings of the Royal Society of London, Series B*, 1977, **198**, 1–59.

Ito, M., Kawabata, M., & Shoji, R. Responses of vibrissa-sensitive cortical neurons in normal and prenatally X-irradiated rat. *Journal of Neurophysiology*, 1979, **42**, 1711–1726.

Jacobson, C. M. A comparative study of the mechanisms by which X-irradiation and genetic mutation cause loss of vibrissae in embryo mice. *Journal of Embryology and Experimental Morphology*, 1966, **16**, 369–379.

Jacobson, M. *Developmental neurobiology* (2nd ed.). New York: Plenum, 1978.

Jeanmonod, D., Rice, F. L., & Van der Loos, H. Mouse somatosensory cortex: Development of the alterations in the barrel field which are caused by injury to the vibrissal follicles. *Neuroscience Letters*, 1977, **6**, 151–156.

Juurlink, B. H., & Fedoroff, S. The development of mouse spinal cord in tissue culture: I. Cultures of whole mouse embryos and spinal-cord primordia. *In Vitro*, 1979, **15**, 86–94.

Killackey, H. P. Anatomical evidence for cortical subdivisions based on vertically discrete thalamic projections from the ventral posterior nucleus to cortical barrels in the rat. *Brain Research*, 1973, **51**, 326–331.

Killackey, H. P., & Belford, G. R. The formation of afferent patterns in the somatosensory cortex of the neonatal rat. *Journal of Comparative Neurology*, 1979, **183**, 285–304.

Killackey, H. P., Belford, G. R., Ryugo, R., & Ryugo, D. K. Anomalous organization of thalamocortical projections consequent to vibrissae removal in the newborn rat and mouse. *Brain Research*, 1976, **104**, 309–315.

Killackey, H. P., Ivy, G. O., & Cunningham, T. J. Anomalous organization of SmI somatotopic map consequent to vibrissae removal in the newborn rat. *Brain Research*, 1978, **155**, 136–140.

Labedsky, L., & Lierse, W. Die Entwicklung der Succinodehydrogenaseaktivität im Gehirn der maus während der Postnatalzeit. *Histochemie*, 1968, **12**, 130–151.

Lee, K. J., & Woolsey, T. A. A proportional relationship between peripheral innervation density and cortical neuron number in the somatosensory system of the mouse. *Brain Research*, 1975, **99**, 349–353.

Lemmon, V., & Pearlman, A. L. Does laminar position determine the receptive field properties of cortical neurons? A study of corticotectal cells in Area 17 of the normal mouse and the reeler mutant. *Journal of Neuroscience*, 1981, **1**, 83–93.

Long, J. A., & Burlingame, P. L. The development of the external form of the rat, with some observations on the origin of the extra-embryonic coelom and foetal membranes. *University of California Publications in Zoology*, 1937, **43**, 143–183.

Long, S. Y. Hair-nibbling and whisker-trimming as indicators of social hierarchy in mice. *Animal Behavior*, 1972, **20**, 10–12.

Lorente de Nó, R. La corteza cerebral del ratón, *Trabajos del Laboratorio de Investigaciones Biologicas de la Universidad de Madrid*, 1922, **20**, 41–78.

Lyon, M. F. Gene action in the X-chromosome of the mouse (*mus musculus L.*). *Nature*, 1961, **190**, 372–373.

McKusick, V. A., Egeland, J. A., Eldridge, R., & Krusen, D. E. Dwarfism in the Amish: I. The Ellis-van Creveld syndrome. *Bulletin of Johns Hopkins Hospital*, 1964, **115**, 306–336.

Nachlas, M., Tsou, K., deSouza, G., Cheng, C., & Seligman, A. Cytochemical demonstration of succinic dehydrogenase by the use of a new p-nitrophenyl substituted ditetrazole. *Journal of Histochemistry and Cytochemistry,* 1957, **5,** 420–436.

Nord, S. G. Somatotopic organization in the spinal trigeminal nucleus, the dorsal column nuclei and related structures in the rat. *Journal of Comparative Neurology,* 1967, **130,** 343–356.

Peters, A. L., Palay, S. L., & Webster, H. deF. *The fine structure of the nervous system: The neurons and supporting cells.* Philadelphia: Saunders, 1976.

Petrovickey, P., & Druga, R. Peculiarities of the cytoarchitectonics and some afferent systems of the parietal cortex. *Folia Morphologica,* 1972, **20,** 161–162.

Pidoux, B., Verley, R., Farkas, E., & Scherrer, J. Projections of the common fur of the muzzle upon the cortical area for mystacial vibrissae in rats dewhiskered since birth. *Neuroscience Letters,* 1979, **11,** 301–306.

Rakic, P. Prenatal development of the visual system in rhesus monkey. *Philosophical Transactions of the Royal Society of London, Series B.,* 1977, **278,** 245–260. (a)

Rakic, P. Effect of prenatal unilateral eye enucleation on the formation of layers and retinal connections in the dorsal lateral geniculate nucleus (LGd) of the rhesus monkey. *Society for Neuroscience Abstracts,* 1977, **3,** 573. (b)

Rice, F. L. Somatosensory cortex of the mouse: Time of origin and postantal migration of neurons in the barrel field. A quantitative and autoradiographic study. *Anatomical Record,* 1974, **178,** 447.

Rice, F. L., & Van der Loos, H. Development of the barrels and barrel field in the somatosensory cortex of the mouse. *Journal of Comparative Neurology,* 1977, **171,** 545–560.

Scheibel, M. E., Davies, T., & Scheibel, A. Ontogenetic development of somatosensory thalamus. I. Morphogenesis. *Experimental Brain Research,* 1976, **25,** 392–406.

Schiffman, H. R., Lore, R., Passafiume, J., & Neeb, R. Role of vibrissae for depth perception in the rat (*Rattus norvegicus*). *Brain, Behavior and Evolution,* 1970, **7,** 360–381.

Shipley, M. T. Response characteristics of single units in the rat's trigeminal nuclei to vibrissa displacements. *Journal of Neurophysiology,* 1974, **37,** 73–90.

Sidman, R. L., Green, M. C., & Appel, S. H. *Catalog of the neurological mutants of the mouse.* Cambridge, Mass.: Harvard University Press, 1965.

Simons, D. J. Response properties of vibrissa units in the rat SI somatosensory neocortex. *Journal of Neurophysiology,* 1978, **41,** 798–820.

Simons, D. J., Durham, D., & Woolsey, T. A. Functional organization of mouse and rat barrel cortex following whisker damage on different postnatal days. *Society for Neuroscience Abstracts,* 1980, **6,** 638.

Simons, D. J., & Woolsey, T. A. Golgi-Cox impregnated barrel neurons in the rat SmI cortex. *Society for Neuroscience Abstracts,* 1978, **4,** 80.

Simons, D. J., & Woolsey, T. A. Functional organization in mouse barrel cortex. *Brain Research,* 1979, **165,** 327–332.

Sokoloff, L., Reivich, M., Kennedy, C., Des Rosiers, M. H., Patlak, C. S., Pettigrew, K. D., Sakurada, O., & Shoinohara, U. The [^{14}C] deoxyglucose method for the measurement of local cerebral glucose utilization: Theory, procedure, and normal values in the conscious and anesthetized albino rat. *Journal of Neurochemistry,* 1977, **28,** 897–916.

Steffen, H. Golgi-stained barrel-neurons in the somatosensory region of the mouse cerebral cortex. *Neuroscience Letters,* 1976, **2,** 57–59.

Steffen, H., & Van der Loos, H. Early lesions of mouse vibrissal follicles: their influence on dendrite orientation in the cortical barrelfield. *Experimental Brain Research,* 1980, **40,** 419–431.

Szentágothai, J. The "module-concept" in cerebral cortex architecture. *Brain Research*, 1975, **95**, 475–496.

Taber, E. Histogenesis of brain stem neurons studied autoradiographically with thymidine-H³ in the mouse. *Anatomical Record*, 1963, **145**, 291.

Theiler, K. *The house mouse*. New York: Springer-Verlag, 1972.

Valentino, K. L., Woolsey, T. A., & Wilson, A. J. Cytoarchitectonic alterations in mouse cortical barrels following different patterns of early vibrissal damage. *Society for Neuroscience Abstracts*, 1978, **4**, 480.

Van der Loos, H. Barreloids in mouse somatosensory thalamus. *Neuroscience Letters*, 1976, **2**, 1–6.

Van der Loos, H., & Dörfl, J. Does the skin tell the somatosensory cortex how to construct a map of the periphery? *Neuroscience Letters*, 1978, **7**, 23–30.

Van der Loos, H., & Woolsey, T. A. Somatosensory cortex: structural alterations following early injury to sense organs. *Science*, 1973, **179**, 395–398.

Van Exan, R. J., & Hardy, M. H. A spatial relationship between innervation and the early differentiation of vibrissa follicles in the embryonic mouse. *Journal of Anatomy*, 1980, **131**, 643–656.

Verley, R., & Axelrad, H. Postnatal ontogenesis of potentials elicited in the cerebral cortex by afferent stimulation. *Neuroscience Letters*, 1975, **1**, 99–104.

Verley, R., & Axelrad, H. Functional maturation of rat trigeminal nerve. *Neuroscience Letters*, 1977, **5**, 133–139. (a)

Verley, R., & Axelrad, H. Organisation en "barils" des cellules de la couche IV du cortex SI chez la souris: Effets de lesions ou de la privation des vibrisses mystaciales. *Comptes Rendus Hebdomadaires des Seances de L'Academie Des Sciences, Serie D, Sciences Naturelles*, 1977, **284**, 1183–1185. (b)

Vincent, S. B. The function of the vibrissae in the behavior of the white rat. *Behavior Monographs*, 1912, **1**, 1–81.

Vincent, S. B. The tactile hair of the white rat. *Journal of Comparative Neurology*, 1913, **23**, 1–36.

Vongdokmai, R. Effect of protein malnutrition on development of mouse cortical barrels. *Journal of Comparative Neurology*, 1980, **191**, 283–294.

Waite, P. M. E. Somatotopic organization of vibrissal responses in the ventrobasal complex of the rat thalamus. *Journal of Physiology*, 1973, **228**, 527–540.

Waite, P. M. E., & Cragg, B. G. The effect of destroying the whisker follicles in mice on the sensory nerve, the thalamocortical radiation and cortical barrel development. *Proceedings of the Royal Society of London, Series B*, 1979, **204**, 41–55.

Waite, P. M. E., & Taylor, P. K. Removal of whiskers in young rats causes functional changes in cerebral cortex. *Nature*, 1978, **274**, 600–602.

Welker, C. Organization of somatosensory cerebral neocortex in micrencephalic rats. *Anatomical Record*, 1973, **174**, 467–468.

Welker, C. Receptive fields of barrels in the somatosensory neocortex of the rat. *Journal of Comparative Neurology*, 1976, **166**, 173–190.

Welker, C., & Woolsey, T. A. Structure of Layer IV in the somatosensory neocortex of the rat: Description and comparison with the mouse. *Journal of Comparative Neurology*, 1974, **158**, 437–454.

Welker, W. I. Analysis of sniffing of the albino rat. *Behaviour*, 1964, **22**, 223–244.

Welker, W. I., & Johnson, J. I. Correlation between nuclear morphology and somatotopic organization in ventro-basal complex of the raccoon's thalamus. *Journal of Anatomy*, 1965, **99**, 761–790.

Weller, W. L. Aspects of the ontogeny of barrels in the sensory neocortex of the deer mouse, *Peromyscus leucopus*. *Anatomical Record*, 1972, **172**, 425.

Weller, W. L. Experimental alteration of neocortex by removal of vibrissa follicles from pouch young Brush-tail Possums, *Trichosurus vulpecula*. *Journal of Anatomy*, 1979, **128**, 659.

Weller, W. L., & Johnson, J. I. Barrels in cerebral cortex altered by receptor disruption in newborn, but not in five-day-old mice. (*Cricitidae* and *Muridae*). *Brain Research*, 1975, **83**, 504–508.

Welt, C. Physiological organization of the rat cortical barrel field following neonatal vibrissal damage. *Neuroscience Abstracts*, 1977, **3**, 494.

Welt, C., & Steindler, D. A. Somatosensory cortical barrels and thalamic barreloids in reeler mutant mice. *Neuroscience*, 1977, **2**, 755–766.

White, E. L. Identified neurons in mouse SmI cortex which are postsynaptic to thalamocortical axon terminals: A combined Golgi-electron microscopic and degeneration study. *Journal of Comparative Neurology*, 1978, **181**, 627–662.

White, E. L., & DeAmicis, R. A. Afferent and efferent projections of the region in mouse SmI cortex which contains the posteromedial barrel subfield. *Journal of Comparative Neurology*, 1977, **175**, 455–482.

Wise, S. P., & Jones, E. G. Developmental studies of thalamocortical and commissural connections in the rat somatic sensory cortex. *Journal of Comparative Neurology*, 1978, **178**, 187–208.

Wong-Riley, M. Cortical barrel fields of adult mice as analyzed with cytochrome oxidase cytochemistry. *Society for Neuroscience Abstracts*, 1980, **6**, 655.

Wong-Riley, M. T. T., & Welt, C. Histochemical changes in cytochrome oxidase of cortical barrels after vibrissal removal in neonatal and adult mice. *Proceedings of the National Academy of Sciences (U.S.A.)*, 1980, **77**, 2333–2337.

Woolsey, T. A. Somatosensory, auditory and visual cortical areas in the mouse. *Johns Hopkins Medical Journal*, 1967, **121**, 91–112.

Woolsey, T. A. Some anatomical bases of cortical somatotopic organization. *Brain, Behavior and Evolution*, 1978, **15**, 325–371.

Woolsey, T. A., Anderson, J. R., Wann, J. R., & Stanfield, B. B. Effects of early vibrissal damage on neurons in the ventrobasal (VB) thalamus of the mouse. *Journal of Comparative Neurology*, 1979, **184**, 363–380.

Woolsey, T. A., & Dierker, M. L. Computer-assisted recording of neuroanatomical data. In Robertson (Ed.), *Neuroanatomical research techniques*. New York: Academic Press, 1978, pp. 47–85.

Woolsey, T. A., Dierker, M. L., & Wann, D. F. Mouse SmI cortex: Qualitative and quantitative classification of Golgi-impregnated barrel neurons. *Proceedings of the National Academy of Science, U.S.A.*, 1975, **72**, 2165–2169. (a)

Woolsey, T. A., & Van der Loos, H. The structural organization of Layer IV in the somatosensory region (SI) of mouse cerebral cortex. *Brain Research*, 1970, **17**, 205–242.

Woolsey, T. A., & Wann, J. R. Areal changes in mouse cortical barrels following vibrissal damage at different postnatal ages. *Journal of Comparative Neurology*, 1976, **170**, 53–66.

Woolsey, T. A., Welker, C., & Schwartz, R. Comparative anatomical studies of the SmI face cortex with special reference to the occurrence of "barrels" in Layer IV. *Journal of Comparative Neurology*, 1975, **164**, 79–94. (b)

Yamakato, M., & Yohro, T. Subdivision of mouse vibrissae on an embryological basis, with descriptions of variations in the number and arrangement of sinus hairs and cortical barrels in BALB/c (nu/+; nude, nu/nu) and hairless (hr/hr) strains. *American Journal of Anatomy*, 1979, **155**, 153–174.

Zucker, E., & Welker, W. I. Coding of somatic sensory input by vibrissae neurons in the rat's trigeminal ganglion. *Brain Research*, 1969, **12**, 138–156.

10

Sensorimotor Development

JOHN C. FENTRESS
Dalhousie University

I. INTRODUCTION

An obvious complement to sensory and perceptual processes is the production of integrated motor output. Indeed, it is often difficult to determine precisely where input and output functions of integrated performance separate, as the two are intimately associated at various levels of nervous system processing (e.g., Evarts, Bizzi, Burke, DeLong, & Thatch, 1971; Granit, 1980). Yet it is upon patterned performance, or in Darwin's term—"expression," that laws of selection in nature operate most directly (e.g., Darwin, 1872; Mayr, 1970; Sperry, 1955). Although performance is important, how the rules of performance emerge during the lifetimes of individual organisms is an issue for which we as yet have surprisingly little basic information.

293

One reason for this dearth of information is that performance characteristics in intact organisms are notoriously difficult to define. We can clearly see that animals move about, and that they do so in various ways. But how many ways; by what criteria? In the abstract such questions are of little utility. What the questions do is remind us that we need to devise methods for separating integrated performance into heuristically appropriate divisions that in turn allow us to determine rules of connection between them over time. The nervous system is quite obviously a temporal machine, as Lashley pointed out some years ago (Lashley, 1951), but the serial nature of its output functions remains a mystery. This mystery is compounded when we expand our time scale to incorporate problems of pattern formation during ontogeny. Performance is process, pattern, and also phenotype (cf. Fentress, 1976b).

A single chapter survey of these issues can only be illustrative, not conclusive. However, concerning these issues, three particularly salient questions can be isolated.

1. How does one separate the action stream into components and their relations in time?

2. How does one determine the relative contributions of certain sensory processes versus central states in the production of this action stream?

3. How does one evaluate genetic predispositions and experience in the developmental formation of this action stream?

To answer these questions, it is useful to consider actions that are relatively modular in their organization, ones that can be related explicitly to well-known sensory inputs, and ones that show clear transitions in their organization during ontogeny. For these reasons, I have for several years examined facial grooming sequences in rodents. These action sequences occur frequently, in predictable contexts, and contain definable subdivisions that permit necessary analyses (e.g., Fentress, 1972). They also tie obviously to sensory processing and go through predictable ontogenetic transitions under various regimes of experience, as I shall show here.

II. THE ACTION STREAM

The first task is one of description, and has two parts: (*a*) What is the context within which motor sequences occur; and (*b*) What is the component structure of these sequences? Of course, these are not questions unique to animal behavioral patterns such as grooming; they apply equally well to action systems over a wide range of complexity, including human language (e.g., Chomsky, 1980; de Villiers & de Villiers, 1978; Luria, 1976). Whereas each action system for each species is in some ways unique, strategies for formulating inquiry can often be generalized (e.g., Fentress, 1980, 1981a).

A. Context

The occurrence of grooming is not haphazard. It often appears between protracted active and inactive states, and during times of relatively undifferentiated (generalized) behavioral "arousal" (e.g., Fentress, 1968a,b, 1972). Hall (1979) has recently shown that infant rats may be rather generally "aroused" by milk injections into the stomach, with the subsequent generation of grooming as well as other forms of motor activity. As the animals mature, more clearly differentiated and restricted feeding responses occur after milk injections, with a correlated decline in grooming, and other behavior. Cohen and Price (1979) have found that self-grooming in rats can be accentuated by the playback of stress cries from which there is no obvious adaptive response (e.g., escape). We have found that voles and mice at various ages groom excessively after exposure to various environmentally produced disturbances when they do not have obviously appropriate courses of action (e.g., Fentress, 1977a, unpublished). There is a close analogy between these observations and what ethologists have described as "displacement activities" in other species, although the mechanisms are likely to be diverse. Their interpretation needs further refinement (e.g., Fentress, 1976a).

Perhaps the single most striking developmental change in the context of grooming is its progressive emancipation from being dictated by sensory cues of the moment, particularly those involving the limb musculature. For example, young mice (6–12 days) may break suddenly into abbreviated grooming sequences when their forepaws pass fortuitously near the face during locomotory attempts, or even during swimming (Fentress, 1972, 1981a). Similarly, Golani and I (unpublished) have found that infant mice can be led to groom almost at will by (a) placing them into an upright sitting posture characteristic of grooming in older animals; and (b) lightly pinching the tail (to awaken—or "arouse"—them). Older animals do not show this posturally generated motor "entrappment," *unless* they have been subjected to various types of central nervous system (CNS) disruption (e.g., Fentress, 1980, 1981a; Golani, Wolgin, & Teitelbaum, 1979). Again one finds interesting analogies to the early ethological literature, this time under the label of "transitional actions." These are actions generated in unexpected functional contexts as a consequence of similarities in motor profiles to aspects of an ongoing movement sequence, such as where a bird that is pecking at its opponent during a fight suddenly switches to pecking at food with similar head movements (e.g., Lind, 1959). Once more the question of mechanism deserves careful exploration.

B. Components

Grooming is not a unitary action. Nearly all adult rodents studied show clearly differentiated and sequentially coupled movements directed to the face, the belly, and the back (e.g., Eisenberg, 1963; Ewer, 1966; Fentress, 1968a,b, 1972). Facial grooming itself consists of definable actions that are hierarchically arranged in time (Fig. 10.1). Interestingly, this modular and hierarchical arrangement appears to be true even though detailed analyses of individual parameters such as forepaw sweep duration, velocity, and area of face contacted by the forepaws are more or less continuously distributed (Woolridge, 1975). This in turn suggests that modular appearance of grooming movements in adult animals depends on definable rules of *synthesis* among individual movement properties (cf. Fentress, 1980, 1981a,b; Polit & Bizzi, 1979).

With that idea in mind, my colleagues and I have sought to unravel developmental profiles of the basic grooming movement dimensions and their rules of synthesis into higher-order structures. We have done this in two ways. The first way has been to utilize the hierarchical arrangement previously determined for adult mice (Fig. 10.1) and to ask (*a*) whether the basic stroke types emerge prior to their sequential coupling; and (*b*) whether the observed developmental transitions have obvious breaking points, or discontinuities. The answer in each case is striking (Figure 10.2).

The smaller and simpler stroke types emerge in a clearly definable form prior to the larger and more elaborate strokes. Nearly as soon as several stroke types have developed they are grouped into recognizable higher-order units that in turn follow one another in the correct overall order, *but* often with rather random strokes being interspersed (see Fig. 10.2). At this time (10–14 days) the strokes, although clearly classifiable using adult criteria, have certain immature characteristics such as irregularity of limb trajectories, imperfect coupling between the limbs, frequent pauses, and so on. By 16 days, these irregularities suddenly disappear and, at the same time, the rules of sequential connection between higher-order units also become adult-like.

Thus the development of individual strokes and their sequential or-

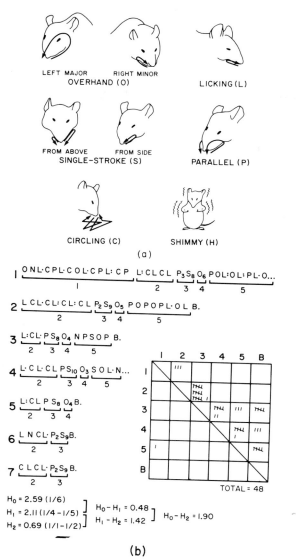

Fig. 10.1 Facial grooming in adult mice consists of a variety of defined stroke types that are combined into hierarchical sequences. (a) Cartoon summary of six forelimb movements found in facial grooming sequences. (b) Examples showing the arrangement of these six movements plus pauses (N) and terminal body grooming (B) into higher-order units (1–5). These higher-order units were defined by abrupt transitions in the sequential arrangement of component strokes, rather like the construction of words from letters in English. The transition matrix shows the sequencing of higher-order units 1–5 plus body grooming in 48 cases. The information statistics (H_0, H_1, H_2) indicate, respectively, the degree of uncertainty of units in a sequence assuming equal probability (H_0), weighted probability (H_1), and sequential dependency of dyads (H_2). Fractions in parentheses are conversions to probabilities of correctly guessing next unit. (Adapted from Fentress, 1972; Fentress & Stilwell, 1973.)

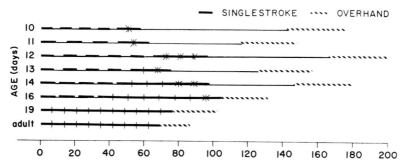

Fig. 10.2 Pictorial summary of grooming ontogeny in 10-day-old to adult mice based on 1500 illustrated profiles of three DBA/2J litter mates. Units (used in Fig. 10.1b) consisting of single-stroke sequences (Unit 3) and overhand stroke sequences (Unit 4) are summarized. Early single-stroke sequences were marked by pauses between successive strokes (indicated by spaces between solid bars) and occasional failure to alternate between major and minor limb excursions on either side of the face (indicated by ×'s). The space between Units 3 and 4 prior to 16 days is indicated. This space was normally filled by miscellaneous strokes that resembled adult Unit 5 movements in their total heterogeneous composition. Note: By Day 16, most spaces between successive single-strokes, most failures to alternate between major and minor paw movements, and the time lapse between the conclusion of Unit 3 and beginning of Unit 4 were all eliminated. By Day 19, protracted adult-like facial grooming sequences were observed, including long trajectory repeated overhands. (Based on Stilwell & Fentress (unpublished) as summarized in Fentress, 1978.)

derings are closely linked, and for each there is a sharp developmental transition after the second postnatal week. It should also be emphasized that, although there is a general cephalocaudal progression of grooming in ontogeny as well as during the performance of long integrated sequences in adult rodents (Fentress, 1972; Richmond & Sachs, 1980), the development of recognizable movement types in facial grooming itself does not correspond perfectly with their order of performance in adult sequences; rather the more simple movements found near the middle of adult mouse facial grooming sequences appear to be perfected earliest (Fentress, 1978, 1981a). This, of course, raises the complex issue of behavioral taxonomy as applied to development, for it is a matter of judgment, and also the criteria employed, as to whether one can state that a movement in infant animals is unambiguously classifiable by standards defined for adults.

Given these taxonomic difficulties, it can be useful to supplement descriptions of action components with descriptions of action dimensions—accelerations, velocity, trajectory, limb coupling, etc. Furthermore, it is often helpful to describe the same features of action from complementary perspectives. For example, facial grooming sequences in rodents can be described either in terms of the kinematic relations among adjacent limb segments or from the perspective of resulting contact pathways between the forepaws and the face. The two descriptions are not necessarily congruent. Thus infant mice may make forearm movements reminiscent of adult facial grooming but without achieving functional contact between the forepaws and the face. Conversely, adult animals may achieve repeated contacts between the forepaws and face through quite variable kinematic configurations.

For these reasons, Ilan Golani and I (in preparation) have recently adopted the Eshkol-Wachmann dance movement notation system (cf. Golani, 1976) to a description of grooming ontogeny from both the perspective of kinematic details and the perspective of functional contacts between the forepaws and the face. Our early intuitions that the kinematic form of facial grooming in mice preceded its successful function (e.g., orientation to specific peripheral irritants) were confirmed. What we had not anticipated was that the young mice first simplified their grooming kinematics upon achieving consistent functional contact with the face (about postnatal Day 5) and then reelaborated these kinematic details some days later (about postnatal Day 10–12). The broad results revealed by high-speed film analyses (100 f.p.s.) were:

1. Newborn mice can occasionally show elaborate grooming-like sequences if given postural support, although the sequences we observed were quite short, involved imperfect coordination within and between individual limb segments (Fig. 10.3), and generated only fortuitous contact between the forepaws and the face.

2. At approximately 5 days, the same mice simplified and coordinated individual kinematic components, and shortened the resulting trajectories across the face.

3. At approximately 10–12 days, there was a marked growth in the richness of kinematic details, now incorporating the head, trunk, and limbs in a flexibly orchestrated and functionally elaborate sequence (cf. Fentress, 1978, 1981a).

That ontogenetically the form of movement may preceed its functionally adequate orientation has been documented in a variety of previous ethological studies, ranging from the opening of nuts by squirrels (Eibl-Eibesfeldt, 1951) to the pouncing on prey objects by wolves (Fentress, 1967). The question of progressive coordination among movement components/dimensions has also received much attention in both the ethological and neurobiological literature (e.g., reviews in Bekoff, 1978; Bullock, 1977; Hinde, 1970; Jacobson, 1978). There are also precedents for the idea of simplification and subsequent elaboration of movement during ontogeny (e.g., Golani et al., 1979; Hines, 1942). Although mechanisms are not clear in most of these cases, they do suggest that control

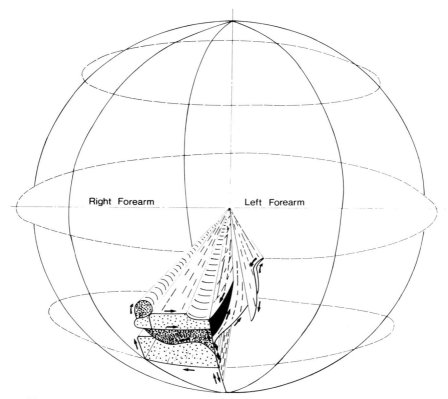

Fig. 10.3 Pictorial representation of facial grooming movements in a 3-day-old mouse. The figure was abstracted from a high-speed (100 frames/sec) film record where the forepaws can be thought of as tracing movements along the surface of a sphere. The asymmetry of right and left forepaw movements at this age is evident, as is the occasional sharp change in trajectory of a single limb due to imperfect coordination of kinematic components. Facial grooming movements at this age are often nonfunctional in the sense that contact between the forepaws and face is sporadic and apparently fortuitous. (Based on Golani and Fentress, unpublished.)

strategies and priorities at different stages of development can be dissected.

We have found that it is possible to mimic some of the earlier developmental stages of grooming by functionally deactivating the cortex with topical application 25% KCl (Fentress, 1981a). For example, adult mice treated in this way are more likely than are control animals to initiate brief facial grooming bouts if their forepaws fortuitously pass near the face, as during locomotion at the edge of a surface (Table 10.1). This is analogous to the transitional behaviors seen in young mice

Table 10.1
Context of Grooming (DBA/2J Mice)

	Motor transitions[b]	Integrative transitions[b]	Totals
Adult normal	7	113	120
(N = 6)	(2/6)	(6/6)	
10-day infant	37	54	91
(N = 6)	(6/6)	(4/6)	
Adult KCl[a]	29	68	97
(N = 6)	(5/6)	(6/6)	
Totals	73	235	308

[a] In the relevant adult group, 25% KCl was administered bilaterally to the cortical surface through small holes in the skull at the beginning of each session.

[b] The number of grooming bouts separated from previous bouts by more than 10 sec is indicated by the integers. The number of mice in each group that showed motor and integrative transitions is given by the numerator of fractions within parentheses.

[c] From Fentress, 1981b.

(previous section). *Motor transitions* are defined as instances in which movement patterns in one functional context become descriptively similar to grooming and suddenly lead to grooming. *Integrative transitions* transitions are defined as instances in which there is not this movement similarity but the animal switches into grooming during transitions between other broadly defined functional states (such as between protracted active and inactive periods). For the data shown in Table 10.1, each animal was tested individually for four contiguous 15-min sessions; each session being initiated by briefly lifting, then placing the animal into a 12 × 12 × 20 cm high observation container. A complete analysis of the component structure of this grooming has not yet been undertaken, but from the work of Teitelbaum and his associates on recovery of movement in CNS-damaged rats (e.g., Golani *et al.*, 1979), I suspect it might be worth pursuing. Levels and priorities among different routes of sensorimotor control do appear to shift in the ontogeny of grooming, and the careful use of developmental profiles can in principle provide useful insights.

III.   SENSORIMOTOR CONTROLS

The most straight-forward initial approach to questions of control is to add and to remove specific sensory inputs. The power of this approach is increased considerably when the manipulations are combined with careful descriptions of ongoing movement patterns. Furthermore, we have found it useful *not* to assume that the behaving animal operates with a fixed set of input–output relations.

A. Addition of Peripheral Stimuli

When adult rodents groom they normally start with their faces, then move to their abdomens, and finally (in prolonged sequences) to their backs (Fentress, 1968a,b, 1972). What would happen, then, if peripheral inputs of different strengths are put directly on the backs of non-grooming animals? The answer is simple and instructive. Mild peripheral irritants, such as light puffs of air or water drops on the back, can generate grooming *but* the sequence in most cases still starts with the face. As the strength, or potency, of the peripheral irritant is increased, the sequence of face–belly–back becomes progressively truncated. With very strong peripheral irritants, such as ether, the back may be groomed directly without the usual preliminaries.

I should mention that this general picture holds when the various irritants are applied in random order (i.e., it is not the result of a simple learning process). The extent to which the sequence might be retrained has not yet been studied systematically, but for other reasons to be discussed, I anticipate quite severe limits to temporal reordering. In this context I should mention that application of peripheral irritants to the face can also increase body grooming due to the normal face–belly–back sequencing. A last point to be noted is that the effectiveness, or potency, of a standard peripheral stimulus can vary widely as a function of the concurrent behavioral state of the animal. Animals that are quiet yet alert are more responsive to a standard stimulus than are animals that are either drowsy or actively engaged in other forms of ongoing behavior (Fentress, 1977a). There is quite clearly a dynamic balance between sensory receptivity, central states, and ongoing action. The precise rules of this balance amongst these dimensions deserve further systematic investigation (Fentress, 1982; see also Chapman & Woodward, 1981; Cohen & Price, 1979).

We have preliminary evidence that young mice (i.e., under 12 days) are less selective in their orientation to localized peripheral irritants than are older animals. Indeed, the most striking data—still rather preliminary—suggest that these young animals are rather generally "aroused" by the application of even quite strong peripheral irritants in the sense that the form of their response is to a large extent predictable by the behavioral "set" of the animals as indicated by body posture, the availability and predominance of other activities such as nursing. This is broadly reminiscent of Anokhin's (1964) model of systemogenesis in development where certain behavioral tendencies are predominant at particular developmental stages and can be engaged by a variety of inputs (also see Hall, 1979). Our data provide an elaboration and refinement on the theme by demonstrating that ongoing postural factors can selectively activate several classes of motor output to standardized stimulus inputs at a given age in young animals (see Fentress, 1979, 1980 for further discussion). In older animals the tight control of response by postural configuration is diminished.

Of related interest in the context of this volume are the striking and progressive changes in an animal's sensory capabilities and integrative capacities with age. Thus, while adult mice have a finely tuned sensory relay system from the mystacial pads and vibrissae through the tactile thalamus (VPM) to the somatosensory cortex (SI) (e.g., Woolsey & Van der Loos, 1970), response patterns to stimulation of the mystacial pads are not obtained in the tactile thalamus prior to postnatal Day 11, and although stimulation of the vibrissae can be picked up as single action potentials in VPM by postnatal Day 5 the adult-characteristic short-latency burst discharges have not been recorded until around postnatal Day 12 (Verley & Onnen, 1981). Similarly, although the striatum has been implicated in the production of temporally integrated sequences of motor activity, including grooming (e.g., Fentress, 1972, 1977; Gispen & Isaacson, 1981; Kolb & Whishaw, 1981), synaptogenesis in this structure does not appear to peak until approximately postnatal Day 12 to 17 (e.g., Butcher & Hodge, 1976; Hattori & McGeer, 1973). Thus, our knowledge of possible anatomical substrates of integrated action today remains at a primitive stage. It has, for example, only recently been demonstrated that the mouse and rat neostriatum (caudate and putamen) develops by neurogenesis along three distinct gradients, with a peak of neuronal proliferation at approximately embryonic Day 14 followed by 25% or so cell death in the first week of postnatal life (Fentress, Stanfield, & Cowan, in press). As we are a long way from establishing precise correlations between such anatomical phenomena and either integrative physiology or behavior, the most efficient and unambiguous source of insight at present often remains at the level afforded by manipulations of sensory processes and observations of motor action in the intact organism (cf. Fentress, 1980).

B.   Removal of Sensory Inputs

The second approach we have taken to clarify sensorimotor relations in grooming is to remove inputs that might be considered necessary, if not sufficient, for the production of integrated movement. For example, by sectioning the sensory branches of the trigeminal nerve (Fentress, 1972, 1977a), it is possible to remove sensations from the face. When this is done with adult animals there is often a momentary *increase* in both face and body grooming in the home cages (Fig. 10.4). The same is true for sham lesions. We expect the observed increases in grooming are due to a combination of (*a*) initial response to the *lack* of normal input from the face; (*b*) stress of the surgery; and (*c*) in-

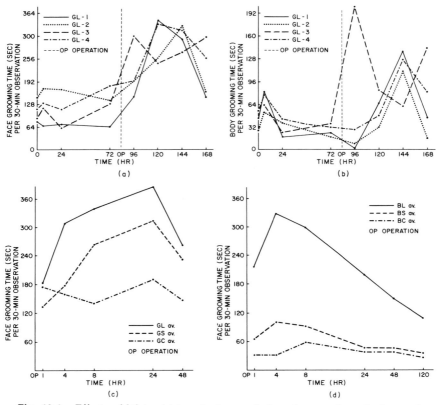

Fig. 10.4 Effects of bilateral trigeminal nerve lesions (sensory branches) on subsequent grooming in adult mice. Face and body grooming in sec/30-min home-cage observation periods for four DBA/2J mice, (a) before and (b) after surgery. Time of operation is designated by vertical---, with OP on the abscissa. A second experiment showing the time course of facial grooming in sec/30-min home-cage observational interval for (c) DBA/2J mice and (d) C57/6J mice. Solid lines (GL/BL) refer to lesioned animals ($N = 6$ for each strain); dashed lines (GS/BS) refer to sham-operated animals ($N = 6$ for each strain), and dot-dash line (GC/BC) refers to controls ($N = 6$ for each strain). The time of operation is designated by OP. (Modified from Fentress, 1977a.)

volvement of body grooming through the normal face–belly–back sequence noted earlier. It would be interesting to know whether the application of body irritants, as just discussed, increases facial grooming even more in newly lesioned animals than in control animals, as might be expected if they truly have a momentary "facial grooming set" (cf. Fentress, 1976a, 1977a, 1981b); unfortunately this experiment was not thought of at the time the lesion studies were conducted.

Between several hours and several days after the lesions, however, we did obtain further evidence for the dynamic relations between sensory and motor processes. When observations were conducted in home cages, the mice were seen to spend an inordinate amount of time grooming their faces as noted. More striking was the frequent observation that the mice would give brief and repeated attention to their faces, pause, and repeat the cycle. Thus the number of brief facial grooming bouts increased even more than is apparent from summed duration scores. However, when these same mice were placed in novel environments we often found it impossible to distinguish their grooming from control animals. Mice in a novel environment tend toward rapid, stereotyped, and abbreviated grooming sequences; the production of these sequences is much less under the control of sensory factors originating from the face than are the more relaxed and elaborate sequences seen in the home cage. These observations have recently received independent support in a study by Chapin and Woodward (1981) who found that rapid motor activity, including grooming, suppresses responses of single somatosensory (SI) cortical neurons to cutaneous stimuli in rats, whereas undifferentiated "arousal" can lead to an increased responsiveness (cf. Fentress, 1977, 1981b; and subsequent sections of this chapter).In brief, context and performance details are extremely relevant to questions of control. Unitary explanations are thus of limited value. These different routes of control in grooming were first reported by Fentress (1972) and confirmed by Woolridge (1975). At present, their differentiation during ontogeny has not been systematically studied, however.

A second line of sensory information that can be removed is the feedback from the limbs via the dorsal roots of the spinal cord. This is relevant to the question of whether grooming is a reflex chain (e.g., Evarts *et al.*, 1971). The first answer (Fentress, 1972) is that grooming movements persisted after unilateral (C4-T4) and bilateral (C6-T2) lesions, and that they were strung together into elaborate sequences. Thus, central programs must be considered in addition to reflex pathways. The second answer is that the larger and more complex grooming movements did show certain irregularities following the lesions, and there was a tonic reduction in movement speed in both the dorsal root lesioned and unlesioned limbs (Fentress, 1972). The mean duration and variance of overhand grooming strokes is shown in film-frame units (64 f.p.s.) and seconds for C57 mice with and without unilateral C4-T4 dorsal root lesions in Table 10.2. Whereas grooming continues after these lesions, the overhand movements both slow down and become more variable. This is true both for the intact and sensory deprived forelimb. Some differences in the detailed sequential structure of stroke types were also seen. The results again stress the subtlety of sensori-motor relations in intact animals; unitary either–or explanations are insufficiently precise for refined analysis.

It would be illuminating to perform these same trigeminal and dorsal root lesions in infant mice. As is the case in many songbird species (Marler, 1976), one might expect that the sensory pathways are necessary for the development of grooming even though they are less important in fully differentiated adult behavior. To date, however, we have not mastered the prerequisite surgical skills. What we can say is that certain routes of experience are not as important to grooming ontogeny as one might anticipate. The clearest example comes from an experiment (Fentress, 1973) where one or both forelimbs of infant mice were surgically removed within a few hours of birth. From previous descriptions of shoulder rotations, eye closures, tongue movements, and body postures, it was possible to trace the development of abortive grooming in these animals. The results were striking. Grooming-type movements in these mice differentiated over the first weeks of life, peaking in probability around 3 weeks of age as was the case for their control littermates (Fig. 10.5). These movements included coordinated eye closures and tongue extensions as well as coupling of the upper

Table 10.2

Duration and Variation of Overhand Grooming Strokes in C-57 Mice following Unilateral Dorsal Root Lesions[a]

	Mean number of frames	Variance (number of frames)	Mean number of seconds
Control mice	13.91	27.7207	0.2172
Dorsal root lesions mice:			
Deafferent limb	20.36	82.2308	0.3181
Intact limb	22.03	70.7207	0.3442

[a] From Fentress, 1972.

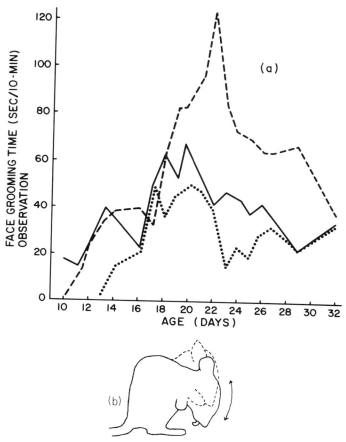

Fig. 10.5 Facial grooming movements develop almost normally in mice who have had one or both forelimbs surgically removed at birth. (a) The three graphs show a developmental peak in "grooming" behavior at approximately 3 weeks in control (—) (N = 3), single-limb removed (---) (N = 2), and both forelimbs removed (·····) (N = 1) DBA/2J animals. (b) The coordination of various movements including eye closure prior to overhand strokes and tongue extension during abortive licking (shown) in operated mice indicates a strong endogenous component to grooming ontogeny. Some alterations in posture as well as an increased tendency to lick other animals or objects in the operated animals indicates the contribution of experiential factors. (From Fentress, 1973.)

arms and head—even though contact between the forepaws and face was *never* possible in postnatal life. Although there were some adjustments, such as an abnormally tight tucking of the body and licking of other objects in the environment as if to obtain "expected" feedback on the tongue, the developmental similarity to normal grooming movements was very striking. It would be of interest to extend these studies through more refined techniques, such as providing collars at birth that would permit only a subset of movements.

C.   Phasic versus Tonic Perturbations

Given the dynamics of behavioral organization, there are limits to the information that can be gained from tonic removal of sensory information. For example, even if an animal continues to perform a given behavior after certain sensory pathways are inactivated, this cannot be taken to imply that the animal is insensitive to *changes* of activity along these same pathways. The point is particularly important if the animal's sensitivity, and direction of response, to specific routes of sensory information varies with the phase of performance in which it is engaged (e.g., Forssberg, Grillner, & Rossignol, 1977). Because of such considerations, Ilan Golani, Michael Woolridge, and I have conducted a series of experiments (unpublished) in which phasic loads are applied to the limbs of mice at different ages, and the consequences upon ongoing sequences of grooming are observed.

The basic idea of these experiments can be seen in Fig. 10.6. The figure shows a young adult mouse that has one forelimb pulled from the face with a thread while it is engaged in face grooming. This disrupts the contact between the pulled forepaw and the face. The result is that the opposite (unpulled) limb also moves to the front of the face, and each limb continues to make several grooming strokes without facial contact. What this reveals is that there is a priority of normal forepaw symmetry over continued ipsilateral facial contact during this phase of the grooming cycle. (Compare to the symmetry of timing of forelimbs in mice with unilateral dorsal root lesions, as well as to the importance of postural and movement "sets" in young mice, discussed earlier.) The point is particularly interesting because by 10 days of age, young mice can perform a variety of body contortions to retain symmetrical facial contacts if one limb segment is prevented from operating in a normal way (e.g., by leaning on a nest mate). Prior to this age disturbance in one kinematic component can lead to a failure in making such adjustments. The particular priorities in adjustment, such as preservation of facial contact versus forelimb symmetry, are possible to dissect

Fig. 10.6 Phasic loading of the limbs of a mouse during different phases of facial grooming has been studied by gently pulling one or both limbs by means of attached threads. In the case illustrated, a single forelimb was pulled outward with the result that the other forelimb joined it, and both forelimbs then continued grooming movements without contacting the face. (Redrawn from Golani & Fentress, in preparation.)

in this way. Changes with age can then be determined (Golani & Fentress, in progress).

A more formal approach to this problem has been initiated by Michael Woolridge in my laboratory (Woolridge & Fentress, in progress). He designed an apparatus whereby one or both forelimbs of the mouse can be horizontally displaced by a set amount during different grooming phases, via elastic threads attached to solinoids. Figure 10.7 shows one of the striking results. During rapid and highly stereotyped phases of grooming, lateral displacement of the forelimbs does not disrupt the normal vertical oscillations of the limbs even though they no longer directly contact the face. One must therefore conclude that there is a strong central component to grooming during this phase. This, however, is in marked contrast to other slower and more variable phases of grooming where precisely the same manipulation produces an abrupt cessation of the grooming sequence. Thus the degree of sensitivity of the animal to sensory perturbations varies systematically with the phase and form of behavior being performed (cf. Chapin & Woodward, 1981).

As in the experiments with the trigeminal and dorsal root lesions mentioned earlier, it would be easy but incorrect to presume that these results indicate a complete lack of influence from the disturbed sensory pathways—at least for the rapid phases of grooming. The horizontal trajectories of the limbs seen in Fig. 10.7a indicate a progressive increase in pressure toward the face with successive strokes, and indeed some overshoot (crossing) of the limbs when the applied load was suddenly removed. Furthermore, Woolridge found that information from the vibrissae may play a role in maintaining grooming during the rapid grooming phase. The vibrissae continue to be contacted by the displaced forelimbs; animals with the vibrissae surgically removed are more likely to interrupt or otherwise modify their grooming behavior when the forelimbs are displaced. Sensorimotor relations in integrated performance are dynamic and subtle.

The question of how these dynamic subtleties are mapped during the ontogeny of the animal remains to be explored. Might we see, for

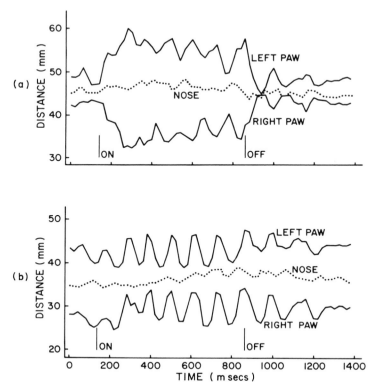

Fig. 10.7 Computer plots of (a) horizontal and (b) vertical vectors during grooming before and after one or both forepaws are laterally displaced permit quantitative evaluation of endogenous–exogenous relations for different phases of the behavior. An instance in which both forepaws were laterally displaced by a predetermined amount (ON) and then released (OFF) during the rapid and stereotyped "single-stroke" phase is shown. It can be seen that, although the limbs were pulled from their initial position of facial contact, the regularity of vertical oscillations of the forepaws continued. Note also the progressive horizontal pressure exerted by the mouse on the elastic threads, with a momentary overshoot when the threads were released. (Redrawn from Woolridge & Fentress, in preparation. Vertical tracings of left and right forepaws have been separated for ease of visual representation.)

example, a shift in the priorities of kinematic and tactile cues as suggested by the aforementioned data on transitional behavior ("motor traps") in young mice? Might adult animals build in a redundancy of cues not available to younger animals? Would sudden displacement of the head in either young or adult animals mimic the results we have obtained to date with phasic limb displacement? It is not difficult to extend such a list of questions. My point is that they indicate the power of combining precise descriptions with systematic manipulations of specific routes of sensory information at different stages of ontogeny. For mammalian behavior, our data base is sadly lacking in this regard. Until it improves, more global speculations about nature versus nurture will remain inconclusive. With these cautions in mind, I shall close with some brief thoughts on the kinds of roles we might expect experience to play in behavioral ontogeny.

IV. GENETIC PREDISPOSITIONS AND EXPERIENCE

A. Diversity of Intrinsic–Extrinsic Relations

As Weiss (1941) pointed out some years ago, a boundary between sensory and motor processes in mammals cannot be sought in absolute and unitary terms, but rather the question is precisely what set of roles sensory processes play in different aspects of motor performance. Thus we might at one extreme anticipate that each of the details of observed action is determined by the pattern of sensory inputs the animal receives, almost as if these inputs are transferred in a one-to-one manner through various intervening stages to the final motor output. Tapping in rhythm to music might be such a case. More commonly we expect that there is a series of transformations in which the details of sensory input play some role but are modulated, translated, or canceled as a function of their interplay with ongoing behavioral states. At a more extreme position on the other side of the spectrum we might expect a stimulus to trigger movement patterns whose details are almost entirely intrinsically ordered. The most extreme case would be movement patterns that occur spontaneously without any reference to extrinsic stimulus (Fig. 10.8). The list could of course be amplified and refined.

The point of view I wish to offer here is that we should explore at least the same diversity of input–output relations in a developmental context as we do in studies of integration per se. Extrapolations of learning theory models to development are basically of the "transfer" type, where a one-to-one relation between experience and performance is anticipated. The failure to recognize that the transformations are often likely to be more subtle than this has led to much of the sterility in the age-old nature *versus* nurture debates (e.g., Fentress, 1977b, 1981a).

B. Gene Activity and Experience

As Davidson (1976) has argued, the cellular biology of development can be viewed most straightforwardly in terms of differential gene

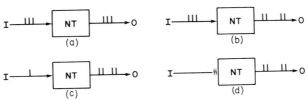

Fig. 10.8 Simplified schematic representation of four classes of input–output relations in behavior. (a) The detailed patterning of sensory information might be *transferred* directly into performance, rather like a simple cable property. Strict stimulus–response models of integration and learning theory approaches to development are couched within this framework. (b) More commonly, one should expect important *transformations* (between input and output due to intervening processes). Ideas such as motivation and attention attempt to capture the variable nature of such processes, as do many models of fluctuating states in development. (c) Stimuli can of be thought of as *triggers* to output patterns whose details reflect intrinsic order with little if any modeling by the input properties. Ethological models of releasers as well as selection models in development are basically of this persuasion. (d) Patterned expression might reflect *intrinsic* processes that can operate in the absence of external factors. Ideas such as vacuum activities, extreme forms of central motor programming, and autonomous maturation stress this viewpoint. (Based on Fentress, 1976b.)

activity. That is, genes are activated or not as a function of the "experience" they gain through interacting with their surround. This means that the product of expression does not necessarily bear any obvious resemblance to the "experience" that is its essential prerequisite. The idea is much closer to the notion of a "trigger" where the stimulus events promote activities that are in some sense already intrinsically encoded. The selection (versus instruction) models of immunology provide the same emphasis upon intrinsically coded capabilities that (metaphorically) are pulled from a file drawer on receipt of an appropriate key (cf. Jerne, 1967).

The application of such models to behavioral development remain curiously absent. This point has recently been emphasized by Chomsky (1980) who discusses the incongruity between the way we think about the development of biological structures and the way we think about the development of behavior. Thus, a child might well need a wide range of experiences to develop linguistic ability, but an important function of these experiences may be to give the child access to potentialities for expression that it in some sense already has available.

It is impossible to judge at present how far such thinking can be carried, or even how it can be translated into concrete experiments (e.g., Fentress, 1977b; 1981a). Yet it does open the issues of what might be critical experience as well as the range of behavioral events that experience might influence. One is reminded here of the study by Birch

(1956) who showed that preventing female rats from self-grooming (by placing a collar around their necks) could lead to a subsequent disruption in maternal behavior. These results are all the more striking in light of observations that female rats do not have to "learn" maternal behavior directly (i.e., by observing other maternal rats). Thus, although they do not learn in any traditional sense, experience from a more broadly defined perspective may still be critical.

C. Comparisons to Biological Development

The biological literature abounds with analogous examples, from which I shall pick two for the point of illustration. Polymorphic social insect species such as ants live in colonies containing a queen, workers, and soldiers (e.g., Wilson, 1975). Now none of these animals has to "learn" the details of its intricate behavioral specializations directly. In that sense, genetic factors are clearly critical. Yet although queens, workers, and soldiers look and behave very differently from one another, they are genetically indistinguishable. What causes them to differentiate down one path versus another is the difference in experience that they have as embryos. This differential experience thus, at least metaphorically, "unlocks" different genetic programs that in turn underlie the complex behavioral specializations that one observes.

Cellular slime molds, such as *Dictyostelium discoideum,* provide an equally dramatic example (e.g., Bonner, 1976). These primitive organisms commonly exist in a free-living amoeboid stage during which they move about at random and feed on bacteria. When food sources become limited the organisms aggregate, forming a sluglike "grex" that migrates in a coordinated manner. The grex then differentiates into a complex stalk with component "organisms" assuming quite varied forms and functions. The stalk gives rise to a fruiting body within which spores are produced, and from which new amoeba are liberated. The transition from amoeboid stage to grex to stalk, etc. reflects differences in experience that somehow tap into different portions of the organisms' genetic potential. Again the behavior is not learned, but experience is critical.

There are numerous related examples that one might cite ranging from transitions between solitary and migratory phases of the locust to the differentiation of organ systems in our own bodies. Yet somehow models of behavioral development have not looked toward these widespread phenomena in constructing new lines of experimentation. I suspect that the liberation of our ideas about behavioral development will generate important new insights.

This, of course, is not to suggest that mice are furry slime molds, nor that extrapolations from simpler creatures can be performed without an eye toward special problems faced by different groups of organisms, different forms of behavior, etc. In particular, there is a danger that these speculations may sound like old-fashioned preformationism in new clothing. I suspect that something more subtle still may be in the offing.

D. Biophysical Models of Differentiation

Recent biophysical models involving the notion of dissipative structures, whereby differentiation is produced through interactions among previously homogeneous ("undifferentiated") systems, provide for such a subtlety (e.g., Katchalsky, Rowland, & Blumenthal, 1974; Nicolis & Prigogine, 1977). Without going into detail here (see Fentress, 1981a) these models have illustrated how it is possible to produce sharp transitions to various highly differentiated states in a way that defies the simple assignment of one role to one element. Once this differentiation occurs, there may be a protective shield of functional inhibition among differentiated parts that prevents their immediate breakdown. Similar conceptualizations have recently been applied to development in "lower" embryonic forms such as hydra (e.g., Gierer, 1977, 1981; Meinhardt, 1979). It will be fascinating to watch their potential applicability to the basic mechanisms underlying more complex neural and behavioral systems such as are the focus of this volume.

V. CONCLUSIONS

Throughout this chapter I have attempted to focus upon the subtle relations between sensory "experience" and the production of integrated patterns of behavioral expression. The first task is to dissect aspects of behavioral performance, see how they relate to one another in time, and then modulate specified sources of potential extrinsic influence. Research on self-grooming in mice illustrates the subtlety of some of these relations as well as their fluidity in time. The data also point, albeit more indirectly, to inadequacies of genetic *versus* experience models of development. To this end I have structured an implicit analogy between "central states" and "sensory inputs" in behavior, and "genetic substrates" and "experience" in biological development. In doing so, it turns out that many of the formal problems involving behavioral integration have their echoes in ontogeny.

If we need to free our thinking about problems of integrated behavior to avoid the sterility of simple compartment models, the same is even truer concerning our present knowledge of development. Dynamic relations as they operate at different levels of order are an essential focus in each case. I have attempted to suggest in later sections of the chapter how we might broaden, as well as make more precise, the questions we pose to developing systems in behavior. I suggest that in all cases we shall have to come to a clearer understanding of control systems that become differentiated through interactions with their surround, and in the process protect themselves from dissipation by that surround. In this way the modular perspective of behavioral control systems can be preserved by viewing these modules as fluid entities that emerge through the context within which they operate.

ACKNOWLEDGMENTS

I thank the editors for their invitation to contribute to this volume, I. Golani and M. Woolridge for allowing me to adapt figures from experiments not yet fully written up, J. Lord, D. Sarty, and F. Stilwell for their assistance with the illustrations, M. MacConnachie for typing the manuscript, and H. Parr for helpful suggestions throughout. The preparation of this manuscript was supported by my NSERC grant (A9787).

REFERENCES

Anokhin, P. K. Systemogenesis as a general regulator of brain development. *Progress in Brain Research*, 1964, **9**, 54–86.

Bekoff, A. A neuroethological approach to the study of the ontogeny of coordinated behavior. In G. M. Burghardt & M. Bekoff (Eds.), *The development of behavior: Comparative and evolutionary aspects*. New York and London: Garland, 1978, pp. 177–202.

Birch, H. G. Sources of order in the maternal behavior of animals. *American Journal of Orthopsychiatry*, 1956, **26**, 279–284.

Bonner, J. T. Signalling systems in Dictyostelium. In C. F. Graham & Wareing (Eds.), *The developmental biology of plants and animals*. London: Blackwell, 1976, pp. 204–215.

Bullock, T. H. *Introduction to the nervous systems*. San Francisco: Freeman, 1977.

Butcher, L. L., & Hodge, G. K. Postnatal development of acetylcholinesterase in the caudate-putamen nucleus and substantia nigra of rats. *Brain Research*, 1976, **106**, 223–240.

Chapin, J. K., & Woodward, D. L. Modulation of sensory responsiveness of single somatosensory cells during movement and arousal behaviors. *Experimental Neurology*, 1981, **72**, 164–178.

Chomsky, N. *Rules and representations*. New York: Columbia University Press, 1980.

Cohen, J. A., & Price, E. O. Grooming in the Norway rat: displacement activity or "boundary-shift"? *Behavioral and Neural Biology*, 1979, **26**, 177–189.

Darwin, C. *The expression of the emotions in man and animals*. London: John Murray, 1872.

Davidson, E. H. *Gene activity in early development* (2nd ed.). New York: Academic Press, 1976.

de Villiers, J. C., & de Villiers, P. A. *Language acquisition*. Cambridge, Mass.: Harvard University Press, 1978.

Eibl-Eibesfeldt, I. Beobachtungen zur fortpflanzungsbiologie und jungendentwicklung des eichörnchens. *Zeitshfift für Tierpsychologie*, 1951, **8**, 370–400.

Eisenberg, J. F. The behavior of heteromyid rodents. *University of California Publications in Zoology*, 1963, **60**, 1–114.

Evarts, E. V., Bizzi, E., Burke, R. E., DeLong, M., & Thach, W. T. (Eds.). Central control of movement. *Neurosciences Research Program Bulletin*, 1971, **9**, No. 1.

Ewer, R. F. The behavior of the African giant rat (*Cricetomys gambianus*, Waterhouse). *Zeitschrift für Tierpsychologie*, 1966, **24**, 6–79.

Fentress, J. C. Observations on the behavioral development of a hand-reared male timber wolf. *American Zoologist*, 1967, **7**, 339–351.

Fentress, J. C. Interrupted on-going behaviour in voles (*Microtus agrestis* and *Clethrionomys britannicus*): I. Response as a function of preceding activity and the context of an apparently "irrelevant" motor pattern. *Animal Behaviour*, 1968, **16**, 135–153. (a)

Fentress, J. C. Interrupted on-going behaviour in voles (*Microtus agrestis* and *Clethrionomys britannicus*): II. Extended analysis of intervening motivational variables underlying fleeing and grooming activities. *Animal Behaviour*, 1968, **16**, 154–167. (b)

Fentress, J. C. Development and patterning of movement sequences in inbred mice. In J. Kiger (Ed.), *The biology of behavior*. Corvallis: Oregon State University Press, 1972, pp. 83–132.

Fentress, J. C. Development of grooming in mice with amputated forelimbs. *Science*, 1973, **179**, 704–705.

Fentress, J. C. Dynamic boundaries of patterned behavior: Interaction and self-organization. In P. P. G. Bateson & R. A. Hinde (Eds.), *Growing points in ethology*. Cambridge: Cambridge University Press, 1976, pp. 135–169. (a)

Fentress, J. C. Behavioral networks and the simpler systems approach. In J. C. Fentress (Ed.), *Simpler networks and behavior*. Sunderland, Mass.: Sinauer, 1976, pp. 5–20. (b)

Fentress, J. C. The tonic hypothesis and the patterning of behavior. *Annals of the New York Academy of Sciences*, 1977, **290**, 370–395. (a)

Fentress, J. C. Constructing the potentialities of phenotype—chairman's opening remarks. *Annals of the New York Academy of Sciences*, 1977, **290**, 220–225. (b)

Fentress, J. C. Mus musicus. The developmental orchestration of selected movement patterns in mice. In M. Bekoff & G. Burghardt (Eds.), *The development of behavior: Comparative and evolutionary aspects*. New York: Garland, 1978, pp. 321–342.

Fentress, J. C. How can behavior be studied from a neuroethological perspective? In H. Pinsker & W. D. Willis, Jr. (Eds.), *Information processing in the nervous system*. New York: Raven, 1980, pp. 263–283.

Fentress, J. C. Order in ontogeny: Relational dynamics. In K. Immelmann, G. Barlow, M. Main, & L. Petrinovich (Eds.), *Behavioral developnent*. London: Cambridge University Press, 1981. (a)

Fentress, J. C. Ethological models of hierarchy and patterning of species-specific behavior. In E. Satinoff & P. Teitelbaum (Eds.), *Handbook of neurobiology: Motivation*. New York: Plenum, 1981. (b)

Fentress, J. C., Stanfield, B. B., & Cowan, W. M. Observations on the development of the striatum in mice and rats. *Anatomy and Embryology* (in press).

Fentress, J. C., & Stilwell, F. P. Grammar of a movement sequence in inbred mice. *Nature*, 1973, **244**, 52–53.

Forssberg, H., Grillner, S., & Rossignol, S. Phasic gain control of reflexes from the dorsum of the paw during spinal locomotion. *Brain Research*, 1977, **132**, 121–139.

Gierer, A. Biological features and physical concepts of pattern formation exemplified by hydra. *Current Topics in Developmental Biology*, 1977, **11**, 16–59.

Gierer, A. Generation of biological patterns and form: some physical, mathematical, and logical aspects. *Progress in Biophysics and Molecular Biology*, 1981, **37**, 1–47.

Gispen, W. H., & Isaacson, R. L. ACTH-induced excessive grooming in the rat. *Pharmacology & Therapeutics*, 1981, **12**, 209–246.

Golani, I. Homeostatic motor processes in mammalian interactions: A choreography of display. In P. P. G. Bateson & P. H. Klopfer (Eds.), *Perspectives in ethology* (Vol. 2). New York: Plenum, 1976, pp. 69–134.

Golani, I., Wolgin, D., & Teitelbaum, P. A proposed natural geometry of recovery from akinesia in the lateral hypothalamic rat. *Brain Research*, 1979, **164**, 237–267.

Granit, R. Reflections on motricity. *Perspectives in Biology and Medicine*, 1980, **23**, 171–178.

Hall, W. G. Feeding and behavioral activation in infant rats. *Science*, 1979, **205**, 206–208.

Hattori, T., & McGeer, P. L. Synaptogenesis in the corpus striatum of infant rat. *Experimental Neurology*, 1973, **38**, 70–79.

Hinde, R. A. *Animal behaviour. A synthesis of ethology and comparative psychology* (2nd ed.). New York: McGraw-Hill, 1970.

Hines, M. The development and regression of reflexes, postures and progression in the young macaque. *Contributions to Embryology Carnegie Institution Washington*, 1942, **196**, 153–209.

Jacobson, M. *Developmental neurobiology* (2nd ed.). New York: Plenum, 1978.

Jerne, N. K. Antibodies and learning: selection versus instruction. In G. C. Quarton, T. Melnechuk, and F. O. Schmitt (Eds.), *The neurosciences: a study program*. New York: The Rockefeller University Press, 1967, pp. 200–208.

Katchalsky, A. K., Rowland, V., & Blumenthal, R. Dynamic patterns of brain cell assemblies. *Neurosciences Research Program Bulletin*, 1974, **12**(1).

Kolb, B., & Whishaw, I. Q. Decortication of rats in infancy or adulthood produced comparable functional losses on learned and species-typical behaviors. *Journal of Comparative and Physiological Psychology*, 1981, **95**, 468–483.

Lashley, K. S. The problem of serial order in behavior. In L. A. Jeffress (Ed.), *Cerebral mechanisms in behavior*. New York: Wiley, 1951, pp. 112–136.

Lind, H. The activation of an instinct caused by a "transitional action". *Behaviour*, 1959, **14**, 123–135.

Luria, A. R. *Basic problems of neurolinguistics*. The Hague: Mouton, 1976.

Marler, P. Sensory templates in species-specific behavior. In J. C. Fentress (Ed.), *Simpler networks and behavior*. Sunderland, Mass.: Sinauer, 1976, pp. 314–329.

Mayr, E. *Populations, species, and evolution*. Cambridge, Mass.: Belknap Press of Harvard University Press, 1970.

Meinhardt, H. The random character of bifurcations and the reproducible processes of embryonic development. *Annals of the New York Academy of Sciences*, 1979, **316**, 188–202.

Nicolis, G., & Prigogine, I. *Self organization in nonequilibrium systems*. New York: Wiley, 1977.

Polit, A., & Bizzi, E. Characteristics of motor programs underlying arm movements in monkeys. *Journal of Neurophysiology*, 1979, **42**, 183–194.

Richmond, G., & Sachs, B. D. Grooming in Norway rats: the development and adult expression of a complex motor pattern. *Behaviour*, 1980, **75**, 82–96.

Sperry, R. W. The neural basis of the conditioned response. *British Journal of Animal Behaviour*, 1955, **3**, 41–44.

Verley, R., & Onnen, I. Somatotopic organization of the tactile thalamus in normal adult and developing mice and in adult mice dewhiskered since birth. *Experimental Neurology*, 1981, **72**, 462–474.

Weiss, P. Does sensory control play a constructive role in the development of motor coordination? *Schwiezerische Medizinische Wochenschrift*, 1941, **71**, 406–407.

Wilson, E. O. *Sociobiology: The new synthesis*. Cambridge, Mass.: Belknap Press of Harvard University Press, 1975.

Woolridge, M. W. *A quantitative analysis of short-term rhythmical behaviour in rodents*. Doctoral dissertation, Wolfson College, Oxford, England, 1975.

Woolsey, T. A., & Van der Loos, H. The structural organization of layer IV in the somatosensory region of mouse cerebral cortex: the description of a cortical field composed of discrete cytoarchitectonic units. *Brain Research*, 1970, **17**, 205–242.

PART D

Development of the Chemical Senses

The five chapters comprising this section offer a remarkably heterogeneous set of examples of current research and thought. Following a period of relative dormancy, there has been a surge of interest in olfaction and taste. Researchers in the chemical senses have diverse origins: Many began with primary interest in animal behavior, discovering that a deeper understanding of the chemical senses was needed to understand the behavior of their animals. Hence, the shape and content of the olfactory literature is, to a large extent, a reflection of questions derived from contemporary ethology, comparative psychology, and sociobiology (e.g., Doty, 1976; Shorey, 1976). Analytic chemists interested in "natural products" have also joined the ranks, and there is a new and much needed sophistication in stimulus control (e.g., Carterette & Friedman, 1978). Workers interested in nutrition, food products, and health have been making significant contributions (Denton & Coghlan, 1976; Kare & Maller, 1967), and a critical number of neuroanatomists and neurophysiologists have discovered (or rediscovered) the utility of the olfactory and taste systems as research models (Carterette & Friedman, 1978; Shepard, 1970). These varied interests are thus forming a lively and creative field.

In a nascent area, it is not surprising that the number of "developmentalists" is still small. It is growing, however, and there is good reason for this. Many mammals begin life with their eyes and ears closed: Olfaction and taste thus represent primary sources of information from the environment. As neonatal behavior is investigated more fully, olfaction and taste emerge as extraordinarily important modalities.

Alberts presents a broad overview of the ontogeny of olfaction in Chapter 11, beginning with a survey of the role of the sense of smell during early life, followed by a discussion of some of the parameters of perceptual development in terms of evolutionary issues and questions of ontogenetic experience. Pedersen and Blass (Chapter 12) present a research chronicle of olfactory control of suckling in infant rats. Theirs is a paradigmatic series of experiments that will undoubtedly set a standard for many future investigators. The study of suckling involves isolation and identification of natural stimuli, exploration of behavioral control, and a fascinating analysis of pre- and early postnatal experiential mechanisms that apparently endow a chemical signal with behavioral meaning. Leonard, in Chapter 13, follows with a helpful introductory survey of olfactory neuroanatomical development and presents a theoretical model accounting for Pedersen and Blass' data in terms of neurobiological processes.

In Chapter 14, Galef focuses on various kinds of postnatal experiences that guide the establishment of gustatory preferences, both in humans and in nonhumans. His treatment of the topic is particularly useful in clarifying the range of concepts that have been invoked to explain individual development and evolution of gustatory choices. Mistretta's contribution (Chapter 15) is a masterful review of the developmental neurophysiology of taste. The uninitiated reader gains a basic understanding of the system, and a special appreciation for the elegant investigations of prenatal function that are described.

REFERENCES

Carterette, E. C., & Friedman, M. P. (Eds.). *Handbook of perception VIA*. New York: Academic Press, 1978.
Denton, D. A., & Coghlan, J. P. (Eds.). *Olfaction and taste* V. New York: Academic Press, 1975.
Doty, R. L. (Ed.). *Mammalian olfaction, reproductive processes and behavior*. New York: Academic Press, 1976.
Kare, M. R., & Maller, O. (Eds.). *The chemical senses and nutrition*. Baltimore, Md.: The Johns Hopkins Press, 1967.
Shepard, G. M. The olfactory bulb as a simple cortical system: Experimental analysis and functional implications. In F. O. Schmitt (Ed.), *The neurosciences: Second study program*. New York: Rockefeller University Press, 1970.
Shorey, H. H. (Ed.). *Animal communication by pheromones*. New York: Academic Press, 1976.

11

Ontogeny of Olfaction: Reciprocal Roles of Sensation and Behavior in the Development of Perception

JEFFREY R. ALBERTS
Indiana University

321

I.   INTRODUCTION

Olfaction is ancient but not primitive. Many "simple," phylogenetically conservative life forms are dominantly olfactory; but so are most
members of our own "complex" class, *Mammalia*. Olfaction is an evo-
lutionarily elaborated, highly refined modality. As researchers have
struggled to become more adept at studying olfactory processes, we
have been rewarded with revelations of a complex and subtle world
of invisible stimuli. Olfactory influences on behavior abound, sometimes as a general tonic modulating force, often as a powerful releaser
of complex behavioral sequences. Many, if not most, forms of animal
life rely on their senses of smell as a primary source of information
about the environment—for recognition, analysis, detection, and the
resurrection of memory.

The ontogeny of olfaction, particularly in species that rely most heavily on their sense of smell, represents a fundamental key to understanding numerous developmental processes. The present chapter is
designed as a general overview of some of the salient phenomena,
features, concepts, and controversies that prevail in research on olfactory ontogenesis. It is written from a "psychobiological perspective",
which means, to me, that it reflects an integrative view of mechanistic,
physiological, behavioral, and evolutionary processes.

A major thesis in this chapter is that to understand *olfactory* development we must include *behavioral* development in our analysis, for
the two are almost inextricably linked. I discuss this linkage in terms
of two major developmental themes: (*a*) the infant's initial adaptation
to the environmental exigencies of early life; and (*b*) successive adaptation to maturational, stage-dependent environmental demands, each
with its own olfactory challenges.

II.   ROLES OF OLFACTION IN EARLY LIFE

To set the stage for the discussion and analyses comprising most of
the present chapter, I will survey the varied and vital roles of olfaction
in early life. The behavioral and physiological processes reviewed here
are not completely inclusive or mutually exclusive, but they illustrate

that olfaction plays an active part in the maintenance and maturation of many vertebrates.

A. Nursing

In his book, *The Expression of Emotion in Man and Animals*, Charles Darwin (1872) described an experiment conducted by a contemporary investigator in which the olfactory axons of young dogs were destroyed. Deprived of their sense of smell, the puppies ceased nursing and in many cases died of inanition. Tobach, Rouger, and Schneirla (1967) revitalized the question of olfactory control of nursing when they surgically removed the olfactory bulbs of newborn rats and produced the same drastic effects described by Darwin (1872). They interpreted their findings to indicate that olfactory input was necessary for the expression of nursing by infant rats, a conclusion shared by others who disrupted rat pups' sense of smell both surgically (Hofer, 1976; Singh & Tobach, 1975) and chemically (Alberts, 1976). Although all of these studies included control procedures, it was nevertheless difficult to make the unqualified conclusion that olfactory input was necessary for successful nursing due to interpretive constraints associated with such disruptive techniques (Alberts, 1974; Murphy, 1976). But, the validity of this conclusion was handily supported when it was reported that careful cleansing of the dam's nipples eliminated the pups' ability to locate and attach to a teat (Hofer, Shair, & Singh, 1976; Teicher & Blass, 1976). Anointing the clean nipple with portions of the substances removed from the nipples or substances believed to be contained therein, reinstated nipple location and nursing; no other substances have been found that can activate this behavior (Teicher & Blass, 1978). Pedersen and Blass (Chapter 12, this volume) provide a detailed account of these elegant and important studies, so I will not describe them further. It is clear from this recent and incisive work, that removal of the cue or interruption of stimulus reception by newborn rats can block nursing behavior.

B. Home Orientation and Approach

The tendency of infant mammals of numerous species to remain nestbound during the mother's absence often reflects active orientation to the odors of the home. If displaced, young rodents and kittens can localize and return to their nests on the basis of olfactory cues.

A variety of tests of "home orientation" and "approach" behavior have been used in the laboratory to analyze aspects of the early olfactory control of behavior. One common behavioral measure is spatial preference. Figure 11.1 depicts a representative testing situation. Young rodents placed on a wire mesh floor above a small divided field display spatial preferences that are determined by the odors emanating from the substrate beneath them. Using this simple measure, it is possible to study maturational, experiential, and stimulus factors that affect this olfactorily guided response tendency.

Odors contained in complex biological products such as urine and feces are sufficient to elicit orientation and approach from rodent pups. Young rodents also respond to the odors of the clean substrate itself (e.g., pine versus cedar shavings) and they can be dramatically affected by artificial scents. Most tests are two-choice, forced-alternative situations. When evaluating such investigations it is usually important to note that the spatial orientation or approach can reflect *either* a preference for one odor over another, or a relative avoidance.

Leon and Moltz (1971) described the rat pup's attraction to "cecotrophe," a soft, volatile, anal excretion passed from the mother rats' cecum (an outpouch in the upper intestine). Testing involved pups' approach to one of two odor streams, created by passing air over bedding material and the residue left by rats. Lactating rats begin to excrete copious amounts of cecotrophe at about the same developmental stage at which pups begin to be attracted to the odor from a distance

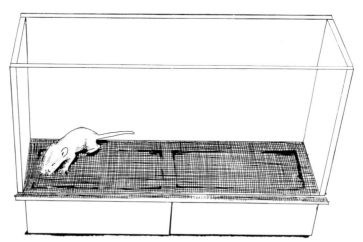

Fig. 11.1 Testing situation used to measure olfactorily guided spatial preferences in young rodents. Scented or nonscented shavings can be presented in separate trays beneath the screen floor; amount of time spent above each odoriferous substrate is recorded as a measure of preference or aversion.

(Leon & Moltz, 1971). Leon found that the so-called "maternal pheromone" is diet-specific; pups are not attracted to the cecotrophic deposits of dams eating a diet different from their own mother's (Leon, 1974). Leon, Galef, and Behse (1972) have argued that *familiarization* with the dam's diet-dependent olfactory qualities was the process underlying specification of the pups' approach reaction. This is an important point of contention because it suggests that olfactory cues are behaviorally active in early life, are multitudinous, and are specified by experience. Indeed, in different testing situations, nonfecal materials have also been found to have behavioral potency (Galef & Heiber, 1976; Nyakas & Endroczi, 1970).

Studies have emphasized the general and seemingly arbitrary nature of the olfactory stimuli that come to control and guide behavior; there is great plasticity in the determination and specification of the cues that become behaviorally active. I will discuss further analyses of the development of odor attraction later in this chapter. Interestingly, it appears that some of the same odors that "tether" the pups to the home, later participate in egression from the nest (Alberts & Leimbach, 1980) and the juveniles' approach to regions of the outside world (Galef & Heiber, 1976).

C. Settling

When an infant mammal is isolated in a novel environment, it often displays signs of agitation and distress. Odors such as those of the home cage or of the mother can exert powerful calming effects. Residual odors of the mother and litter attract kittens, and cause them to settle and cease cries of distress (Freeman & Rosenblatt, 1978a,b; Rosenblatt, Turkewitz, & Schneirla, 1969).

Squirrel monkeys recognize and cling to soft surfaces that bear familiar odors (Kaplan & Russell, 1974). In rat pups, emission of high-frequency ("ultrasonic") vocalizations stimulated by isolation distress and cold, are attenuated by nest odors (Conely & Bell, 1978). Bursts of locomotor hyperactivity in weanling rats tested in the novel cage are eliminated by the presence of nest-typical scents (Campbell & Raskin, 1978). Similarly, cardiac indices of distress and depression can be attenuated in infant rats by the odors of the nest (Hofer, 1970).

D. Contact Behavior

Infant mammals, especially those born in litters of multiple offspring, engage in numerous activities with siblings and adults that involve cutaneous contact. Young rodents, for example, remain clumped in the nest and huddle almost continuously with one another. Initially, the newborns' contact behavior appears to be dominated by thermotactile cues (Cosnier, 1965; Jeddi, 1970; Rosenblatt, 1976) and is affected only secondarily by olfactory input. Young rat pups are relatively unaffected by the nonthermal properties of a stimulus object (animate or inanimate) with which it will huddle. In short, infant rats are promiscuous and indifferent huddlers. Around Day 15 (the onset of weaning), there occurs a profound change in the sensory control of huddling. Although warm cyclinders, members of other species, and furry, inanimate objects remain acceptable stimuli for huddling, the 15-day-olds display reliable and robust preferences for huddling with conspecific (of the same species) stimuli. In short, the weanlings are promiscuous but selective huddlers.

Figure 11.2 shows the results of one such experiment (Alberts & Brunjes, 1978). Standardized huddling preference tests were administered to 5-, 10-, 15-, and 20-day-old rat pups. Each pup was presented with a 40-day-old rat pup at one end of a small test cage and a like-sized gerbil at the other. Both stimulus animals were anesthetized and

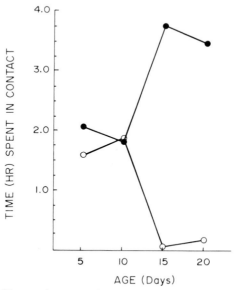

Fig. 11.2 Huddling preferences of rat pups given a simultaneous choice between an anesthetized conspecific (●) and an anesthetized gerbil (○). Time spent huddling was measured from time-lapse videotape recordings in a standard test. (From Alberts & Brunjes, 1978.)

when available singly, were known to be acceptable stimuli for huddling. We observed and quantified the amount of contact behavior exhibited toward each adult stimulus animal during a continuous 4-hr huddling test. Five- and 10-day-old pups were equally attracted to the two stimulus animals, as indicated by the total amount of time they spent huddling. In contrast, the 15- and 20-day-olds barely contacted the gerbil after encountering it early in the session and instead huddled for the vast majority of the test period with the anesthetized rat. It can be seen in this figure that the total amount of time spent huddling was equal across all of the ages tested so that the differences shown were in age related huddling preferences rather than amount of time spent huddling. In other experiments, chemically induced olfactory disruption (by intranasal zinc sulfate) eliminated the specificity of the weanlings' preference without reducing overall huddling, thus supporting the conclusion that the *filial* aspects of the conspecific were determined by olfaction.

E. Weaning and Recognition of Food

Weaning, the developmental epoch during which dependence on mother's milk is gradually replaced by independent ingestion of solid food, can involve several olfactory processes. Little is known about the factors that terminate suckling in developing mammals, but it has been shown that olfactory cues help to determine the site at which weanling rats first eat, and the substances that they recognize and prefer as food. Galef and his associates have elucidated many of the olfactory and behavioral processes that support and guide the maturation of feeding independence. To summarize briefly some of the pertinent features of this work: Infant rats, while suckling, acquire chemical information about specific food substances via flavors that survive metabolic degradation and are present in mother's milk. The pups can later recognize specific food substances contained in their mother's diet on the basis of milk-borne cues (Bronstein & Crockett, 1976; Galef & Henderson, 1972; Galef & Sherry, 1973). Whereas the precise contribution of olfaction (versus taste) to food recognition is now known, analyses such as that of Martin and Lawrence (1979) suggest that in rodents, the sense of smell may be the primary mode of discrimination.

Galef & Heiber (1976) have also shown that exploration of the area outside the maternal den and the selection of feeding site by pups is determined by residual odors deposited by conspecifics. These odors can be quite general in nature; urine, feces, cecotrophe, and other odorants are all effective in this important developmental transition.

Galef has reviewed this work in detail (Galef, 1976; Chapter 14, this volume) and the interested reader should examine those discussions for a more complete treatment.

Newborn reptiles generally receive no parental care whatever and, of course, they do not nurse. Nevertheless, there is marked species-specificity in their feeding topography and diet preferences that are derived without direct parental influence. The primary afferent channel guiding serpentine feeding is a specialized portion of the olfactory epithelium called the vomeronasal, or Jacobsen's organ (see Section III.A, following). Olfactory stimuli are carried from the environment to the chemosensitive vomeronasal nerves by the flicking tongue and reach the nasal organ through foramen in the roof of the mouth.

Burghardt and his associates have performed broadly comparative analyses of the developmental origins of feeding specificity in the largest serpent family, Colubridae (Burghardt, 1970; 1978). For example, the dietary preferences of adult midland brown snakes, Butler's garter snake, and the aquatic garter snake are distinct and species-specific, even though the three species are closely related. Burghardt (1967) presented to inexperienced newborn snakes, extracts from the surface substances of the classes of preferred prey for each species. Figure 11.3 shows the responses made by these neonates to fish, worm, and slug extracts. In each case, the feeding responses of the naive newborns paralleled the adult species-typical pattern. In contrast to rats, the initial recognition of preferred food was independent of prior experience and was not modified by maternal diet. Nevertheless, the young snakes' responses to prey cues were remarkably malleable and could be altered by prior experience with other extracts, differential feeding, and conditioned aversions (Burghardt, 1978). The genetic foundations of chemical cue recognition and its evolutionary implications are beginning to receive attention. For instance, Arnold (1977) and Burghardt (1975) have analyzed patterns of differences in chemical cue preferences within litters and in geographically separate groups of snakes of the same species.

F. Identification of Individuals, Groups, and Kin

Within a few days of parturition, mother rats (*R. norvegicus*) can discriminate their own pups from those of another, same-aged litter on the basis of odors (Beach & Jaynes, 1956). Moore (1981) recently reported that rat dams can also distinguish the gender of infant rats, as early as Day 3 postpartum. This discrimination is based on androgen-

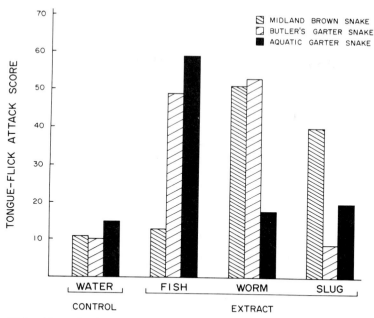

Fig. 11.3 Normalized response scores of naive, newly hatched snakes of three closely related species to chemical cues derived from typical prey. In each case the naive newborns showed their species-typical prey preference. (Adapted from Burghardt, 1967.)

dependent urinary cues that can be transferred across individuals and masked by perfumes.

Rodent pups display the capacity to discriminate home odors. Initially, rat pups are generally and nonselectively attracted to soiled nesting material, but by 2 weeks of age they choose their *own* home odors over those of another same-aged nest, even from the same strain of rats maintained on the same diet (Gregory & Pfaff, 1971). Kittens display a similar developmental pattern (Freeman & Rosenblatt, 1978a).

Human infants can also recognize maternal odors. The 1-week-old human infant orients by turning its head preferentially toward a hidden breast pad imbued with the odors of a lactating woman versus a clean pad. Like the olfactorily guided home orientation response of infant rats, the human neonate is indiscriminately responsive to *any* milk-soiled maternal breast pad. By 2 weeks of age, however, human infants react preferentially to the odors of their *own mother's* breast pad, relative to that of another, unrelated woman (McFarlane, 1975).

In addition to odor identification between parents and offspring, which may help to expedite the formation and maintenance of early attachments, there is now evidence from a variety of nonhuman species that group members can recognize kin—individuals of close genetic relationship. (Olfactory cues appear to provide the familial signature for a number of mammals). Supporting data exists from both field and laboratory studies and are of considerable theoretical interest to evolutionary or sociobiological theorists (Alexander, 1974; Barash, 1977). Hamilton's (1964) "kin selection" hypothesis predicts that, in social interactions, individuals will favor others according to their genetic relatedness. Such factors can strongly influence the structure of social organization and guide its evolution (Dawkins, 1978). Thus, Michener's (1974) finding that wild Richardson's ground squirrels can recognize close relatives after 8 months of separation, and are differentially "cohesive" with genetic relatives, demands that these mammals detect and discriminate cues of kinship. Sherman (1980) has described extensive and elegant field analyses of kin recognition in Belding's ground squirrels and concluded that recognition is dependent on early social–olfactory experiences. Similarly, the work of Porter and his associates on sibling recognition in the Egyptian Spiny Mouse, *Acomys caharinus*, indicates that this precocious murid rodent acquires olfactory information from early familial interactions relevant to recognition of sibs (Porter & Wyrick, 1979; Porter, Wyrick, & Pankey, 1978). It is becoming evident that early olfactory experiences are important functional components in evolutionary systems.

G. Sexual Maturation and Mating Preference

Specific urinary constituents, excreted by adult mice have been shown to affect the *rate* of sexual maturation of conspecific young. Normally, female mouse pups (*Mus musculus*) in the laboratory reach sexual maturity at about 56 days of age. If a litter of mouse pups is reared in the presence of a sexually active male mouse—or just his urine—the females will reach full sexual maturity as early as 39 days of age! Vandenbergh and his associates have examined maturation acceleration in female mice quite extensively (Vandenbergh, 1967; 1969; Vandenbergh, Whitsett, & Lombardi, 1975). Their analyses suggest that adult male mouse urine contains a relatively heavy, androgen-dependent protein molecule that is, or carries, the maturation accelerating pheromone, although precise chemical identification remains a matter of debate.

Adult female mice can play a biological balancing act by exerting an inhibitory effect on the rate of sexual maturation of female pups (Drickamer, 1974). Specifically, pregnant and lactating mice excrete a urinary chemical that significantly delays the onset of the first vaginal estrus in nearby female pups (Drickamer & Hoover, 1979). It appears that such a chemical is present in the bladder urine of all female mice, but that it is usually deactivated by urethral gland constituents before it is passed into the environment (McIntosh & Drickamer, 1977). The ecological import of these oppositional processes has yet to be documented, but the potential pattern is clear. Adult members of mouse colonies possess the ability to regulate the rate at which offspring join the pool of reproductively active individuals. The juveniles' olfactory system appears to be the window through which these messages pass. It is not known what, if any, role the pups may play in this process.

Early olfactory stimulation not only regulates the time of onset of sexual activity in rodents, but it also functions to determine the choice of partner. In a variety of laboratory studies involving cross-fostering and perfuming procedures it has been reported that the odors experienced during early life can have a lasting influence on mating preferences in adulthood (see Alberts, 1976; Doty, 1974 for summaries). In contemporary evolutionary theorizing it is predicted that if one gender makes a larger investment of energy in reproduction, that sex will be more selective in its mating choices. Female mammals invest disproportionately large amounts of energy in reproduction, mainly through the demands of gestation and lactation, as well as other forms of postpartum care. Doty (1974) has noted that the predicted pattern of results appears in the data on early olfactory preferences. Mating choices of female rodents appear to be differentially influenced by early odor exposures. Males remain relatively unaffected by their early olfactory exposures, whereas females' later mating preferences can be guided significantly by olfactory experiences of early life. In these realms of olfactory ontogenesis we can see immediate, tonic-continuous, and delayed effects of early olfactory experience.

III. DEVELOPMENT OF SENSORY–PERCEPTUAL FUNCTION

How, and to what extent does the processing of olfactory input change over the course of development? Do the "operating characteristics" of olfactory sensory–perceptual function evolve during the process of maturation? Answers to such questions are crucial to our understanding of olfactory perception in general and even more pervasively, to our ability to analyze the development of behavior. The development of olfaction and the development of behavior are delightfully confounded. As we have seen, behavioral development in macrosmatic species is largely comprised of the development of olfactorily guided activities. Thus, when a new behavioral capability emerges ontogenetically, we must ask (very simplistically), what is developing—perceptual analyzers or motor capacities? Our task then, is to separate olfactory ontogenesis from behavioral ontogenesis.

There is already ample evidence for ontogenesis in olfactory function. At present we seem to be facing a montage of compelling, but rather isolated shreds of knowledge. However, there are threads of connection and the promise of a coherent picture of olfactory development. Surveyed in the next section is an organization of olfactory ontogenesis that, to me, represents a foundation for future analyses. I will describe anatomical and behavioral data that reflect the nature and parameters of olfactory development. It will be noted that there is a paucity of basic psychophysical data in the forthcoming review. Olfactory stimuli remain elusive tools, difficult to control in "pure," reagent form and generally defiant to identification as natural, biological products. In addition to problems of stimulus control, sensitive dependent measures are still needed. Methodological sophistication is improving, but the olfactory world is difficult to enter with a technology suitable to the high level of performance common to the "simplest" animals.

A. The Olfactory Apparatus and Its Development

Although we are accustomed to speaking of "the sense of smell" as a singular perceptual system, the nasal chemoreceptive apparatus is divisible into at least three separate channels of input. Each of these afferent subsystems is anatomically distinct and each has an exclusive receptor organ, projection pathway, and central target region in the brain. The three primary mammalian subsystems are: (a) nasal branches of the trigeminal nerve (CN V) and central pathways of the trigeminus; (b) the olfactory nerve (CN I) and main olfactory bulb; and (c) the vomeronasal organ and accessory olfactory bulb. The developmental neurobiology of the olfactory apparatus is entirely consistent with these anatomical divisions. That is, each component subsystem arises from a different embryological placode and then matures according to virtually nonoverlapping schedules of mitosis, differentiation, and synaptogenesis (for reviews, see Alberts, 1976; Leonard, Chapter 13, this volume). Figure 11.4 depicts the time of origin of the three classes of neurons comprising the main olfactory bulb, as revealed by standard autoradiographic techniques (Hinds, 1968a,b). Olfactory bulb neurons

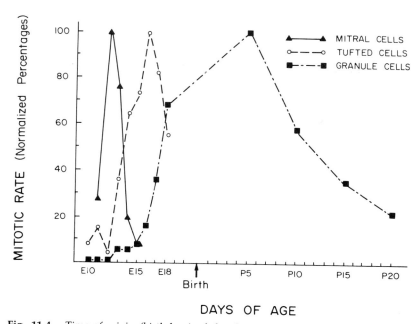

Fig. 11.4 Time-of-origin (birthdays) of the three types of neurons comprising the olfactory bulb of the mouse, as revealed by autoradiography. Mitotic rate is expressed as the percentage of the peak rate for each cell type, to equate for differences in absolute size of each neuron population. (Based on data presented by Hinds, 1968a.)

adhere to the general rule of CNS neurogenesis, namely, that cells arise in order according to final size. The mitral cells are the largest olfactory bulb neurons. Mitosis of future mitral cells peaks about midway through embryogenesis in the mouse and is followed by the birth of the midsized olfactory neuron class, the tufted cells. The small granule cells appear last; these neurons are unusual because they do not begin to arise in significant numbers until *after* the time of birth, when most neuron groups have finished dividing and are migrating or are busy forming synaptic relationships.

Jacobsen (1974) has suggested that small neurons, as a class (termed *Type II* neurons) are differentially sensitive to extrinsic stimulation, relative to larger, and earlier-arising neurons that comprise the *Type I* class. The postnatal appearance of large populations of granule cell *interneurons* implies that the olfactory system may be particularly susceptible to experience. Indeed, the discovery that reduced postnatal olfactory input dramatically reduces both neurochemical activity and anatomical development in the olfactory bulb (Meisami, 1974) suggested that *general* olfactory stimulation is intimately involved in olfactory system maturation. Additional evidence, discussed later in this chapter and elsewhere in this volume (Pedersen & Blass) further indicates that *specific* stimulation also guides olfactory development. Leonard (Chapter 13, this volume) offers a tantalizing neuroanatomical model for the action of perinatal olfactory stimulation that conforms to known anatomical and functional processes.

From a functional point of view, the heterochronous development of the olfactory apparatus heralds a number of intriguing problems. For instance, the three-component subsystems of the olfactory organ arise at different times and mature at different rates. Therefore, the combination and array of chemosensitive inputs carrying olfactory information changes throughout ontogenesis. Moreover, olfactory system development extends well into postnatal life in altrically born, macrosmatic species. Together with the known experiential influences in olfactory development mentioned above, such considerations strongly suggest that the *operating characteristics* of the perceptual system, as a whole, are likely to display important postnatal changes. Reviewed in what follows is a brief appraisal of the functional status and developmental landmarks of olfaction in early life.

B. Sensitivity

Willard Small's (1899) classic study of the development of the rat included longitudinal tests in which rat pups were presented with a number of odorants on cotton swabs held near their noses. Small's vivid descriptions of the infants' affective reactions are barely amenable to empirical replication, but his basic finding that neonatal rats detect numerous complex olfactory stimuli has been repeatedly verified. Human newborns also can detect odorants and, like rats, can localize the source of airborne stimuli, presumably by differences in perceived olfactory gradients (Reiser, Yonas, & Wikner, 1976).

We have described a cross-sectional, olfactometric study of the early development of odor sensitivity in rat pups (Alberts & May, 1980b). Controlled quantities of amyl acetate, a broad-spectrum olfactant, were delivered via a dilution olfactometer to rat pups from 1- to 17-days of age. Ascending concentrations of the test odor were added to a background stream of clean air. Detection of the cue was measured by alterations in respiratory rhythms recorded by strain gauge plethysmography (Alberts & May, 1980a). Figure 11.5 shows the results of this study, which indicate that nasal chemosensitivity improves dramatically and steadily during the first few postnatal weeks.

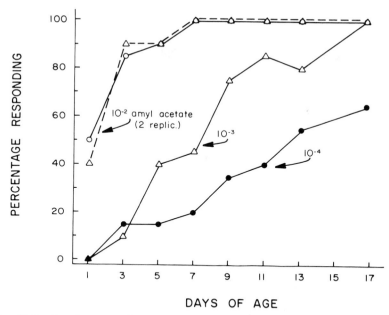

Fig. 11.5   Development of sensitivity to three concentrations of amyl acetate presented in ascending order of concentration. Independent groups of pups were tested with the 10^{-4} and 10^{-2} dilutions (circles) and the 10^{-3} and 10^{-2} dilutions (triangles). N = 20 per age for both replicates. (From Alberts & May, 1980b.)

In humans also, olfactory sensitivity increases markedly during the early postnatal periods (Lipsitt, Engen, & Kaye, 1963). Rovee, Cohen, and Shlapack (1975) have suggested that the dulling and deterioration of perceptual function during aging, typical of other sensory modalities (e.g., vision and audition), does *not* occur with olfaction. In rats, the olfactory system displays cellular renewal both peripherally (Moulton, 1975) and centrally (Hinds & McNelly, 1977) which may be related to its resiliance of function. Such possibilities are highly speculative, but warrant continued investigation.

Early development of chemosensitivity is related to circulating levels of thyroid hormones. Using the same olfactometric tests as those described earlier (see Fig. 11.5), Brunjes and Alberts (1980) found that early olfactory sensitivity is greater in pups administered exogenous thyroxin on postnatal Days 1–4, than in the normal littermate controls. Thyroid accelerated chemosensory development did not appear to affect the final level of sensitivity attained. By 19 days of age, experimental and control pups were about equivalently sensitive to amyl acetate.

In most of this discussion I have referred to detection of olfactants as nasal *chemosensitivity*, rather than olfactory sensitivity, to acknowledge the uncertainty regarding which chemosensitive receptor system(s) mediate odor detection during life. Recall that the various subsystems of olfaction are differentially mature at birth and that they develop at variable rates. Detection could be mediated by any subsystem, singly, or in different combinations. Even the trigeminal nerve, acting alone, could mediate the neonates' detection responses. The trigeminus is an early-maturing sensory afferent (Alberts, 1976) that is broadly sensitive (Tucker, 1971) and capable of mediating odor recognition (Doty, 1975).

C. Discrimination

In addition to detecting the presence of olfactory stimuli, newborn rats and newborn humans can discriminate among a variety of odors. A particularly dramatic instance of olfactory discrimination by a newborn was reported by Johanson and Hall (1979), who found that 1-day-old rats could learn to push either of two, scented overhead paddles in an operant conditioning situation. In this case, the neonates were performing a simultaneous discrimination between the odors of lemon and cloves to receive an injection of milk through an oral cannula.

There is further evidence that the ability to perform other, seemingly more difficult olfactory discriminations, develops early in life. For example, consider the so-called home orientation responses of young rodents discussed earlier (Section II.B). Initially, rodent pups are attracted to the odors of soiled bedding material compared to clean bedding. Neonatal pups do not appear to be differentially attracted to the odors of their *own home* versus the odors of some *other home*. Around Days 9–12, however, rats begin to show a strong preference for the familiar odor of their *own* home in a two-choice test between own and other home shavings. This is a remarkable discrimination, given that the 2-week-old is examining odors derived from the same inbred strain maintained on the same diet, under identical conditions.

Such feats of early olfactory finesse are not confined to rodents. MacFarlane (1975) has shown a similar development of perceptual performance in human olfaction. The results of his experiments indicate that human newborns can detect the odors of human breast pads. Evidence for the development of discrimination came from the observation that by 2 weeks of age, human infants turn preferentially toward the odor of their own mother's breast pad *versus* that of another woman.

D. Recognition and Retention

There is also evidence that rat pups are capable of recognition of odors (successive, as opposed to simultaneous discrimination) and that they may be particularly adept at remembering olfactory stimuli. Odor stimuli evoke distinct cardiac reactions from infant rats. The form of this modulated heart rate reaction can be determined by a single conditioning experience with that odor (Martin & Alberts, 1979a) on Day 3 of life. Analysis of the form of the cardiac response differentiates between odors that are familiar, novel, neutral, and aversive to the infants.

Rudy and Cheatle (1978) found exceptional long-term memory for odors in 2-day-old rats, also using a conditioning procedure. Several sets of studies suggest that the rat pups' memory for odors develops earlier than its memory for other learned, nonolfactory associations (Campbell & Alberts, 1979; Martin & Alberts, 1979b; Wayne, Martin, & Alberts, 1979).

E. Stimulus Sampling

Olfactory perception depends on active sampling of the environment, usually by nasal respiration. The normal inhalation–exhalation cycle of nasal respiration creates repetitive "nasal sampling epochs" during which airborne molecules are swept across the olfactory epithelium. When there is a sudden change in the environment, most animals emit a more rapid and regular respiratory rhythm; "sniffing" is said to occur.

Rats are obligate nose breathers. Respiration thus provides continuous odor sampling. We have studied the development of nasal respiration and rapid, stereotyped sniffing (polypnea) in the rat pup. Rapid sniffing was relatively rare and poorly maintained in pups less than 1 week old. With age, however, there was a notable increase in the baseline rate of respiration, concomitant with more frequent episodes of regular and rhythmic "spontaneous" acceleration (i.e., bursts of polypnea not correlated with any known external stimuli). Such emissions of high-frequency sniffing became more stereotyped in form, more frequent in occurrence, and longer in duration during development.

The development of nasal respiration and sniffing correlates with a marked increase in sensitivity to odor stimuli in the rat pup (Alberts & May, 1980b). To what extent is the development of respiratory "competence" (rate, lability, regularity, amplitude, modulation, etc.) related to the development of olfactory–perceptual input? To what extent is the development of olfactory input related to the appearance of more controlled and stereotyped odor-induced sniffing reactions? Various kinds of spatiotemporal hypotheses of olfactory function posit that rate and pattern of airflow across the olfactory epithelium are integral aspects of neuronal coding (Moulton, 1976; Mozell, 1971) and there is empirical support for such notions. Ontogenetic changes in sniffing (Alberts & May, 1980a) may be important precursors to the development of olfactory–perceptual functions. Because of potential reciprocity in these functions, the alternatives are not necessarily mutually exclusive.

IV. MEANS AND ENDS IN OLFACTORY DEVELOPMENT

A. Function during Development versus Development of Function

Two distinct levels of analysis have been explored in this attempt to characterize the development of olfaction. In the first analysis, the *adaptive functions* of sensory–perceptual events in the life of the young mammal were evaluated. Broadly speaking, olfaction makes two kinds of contributions to the adaptational systems of development: (*a*) olfactory perceptual function *maintains* the organism by mediating behavioral adjustments to numerous moment-to-moment, proximate demands of the environment (e.g., nipple location, attraction to the nest); and (*b*) olfactory stimulation during early life *prepares* the developing organism for the bevy of later, olfactorily guided activities, many of which relate directly to the organism's reproductive success and, hence, its inclusive fitness (e.g., rate of sexual maturation, sexual preference). The preparatory roles of olfactory function appear as delayed or remote effects, expressed after some amount (in time or degree) of specific olfactory system activity has accrued, or after the maturation of other response systems (e.g., locomotor).

The second analysis was concerned with the *operating characteristics* of the sense of smell during ontogenesis. Here we focused on the parameters and perceptual capacities for processing olfactory input. Such concerns probably best represent the kinds of issues that have traditionally been examined by workers interested in perception. The olfactory system was found to be functional in the newborn mammal and, although systematic analyses are limited in number, there is good evidence that the power and intricacy of olfactory processing increases markedly during early postnatal life. Thus olfaction, like all other sensory systems that have been analyzed, manifests "function prior to complete maturation," a characteristic pattern of sensory development documented and explored by Gottlieb (1971).

Both of these levels of analysis—the early adaptive roles of olfaction (function during development) and the changing parameters of perception (development of function)—are essential for a full appreciation of the development of olfaction. To discuss behavioral development without paying explicit attention to the changes of perceptual inputs or, to consider the process of sensory development devoid of its behavioral implications, diminishes unnecessarily the meaning and interpretability of empirical data.

Although these two levels of analysis are closely related and interdependent, their relationship is fundamentally asymmetrical. As shown in the early sections of this chapter, most newborn mammals rely on olfactory input to adapt to their postuterine world; without it they would die. Thus, to the extent that olfactory perceptual function fulfills vital, adaptational functions, I regard the maturation of perceptual processing in macrosmatic infants as a *means* to the adaptive *ends* of nursing, huddling, and mating. We can consider the development of olfactory–perceptual processing in all its pre- and postnatal aspects to be the means to some specific olfactory guided adaptations. We should certainly expect to discover significant bidirectionality in structure–function and sensory maturation–behavioral development relationships involving the olfactory system. Data to be presented later in this chapter and elsewhere in this volume address such issues.

B. Specialization and Induction

Perhaps the most important general aspect of olfactory system maturation is the establishment of perceptual preferences that serve the ontogenetic adaptations of the newborn and the juvenile. Such perceptual preferences are usually recognized through *behavior*: The developing organism is attracted to certain stimuli and is repelled or unaffected by others. At each stage in development, there are significant alterations in the stimuli that are relevant to the organism, and in the responses that are relevant to the situation. Perceptual preferences must therefore appear, disappear, and evolve at the proper time and in the correct sequence.

It is possible to conceive of two kinds of processes that could serve as ontogenetic pathways in the formation of stage-appropriate perceptual preferences. I shall use the terms specialization, and induction to describe the two processes.

Specialization refers to perceptual preferences based on predetermined receptor or CNS mechanisms whose operating characteristics are relatively insensitive to appearance.

Induction refers to processes by which extrinsic stimulation acts on receptor or CNS mechanisms to bias the organism's response to certain stimuli; it is based on experience-sensitive changes. Gottlieb (1976) introduced the term induction into the behavioral literature, drawing on its historical importance to embryologists. Defined operationally, induction of a behavioral activity occurs when the presence or absence of particular stimuli determine whether the activity will manifest itself. Similarly, induction can also be recognized when the development of a perceptual preference or perceptual capacity is dependent on antecedent stimulus events.

1. Specialization of Olfactory Function

During olfactory development, when the sensory system is grossly incomplete and function is limited, the survival of the organism is nonetheless dependent on reliable performance of olfactory feats. It would seem that the incomplete olfactory system of rats is probably highly refined and specialized for specific tasks—such as olfactory detection of nipples. Such specializations could be based on genetic predetermination of specific receptors.

Genetic factors can limit, determine, or bias olfactory perception. There are documented examples of "specific anosmias" in which subjects appear olfactorily normal except for their inability to detect certain odors (Amoore, 1971). To the extent that these specific anosmias are cases of "odor blindness," akin to cases of genetically linked color blindness, we may someday be able to recognize the development of specific types of olfactory receptors.

Galef and Kaner (1980) have suggested that "The preference of rat pups for biologically important odors might well be less dependent on experience than is the development of preferences for odors of less biological relevance [p. 593]." In my laboratory, we have asked whether rat pups, exposed for equal amounts of time to unadulterated conspecific odors of a mother rat *and* to an artificial odor superimposed on a mother rat, would tend to develop a stronger attraction to the "natural" olfactory stimulus. Our results indicated that pups developed equal attachments to the two test odors (natural versus artificial), as measured by their huddling preferences: No specialized bias (preference) for the natural stimulus was revealed (Alberts, Addison, & May, 1980). These results, then, suggest that the rats' immature olfactory system may *not* be specialized to prefer conspecific odors as attractants for huddling. Other factors and other mechanisms, however, could create a species-typical perceptual specialization.

For instance, differential sensitivity could also be a source of perceptual bias. Using our olfactometric techniques described earlier, we have investigated whether the rat pups' olfactory system is biased or specialized during development to be differentially sensitive to odors of the species. The development of chemosensitivity to natural, species-relevant cues (rat urine odors) was compared with sensitivity to an "arbitrary" chemical odorant (amyl acetate). The strength of the two stimuli was "normalized" empirically for just one age group and then we compared the course of development of sensitivity for these cues. Figure 11.6 shows the results. Note that the broken lines in Fig. 11.6 are the sensitivity values for 10^{-4} and 10^{-3} concentrations of amyl acetate that were presented in Fig. 11.5, earlier. The development of the rat pup's sensitivity to urine odors appeared equivalent to the development of sensitivity to the chemical odorant amyl acetate. In short, there was no evidence for a bias in chemosensitivity between a real, relevant, biological product and the reagent odor of amyl acetate.

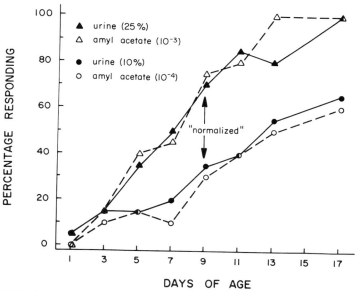

Fig. 11.6   Development of sensitivity to two concentrations of urine odors (solid lines), compared to the development of sensitivity to amyl acetate. Strength of urine stimuli was adjusted empirically to match the strength of amyl acetate for the 9-day-olds. (From Alberts & May, 1980b.)

It is impossible to reject the important possibility of olfactory specialization in infancy on the basis of sensitivity tests with only two odorants
(see discussion, Alberts & May, 1980b). Additional tests with a broader
range of stimuli and measurements are called for. Given the marked
behavioral preferences for specific prey types, it would seem particularly
instructive to have further insight into the means by which reptilian
young derive their vomeronasal biases for the chemical cues of species-
typical prey types (cf., Arnold, 1977; Burghardt, 1978) described earlier.

2. Induction of Olfactory Function

There is abundant evidence for the progressive establishment of olfactory preferences during early life (for examples, see Section II) In
fact, the bulk of postnatal olfactory development seems to involve formation of experience-dependent perceptual preferences. The literature
is now replete with numerous demonstrations of experience-dependent
effects derived from olfactory stimulation. Researchers have proceeded
to unravel the variety of mechanisms underlying the development of
olfactorily guided preferences and aversions. These mechanisms can
vary in specificity, in the type of responses they support, and in the
endurance of their effects. Such considerations have been discussed by
Brunjes and Alberts (1979) and Galef and Kaner (1980). In the following
section I shall further explore some of these issues.

V. ROUTES TO BEHAVIORAL SPECIFICITY

In the foregoing paragraphs, I have made frequent use of "perceptual
preferences" as a type of developmental endpoint. I suggested that
olfactory stimulation can act to "specify" such preferences. I have also
made the point, however, that sensory–perceptual development is a
means to the end of adaptive, developing behavior. Thus, the establishment of perceptual preferences suitable for different ontogenetic
situations, whether by "specialization" or "induction" or any other
hypothesized process, is a means of producing stage-appropriate behavioral specificity (i.e., endowing behavior with a dynamic organization
that functions adaptively). As maturation proceeds, there is a marked
increase in the range of stimuli that affect behavior, but there is also
an increase in the specificity of the stimuli that come to regulate particular behavioral activities. We have repeatedly noted this theme in
our considerations of the development of olfactorily controlled behavior.
Whatever the means, behavioral specificity is the outcome, and, as
Lehrman (1970, p. 36) eloquently stated:

Nature selects for *outcomes.* Natural selection acts to select genomes that, in a normal environment, will guide development into organisms with the relevant adaptive characteristics. But the path of development from the zygote stage to the phenotypic result is devious, and includes many developmental processes including, in some cases, experience.

In the present section I shall discuss some cases in which experience does, in fact, play a major role in the developmental production of the "phenotypic result." It appears to me that in rodents at least, such cases represent the rule rather than the exception, for the development of behavioral specificity based on olfactory stimuli. I should reiterate that this section is not intended to be a review; instead, I have chosen to describe a set of experiments, mostly from my own laboratory, that illustrate some of the conceptual issues at hand. The focus of the discussion is on the different, "devious" routes that experiential processes can take to create the phenotypic result. In this case the phenotypic result is a perceptual preference of rats that is manifest in the specificity of their social contact behavior.

A. The Phenomenon: Olfactory Induction of Filial Huddling

Contact behavior (huddling) by rats, introduced earlier in this chapter (Sections II.D; IV.B), provides a clear behaviorial phenotype for developmental analysis and can serve as a "model system" for an analysis of the development of behavioral specificity. Huddling begins in the nest immediately after birth, as the infants clump together with their littermates and mother. During the first 2 weeks of life huddling by rats is dominated by thermotactile cues (Alberts, 1978; Alberts & Brunjes, 1979; Cosnier, 1965; see Rosenblatt, 1976 for a thorough review). However, by Day 15 and thereafter olfaction dominates huddling; rats express their olfactory–perceptual preference by huddling preferentially with targets that bear conspecific olfactory cues (Alberts & Brunjes, 1978; see Fig. 11.2).

The development of the rats' olfactory preferences, then, results in expression of "normal" affiliative tendencies, a form of behavioral specificity in the young rat—that we refer to as "filial huddling" (Alberts & Brunjes, 1979). We suggested that the development of preference for conspecific odors might be an acquired preference, derived from experiences in the nest with conspecific odors.

To examine whether the rats' filial huddling preferences are malleable by experience, we applied a novel, nonbiological odor (Coty's "Wild Musk" perfume) to the ventrum of mother rats and allowed the litters

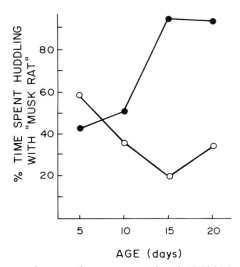

Fig. 11.7 Rat pups whose mother was scented with "Wild Musk" perfume showed a preference for huddling with a musk-scented anesthetized stimulus rat (●), relative to a non-scented, "normal" rat (○), beginning around Day 15. Control animals begin to prefer the normal stimulus at that age.

to be raised normally (Brunjes & Alberts, 1979). Pups of various ages were given a standardized two-choice preference test for huddling with an unaltered rat (the species-typical stimulus) and a "Wild Musk rat" (i.e., a stimulus rat scented with the "Wild Musk" perfume). Figure 11.7 shows that pups reared by musk-mothers showed no significant preference for huddling with a "musk rat" versus a "normal" rat until Day 15, at which time they strongly preferred "musk rats" to the "normal" species-typical stimulus. Control subjects, pups from litters whose mothers were treated every day with water, not perfume, developed the typical conspecific preference—also by Day 15. The time course of experimentally induced odor preference thus parallels the normal appearance of olfactorily guided filial huddling, supporting the view that the rats' first affiliative responses to species odors are *acquired* from early experiences in the nest. Therefore, we should be able to isolate and to identify the *kinds of experiences* that are necessary and sufficient to determine the development of such behavioral specificity. Described in the following sections are a series of recent experiments, largely from my laboratory, designed to titrate the nest environment into separable sources of experience.

B.   Familiarity and "Mere Exposure"

In the experiments to be described, variants of the following procedure were used: Each day, from Days 1–14, rat pups are taken from their own mothers and given for 4 hr to a foster mother. The foster dam bears a novel scent (Odor A). The attractiveness of Odor A is compared to another novel nonbiological odor (Odor B) in a standard two-choice test of huddling preference. Huddling stimuli in the preference tests are inanimate, furry cylinders containing measured quantities of Odor A, or the other synthetic scent, Odor B. Pups readily huddle with such stimuli presented singly. Relative *preferences* between two stimuli are measured by presenting both simultaneously, positioned at opposite ends of a small chamber (Alberts, 1978). Time-lapse videographic recordings provide a quantifiable, continuous measures of huddling by the pups. All experiments described were run with Odors A and B counterbalanced. I will treat these olfactants as interchangeable and equipotent, as they seem to be (Alberts, Addison, & May, 1980).

I.   *Induction of Huddling Preferences*

We have replicated the basic effect reported by Brunjes & Alberts (1979) with daily, 4-hr exposures to a scented foster dam. Figure 11.8a shows that 15-day-old pups that received maternal care in the nest of

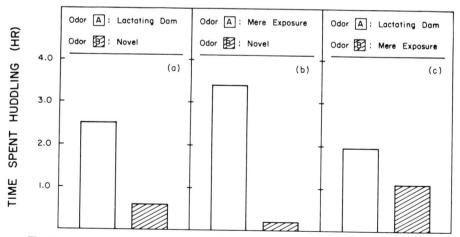

Fig. 11.8   Huddling preferences of individual rat pups choosing between two "pelts" of scented, artificial fur. Odors were associated with different daily experiences or were unfamiliar to the subjects.

a scented foster dam exhibited a strong huddling preference for a pelt bearing the foster dam's perfume (Odor A) relative to another pelt scented with a different fragrance (Odor B). (These pups would nevertheless prefer the odor of rat to either perfume; but they had experienced unadulterated rat scent at least 20 hr/day). This replication of induced filial preference set the stage for the series of experiments to follow.

2.   "Mere Exposure" Produces Behavioral Preferences

Is it necessary that rat pups experience olfactants on the fur of a lactating maternal rat for them to acquire a filial preference for that odor or would mere exposure be sufficient? We placed litters in small, odoriferous containers for 4 hr/day. By Day 15 these pups were experienced with the nonbiological odor, as were their counterparts in the foster mother study just described. The huddling preference tests revealed the same robust filial attraction (Fig. 11.8b as that seen after foster maternal care.

Leon *et al.* (1979) have described a similar finding relevant to the extensive investigations of the "maternal pheromone." In their study pups were exposed to an airstream containing the odor of peppermint for 3 hr/day while isolated in a chamber (equivalent to our "mere exposure" condition). Their preexposed pups responded to a peppermint airstream in Leon's standard approach test as though it was their mother's cecotrophic scent (Section II.B.; Leon, 1975).

Such results demonstrate that the consequences of simple exposure to an olfactory cue are sufficient to establish an apparent preference for that odor. What is the nature of this experience-dependent process? Sluckin (1964) has postulated that there is a general, nonassociative acquisition process, termed *exposure learning,* which involves "perceptual registration by the organism of the environment of which it is exposed [p. 109]."

However, instances of presumed exposure learning can also be explained in terms of *mere exposure,* experiences that familiarize the subject with a cue and act to decrease novelty reactions (avoidance) toward those features of the environment. Unfortunately, most testing protocols do not differentiate whether an animal is showing a diminished aversion to one stimulus, or if a behavioral preference actually represents a response of active, positive valence. This is a fundamental distinction that can significantly affect the accuracy of our formulations of developmental processes (see Brunjes & Alberts, 1979). We should consider these distinctions in the design and interpretation of our measures of preference.

C. Beyond the Effects of "Mere Exposure"

Perceptual preferences for an artificial odor can be established by *either* experiences with that odor on a foster mother, *or* mere exposure to the odor on an equivalent schedule (Fig. 11.8a,b). It is not safe to assume, however, that the strength, endurance, or nature of the preferences are similar or equivalent (Alberts & Brunjes, 1978; Galef & Kaner, 1980). We have derived a procedure that can be used to compare the strength of olfactory preferences induced by different kinds of experiences within the same animal. The basic paradigm is as follows: Litters of rat pups are given alternating bouts of daily exposure to two odorants, from Days 1–14, postpartum. Each odor is experienced for 4 hr/day on alternate days. Thus, on Day 15 (when olfactorily guided, filial huddling emerges in our tests) the pups have had equal experience with the two odors. By manipulating the conditions of odor exposure (e.g., on a dam, mere exposure) we can evaluate, by testing olfactory guided filial huddling choices, the relative degree of odor preference established by the two kinds of experience.

The procedure revealed an important finding. When one odor was presented on the ventrum of a lactating foster dam, the odor associated with the foster mother was strongly preferred to the odor of exposure. (All treatments are counterbalanced for olfactants.) The histograms in Fig. 11.8c show the results. Exposure learning is sufficient to alter the pups' behavioral response, but it does *not* induce the same kind or degree of attraction as that derived from olfactory experience contiguous with some aspect(s) of maternal care. It is exciting to note Galef and Kaner's (1980) recent report that odor preferences established by simple exposure conditions are not as long-lasting as odor preferences established by contact with a foster dam.

D. Identification of Inductive Experiences

We have asserted previously (Brunjes & Alberts, 1979) that the normal, species-typical huddling preference of rat pups is probably established by a process of induction, as defined by Gottlieb (1976). Briefly, the induction of a species-typical behavioral activity (such as filial huddling) is said to occur when a sensory–perceptual preference that directs or canalizes the behavior is determined (induced) by previous stimulus events (Gottlieb, 1976, Pp. 37–38; see Gottlieb, Chapter 1, this volume and Aslin, Volume 2, for discussions that amplify these conceptual issues). According to this view, rats prefer rats because an olfactory preference that directs their affiliative behavior is induced by early experience. The "normal" or species-typical phenotype arises not because it is an invariant feature of the organism, but because there are species-typical features of the early environment that produce the phenotype. What are the inductive features of the pups' early environment.

Clearly, some of the stimuli presented by a foster dam make significant contributions to the establishment of filial odor attachments. We can now proceed to assess the effects of various components of the maternal complex as factors that can enhance the affective value of odors.

1. Is Nutritive Reward Necessary for the Formation of Filial Attachment?

In the next experiment, rat pups were again given alternating odor experiences. As in previous study, one olfactant was an "odor of exposure" presented in the atmosphere of a plastic chamber. The second odor was presented on the ventrum of a nonlactating but maternally responsive rat.

It is known that nonreproductive female (or male) rats can be induced into a condition of "maternal responsiveness" by continuously exposing the subject to litters of active infant rats. With 4–7 days of such exposure, the adult builds a nest, retrieves the pups, licks them, and crouches over the litter in the stereotyped nursing posture (Rosenblatt, 1969). Normal levels of maternal care are provided, but no milk is delivered and, in most cases, the female's nipples remain sufficiently involuted so that nipple attachment does not occur. We exploited this phenomenon and associated the second odor with such nonnutritive maternal services.

The results indicated that the nutritive consequences of suckling are not necessary for pups to form a filial preference for an odor because odors associated with nonnutritive maternal care were vastly more attractive than odors of exposure.

2. Does Mother's Milk Make a Difference?

In the next experiment, rat pups were given equivalent exposure to two odorants on alternative days. Odor A was borne by a *lactating* foster dam that brooded the test litter, licked them, and delivered milk when they suckled. On the alternate days, the same subjects went for 4 hr to a *nonlactating* foster dam, rendered maternal as described, and bearing Odor B. Thus, both odors were associated with maternal care but only one odor was associated with nipples to suckle and delivery of milk. Figure 11.9a shows that there was no difference in the pups' affiliative attraction to these odors. The rewards of suckling, although

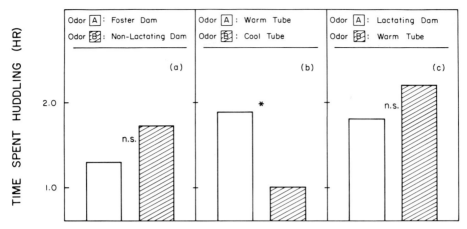

Fig. 11.9   Huddling preferences of rat pups choosing between two "pelts" of scented, artificial fur. Odors were presented for 4 hr/day under different conditions shown at top of each panel. $N = 12$ per group. Subjects were 15–16 days old. *$p < .05$.

powerful in other situations (Kenny & Blass, 1977), made no measurable, additive differences in the formation of rats' filial huddling preferences.

3.   The Odor-Heat Hypothesis

Taken together, the results of our analysis suggest that filial odor attachments arise when odors are experienced in concert with a maternal dam; the effective inductive experiences, however, are not dependent on nursing interactions. The thermal properties of the rodent nest have recently been demonstrated to exert powerful influences on behavioral and physiological relations of the mother and offspring, particularly at early developmental stages when the young are thermally fragile (Alberts, 1978a; Cosnier, 1965; Leon, Crosskerry, & Smith, 1979; Rosenblatt, 1976). We therefore investigated the possibility that odor attachments could develop through association with thermal energy.

Pups received alternating 4-hr odor exposures from inanimate, immobile, odorized cylinders, one of which was left at room temperature (22°C) and the other warmed to the surface temperature approximating that of an adult rat (32°C). As shown in Fig. 11.9b, the huddling preference tests revealed that the odor borne on the warm cylinder was strongly preferred.

We again used the within-subject, alternating odor procedure to determine the relative potency of perceptual preferences produced by experience with a warm tube versus a lactating dam. The results, shown in Fig. 11.9c, suggest that the magnitude of the odor preferences derived from the warm cylinder are equivalent to those induced by experience with a lactating foster mother! Before concluding that a mother rat can be reduced to a thermostatically controlled tube, we are undertaking further analyses. It is instructive to note that we have also discovered that neonatal rat pups rapidly acquire odor–temperature associations after brief (10 min) exposures to a test odor paired with severe cold (10°C). Using a measure of cardiac responsivity to odor cues, we found that infant rats had formed conditioned aversive associations to odors on the basis of the brief temperature pairings (Martin & Alberts, 1979a). The rapidity and strength of this odor–temperature conditioning rivals that of conditioned taste and odor aversions (Campbell & Alberts, 1979; Rudy & Cheatle, 1977). Together, these findings imply that odor–temperature associations are readily formed in the infant rat and that the maternal nest represents a learning milieu in which the infant can acquire its olfactory identity. With analyses such as these, we are penetrating into the experiential mechanisms whereby olfactory stimuli acquire behavioral meaning through identified developmental processes.

VI. SUMMARY AND CONCLUDING REMARKS

Olfaction is functional at birth and provides life-sustaining information to even the most altricial neonates. In light of the salience and crucial importance of the sense of smell during early life it seems paradoxical that olfaction is mediated by a sensory system that is anatomically and functionally incomplete. I have attempted in this chapter to delineate and to resolve at least partially the paradox of function during development *versus* the development of function.

Function-during development refers to the varied roles of olfaction in guiding behavioral adjustments to the immediate environment during early life, as well as preparing perceptual preferences for later expression. Olfactory control of nursing is an example of an immediate functional role of olfaction during development. The formation of odor preferences for mate selection is an example of a more remote functional role of early olfactory experiences.

Coincident with the early involvement of olfactory stimuli in behavioral control is a dramatic improvement of olfactory perceptual processing, i.e., the *development of function*. Although complete empirical accounts are sorely lacking, there is evidence that perceptual function improves considerably during early life. In the rat pup, olfactory sensitivity, odor discrimination, and stimulus sampling (sniffing) have been found to improve during the preweaning period. At this time there also appears throughout the olfactory apparatus dramatic structural changes, involving the birth and differentiation of neuron populations, widespread synaptogenesis, and the establishment of telencephalic connections. Virtually no correlative or manipulative studies have been attempted to relate structural features of the developing olfactory system to increments in perceptual capacity. Nevertheless, Shepard (1970) and others have touted the olfactory system as anatomically favorable for analyses of structure–function relationships, and the ontogenetic features of the system, as discussed in this chapter reinforce the overall utility of the olfactory system for neurobiological "models."

During the course of this chapter, I have argued that there *is* a resolution to the paradox of why a sensory system crucial to survival would be blatantly incomplete and functionally immature. The resolution is found in the context of considering olfactory ontogenesis as a *means* to the *adaptational ends* of early life. The developing olfactory system can be viewed not so much as *incomplete* (in comparison to that of the adult), but as sufficiently and selectively organized to accomplish the perceptual tasks required for adaptation to each stage-dependent problem encountered by the maturing organism. Taking the neonatal rat as an example, the normal sequence of stage-dependent challenges would include: nipple location and nursing, orientation to the home nest, attraction to social cohorts, selection of safe foods and rejection of dangerous ones, exploring the environment around the natal nest, and choice of optimal mates.

Within an adaptive evolutionary framework, emphasis is on *outcomes*, the so-called phenotypic results. I have asserted that in the context of olfaction, behavioral outcomes (or behavioral phenotypes) are the adaptive ends, shaped by natural selection. Behavioral phenotypes can also provide evidence for perceptual preferences. Organisms detect, react to, approach, and avoid olfactory stimuli. There is often great species-specificity in the form of odor-elicited responses, and in the stimuli that evoke the responses. Two kinds of developmental processes can lead to behavioral manifestation of a perceptual preference. It is conceivable that natural selection could provide a genetic foundation for *specialization* in stimulus reception to bias the organism toward or away from certain olfactory cues. Given a sufficient level of perceptual capacity and appropriate response tendencies, perceptual preferences will have clear behavioral manifestations. However, identical behavioral biases can also be *induced* by *experience*. Indeed, it appears that numerous species-specific olfactory reactions are established by species-typical experiences, rather than by a genetically based predetermination.

The ontogeny of olfaction, as I have characterized it in the present chapter, involves several, simultaneous ontogenetic processes. Two of these deserve special attention because they appear to be mutually interdependent; through their reciprocal effects the development of olfactory perception can be better understood. First I reviewed evidence suggesting that the sensitivity and complexity of stimulus transduction in the olfactory system increases with maturation. Second, I showed that an additional, complex level of experiential input to the organism is provided by the development of behavior. Sensory input evokes behavioral reactions that help to modulate the quantity and quality of sensory stimulation. Together, these two processes unite to channel and shape the development of olfactory perception.

Nonolfactory experiences also contribute importantly to the development of olfactory perceptual preferences. The powerful role of thermal stimulation as a determinant of olfactory filial attraction is an example of the formation of a perceptual preference based on sensory–behavior reciprocities. This kind of effect can be differentiated from simple sensory effects, reflected in processes such as familiarization, and from other kinds of preferences such as those that activate and guide suckling.

It is "natural" that olfactory studies have become distinctly intertwined with behavioral concerns. It is, I think, the nature of the system. Olfactory influences on behavior are profound and widespread. Neonates, particularly those with limited sensory channels, rely on olfactory input to such an extent that we cannot appreciate their behavior without understanding the roles of olfaction. Similarly, the ontogeny of olfaction can only be appreciated by understanding its reciprocal connections with behavior.

ACKNOWLEDGMENTS

Preparation of this chapter and much of the cited research was supported by Grant MH 28355 from the National Institute of Mental Health and Research Scientist Development Award MH 00222 from the NIMH to the author. The interest and helpful comments of K. Addison, R. Aslin, S. Bollinger, R. Doty, D. Gubernick, and L. Martin are gratefully acknowledged.

REFERENCES

Alberts, J. R. Interpreting experimental olfactory deficits. *Physiology and Behavior*, 1974, **12**, 657–670.

Alberts, J. R. Huddling by rat pups: Multisensory control of contact behavior. *Journal of Comparative and Physiological Psychology*, 1978, **92**, 220–230. (a)

Alberts, J. R. Huddling by rat pups: Group behavioral mechanisms of temperature regulation and energy conservation. *Journal of Comparative and Physiological Psychology*, 1978, **92**, 231–240. (b)

Alberts, J. R. Olfactory contributions to behavioral development in rodents. In: R. L. Doty (Ed.), *Mammalian olfaction, reproductive processes and behavior*. New York: Academic Press, 1976.

Alberts, J. R., Addison, K. S., & May, B. Developmental specification of olfactory preferences for filial huddling. Presented at meeting of International Society for Developmental Psychobiology, Cincinnati, 1980.

Alberts, J. R., & Brunjes, P. C. Ontogeny of thermal and olfactory determinants of huddling in the rat. *Journal of Comparative and Physiological Psychology*, 1978, **92**, 897–906.

Alberts, J. R., & Leimbach, M. The first foray: Maternal influences on nest egression in the weanling rat. *Developmental Psychobiology*, 1980, **13**, 417–429.

Alberts, J. R., & May, B. Development of nasal respiration and sniffing in the rat. *Physiology and Behavior*, 1980, **24**, 957–963. (a)

Alberts, J. R., & May, B. Ontogeny of olfaction: Development of the rat's sensitivity to urine and amyl acetate. *Physiology and Behavior*, 1980, **24**, 965–970. (b)

Alexander, R. The evolution of social behavior. *Annual Review of Ecology and Systematics*, 1974, **5**, 325–383.

Amoore, J. E. Olfactory genetics and anosmia. *Handbook of sensory physiology* IV, Chemical senses, Part 1, L. M. Beidler (Ed.). New York: Springer-Verlag, 1971, pp. 245–256.

Arnold, S. J. Polymorphism and geographic variation in the feeding behavior of the garter snake. *Science*, 1977, **197**, 676–678.

Barash, D. P. *Sociobiology and behavior*. New York: Elsevier, 1977.

Beach, F., & Jaynes, J. Studies of maternal retrieving in rats I: Recognition of young. *Journal of Mammalogy*, 1956, **37**, 177–180.

Bronstein, P. M., & Crockett, D. P. Maternal rations affect the food preferences of weanling rats: II. *Bulletin of the Psychonomic Society*, 1976, **8**, 227–229.

Brunjes, P. C., & Alberts, J. R. Olfactory stimulation induces filial huddling preferences in rat pups. *Journal of Comparative and Physiological Psychology*, 1979, **93**, 548–555.

Brunjes, P. C., & Alberts, J. R. Precocious nasal chemosensitivity in hyperthyroid rat pups. *Hormones and Behavior*, 1980, **14**, 76–85.

Burghardt, G. M. Chemical-cue preferences of inexperienced snakes: Comparative aspects. *Science*, 1967, **157**, 718–721.

Burghardt, G. M. Chemical perception in reptiles. In J. W. Johnston, Jr., D. G. Moulton, & A. Turk (Eds.), *Communication by chemical signals*. New York: Appleton-Century-Crofts, 1970, pp. 241–308.

Burghardt, G. M. Chemical prey preference polymorphism in newborn garter snakes, *Thamnophilus sirtalis*. *Behaviour*, 1975, **52**, 202–225.

Burghardt, G. M. Behavioral ontogeny in reptiles: Whence, whither, and why. In G. M. Burghardt & M. Bekoff (Eds.), *The development of behavior: Comparative and evolutionary aspects*. New York: Garland, 1978, pp. 149–174.

Campbell, B. A., & Alberts, J. R. Ontogeny of long-term memory for learned taste aversions. *Behavioral and Neural Biology*, 1979, **29**, 139–156.

Campbell, B. A., & Raskin, L. Ontogeny of behavioral arousal: Effects of environmental cues. *Journal of Comparative and Physiological Psychology*, 1978, **92**, 176–184.

Conely, L., & Bell, R. W. Neonatal ultrasounds elicited by odor cues. *Developmental Psychobiology*, 1978, **11**, 193–197.

Cosnier, J. Le comportement grégaire du rat d'élevage. Doctoral dissertation, L'Université de Lyon, 1965.

Darwin, C. [*The expression of the emotions in man and animals*]. Chicago: The University of Chicago Press, 1965. p. 47. (Originally published, 1872.)

Dawkins, R. *The selfish gene*. Oxford: Oxford University Press, 1976.

Doty, R. L. A cry for the liberation of the female rodent: Courtship and copulation in *Rodentia*. *Psychological Bulletin*, 1974, **81**, 159–172.

Doty, R. L. Intranasal trigeminal detection of chemical vapors by humans. *Physiology and Behavior*, 1975, **14**, 855–859.

Drickamer, L. C. Sexual maturation of female house mice: Social inhibition. *Developmental Psychobiology*, 1974, **7**, 113–115.

Drickamer, L. C., & Hoover, J. E. Effects of urine from pregnant and lactating female house mice on sexual maturation of juvenile females. *Developmental Psychobiology*, 1979, **12**, 545–551.

Engen, T., Lipsitt, L. P., & Kaye, H. Olfactory responses and adaptation in the human neonate. *Journal of Comparative and Physiological Psychology*, 1963, **56**, 73–77.

Freeman, N. C. G., & Rosenblatt, J. S. Specificity of litter odors in the control of home orientation among kittens. *Developmental Psychobiology*, 1978, **11**, 459–468. (a)

Freeman, N. C. G., & Rosenblatt, J. S. The interrelationship between thermal and olfactory stimulation in the development of home orientation in newborn kittens. *Developmental Psychobiology* 1978, **11**, 437–457. (b)

Galef, B. G., Jr. Social transmission of acquired behavior: A discussion of tradition and social learning in vertebrates. In J. S. Rosenblatt, R. A. Hinde, E. Shaw, & C. Beer (Eds.), *Advances in the study of behavior* (Vol. 6). New York: Academic Press, 1976.

Galef, B. G., & Heiber, L. The role of residual olfactory cues in the determination of the feeding site selection and exploration patterns of domestic rats. *Journal of Comparative and Physiological Psychology*, 1976, **90**, 727–739.

Galef, B. G., Jr., & Henderson, P. Mother's milk: A determinant of the feeding preferences of weaning rat pups. *Journal of Comparative and Physiological Psychology*, 1972, **78**, 213–219.

Galef, B. G., Jr., & Kaner, H. C. Establishment and maintenance of preference for natural and artificial olfactory stimuli in juvenile rats. *Journal of Comparative and Physiological Psychology*, 1980, **94**, 588–596.

Galef, B. G., Jr., & Sherry, D. F. Mother's milk: A medium for transmission of cues reflecting the flavor of mother's diet. *Journal of Comparative and Physiological Psychology*, 1973, **83**, 374–378.

Gottlieb, G. Introduction to behavioral embryology. In G. Gottlieb (Ed.), *Studies on the development of behaviors and the nervous system* I. New York: Academic Press, 1973.

Gottlieb, G. Ontogenesis of sensory function in birds and mammals. In E. Tobach, L. R. Aronson, & E. Shaw (Eds.), *The biopsychology of development*. New York: Academic Press, 1971.

Gottlieb, G. The roles of experience in the development of behavior and the nervous system. In G. Gottlieb (Ed.), *Studies in the development of behavior and the nervous system* (Vol. 4). New York: Academic Press, 1976.

Gregory, E., & Pfaff, D. Development of olfactory guided behavior in infant rats. *Physiology and Behavior*, 1971, **6**, 573–576.

Hamilton, W. D. The genetical evolution of social behaviour I & II. *Journal of Theoretical Biology*, 1964, **7**, 1–52.

Hinds, J. W. Autoradiographic study of histogenesis in the mouse olfactory bulb: I. Time of origin of neurons and neuroglia. *Journal of Comparative Neurology*, 1968, **134**, 287–304. (a)

Hinds, J. W. Autoradiographic study of histogenesis in the mouse olfactory bulb: II. Cell proliferation and migration. *Journal of Comparative Neurology*, 1968, **134**, 305–322. (b)

Hinds, J. W., & McNelly, N. A. Aging of the rat olfactory bulb: Growth and atrophy of constituent layers and changes in size and number of mitral cells. *Journal of Comparative Neurology*, 1977, **171**, 345–368.

Hofer, M. A. Physiological responses of infant rats to separation from their mothers. *Science*, 1970, **168**, 871–873.

Hofer, M. A. Olfactory denervation: Its biological and behavioral effects in infant rats. *Journal of Comparative Physiological Psychology*, 1976, **90**, 829–838.

Hofer, M. A., Shair, H., & Singh, P. Evidence that maternal ventral skin substances promote suckling in infant rats. *Physiology and Behavior*, 1976, **17**, 131–136.

Jacobsen, M. A plentitude of neurons. In G. Gottlieb (Ed.), *Aspects of neurogenesis: Studies of behavior and the nervous system (Vol. 2)*. New York: Academic Press, 1974, pp. 151–168.

Jeddi, E. Confort du contact et thermoregulation comportementale. *Physiology and Behavior*, 1970, **5**, 1487–1493.

Johanson, I. B., & Hall, W. G. Appetitive learning in 1-day-old rat pups. *Science*, 1979, **205**, 419–421.

Kaplan, J., & Russell, M. Olfactory recognition in the infant Squirrel Monkey. *Developmental Psychobiology*, 1974, **7**(1), 15–19.

Kenny, J. T., & Blass, E. M. Suckling as an incentive to instrumental learning in preweanling rats. *Science*, 1977, **196**, 898–899.

Lehrman, D. S. Semantic and conceptual issues in the nature–nurture problem. In L. R. Aronson, E. Tobach, D. S. Lehrman, & J. S. Rosenblatt (Eds.), *Development and evolution of behavior*. San Francisco: Freeman, 1970.

Leon, M. Maternal pheromone. *Physiology and Behavior*, 1974, **13**, 441–443.

Leon, M., Crosskerry, P. G., & Smith, G. K. Thermal control of mother–young contact in rats. *Physiology and Behavior*, 1979, **21**, 793–811.

Leon, M., Galef, B. G., & Behse, J. H. Establishment of pheromonal bonds and diet choice in young rats by odor pre-exposure. *Physiology and Behavior*, 1972, **18**, 387–391.

Leon, M., & Moltz, H. Maternal pheromone: discrimination by preweanling albino rats. *Physiology and Behavior*, 1971, **7**, 265–267.

Leon, M., & Moltz, H. The development of the pheromonal bond in the albino rat. *Physiology and Behavior*, 1972, **8**, 683–686.

Lipsitt, L. P., Engen, T., & Kaye, H. Developmental changes in the olfactory threshold of the neonate. *Child Development*, 1963, **34**, 371–376.

Martin, L. T., & Alberts, J. R. Taste aversions to mother's milk: The age-related role of nursing in acquisition and expression of a learned association. *Journal of Comparative and Physiological Psychology*, 1979, **93**, 430–445. (a)

Martin, L. T., & Alberts, J. R. *Heart rate change as a measure of associative learning in neonatal rodents.* Paper presented at the meetings of the International Society of Developmental Psychobiology, Atlanta, Ga., 1979. (b)

Martin, L. T., & Lawrence, C. D. The importance of odor and texture cues in food aversion learning. *Behavioral and Neural Biology*, 1979, **27**, 503–515.

McFarlane, J. A. Olfaction in the development of social preferences in the human neonate. In M. A. Hofer (Ed.), *Parent–infant interaction*. Amsterdam: Elsevier, 1975.

McIntosh, T. K., & Drickamer, L. C. Excreted urine, bladder urine, and the delay of sexual maturation in female house mice. *Animal Behavior*, 1977, **25**, 999–1004.

Meisami, E. Early sensory influences on regional activity of brain ATPases in developing rats. In M. A. B. Brazier (Ed.), *Growth and development of the brain* I. New York: Raven, 1975, pp. 51–74.

Michener, G. R. Development of adult–young identification in Richardson's ground squirrel. *Developmental Psychobiology,* 1974, **7**(4), 375–384.

Moore, C. L. An olfactory basis for maternal discrimination of sex of offspring in rats (*Rattus norvegicus*). *Animal Behaviour,* 1981, **29**, 383–386.

Moore, C. L., & Morelli, G. A. Mother rats ineract differently with male and female offspring. *Journal of Comparative and Physiological Pyschology,* 1979, **93**, 677–684.

Moulton, D. G. Cell renewal in the olfactory epithelium of the mouse. In D. A. Denton & J. P. Coghlan (Eds.), *Olfaction and Taste* V. New York: Academic Press, 1975, pp. 111–114.

Moulton, D. G. Spatial patterning of response to odors in the peripheral olfactory system. *Physiological Reviews,* 1976, **56**, 578–593.

Mozell, M. M. Spatial and temporal patterning. In L. M. Beidler (Ed.), *Handbook of Sensory Psychology IV: Chemical Senses.* New York: Springer-Verlag, 1971, pp. 205–215.

Murphy, M. Olfactory impairment, olfactory bulb removal, and mammalian reproduction. In R. L. Doty (Ed.), *Mammalian olfaction, reproductive processes and behavior.* New York: Academic Press, 1976, pp. 96–118.

Nyakas, C., & Endroczi, E. Olfaction guided approaching behavior of infantile pups to the mother in a maze box. *Acta Physiologica Academia Scientiarum Hungaricae,* 1970, **38**, 59–65.

Porter, R. H., & Wyrick, M. Sibling recognition in spiny mice (*Acomys cahirinus*): Influence of age and isolation. *Animal Behaviour,* 1979, **27**, 761–766.

Porter, R. H., Wyrick, M., & Pankey, J. Sibling recognition in spiny mice (*Acomys cahirinus*). *Behavioral Ecology and Sociobiology,* 1978, **3**, 61–68.

Reiser, J., Yonas, A., & Wikner, K. Radial localization of odors by human newborns. *Child Development,* 1976, **47**, 850–859.

Rosenblatt, J. S. The basis of early response to the mother, siblings, and the home and nest in altricial young of selected species of subprimate nammals. In R. A. Hinde & P. P. G. Bateson, (Eds.), *Growing points in ethology.* New York: Cambridge University Press, 1976, pp. 345–386.

Rosenblatt, J. S. The development of maternal responsiveness in the rat. *American Journal of Orthopsychiatry,* 1969, **39**, 36–56.

Rosenblatt, J. S., Turkewitz, G., & Schneirla, T. C. Development of home orientation in newly born kittens. *Transactions of the New York Academy of Sciences,* 1969, **31**, 231–250.

Rovee, C. K., Cohen, R. Y., & Shlapack, W. Life-span stability in olfactory sensitivity. *Journal of Experimental Child Psychology,* 1975, **11**, 311–318.

Rudy, J. W., & Cheatle, M. D. Odor-aversion learning in neonatal rats. *Science,* 1978, **198**, 845–846.

Shepard, G. M. The olfactory bulb as a simple cortical system: Experimental analysis and functional implications. In F. O. Schmitt (Ed.), *The neurosciences: Second study program.* New York: Rockefeller University Press, 1970, pp. 539–552.

Sherman, Paul. W. The limits of ground squirrel nepotism. In G. W. Barlow & J. Silverberg (Eds.), *Sociobiology: Beyond nature/nurture.* Boulder, Colo.: Westview Press, 1980, pp. 505–544.

Singh, P., & Tobach, E. Olfactory bulbectomy and nursing behavior in rat pups (Wistar DAB). *Developmental Psychobiology,* 1975, **8**, 151–164.

Sluckin, W. *Imprinting and early learning.* Chicago: Aldine, 1964.

Small, W. S. Notes on the psychic development of the albino rat. *American Journal of Psychology,* 1899, **11**, 80–100.

Teicher, M. H., & Blass, E. M. Suckling in newborn rats: Eliminated by nipple lavage, reinstated by pup saliva. *Science,* 1976, **193**, 422–425.

Teicher, M. H., & Blass, E. M. The role of olfaction and amniotic fluid in the first suckling response of newborn albino rats. *Science*, 1978, **198**, 635–636.

Tobach, E., Rouger, Y., & Schneirla, T. C. Development of olfactory function in the rat pup. *American Zoologist*, 1967, **7**, 792.

Tucker, D. Nonolfactory responses from the nasal cavity: Jacobson's organ and the trigeminal system. In L. M. Beidler, (Ed.), *Handbook of sensory physiology* IV, (Part 1). New York: Springer-Verlag, 1971.

Vandenbergh, J. G. Effect of the presence of a male on the sexual maturation of female mice. *Endocrinology*, 1967, **81**, 345–349.

Vandenbergh, J. G. Male odor accelerates female sexual maturation in mice. *Endocrinology*, 1969, **84**, 658–660.

Vandenberg, J. G., Whitsett, J. M., & Lombardi, J. R. Partial isolation of a pheromone accelerating puberty in female mice. *Journal of Reproduction and Fertility*, 1975, **43**, 515–523.

Wayne, M. L., Martin, L. T., & Alberts, J. R. Ontogeny of long-term memory for learned odor aversions. Presented at meetings of International Society for Developmental Psychobiology, Atlanta, November, 1979.

12

Olfactory Control
over Suckling in Albino Rats

PATRICIA E. PEDERSEN
ELLIOTT M. BLASS
Johns Hopkins University

I. INTRODUCTION

Chemical signals are part of a major communication network that is used by animals ranging from paramecia to primates. These signals are transmitted in air or water and are transduced peripherally and centrally to provide information concerning, among other things, conspecifics, predators, prey, physiological status, food, and territory (for review, see: Birch, 1974; Doty, 1976; Müller-Schwarze & Mozell, 1977; Shorey, 1976). The obvious importance of this network in conjunction with advances in microanalytical, behavioral, and neurological techniques has generated multidisciplinary collaborations dedicated to identifying

359

chemical signals, their receptors, the behaviors they elicit, and the central and peripheral neurologies that manage these behaviors. The critical role of chemical communication during development is now recognized and has been described in recent reviews (Alberts, 1976, Chapter 11, this volume; Cheal, 1975; Rosenblatt, 1976). Four fundamental issues are apparent:

1. What behaviors are under olfactory control during ontogeny?
2. What specific odors are involved?
3. What are the mechanisms that mediate this olfactory control?
4. What is the relative contribution of early experience in the recognition of chemical stimuli during development?

The present chapter addresses these issues by focusing on the olfactory cues that elicit suckling in albino rats and some of the mechanisms that mediate this olfactory control. Specific odors not only direct rat pups to a nipple, but also elicit an elaborate sequence of movements that terminate with nipple attachment. Suckling is an appropriate behavior to study for delineating the ontogeny of chemical communication for a number of reasons. First, suckling is present at birth. This allows neural, behavioral, and chemical analyses of the properties of the olfactory system, which is relatively well developed at birth in albino rats. Second, suckling is a well-defined response. Therefore, olfactory control over a fairly complex motor sequence can be studied in some detail. Third, suckling is the predominant behavior of awake infant rats. Analyses of its olfactory controls would enhance a more general understanding of a developmental process.

II. PARADIGM FOR ANALYSES OF OLFACTORY CONTROL OVER BEHAVIOR

In seeking guidance for the study of chemical control over suckling, we have turned to the general paradigms and criteria that have revealed the contributions of olfactory processes in controlling reproductive behavior in male golden hamsters. This behavior consists of approaching, sniffing, licking, and investigating the female vaginal area, mounting, and intromission (Darby, Devor, & Chorover, 1975). Intact olfactory systems are necessary for the initiation of reproductive activities in male golden hamsters. Blocking or destroying the primary olfactory and vomeronasal systems essentially eliminates male reproductive behavior in this species (Murphy & Schneider, 1970; Powers, Fields, & Winans, 1979). Such deficits could be due to lack of necessary olfactory input and/or nonspecifically related damage to nonsensory circuits in the brain (Alberts, 1974). The importance of olfactory input has been assessed by observing the response of neurologically intact males to scents and their fractions that are deposited by the estrus female. A number of studies have demonstrated that males attend to female hamster vaginal discharge (FHVD) (for review, see Johnston, 1977). Indeed, because of the male's powerful attraction to FHVD, and the deposition of FHVD by the female exclusively during epochs of maximum sexual receptivity (Johnston, 1977), FHVD has been implicated as a control of male sexual behavior. The attractive properties of FHVD are such that males approach, sniff, and lick even inanimate objects such as furry models or glass plates scented with FHVD (Darby et al., 1975; Johnston, 1974; Murphy, 1973). FHVD also increases sexual arousal as scented anesthetized males or females elicit mounting and pelvic thrusting in males (Darby et al., 1975; Johnston, 1975; Murphy, 1973). Attraction to vaginal secretions from lactating females suggests that some facet of the mother–infant interaction may induce the preference for FHVD in males (Macrides, Johnson, & Schneider, 1977).

More direct evidence for the role of FHVD as an olfactory stimulant has been obtained by combining chemical with behavioral strategies of investigation. It has been fractionated and its constituents identified (Singer, Agosta, O'Connell, Pfaffmann, Bowen, & Field, 1976). One of FHVD's volatile constituents, dimethyl disulfide (DMDS), appears to serve as a general attractant for the male. DMDS elicits approach and sniffing by male hamsters and thus may function to bring them into close proximity with receptive females. Mounting and pelvic thrusting do not occur toward anesthetized male hamsters scented with DMDS (Macrides et al., 1977). Undoubtedly, the presence of some 300 compounds in FHVD suggests that more compounds will be implicated in the modulation of other aspects of male reproductive behavior (one nonvolatile portion already has been) (Johnston, 1977). In any event, isolation and identification of DMDS provides a first step toward characterizing the odors that mediate the reproductive activities of male golden hamsters.

These analyses provide a paradigm for studying other classes of behavior that might be under olfactory control. The approach may be characterized as consisting of four phases, each with its own set of behavioral and chemical criteria that assesses behavior elicited by an isolated substance relative to the behavior as it appears spontaneously. These phases address the fundamental issues raised earlier. Each step and its exemplar from the analyses of male hamster reproductive behavior follows:

A. Documentation of Olfactory Control over the Behavior

Intact olfactory systems are necessary for the initiation of reproductive activities in male golden hamsters (Murphy & Schneider, 1970; Powers *et al.*, 1979). One important source of olfactory input appears to be FHVD, which (*a*) provides information regarding the physiological status of the female; and (*b*) promotes behaviors that direct and maintain some aspects of the reproductive activities of the female.

B. Fractionation of the Behaviorally Active Secretions

A volatile compound, DMDS, has been isolated from vaginal secretions of hamsters in estrus by the techniques of gas chromatography–mass spectrometry. DMDS appears to have general attractive properties because, by itself, DMDS will elicit approach and sniffing in males but not mounting or pelvic thrusting (Macrides *et al.*, 1977). Behavioral comparison of whole vaginal secretions to DMDS shows DMDS to be 60–80% as effective as whole secretions in eliciting approach and sniffing in males.

C. Mechanism of Action

Dummy objects scented with FHVD elicit little or no mounting and pelvic thrusting in comparison to scented anesthetized males or females. Indeed, the ability of vaginal secretions to facilitate copulatory behaviors depends on how the features of the scented stimulus objects approximates those of the receptive female (Darby *et al.*, 1975). Thus, FHVD plays a facilitatory role for male reproductive behaviors in the context of other olfactory and nonolfactory characteristics of the receptive female. DMDS accounts for one particular aspect of that facilitatory role, namely, it serves as an attractant.

D. Assessment of the Role of Experience in Response to These Secretions

Sexually naive male hamsters spend equal amounts of time sniffing vaginal secretions as do sexually experienced male hamsters. (Gregory, Engel, & Pfaff, 1975). Pups show a marked attraction to vaginal secretions over other chemical stimuli at 14 days of age as indicated by time spent sniffing and licking vaginal secretions. However, neither younger nor older pups show this responsivity to vaginal secretions. The response reappears at about 40 days of age (Johnston & Coplin, 1979).

III. SUCKLING

A. Documentation of Olfactory Control over the Behavior

To attach a nipple, pups must orient to their mother, locate her ventrum, find a nipple, and seize it. Although the mother makes herself available to the pups by crouching over them in a nursing posture, she does not help pups onto her nipples. Mothers are suckled shortly (less than 2 hr) after birth (Rosenblatt & Lehrman, 1963). Thus suckling integrated the full sensory and motor capacities available at birth and represents the earliest, most fully formed pattern of behavior exhibited by altricial neonates. Moreover, internal cues do not appear to modulate nipple attachment until well into the second week of life. Young pups deprived of food, water, and their mother for 24 hr attach as quickly to an available nipple as do nondeprived siblings (Hall, Cramer, & Blass, 1975, 1977). It is clear that some characteristics of the mother draw the pups to the nipple.

To assess the maternal sensory features that elicit nipple attachment, it was necessary to eliminate the dam's active contribution to suckling. To achieve this, the mother was anesthetized. By definition, anesthetization eliminates active and differential responding and also blocks milk letdown. This preparation is ideal for sensory determinants of nipple attachment because a full spectrum of maternal sensory features—fur, temperature, texture, and odor—can be experimentally manipulated. One of these sensory features, odor, was first implicated in suckling by Tobach and her colleagues (Tobach, Rouger, & Schneirla, 1967; Singh & Tobach, 1975). They demonstrated that complete bilateral bulbectomy was fatal to the pups because it interfered with their ability to suckle. These data encouraged Teicher and Blass (1976, 1977) to assess more directly the role of olfaction by studying suckling on an anesthetized rat mother whose nipples were cleaned of olfactory cues. Accordingly, a wash technique was devised by Teicher (1977) that cleaned the nipple of organic substances without changing the nipple's morphology. A Teflon tube connected by a lead to a vacuum pump gently suctioned off a solution of methylene chloride and ethanol, that was pipetted at the base of the teat, into a collecting tube for subsequent distillation. This wash essentially eliminated nipple attachment in rat pups 2–28 days of age. Returning a vacuum distillate of the wash to the nipples restored attachment to prewash levels. Thus, pups that demonstrate internal physiological control by modifying their nipple attachment according to deprivational status still relied on olfactory cues to attach to the nipple. Furthermore, attachment could be rein-

stated by painting saliva or salivary gland extract obtained from deprived siblings on the nipples. Hofer, Shair, and Singh (1976) independently found that washing the anesthetized mother's entire ventrum
eliminated nipple attachment in 9- and 14-day-old rats.

Other sensory features of the mother (i.e., tactile or thermal stimuli)
have been found to be of little importance in helping pups locate and
attach to the nipples (Blass, Teicher, Cramer, Bruno, & Hall, 1977;
Bruno, Teicher, & Blass, 1980). Throughout the nursing period (i.e.,
2–30 days of age (first nipple attachment will be discussed later)) pups
attached to their anesthetized mother whether she was shaved, thereby
eliminating the contrast between fur and nipple; whether her peripheral
and nipple skin temperature was cooled to 31° or 28°C, thereby eliminating the gradients between nipple and skin; or whether the dam
was both shaved and cooled. As shown in Fig. 12.1, only alteration of
the olfactory properties of the nipples consistently disrupted nipple
attachment in these pups. This deficit was particularly striking in older
rats that were capable of visually guided behavior.

In summary, olfactory cues on the mother's nipples elicit nipple
attachment, rat pups do not suckle in the absence of these cues, 15
days of age being an exception; and painting an extract of the nipple
wash solution, saliva, or salivary gland extract on the washed nipples
restores attachment to almost normal levels.

B.   Fractionation of Behaviorally Active Secretions

The olfactory cues that mediate suckling appear to be highly specific
because suckling is elicited only by a narrow range of substances (pup

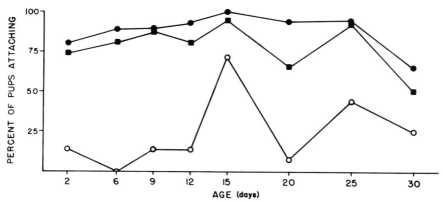

Fig. 12.1   Percentage of 22-hr deprived pups, 2–30 days of age, that attach to the
nipples of their fresh (●) washed (○) and reinstated (■) anesthetized mothers.

saliva, pup salivary gland extract, and nipple wash extract). These findings justified further analysis of the chemical properties of these substances. First, we had identified an accessible biological fluid. Second, the bioassay for nipple attachment was unambiguous—almost all pups 3–5 days of age attach to normal nipples or those coated with saliva, and very few attach to washed nipples. Thus, the behavioral effects of compounds chemically isolated from saliva (or synthetic analogues of these) could be measured by their ability to elicit nipple attachment.

Research from biochemical, behavioral, and peridontal fields provided converging lines of evidence that a sulphur compound (possibly DMDS) might be a critical salivary cue controlling nipple attachment. These lines of evidence may be briefly summarized: First, the capability of DMDS to elicit behavior has already been established. It has been isolated from the vaginal secretions of estrus female hamsters and found to be an attractant to the male (Singer *et al.*, 1976). Second, sulphur compounds contribute to common mammalian odors (Wheeler, 1977). Specifically, they have been isolated in the scent glands of hyenas (Wheeler, Von Endt, & Wemmer, 1975), skunks (Anderson & Bernstein, 1975), preputial glands of males and female rats (Gawienowski, Orsulak, Stacewicz-Sapuntzakis, & Joseph, 1975; Gawienowski, Orsulak, Stacewicz-Sapuntzakis, & Pratt, 1976) and the urine of humans (Ellin, Farrand, Oberts, Crouse, Billups, Koon, Musselman, & Sidell, 1974). Third, constituents in the salivary glands and saliva may serve as substrates for the formation of DMDS in rat saliva. These include disulphide groups, sulpholipids, and cysteines. Disulfides are present in the secretory granules of the duct system in the rat submandibular gland (Montero, 1972). Tissue slices from submandibular glands of rats as young as 10 days of age incorporate radiosulphate, indicating that sulpholipid metabolism occurs during early growth in these tissues (Pritchard, 1975). Cysteine, a substrate containing free thiol groups (sulphur analogs of alcohols), is a common oral compound (Dewey, 1958). Accordingly, we first attempted to detect the presence of DMDS in rat pup saliva and second, we tested whether DMDS could elicit nipple attachment in rat pups.

Saliva was obtained, by aspiration, from the mouths of 50, 3 to 5-day-old rat pups anesthetized by hypothermia. The saliva was extracted in methylene chloride and vacuum distilled to near dryness at 35°C. The saliva sample, redissolved in methylene chloride, was then subjected to gas chromatography–mass spectrometry analysis. Gas chromatography separates a mixture into its component parts by selectively retaining these components on adsorptive materials packed in a column according to the physicochemical properties of each component. The time it takes components to elute from the column (i.e., the retention time), helps to identify the chemical properties of the components. Components are more finely analyzed by a mass spectrometer that gives relative atomic weights in a mass spectra. Further information regarding the chemical identification of a component is thus gained by knowledge of the molecular weight of its constituents. Therefore, to confirm the presence of DMDS in rat pups saliva, one of its components must have an identical retention time and an identical mass spectra to a standard sample of DMDS.

Figure 12.2a shows a gas chromatogram of 3 to 5-day-old rat pup saliva and in Fig. 12.2b, a standard sample of DMDS. The peak representing DMDS in the chromatogram of the standard has a retention time identical to the peak indicated by an arrow in the chromatogram of the saliva sample. Thus, gas chromatography analysis indicates that one component of pup saliva is similar in chemical property to DMDS. The next stage of analysis, mass spectrometry, gives the atomic mass units of this component. Figure 12.3a depicts our preliminary findings on the mass spectra of the peak having the identical retention time as DMDS and in Fig. 12.3b of the peak representing DMDS in the standard sample. Both mass spectra indicate ions at 94 (the molecular weight of DMDS) and 79 (DMDS minus one methyl group). The retention time and mass spectra of a standard sample of DMDS and a constituent of pup saliva yield identical results, indicating the presence of DMDS in pup saliva.

We then attempted to determine if DMDS was a behaviorally active component of pup saliva. To do this, we coated the washed nipples of an anesthetized dam with DMDS to test if 3 to 5-day-old rat pups could attach to these nipples. The findings of this study are presented in Fig. 12.4, which shows the percentage of pups that attach to nipples cleaned of olfactory cues (wash condition), nipples painted with DMDS (DMDS condition), and nipples unmanipulated (fresh condition). Portion b shows mean attachment latency in each of these conditions. Cleaning the nipple of organic substances eliminated nipple attachment. This replicates the main finding of Teicher and Blass (1976, 1977). Painting a synthetic sample of DMDS on the same washed nipples restores

---

Fig. 12.2 Gas chromatogram of (a) 3–5-day-old rat pup saliva and (b) of a standard sample of dimethyl disulfide (DMDS) both in methylene chloride. The peak of interest (indicated by arrow in each chromatogram) was analyzed further by mass spectrometry. The other peaks represent solvents used in the extraction procedure of pup saliva.

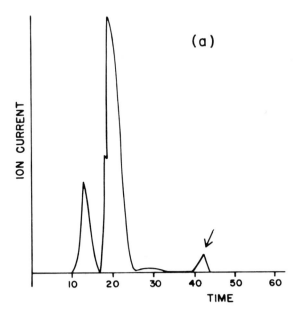

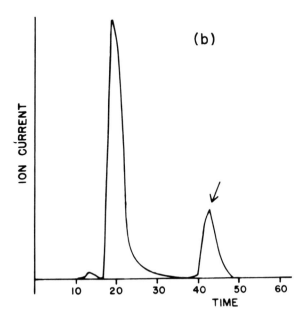

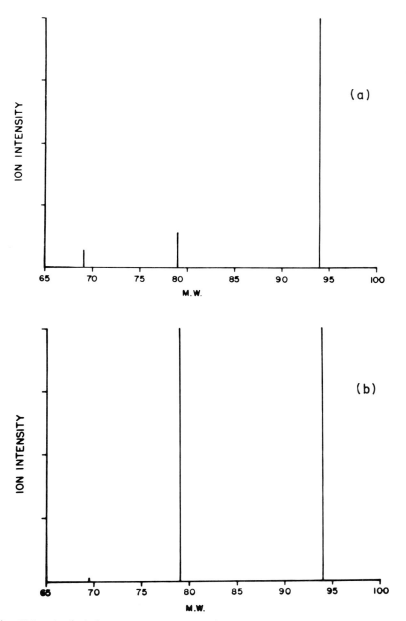

Fig. 12.3   Analysis by mass spectrometer of gas chromatogram peak (a) in 3–5-day-old rat pup saliva having the identical retention time as DMDS and (b) of a gas chromatogram peak representing DMDS in the standard sample, both in methylene chloride.

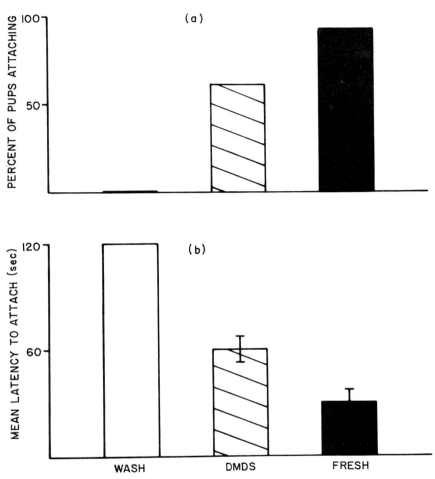

Fig. 12.4   (a) Percentage of pups attaching and (b) mean attachment latency to nipples washed, washed and painted with DMDS, and fresh. Each pup was tested on all three nipple conditions by the experimenter holding the pup to a nipple for a 2-min period.

nipple attachment in 61.7% of the pups. Although this percentage of pups that attach to nipples is not as high as it is in the fresh condition (93%), it is significantly different from the percentage of pups that attach to nipples in the wash condition (0%). The same results are reflected in mean attachment latencies. No pups attached to washed nipples in the 2-min period of testing. In the DMDS condition, pups attached with a mean attachment latency of 59.8 sec and in the fresh condition, pups attached with a mean attachment latency of 29.1 sec. Overall, it appears that DMDS is 50–60% as effective in eliciting nipple attachment as the substances that coat the nipples of lactating dams.

In conclusion, DMDS appears to be in pup saliva and is a potent elicitor of nipple attachment in rat pups 3–5 days of age. Evidence from both behavioral and chemical analyses converge to suggest that a salivary sulphur compound is sufficient to elicit nipple attachment in neonatal rat pups. Thus, an encouraging start on characterizing the olfactory cues for nipple attachment has been made. Further analysis to characterize fully this system must entail: (a) confirmation that DMDS uniquely controls nipple attachment by testing saliva from which DMDS has been extracted and by testing the efficacy of other sulphur compounds (e.g., methyl disulfide); (b) determination of the physiological range by obtaining dose–response curves for DMDS; and (c) determination of other odors that may be involved in location of the mother and her nipples.

C. Mechanism of Action

We have documented that saliva controls nipple attachment. However, nipple attachment actually involves complex motor patterns beyond just seizure of the nipple. When pups first establish contact with a nipple of an anesthetized mother, they usually root, probe, open their mouths, extend their tongues, and lick the nipple to erect it. This mouthing or licking invariably results in the pup taking the nipple into its mouth. How does salivary cue influence these facets of nipple attachment? We will now demonstrate that saliva influences at least four facets of nipple attachment: activity, orientation, control of motor pattern, and allowance of tactile stimulation to elicit mouth opening, tongue extension, and licking of the nipple.

1. Activity

The most direct evidence for an arousing quality of the substances coating the nipple comes from our observations that rat pups, hand-held 1–2 cm from a recently suckled nipple, will become so active that they occasionally propel themselves out of the experimenter's loose grasp. Control substances do not have this effect. Activity is also significantly increased by adding the extract to the washed mother's ventrum. When contact is established with the scent, the pup's behavior becomes extremely vigorous as it roots and probes into the "painted" area.

2.   *Orientation*

In collaboration with Carol Cornell, we have utilized the following paradigm to demonstrate that the volatiles emanating from the nipple exert control over orientation. The mothers' nipples were washed, as described earlier, but the extract from the wash was painted on the midline, thereby leaving the nipple region clean. Pups were tested on the mother prior to washing, following the wash, and after the nipple wash extract was painted on the midline. Location and activity were determined every 15 sec during the 5-min test period. To be considered on the midline, a pup had to spend at least 50% of two successive 15-sec epochs in contact with the midline. The mother was positioned on her side in a manner that required effort by the pup to establish and hold contact for even a few seconds. Figure 12.5 demonstrates that placing the nipple-wash extract on the midline markedly increased the number of pups that maintained contact with the extract. This suggests that 3 to 5-day-old rat pups can orient to and approach an extract of the nipple-wash solution. Further support for this idea comes from observations that rats hand-held midway between a washed and un-washed nipple, orient and move toward the *un*washed nipple. It is important to note that orientation does not occur at distances greater than 2 cm.

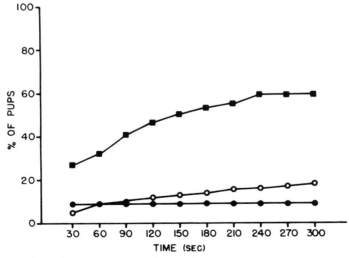

Fig. 12.5   Cumulative percentage of pups that maintain contact with the midline of their anesthetized mother unwashed (●), after nipple wash (○), and after painting nipple wash extract on the midline (■).

3. Control of Motor Patterns

These observations of probing into fur painted with nipple-wash extract led Cornell to modify her basic paradigm by painting salivary gland extract on the flank about 2 cm above the substrate. In this situation, pups displayed a variety of behaviors without losing contact with the "scented" area. Cornell established 15 behavioral categories in this test situation. Figure 12.6 demonstrates the marked change in motor behavior that occurred when contact was established with the flank. Patterns such as rooting and probing that were fragmented when pups contacted washed dams appeared with regularity and in sequence when pups contacted dams with salivary gland extract on the flank. In fact, all these behaviors observed are facets of the motor sequence that normally occurs when contact is established with unwashed nipples. It is of considerable interest that, although some of the major components of the nipple attachment sequence occurred on the flank painted with saliva scent, the terminal aspects of the suckling act, mouth opening, tongue extension, and licking, were observed very rarely. There were few differences between the wash condition and other conditions in overall behavior of the pups. Saliva, therefore, appears to prolong and possibly to organize the sequence of behaviors

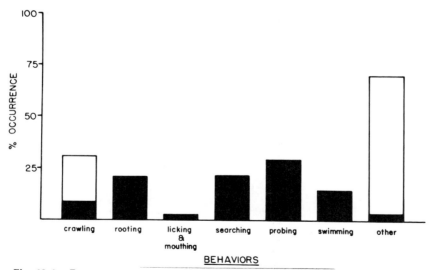

Fig. 12.6 Percentage occurrence of behaviors on an anesthetized mother after nipple wash (white bar) and after painting salivary gland extract on the flank (black bar). Other category includes behaviors such as sleeping, grooming, yawning, and twitching.

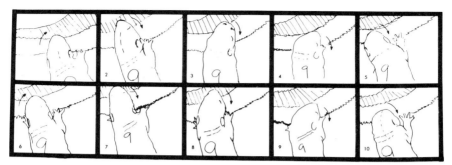

Fig. 12.7 Response of *rooting* on an anesthetized mother after painting her flank (striped area) with salivary gland extract. This sequence took 10 sec to complete.

leading to nipple attachment stopping at the penultimate act of mouth opening.

Cornell has studied the sequences further by video taping the pups' behavior on the mother. Figure 12.7 demonstrates the response of *rooting* on the scented flank. The quadrapedal locomotion that had propeled the pup across the mother was arrested, the hind legs were extended, and the pup circled its head into the extract. Each 360° arc took about 5 sec to complete. Two 5-sec sequences are presented in the figure (the remaining three 5-sec sequences can be virtually superimposed on the presented ones). This behavioral sequence is almost identical to the one seen during attachment. It differs in that the circle subtended by the rotary actions of the head becomes increasingly smaller with successive circular movements as the pup focuses in on the nipple.

4. Mouth Movements

The fourth major mechanism of action of saliva concerns a permissive role. When pups are hand-held to a washed nipple, the behaviors just described are rarely elicited. When the nipple is saliva-coated, it elicits mouth opening, tongue extension, and licking. Thus, saliva allows the tactile properties of the nipple to gain control over the area served by the trigeminal field and to elicit behaviors leading to seizure of the nipple. The importance of the trigeminal sensory field in nipple attachment has been convincingly demonstrated by Hofer, Fisher, and Shair (1979) who eliminated the last three stages of the nipple attachment sequence (mouth opening, tongue extension, and licking) but preserved rooting and probing by bilateral destruction of the trigeminal nerve in 7-day-old rat pups.

Pups can rely exclusively on tactile cues for nipple attachment if they are made anosmic soon after birth. Teicher, Flaum, Williams, Eckhert, and Lumia (1978) performed complete bilateral bulbectomies on pups 2 days postnatally and found that pups were able to suckle and thus survive when raised in an ambiance of 28°C. When these same pups were tested on their anesthetized mothers at Day 10, they were unable to locate her nipples but could attach if their snouts were placed in contact with the nipples. Washing the nipples did not disrupt nipple attachment for these anosmic pups. Although these pups sufficiently compensated for their olfactory loss by relying on tactile cues for nipple attachment, we suggest that intact rat pups do need the appropriate cue for the nipple's textural qualities to gain control over the final phase of the nipple-attachment sequence.

In summary, the salivary cue arouses and directs the pup to the nipple area. Once in the immediate vicinity of the nipple, the cue elicits rooting and probing in sequence which brings the pup's snout into contact with the nipple. Then the textural properties of the nipple releases mouth opening, tongue extension, and licking, which results in nipple attachment.

D. Role of experience

Thus far, we have discussed suckling elicited by pup saliva, a cue that pups themselves deposit on the nipple when they suckle. Because pups at birth are not presented with nipples that have been suckled, we asked how do newborns locate and attach to their first nipple? Teicher and Blass (1977) addressed this by demonstrating that the first nipple attachment in newborn rats is also disrupted by removal of olfactory cues from the nipple. Figures 12.8 and 12.9 depict these data. Painting newly parturient maternal saliva or amniotic fluid on the nipple elicits attachment, but painting urine, isotonic saline, virgin female saliva, as well as a number of nonphysiological substances, does not. Because preparturient female rats spend a great amount of time licking the nipple, pelvic, and anogenital regions, and the vagina (Roth & Rosenblatt, 1967), it is likely that the mother is applying this amniotic–maternal saliva mix to her nipples.

We have tested the hypothesis that amniotic fluid is an effective elicitor of suckling by virtue of the animal's prenatal and/or immediate postnatal experience with it. A number of considerations made this hypothesis reasonable. First, the chemical composition of amniotic fluid is continually changing by its passage through the developing fetal alimentary canal as a result of fetal swallowing and excreting in utero

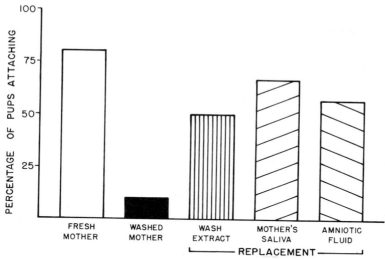

Fig. 12.8 Percentage of pups attaching to nipples: fresh, washed, and reinstated with nipple wash extract, newly parturient mother's saliva, or amniotic fluid.

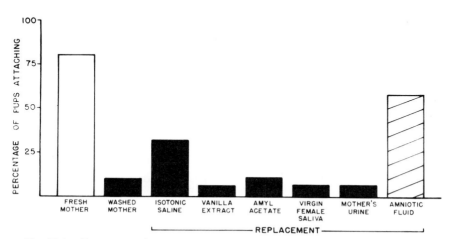

Fig. 12.9 Percentage of pups attaching to nipples fresh, washed, and reinstated with one of the following: virgin female saliva, parturient mother's urine, isotonic saline, amyl acetate, vanilla extract, or amniotic fluid.

(Lev & Orlic, 1972; Narayanan, Fox, & Hamburger, 1971). Furthermore, amniotic fluid is a plasma filtrate and therefore reflects the mother's altered diet and endocrine status. Third, as taste buds in the rat fungiform papillae are present in 20-day-old rat fetuses (Farbman, 1965), they may be functional. This possiblity is supported by the observed increase in human fetal swallowing after injections of sugar into the amniotic sac (DeSnoo, 1937) and its decrease after injections of quinine (Liley, 1972). Third, rat fetuses may actually detect odorous molecules in amniotic fluid such as citric, lactic, uric, fatty, and amino acids (Bradley & Mistretta, 1975). The vomeronasal organ, an important component of the olfactory system, is morphologically mature at birth in some rodents, mice for example (Hinds & Hinds, 1976).

Accordingly, we altered the amniotic fluid environment of rat fetuses by intrauterine injections of a sterile citral solution (tasteless lemon odor) on Day 20 of gestation. Fetuses therefore experienced amniotic fluid of a differing composition and odor. On Day 22 of gestation, pups were delivered by caesarean section and placed in a warm humid ambiance (33–34°C) scented with citral. To approximate the natural environment after birth when the mother actively cleans and licks the newborn pups, the postnatal environment was manipulated as follows: During the first hour after birth, in the presence of citral, pups were stroked with an artist's brush thereby mimicking maternal stimulation that naturally occurs immediately after delivery. Pups were then permitted to attach to normally scented or washed nipples of a test mother in a chamber that was either scented with citral or was citral-free.

Figure 12.10 depicts percentage attachment to washed and unwashed nipples in a citral and citral-free environment for pups both normally delivered and pups experiencing citral in utero and after birth. As Teicher and Blass demonstrated, removing olfactory cues disrupts nipple attachment of normally reared pups (Fig. 12.10a). However, pups experiencing citral both in utero and postnatally for 1 hour show low percentages of attachment on washed nipples and even on recently suckled nipples when tested in a citral-free environment. Conversely, these "citral-reared" and stimulated pups rapidly attached to washed or recently suckled nipples *provided citral was present in the test chamber.*

These results suggested that citral had acquired its ability to elicit nipple attachment as a result of pre- and postnatal exposure to citral. To assess the relative contributions of pre- and postnatal exposure, the experiment was repeated; this time either citral or isotonic saline was injected into the amniotic sac on Day 20 of gestation. The pups were subsequently stroked for the first hour after caesarean delivery in the presence of citral and isotonic saline. In this way we could determine

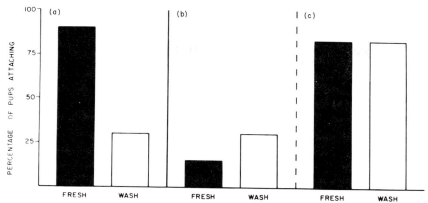

Fig. 12.10   Percentage of pups attaching to fresh or washed nipples in either a citral-free (a,b) or citral environment (c). Pups were either normally delivered (a), or had experienced citral in utero and after birth (b,c).

the necessary and sufficient conditions to bias the pups' attachment to citral-scented nipples. Figure 12.11 demonstrates that only those pups experiencing citral *both* in utero and within 1 hour after delivery attach to unwashed and washed nipples in a citral-scented environment. Exposure to citral exclusively prenatally or postnatally was not sufficient to allow attachment on a nipple scented with citral.

Together, these experiments support previous findings that pups rely on olfactory cues for their first nipple attachment. Moreover, altering

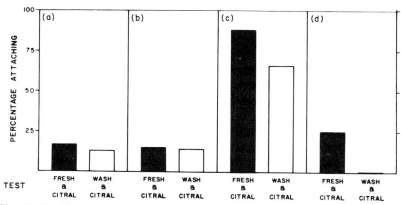

Fig. 12.11   Percentage of pups, attaching to fresh or washed nipples in a citral environment after experiencing either citral or saline prenatally and either citral or saline postnatally for 1 hr: (a) saline, pre- and postnatal; (b) saline prenatal, citral postnatal; (c) citral, pre- and postnatal; (d) citral prenatal, saline postnatal.

pre- and postnatal sensory environments markedly alters the stimuli that elicit the initial nipple attachment. Accordingly, we suggest that the circumstances that normally permit amniotic fluid to elicit nipple attachment are its exposure to the fetus during the last 2–3 days of gestation in conjunction with postnatal stimulation by the mother in the amniotic-rich environment.

IV. SUMMARY

Suckling is a well-defined behavior at birth that is under olfactory control in albino rats. Pups rely heavily upon specific olfactory cues for location and attachment to their mother's nipples throughout the nursing period. Prior to parturition, the mother spreads amniotic fluid over her nipples to which pups attach for the first time. Thereafter pups deposit their own saliva on the nipple. Whether components common to amniotic fluid and saliva elicit nipple attachment remains to be determined. We have isolated and identified one component of pup saliva, DMDS, that is sufficient to elicit nipple attachment. Further chemical analyses will document the specificity and uniqueness with which DMDS controls nipple attachment.

Presently we have restricted our study to pups less than 7 days of age. Salivary secretions do change with age, most markedly about the time of weaning (Leeson & Booth, 1961). These changes in salivary secretions suggest that, during development, the saliva cue for nipple attachment may change or perhaps be masked by the presence of other salivary components. This is supported by Teicher and Blass's (1977) findings that adult rat saliva does not elicit nipple attachment. If the critical characteristics of saliva lose their behavioral properties as far as suckling is concerned, perhaps those characteristics become meaningful later on in another context. In other words, does experience with saliva cues that elicit nipple attachment during development circumscribe a range of chemical stimuli that may gain control over postweaning behaviors, mediated in part by olfactory processes? Although we cannot address this issue directly now, it is of considerable interest that dimethyl sulfite has been isolated and identified in male rat preputial glands and other sulphur compounds (e.g., hexyl mercaptan) have been identified in both male and female preputial glands (Gawienowski et al., 1975, 1976). Moreover, preference tests have revealed that these sulphur compounds, including DMDS, are highly attractive to both sexes (Gawienowski & Stacewicz-Sapuntzakis, 1978). This suggests that certain sulphur compounds may play some part (not a specific one

because sulphur compounds are not unique to albino rats) in finding
a mate, and this attraction is induced early in development.

ACKNOWLEDGMENTS

The authors thank Dr. C. F. Fenselau and Ms. Sharon Polanti for their assistance with
the gas chromatography–mass spectrometry analysis; and Dr. C. L. Williams for her
helpful criticisms in reviewing a preliminary draft of this chapter.

REFERENCES

Alberts, J. R. Producing and interpreting experimental olfactory deficits. *Physiology and
   Behavior*, 1974, **12**, 657–670.
Alberts, J. R. Olfactory contributions to behavioral development in rodents. In R. L. Doty
   (Ed.), *Mammalian olfaction: Reproductive processes and behavior*. New York: Academic
   Press, 1976, pp. 67–94.
Anderson, K. K., & Bernstein, D. T. Some chemical constituents of the scent of the
   striped skunk (*Mephitis mephitis*). *Journal of Chemical Ecology*, 1975, **1**, 493.
Birch, M. C. (Ed.). *Pheromones*. New York: Elsevier, 1974.
Blass, E. M., Teicher, M. H., Cramer, C. P., Bruno, J. P., & Hall, W. G. Olfactory,
   thermal, and tactile controls of suckling in preauditory and previsual rats. *Journal
   of Comparative and Physiological Psychology*, 1977, **91**, 1248–1260.
Bradley, R. M., & Mistretta, C. M. Fetal sensory receptors. *Physiology Reviews*, 1975, **55**,
   352–382.
Bruno, J. P., Teicher, M. H., & Blass, E. M. Sensory determinants of suckling behavior
   in weanling rats. *Journal of Comparative and Physiological Psychology*, 1980, **94**, 115–127.
Cheal, M. L. Social olfaction: A review of the ontogeny of olfactory influences on vertebrate behavior. *Behavioral Biology*, 1975, **15**, 1–25.
Darby, E. M., Devon, M., & Chorover, S. L. A presumptive set pheromone in the
   hamster: Some behavioral effects. *Journal of Comparative and Physiological Psychology*,
   1975, **88**, 496–502.
DeSnoo, K. Das trinkende kind im uterus. *Montasschrift für Geburtshulfe und Gynaecologie*,
   1937, **105**, 88–97.
Dewey, M. M. A histochemical and biochenical study of the parotid gland in normal
   and hypophysectomized rats. *American Journal of Anatomy*, 1958, **102**, 243–262.
Doty, R. L. (Ed.). *Mammalian olfaction: Reproductive processes and behavior*. New York:
   Academic Press, 1976.
Ellin, R. I., Farrand, R. L., Oberst, F. W., Crouse, C. L., Billups, N. B., Koon, W. S.,
   Musselman, N. P., & Sidell, R. F. An apparatus for the detection and quantitation
   of volatile human effluents. *Journal of Chromatography*, 1974, **100**, 137–152.
Farbman, A. I. Electron microscope study of the developing taste bud in rat fungiform
   papillae. *Developmental Biology*, 1965, **11**, 110–135.
Gawienowski, A. M., Orsulak, P. J., Stacewicz-Sapuntzakis, M., & Joseph, B. M. Presence
   of sex pheromone in preputial glands of male rats. *Journal of Endocrinology*, 1975,
   67, 283–288.

Gawienowski, A. M., Orsulak, P. J., Stacewicz-Sapuntzakis, M., & Pratt, J., Jr. Attractant effect of female preputial gland extracts on the male rat. *Psychoneuroendocrinology,* 1976, **1,** 411–418.

Gawienowski, A. M., & Stacewicz-Sapuntzakis, M. Attraction of rats to sulfur compounds. *Behavioral Biology,* 1978, **23,** 267–270.

Gregory, K., Engel, K., & Pfaff, D. Male hamster preference of female hamster vaginal secretions: Studies of experimental and hormonal determinants. *Journal of Comparative and Physiological Psychology,* 1974, **89,** 442–446.

Hall, W. G., Cramer, C. P., & Blass, E. M. Developmental changes in suckling of rat pups. *Nature,* 1975, **258,** 319–320.

Hall, W. G., Cramer, C. P., & Blass, E. M. The ontogeny of suckling in rats: Transitions toward adult ingestion. *Journal of Comparative and Physiological Psychology,* 1977, **91,** 1141–1155.

Hinds, J. W., & Hinds, P. L. Synapse formation in the mouse olfactory bulb I. Quantitative studies. *Journal of Comparative Neurology,* 1976, **169,** 15–40.

Hofer, M. A., Fisher, A., & Shair, H. *Snout denervation disrupts suckling in young rats.* Paper presented at International Society in Developmental Psychobiology, 1979, Atlanta, Ga.

Hofer, M. A., Shair, H., & Singh, P. Evidence that maternal skin substances promote suckling in infant rats. *Physiology and Behavior,* 1976, **17,** 131–136.

Johnston, R. E. Sexual attraction function of golden hamster vaginal secretion. *Behavioral Biology,* 1974, **12,** 111–117.

Johnston, R. E. Sexual excitation function of hamster vaginal secretion. *Animal Learning and Behavior,* 1975, **3,** 161–166.

Johnston, R. E. Sex pheromones in golden hamsters. In D. Muller-Schwarze & M. M. Mozell (Eds.), *Chemical signals in vertebrates.* New York: Plenum, 1977, pp. 367–375.

Johnston, R. E., & Coplin, B. Development of responses to vaginal secretion and other substances in golden hamsters. *Behavioral and Neural Biology,* 1979, **25,** 473–489.

Lev, R., & Orlic, O. Protein absorption by the intestine of the fetal rat in utero. *Science,* 1972, **177,** 522–524.

Liley, A. W. Disorders of amniotic fluid. In N. S. Assali (Ed.), *Pathophysiology of gestation: Fetal-placental disorders* (Vol. II). New York: Academic Press, 1972.

Leeson, C. R., & Booth, W. G. Histological histochemical, and electron-microscopic observations on the postnatal development of the major sublingual gland of the rat. *Journal of Dental Research,* 1961, **40,** 838–845.

Macrides, R., Johnson, P. A., & Schneider, J. P. Responses of the male golden hamster to vaginal secretion and dimethyl disulfide: Attraction versus sexual behavior. *Behavioral Biology,* 1977, **20,** 377–386.

Montero, C. Histochemistry of protein-bound disulfide groups in the duct secretory granules of the rat submandibular gland. *Histochemistry Journal,* 1972, **4,** 259–266.

Müller-Schwarze, D., & Mozell, M. M. (Eds.). *Chemical signals in vertebrates,* New York: Plenum, 1977.

Murphy, M. R. Effects of female hamster vaginal discharge on the behavior of male hamsters. *Behavioral Biology,* 1973, **9,** 367–375.

Murphy, M. R., & Schneider, G. E. Olfactory bulb removal eliminates mating behavior in the male golden hamster. *Science,* 1970, **167,** 302–304.

Narayanan, C. H., Fox, M. W., & Hamburger, V. Prenatal development of spontaneous and evoked activity in the rat (*Rattus norvegicus albinus*), *Behavior,* 1971, **40,** 100–134.

Powers, J. B., Fields, R. B., & Winans, S. S. Olfactory and vomeronasal system participation in male hamster's attraction to female vaginal secretions. *Physiology and Behavior,* 1979, **22,** 77–84.

Pritchard, E. T. Variations in sulpholipid metabolism during early growth in some rat tissues. *International Journal of Biochemistry*, 1975, **6**, 353–359.

Rosenblatt, J. S. Stages in the early behavioral development of altricial young of selected species of nonprimate mammals. In P. P. G. Bateson & R. A. Hinde (Eds.), *Growing points in ethology*. Cambridge: Cambridge University Press, 1976, pp. 345–383.

Rosenblatt, J. S., & Lehrman, D. S. Maternal behavior of the laboratory rat. In H. L. Rheingold (Ed.), *Maternal behavior in mammals*. New York: Wiley, 1963, pp. 8–57.

Roth, L. L., & Rosenblatt, J. S. Changes in self-licking during pregnancy in the rat. *Journal of Comparative and Physiological Psychology*, 1967, **63**, 397–400.

Shorey, H. H. *Animal communication by pheromones*. New York: Academic Press, 1976.

Singer, A. C., Agosta, W. C., O'Connell, R. J., Pfaffman, C., Bowen, D. V., & Field, F. H. Dimethyl disulfide: An attractant pheromone in hamster vaginal secretion. *Science*, 1976, **191**, 948–950.

Singh, P. J., & Tobach, E. Olfactory bulbectomy and nursing behavior in rat pups (Wistar DAB), *Developmental Psychobiology*, 1975, **8**, 151–164.

Teicher, M. H. *Suckling in the developing rat: The importance of olfaction and a putative nursing pheromone*. Unpublished doctoral dissertation, The Johns Hopkins University, 1977.

Teicher, M. H., & Blass, E. M. Suckling in newborn rats: Eliminated by nipple lavage, reinstated by pup saliva. *Science*, 1976, **193**, 422–425.

Teicher, M. H., & Blass, E. M. First suckling response of the newborn albino rat: The roles of olfaction and amniotic fluid. *Science*, 1977, **198**, 635–636.

Teicher, M. H., Flaum, L. E., Williams, M., Eckhert, S. J., & Lumia, A. R. Survival, growth, and suckling behavior of neonatally bulbectomized rats. *Physiology and Behavior*, 1978, **21**, 553–561.

Tobach, E., Rouger, Y., and Schneirla, T. C. Development of olfactory function in the rat pup. *American Zoologist*, 1967, **1**, 792–793.

Wheeler, J. W. Properties of compounds used as chemical signals. In D. Müller-Schwarze & M. M. Mozell (Eds.), *Chemical signals in vertebrates*. New York: Plenum, 1977, pp. 61–70.

Wheeler, J. W., Von Endt, D. W., Wemmer, C. 5-Thiomethyl-pentan-2, 3-dione: A unique natural product from the striped hyena. *Journal of American Chemical Society*, 1975, **97**, 441.

13

Some Speculations concerning Neurological Mechanisms for Early Olfactory Recognition

CHRISTIANA M. LEONARD
University of Florida

I. INTRODUCTION

Organisms can respond to their environments in ways that are adaptive because they "recognize" critical stimulus elements and emit appropriate responses to them. The olfactory worlds of mammals contain numerous odor cues that are critical for life-sustaining behavioral and physiological regulations (cf. Doty, 1976). What factors determine recognition of these olfactory signals?

383

In general, one of two broad types of processes are considered to constitute the ontogenetic determinants of odor recognition. The more common process involves some form of experience. For example, rat pups are more attracted to familiar odors than to novel ones (Leon, Galef, & Behse, 1972) and fairly specific preferences can be formed on the basis of chemical cues contained in the mother's milk (Galef & Sherry, 1973). Juvenile rodents respond differentially to odors, as a function of the olfactory characteristics of the materials of the home nest (Cornwell, 1975; Cornwell-Jones & Sobrian, 1977). Odor–temperature contingencies that exist in the maternal nest appear to constitute a natural basis for associative conditioning that establishes olfactory preferences for social huddling by rats (Alberts, Chapter 11, this volume). Numerous terms are used to describe the experience-dependent processes that determine recognition of and responses to odors. A partial list would include: *familiarization, adaptation, exposure learning, associative learning, imprinting,* and *induction.*

Odor recognition can also be mediated by processes that are relatively *insensitive* to experience. In more brazen terminology these would be cases of so-called *innate, instinctive, prewired,* or *predetermined* recognition. Such terms are often invoked when a capacity is present immediately upon birth. "Isolation" experiments are also used to demonstrate that a capacity can develop in the absence of specific, seemingly relevant experiences.

Dieterlen (1959) attempted to examine the ontogenetic basis of recognition of sex odors by hamsters using an isolation paradigm. Noting that adult male hamsters are powerfully attracted by the odor of female hamster vaginal discharge (FHVD), he asked whether a male hamster isolated at birth from its mother would show the characteristic species-specific response that the odor induces in normally reared adults— excitement, approach, vigorous licking and consumption of the discharge, and in the proper circumstances, mounting and copulation. Unfortunately, he only succeeded in rearing one hamster isolated at Day 3; all hamsters isolated at birth died. The hamster isolated at Day 3 went wild when he encountered the odor in adulthood. It took him a long time to copulate because he was very excitable and fearful, and the female appeared to become impatient, but he was clearly responsive to the odor. Because he had at least 3 days of experience with conspecific smells, however, the experiment did not answer unequivocally the basic question. Such methodological difficulties are common to early isolation studies. Lehrman (1970) and others have discussed further interpretive limitations of the isolation paradigm.

In contrast to the simple dichotomies of postnatal learning versus innate determinism are the results of recent and elegant research on the olfactory control of nipple location in newborn rats. It has been discovered that careful cleansing of a rat dam's ventrum eliminated nipple attachment by rat pups. Suckling could be reinstated with oxytocin injection (Hofer, Shair, & Singh, 1976) or by painting the nipples with maternal saliva, pup saliva, or amniotic fluid (Chapter 12, this volume).

Blass and his colleagues recently discovered that dimethyl disulfide (DMDS), is sufficient to elicit nipple attachment in newborn rat pups (Pedersen & Blass, 1980). DMDS is present in pup saliva and thus may be present in the prenatal environment of the pup. [Ironically, DMDS is also an attractant contained in FHVD (Singer, Agosta, O'Connell, Pfaffmann, & Field, 1976)]. The possibility that prenatal experience might influence pups' nipple attachment has been further investigated by Pedersen & Blass (Chapter 12, this volume). They injected citral into the womb two days before cesarean delivery. Citral then elicited nipple attachment if the pup experienced the odor postnatally as well. The conditions of postnatal exposure were critical—the pup was placed in a citral-rich atmosphere and stroked with a camel's hair brush in an attempt to mimic normal postnatal maternal licking. This treatment caused the pup to locomote or "sit up and take notice." In the absence of stroking the pups lay quietly and citral did not acquire new properties. Pups that had been exposed to the double treatment (citral + stroking) subsequently attached to washed nipples provided they were in a citral atmosphere. This last fact is especially important, for normally delivered and reared pups never attach to washed nipples (Teicher & Blass, 1977). Blass has shown that the treated pups have acquired a preference for the odor for they will orient to it in an open field. Even more interesting, treated pups no longer attach to nipples painted with saliva. Citral has apparently suppressed or surpassed the efficacy of saliva.

The findings of Blass's group have illuminated the phenomenon of early olfactory learning in several ways:

1. They have shown that a species-specific response can be brought under the control of a synthetic odor, using proper prenatal and postnatal manipulations.

2. Both pre- and postnatal exposure are necessary.

3. Exposure is not sufficient, the pup must be in a particular state during the postnatal exposure.

4. The odor does not serve as a simple localizer for reflex attachment, but as a sign of some kind.

Presented with an anesthetized dam, a citral atmosphere allows the pup to search for and attach to the nipple. Why does citral have this effect? Does the pup relax and allow the dominant response in the hierarchy (presumably nipple attachment) to proceed? Does citral activate the pup, causing it to locomote and accidentally come in contact with the nipple where trigeminal stimulation causes reflex attachment? Or does citral create an image of good times, the memory of reward of being rocked in the womb, and a concomitant desire to seek further reinforcement through oral gratification? Whether one prefers the behaviorist or psychoanalytic formulation, it is clear that olfactory imprinting provides an excellent model system for the speculative neuroanatomist. Because the brain of the late gestational pup is exceedingly undeveloped, many brain regions can be excluded from a possible neural substrate by virtue of their immaturity. One might naively hope, indeed, that the only functional systems would be those involved in essential life support processes and the behaviors needed immediately postnatally. It is thus possible that a study of the neural mechanisms involved in early olfactory learning might reveal a skeletal reinforcement system that becomes obscured by redundant systems in later life. In this chapter I will discuss anatomic, physiological, and developmental aspects of olfaction that might be relevant to the phenomena of early olfactory learning and suggest some hypotheses concerning its neural substrate.

II. FUNCTIONAL NEUROANATOMY OF THE OLFACTORY SYSTEM

In this section, I review some of the anatomical features and structural relations of the mammalian olfactory system. The review begins with consideration of separate receptor systems in the nasal cavity, then follows the afferents into the brain and traces subsequent central projections. Functional implications are discussed throughout this survey, as well as a consideration of the coding mechanisms for olfactory information. The aim of this noncomprehensive review is to introduce the reader to basic features of the mammalian olfactory system with emphasis on aspects relevant to the developmental model to be presented later in this chapter.

A. Receptor Organs and Peripheral Processes

Most mammals have two discrete regions of receptive epithelium in their snouts: the olfactory epithelium (OE) lining a small portion of the nasal septa and the vomeronasal epithelium contained in the vomeronasal organ (VM), a small blind pocket above the roof of the mouth.

The VM has access to the oral or nasal cavity or both, depending on the species. It is apparently specialized to receive nonvolatile odor components (Ladewig & Hart, 1980; Meredith & O'Connell, 1979; Wysocki, Beauchamp, Wellington, Erisman, & Barth, 1980). The primary receptor cells in the receptive epithelia are unique in two ways; (a) they are continually replaced throughout the life of the organism (Graziadei & Monti-Graziadei, 1978); and (b) they have axons that terminate directly in the brain. By contrast, other epithelial receptive cells synapse in the periphery with long processes of spinal and cranial root ganglia and do not enter the brain directly.

The olfactory cells are ciliated, whereas the VM cells have microvilli but no cilia (Graziadei, 1971). The OE has been extensively studied in the amphibian since the pioneering work of Gesteland, Lettvin, and Pitts (1965). Olfactory receptors respond to a wide variety of chemicals with a generator potential followed by a series of action potentials. No inhibitory responses are found when stimulus delivery is carefully controlled and no adaptation occurs in the peripheral receptor (Getchell & Shepherd, 1978). The present consensus is that olfactory molecules stimulate receptor cells by lodging in receptor sites on cilia or microvilli after dissolving in the epithelial mucus (Van Drongelen, 1978). A particular cell has receptive sites for a variety of odors and its threshold for different odors may vary tremendously, presumably because the number of sites varies from cell to cell (Getchell & Shepherd, 1978).

B. The Olfactory Bulbs

The topography of the receptor sheet is reasonably faithfully preserved in the main olfactory bulb, the brain structure to which the olfactory axons project (Clark, 1951; Land, 1973). Sensory afferents of the vomeronasal organ project exclusively to the accessory olfactory bulb, a separate structure with similar cellular organization but distinct efferent projections. A schematic drawing of neural organization within the olfactory bulb is shown in Fig. 13.1. The outermost layer of the bulb contains the thin (0.2μ unmyelinated olfactory fila) axons. They terminate in glomeruli that contain the dendritic tufts of the principal olfactory bulb cell, the mitral cell. There are about 25,000 times as many receptors as glomeruli, thus there is tremendous convergence at the glomerular level (Allison & Warwick, 1949). Glomeruli are linked by short-axon periglomerular (PG) cells that have their dendrites in one glomerulus and their axon terminals in several adjacent ones. Recent evidence (Davis, Hoffman, & Macrides, 1980; Halasz, Llungdahl, Hokfelt, Johansson, Goldstein, Park, & Biberfeld, 1977) suggests that the

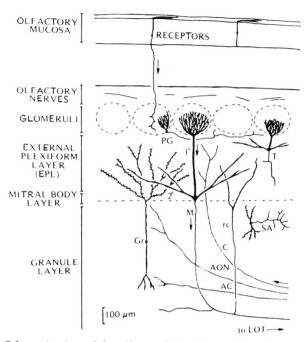

Fig. 13.1 Schematic view of the olfactory bulb. The peripheral receptor terminates in a glomerulus on dendrites of the principal mitral cell (M) or tufted cell (T) and periglomerular cells (PG). Intrinsic granule cells (Gr) make inhibitory dendrodentritic synapses with M. Centrifugal fibers (C) from the anterior commissure (AC) and anterior olfactory nucleus (AON) are also shown. The mitral and tufted cells send their axons into the lateral olfactory tract (LOT) and almost make recurrent collateral connections (rc) in the bulb. 1°: primary dendrites; 2°: secondary dendrites. (Reprinted from Shepherd, 1979, by permission of Oxford University Press.)

glomeruli are surrounded with PG cells containing specific neuropeptides (enkephalins, releasing factors, or dopamine).

Postglomerular processing is complex. Internal to the glomerular layer is the external plexiform layer that contains the primary (apical) and secondary (lateral) dendrites of the mitral cell and countless granule cell dendrites. The granule cell is an intrinsic inhibitory (GABAergic) neuron that lies in the core of the bulb below the mitral cell layer and has the dinstinction of being one of the few neurons that is produced throughout the life of the animal (Kaplan & Hinds, 1977). The granule cell has no axon and thus has been compared by Shepherd (1979) to the amacrine cell of the retina. It makes reciprocal synapses with the mitral cell dendrite and, as a result, causes a feedback inhibition. The

external plexiform layer also contains tufted cells, large projection neurons that may differ significantly from mitral cells in their response
properties (Macrides, personal communication, 1980).

C. Olfactory Projections

The mitral and tufted cells are the only bulb cells with extrinsic
projections. Their axons form the lateral olfactory tract which is the
sole olfactory projection tract (Devor, 1976; White, 1965) and spread
out over the entire ventral forebrain medial to the rhinal sulcus (see
Fig. 13.2). The main olfactory bulb projects to the anterior olfactory
nucleus, hippocampal rudiment, piriform (olfactory) cortex, olfactory
tubercle, entorhinal area, and anterior amygdala. The accessory olfac-

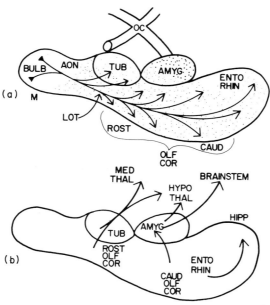

Fig. 13.2 (a) Schematic view of secondary olfactory projections (fine stipple) from
main and accessory olfactory bulb (coarse stipple). Mitral (M) and tufted cells from the
main bulb send their axons into the lateral olfactory tract (LOT) to the rostral and caudal
olfactory cortex (ROST and CAUD OLF COR), olfactory tubercle (TUB), a small lateral
part of the amygdala (AMYG), and entorhinal area (ENTORHIN). The mitral cells in the
accessory olfactory bulb also send their axons into LOT. They terminate in the medial
and cortical amygdaloid nuclei. OC: optic chiasm. (b) Schematic view of the tertiary
olfactory projections. Abbreviations: MED THAL, dorsomedial nucleus of the thalamus;
HIPP, hippocampus.

tory bulb projects to the medial and cortical amygdaloid nuclei (Winans & Scalia, 1970).

Mitral and tufted cell axons terminate in a discrete outer lamina of the molecular layer of olfactory cortex. The inner lamina is filled with terminals from association fibers originating in other olfactory regions (Heimer, 1968; Price, 1973). Both projections terminate in round-vesicled asymmetric synaptic specializations (Caviness, Korda, & Williams, 1977; Westrum, 1975). The olfactory tubercle contains an additional projection from the dopaminergic cells of the ventral tegmental area and possibly substantia nigra (Fallon & Moore, 1978; Ungerstedt, 1971). Because the tubercle contains the highest concentration of cholinergic markers in the forebrain (Hoover, Muth, & Jacobowitz, 1978), it bears a strong resemblance to the more dorsal caudate and putamen. Heimer and Wilson (1975) have speculated that the tubercle is not primarily an olfactory structure but a "ventral striatum" bearing the same functional relation to olfactory cortex that the dorsal striatum (caudate–putamen) does to neocortex.

In view of the heterogeneous nature of the olfactory projection areas, it is disappointing to learn that very little evidence has been found for topographical specificity in the efferent bulb projections. Individual mitral cells apparently collateralize widely and may project to many different regions (Devor, 1976). A single region of olfactory cortex may thus receive projections from widely separate regions of the bulb (Haberly & Price, 1977). This convergence and divergence has led Devor (1977) to speculate that olfactory coding at the cortical level must be contained in a spatiotemporal "fingerprint." Few experiments have been performed on the coding properties of olfactory cortex.

It is unfortunate that so little is understood about cortical processing, because a great deal of anatomical evidence suggests that the efferent projections of the various olfactory areas are distinct and almost exclusively to the limbic system, the region of the brain involved in emotional, autonomic, endocrine, and reproductive control (Maclean, 1949). Efferent projections from the rostral olfactory cortex go to the lateral hypothalamus and mediodorsal nucleus of the thalamus, the projection nucleus for orbital prefrontal cotex (Powell, Cowan, & Raisman, 1965); from caudal olfactory cortex they go to the central nucleus of the amygdala (Heimer & Wilson, 1975) which projects to cranial parasympathetic nuclei (Hopkins, 1975); the olfactory tubercle projects to a posterior hypothalamic region adjacent to the ventral tegmental area (Scott & Chafin, 1975; Scott & Leonard, 1971); the entorhinal area is the major afferent to the hippocampal formation (Cajal, 1906); and the medial and cortical amygdala contain estrogen receptors (Pfaff & Keiner,

1973) and project to the medial hypothalamic areas involved in reproductive endocrine and behavioral control. Figure 13.2 shows a summary of the tertiary olfactory projections.

The anatomical evidence strongly suggests that different olfactory projection regions are involved in different behavioral control mechanisms. The tubercle has been implicated in locomotor and exploratory behavior (Fink & Smith, 1980; Ormond & Van Hartesveldt, 1979); the entorhinal area in discrimination learning, memory, and spontaneous alternation (Loesche & Steward, 1977); and the amygdala in a variety of species-specific, social, reproductive, aggressive, and alimentary behaviors (Valenstein, 1973). Although there is considerable evidence that the ventromedial (VM) projection has specific behavioral functions (Powers, Fields, & Winans, 1979; see Halpern, 1980, for other examples) there is no evidence for specificity in other bulb projections.

D. Olfactory Coding

Like receptor cells, individual mitral cells respond to a variety of odors. To date, little evidence for stimulus specificity has been obtained. Unlike receptor cells, however, mitral cells can respond to different odors with either excitation or suppression and they do show adaptation (Kauer, 1974). These latter responses are presumably caused by inhibitory connections from intrinsic bulbar cells. Shepherd and his colleagues propose that the suppressive response is due to postglomerular influences from granule and PG cells and liken it to the phenomenon of lateral inhibition in the retina (Shepherd, 1979). The function of lateral inhibition in the retina is to enhance contours. It is difficult to define the dimension along which discrimination would be enhanced by lateral inhibition in the bulb, because the rules governing the formation of inhibitory connections are not understood.

The coding of odor quality is a major unsolved problem. It is difficult for us to reconstruct our rich and varied olfactory world from receptors that respond to all odors in the same way and bulb cells that receive connections from thousands of receptor cells and respond in two ways. Theorizing in this field is not advanced but there are a few experimental observations that can somewhat constrain our hypotheses.

Amoore (1975) has collected evidence for specific anosmias: human cases that cannot smell specific odors. Interestingly enough, he has found four categories of anosmia for simple molecules emitted by humans. Amoore classifies these odors as sweaty, fishy, musky, and semenous. He believes that a specific anosmia results from the absence of a specific type of receptor site. Receptors lacking these sites would obviously not fire in the presence of these odors and the organism would be unresponsive. This theory explains the failure of discrimination but it does not explain how a receptor cell with innumerable sites transmits the signal for a specific odor. Most theories invoke some type of spatial or temporal summation.

Because the olfactory receptor sheet has a topographic representation in the bulb, a spatial olfactory code could be transmitted if different odors stimulated different regions of the mucosa. Mozell (1966) has shown that this is indeed the case. Different odorants flow through the nose at different rates and have peak concentrations at different locations along the receptor sheet. In addition, Macrides (1977) has shown that bulb units respond to odors in different phases of the sniff cycle. Since flow rate is a function of the physical characteristics of the stimulus, it is reasonable to suppose that chemicals with different properties would stimulate different epithelial areas and this could form the basis for odor discrimination.

Another spatial hypothesis has been proposed by Kauer and Moulton (1974). Using punctate odor stimulation of the epithelium (thus eliminating the factor of airflow) they recorded the responses of olfactory bulb cells in the salamander. Their results support the view that receptor cells from discrete regions of epithelium converge on particular mitral cells and, in addition, that these epithelial cells share similar response properties. Van Drongelen (1978) has proposed an explanation for a particularly puzzling characteristic of olfaction. There are literally millions of receptor sites in the mucosa, yet one or two molecules of odorant may evoke a behavioral response. He suggests that a molecule of odorant can skip from cilium to cilium, depolarizing each in turn. If similarly responsive cells are grouped in the epithelium and converge on a glomerulus in which there are primary tufts from many mitral cells, tremendous focusing and amplification of the response is possible.

These results suggest that olfactory stimuli may be coded at the glomerular level. This view has received additional support from work in Shepherd's laboratory (Stewart, Kauer, & Shepherd, 1979) suggesting that glomeruli are differentially active under different odor conditions. They used the recently developed 2-deoxyglucose technique that allows the histological demonstration of regions of high synaptic activity. Different odors reliably produced different patterns of activity in the glomeruli and the response to a given odor was reasonably similar from animal to animal. All odors appeared to have both medial and lateral foci of activity extending from the rostral to the caudal tip of the bulb. Such a pattern of activity could result from either (a) differential receptor stimulation due to airflow over the mucosa; or (b) convergence of similarly responsive receptor cells onto particular glomeruli.

Like many sensory processing stations, the bulb is subject to numerous centrifugal inputs: cholinergic fibers from the ventral forebrain (olfactory tubercle, lateral preoptic area, and diagonal band; Godfrey, Ross, Hermann and Matshinsky, 1980); serotonergic fibers from the raphé and noradrenergic fibers from locus coeruleus (Shepherd, 1979). As these neurochemicals all play major roles in modifying behavioral states, and their sites or origin are well known limbic structures (Nauta & Domesick, 1977), it seems reasonable to suppose that information concerning central state and reinforcement variables may be conveyed to the bulb through these pathways and that they may play a role in modifying glomerular activity. Cornwell-Jones (1980) has shown that male rats depleted of norepinephrine do not show typical preferences for estrus urine, although their odor discrimination was presumed to be unimpaired.

To retierate and expand the questions asked in the introduction: How do olfactory stimuli acquire their behavioral significance? How does the entorhinal cortex or the olfactory tubercle know what to do with the incoming signal? If one mitral cell projects to all or nearly all target areas, why do particular olfactory stimuli cause particular behavioral responses? Perhaps the answer to this question lies in the manner in which olfactory connections develop.

III. FUNDAMENTALS OF OLFACTORY NEURAL DEVELOPMENT

Some of the sequences and patterns of neural development found in the mammalian olfactory system are reviewed in this section. Emphasis is on the time of origin and possible onset of function at different organizational levels of the developing olfactory system. Again, this is a selective review, aimed at providing a basic neurobiological framework for a functional model. As you will note, many events in the establishment of neuronal circuitry take place before birth, providing a basis for prenatal effects on olfactory processing.

A. Birth and Differentiation of Neural Elements

The development of the olfactory mucosa has been studied in the mouse by Hinds (1972a,b) and by Cuschieri and Bannister (1975a,b).

Differentiated epithelial cells can be identified on prenatal Day 10, about midway through gestation. Their axons immediately leave the epithelium and reach the bulb on Day 11, the day the first mitral cells are born. Different techniques were used to determine the date of mitral cell appearance and axonal outgrowth, so it is not known whether the first axons to reach the bulb contact the first mitral cells to be born.

Hinds has done a thorough study of bulb-cell birth dates (1968a,b), which has been recently summarized by Alberts (1976). Most of the principal cells in the main and accessory bulbs are born between Days 10 and 16 of prenatal life. The principal cells of the accessory bulb are born slightly earlier and the tufted cells of the main bulb slightly later, but there is a large degree of overlap. Granule cells are born over a much longer time period, starting soon after the first mitral cells but continuing to proliferate rapidly for the first postnatal month and then continuing to turn over at a slow rate throughout life. It is odd that the principal cells of the accessory bulb are the first to be born, as the vomeronasal epithelium starts to differentiate later than the olfactory epithelium (Cuschieri & Bannister, 1975a).

Hinds did not report any regional differences in mitral or tufted cell birth dates (1968a), although his drawings show that the earliest born cells tend to be clumped on the medial aspect of the bulb. Similarly, in the newborn hamster, the olfactory fila appear to be most numerous on the medial aspect of the bulb and the mitral cells in this region are the first to send their axons into the lateral olfactory tract (Grafe & Leonard, 1980).

B. Structural and Functional Specification

In view of the apparent coupling of epithelial and bulbar development, it is interesting that synapses are not found in the glomerular layer until several days after the first olfactory axon enters. Hinds speculates that this period is occupied by mitral cell differentiation. The dendritic processes of the mitral cells are initially oriented tangentially in the external plexiform layer. After the olfactory fila have penetrated the bulb, Hinds found mitral cells with radially oriented primary dendrites that extended into glomeruli. He speculated that the reorientation was induced by some chemical or electrical influence emanating from the olfactory fila and called the process anterograde instruction or specification (1972a).

The findings of Cuschieri and Bannister (1975b) suggest that there is also a retrograde influence emanating from the bulb that affects epithelial development. Although the epithelial axons penetrate the bulb on Day 11, and the first cilia are seen on Day 13, the epithelial cells do not have a mature appearance until Day 17, 2 days before birth. At this time, they acquire abundant endoplasmic reticula, Golgi apparatus, mitochondria, and develop mature looking cilia.

Gesteland (personal communication, 1980) reports that cultured epithelial cells show no response specificity until they have developed cilia. It seems that there may be a stepwise reciprocal oscillating form of induction acting between bulb and epithelium. First the entering receptor axon induced mitral-cell reorientation, then information passed retrogradely from the mitral cell induces further receptor differentiation. It would be particularly interesting to know whether the hypothetical retrograde influence could be specific enough to induce the differentiation of particular receptive properties in the epithelial cells. Such a mechanism could operate throughout life, ensuring that the newly formed receptor cells had specificities appropriate for the glomeruli to which they were connected.

Cuschieri and Bannister (1975) report that differentiating receptor cells are closely apposed early in development (see Fig. 13.3) and suggest cell–cell coupling for the transfer of information. This could be a mechanism by which epithelial cells specialized for the reception of similar information could become clumped together and project to the same glomerulus. One wonders if it is significant that in the mouse the first epithelial cells acquire a mature appearance and lose their close appositions 2 days before birth—the period, when in the rat, Pedersen and Blass find that prenatal experience can influence postnatal development. Unfortunately, no comparable information on rat epithelial development is available.

Hinds has shown that each step in the synaptic circuitry of the bulb is complete by late fetal life (Hinds & Hinds, 1976a,b). This does not mean that the bulb as a whole is mature (see Fig. 13.4). The layers are undifferentiated, and granule cells are being added continually in postnatal life. The Hinds estimate that 1% of the eventual complement of synapses is present at birth. Inspection of the bulb does not suggest that individual glomeruli are larger or better developed than are their neighbors, or that a few mitral cells have a mature appearance. This is odd because it is hard to imagine that glomeruli with 1% of their adult complement of synapses could be particularly functionally effective.

There is some evidence that postnatal stimulation can affect the histological maturation of the bulb. Doving and Pinching (1973) exposed 14-day-old rats to single odors for periods of 2 weeks to 2 months and

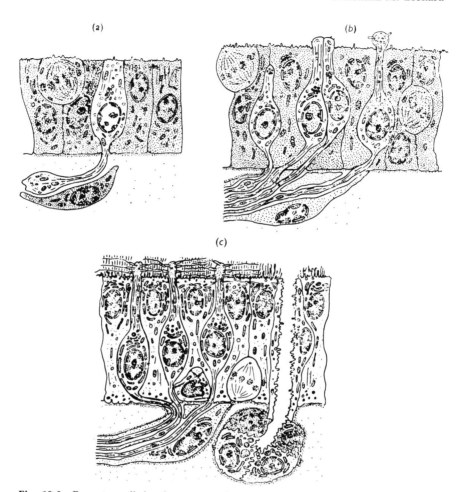

Fig. 13.3 Receptor cell development in the mouse. Cuschieri and Bannister (1975b) found evidence of close appositions between receptor cells in development and hypothesized that this provided a means for cell to cell communication. (a) On gestational Day 10 receptor cell axons can be seen leaving the epithelium. (b) On Day 13, some axons are seen traveling together in bundles enveloped by a glial sheath. The first dendrites push up into the nasal cavity and cilia sprout laterally. (c) By gestational Day 17, mature cilia fill the mucosal layer and mature receptors show no signs of close appositions. Mature gland cells below the epithelial layer secrete mucosal substance. (From Cuschieri and Bannister, 1975b, reprinted by permission from Cambridge University Press.)

then examined their olfactory bulbs. They found patches of degenerating mitral cells in specific regions of the olfactory bulbs. These regions were the same in rats exposed to the same odor but different in rats exposed to other odors (Pinching & Doving, 1974). A second piece of evidence comes from the work of Meisami (1978). He closed one nostril of a mouse on the day of birth and then examined the olfactory bulb at 1 month of age. Although the number of glomeruli on the two sides were comparable, the number of mitral cells on the unstimulated side was reduced by 20%. If postnatal manipulations cause such a marked change, one can imagine that prenatal manipulations might be even more effective.

The available evidence suggests, then, that by 2 days before birth, peripheral olfactory structures are sufficiently mature to support function. The tissue, however, still appears immature. Identifying functional circuits in immature tissue is a major problem in developmental anatomy. Most anatomical methods are appropriate for describing the appearance of tissues as a whole. Function, however, particularly nervous function, may not be a property of the tissue as a whole, but of specific elements in that tissue and their connections with far-distant regions. We need a method that will allow functionally competent circuits to stand out in an immature and developing neuropil.

One method for assessing functional maturity is the 2-DG technique for measuring glucose utilization or synaptic activity. Shepherd and his associates (Teicher, Stewart, Kauer, & Shepherd, 1980) have applied this technique to the neonatal rat but have been unable to obtain consistent results in pups less than 1 week old. Older pups who are suckling show a specific focus of activity in a macroglomerulus at the posterior junction of the accessory and main olfactory bulbs. Whether activity in this glomerulus is particularly related to olfactory stimuli from the nipple is not yet known. Pups sniffing room-air sometimes show activity in this glomerulus, but Teicher feels this may be a confounding effect of a pup's sniffing itself and its own saliva. Clearly, it will be of great interest to investigate the developmental history of this region of the bulb and its epithelial projection. One method for investigating the maturity of the epithelial cells that has not been tried would be to look at the appearance of the olfactory receptor protein (Margolis, 1974). Monti-Graziadei (1980) has shown that it appears in epithelial cells regenerating after nerve section at the time that the epithelial axons make connections with the bulb. It would be interesting if there were some kind of topographical gradient in the appearance of the protein in development. Perhaps it peaks first in cells making contact with the macroglomerulus.

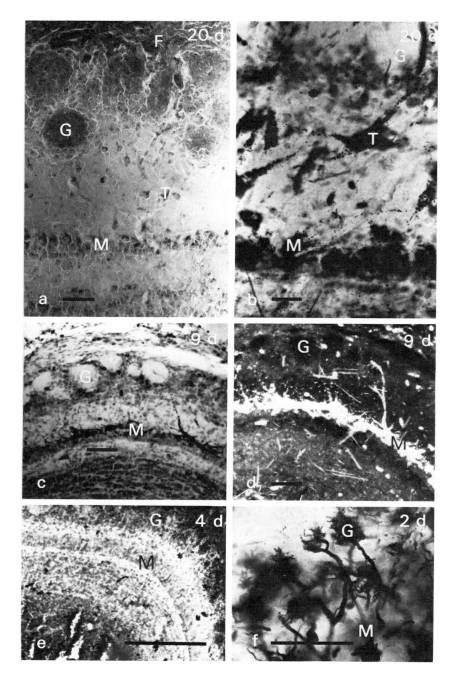

C. Development of Central Olfactory Projections

The maturation of the olfactory projection has been studied with three techniques: (a) electron-microscopy (Westrum, 1975); (b) autoradiography (Schwob & Price, 1978); and (c) degeneration (Leonard, 1975; Singh, 1977a,b). Using the electron microscope, Hinds, (1972) and Westrum (1975) have shown that there are synapses in the piriform cortex by birth although the number increases greatly during subsequent weeks. For information about whether different regions of the olfactory projection differ in their maturational level at birth, however, a light microscopic method is necessary. It is simply too time consuming to sample several regions and ages with ultrastructural methods.

The two commonly used methods for tracing tracts—autoradiography and degeneration—give different results concerning the state of development of the olfactory projection at birth, probably because of intrinsic differences in the two techniques. When a radioactive amino acid is injected into a cellular field, it is incorporated into protein in the cell body and transported down the axon to the terminals. Because the label fills every terminal ramification whether it has made a synapse or not, an overestimation of the functional significance of the projection may result.

Such an overestimation has been documented in the visual systems of the kitten and the rodent. Mize and Sterling (1977) found that although the retinal projection to the superior colliculus of the kitten appeared to be well developed at birth, when they examined the projection with EM-autoradiography they found very few synapses of retinal origin. They concluded "it is impossible to gauge synapse formation by light microscope autoradiography [p. 658]." The retinal projection to the colliculus of the hamster as demonstrated by autoradiography

---

Fig. 13.4 Olfactory bulb of the hamster at different stages of development. Bar = 100 μm. (a) Twenty days of age: receptor axons (F) stained with acid phosphatase (AP) fill glomeruli (G). Well-differentiated mitral (M) and tufted cells (T) are seen; external plexiform layer is well developed. Barka AP technique counterstained with methyl green. (b) Twenty days of age. Mitral and tufted cells are labeled with HRP placed in olfactory projection cortex; Mesulam TMB technique counterstained with neutral red. (c) Nine days of age. Bulb is much smaller and less differentiated. Mitral cell with well-developed secondary and primary dendrites is labeled by an HRP injection in projection cortex. Note the primary dendrites extending into the glomerulus. (d) A dark field photograph in another region of the bulb shown in (c). At this age, all mitral cells have sent axons into the lateral olfactory tract as is evidenced by heavy labeling in the mitral cell layer; (e) four days of age. Bulb is very small, mitral cell layer is very poorly differentiated. Receptor axons have been filled anterogradely with HRP to show glomeruli. (f) Two days of age. Although the bulb is very undifferentiated, a Golgi preparation shows that some mitral cells have well-developed dendritic tufts extending into glomeruli.

is mature at 8 days (So, Schneider, & Frost, 1978) yet the eyes do not open until 14 days of age, at which time the first typical optic tract synapses are found (Lund & Lund, 1972).

The traditional method of tract tracing—degeneration argyrophilia—or "Nauta degeneration" in young brains shows a very different picture from that seen with autoradiography. Many axons degenerate and disappear within hours of transection (Leonard, 1975) and thus can not be stained with silver. Interestingly enough, in many pathways, the age at which one can first see "long-lasting degeneration" (72 hours or longer after transection) coincides with the age at which one sees degenerating synapses with the electron microscope (Singh, 1977a). At younger ages, the axons seem to swell and disintegrate, without going through the normal adult sequence of shrinkage, increased electron density, and glial investiture (Schoenfeld, Street, & Leonard, 1979). Apparently, a maturing neuron acquires stability and resistance to degeneration. I have suggested elsewhere (Leonard, 1974, 1975) that the onset of function, synaptogenesis, and long-lasting degeneration may coincide in time, and that, in fact, there may be some causal relation. One can hypothesize that a "functionally validated" synapse (Jacobson, 1970) may acquire special adhesive properties, or particles in the post-synaptic membrane (Landis & Reese, 1977) that serve to protect it from disintegration. An expanding growth cone, however, would have no such protective mechanisms.

Whether or not the onset of long-lasting degeneration signals the onset of function or some shift in the rate of synaptogenesis, it does provide a maturational yardstick that can be used to compare the developmental state of various projection systems. If one examines the olfactory bulb projection in the golden hamster with this method at birth, one finds that only a restricted region in the caudal olfactory cortex (see Fig. 13.5) shows long-lasting degeneration (Leonard, 1975). It is interesting that this region is the first to show evidence of synaptic connections because these cells project to the central nucleus of the amygdala and thus could influence early maturing behavioral mechanisms organized in the brainstem.

The vomeronasal projection to the amygdala is one of the last projections to show long-lasting degeneration argyrophilia (Leonard, 1975). This is surprising, because Hinds had reported that the mitral cells here are the earliest to be born. In view of Cuschieri and Bannister's (1975a) finding that the vomeronasal epithelium develops after the olfactory epithelium and Teicher et al.'s (1980) finding that a macroglomerulus between the accessory olfactory bulb and main olfactory bulb shows activity early in development, it seems possible that the early appearing

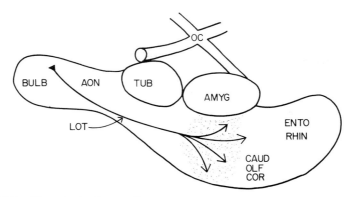

Fig. 13.5   Fine stipple shows olfactory projection region that shows histological evidence of synaptic development at birth in the hamster. The remainder of the bulb projection shows evidence of immaturity at birth.

mitral cells of the accessory bulb could be stimulated by the olfactory epithelium and perhaps send their axons into the main olfactory tract. A Golgi study of this region in the rat might identify the location of mitral cells that extend their dendrites into the macroglomerulus.

Little is known about fetal receptor sensitivity in the olfactory system. The fetus, lying in the womb, is continually perfused with amniotic fluid, a complex mixture of proteins, salts, and sugars (Bradley & Mistretta, 1975), molecules capable of depolarizing receptor cells in the olfactory or vomeronasal mucosa. Whether or not fetal receptors are actually sensitive to, or transmit information about, these stimuli is unknown. At this point, we shall leave the realm of reality and concrete data to postulate a possible mechanism by which prenatal stimulation could come to control postnatal responsiveness.

IV. SPECULATIONS ON THE DEVELOPMENT OF A NEURAL SUBSTRATE FOR NIPPLE LOCATION AND SUCKLING

Having reviewed some fundamentals of olfactory system ontogenesis, we are equipped to consider the simple, but practical problem of functional development introduced earlier. Specifically, I shall offer a model of neural development that can account for the ability of a newborn rat, just minutes after being expelled from the uterine environment, to orient to the dam, "recognize" the odor of her and her nipples, apprehend a teat, and suckle. In addition, this model can accommodate the data from Blass's laboratory concerning perinatal manipulations that establish olfactory controls over suckling in the newborn rat (Chapter 12, this volume). It should be emphasized that this is a highly speculative model, but that it is based on established phenomena and data in neurogenesis. The reader who is unfamiliar with the background or procedural details of the relevant behavioral studies should read Section I of this chapter or examine Chapter 12 by Pedersen and Blass.

Exposure to citral in the presence of an arousing stimulus, such as stroking, changes the significance of citral and causes it to acquire reinforcing properties. There are five questions:

1. Why is prenatal stimulation with citral necessary?
2. What is the neural equivalent of arousal, excitement, stroking, and so on?
3. How does excitement affect citral processing in the olfactory system?
4. Why is the net effect, nipple attachment?
5. Why does saliva and/or amniotic fluid normally elicit nipple attachment?

Let us take the last question first. If the pup in the womb is continually exposed to molecules contained in amniotic fluid, the most active olfactory receptors will be those with the most receptive sites for those molecules. Active receptors will increase their metabolic rate, protein synthesis, and, perhaps, their rate of growth. Axonal growth of receptors sensitive to amniotic fluid will therefore exceed growth of axons from less sensitive receptors in the race to the olfactory bulb. If Hind's postulate of anterograde specification is correct, mitral cells will be more likely to reorient their dendrites to amniotic-fluid-sensitive glomeruli than to their neighbors (see Fig. 13.6). Thus the first functional receptor–mitral cell connections would be those activated by the components of amniotic fluid (and/or pup saliva).

Which mitral cells will be most likely to reorient their dendrites? Probably those mitral cells that have already made axonal connections in olfactory cortex. Cajal (translated 1959) has postulated a principle of retrograde development stating that a neuron's dendrites proliferate after its axon has made terminal connection. This principle has been found to be valid for motor neurons in the spinal cord but is difficult to test for individual neurons in the central nervous system (CNS). Assuming that this principle is valid, we would predict that mitral cells that had made synaptic connections in olfactory projection areas would be the most likely to have sprouted dendrites and thus would be most likely to make their connections with amniotic-fluid-sensitive receptor

I. RETROGRADE DEVELOPMENT :
PRENATAL : DAY 9-11

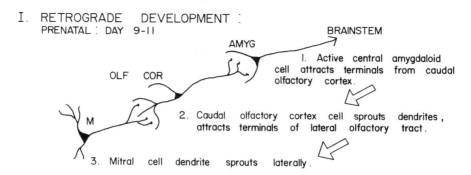

1. Active central amygdaloid cell attracts terminals from caudal olfactory cortex.

2. Caudal olfactory cortex cell sprouts dendrites, attracts terminals of lateral olfactory tract.

3. Mitral cell dendrite sprouts laterally.

II. ANTEROGRADE SPECIFICATION :
PRENATAL : DAY 13-BIRTH

1. Active receptor sites

2. Terminal proliferation

3. Mitral dendrite reorientation

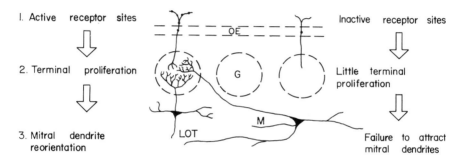

Inactive receptor sites

Little terminal proliferation

Failure to attract mitral dendrites

III. REINFORCEMENT :
POSTNATAL

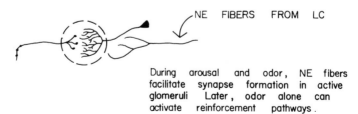

NE FIBERS FROM LC

During arousal and odor, NE fibers facilitate synapse formation in active glomeruli Later, odor alone can activate reinforcement pathways.

Fig. 13.6 Hypothetical schema for the development of functional olfactory pathways. Events in I and II occur simultaneously and more or less independently during prenatal development. Step III occurs after birth. Synaptic formation by periglomerular cells, granule cells, and mitral cell collaterals could also be involved but are not shown. See text for details.

axons. The evidence presented in the preceeding section suggested that the first synaptic connections (in the hamster, at least) are in the caudal olfactory cortex that projects to the central nucleus of the amygdala. It is perhaps not surprising that this should be the first region of the olfactory cortex to mature, because the central nucleus has long descending connections into cranial motor and visceral nuclei that mature early in development. Invoking Cajal's retrograde principle we might suppose that the central nucleus sprouts dendrites relatively early compared to forebrain regions whose projections terminate more rostrally in less rapidly maturing regions. The sprouting dendrites of the central nucleus would attract axons from the caudal olfactory cortex and, after terminal formation, the dendrites of the cortical neurons would be ready to receive the first olfactory tract axons. To recapitulate, the first functional olfactory circuits would be from amniotic-fluid-sensitive receptors to mitral cells with terminations in caudal olfactory cortex. These cortical cells would have access to functionally mature brainstem circuits through synapses in the central nucleus of the amygdala.

Unfortunately, we do not know what brainstem mechanisms are affected by the central nucleus of the amygdala, in either the neonate or the adult. The nucleus is, however, rich in catecholamines (Jacobowitz & Palkovits, 1974), enkephalins (Johansson, Hokfelt, Elde, Schultzberg, & Terenius, 1978), supports self-stimulation, receives visceral and taste input (Norgren, 1976), and thus could be an important substrate for reinforcement and appetitive mechanisms. If amniotic fluid receptors gain early access to this region, it is reasonable to speculate that they would come to control some forms of appetitive behavior or reinforcement, simply by virtue of being there first.

Now we come to Pedersen and Blass, trying to upset the normal course of development by stimulating citral receptors in the womb. Following the argument laid out, the addition of citral prenatally should accelerate the growth of citral-sensitive receptors and their axons should capture some of the dendrites of mitral cells which would ordinarily be attracted by amniotic-fluid-receptive cells. At birth the bulb would contain two populations of functional glomeruli, neither of which is quite large enough to control behavior. During the hour of postnatal stroking, a reorganization occurs, possibly as a result of lateral inhibition. Citral-sensitive glomeruli acquire the capacity to activate mitral cells and the PG cells with dendritic tufts in citral-sensitive glomeruli elaborate inhibitory connections in neighboring glomeruli, including those with amniotic-fluid-sensitive receptors. Amniotic fluid thus loses its capacity to elicit attachment. The function of the stroking or arousal is to elicit activity in the centrifugal projections to the bulb. The centrifugal projections, particularly the norepinephrine (NE) projections, somehow shape the emerging lateral inhibition so that citral activity is enhanced and amniotic fluid activity is depressed. The hypothesis that NE projections are involved is supported by the work of Kasamatsu and Pettigrew (1979) who found that NE projections to visual cortex are required for plastic changes in visual units.

Can this theory be tested? What are its predictions? One prediction is that there should be discrete foci of activity in the bulbs of pups exposed to amniotic fluid, and that although these foci would be weaker in pups stimulated with citral, there would be additional strong foci for citral. Pups depleted of NE with 6-OHDA should not show the plastic response in the presence of citral. Perhaps one could even predict that turnover of NE would be increased in the bulbs of pups exposed to citral.

Another line of experiment could analyze the projections between the epithelium and bulb using horse radish peroxidase (HRP) injection at different ages and perhaps determine whether information is indeed retrogradely transported to the mucosa and then passed from cell to cell. Perhaps one could pick up differences between the connections in normal and citral-exposed pups. It would also be interesting to try recording from epithelia of treated and untreated pups to see whether foci of sensitivity to citral were increased after treatment.

In summary, it is proposed that olfactory information received in utero induces differentiation of epithelial cells with specific receptors and these cells become plugged into reinforcement pathways postnatally. The anatomical sites of the plastic changes and the anatomical pathways responsible for olfactory reinforcement have been suggested together with specific experiments that could test the hypothesis. Whether the experiments will prove to be too difficult to accomplish in the neonatal rodent, only time will tell.

ACKNOWLEDGMENTS

Much of the work discussed in this chapter was supported by grant NS 13516.

I am grateful to Robert MacLeod for the illustrations and to Marjorie Grafe, James Crandall, Marieta Heaton, Robert Morison, Jeffrey Alberts, Christina Williams, Patricia Pederson, and Elliott Blass for providing unpublished data, and stimulating discussions and advice on the manuscript.

REFERENCES

Alberts, J. R. Olfactory contributions to behavioral development in rodents. In R. L. Doty (Ed.), *Mammalian olfaction, reproductive processes and behavior.* New York: Academic Press, 1976.

Allison, A. C., & Warwick, R. T. T. Quantitative observations on the olfactory system of the rabbit. *Brain*, 1949, **72**, 186–197.

Amoore, J. E. Four primary odor modalities of man, experimental evidence and possible significance. In D. A. Denton & J. P. Coghlan (Eds.), *Olfaction and Taste V*. New York: Academic Press, 1975. pp, 283–290.

Bradley, R. M., & Mistretta, C. M. Fetal sensory receptors. *Physiological Reviews*, 1975, **55**, 325–382.

Cabanac, M. Sensory Pleasure. *The Quarter Review of Biology*, 1979, **54**, 1–29.

Cajal, S. Ramon y. [Histologie du systeme nerveux de l'Homme et des vertebres]. Madrid: Consejo superior de investigaciones scientificas, 1955. (Originally published, 1906.)

Cajal, S. Ramon y. Studies on vertebrate neurogenesis (L. Guth, Trans.). Springfield, Ill.: Charles C. Thomas, 1959.

Caviness, V. S., Korda, M. G., & Williams, R. S. Cellular events induced in the molecular layer of the piriform cortex by ablation of the olfactory bulb in the mouse. *Brain Research*, 1977, **134**, 13–34.

Clark, W. E. LeGros. The projection of the olfactory epithelium on the olfactory bulb in the rabbit. *Journal of Neurology Neurosurgery and Psychiatry*, 1951, **14**, 1–10.

Cornwell, C. A. Golden hamster pups adapt to complex rearing odors. *Behavioral Biology*, 1975, **14**, 175–188.

Cornwell-Jones, C. A. Intracerebral 6-hydroxydomamine reverses conspecific odor preferences of male albino rats. Association for Chemoreception Sciences, Sarasota, Fla., 1980.

Cornwell-Jones, C. A., & Sobrian, S. K. Development of odor-guided behavior in Wistar and Sprague-Dawley rat pups. *Physiology and Behavior*, 1977, **19**, 685–688.

Cuschieri, A., & Bannister, L. H. The development of the olfactory mucosa in the mouse: Light microscopy. *Journal of Anatomy*, 1975, **119**, 277–286. (a)

Cuschieri, A., & Bannister, L. H. The development of the olfactory mucosa in the mouse: Electron microscopy. *Journal of Anatomy*, 1975, **119**, 471–498. (b)

Davis, B. J., Hoffmann, G. E., & Macrides, F. Somatostatin and LHRH perikarya and axons are present in the olfactory system in the hamster. Association for Chemoreception Sciences, Sarasota, Fla., 1980.

Devor, M. Fiber trajectories of olfactory bulb efferents in the hamster. *Journal of Comparative Neurology*, 1976, **166**, 31–48.

Devor, M. Central processing of odor signals. In D. Muller-Schwarze and M. M. Mozell (Eds.), *Chemical signals in vertebrates*. New York: Plenum, 1977, pp. 531–545.

Dieterlen, Fritz. Das verhalten des syrischen Gold hamsters (*Mesocricetus auratus* Waterhouse). *Zeitschrift Fuer Tierpsychologie*, 1959, **16**, 47–103.

Doving, D. R., & Pinching, A. J. Selective degeneration of neurones in the olfactory bulb following prolonged odour exposure. *Brain Research*, 1973, **52**, 115–129.

Engen, T. Controlling food preferences in children. In F. Horowitz (Ed.), *Early developmental hazards: Predictors and precautions*, Boulder, Col.: Westview Press, 1978.

Fallon, J. H., & Moore, R. Y. The Catacholamine innervation of the basal forebrain IV. Topography of dopamine cell projections to the basal forebrain and striatum. *Journal of Comparative Neurology*, 1978, **180**, 545–580.

Fink, J. S., & Smith, G. P. Mesolimbic and mesocortical dopaminergic neurons are necessary for normal exploratory behavior in rats. *Neuroscience Letters*, 1980, **17**, 61–65.

Galef, B. B., Jr., & Sherry, D. F. Mother's milk: A medium for the transmission of cues reflecting the flavor of mother's diet. *Journal of Comparative and Physiological Psychology*, 1973, **83**, 374–378.

Gesteland, R. C., Lettvin, J. Y., & Pitts, W. H. Chemical transmission in the nose of the frog. *Journal of Physiology*, 1965, **181**, 525–599.

Getchell, T. V., & Shepherd, G. M. Responses of olfactory receptor cells to step pulses of odour at different concentrations in the salamander. *Journal of Physiology*, 1978, **282**, 521–540.

Godfrey, D. A., Ross, C. D., Herrmann, A. D., & Matshinsky, F. M. Distribution and derivation of cholinergic elements in the rat olfactory bulb. *Neuroscience*, 1980, **5**, 273–292.

Grafe, M. E., & Leonard, C. M. Developmental changes in the topographical distribution of cells contributing to the lateral olfactory tract. Society for Neurosciences Abstracts, 1980.

Graziadei, P. P. C. The olfactory mucosa of vertebrates. In *Handbook of sensory physiology IV*. New York: Springer-Verlag, 1971.

Graziadei, P. P. C., & Monti-Graziadei, G. A. Continuous nerve cell renewal in the olfactory system. In *Handbook of sensory physiology IX*. New York: Springer-Verlag, 1978, pp. 55–83.

Haberly, L. B., & Price, J. L. The axonal projections of the mitral and tufted cells of the olfactory bulb of the rat. *Brain Research*, 1977, **129**, 152–157.

Halalsz, N., Lungdahl, A., Hokfelt, T., Johansson, O., Goldstein, M., Park, D., and Biberfeld, P. Transmitter histochemistry of the rat olfactory bulb. Immuno histochemical localization of monoamine synthesizing enzymes. Support for intrabulbar, periglomerular dopamine neurons. *Brain Research*, 1977, **126**, 455–474.

Halpern, M. Chemical ecology of terrestrial vertebrates. In R. Gilles (Ed.), *Animals and environmental fitness*. New York: Pergamon, 1980.

Heimer, L. Synaptic distribution of centripetal and centrifugal nerve fibers in the olfactory system of the rat. An experimental anatomical study. *Journal of Anatomy*, 1968, **103**, 413–432.

Heimer, L., & Wilson, R. D. The subcortical projection of the allocortex: Similarities in the neural associations of the hippocampus, the piriform cortex and the neocortex. In M. M. Santini (Ed.), *The Golgi centennial symposium: Perspectives in neurobiology*, New York: Raven, 1975.

Hinds, J. W. Autoradiographic study of histogenesis in the mouse olfactory bulb I: Time of origin of neurons and neuroglia. *Journal of Comparative Neurology*, 1968, **134**, 287–304. (a)

Hinds, J. W. Autoradiographic study of histogenesis in the mouse olfactory bulb II: Cell proliferation and migration. *Journal of Comparative Neurology*, 1968, **134**, 305–322. (b)

Hinds, J. W. Early neuron differentiation in the mouse olfactory bulb I: Light microscopy. *Journal of Comparative Neurology*, 1972, **146**, 233–252. (a)

Hinds, J. W. Early neuron differentiation in the mouse olfactory bulb II. Electron microscopy. *Journal of Comparative Neurology*, 1972, **146**, 253–276. (b)

Hinds, J. W., & Hinds, P. L. Synapse formation in the mouse olfactory bulb I: Quantitative studies. *Journal of Comparative Neurology*, 1976, **169**, 15–40. (a)

Hinds, J. W., & Hinds, P. L. Synapse formation in the mouse olfactory bulb II: Morphogenesis. *Journal of Comparative Neurology*, 1976, **169**, 41–62. (b)

Hofer, M. A., Shair, H., & Singh, P. Evidence that maternal ventral skin substances promote suckling in infant rats. *Physiology and Behavior*, 1976, **17**, 131–136.

Hoover, D. B., Muth, E. A., & Jacobowitz, D. M. A mapping of the distribution of acetylcholine, choline acetyltransferase, and acetylcholinesterase in discrete areas of rat brain. *Brain Research*, 1978, **153**, 295–306.

Hopkins, D. A. Amygdalo-tegmental projection in the rat, cat, and rhesus monkey. *Neuroscience Letters*, 1975, **1**, 263–273.

Jacobowitz, D. M., & Palkovits, M. Topographic atlas of catecholamine and acetylcholinesterase-containing neurons in the rat brain I: Forebrain (telencephalon, diencephalon). *Journal of Comparative Neurology*, 1974, **157**, 13–28.

Jacobson, M. *Developmental neurobiology*. New York: Holt, Rinehart & Winston, 1970.

Johansson, I. B., & Hall, W. G. Appetitive learning in 1-day-old rat pups. *Science*, 1979, **205**, 419–421.

Johansson, O., Hokfelt, T., Elde, R. P., Schultzberg, M., & Terenius, L. Immunohistochemical distribution of enkephalin neurons. *Advances in Biochemical Psychopharmacology*, 1978, **18**, 51–70.

Kaplan, M. D., & Hinds, J. W. Neurogenesis in the adult rat: Electron microscopic analysis of light autoradiographs. *Science*, 1977, **197**, 1092–1094.

Kauer, J. S. Response patterns of amphibian olfactory bulb neurones to odour stimulation. *Journal of Physiology*, 1974, **243**, 695–715.

Kauer, J. S., & Moulton, D. G. Responses of olfactory neurones to odour stimulation of small nasal areas in the salamander. *Journal of Physiology*, 1974, **243**, 717–737.

Kasamatsu, T., & Pettigrew, J. D. Preservation of binocularity after monocular deprivation in the striate cortex of kittens treated with 6-hydroxydopamine. *Journal of Comparative Neurology*, 1979, **185**, 139–162.

Ladewig, J., & Hart, B. L. Flehmen and vomeronasal organ function in male goats. *Physiology and Behavior*, 1980, **24**, 1067–1071.

Land, L. J. Localized projection of olfactory nerves to rabbit olfactory bulb. *Brain Research*, 1973, **63**, 153–166.

Landis, D. M. B., & Reese, T. S. Structure of the Purkinje cell dendritic membrane during synaptogenesis. *Neuroscience Abstracts*, 1977, **3**, 57.

Lehrman, D. S. Semantic and conceptual issues in the nature–nurture problem. In L. R. Aronson, E. Tobach, D. S. Lehrman, & J. S. Rosenblatt (Eds.), *Development and evolution of behavior*. San Francisco: Freeman, 1970.

Leon, M., Galef, B. G., & Behse, J. Establishment of pheromonal bonds and diet choice in young rats by odor pre-exposure. *Physiology and Behavior*, 1972, **18**, 387–391.

Leonard, C. M. Degeneration argyrophilia as an index of neural maturation: Studies on the optic tract of the golden hamster. *Journal of Comparative Neurology*, 1974, **156**, 435–458.

Leonard, C. M: Developmental changes in olfactory bulb projections revealed by degeneration argyrophilia. *Journal of Comparative Neurology*, 1975, **162**, 467–486.

Loesche, J., & Steward, O. Behavioral correlates of denervation and reinnervation of the rat: Recovery of alternation performance following unilateral entorhinal cortex lesions. *Brain Research Bulletin*, 1977, **2**, 31–39.

Lund, R. D., & Lund, J. S. Development of synaptic patterns in the superior colliculus of the rat. *Brain Research*, 1972, **42**, 1–20.

Maclean, P. D. Psychosomatic disease and the "visceral brain." Recent developments bearing on the Papez theory of emotion. *Psychosomatic Medicine*, 1949, **11**, 338–353.

Macrides, F. Dyanmic apsects of central olfactory processing. In D. Muller-Schwarze & M. M. Mozell (Eds.), *Chemical signals in vertebrates*, New York: Plenum, 1977, pp. 499–514.

Margolis, F. L. Carnosine in the primary olfactory pathway. *Science*, 1974, **184**, 909–911.

Meisami, E. Influence of early anosmia on the developing olfactory bulb. *Progress in Brain Research*, 1978, **48**, 211–230.

Meredith, M., & O'Connell, R. J. Efferent control of stimulus access to the hamster vomeronasal organ. *Journal of Physiology*, 1979, **286**, 301–316.

Mize, R. R., & Sterling, P. Synaptic development in the superficial gray layer of the cat superior colliculus. *Anatomical Record*, 1977, **187**, 658.

Monti-Graziadei, G. A. The olfactory marker protein (OMP) in the neuroepithelium of adult mice after bulbectomy. Association for Chemoreception Sciences, Sarasota, Fla., 1980.

Mozell, M. The spatiotemporal analysis of odorants at the level of the olfactory receptor sheet. *Journal of General Physiology*, 1966, **50**, 25–41.

Nauta, W. J. H., & Domesick, V. B. Crossroads of limbic and striatal circuitry: hypo-thalamo–nigral connections. In K. E. Livingston & O. Hornykiewicz (Eds.), *Limbic mechanisms: The continuing evolution of the limbic system concept*, New York: Plenum, 1977.

Norgren, R. Taste pathways to hypothalamus and amygdala. *Journal of Comparative Neurology*, 1976, **166**, 17–30.

Ormond, D. L., & Van Hartesveldt, C. Functional development of dopamine receptors in the cat forebrain. *Pharmacology, Biochemistry and Behavior*, 1979, **10**, 855–860.

Pedersen, P. E., & Blass, E. M. Dimethyl disulfide: A cue for nipple attachment in albino rats. Association for Chemoreception Sciences, Sarasota, Fla., 1980.

Pfaff, D. W., & Keiner, M. Atlas of estradiol-concentrating cells in the central nervous system of the female rat. *Journal of Comparative Neurology*, 1973, **151**, 121–158.

Pinching, A. J., & Doving, K. B. Selective degeneration in the rat olfactory bulb following exposure to different odors. *Brain Research*, 1974, **82**, 195–204.

Powell, T. P. S., Cowan, W. M., & Raisman, G. The central olfactory connections. *Journal of Anatomy (London)*, 1965, **99**, 791–813.

Powers, J. B., Fields, R. B., & Winans, S. S. Olfactory and vomeronasal system partic-ipation in male hamsters' attraction to female vaginal secretions. *Physiology and Behavior*, 1979, **22**, 77–84.

Price, J. L. An autoradiographic study of complementary laminar patterns of termination of afferent fibers to the olfactory cortex. *Journal of Comparative Neurology*, 1973, **150**, 87–108.

Schoenfeld, T. A., Street, C. K., & Leonard, C. M. Maturation of Wallerian Degeneration: An EM study in the developing olfactory tubercle. *Neurosciences Abstracts*, 1979, **5**, 177.

Schwob, J. E., & Price, J. L. The cortical projection of the olfactory bulb development in fetal and neonatal rats correlated with quantitative variations in adult rats. *Brain Research*, 1978, **151**, 369–374.

Scott, J. W., & Chafin, B. R. Origin of olfactory projections to lateral hypothalamus and nuclei gemini of the rat. *Brain Research*, 1975, **88**, 64–68.

Scott, J. W., & Leonard, C. M. The olfactory connections of the lateral hypothalamus in the rat, mouse, and hamster. *Journal of Comparative Neurology*, 1971, **141**, 331–344.

Shepherd, G. M. *The synaptic organization of the brain* (2nd ed.). New York: Oxford University Press, 1979.

Singer, A. G., Agosta, N. C., O'Connell, R. J., Pfaffmann, D. V., & Field, F. Dimethyl disulfide: An attractant pheromone in hamster vaginal secretion. *Science*, 1976, **191**, 948–950.

Singh, S. C. Comparison of electron microscopy and silver staining for the detection of the first entorhinal synapses to develop in the dentate gyrus. *Anatomy and Embryology (Berlin)*, 1977, **151**, 71–79. (a)

Singh, S. C. The development of olfactory and hippocampal pathways in the brain of the rat. *Anatomy and Embryology*, 1977, **151**, 183–199. (b)

So, K. F., Schneider, G. E., & Frost, D. O. Postnatal development of retinal projection to the lateral geniculate body of Syrian hamsters. *Brain Research*, 1978, **142**, 343–352.

Stewart, W. B., Kauer, J. S., & Shepherd, G. M. Functional organization of rat olfactory bulb analyzed by the 2-deoxyglucose method. *Journal of Comparative Neurology,* 1979, **185,** 715–734.

Teicher, M. H., & Blass, E. M. First suckling response of the newborn albino rat: the roles of olfaction and amniotic fluid. *Science,* 1977, **198,** 635–636.

Teicher, M. H., Stewart, W. B., Kauer, J. S., & Shepherd, G. M. Developmental studies of the olfactory bulb: 2-deoxyglucose uptake patterns in suckling rat pups. Association for Chemoreception Sciences, Sarasota, Fla., 1980.

Ungerstedt, U. Stereotaxic mapping of monoamine pathways in the rat brain. *Acta Physiologica Scandinavica Suppl.,* 1971, **367,** 1–44.

Valenstein, E. S. *Brain control.* New York: Wiley-Interscience, 1973.

Van Drongelen, W. Unitary recordings of near threshold responses of receptor cells in the olfactory mucosa of the frog. *Journal of Physiology,* 1978, **277,** 423–435.

Westrum, L. E. Axonal patterns in olfactory cortex after olfactory bulb removal in new born rats. *Experimental Neurology,* 1975, **47,** 442–447.

White, L. E., Jr. Olfactory bulb projection of the rat. *Anatomical Record,* 1965, **152,** 465–480.

Winans, S. S., & Scalia, F. Amygdaloid nucleus: New afferent input from the vomeronasal organ. *Science,* 1970, **170,** 330–332.

Wysocki, C. J., Beauchamp, G. K., Wellington, J. L., Erisman, S., & Barth, M. L. Access of low volatile stimuli to and clearance rates from the mammalian vomeronasal organ. Association for Chemoreception Sciences, Sarasota, Fla., 1980.

14

Development of Flavor
Preference
in Man and Animals:
The Role of Social
and Nonsocial Factors

BENNETT G. GALEF, JR.
McMaster University

The present chapter concerns the ontogeny of response to gustatory stimuli in both animals and man.[1] More specifically, it is about the

---

[1] Whereas it is both convenient and conventional to compare the behavior of man and animals, any conclusions drawn from such comparisons must be extremely tentative. Nearly a century of study has provided an incomplete picture of the feeding behavior of a few mammalian species, an inadequate sample, selected in large measure for reasons of experimental convenience, from among the 4237 extant mammalian species (Morris, 1965). It would have been more accurate, if less interesting, to title the present chapter "Preference development in domesticated Norway rats and man."

DEVELOPMENT OF PERCEPTION
Volume 1

development of acceptance and rejection responses to gustatory sensation; and more specifically still, it concerns the contribution of both nonsocial experiences and of social interactions to the ontogeny of diet preference.

The organization of the chapter reflects the fact that it is the individual organism that ultimately selects items for ingestion. Social influence acts only indirectly in the development of taste acceptance or rejection by affecting processes that channel flavor preference development in the individual. Thus, discussion of the mechanisms underlying development of flavor preference in individuals is a necessary antecedent to discussion of the ways in which social factors influence the development of individual response to gustatory stimuli.

I. INTRODUCTION: BEHAVIORISM, HEDONICS, BIOLOGY, AND FLAVOR PREFERENCE DEVELOPMENT

The major function of the sense of taste is to enable organisms to use chemical cues to select appropriate items for ingestion from among the multitude of nutritive, nonnutritive and toxic objects encountered in natural habitats. Possession of a sensory system able to detect chemical properties of potential ingesta would be of little use to the detecting organism without a concomitant behavioral capacity to either accept or reject items as food on the basis of their sensed chemical properties. Consequently, discussion of the development of the functioning ingestive system requires consideration of the development of two capacities: the capacity to sense gustatory stimuli and the capacity to respond behaviorally to gustatory sensations. The present chapter concerns the development of behavioral response to gustatory stimuli. (For a discussion of the development of gustatory sensation per se, see Mistretta, Chapter 15, this volume.)

The phenomenon with which I am concerned is easily described: any organism will more readily accept some items for ingestion than others. Clearly, the ontogeny of such flavor preferences can be discussed in terms of observable behavior without reference to hypothetical underlying internal states. However, recent interest in internal process oriented interpretations of behavior (Griffin, 1976) and hedonic models (Cabanac, 1979) has produced a second vocabulary of use in discussion of data relevant to questions concerning development of flavor preference. Although there is reason to prefer explanations of behavior stated in terms of observable events to those invoking hypothetical internal states as explanatory concepts, the vocabulary of hedonic models can be useful in clarifying conceptual issues relevant to the ontogeny of responses to gustatory stimuli.

In particular, I find it helpful in thinking about the ontogeny of response to tastes to conceive of gustatory stimuli as evoking response in two relatively independent dimensions: a discriminative dimension and an affective one (Cabanac, 1979; Young, 1959). The discriminative dimension describes the detectability and identifiability of a stimulus, whereas the affective dimension describes the amount of pleasure or displeasure that a stimulus arouses in a sensing organism. Within hedonic models of perception, it is usually assumed that there is a direct relationship between the affective dimension of perception and behavior. Pleasurable stimuli elicit approach and acceptance, whereas displeasure induces avoidance and rejection. One advantage of conceptualizing the discriminative and affective responses to gustatory stimuli as distinct from one another is that such conceptualization permits separate discussion of the ontogeny of each dimension of response.

The assumption that organisms respond affectively to gustatory stimuli implies the existence of physiological systems that produce sensations of pleasure and displeasure in response to taste. These physiological systems may be conceived of as species-typical features, evolved to promote efficient utilization of food resources by species members in their natural habitats. On this model, natural selection is seen as having acted to produce physiological systems that cause sensations of pleasure in response to gustatory stimuli frequently predicting the presence of needed nutrients and sensations of displeasure in response to gustatory stimuli frequently predicting the presence of toxins. Within such a framework, one can consider organisms as selected to choose ingesta maximizing pleasant, and minimizing unpleasant, gustatory sensation.[2]

As a general rule, molecules that serve as energy carriers, such as sugars, are perceived as pleasant tasting by man and tend to be accepted by both humans and animals. Unpleasant sensations and rejection responses are induced by bitter substances, for example, alkeloids and glycosides that are characteristically useless or even dangerous to ingest. This tendency to accept substances described by man as "sweet" (Pfaffman, 1975) and to reject those perceived as "bitter" is extremely widespread phylogenetically (Garcia & Hankins, 1975; Young, 1968) and probably represents a set of convergent mechanisms for biasing diet

---

[2] On this model, homeostatic or regulatory influences on dietary selection are conceived of as acting via changes in perceived palatability (see Cabanac, 1979, for relevant discussion).

selection in natural habitats in adaptive directions (Longhurst, Oh, Jones, & Kepner, 1968). Evidence that species introduced by man into alien ecosystems often succumb to unfamiliar toxic plants that are rejected native species is consistent with the hypothesis that at least some biases in diet preference are the product of natural selection (Arnold & Dudzinski, 1978, p. 119). Species that typically do not respond positively to sweet tastes, such as sucrose (e.g., cats and chickens) (Beauchamp, Maller, & Rogers, 1977; Gentle, 1972; Kare, 1961), or respond positively to generally aversive tastes, such as bitter, pose interesting but as yet unresolved problems in behavioral ecology and comparative physiology (see Young, 1968).

II.   INHERENT SENSORY–AFFECTIVE BIAS

If natural selection has acted to produce physiological mechanisms that bias naive individuals toward experiencing certain gustatory stimuli as more pleasurable than others, one would expect to observe species-typical acceptance and rejection responses to various flavors in the newborn.

Although empirical evidence of affective bias in response to taste in neonates is rare, the results of studies with human infants are consistent with the view that such biases are present immediately following birth. Steiner (1974, 1977) has photographed the facial expressions of human infants in response to their first extrauterine gustatory experiences. He reports that application of 0.5 ml of concentrated solutions of sweet, bitter, and sour flavorants onto the central area of the dorsal tongue surface elicits reliably different responses. Administration of a 25% sucrose solution produced a slight smile, followed by licking and sucking; similar exposure to 0.25% quinine-sulfate solution elicited tongue protrusion, splitting, and depression of the mouth angles. Sour taste (2.5% citric acid) elicited pursing and protusion of the lips, accompanied by nose wrinkling.

Such observations are consistent with the hypothesis that the physiology of the organism, as it develops in the normal uterine environment, predisposes the infant to experience certain gustatory sensations as more pleasurable than others. It is admittedly an extrapolation from these data to infer that the facial expressions of human neonates reflect affective states similar to those of adults. However, the observed differential response to sweet, sour, and bitter certainly indicates an ability of human infants to discriminate among the various flavors immediately following birth and suggests that some of these flavors may be more pleasurable to infants than are others.

If human infants are born with affective biases with respect to gustatory sensation, they should exhibit alterations in intake as well as changes in facial expression in response to the taste of potential ingesta. Surprisingly, investigators of the ingestive responses of human neonates to sweet, bitter, and sour solutions have found that, although addition of sugars to water results in enhanced solution intake, the addition of urea (bitter taste) or of citric acid (sour taste) does not reliably result in decreased intake (Desor, Maller, & Andrews, 1975; Desor, Maller, & Turner, 1973; Maller & Desor, 1974; also see Nisbett & Gurwitz, 1970).

Two conclusions are suggested by Desor and Maller's and Steiner's data considered together. First, receptor response, hedonic response, and augmentation of intake in response to sweet sensation are all intact and functional in the human neonate shortly after birth. Second, response to bitter flavor, and perhaps to sour as well, are not in the adult state in the infant. Although, as Steiner's data show, the infant human can detect sour and bitter, either the neonate does not find sour or bitter aversive or the sucking mechanism is not subject to inhibition by unpalatability. One might therefore expect a postnatal development of the sour–bitter rejection system in humans absent in the sweet acceptance system.

Comparable evidence on the development of response to tastes in infrahuman species is not presently available. However, a series of recently devised techniques should greatly facilitate future study of the development of response to gustatory stimuli in infant animals.

Johanson and Hall (1979) have developed a procedure allowing a 1-day-old rat pup to exhibit discriminated learning of a lever press response for rewards of small infusions of fluid into its mouth. Minor modifications in apparatus, providing the opportunity for pups to choose between infused solutions of varying taste, would permit both determination of flavor preferences shortly after birth and study of the development of both discriminative and affective functioning. Grill and Norgren (1978a,b) developed a system for describing the movements of the tongue, jaw, and face of adult rats in response to the infusion of small quantities of flavored solutions into their mouths. Extension of this descriptive system to neonatal rats would permit experiments with infrahuman subjects analogous to Steiner's previously described work with human infants.

Also, recent innovations in the measurement of the heart rate profiles of neonatal rats in response to olfactory stimuli could be adapted to the study of response to gustatory cues, permitting the monitoring of alterations in response to tastes resulting from experience (see Martin & Alberts, 1979; Alberts, Chapter 11, this volume). The development of such techniques for behavioral measurement in neonatal animals provides the opportunity for a very rapid expansion of information concerning both the taste preferences of organisms immediately after birth and the effectiveness of experience in altering infantile preferences.

III. EFFECTS OF POSTNATAL EXPERIENCE ON FLAVOR PREFERENCE

Even if neonates experience certain gustatory sensations as pleasant and others as unpleasant, this does not mean that response to gustatory sensation at either the hedonic or behavioral level cannot change as the result of experience. Genotypes predisposing the individual to develop palatability preferences typical of its species can only be adaptive with respect to the mean properties of that species' ecological niche (Williams, 1966). Behavioral plasticity in response to gustatory cues enables individuals to adapt to the special demands of the particular area in which they are located. Because potential ingesta are frequently heterogeneous across a species' range, one would expect the physiological systems underlying affective response to taste to be "open-programs" in Mayr's (1974) sense. That is, one would expect these systems to be subject to modification by experience during the life of the organism so that the individual would have the capacity to learn to ingest nutritive substances or to avoid toxic substances idiosyncratic to its particular home range.

A wide variety of studies indicate that the same gustatory stimulus may be responded to by an individual as either pleasant or unpleasant depending on that individual's previous experience. The term "alliesthesia" has been suggested as a label for such changes in hedonic response, a "negative alliesthesia" being an increase in the perceived unpleasantness of a fixed stimulus and a "positive alliesthesia" the reverse (Cabanac, 1979). Current evidence suggests that two very different types of experience can produce profound alliesthesias.

A. Simple Exposure

Data from studies of both animals and humans indicate that, as a general rule, familiar tastes are preferred to novel ones. Effects of familiarity on taste preference, measured either in terms of intake (in infants or animals) or by preference ratings (in adult humans), can be profound and familiarity can result in what those of us lacking a given exposure-induced preference might consider perverse hedonic response. For example, Moskowitz has reported that north Indian laborers describe quinine-sulfate (bitter) solutions as exceptionally pleasant at low concentrations and find citric acid, a sour taste, like sweet taste (sucrose), increasingly pleasant with increasing concentration. These hedonic responses contrast markedly with those generally exhibited by other human subjects. (Both Americans and Indian medical students report that sourness and bitterness become increasingly unpleasant with increasing concentration and neither finds bitter taste highly palatable at any concentration).

The north Indian laborers studied by Moskowitz and his colleagues subsist on a sparse diet that contains many sour fruits. The tamarind fruit, which tastes extremely sour and slightly bitter, is chewed by the laborers as a confection and is used by them as a flavorant in staple foods (Moskowitz, Kumraiah, Sharma, Jacobs, & Sharma, 1975). Whereas it is possible that genetic inbreeding among the laborers has yielded a population with anomalous inherent biases toward sour and bitter, it seems more likely that they, like Mexican peasant populations whose members exhibit strong preference for "hot" foods, do so as a result of gradual familiarization with the relevant flavorants (Rozin, 1977; Rozin & Schiller, 1980).

Data from animals support the generalization that simple exposure to a diet can enhance intake of that diet and, presumably, change hedonic response to it. In a particularly striking demonstration of the effects of brief exposures on preference in animals, Siegel (1974) exposed different groups of rats to either coffee or vinegar solutions for 30 min and either 7 or 24 days later measured the intake of all subjects of the two solutions in a series of five daily simultaneous choice tests. Subjects ingested approximately twice as much of the preexposed flavor as the novel one in each test. Although Siegel's methods resulted in the demonstration of long-lasting and robust effects of brief exposure to a flavor, his results are, so far as I know, exceptional in the druation of the effects observed. Attempts to demonstrate long-term changes in taste preference in animals as the result of simple exposure to a flavor generally have not been successful (Capretta, 1977; Capretta & Rawls, 1974; Rozin, Gruss, & Berk, 1979; Warren & Pfaffman, 1959). The effects of exposing animals to a given flavor seem to gradually dissipate if the subject has the opportunity to sample other flavors of greater species-typical acceptability. Information on the factors effecting the duration of exposure effects on palatability and preference in animals are both lacking and much needed.

B. Association Learning

There are, of course, experiences other than simple exposure to a gustatory stimulus that can profoundly affect an organism's acceptance or rejection of that stimulus. A flavor, even a highly palatable one, that has been experienced prior to an experimentally induced illness, will subsequently be rejected (Garcia & Ervin, 1968; Garcia & Koelling, 1966). Whether this rejection results from an hedonic shift (e.g. a sweet taste actually becoming perceptually unpleasant), as Garcia and Hankins (1977) have argued (see also Rozin, 1967; 1979), or from an association of the flavor with illness (Revusky, 1977), or from a more cognitive process in which the subject learns that a flavor is not safe (Kalat & Rozin, 1973) is not yet clear.

Just as the association of a flavor with illness reduces subsequent ingestion of the illness-associated flavor, association of a flavor with recovery from illness can enhance intake of the recovery-associated flavor (Zahorik, 1977; Zahorik, Maier, & Pies, 1974). Demonstrations of enhanced intake of a flavor as the result of association of that flavor with beneficial postingestional consequences such as recovery from illness (Green & Garcia, 1971), recovery from morphine withdrawal (Parker, Failor, & Weidman, 1973), or reduction of caloric deficit (Holman, 1969; Siqueland, 1965), are far less common in the literature than demonstrations of reduced intake following flavor-illness pairing and are generally of lesser magnitude and duration (Zahorik, 1977). Again it is not known whether the alteration in intake subsequent to flavor–beneficial consequence pairings results from an alleisthesia or some other process.

IV. SOCIAL FACTORS IN THE DEVELOPMENT OF FLAVOR PREFERENCE

Whereas much of the development of flavor preference in animals depends on the experience of individuals feeding in isolation, members of many vertebrate species eat in the presence of conspecifics and all mammals experience their first ingestive episodes during periods of interaction with their dam. Such social interactions during feeding can profoundly affect flavor preference and diet selection.

The field literature is rich in examples of animal social groups which feed in an unusual way or select unusual items for ingestion (Galef, 1976). There is a tendency on the part of field observers to attribute such idiosyncratic group behaviors to the action of social learning processes. However, the range of possible causes of differences in feeding behavior among members of different subpopulations of a species living in uncontrolled environments is too great to permit uncritical attribution of idiosyncratic patterns of food selection to social causes. In fact, recent evidence suggests that several well-known instances of idiosyncratic group feeding patterns, frequently discussed in the literature as examples of social learning in animals, may be due to other causes. For example, Green (1975) has reported observations suggesting that the behavior of dipping sweet potatoes in saltwater, exhibited by a long-studied troop of Japanese macaques (Kawai, 1965; Kawamura, 1959), results from shaping by human provisioners rather than observational learning among the monkeys. Similarly, it has been suggested that apparently traditional patterns of feeding on molluscs in colonies of wild rats (Gandolfi & Parisi, 1972, 1973; Parisi & Gandolfi, 1974) may result from differences in colony access to alternative food resources, rather than to learning by imitation (Galef, 1980). One must be cautious in attributing the development of feeding behaviors to social processes, particularly observational learning or imitation, until alternative explanations have been excluded (Hall, 1963).

As we shall see from what follows, animal analogues of human traditions in feeding behavior do exist. However, those instances that have been carefully studied seem to depend on rather subtle social influences acting on simple exposure and associational processes of the type discussed in the preceding section, rather than on processes such as observational learning or direct imitation.

A. Social Factors in the Development of Flavor Acceptance

One of the more extensively studied cases of naturally occurring differences among populations in diet selection, involves the development of food preferences in wild rats. Fritz Steiniger, who worked for many years on problems of rat extermination, reported in 1950 that naive young rats, born to colonies that have learned to avoid ingesting a particular poison bait, absolutely reject the diet that their progenitors have learned to avoid without ever even sampling it.

In our laboratory analogue of Steiniger's field situation, colonies of adult wild rats were trained to eat one of two distinctive, nutritionally adequate diets (Diets A and B) and to avoid the other by introducing sublethal concentrations of poison into the samples of one of the two diets offered to each colony (Galef & Clark, 1971). Under these conditions, members of our adult colonies rapidly learned to avoid ingesting the diet into which poison was introduced and continued to avoid uncontaminated samples of that diet for several weeks.

Experiments began when pups born to colony members left their nest sites to feed on solid food for the first time. We observed adults

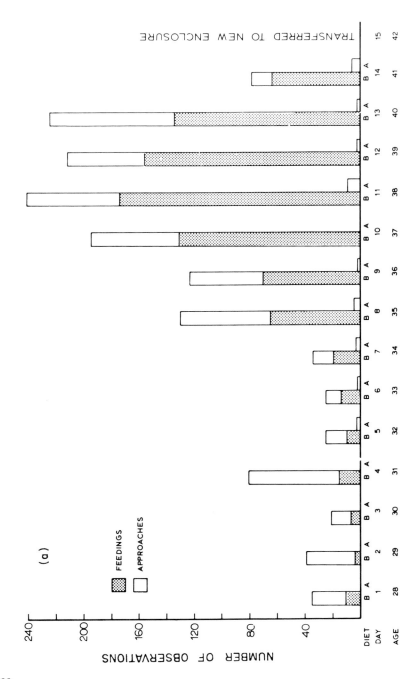

420

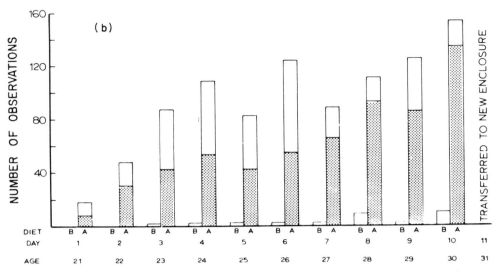

Fig. 14.1   Number of observed approaches to and feedings from Diets A and B by wild rat pups whose parents had been poisoned on either (a) Diet A or (b) Diet B. Shaded area indicates feedings; white area, approaches.

and pups throughout daily 3-hr feeding periods and recorded the number of times pups approached and ate each of the two available uncontaminated diets. After the pups had been feeding with the adults for several days, they were transferred to new enclosures, separate from the adults, and again offered uncontaminated samples of Diets A and B.

Typical results of these experiments are presented in Figs. 14.1 and 14.2. Figure 14.1a presents data describing the feeding behavior of a litter of wild rat pups born to a colony trained to eat Diet B; Fig. 14.1b presents data describing the behavior of a litter of pups born to a colony trained to eat Diet A. As is clear from comparison of the data presented in the two histograms, the learned feeding preferences of adult colony members profoundly affected the feeding preferences of their young. While in contact with adults of their colony, wild rat pups ingested only the diet that the adults of their colony ate and rejected alternatives.

Furthermore, as shown in Fig. 14.2, the acquired diet preference of adults continued to affect the feeding preferences of their young for 8–10 days following transfer of the pups to enclosures separate from adults. As can also be seen in Fig. 14.2, the effects of interaction with adults were transitory. All subjects, independent of rearing experience,

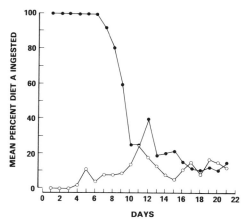

Fig. 14.2 Amount of Diet A eaten, as a percentage of total intake of Diets A and B, by pups following removal to a new enclosure isolated from adults. Pups whose parents were poisoned on Diet A indicated by ○; parents poisoned on Diet B, by ●.

eventually showed a stable preference for Diet B rather than for Diet A, presumably reflecting an inherent sensory–affective bias.

The analytic problem is to determine the behavioral mechanisms that: (a) lead rat pups to wean onto a diet that adult members of their colony are exploiting; and (b) cause the juveniles to exhibit continued avoidance of alternative diets even after they have been removed from direct adult influence. To begin, it is important to determine whether the juveniles are learning to avoid the diet that the adults of their colony have learned to avoid or are learning to eat the diet that the adults of their colony have learned to eat. The mechanisms responsible for each of these types of learning, either of which would be sufficient to produce the homogeneity of adult and pup dietary preference observed in our basic experiment, obviously would differ markedly.

Our data (Galef & Clark, 1971) are consistent with the view that rat pups learn to eat the diet that the adults of their colony are eating rather than to avoid the colony-avoided diet. If, for example, one rears wild rat pups in a colony having access only to Diet A and subsequently tests these pups with a choice between Diets A and B, they are just as hesitant to eat Diet B as are pups reared by a colony trained to eat Diet A and avoid Diet B. The important environmental factor during ontogeny, influencing pups diet preference in our experimental situations, appears to be socially induced exposure to the diet that adult colony members are eating.

My co-workers and I have found three ways in which adult rats can influence pups of their colony to wean to a diet that they are exploiting:

1. The physical presence of adult rats at a feeding site attracts pups to that feeding site and markedly increases the probability of young rats initiating weaning on the foodstuff located there (Galef & Clark, 1971, 1972).

2. Adult rats deposit residual olfactory cues in areas that they visit and pups prefer to explore and eat in an area soiled by conspecifics rather than in a clean area (Galef & Heiber, 1976).

3. The milk of a lactating female rat contains gustatory cues directly reflecting the flavor of her diet and, at weaning, isolated pups exhibit a preference for a diet of the same flavor as the diet that its mother has been eating during lactation (Galef & Clark, 1972; Galef & Henderson, 1972; Galef & Sherry, 1973).

We have also examined a number of potential routes by which adult rats could influence the food choices of their young, but which do not, in fact, appear to be effective. For example, it does not seem to be the case that pup ingestion of the anal excreta of adult colony members results in an enhanced preference for the diet of those adults (Galef & Henderson, 1972; Galef, 1979a).

There is a sense in which each of the three mechanisms effective in modifying pups' food preferences is simply a way in which adult rats can influence their young to become familiar with the properties of one diet rather than another. If, as is the case (see, e.g., Galef, 1977c), young rats exhibit a preference for a familiar diet when selecting items for ingestion, anything that an adult rat does to increase pup familiarity with the properties of a given diet will increase pup ingestion of it. I believe one can understand the initial preference of pups for the diet that the adults of the colony are exploiting as a result of an enhanced familiarity with that diet consequent on social interaction with adult colony members (Galef, 1977a,b; 1979b).

Adults of a number of species other than the rat are also known to be able to bring their young to wean to diets that they would otherwise avoid. For example, mother hens use a special food call to attract their young to a feeding site, and a food-calling hen can induce her chicks to ingest mealworms, a food that they would otherwise avoid (Hogan, 1966). Similarly, meerkat females with weanling young will run to and fro in front of their kits holding food in their mouths and elicit a food-snatching response from the young, thereby inducing the kits to ingest food, such as bananas, that they would normally ignore (Ewer, 1969).

And both kittens and 3½-year-old human infants can be induced to eat novel foods that they would otherwise reject, by interaction with a conspecific adult eating those foods (Harper & Sanders, 1975; Wyrwicka, 1978). The ability of adults to bias young of their species to wean to diets that they are exploiting and, as a result, to become familiar with those diets appears to be a common mode of social influence on the development of flavor preference in vertebrates.

B. Social Factors in Development of Flavor Rejection

If members of a given group tend to select the same foods for ingestion, then by definition, they also tend to reject the same potential ingesta. Whether the mechanisms serving to produce homogeneity in group typical rejection responses are dependent upon or independent of those producing group-typical acceptance responses is open to question. Rozin (1977) has suggested, following examination of the anecdotal evidence, that human reluctance to ingest unusual foods results in large part from an aversion to novelty itself when selecting items for ingestion. Similarly, I have proposed (Galef, 1971; 1977b) that the prolonged avoidance by wild rat pups of alternative diets, once they have become familiar with the diet that the adults of their colony are eating, is the result of their extreme reluctance to ingest novel foods (Barnett, 1958; Galef, 1970; Rozin, 1968). The general line of argument, based on the animal experiments and extrapolated to humans, is that individuals do not learn to avoid specific flavors as a result of interacting with conspecifics; rather, they are socially induced to eat some subset of potential ingesta and subsequently reject other ingesta because they are hesitant to ingest unfamiliar foods.

Although there is convincing data that animals can indirectly influence conspecifics to avoid one food simply by directly influencing them to eat an alternative, evidence suggesting direct social transmission of food avoidance is not available. Lavin, Freise, and Coombes (1980); Coombes, Revusky, and Lett (in press); and Freise and Lavin (1978) have found that a naive rat that ingests a novel palatable food and is then exposed to a conspecific made ill by poisoning, will subsequently reject that palatable food. Cues emitted by a sick conspecific can serve, as does illness itself, as an unconditioned stimulus producing a learned aversion to a novel, palatable flavor with which it is associated. However, it is not known how such a mechanism might act in natural circumstances to reduce the probability of naive group members ingesting a diet that their more knowledgeable fellows found toxic.

Active physical interference in the ingestive behavior of others to prevent them from ingesting potentially noxious foods has not been unequivocally demonstrated in any animal species. Danguir and Nicolaidis (1975) have reported that rats trained to avoid ingesting a toxic solution will physically restrain naive conspecifics and actively interfere with their ingestion of a similar-tasting safe solution. Unfortunately, replication with additional controls has indicated that the observed reduced ingestion of the safe solution by naive subjects did not result from actions of the trained conspecifics (Galef & Dalrymple, 1978). Menzel (1966, p. 134) and Stephenson (1967) have both reported instances of nonhuman primates pulling naive conspecifics away from potentially dangerous objects. These observations deserve further examination, as they suggest a means by which primates might directly induce naive conspecifics to avoid ingesting dangerous foods.

The absence of any animal model of the direct transmission of food aversions appears to have limited consideration of the importance of such processes in the development and maintenance of human traditions of flavor preference. Although there is, so far as I know, no experimental evidence that human facial expressions signaling disgust inhibit others from ingesting substances they might otherwise eat, I would be surprised if disgust signals did not act in this way. Similarly, the active intervention of human parents to prevent their offspring from ingesting substances that the parents' social group defines as unedible (for example, worms, or insects) must influence the child's subsequent selection of items for ingestion (see Rozin, 1978, for discussion). The investigation of such phenomena in both humans and other primates should prove to be fruitful.

V. CONCLUSION: PREFERENCE DEVELOPMENT IN ANIMALS AND MAN

The development of gustatory preference is clearly a multiply determined process.

1. Organisms are born with preferences for certain flavors and aversions to others.

2. Such species-typical affective responses to tastes are modifiable by gustatory experience.

3. Interaction with conspecifics can determine the gustatory experiences that an individual has during ontogeny. Furthermore, both the extent to which postnatal experience can alter gustatory preferences

present at birth and the extent to which social interactions influence postnatal experience probably vary among species.

Present evidence suggests that development of flavor preference in our own species may be more profoundly affected by experiential and social factors than is flavor preference development in other mammals. Humans appear to be unusual in their formation of long-lasting and extremely robust preferences for familiar but inherently unpalatable flavors. For example, human infants, naive children, and adults typically reject bitter or "hot" flavorants, as do naive animals. However, following repeated exposure to horseradish, quinine water, or chili peppers, humans reverse their initial rejection and develop positive responses to such inherently unpalatable substances (Rozin, 1978; Rozin & Schiller, 1980). As can be seen in Fig. 14.2, nonhuman animals have not been found to exhibit analogous long-term reversals in response as a result of simple exposure (see also Rozin et al., 1979). Thus, the effects of exposure to a flavor on preference for it appear markedly different in humans and animals, the former exhibiting far more long-lasting and profound effects of familiarity on taste preference than the latter.

Also, humans appear to exhibit greater effects of social interaction on diet selection than do members of other mammalian species. Food selection in human social groups is profoundly shaped by social tradition, whereas members of other species seem to depend largely on individual experience to select palatable or nutritional substances. Non-human omnivores, like rats, frequently chew and taste available objects. The absence of analogous patterns of oral exploration in human adults, permitting discovery of previously unexploited food resources, must increase human dependence on social interaction for successful identification of foods.

In summary, two of the central factors influencing human flavor preference development, social tradition and repeated exposure, may be of considerably less importance in the development of long-term animal feeding preferences. Animal food selection probably depends to a far greater extent than human food selection on individual sampling and subsequent evaluation of postingestional consequences.

The ultimate causes of anomalous patterns of flavor preference development in man remain obscure, but offer fertile grounds for speculation. One would suspect that there must be some features of human exploitation of food resources, not seen in most other animals, that would require both flexibility and homogeneity in flavor preference among members of a social group. The food sharing, typical of human social groups, would appear to require at least a degree of homogeneity in group flavor preference. Furthermore, an ability to come to favor whatever foods are readily available would seem appropriate to the opportunistic foraging of a geographically widely dispersed hunter–gatherer species such as our own.

In any case, the importance of social interaction and of postnatal exposure as factors in the determination of human diet selection and their relative lesser importance in other vertebrate species studied to date, casts some doubt on the adequacy of animal models to illuminate some of the most important processes underlying human flavor preference development. Although our species shares with others many features of its food selection behavior (e.g., a reluctance to ingest novel foods, a capacity to form associations between flavors and illness, inherent aversions to some flavors, etc.), at least two important factors in human flavor preference development may be uniquely human. A major part of the contribution of the study of the development of animal flavor preference to the understanding of the same process in man may lie in the identification of those features of the process that are unique to, and can only be studied in, *Homo sapiens*.

ACKNOWLEDGMENTS

Preparation of this chapter was greatly facilitated by financial support provided by the National Science and Engineering Research Council of Canada and the McMaster University Research Board. I thank Harvey Weingarten, Paul Rozin, Mertice Clark, and Jeff Alberts for their thoughtful reviews of earlier drafts of this manuscript.

REFERENCES

Arnold, G. W., & Dudzinski, M. L. *Ethology of free-ranging domestic animals.* Amsterdam: Elsevier, 1978.

Barnett, S. A. Experiments on "neophobia" in wild and laboratory rats. *British Journal of Psychology,* 1958, **49,** 195–201.

Beauchamp, G. K., Maller, O., & Rogers, J. G., Jr. Flavor preferences in cats (*Felis catus* and *Panthera* sp.). *Journal of Comparative and Physiological Psychology,* 1977, **91,** 1118–1127.

Bronstein, P. M., & Crockett, D. P. Maternal rations affect the food preferences of weanling rats: II. *Bulletin of the Psychonomic Society,* 1976, **8,** 227–229.

Cabanac, M. Sensory pleasure. *The Quarterly Review of Biology,* 1979, **54,** 1–29.

Capretta, P. J. Establishment of food preferences by exposure to ingestive stimuli early in life. In L. M. Barker, M. R. Best, & M. Domjan (Eds.), *Learning mechanisms in food selection.* Waco, Tex.: Baylor University Press, 1977.

Capretta, P. J., & Rawls, L. H., III. Establishment of flavor preference in rats: Importance of nursing and weaning experience. *Journal of Comparative and Physiological Psychology,* 1974, **86,** 670–673.

Coombes, S., Revusky, S., & Lett, B. T. Long-delay taste aversion learning in an unpoisoned rat: Exposure to a poisoned rat as the US. *Learning and Motivation,* in press.

Danguir, J., & Nicolaidis, S. Protection d'un rat naif de la consummation d'une solution par des congeneres ayant appris a la refuser. *Acadamie des Sciences. Comptes Rendus Hebdomadaires des Seances. Series D.,* 1975, **280,** 2595–2598.

Desor, J. A., Maller, O., & Andres, K. Ingestive response of human newborns to salty, sour, and bitter stimuli. *Journal of Comparative and Physiological Psychology,* 1975, **89,** 966–970.

Desor, J., Maller, O., & Turner, R. Taste in acceptance of sugars by human infants. *Journal of Comparative and Physiological Psychology,* 1973, **84,** 496–501.

Ewer, R. F. The "instinct to teach." *Nature,* 1969, **222,** 698.

Freise, B. G., & Lavin, M. J. *The effects poisoned rats have on modifying flavor choices in nonpoisoned conspecifics.* Paper presented at the meetings of the Eastern Psychological Association, Washington, D.C. March, 1978.

Galef, B. G., Jr. Aggression and timidity: Responses to novelty in feral Norway rats. *Journal of Comparative and Physiological Psychology,* 1970, **71,** 370–381.

Galef, B. G., Jr. Social transmission of acquired behavior: A discussion of tradition and social learning in vertebrates. In J. S. Rosenblatt, R. A. Hinde, E. Shaw, & C. Beer (Eds.), *Advances in the study of behavior* (Vol. 6). New York: Academic Press, 1976.

Galef, B. G., Jr. Mechanisms for the social transmission of food preferences from adult to weanling rats. In L. M. Barker, M. R. Best, & M. Domjan (Eds.), *Learning mechanisms in food selection.* Waco, Tex.: Baylor University Press, 1977. (a)

Galef, B. G., Jr. Mechanisms for the transmission of acquired patterns of feeding from adult to weanling rats. In J. M. Weiffenback (Ed.), *Taste and development: The genesis of sweet preference.* Washington, D.C.: U.S. Government Printing Office, 1977. (b)

Galef, B. G., Jr. Social transmission of food preferences: An adaptation for weaning in rats. *Journal of Comparative and Physiological Psychology,* 1977, **91,** 1136–1140. (c)

Galef, B. G., Jr. Investigation of the functions of coprophagy in juvenile rats. *Journal of Comparative and Physiological Psychology,* 1979, **93,** 295–305. (a)

Galef, B. G., Jr. Social transmission of learned diet preferences in wild rats. In J. H. A. Kroeze (Ed.), *Preference behavior and chemoreception.* London: Information Retrieval, 1979. (b)

Galef, B. G., Jr. Diving for food: Analysis of a possible case of social learning in rats (*Rattus norvegicus*). *Journal of Comparative and Physiological Psychology,* 1980, **94,** 416–425.

Galef, B. G., Jr., & Clark, M. M. Social factors in the poison avoidance and feeding behavior of wild and domesticated rat pups. *Journal of Comparative and Physiological Psychology,* 1971, **75,** 341–357.

Galef, B. G., Jr., & Clark, M. M. Mother's milk and adult presence: Two factors determining initial dietary selection by weaning rats. *Journal of Comparative and Physiological Psychology,* 1972, **78,** 220–225.

Galef, B. G., Jr., & Dalrymple, A. J. Active transmission of poison avoidance among rats? *Behavioral Biology,* 1978, **24,** 265–271.

Galef, B. G., Jr., & Heiber, L. The role of residual olfactory cues in the determination of feeding site selection and exploration patterns of domestic rats. *Journal of Comparative and Physiological Psychology,* 1976, **90,** 727–739.

Galef, B. G., Jr., & Henderson, P. W. Mother's milk: A determinant of the feeding preferences of weaning rat pups. *Journal of Comparative and Physiological Psychology*, 1972, **78**, 213–219.

Galef, B. G., Jr., & Sherry, D. F. Mother's milk: A medium for the transmission of cues reflecting the flavor of mother's diet. *Journal of Comparative and Physiological Psychology*, 1973, **83**, 374–378.

Gandolfi, G., & Parisi, V. Predazione su *Unio pictorum* L. da parte del Ratto, *Rattus norvegicus* (Berkenhout). *Acta Naturalia*, 1972, **8**, 1–27.

Gandolfi, G., & Parisi, V. Ethological aspects of predation by rats, *Rattus norvegicus* (Berkenhout), on bivalves *Unio pictorum* L. and *Cerastoderma lamarckii* (Reeve). *Bollettino di Zoologia*, 1973, **40**, 69–74.

Garcia, J., & Ervin, F. R. Gustatory–visceral and telereceptor–cutaneous conditioning—adaptation to internal and external milieus. *Communications in Behavioral Biology*, 1968, **1** (Part A), 389–415.

Garcia, J., & Hankins, W. G. The evolution of bitter and the acquisition of toxiphobia. In D. A. Denton & J. P. Coghlan (Eds.), *Olfaction and taste V*. Academic Press: New York, 1975.

Garcia, J., & Hankins, W. G. On the origin of food aversion paradigms. In L. M. Barker, M. R. Best, & M. Domjan (Eds.), *Learning mechanisms in food selection*. Waco, Tex.: Baylor University Press, 1977.

Garcia, J., & Koelling, R. A. Relation of cue to consequence in avoidance learning. *Psychonomic Science*, 1966, **4**, 123–124.

Gentle, M. J. Taste preference in the chicken (*Gallus domesticus* L.). *British Poultry Science*, 1972, **13**, 141–155.

Green, K. F., & Garcia, J. Recuperation from illness: Flavor enhancement in rats. *Science*, 1971, **173**, 749–751.

Green, S. Dialects in Japanese monkeys: Vocal learning and cultural transmission of locale-specific vocal behavior? *Zeitschrift fur Tierpsychologie*, 1975, **38**, 304–314.

Griffin, D. R. *The question of animal awareness*. New York: Rockefeller University Press: 1976.

Grill, H. J., & Norgren, R. The taste reactivity test I. Mimetic responses to gustatory stimuli in neurologically normal rats. *Brain Research*, 1978, **143**, 263–279. (a)

Grill, H. J., & Norgren, R. The taste reactivity test II. Mimetic responses to gustatory stimuli in chronic thalamic and chronic decerebrate rats. *Brain Research*, 1978, **143**, 781–797. (b)

Hall, K. R. L. Observational learning in monkeys and apes. *British Journal of Psychology*, 1963, **54**, 201–226.

Harper, L. V., & Sanders, K. M. The effect of adults' eating on young children's acceptance of unfamiliar foods. *Journal of Experimental Child Psychology*, 1975, **20**, 206–214.

Hogan, J. A. An experimental study of conflict and fear: An analysis of behavior of young chicks towards a mealworm II: The behavior of chicks which eat the mealworm. *Behaviour*, 1966, **27**, 273–289.

Holman, G. H. Intragastric reinforcement effect. *Journal of Comparative and Physiological Psychology*, 1969, **69**, 432–441.

Johanson, I. B., & Hall, W. G. Appetitive learning in 1-day-old rat pups. *Science*, 1979, **205**, 419–421.

Kalat, J. W., & Rozin, P. "Learned safety" as a mechanism in rats' long-delay taste-aversion learning. *Journal of Comparative and Physiological Psychology*, 1973, **83**, 198–207.

Kare, M. R. Comparative aspects of the sense of taste. In M. R. Kare & B. P. Halpern (Eds.), *Physiological and behavioral aspects of taste.* Chicago: University of Chicago Press, 1961.

Kawai, M. Newly acquired pre-cultural behavior of the natural troop of Japanese monkeys on Koshima inlet. *Primates,* 1965, **6,** 1–30.

Kawamura, S. The process of sub-culture propagation among Japanese macaques. *Primates,* 1959, **2,** 43–54.

Lavin, M. J., Freise, B., & Coombes, S. Transferred flavor aversions in adult rats. *Behavioral and Neural Biology,* 1980, **28,** 15–33.

Longhurst, W. M., Oh, H. K., Jones, M. B., & Kepner, R. E. A basis for the palatability of deer forage plants. *North American Wildlife and Natural Resources Conference Transactions,* 1968, 181–192.

Maller, O., & Desor, J. Effects of taste on ingestion by human newborns. In J. Bosma (Ed.), *Oral sensation and perception: Development in the fetus and infant.*Washington, D.C.: U.S. Government Printing Office, 1974.

Martin, L. T., & Alberts, J. R. *Heart rate change as a measure of associative learning in neonatal rodents.* Presented at the meetings of the International Society of Developmental Psychobiology, Atlanta, Ga., 1979.

Mayr, E. Behavior programs and evolutionary strategies. *American Scientist,* 1974, **62,** 650–659.

Menzel, E. W., Jr. Responses to objects in free-ranging Japanese monkeys. *Behaviour,* 1966, **26,** 130–150.

Morris, D. *The mammals.* New York: Harper & Row, 1965.

Moskowitz, H. R., Kumraiah, V., Sharma, H., Jacobs, L., & Sharma, S. D. Cross cultural differences in simple taste preference. *Science,* 1975, **190,** 1217–1218.

Nisbett, R. E., & Gurwitz, S. B. Weight, sex, and the eating behavior of human newborns. *Journal of Comparative and Physiological Psychology,* 1970, **73,** 245–253.

Parker, L., Failor, A., & Weidman, K. Conditioned preferences in the rat with an unnatural need state: Morphine withdrawal. *Journal of Comparative and Physiological Psychology,* 1973, **82,** 294–300.

Parisi, V., & Gandolfi, G. Further aspects of the predation by rats on various mullusc species. *Bollettino di Zoologia,* 1974, **41,** 87–106.

Pfaffmann, C. Phylogenetic origins of sweet sensitivity. In D. A. Denton & J. P. Coghlan (Eds.), *Olfaction and taste V.* New York: Academic Press, 1975.

Revusky, S. The concurrent interference approach to delay learning. In L. M. Barker, M. R. Best, & M. Domjan (Eds.), *Learning mechanisms in food selection.* Waco, Tex.: Baylor University Press, 1977.

Rozin, P. Specific aversions as a component of specific hungers. *Journal of Comparative and Physiological Psychology,* 1967, **64,** 237–242.

Rozin, P. Specific aversions and neophobia resulting from vitamin deficiency or poisoning in half-wild and domestic rats. *Journal of Comparative and Physiological Psychology,* 1968, **66,** 82–88.

Rozin, P. The significance of learning mechanisms in food selection: Some biology, psychology and sociology of science. In L. M. Barker, M. R. Best, & M. Domjan (Eds.), *Learning mechanisms in food selection.* Waco, Tex.: Baylor University Press, 1977.

Rozin, P. The use of characteristic flavorings in human culinary practice. In C. M. Apt (Ed.), *Flavor: Its chemical, behavioral, and commercial aspects.* Boulder, Colo.: Westview Press, 1978.

Rozin, P. Preference and affect in food selection. In J. H. A. Kroeze (Ed.), *Preference behaviour and chemoreception.* London: Information Retrieval, 1979.

Rozin, P., & Kalat, J. W. Specific hungers and poison avoidance as adaptive specializations of learning. *Psychological Review,* 1971, **78,** 459–486.

Rozin, P., Gruss, L., & Berk, G. Reversal of innate aversions: Attempts to induce a preference for chili peppers in rats. *Journal of Comparative and Physiological Psychology,* 1979, **93,** 1001–1014.

Rozin, P., & Schiller, D. The nature and acquisition of a preference for chili pepper by humans. *Motivation and Emotion,* 1980, **4,** 77–101.

Siegel, S. Flavor preexposure and "learned safety." *Journal of Comparative and Physiological Psychology,* 1974, **87,** 1073–1082.

Siqueland, E. R. Experimental modification of taste preference. *Journal of Comparative and Physiological Psychology,* 1965, **59,** 166–170.

Steiner, J. E. The human gustofacial response. In J. F. Bosma (Ed.), *Oral sensation and perception: Development in the fetus and infant.* Washington, D.C.: U.S. Government Printing Office, 1974.

Steiner, J. E. Facial expressions of the neonate infant indicating the hedonics of food-related chemical stimuli. In J. M. Weiffenback (Ed.), *Taste and development: The genesis of sweet preference.* Washington, D.C.: U.S. Government Printing Office, 1977.

Steiniger, F. von. Beitrage zur Soziologie und sonstigen Biologie der Wanderratte. *Zeitschrift fur Tierpsychologie,* 1950, **7,** 356–379.

Stephenson, G. R. Cultural acquisition of a specific learned response among rhesus monkeys. In D. Starek, R. Scheider, & H. J. Kuhn (Eds.), *Progress in primatology,* Stuttgart: Fischer, 1967.

Warren, R. P., & Pfaffman, C. Early experience and taste aversion. *Journal of Comparative and Physiological Psychology,* 1959, **52,** 263–266.

Williams, G. C. *Adaptation and natural selection: A critique of some current evolutionary thought.* Princeton, N.J.: Princeton University Press, 1966.

Wyrwicka, W. Imitation of mother's inappropriate food preference in weanling kittens. *Pavlovian Journal of Biological Science,* 1978, **13,** 55–72.

Young, P. T. The role of affective processes in learning and motivation. *Psychological Review,* 1959, **66,** 104–125.

Young, P. T. Evaluation and preference in behavioral development. *Psychological Review,* 1968, **75,** 222–241.

Zahorik, D. M. Associative and non-associative factors in learned food preferences. In L. M. Barker, M. R. Best, & M. Domjan (Eds.), *Learning mechanisms in food selection.* Waco, Tex.: Baylor University Press, 1977.

Zahorik, D. M. Learned changes in preferences for chemical stimuli: Asymmetrical effects of positive and negative consequences and species differences in learning. In J. H. A. Kroeze (Ed.), *Preference behaviour and chemoreception.* London: Information Retrieval, 1979.

Zahorik, D. M., Maier, S. F., & Pies, R. W. Preferences for tastes paired with recovery from thiamine deficiency in rats: Appetitive conditioning or learned safety. *Journal of Comparative and Physiological Psychology,* 1974, **87,** 1083–1091.

15

Neurophysiological
and Anatomical Aspects
of Taste Development

CHARLOTTE M. MISTRETTA
The University of Michigan

I. INTRODUCTION

Taste perception plays a primary role in identifying and selecting food to be ingested. So powerful are the influences of taste on ingestion that hungry animals will refuse foul-tasting substances and satiated mammals will overindulge in highly palatable foods (e.g., Epstein, 1967). Mammalian taste preferences and aversions are to some extent universal. For example, all species studied exhibit a preference for sucrose[1] and sodium chloride at certain concentrations, and tend to reject

---

[1] Although some investigators contend that cats represent an exception to the "universal" mammalian preference for sucrose (Beauchamp, Maller, & Rogers, 1977), others report that cats *do* display sucrose preference when tested with solvents to mask the water taste (Bartoshuk, Harned, & Parks, 1971). Those interested in this issue should read both papers.

433

sour and bitter-tasting chemicals (Denton & Coghlan, 1975). Other preferences and aversions are idiosyncratic, as evinced by dramatic cultural differences in taste behaviors (Jerome, 1977; Moskowitz, Kumaraiah, Sharma, Jacobs, & Sharma, 1975). Galef's discussion in the previous chapter on development of taste preference indicates that the combined universal and idiosyncratic nature of preferences and aversions derive from identifiable genetic and environmental influences. But to understand the effects of innate and environmental factors, it is essential to have information on how the sense of taste develops, structurally and functionally, and on the sequence and time course of development in the gustatory system. Only during the last 10 to 15 years have such data become available and complete studies for any one species are still lacking. Therefore it is timely and exciting to discuss the topic of taste development while the area is new and the choice of future directions can be carefully considered.

II. GENERAL BACKGROUND ON TONGUE TASTE BUDS AND INNERVATION

The chemoreceptors that mediate gustatory sensation, called taste buds, are collections of about 40 cells contained in the epithelium of the tongue, soft palate, and epiglottis (Bradley, 1971; Miller, 1977; Mistretta, 1972). Because this chapter focuses on responses from *lingual* taste buds, a brief description of the location, structure, and innervation of these receptors in the adult tongue is included as background. The rat and sheep tongue are discussed, because much of the data on structural and functional development derive from these species; but some available data on the human tongue are included.

Lingual taste buds are located in structures called papillae, including fungiform, circumvallate, and foliate. Fungiform papillae are distributed over the anterior two thirds of the mammalian tongue (Fig. 15.1). One taste bud is found in the apex of each fungiform papilla in the rat tongue, whereas sheep fungiform contain 1 to 8 taste buds and human fungiform papillae contain up to 27 buds each (Arvidson, 1979).

In contrast, taste papillae on the posterior tongue usually contain 100 or more taste buds. The single circumvallate papilla on the back of the rat tongue has about 400–500 taste buds. In sheep, 20–30 circumvallate papillae on either side of the posterior tongue contain from 50 to 200 taste buds each. Human circumvallate papillae, 8–12 arranged in a V-shape across the posterior tongue, contain about 250 taste buds each.

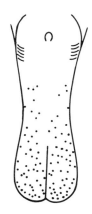

Fig. 15.1 Diagram of the rat tongue. Fungiform papillae (indicated by dots) are distributed over the anterior two thirds of the mammalian tongue. In the rat, there is a single circumvallate papilla in the midline of the posterior tongue, and a set of foliate papillae on each lateral border (indicated by diagonal lines).

The posterior mammalian tongue also contains foliate papillae, one set on each lateral border. Rat foliate papillae contain about 200 taste buds per set (Oakley, 1974), human about 1280 (Bradley, 1971). These papillae are not apparent on the sheep tongue.

The gustatory papillae, fungiform, circumvallate, and foliate, are distributed among filiform papillae on the tongue. The filiform do not have taste buds but rather serve a tactile and mechanical function in food detection and manipulation.

Each taste bud contains about 40 modified epithelial cells oriented in an ovoid collection that is readily distinguished from the surrounding epithelium in standard histological sections (Fig. 15.2). Although some histochemical differences have been described among taste buds in the various gustatory papillae (Iwayama & Nada, 1969), obvious structural differences are not apparent at the light microscopic level. The cells of an individual taste bud have been categorized into "types" by some investigators (Farbman, 1965; Murray 1973), but there is no clear indication of what function each cell type might serve. Murray (1973) has reported synapses between "type 3" cells and nerve fibers. "Type 2" cells have extensive contacts with nerves but no classical synapses. The roles of these cells in taste transduction is not understood. Certainly, though, the older classical description of "sustentacular" versus "neuroepithelial" cells is oversimplified and is not substantiated by recent studies.

Cells of the taste bud end in apical specializations called microvilli. These microvilli may be 2.5–7.0 μ in length (Jahnke & Baur, 1979) and they extend into the pore region of the taste bud (Fig. 15.3). The pore is a channel that penetrates through surrounding epithelial cells and cornified layers to form a direct communication between taste bud cells

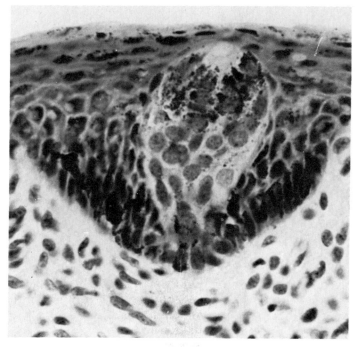

Fig. 15.2 Photomicrograph of a taste bud from the tongue of a newborn lamb (×500). The cells of the taste bud are oriented in an ovoid collection, about 45 to 60 μ in diameter. The wide bottom of the taste pore is apparent at the apex of this bud.

and the oral environment. It is thought that chemical stimuli enter the taste pore and stimulate receptor membranes on the microvilli (Beidler, 1961).

An important physiological characteristic of the taste bud is its potential for renewal. Individual taste bud cells are continuously replaced, presumably by modified, surrounding epithelial cells; those in the rat turn over with a half-life of about 10 days (Beidler and Smallman, 1965). This property of normal replacement reflects a plasticity that is also exhibited during lesions. If a taste nerve in the adult mammal is cut, associated taste buds degenerate, and subsequently regenerate on reinnervation as the nerve grows into the epithelium again (Guth, 1971).

Taste buds in fungiform papillae on the anterior mammalian tongue are innervated by the chorda tympani nerve, a branch of the seventh cranial nerve. Circumvallate taste buds are innervated by the lingual branch of the glossopharyngeal or ninth cranial nerve. Anterior and

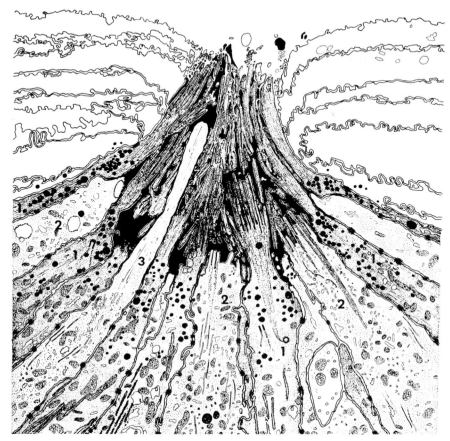

Fig. 15.3 Drawing of the pore region of a taste bud. Microvilli of the taste cells extend into the pore which forms a channel between the oral cavity and the taste cells. Numbers in the drawing refer to cell types in Murray's classification. (From Murray, 1973.)

posterior aspects of the foliate papillae are innervated by chorda tympani and glossopharyngeal nerves, respectively. All of the first-order taste neurons synapse in the brainstem in the nucleus of the tractus solitarius. From this nucleus, fibers extend to the pontine taste area; some pontine neurons project to the amygdala in an area important for control of feeding and drinking. Other neurons project to the dorsal thalamus and then to the cortex (see Norgren, 1977, for a detailed description of rat taste pathways).

At all levels of the taste system, from peripheral receptor cells to various central relays, single taste neurons usually respond to more than one chemical stimulus and to more than one chemical *class* of stimuli. Therefore, strict "salt neurons" or "sugar neurons," and so on, do not exist. This makes gustatory quality coding a difficult and much-debated issue (the interested reader should see discussions in Bartoshuk, 1978; McBurney, 1974; Pfaffmann, Frank, & Norgren, 1979, for examples).

With this brief general description as a background, the topic of taste development can be approached. The time course of taste bud formation will be described first, but further details of structural development are incorporated in Sections IV and V on taste function.

III.   TIME COURSE OF TASTE BUD DEVELOPMENT

It has been known for many years that taste buds begin to develop structurally in utero, first appearing at about 20 days of gestation in the rat (Farbman, 1965; Mistretta, 1972), before 50 days of gestation in sheep (Bradley & Mistretta, 1973a), and at about 55 days in the human fetus (Bradley, 1972; Bradley & Stern, 1967). Gestation in the rat is rather short (21 days) and because taste buds only begin to form near term, structural development is completed postnatally. However, in the sheep, with a gestation of about 150 days, and human, with a gestation of 40 weeks, adult taste bud morphology is acquired in utero.

But although structural maturation may be achieved prenatally, the number of taste buds in sheep continues to increase after birth (Bradley & Mistretta, 1972; Bradley, Cheal, & Kim, 1980). It is reasonable to assume that this occurs in the human as well because there are other similarities in the taste systems of these two species. Therefore the combined pre- and postnatal components in structural development suggest that function will also have intra- and extrauterine components.

In the human there has long been a good indication that prenatal taste buds are functional, since Peiper (1925) reported that the newborn human makes facial expressions that indicate an ability to discriminate among taste solutions. Steiner (1973) has more recently extended these observations on newborn facial expressions, and Desor and Maller (1973) have reported quantitative data on solution intake, demonstrating taste sensitivity within a few hours after birth. It is unlikely that the ability to taste would suddenly "switch-on" at birth, and therefore the fetus must have a gustatory system that functions to some extent.

IV. TASTE DEVELOPMENT IN SHEEP: PRENATAL AND POSTNATAL

To determine whether the taste system is indeed functional prenatally and to study the time course of taste development, Robert M. Bradley and I began neurophysiological experiments in fetal sheep in 1970. Sheep were chosen because gestation is lengthy; the fetus is relatively large; the pregnant ewe readily withstands surgical manipulations; sheep are extensively used in studies of reproductive endocrinology and perinatal physiology, and therefore a wealth of data exists on the physiology of the pregnant ewe and fetus; and, taste buds undergo structural development in utero, as they do in the human.

From studies of taste responses recorded from the chorda tympani nerve during chemical stimulation of the fetal tongue, we concluded that the peripheral gustatory system of the sheep is functional for at least the last third of gestation (Bradley & Mistretta, 1973a). To learn whether neurophysiological taste response characteristics alter as the taste system matures, we began to record from taste neurons in the medulla (Bradley & Mistretta, 1975; 1980; Mistretta & Bradley, 1975a, 1977, 1978a). Central nervous system (CNS) studies enabled us to record from younger fetuses and to obtain more single and few unit responses. We found that taste function does indeed change during development. Taste neurons in young fetuses (84 to about 110 days of gestation) respond to stimulation of the tongue with fewer salts and acids than do cells in older fetuses (greater than 114 days of gestation) (Mistretta & Bradley, 1978a). Furthermore, responses to specific chloride salts develop in a particular sequence, not randomly. Responses to NH_4Cl and KCl appear first, and only in older fetuses do units respond during stimulation of the tongue with NaCl or LiCl (Fig. 15.4). We hypothesized that these changes may relate to receptor development, whereas other changes in response latency and discharge duration probably relate to development of taste fibers and CNS synapses (Bradley & Mistretta, 1980; Fig. 15.5).

If the changes in CNS response characteristics do relate to receptor maturation, a return to investigations of *peripheral* taste nerve responses should help to delimit the origin and nature of the developmental phenomenon. Therefore, we are presently recording from the chorda tympani nerve in sheep fetuses, lambs, and adults.

When recording from the chorda tympani nerve in fetuses at about 110 days of gestation, NH_4Cl and KCl are very effective taste stimuli whereas NaCl and LiCl either elicit no response or a minimal response

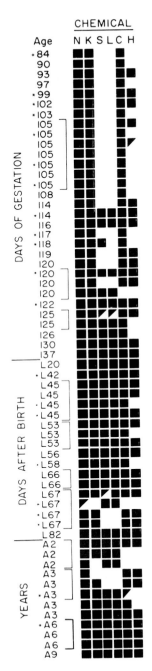

Fig. 15.4 Response of 61 taste neurons in the nucleus of the solitary tract in the medulla of fetuses, lambs, and adult sheep. Six chemical stimuli were applied to the anterior tongue: 0.5 M NH$_4$Cl (N), 0.5 M KCl (K), 0.5 M NaCl (S), 0.5 M LiCl (L), 0.1 M citric acid (C), and 0.01 M HCl (H). Fetal and lamb ages are given in days of gestation or days after birth; adult ages are given in years. Responses to each chemical are indicated by a closed square (■); no response is indicated by a blank. If a unit was inconsistent (sometimes responded, sometimes did not), a half-square is noted (◪). Dots at the far left signify single-unit recordings. Bracketed ages indicate that these units were recorded from one animal.

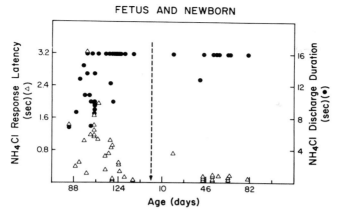

Fig. 15.5   Response latency ($\triangle$) and discharge duration ($\bullet$) for fetal and lamb taste units in the medulla during stimulation of the tongue with NH_4Cl. An arrow marks the time of birth. Fetal ages are in days of gestation and lamb ages in days after birth. The functions for latency and discharge duration follow a similar time course. (From Bradley & Mistretta, 1980.)

(Fig. 15.6). The NH_4Cl response is on average six times greater than the NaCl response, and the KCl response is three times greater. In lambs after birth NaCl and LiCl are equally as effective as KCl, and NH_4Cl now elicits a response only about one and a half times greater than NaCl (Fig. 15.7). Although no responses were recorded to NaCl and LiCl in young taste neurons in the medulla and a weak response is sometimes recorded in peripheral nerves, the phenomenon is essentially the same (i.e., relative to NH_4Cl, NaCl and LiCl gradually become more effective stimuli as development progresses).

Preliminary data on older fetuses and perinatal animals now indicate that the changes in taste function continue postnatally, between birth and about 2 months after birth. Ratios of responses to stimulation of the tongue with KCl, NaCl, and LiCl, relative to the NH_4Cl response, are plotted for animals in five age groups (Fig. 15.8). Although these data are preliminary, they suggest a gradual change in taste function that has pre- and postnatal components. This continued, postnatal alteration in taste function is extremely important because it demonstrates the existence of a changing neurophysiological substrate for changing behavioral responses.

These studies on development of taste function have demonstrated that the gustatory system is functional prenatally (from at least 84 days or about 0.60 of gestation in the sheep) and that prenatal and postnatal changes occur in taste response characteristics. Because taste buds in

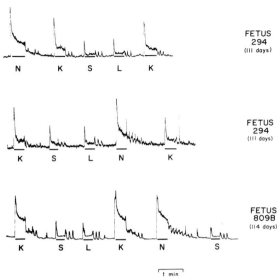

Fig. 15.6 Integrated responses from the chorda tympani nerve in fetuses at 111 and 114 days of gestation. The chemical stimuli applied to the anterior tongue were 0.5 M NH$_4$Cl (N), 0.5 M KCl (K), 0.5 M NaCl (S), and 0.5 M LiCl (L). Black lines under each trace indicate when the chemical was applied to the tongue; between stimulation periods the tongue was rinsed with distilled water. The absolute height of the integrated responses should not be compared between animals, but the ratio of responses in each animal relative to other animals. For example, in the first trace, the NaCl–NH$_4$Cl response ratio is 0.14; in the second trace, it is 0.29; in the third, 0.13.

the fetal sheep are not structurally mature at 84 days (Bradley & Mistretta, 1972; 1973a), functional changes in responses to taste stimuli accompany morphological changes in taste buds. As Gottlieb (1971) indicated, function precedes structural maturation in many sensory systems. Our knowledge of ultrastructural development of taste buds is not sufficient to permit speculation on particular structures that might relate to functional alterations. Electron microscopic studies of taste bud development in the sheep are in progress in our laboratory with Dr. Soo Duk Lee. We know that, as early as 80 days of gestation, when taste response characteristics are still immature, taste bud cells already possess microvilli that extend into the taste pore region (Fig. 15.9). Also, distinct types of microvilli similar to those described in the adult rabbit (Jahnke & Baur, 1979), are present at 80–100 days. The presence of microvilli is important because it is generally assumed that the initial

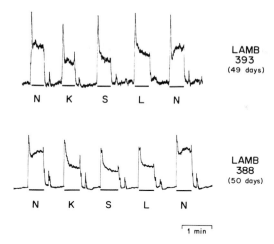

Fig. 15.7 Integrated responses from the chorda tympani nerve in lambs aged 49 and 50 days after birth. The chemical stimuli applied to the anterior tongue were 0.5 *M NH₄Cl* (N), 0.5 M KCl (K), 0.5 M NaCl (S), and 0.5 M LiCl (L). Black lines under each trace indicate when the chemical was applied to the tongue; between stimulation periods the tongue was rinsed with distilled water. Compared to the NaCl and NH₄Cl responses from fetuses in Fig. 15.6, the NaCl–NH₄Cl response ratios have now increased, to average ~ 0.44.

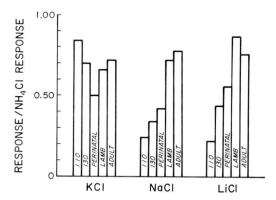

Fig. 15.8 Ratios of chorda tympani nerve responses in fetuses (at 110 and 130 days of gestation and near birth), lambs, and adults. The ratios of KCl, NaCl, and LiCl responses *relative* to the NH₄Cl response are compared. With increasing age in the sheep, NaCl and LiCl become more effective stimuli relative to NH₄Cl. For the five groups in this figure, data from 8, 6, 4, 4, and 2 animals, respectively, are presented.

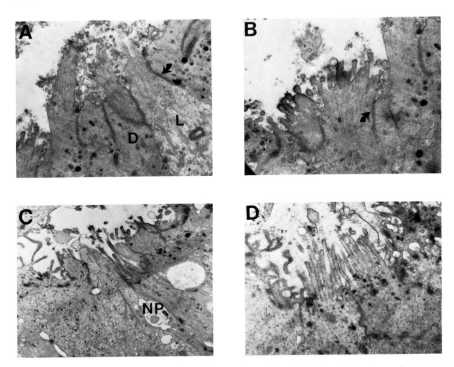

Fig. 15.9 Electron micrographs of the apices of taste bud cells in sheep fetuses at (A) and (B) 80 days (× 6800), (C) 90 days (× 5440), and (D) 100 days of gestation (× 2720). As early as 80 days, tight juntions (arrows) are found between the cell apices. Nerve profiles (NP) and light (L) and dark (D) cells are also seen in these young fetuses. Clublike microvilli are present, as well as several fingerlike microvilli on one cell.

step in the taste transduction process occurs on the microvilli membranes (Beidler, 1961), the most accessible portions of the taste bud. Another characteristic of the 80-day taste bud is the presence of tight junctions between the apices of the taste cells and between taste bud and surrounding epithelial cells (Fig. 15.9). This suggests that the immature taste bud is not readily susceptible to direct penetration of chemicals (Murray, 1973) but that chemicals probably bind to microvilli membranes as in the adult. Finally, at least two cell types are already apparent in the taste bud, including those that correspond to "light" and "dark" cells in other species (Farbman, 1965; Murray, 1973), and numerous nerve profiles are present.

But ultrastructural information will not elucidate the underlying physicochemical alterations that must take place during receptor development. Dr. John DeSimone of the Medical College of Virginia, Richmond, is at present isolating phospholipids from fetal, newborn, and adult sheep tongues after we record taste responses from the chorda tympani nerve. Phospholipids are proposed as key elements in the process of binding salts in the taste transduction mechanism (DeSimone & Price, 1976). DeSimone hypothesizes that developmental changes in phospholipid composition relate to changes in the ability of taste receptor membranes to bind various cations. Eventually we hope to have data on physicochemical, ultrastructural, and neurophysiological development of the taste system in sheep. Comparisons among these data should clarify which structures and chemical components are necessary for responses to different taste stimuli. Such information will then make it possible to design sound behavioral experiments to investigate development of taste preferences and aversions. Behavioral investigations of taste preferences and aversions are feasible *prenatally* in sheep since the fetus swallows large volumes of amniotic fluid each day (Bradley & Mistretta, 1973b,c; Mistretta & Bradley, 1975b), and *postnatally* because the lamb is precocious and able to feed itself from a bottle soon after birth.

V.   POSTNATAL TASTE DEVELOPMENT IN THE RAT

Dr. Fay Ferrell, working as a postdoctoral fellow in our laboratory, reported changes in neurophysiological taste response characteristics during *postnatal* development in the rat (Ferrell, Bradley, Mistretta, & Miklossy, 1979; Ferrell, Mistretta, & Bradley, 1981). Working independently on his dissertation research in another laboratory, David Hill simultaneously reported similar findings (Hill & Almli, 1979; 1980). Essentially both Ferrell and Hill found that in preweaning rats NH_4Cl is a more effective taste stimulus (i.e., elicits a greater magnitude neural response) than NaCl or LiCl, whereas in rats older than about 20–30 days, NaCl and LiCl are more effective than NH_4Cl (Figs. 15.10 and 15.11). In Fig. 15.12, relative responses to LiCl, NH_4Cl and KCl are plotted as a function of age to illustrate the gradual nature of this change in effectiveness of taste stimuli.

We now know, therefore, that in two species with very different developmental time periods, similar changes take place in taste function. In both rat and sheep, as development progresses NaCl and LiCl become more effective taste stimuli, relative to NH_4Cl and KCl (or NH_4Cl and KCl become less effective, relative to NaCl and LiCl). In the sheep, these changes have important prenatal and postnatal components; in the rat they are postnatal. Therefore the changes are probably not directly related to any alterations in the external environment of the organism, but rather to other, physiological phenomena.

(a)

S L K N S

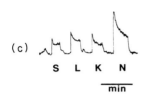

(b)

S   L   K   N   S

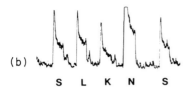

(c)

S L K   N

min

Fig. 15.10 Integrated responses from the chorda tympani nerve in rats at 12 (a,b) and 15 (c) days after birth. Chemical stimuli applied to the anterior tongue were 0.5 M NaCl (S), 0.5 M LiCl (L), 0.5 M KCl (K) and 0.5 M NH$_4$Cl (N). Ratios of NH$_4$Cl–NaCl responses average ~ 2.20 in these preparations, indicating that NH$_4$Cl is a more effective stimulus than NaCl.

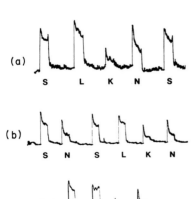

(a)

S   L   K   N   S

(b)

S   N   S   L   K   N

(c)

S   L   K   N

(d)

S L K N S

min

Fig. 15.11 Integrated responses from the chorda tympani nerve in rats aged (a) 26 days after birth, (b) 32 days, (c) 58 days, and (d) adult age. Chemical stimuli applied to the anterior tongue were 0.5 M NaCl (S), 0.5 M LiCl (L), 0.5 M KCl (K), and 0.5 M NH$_4$Cl (N). Whereas the NH$_4$Cl–NaCl response ratio averaged 2.20 in younger rats (Fig. 15.10), the ratio declines to approximately 0.44 in the adult data presented here. That is, NaCl is now a more effective stimulus than NH$_4$Cl.

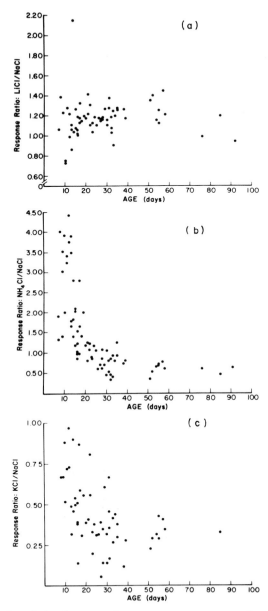

Fig. 15.12   Ratios of chorda tympani nerve responses to stimulation of the tongue with (a) LiCl, (b) NH$_4$Cl, and (c) KCl *relative* to the NaCl response plotted as a function of age in postnatal rats. Although the LiCl–NaCl ratios are relatively constant, NH$_4$Cl and KCl ratios decrease during development. (From Ferrell *et al.*, 1981.)

Ferrell and Hill also found developmental changes in responses to acids and Ferrell described altering responses to sucrose, extending the phenomenon beyond the range of salts only (Fig. 15.13). The postnatal changes in rat taste function occur simultaneously with structural development of the taste bud (Farbman, 1965; Mistretta, 1972). Taste buds begin to form in the rat fetus near term (about 20 days of gestation) and acquire structural characteristics similar to the adult during the first 2 weeks after birth. Development in the first postnatal week is characterized by differentiation of cells into types called peripheral, basal, and Type I (Farbman, 1965). Farbman (1965) reported that he first observed taste buds of an adult configuration at 12 days after birth. That is, Type II cells and a taste pore had appeared. However, using the presence of a taste pore as an index of maturity, Mistretta (1972) reported that not all taste buds mature simultaneously. At 1 day after birth, about 2% of taste buds in fungiform papillae have taste pores, whereas by 12 days postnatally, about 70% have pores (Fig. 15.14).

Interestingly, Hill has recorded from rat pups as young as 2 days after birth, when presumably the majority of taste buds are still very

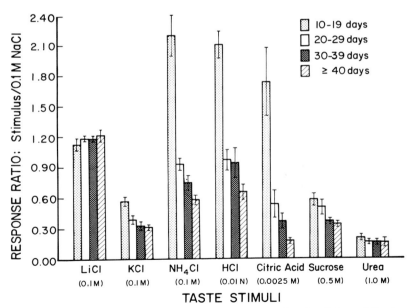

Fig. 15.13 Ratios of chorda tympani nerve responses to stimulation of the tongue with four salts, two acids, sucrose, and urea. Animals are arbitrarily divided into four age groups. Changes in responses to citric acid, hydrochloric acid, and sucrose also occur during development in rat.

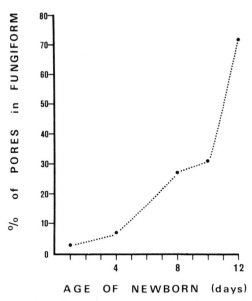

Fig. 15.14   The number of taste pores seen in fungiform papillae on newborn rat tongues examined with scanning electron microscopy. The number of pores is expressed as a percentage of the total number of fungiform papillae that were examined on any individual tongue. One tongue was scanned at each indicated age. (From Mistretta, 1972.)

immature structurally. Although some early behavioral experiments suggest that the newborn rat does not discriminate among taste solutions until about 6 days after birth (Jacobs & Sharma, 1969), Hall (1979; Hall & Bryan, 1981) has recently found that rat pups as young as 1–3 days after birth differentially ingest chemical stimuli. And other investigators have reported that the newborn rabbit, less than 24 hours old, discriminates among taste solutions by making different facial motor displays (Ganchrow, Oppenheimer, & Steiner, 1979). So in altricial species like rat (gestation = 21 days) and rabbit (gestation = 32 days), neurophysiological and behavioral taste responses are probably present from birth or late fetal life.

VI. POTENTIAL ROLE OF EARLY EXPERIENCE IN TASTE DEVELOPMENT

Because mature taste response characteristics are gradually acquired during development, as structural maturation proceeds, there is a possibility that the gustatory system could be modified by early taste stimuli. Components in the maternal diet that reach the developing gustatory system via amniotic fluid and/or breast milk during critical, early periods when structure and function are changing, may stimulate, and thereby influence, development of the taste system (Fig. 15.15). Physiological changes could then lead to alterations in taste preference–aversion behavior.

One way to test this hypothesis is to deliberately modify fetal or newborn taste stimuli and subsequently test for results of the modification. However, in many attempts to alter the developing taste system, modifying stimuli have not been introduced at the time of predictably optimal effectiveness. For example, Warren and Pfaffmann (1959) exposed newborn guinea pigs to a bitter stimulus and later tested to learn if there was a reduced aversion to bitter in exposed animals. But the guinea pig has a rather lengthy gestation (63 days) and is precocial in

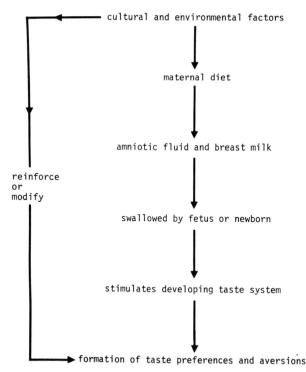

Fig. 15.15 Outline for possible influence of early taste experience on the developing sense of taste. The role of genetics is not meant to be ignored in this outline, but is implicitly included as directing early formation of the substrate of the taste system. The outline can be applied to pre- or postnatal influences, or a combination of both.

sensory system development at birth (Gottlieb, 1971); so the taste system is probably undergoing major development, and is therefore most susceptible to change *prenatally* rather than after birth.

Wurtman and Wurtman (1979) fed rats aged 16–30 days with a diet artificially high in sucrose. There was no relationship between the sucrose content of the diet consumed prior to Day 30 and the amount of sucrose subsequently eaten. Again, taste experience was manipulated well after the gustatory sense begins to function rather than during a period when the most dramatic neurophysiological changes are occurring. Earlier exposure might have produced different results. Of course, additional factors including stimulus quality and concentration, method of testing, and total length of the exposure period may also influence the results of such experiments (Mistretta & Bradley, 1978b). Unfortunately, negative results in such experiments contribute little to understanding the issue under investigation.

In other experiments in which rodents were exposed to distinctive chemicals during all of the nursing period, some degree of modification of later taste behavior has been observed (Capretta & Rawls, 1974; Galef & Henderson, 1972; LeMagnen & Tallon, 1968). And Capretta and Rawls (1974) found that exposure during nursing *and* after weaning is more effective than during either period alone. London, Snowden, and Smithane (1979) reported that either preweaning or postweaning exposure may be more effective in producing modifying effects, depending on the taste stimulus in question. But although some efforts to alter taste preferences and aversions through early exposure have been partially successful, there has been no demonstration of a lasting change in taste attributable to stimulation during development. Indeed one should carefully consider whether the gustatory sense should be expected to undergo irreversible modification due to early experience. For example, whereas a variety of "selective advantages" can be listed that may relate to the early plasticity and irreversible changes that can be produced in the visual system (Blakemore, 1974), it is relatively easy to argue that the taste system should be *resistant* to irreversible change (Rozin, 1976). Once certain broad preferences and aversions are "built-in" (e.g., an aversion for bitter chemicals including poisons, a preference for sugars which are nutritious, etc.) an organism that will alter its taste behavior to eat available food is more adaptive than one that will forever reject certain items. Because taste buds turn over, or are renewed in the adult (Beidler & Smallman, 1965), additional plasticity may perhaps be expected in the taste system.

Furthermore, it may be that the sorts of changes expected in taste preference–aversion behavior as a result of early experience have been too gross. Perhaps lasting, subtle changes do indeed occur. In the visual system there are examples of the influence of early experience at the neurophysiological level; but there is disagreement on the extent to which behavioral correlates of the neural changes have been shown. Investigators of gustatory plasticity have focused on behavioral effects without any indication that changes occur at the cellular level. And of course it is difficult to pursue neurophysiological or anatomical investigations of *taste plasticity* in the absence of detailed understanding of the taste transduction process, taste coding at peripheral and central levels, central neural pathways, and so on.

What, then, can be concluded about the potential for modifying the taste system through early experience? It is now known that taste function changes during development—the system is not "set" to respond in an adult manner from the moment function begins. This is true for two species with very different developmental time courses: rat and sheep. In the rat, much of taste development occurs postnatally, in the sheep, prenatally and postnatally. Because alterations in response characteristics occur, it is possible that stimulation during the early periods of functional and structural maturation may influence the development of the taste system. It is not, then, unreasonable to hypothesize that early taste experience may affect later taste preference–aversion behavior. Galef (Chapter 14, this volume) summarizes literature on taste preference development and concludes that mammals are born with some preferences and aversions and yet such taste responses may be modified by gustatory experience. It is now apparent that a changing neural substrate exists as a basis for proposed behavioral changes.

If the effects of early taste experience are to be tested, it should be in the context of knowledge of neurophysiological development. From the work of Ferrell and Hill, it is apparent that attempts to alter rodent taste preferences and aversions through early experience should be instituted as soon as possible after birth and continued through at least 35 days postnatally. For animals that are precocial in sensory development, such as sheep, *prenatal* exposure to taste stimuli may be as effective as postnatal. Or a combination of pre- and postnatal experience may be most effective. Because the structural development of human taste buds has a similar time course to that in sheep, the human taste system is presumably also susceptible to modifying stimuli before and after birth. Until more basic information is acquired on development of gustatory physiology, anatomy, and physicochemistry, any behavioral changes that are observed will be difficult to interpret. It will also remain difficult to choose appropriate chemical stimuli and exposure concentrations, and to identify precisely periods when modifying influences might be most effective.

ACKNOWLEDGMENTS

Preparation of this manuscript was partially funded by National Science Foundation Grant BNS 77-09920 and National Institute of Health Grant DE 04491. The author holds a Research Career Development Award from the National Institutes of Dental Research (Grant DE 00066).

REFERENCES

Arvidson, K. Location and variation in number of taste buds in human fungiform papillae. *Scandinavian Journal of Dental Research*, 1979, **87**, 435–442.

Bartoshuk, L. Gustatory system. In R. B. Masterton (Ed.), *Handbook of behavioral neurobiology* (Vol. 1). *Sensory integration*. New York: Plenum, 1978, pp. 503–567.

Bartoshuk, L., Harned, M. A., & Parks, L. H. Taste of water in the cat: Effects on sucrose preference. *Science*, 1971, **171**, 699–701.

Beauchamp, G. K., Maller, O., & Rogers, J. G. Flavor preferences in cats. *Journal of Comparative and Physiological Psychology*, 1977, **91**, 1118–1127.

Beidler, L. M. Taste receptor stimulation. In *Progress in biophysics and biophysical chemistry*. Oxford: Pergamon, 1961, pp. 107–151.

Beidler, L. M., & Smallman, R. L. Renewal of cells within taste buds. *Journal of Cell Biology*, 1965, **27**, 263–272.

Blakemore, C. Development of functional connexions in the mammalian visual system. *British Medical Bulletin*, 1974, **30**, 152–157. (a)

Bradley, R. M. Tongue Topography. In L. M. Beidler (Ed.), *Handbook of sensory physiology IV: Chemical senses (Part 2), Taste*. Berlin: Springer-Verlag, 1971, pp. 1–30.

Bradley, R. M. Development of the taste bud and gustatory papillae in human fetuses. In J. F. Bosma (Ed.), *Third symposium on oral sensation and perception. The mouth of the infant*. Springfield, Ill.: Charles C Thomas, 1972, pp. 137–162.

Bradley, R. M., Cheal, M. L., & Kim, Y. H. Quantitative analysis of developing epiglottal taste buds in sheep. *Journal of Anatomy*, 1980, **130**, 25–32.

Bradley, R. M., & Mistretta, C. M. The morphological and functional development of fetal gustatory receptors. In N. Emmelin & Y. Zotterman (Ed.), *Oral physiology*. Oxford: Pergamon, 1972, pp. 239–253.

Bradley, R. M., & Mistretta, C. M. The gustatory sense in foetal sheep during the last third of gestation. *Journal of Physiology*, 1973, **231**, 271–282. (a)

Bradley, R. M., & Mistretta, C. M. Swallowing in fetal sheep. *Science*, 1973, **179**, 1016–1017. (b)

Bradley, R. M., & Mistretta, C. M. Investigations of taste function and swallowing in fetal sheep. In J. F. Bosma (Ed.), *Development in the fetus and infant*. Bethesda, Md.: DHEW Publication No. (NIH) 73-546, 1973, pp. 185–205. (c)

Bradley, R. M., & Mistretta, C. M. The developing sense of taste. In D. A. Denton & J. P. Coghlan (Eds.), *Olfaction and taste V*. New York: Academic Press, 1975, pp. 91–98.

Bradley, R. M., & Mistretta, C. M. Developmental changes in neurophysiological taste responses from the medulla in sheep. *Brain Research*, 1980, **191**, 21–34.

Bradley, R. M., & Stern, I. B. The development of the human taste bud during the foetal period. *Journal of Anatomy*, 1967, **101**, 743–752.

Capretta, P. J., & Rawls, L. H. Establishment of a flavor preference in rats: Importance of nursing and weaning experience. *Journal of Comparative and Physiological Psychology*, 1974, **86**, 670–673.

Denton, D. A., & Coghlan, J. P. *Olfaction and taste V*. New York: Academic Press, 1975.

DeSimone, J. A., & Price, S. A model for the stimulation of taste receptor cells by salt. *Biophysical Journal*, 1976, **16**, 869–881.

Desor, J. A., Maller, O., & Turner, R. E. Taste in acceptance of sugars by human infants. *Journal of Comparative Physiological Psychology*, 1973, **84**, 496–501.

Epstein, A. N. Oropharyngeal factors in feeding and drinking. In C. F. Code (Ed.), *Handbook of physiology, section 6, alimentary canal* (Vol. 1): *Control of food and water intake*. Washington, D.C.: American Physiological Society, 1967, pp. 197–218.

Farbman, A. I. Electron microscope study of the developing taste bud in rat fungiform papilla. *Developmental Biology*, 1965, **11**, 110–135.

Ferrell, M. F., Bradley, R. M., Mistretta, C. M., & Miklossy, K. Developmental changes in neural taste responses in postnatal rats. *Neuroscience Abstracts*, 1979, **5**, 127.

Ferrell, M. F., Mistretta, C. M., & Bradley, R. M. Chorda tympani taste responses during development in rat. *Journal of Comparative Neurology*, 1981, **198**, 37–44.

Galef, B. G. Jr., & Henderson, P. W. Mother's milk: A determinant of the feeding preferences of weaning rat pups. *Journal of Comparative and Physiological Psychology*, 1972, **78**, 213–219.

Ganchrow, J. R., Oppenheimer, M., & Steiner, J. E. Behavioural displays to gustatory stimuli in newborn rabbit pups. *Chemical Senses and Flavour*, 1979, **4**, 49–61.

Gottlieb, G. Ontogenesis of sensory function in birds and mammals. In E. Tobach, L. R. Aronson, & E. Shaw (Eds.), *The biopsychology of development*. New York: Academic Press, 1971, pp. 67–128. (b)

Guth, L. Degeneration and regeneration of taste buds. In L. M. Beidler (Ed.), *Handbook of sensory physiology, IV: Chemical senses* (Part 2), *taste*. Berlin: Springer-Verlag, 1971, pp. 63–74.

Hall, W. G. Feeding and behavioral activation in infant rats. *Science*, 1979, **205**, 206–208.

Hall, W. G., & Bryan, T. E. The ontogeny of feeding in rats: II. Independent ingestive behavior. *Journal of Comparative and Physiological Psychology*, 1981, **95**, 240–251.

Hill, D. L., & Almli, C. R. Neural ontogeny of chorda tympani taste responses in the rat. *Neuroscience Abstracts*, 1979, **5**, 128.

Hill, D. L., & Almli, C. R. Ontogeny of chorda tympani nerve responses to gustatory stimuli in the rat. *Brain Research*, 1980, **197**, 27–38.

Iwayama, T., & Nada, O. Histochemical observation on phosphatase activities of degenerating and regenerating taste buds. *Anatomical Record*, 1969, **163**, 31–38.

Jacobs, H. L., & Sharma, K. N. Taste versus calories: sensory and metabolic signals in the control of food intake. *Annals of the New York Academy of Sciences*, 1969, **157**, 1084–1125.

Jahnke, D., & Baur, P. Freeze-fracture study of taste bud pores in the foliate papillae of the rabbit. *Cell and Tissue Research*, 1979, **200**, 245–256.

Jerome, N. W. Taste experience and the development of a dietary preference for sweet in humans: Ethnic and cultural variations. In J. M. Weiffenbach (Ed.), *Taste and development: The genesis of sweet preference*. Washington, D.C.: U.S. Government Printing Office, DHEW Publication Number (NIH) 77-1068, 1977, pp. 235–248.

LeMagnen, J., & Tallon, S. Preference alimentaire du jeune rat induite par l'allaitement maternel. *Comptes Rendus des Seances de la Societe de Biologie et de ses Filiales*, 1968, **162**, 387–390.

London, R. M., Snowdon, C. T., & Smithane, J. M. Early experience with sour and bitter solutions increases subsequent ingestion. *Physiology & Behavior*, 1979, **22**, 1149–1155.

McBurney, D. H. Are there primary tastes for man? *Chemical Senses and Flavor*, 1974, **1**, 17–28.

Miller, I. J. Gustatory receptors of the palate. In Y. Katsuki, M. Sato, S. Takagi, & Y. Oomura (Eds.), *Food intake and chemical senses*. Japan: Japanese Scientific Societies, 1977, pp. 173–185.

Mistretta, C. M. Topographical and histological study of the developing rat tongue, palate and taste buds. In J. F. Bosma (Ed.), *Third symposium on oral sensation and perception: The mouth of the infant*. Springfield, Ill.: Charles C Thomas, 1972, pp. 163–187.

Mistretta, C. M., & Bradley, R. M. Taste responses in fetal sheep medulla. *Neuroscience Abstracts*, 1975, **1**(8). (a)

Mistretta, C. M., & Bradley, R. M. Taste and swallowing in utero. *British Medical Bulletin*, 1975, **31**, 80–84. (b)

Mistretta, C. M., & Bradley, R. M. Maturation of CNS taste responses during fetal development. *Annales Récherches Vétérinaries*, 1977, **8**, 495–496.

Mistretta, C. M., & Bradley, R. M. Taste responses in sheep medulla: changes during development. *Science*, 1978, **202**, 535–537. (a)

Mistretta, C. M., & Bradley, R. M. Effects of early sensory experience on brain and behavioral development. In G. Gottlieb (Ed.), *Studies on the development of behavior and the nervous system*. New York: Academic Press, 1978, pp. 215–247. (b)

Moskowitz, H. W., Kumaraiah, V., Sharma, K. N., Jacobs, H. L., & Sharma, S. D. Cross-cultural differences in simple taste preferences. *Science*, 1975, **190**, 1217–1218.

Murray, R. G. The ultrastructure of taste buds. In I. Friedman (Ed.), *The ultrastructure of sensory organs*. New York: Elsevier, 1973, pp. 1–82.

Norgren, R. A synopsis of gustatory neuroanatomy. In J. LeMagnen & P. Macleod (Eds.), *Proceedings of the sixth international symposium on olfaction and taste*. London: Information Retrieval, 1977, pp. 225–232.

Oakley, B. On the specification of taste neurons in the rat tongue. *Brain Research*, 1974, **75**, 85–96.

Peiper, A. Sinnesempfindungen des kindes vor seiner geburt. *Monatsschr. Kinderheilk.*, 1925, **29**, 236–241.

Pfaffmann, C., Frank, M., & Norgren, R. Neural mechanisms and behavioral aspects of taste. *Annual Reviews of Psychology*, 1979, **30**, 283–325.

Rozin, P. The selection of foods by rats, humans, and other animals. *Advances in the Study of Behavior*, 1976, **6**, 21–76.

Steiner, J. The human gustofacial reflex. In J. F. Bosma (Ed.), *Fourth symposium on oral sensation and perception: Development in the fetus and infant*. Bethesda, Md.: NIH Publication No. 73-546, 1973, pp. 254–278.

Warren, R. P., & Pfaffmann, C. Early experience and taste aversion. *Journal of Comparative and Physiological Psychology*, 1959, **52**, 263–266.

Wurtman, J. J., & Wurtman, R. J. Sucrose consumption early in life fails to modify the appetite of adult rats for sweet foods. *Science*, 1979, **205**, 321–322.

Index